D1740747

PRIVATE BEHAVIOUR AND GOVERNMENT POLICY IN INTERDEPENDENT ECONOMIES

PRIVATE BEHAVIOUR AND GOVERNMENT POLICY IN INTERDEPENDENT ECONOMIES

Edited by
A. S. COURAKIS
and M. P. TAYLOR

CLARENDON PRESS · OXFORD
1990

Oxford University Press, Walton Street, Oxford OX2 6DP
Oxford New York Toronto
Delhi Bombay Calcutta Madras Karachi
Petaling Jaya Singapore Hong Kong Tokyo
Nairobi Dar es Salaam Cape Town
Melbourne Auckland
and associated companies in
Berlin Ibadan

Oxford is a trade mark of Oxford University Press

Published in the United States
by Oxford University Press, New York

British Library Cataloguing in Publication Data
Courakis, Anthony S.
Private behaviour and government policy in interdependent economies
1. Macroeconomic policies
I. Title II. Taylor, Mark P. 1958–
339

ISBN 0–19–828350–4
ISBN 0–19–828325–3 (Pbk)

Library of Congress Cataloging in Publication Data
Private behaviour and government policy in interdependent economies/[compiled by] A. S. Courakis and M.P. Taylor.
p. cm.
Includes bibliographicsl references and index.
1. International economic relations. 2. International finance.
3. Economic forecasting. 4. Economic history—1971– I. Courakis.
Anthony S. II. Taylor, Mark P., 1958–
HG3881.P575 1990 337—dc20 90–47077

ISBN 0–19–828350–4
ISBN 0–19–828325–3 (Pbk)

Typeset by The Greek Economic Review
Printed and bound in Great Britain by
Biddles Ltd, Guildford and King's Lynn

CONTENTS

AN OVERVIEW

By Anthony S. Courakis

This volume comprises fourteen studies on various aspects of the complex milieu that confronts policy makers in the context of international economic interdependence. It is divided into four less than 'weakly separable' parts. Part I focuses on exchange rate determination; Part II is concerned with exchange controls, financial integration, and the European Monetary System; Part III examines aspects of interdependence relating to the degree of substitutability between countries' products, North-South interactions, and savings-investment behaviour and fiscal imbalances; and Part IV is concerned, more specifically, with the design of macroeconomic policy in open economies and with aspects of international policy coordination.

The Exchange Rate Environment

Experience under floating has continuously defied the evolving theories of exchange rate behaviour. As Frankel and Froot note in their contribution in this volume, 'the proportion of exchange rate changes that we are able to predict seems to be not just low but zero'; and 'the proportion of exchange rate movements that can be explained even after the fact, using contemporaneous macroeconomic variables, is disturbingly low.[1] Yet, a close understanding of exchange rate behaviour is clearly essential for policy design in a world of floating or managed floating exchange rates. Experience, moreover, has not dealt kindly with the notion[2] that private behaviour in foreign exchange markets shall always be such as to prevent substantial exchange rate misalignments.[3]

1. This vacuum is acknowledged by other authors in the area, most recently Meese, R., 'Currency Fluctuations in the Post-Bretton Woods Era', *Journal of Economic Perspectives*, Vol. 4, 1990, pp. 117-134.

2. Generally traced to Friedman, M., 'The Case for Flexible Exchange Rates', in his *Essays in Positive Economics*, (Chicago: Chicago University Press, 1953).

3. I use the term here in the sence of Williamson, J., 'The Exchange Rate System', (Washington: Institute of International Economics, 1983), thus distinguishing between *volatility* (i.e. short-term variations) and *misalignments* (i.e. persistent departures from long-term equilibrium).

Much of the existing literature on exchange rate determination is based, explicitly or implicitly, on a number of international parity conditions – notably covered or uncovered interest parity, real interest parity and short or long-run purchasing power parity.[4] In *chapter one*, Ronald MacDonald and Mark Taylor survey the empirical evidence on these international parity conditions and present some new evidence on covered interest parity and real interest parity. They show that, with the exception of covered interest parity, the empirical evidence has tended to reject the international parity conditions. Specifically, they conclude that uncovered interest parity is 'resoundly rejected for the recent experience with floating exchange rates', a fact which (on the available evidence) they are inclined to attribute more to failure of the rational expectations component of this hypothesis than to its risk neutrality component. Similarly, with regard to purchasing power parity (PPP), they conclude that 'the evidence convincingly supports the view that *continuous* PPP has not held for the recent floating period', and it is doubtful whether it has held in the interwar years either. Rather, the evidence suggests that the real exchange rate follows a random walk process. Correspondingly, moreover, the evidence under floating rates reveals that real interest parity does not hold.

Rejection of these parity conditions, MacDonald and Taylor note, has important implications for exchange rate modelling; for at the very least it implies that future modelling should take proper account of the time series properties of uncovered interest parity and purchasing power parity.

Careful modelling of dynamics in models of exchange rate determination is also stressed in *chapter two* by Peter Smith and Michael Wickens, whose work though presents a more sanguine picture for rationality in the context of uncovered interest parity than the analysis of McDonald and Taylor encourage us to expect.

The poor performance of empirical exchange rate models, Smith and Wickens argue, may be largely due to inadequacies in econometric specification as many of the tests carried out are based on unrestricted reduced form equations, rather than restricted reduced forms, or, better still, structural equations. Accordingly, they define and estimate on UK data a five equation structural model of the exchange rate. The model is of the 'overshooting'

4. See, for instance, the chapters by Frenkel and Mussa and by Levich, in R. W. Jones and P. B. Kenen (eds), *Handbook of International Economics*, Vol. II (Amsterdam: North Holland, 1985); the chapter by MacDonald and Taylor, in R. MacDonald and P. Taylor (eds), *Exchange Rates and Open Economy Macroeconomics*, (Oxford: Basil Blackwell, 1989); and Meese, R., 'Currency Fluctuations...' op. cit.

exchange rate kind.[5] A 'flexible dynamic structure' affords a specification that is consistent with the data. The estimated model is used to examine the extent to which the 1979-1980 appreciation of the effective sterling exchange rate can be attributed to domestic monetary shocks. In this context, the results suggest that around half of the nominal appreciation and a quarter of the real appreciation in the effective sterling exchange rate can be attributed to unanticipated *temporary* shocks in the rate of growth of the money stock, and that these proportions double if the shocks are perceived as *permanent*.

In *chapter three*, Jeffrey Frankel and Kenneth Froot aim to explain the large real appreciation of the dollar in the period 1981-1985, and its subsequent depreciation, a phenomenon also discussed later in this volume by Masson and Knight. They examine a number of hypotheses that have been commonly proposed to account for the rise in demand for dollars in the first half of the 1980s. Three of these hypotheses relate to economic fundamentals and point either to reduced US monetary growth (the 'monetarist' hypothesis), or to an increase in the real interest rate differential (the 'overshooting' hypothesis), or to an increase in the perceived relative safety of US assets (the 'safe haven' hypothesis). A fourth hypothesis considered is that of a self-confirming increase in the expected rate of dollar appreciation, or fall in the expected rate of depreciation (the 'speculative bubble' hypothesis). Of the three that rely on fundamentals, Frankel and Froot argue that only the overshooting hypothesis goes some way towards explaining the path of the dollar, but that this too cannot track the last 20 per cent of appreciation preceding the February 1985 peak and the subsequent rapid decline. Moreover, the evidence suggests that the probability that can be assigned to such a protracted appreciation being due to a rational expectations bubble is very small. To fill the void they propose a model of speculative bubbles in foreign exchange markets which does not rely on the usual Blanchard-type[6] rational expectations sequence of temporary equilibria. Rather, the model defined treats exchange rates as determined by the roles of three groups of actors, notably fundamentalist forecasters, chartists (technical analysts) and portfolio managers. *Fundamentalists* forecast, by means of the overshooting model, a depreciation

5. Dornbush, R., 'Expectations and Exchange Rate Dynamics', *Journal of Political Economy*, Vol. 84, 1976, pp. 1161-1176; Buiter, W. H. and Miller, M. H., 'Monetary Policy and International Competitiveness', *Oxford Economic Papers*, Vol. 33 (supplement), 1981, pp. 143-175.

6. Blanchard, O. J. and Watson, M. W., 'Bubbles, Rational Expectations and Financial Markets', in P. Wachtel (ed), *Crisis in Economics and Financial Structure*, (Lexington, Mass: Lexington Books, 1982).

of the dollar that would be rational if there were no chartists. *Chartists* extrapolate recent trends based on an information set that includes no fundamentals. *Portfolio managers* take positions in the market and thus determine the exchange rate based on expectations that are a weighted average of the fundamentalists' and chartists' forecasts.

The first stage of the dollar appreciation after 1980 is explained by increases in real interest rate differentials. The second stage is explained by the endogenous take off of the speculative bubble. As fundamentalists' forecasts of depreciation prove incorrect month after month, the portfolio managers decrease the weight they assign to those forecasts and increase the weight they assign to those of the chartists; in doing so they reduce their weighted-average expectations of dollar depreciation, raise their demands for dollars, and thus bring about the continued appreciation of the dollar. In 1985 the dollar enters a third stage where an ever worsening current account deficit reverses the overvaluation caused by the bubble.

The Frankel and Froot model accounts for the movements of the dollar in the 1980s in a way that reconciles some seemingly paradoxical or contradictory evidence about behaviour in foreign exchange markets. In the event they show how, in a world that does not afford unanimity of expectations, ('non-rational' but) *sensible behaviour*[7] can generate not simply short run volatility in exchange rates but also, and more importantly, large and cumulative exchange rate misalignments.

Capital Controls, Financial Integration, and the European Monetary System

Sharp movements in exchange rates in response to news, and bubbles both of the 'rational' and 'non-rational' kind, it is agreed, reflect high international capital mobility. Moreover, high international capital mobility limits the policy choices available to national authorities. On both these counts reinforcing barriers to capital movements or 'throwing sand in the

7. Encompassing 'short-termism', 'noise-trading', and the like—features of experience that we have always known, but only recently begun to pay due attention to — see in particular, Black, F., 'Noise', *Journal of Finance*, Vol. 41, 1986, pp. 529-543; De Long, J.B. *et al*, 'The Economic Consequences of Noise Traders', NBER Working Paper, No. 2395, October 1987; Schulmeister, S., 'Currency Speculation and Dollar Fluctuations', *Banca Nationale del Lavoro Quarterly Review*, No. 167, 1988, pp. 343-365. See also de Grawe, P., 'The Long Swings in Real Exchange Rates : Do They Fit Our Theories?', *Bank of Japan Monetary and Economic Studies*, Vol. 6, 1988, pp. 37-60.

wheels',[8] has been a view much applauded in some quarters in recent years. Yet, since the late 1970's many countries, encouraged by arguments of gains in efficiency, have, not always felicitously, relaxed long standing exchange controls, and the members of the European Community are well on the way towards *complete* liberalisation of capital movements.

In *chapter four*, Michael Artis and Mark Taylor examine the consequences of the abolition of UK exchange controls in 1979, for overseas direct and portfolio investment, for the composition of monetary aggregates, for off-shore/on-shore interest rate differentials, for bank regulation and the conduct of monetary policy, for exchange rates and the stock market. Precise inferences, they note, are complicated by the fact that the abolition of controls coincides with the advent of the Thatcher government and changes in monetary regime (both in terms of controls on banks' choices and in the orientation of policy), with the second OPEC oil shock, and with the move of the UK from oil deficit to self-sufficiency in oil production. Nevertheless, Artis and Taylor are able to draw a number of conclusions. Exchange controls, they argue, appear to have been more of a hindrance to financial integration than was perhaps realised before their abolition. Conversely, their abolition has radically altered the nature of monetary policy that is practicable, reducing the scope for sterilized intervention and for direct controls on bank portfolio choices. Yet, 'the potential for currency substitution', they remark, 'has still to be revealed'. Amongst their other findings, Artis and Taylor also adduce evidence to suggest that the abolition of exchange controls may have led to an increased degree of internationalisation of the UK stock market after 1979, in terms of factors affecting asset prices.

The year 1979 also marks the beginning of operation of the European Monetary System (EMS). The object of the EMS was to create a 'zone of monetary stability' within the European Community, through close monetary cooperation and coordinated exchange rate management. In line with this objective, the last ten years have seen a reduction in the variability of nominal and real exchange rates among countries participating in the Exchange Rate Mechanism (ERM), as well as in levels of, and differentials between, the rates of inflation among these countries. However, while the evidence suggests that this experience was not coincidental, and that due credit therefore must go

8. Notably Tobin, J., 'A Proposal for International Monetary Reform', in his *Essays in Economics: Theory and Policy*, (Cambridge, Mass: MIT Press, 1982); Kareken, J. and Wallace, N., 'On the Indeterminancy of Equilibrium Exchange Rates', *Quarterly Journal of Economics*, Vol. 96, 1981, pp. 207-220; and Dornbusch, R., 'Flexible Exchange Rates and Interdependence', *IMF Staff Papers*, Vol. 30, 1983, pp. 3-38.

to the EMS and ERM arrangements,[9] it has also been argued that this performance owes much to the presence of capital controls, and that the system may not survive their abolition.[10] In addition, doubts about the future of the EMS have been expressed, in that with rates of inflation having subsided more emphasis is now likely to be placed by members on national output and employment objectives (apparently sacrificed on the inflation control and ERM altars in recent years), and correspondingly on the grounds that the fundamental ambiguity involved in a system with a formal objective of stabilising *nominal* rates but with a long-run rationale that involves a requirement on *real* exchange rates, will eventually claim its toll.[11]

In *chapter five*, Giorgio Radaelli, provides further evidence in support of the position that the EMS has contributed to improving the stability of intra-EMS real and nominal exchange rates, yet argues that these achievements have been less due to the presence of capital controls and more due to foreign exchange intervention combined with greater coordination of monetary policies among member countries. Given that a sufficient condition for sterilized intervention to be effective is that economic agents regard domestic and foreign assets as imperfect substitutes, he reasons that 'detection of a systematic risk premium *independent* from capital controls would support effective EMS intervention being carried out in the absence of controls'. Testing the null hypothesis of perfect asset substitutability on French /German data, with the dependent variable so selected as to permit the identification of a risk premium independently of French capital controls, Radaelli confirms the presence of a risk premium which depends on the relative quantities of domestic and foreign government bonds held by the private sector. With the sufficient condition for sterilised intervention thus satisfied, he then proceeds

9. See, for example, Ungerer, H. *et al, The European Monetary System: Recent Developments*, (Washington: IMF, Occasional Paper No. 48, 1986); Rogoff, K., 'Can Exchange Predictability be Achieved Without Monetary Convergence? Evidence from the EMS', *European Economic Review*, Vol. 28, 1985, pp. 93-115; Guitian, M., and Russo, M. and Tullio, G., *Policy Coordination in the European Monetary System*, (Washington: IMF, Occasional Paper No. 61, 1988); and the chapters by Artis and Taylor and by Collins in F. Giavazzi, S. Micossi and M. Miller (eds), *The European Monetary System*, (Cambridge: Cambridge University Press, 1988).

10. For example Rogoff, op. cit.

11. de Grawe, P., 'International Trade and Economic Growth in the European Monetary System', *European Economic Review*, Vol. 31, 1987, pp. 389-398; Vona and Bini Smaghi in Giavazzi, Micossi and Miller (eds), *The European Monetary System*, op. cit; Artis and Taylor, in MacDonald and Taylor (eds), *Exchange Rates and Open Economy Macroeconomics*, op. cit; and F. Giavazzi and A. Giovannini, *Limiting Exchange Rate Flexibility : The European Monetary System*, (Cambridge Mass : MIT Press, 1989).

to present also empirical evidence that exchange rate behaviour since 1979 is consistent with the proposition that central banks deployed sterilised intervention in pursuit of their EMS exchange rate undertakings. Radaelli does not dispute the fact that exchange controls have had a role to play in achieving exchange rate stability over the period. But on the available evidence he is disposed to conclude that foreign exchange intervention has been more important than capital controls, and that a gradual removal of capital controls should not jeopardise the EMS.

In the context of the advancing liberalisation of capital movements, mentioned above, the Radaelli findings are encouraging for the near future viability of the system. Yet, insofar as the emphasis on inflation control can now be said to be giving way to output and employment objectives, the nexus between capital controls and (more generally) degree of financial integration, on the one hand, and structural asymmetries, on the other hand, merits particular attention.

Considerations of the latter kind motivate the analysis in *chapter six*, by Michael Artis and Shaziye Gazioglu. Noting that empirical evidence reveals differences in wage-price behaviour (in the sense of differences in the sensitivity of wage inflation to pressure of demand, and in responsiveness of wages to prices) as between Germany and other EMS countries,[12] Artis and Gazioglu proceed, in terms of a detailed two-country model, to examine the implications of wage-price asymmetries for the effects of various shocks on rates of inflation, levels of output, and the real exchange rate. The authorities are assumed to intervene in the foreign exchange market to stabilize competitiveness (the real exchange rate), and to be able to deploy (if they choose) exchange controls. The effects of exchange market intervention, the consequences of wage-price asymmetries and the putative effect of exchange controls in offsetting them, are assessed by evaluating the responses of the system to the various shocks under alternative assumptions regarding the degree of wage price asymmetries and the severity of the controls. Artis and Gazioglu find that Phillips curve asymmetries lead to pronounced differences in the effects of the various disturbances considered. However, they also find that removing exchange controls, or, more generally, attaining a higher level of international financial integration, does not always lead to,

12. The pattern is rather complex; see for example, also the chapter by van der Ploeg in this volume and the OECD study on *Economies in Transition: Structural Adjustment in the OECD Countries*, (Paris: Organisation for Economic Cooperation and Development, 1989). Some of the problems that Philips curve asymmetries pose for European monetary integration were stressed long ago in Corden, W. M., *Monetary Integration*, (Princeton: Princeton University, Essays in International Finance, No. 93, 1972).

or exacerbate, exchange rate instability. Whether it does so or not depends on the kind of shock considered. Indeed, the results presented show that some shocks can be more disruptive in their real exchange impacts under a low than under a high degree of financial integration; and the same is true of most shocks in terms of effects on output. Again, for some combinations of parameters the largest degree of exchange rate overshooting following certain shocks is to be found in the 'middle' range of financial integration. Such results commend caution in appealing to the 'second best' theorem to justify the use of exchange controls in a world of sticky wages and prices.[13] They also warn against overt reliance on the seemingly more unequivocal conclusions afforded by some simple models.

The role of capital controls in circumstances where, as with France and Italy in yesteryears and as with Britain, Greece, Portugal and Spain today, participation in the EMS and ERM is seen as a way for a high inflation country to obtain and sustain a low inflation rate, is examined in *chapter seven*, by Michael Moore. Characterizing the decision to join the EMS as a movement from a fixed exchange rate with a *high* inflation country to a fixed exchange rate with a *low* inflation country, Moore constructs three variants of a two-period, two goods (traded and non-traded) model of a small open economy. He then traces, and compares, the implications of the change to the hard currency peg in circumstances where the economy is (a) 'distortion-free', or (b) characterized by capital controls and market clearing, or (c) characterized by capital controls and price stickiness in the non-traded goods (labour) market. Analysing the consequences of the hard currency peg for the real interest rate, the real exchange rate, output, and welfare, Moore shows that the key source of non-neutrality for this disinflationary shift is the presence of capital controls, and that when capital controls are present in circumstances of demand deficiency output and possibly welfare losses will arise.

The Nature of Economic Interdependence

Whether for fixed or for floating exchange rates, on issues of macroeconomic interdependence much of our trained intuition springs from Mundell's two-country IS-LM model.[14] Assuming perfect capital mobility,

13. See also Edwards, S. and Ostry, J. D., 'Terms of Trade Disturbances, Real Exchange Rates, and Welfare: The Role of Capital Controls and Labour Market Distortions', (Washington : IMF Working Paper, March 1989).

14. Mundell, R. A., *International Economics*, (New York: Macmillan Press, 1968).

Mundell showed that under floating exchange rates a fiscal expansion in one country has an expansionary effect abroad, while a monetary expansion in one country has a contractionary effect abroad.

In *chapter eight*, Neil Rankin re-examines these conclusions in the context of an intertemporal disequilibrium version of Mundell's model, with floating exchange rates and perfect capital mobility. The world lasts two periods and consumers optimize intertemporally with perfect foresight. First period nominal wages and prices are rigid, causing excess supply in both goods and labour markets 'in the short run'; in the second period they are flexible, ensuring full employment 'in the long run'. Countries are approximately symmetric and produce single specialised outputs that are imperfect substitutes in consumer's preferences in both countries. Rankin shows, that the degree of substitutability between the two countries' products is crucial to the nature of macroeconomic interdependence. When the products are gross substitutes, both monetary and fiscal policy have contractionary effects abroad. When they are gross complements both policies have expansionary effects abroad. In the intermediate case, there are no foreign effects at all. The contrast with Mundell is striking. And though, as Rankin remarks, one should not forget that the results are drawn from a model that 'still omits many important factors' and cannot therefore be construed as general propositions, they provide eloquent testimony that 'much more remains to be learnt about interdependence, and that any general propositions may have to give way to more complex statements'.

Unlike Rankin's 'two-country' model, which as noted above assumes that the countries are approximately symmetric, with regard to interdependence between North and South structural differences have long been stressed as a key feature of reality. Thus, with the North assumed to specialise in the production of manufactures and the South in the production of primary commodities, models of North-South interaction are generally fashioned to involve asymmetries in goods and factor markets, and so to render patterns of 'asymmetric interdependence' or 'non-reciprocal dependence'.[15]

In the model constructed by S. Mansoob Murshed and Somnath Sen in *chapter nine*, the North is characterized by fix-price markets, while the South is characterized by flex-price markets. As with models in the 'structuralist

15. Needless to say models differ in their contrasts between North and South; see, for instance, the survey paper of Findlay, in R.W. Jones and P. B. Kenen (eds), *Handbook of International Economics*, Vol. 1, (Amsterdam: North Holland, 1984), and D. Currie and D. Vines (eds), *Macroeconomic Interactions Between North and South*, (Cambridge: Cambridge University Press, 1988).

tradition',[16] therefore, changes in effective demand result in changes in employment and output in the North, whereas, in the medium-run, in the South they cause mainly changes in prices. However, though prices in the North are determined by wages in the North, the fact that the Northern consumption basket includes Southern commodities combines with real wage resistance in the North to imply that prices in the North are not determined independently of prices in the South. Murshed and Sen examine the effects of various 'exogenous' (to the model) changes, suggested by the experience of the last forty years. Productivity increases North or South confer gains on the North; but only productivity increases in the North can benefit the South, via improved terms of trade. Northern protection can have deleterious effects upon both North and South. Expansionary policies confer output gains in the North and increase prices North and South. Contractionary policies in the North imply smaller costs of disinflation for the North than these costs would be were it not for the fact that some of the costs are carried, though lower terms of trade, by the South. Over time, a tendency for real wages to rise (and for real wage resistance to stiffen) in the North, is shown to be consistent with the apparent secular decline[17] in the terms of trade of the South.

From a broader standpoint, and focussing more on the experience of the 1970's and the 1980's, it should be noted that the model of chapter nine abstracts from capital movements and hence from a set of conspicuously important aspects of North-South economic relations in recent years.[18] On the other hand, capital movements play a key role in the analysis of experience in the 1980's of the major industrial countries (the G-3), presented in *chapter ten*, by Paul R. Masson and Malcolm Knight.

Unusually high (though changing over time both in levels and in differentials between countries) real interest rates, large movements in the dollar (as already mentioned above in connection with chapter three), and large current account imbalances (with the US in persistent deficit and Japan and Germany in persistent surplus), mark the international scene of the major

16. Notably Taylor, L., *Structuralist Macroeconomics*, (New York: Basic Books, 1983).

17. See, for example, Spraos, J., 'The Statistical Debate on the Net Barter Terms of Trade Between Primary Commodities and Manufacturers', *Economic Journal*, Vol. 90, 1980, pp. 107-128; and Evans, D., 'The Long Run Determinants of North-South Terms of Trade and Some Recent Empirical Evidence', *World Development*, Vol. 15, 1987, pp. 657-671.

18. See, for example, Van Wijnbergen, S., 'Interdependence Revisited: A Developing Countries Perspective on Macroeconomic Management and Trade Policy in the Industrial World', *Economic Policy*, Vol. 1, 1985, pp. 81-137.

OECD economies in the 1980's. Masson and Knight examine how in principle, and to what extent in fact, these aspects of recent experience can be said to follow the major shifts in fiscal stance recorded during this period in the US, Japan, and Germany. They show that, under plausible assumptions (regarding particularly savings and investment behaviour), a simple classical model of savings and investment, capital transfers and net exports, yields a pattern of medium run (comparative static) responses to changes in government deficits and private desired investment expenditures that is qualitatively consistent with the exchange rate and current account patterns described, while if these autonomous changes are sufficiently large they will also induce corresponding movements in real interest rates world wide. Empirical estimates – drawn from an extended version of the model, which with a view to the long-run also allows for the accumulation of assets that are the counterparts of the flows emphasized in the simple model – suggest that the behavioural characteristics necessary to render the desired pattern of responses are consistent with the data. Moreover, simulations of the combined effects of tax incentives for increased US investment and of movements in inflation-adjusted deficits in all three countries, suggest that interest rate and exchange rate movements in the 1980's were importantly related to shifts in fiscal policy.

The Setting of Policy in the Open Economy

With regard to policy design, much emphasis in recent years has been placed on the significance of private agents perceptions of future policy, and, similarly, at the international level, on perceptions between governments about each others policy strategies. Policy credibility, reputation, choices of rules versus discretion, more generally 'game-theoretic' aspects of policy design, (always perhaps in the conscious of policy makers), have moved from the status of afterthought and footnote qualifications, or the fringe, which they have previously occupied in analytical treatments of policy, to hold the centre of the stage.

In *chapter eleven*, Patrick Minford draws attention to various limitations of existing treatments of policy credibility in open economies, and then proceeds to develop an empirical model of government behaviour that, like private behaviour, is derived from maximising principles. The model, being solved alongwith the model of private behaviour, assumes that the government is a Stackelberg leader, that both the government and the private sector have rational expectations, and that both know the full model (including the government's preferences and constraints). Governments can choose between two types of plan, discretionary or pre-committed; but rational expectations rules out time inconsistent strategies, since everyone knows the circumstances under which the government will find it in its interests to 'renege' and so any plan containing such circumstances will not be viable. Thus, in any pre-commitment the government also specifies the punishments to be inflicted upon it for deviant behaviour, and these punishments are taken into account by private agents in computing what the government will actually do in pursuing its own objectives. In this way, Minford notes, one and only one (entirely credible) strategy will be optimal chosen and of course, expected. The paper presents estimates, for the UK, based on the Liverpool model, of the differences between pre-committed and discretionary strategies, and shows how party affiliation matters by contrasting the policy choices of two parties, each bent to maximize a weighted average of the utilities of its supporters and of floating voters, where one party's support is drawn from 'workers' and the other's from 'capitalists'.

With pre-commitment defined as a manifesto undertaking to pursue some particular policy for four years, subject to penalties for digression, and with discretion as the option to set policy as the government chooses in each of the four years, according to the circumstances of the time, Minford shows that the welfare of both parties is higher under pre-committed than under discretionary policies. The contrast with what we presume to be true of reality, he explains, is more apparent than real; since historically discretion has in fact been the exception rather than the rule. As for the costs of pre-commitment, these relate partly to provisions for monitoring and punishing, where a government makes arrangements of the 'nailing itself on the mast' kind, and partly to loss of flexibility of response which is not total but rather involves surrendering some of the potential freedom to the judgement of the moritoring agency—viz public opinion (the electorate), or some supranational body or international agreement (the IMF or the EMS). As an example of such pre-commitment Minford cites the UK Medium Term Financial Strategy. The government survived overruns in the monetary target and convenient re-definitions in the public sector borrowing requirement as it was able to deliver its 'lower inflation' pledge.

One particular kind of monetary 'overrun', we are reminded by Emmanuel Pikoulakis in *chapter twelve*, will in general be desirable to entertain in the context of a policy that involves a lower rate of growth of the money stock with a view to reducing inflation. For if this policy is not to cause overshooting of the real exchange rate and loss of output, the announced reduction of *the rate of growth* of the money stock ought to be coupled with an immediate increase in *the level* of the nominal money stock, so as to meet the increased demand for real money balances that the reduction in the anticipated rate of inflation entails.

The credibility problem inherent in such a strategy is obvious. Yet, this problem Pikoulakis argues can be overcome if the authorities announce and pursue a policy that combines a reduction in the rate of growth of the domestic ('core') component of the money stock together with a (McKinnon-like)[19] commitment to engage in non-sterilized intervention at whatever nominal exchange rate yields a real exchange rate equal to the long-run equilibrium real exchange rate. Such 'an adjustable PPP policy', he explains, implies that the money supply is perfectly elastic at the targeted exchange rate, being fully accommodating to the demand for real money balances, so that the disinflation policy involves no output loss.

The implications of credibility/reputation for international policy coordination are examined by David Currie and Ullrich Hoffmeyer in *chapter thirteen*. They analyse the joint setting of fiscal and monetary policies in a two country, strictly symmetric, natural rate world. Policies can be cooperative or non-cooperative, reputational or non-reputational. Focussing on the four (symmetric across countries) of the eight possible regimes that different combinations of those two aspects of policy define, they show that on a common criterion for evaluating the relative success of the chosen policies, cooperation and reputation are mutually dependent. A complete breakdown of both cooperational and reputational forces may, in certain circumstances, lead to better outcomes than a partial breakdown.

In the setting of fiscal policy, in particular, Currie and Hoffmeyer find that non-cooperative relations between governments with ambitious targets encourage too high levels of government spending, as governments seek beneficial supply side effects through real exchange appreciation induced by fiscal expansion. The absence of reputation exacerbates this overspending bias. On the other hand reputation is not unambiguously desirable, since governments that discount the future heavily may act in a way that destabilizes the system.

The analysis presented in this chapter also provides some useful pointers on how best to cooperate in the setting of monetary and fiscal policy. In practice, Currie and Hoffmeyer note, we observe cooperation in monetary

19. McKinnon, R. I., *An International Standard for Monetary Stabilisation*, (Washington: Institute for International Economics, 1984), and 'Monetary and Exchange Rate Policies for International Financial Stability; A Proposal', *Journal of Economic Perspectives*, Vol. 2, 1988, pp. 83-103. Some of the comments by Dornbusch and Williamson that follow the 1988 McKinnon paper (op. cit, pp. 105-119) are also revelant to the Pikoulakis story.

policy, but not so much in fiscal policy – the EMS countries being a case in point, both with regard to the last ten years and with regard to near future intentions.[20] Yet, the analysis in this paper emphasizes the key role of fiscal policy coordination. In the absence of reputation, the authors argue, it might be most advantageous to coordinate fiscal policy while setting monetary policy non-cooperatively.

Many of the themes that run through the rest of the book re-surface in *chapter fourteen*. In this last chapter of the book, Frederick van der Ploeg: (i) provides new empirical evidence on real and nominal wage rigidity in the seven major OECD economies; (ii) develops a useful diagrammatic exposition or spill-over effects of fiscal, monetary and supply side policies in a two country model with floating exchange rates, perfect capital mobility and real and/or nominal wage rigidity; (iii) analyses in a game-theoretic context the nature of the bias in economic policies arising from lack of international policy co-ordination; and (iv) examines the effects of an oil shock in a two country model with real wage rigidity at home and nominal wage rigidity abroad.

At the empirical level van der Ploeg's results reveal that real wage rigidity cannot be rejected for France, Germany, Italy and Japan, whereas the UK, the US and Canada display a significant degree of nominal wage rigidity. At the analytical level it is shown, in the context of a two country model with floating rates, uncovered interest parity, and imperfect substitution between home and foreign goods, that the nature of the labour markets is crucial for policy design. If both countries have nominal wage rigidity, lack of coordination leads to monetary policy being too loose, fiscal policy being too tight, and supply-side improvements that are too far reaching. If both countries have real wage rigidity, lack of coordination leads to fiscal policy being too loose, and to tax wedges that are too high. If we take Europe to have real wage rigidity and the US to have nominal wage rigidity, as the empirical evidence presented suggests, then US monetary policy is too tight while the US fiscal stance is too loose. As for the European fiscal stance, that is too tight as far as US welfare is concerned, while in terms of European welfare it is too loose.

20. See, for instance, Tanzi and Ter-Minassian, in S. Cnossen (ed), *Tax Coordination in the European Community* (London: Kluwer Law and Taxation Publishers, 1987); Delors Report, *Report on Economic and Monetary Union in the European Community*, (EC, April 1989); and R. Portes and J. Vinals (eds), *The European Monetary System in Transition*, (London : Centre for Economic Policy Research, 1989).

Background and Acknowledgements

Earlier versions of six of these papers were presented at the 16th *Money Study Group – Oxford Conference*, as usual organized by me and held at Brasenose College, Oxford. The remainder were solicited by Mark Taylor and myself. All papers were refereed for publication in the *Greek Economic Review* whence they are reprinted. On behalf of the Money Study Group, the Greek Economic Review, and the Editors of this volume, I wish to thank the referees for their assessments, and the authors for their cooperation in revising their papers for publication. My thanks are also due to Verra Rodis of the Greek Economic Review, and to Anna Zaranko and Andrew Schuller of Oxford University Press for their kind support and for their efficiency in dealing with production matters.

Brasenose College and Institute of Economics and Statistics, University of Oxford.

PART I
THE EXCHANGE RATE ENVIRONMENT

INTERNATIONAL PARITY CONDITIONS

By Ronald MacDonald and Mark P. Taylor*

I. INTRODUCTION

Economic reasoning ultimately depends on formulating some kind of economic model. This is ultimately true of even the most hard-nosed practitioners in the business and financial world – this was the message of Keynes' now famous words concerning 'practical men of affairs'. Economic models, in turn, have to start somewhere, with some 'self-evident truths' which can be used as the foundations for a theory. Perhaps one of the clearest examples in economics are the axioms of consumer choice theory (see e.g. Varian (1978)). In international monetary economics, a set of international parity relationships is often used much as an axiom set, particularly in deriving empirical models. For example, most international monetarists would argue that some form of purchasing power parity (PPP) is a *prediction* of monetarist analysis; yet, on deriving empirical models of the exchange rate, early, flex-price monetary analyses (MacDonald and Taylor (1988)) generally use PPP much as an axiom. Later, sticky-price monetary models generally treat uncovered interest parity and long-rum purchasing power parity in much the same way.

This paper is concerned with the empirical evidence for a number of international parity conditions – namely, covered and uncovered interest rate parity, real interest rate parity and purchasing power parity. Whilst much of what follows is a straightforward survey of the existing literature, we also present some new evidence on covered interest rate parity, using high-quality, high-frequency data, and on real interest rate parity, using vector autoregressions.

II. COVERED INTEREST RATE PARITY

If foreign exchange markets are operating efficiently then arbitrage should ensure that the covered interest differential on similar assets

* Any views expressed in this paper are those of the authors and are not necessarily those of the Bank of England.

denominated in different currencies be continually equal to zero – i.e., covered interest rate parity should hold. In any computation of covered interest parity (CIP) it is clearly important to consider home and foreign assets which are comparable in terms of maturity and also in terms of other characteristics, such as default and political risk. For example, Aliber (1973) has argued that considering 90-day treasury bills may introduce a bias into the computation of interest parity since such assets are liable to sovereign, or political, risk – e.g. the possibility that the foreign country may impose exchange controls before the bill matures. Thus, in computing covered interest differentials, assets should be considered which do not suffer from sovereign risk; euro-assets are regarded as free of sovereign risk.

Essentially two types of tests of covered interest parity have been conducted. The first relies on computing the actual deviations from interest parity to see if they differ 'significantly' from zero. The significance level is usually defined with respect to a neutral band, which is determined by transaction costs. Thus, Frenkel and Levich (hereafter FL) (1975) distinguish four types of *transaction* costs associated with a covered outflow: the transaction cost of selling a domestic security; the transaction costs associated with the purchase of spot foreign exchange; the transaction costs of forward cover; and the transaction costs of buying a foreign security. (FL calculated foreign exchange costs as deviations from the triangular arbitrage condition, and the total cost of transacting in securities was computed to be 2.5 times the ask-bid spread.) These costs give an upper and a lower band within which deviations from covered interest parity do not conflict with efficiency. For the period January 1962-November 1967, FL find that 85 per cent of apparent profit opportunities are within the neutral band when one considers treasury bill interest rates (UK-US and Canada-US) and almost 100 per cent lie within the neutral band when euro-rates are considered (euro-dollar vis-a-vis euro-sterling). FL concur with Aliber that the higher deviations from interest parity discovered using the treasury bill rates may be due to sovereign risk, but they also argue that the residual can alternatively be explained by a time differential between observing a profit opportunity and the execution of the arbitrage activity, or in terms of arbitrage elasticity schedules which are less than infinite. In a further paper, Frenkel and Levich (1977) apply the analysis of the neutral band to three different time periods, which they categorise as: 'the tranquil pegged exchange rate period' (January 1962-November 1967); the 'turbulent pegged exchange rate period' (1968-1969); and 'the managed float period' (1973-1975). Using the methodology of FL (1975), neutral bands are calculated for these three separate periods and it is shown that the tranquil and managed float periods exhibit similar characteristics, with over 80 per cent of the deviations for the treasury bills considered within the neutral band and almost 100 per cent for the euro-rates; however, for the turbulent period a much smaller percentage of the deviations is explained in terms of transaction costs and this is regarded as a reflection of the financial uncertainty in the period.

FL's results, however, depend crucially on the method used to calculate their transaction costs and McCormick (1971) has shown that if one uses 'better' quality data, most of the deviations from interest parity for UK-US treasury bills lie *outside* the neutral band (70%-80%). Taylor (1987a, 1988a) goes further than McCormick and argues that in order to provide a true test of CIP it is important to have data on the appropriate exchange rates and interest rates recorded at the same instant in time and at which a trader could have dealt. Taylor (1987a) analyses a data set, collected personally in the London foreign exchange market during three days in November 1985, covering ten-minute contemporaneous observations of brokers' quotations on spot and forward dollar-sterling and dollar-mark exchange rates and the appropriate euro-deposit rates, for maturities of one, three, six and twelve months maturities. Calculations are then made as to the profitability of arbitrage from any one of the currencies into either of the other two for all maturities. In the course of 3,456 covered arbitrage calculations (144 data points, six different borrowing-lending combinations, four maturities) only one, very tiny, profit opportunity is observed, which is more than accounted for by brokerage costs. In a further paper, Taylor (1988a) carries out the same sort of analysis for a number of historical periods known to have introduced uncertainty and turbulence into the markets. The data base consists of high-quality, contemporaneous recordings of dollar-sterling spot and forward rates and the appropriate euro-deposit rates, recorded by the dealers at the Bank of England three times a day, for a number of weeks around the following 'news' events: the 1967 devaluation of sterling, the 1972 flotation of sterling, the 1979 UK general election, the 1979 inception of the European Monetary System, and the 1987 UK general election. In addition, the 1984 US presidential election is used as a 'quiet', control period: Reagan's re-election was largely discounted and no major news items occurred during this sample period. The results indicate that tiny, profitable arbitrage opportunities do occasionally occur during turbulent periods (no profitable opportunities are observed during the control period), even after allowing for brokerage costs. In addition, Taylor identifies a 'maturity effect'– the frequency, size and persistence of profitable arbitrage opportunities appear to be an increasing function of the length of maturity of the underlying financial instruments. This is itself something of a paradox – one cannot appeal to a Hicksian notion of liquidity preference to explain this 'term structure' of arbitrage opportunities since no actual endowments of funds are required and no significant risk is involved on pure covered interest arbitrage. Taylor offers a rationale for the maturity effect in terms of banks' prudential credit limits. Banks will generally have an internal limit, laid down by the management, with respect to the outstanding credit exposure it wishes to have with any other bank at any point in time. Once these limits are 'full', dealers have to wait until outstanding assets mature before any further trading can take place with the bank or banks in question. This may effectively operate as a budget constraint on dealers; they will therefore prefer to operate in the 'short end' of the market in order to avoid filling up credit limits for extended periods of time. Moreover, if dealers wish to keep a certain amount of 'credit liquidity' in order to be able to take advantage of exceptional arbitrage opportunities which they believe may arise from time to time, they may even ignore small profit opportunities which they believe to be available in the long term maturities. The largest arbitrage opportunities identified by Taylor (1988a) were generally less than one per cent.

Another method for empirically testing the validity of covered interest parity is with the aid of regression analysis. Thus, if covered interest parity holds, and in the absence of transactions costs, estimation of equation (1)

$$f_t - s_t = \alpha + \beta(i - i^*)_t \tag{1}$$

(where s_t is the logarithm of the spot rate (domestic price of foreign currency), f_t is the logarithm of forward rate at time t for maturity a certain number of periods ahead, and i_t and i_t^* denote domestic and foreign interest rates on appropriate financial assets of same maturity as the forward rate), should result in the constant, α, being insignificantly different from zero and the slope coefficient, β, being insignificantly different from unity. In the presence of FL-type transaction costs, α is expected to be significant and should capture the mean transaction costs over the estimated period.

Branson (1969) tests equation (1) for the UK-US and Canada-US using treasury bill rates for the period July 1962-December 1964. For the former relationship Branson cannot reject the null hypothesis of $\alpha = 0$ and $\beta = 1$, but for the latter he finds the constant to be significant and the value of the slope coefficient to be less than unity. In the light of our previous discussion it is important to note that Branson uses treasury bill rates in his computations. A series of papers by Marston (1976), Cosandier and Laing (1981) and Fratianni and Wakeman (1982) test equation (1) using Euro-deposit rates. For example, Fratianni and Wakeman test equation (1) for six Euro-rates vis-a-vis the Euro-dollar, using three maturities (one, three and six months), for the period 1967-1978. They find that for 13 out of 18 cases α is significantly positive and β is insignificantly different from unity. The estimated value of α gives a measure of transaction costs which is supportive of FL's estimate. Fratianni and Wakeman do not, however, find support for the FL distinction between 'tranquil' and 'turbulent' periods.

As noted by Taylor (1987a, 1988a), however, it is not clear what regression-based analyses of CIP are actually testing. It may be that the researcher cannot reject the hypothesis that $\alpha = 0$ and $\beta = 1$ in equation (1) but that the fitted residuals themselves represent substantial arbitrage opportunities. The value of regression-based tests can only lie in being able to determine whether or not CIP has held *on average* over a particular period—and therefore, for example, whether it is reasonable to assume CIP in models of exchange rate determination; they can tell us very little about market efficiency.

A novel application of the CIP concept has been given by a number of researchers trying to determine whether, in a regime of monetary targetting, monetary overshoots result in a change in the real interest rate—the so-called policy anticipation effect (see Cornell (1983)) - or leave it unaffected— the Fisher hypothesis. Thus researchers in the US (see Cornell (1983)) and UK (see MacDonald and Torrance (1987)) have documented that short term normal interest rates unambiguously rise after the announcement of a monetary overshoot, which is consistent with both the policy anticipation view and the Fisher hypothesis. One way of discriminating between the two hypothesis is to examine the effect of a monetary overshoot on the spot exchange rate (see Engel and Frankel (1982)): if the spot rate appreciates this supports the policy anticipation effect (higher real interest rates), but if it depreciates this is supportive of the Fisher effect (real interest rates constant, expected inflation higher). If monetary overshoots are associated with movements in short-term interest rates and exchange rates then this implies that there may be a change in the CIP relationship after a monetary movement. Husted and Kitchen (1985) test this hypothesis for the US experience with monetary targetting and found that US money surprises are associated with increases in the forward premium of the Canadian dollar and the German mark against the US dollar, and also that the pattern of response is in conformity with CIP. Similar results are reported for part of the UK experience with monetary targets by MacDonald and

Torrance (1988c): an unanticipated increase in UK money (sterling M3) results in an increase in the domestic interest rate and an increase in the forward discount on the sterling-dollar rate. Interestingly, the latter authors' results suggest that CIP does not hold exactly following a monetary shock (although this hypothesis in not tested formally).

II.1 *Some Additional Evidence on Covered Interest Rate Parity*

In this section we present some additional empirical evidence on CIP using high-frequency, high-quality data and following the approach of Taylor (1987a, 1988a). We use thrice-daily contemporaneous data (7.30 a.m., 12.00 noon and 4.00 p.m. London time) on dollar-sterling spot and forward rates and Euro-dollar and Euro-sterling interest rates for one, two, three, six and twelve months maturities. These data were recorded by dealers at the Bank of England during the period surrounding the famous 'Plaza Accord' of the weekend of 21-22 September 1985 when the finance ministers of the 'Group of Five' (Britain, France, USA, Germany and Japan) announced their intention to stem further rises in the dollar. The data set covers the period from Tuesday 17 September to Thursday 26 September (excluding the weekend).

In other to test CIP, we used the 'no-profit conditions' discussed in Taylor (1988a). These are derived as follows. Let the superscripts B and O denote 'bid' and 'offer'. Then $i_{\pounds}^{B}$ will be the (annualised) interest rate available in the market for placements of Euro-sterling deposits for, say, D days. Similarly, $i_{\pounds}^{o}$ will be the rate at which Euro-sterling can be borrowed for D days, with the D-day dollar rates $i_{\$}^{B}$ and $i_{\$}^{o}$ defined similarly. We denote the spot bid and offer dollar-sterling rates (dollars per pound) as S^{B} and S^{o} (so S^{B} is the spot market bid for sterling) and the corresponding D-day forward rates as F^{B} and F^{o}.

It is easy to establish that covered arbitrage from sterling to dollars (i.e. borrow sterling, lend dollars) will be unprofitable when the following inequality holds:

$$\frac{S^{B}}{F^{o}}\left(1+i_{\$}^{B}\frac{D}{360}\right)\leqslant\left(1+i_{\pounds}^{o}\frac{D}{365}\right) \qquad (2)$$

The left-hand side of (2) gives the sterling value of the maturing dollar asset where dollars have been lent at an annualised interest rate of $i_{\$}^{B}$ for D days.

The right hand side of the inequality is the value of the maturing sterling liability, where pounds have been borrowed at an annualised rate of $i_{£}^{0}$ for D days. Note that (2) reflects the peculiarly British habit of basing interest payments on a 365-day basis, as opposed to the more usual 360 days.

Similarly, covered arbitrage from dollars to sterling will be unprofitable whenever inequality (3) holds :

$$\frac{F^B}{S^0}\left(1+i_{£}^{B}\frac{D}{365}\right) \leqslant \left(1+i_{\$}^{0}\frac{D}{360}\right) \tag{3}$$

The actual calculations carried out to test CIP are slight variants of (2) and (3), viz :

$$\$\text{ Return} = 100\left\{\frac{S^B}{F^0}\left((1+i_{\$}^{B}\frac{D}{360}\right)-\left(1+i_{£}^{0}\frac{D}{365}\right)\right\} \tag{4}$$

$$£\text{ Return} = 100\left\{\frac{F^B}{S^0}\left(1+i_{£}^{B}\frac{D}{365}\right)-\left(1+i_{\$}^{0}\frac{D}{360}\right)\right\} \tag{5}$$

Thus, (4) gives the percentage period return in sterling from arbitraging from sterling to dollars. For example, if (4) is equal to x, then a profit of £Nx/100 could have been realised from arbitraging an amount £N in this way. Similarly, (5) is the percentage period return in dollars from arbitraging from dollars to srerling.

The results of analysing the data set using (4) and (5) are given in Table 1. Table 2 gives results of a similar analysis but where allowance has been made for brokerage costs on the taking and placing of deposits (this amounts to subtracting $b\%$ from the bid price and adding $b\%$ to ask the price, with $b = 1/50$ for Euro-dollars and $b = 1/32$ for Euro-sterling).

Tables 1 and 2 are interesting for at least two reasons. First, they show that the markets are generally quite efficient in arbitraging away profitable opportunities-no profitable arbitrage opportunities occur at all in maturities of three months or less. Secondly, they illustrate the 'maturity effect' first noted by Taylor (1988a) and discussed above: no profitable arbitrage opportunities occur in maturities up to and including three months, one or two small profit opportunities occur quite randomly in the six months maturity and larger and more frequent and persistent profit opportunities occur in the twelve months maturity. Although the number of profitable opportunities falls substantially when allowance is made for brokerage costs, they are still reasonably large and persistent. For example, on September 19 1985, between \$1,500 and \$32,000 net of brokerage costs could have been risklessly earned on a \$10mn dollar arbitrage into sterling.

If one accepts Taylor's (1988a) credit constraint argument as a rationalisation of the maturity effect, these results offer qualified support for CIP and market efficiency.

III. UNCOVERED INTEREST RATE PARITY

Subject to one or two qualifications, the discussion and empirical analysis of the previous section suggest that CIP probably holds quite well, at least for Euro-deposit rates. Uncovered interest parity (UIP) is the proposition that the interest differential should be exactly equal to the expected rate of depreciation of the exchange rate. Given CIP, this means that the forward premium should in fact be equal to the expected rate of depreciation. Clearly, this will only hold if market participants are risk-neutral, so that they are indifferent to seeking forward cover so long as the forward premium is equal to the expected depreciation. In the absence of a direct measure of expectations, it is then necessary to formulate an auxiliary hypothesis concerning expectations formulation before UIP becomes testable, and it is usual to assume that expectations are rational. In this case, the forward rate should act as an optimal predictor of the future spot rate. But this of course takes us back to the literature on forward market efficiency which is discussed extensively in MacDonald and Taylor (1988). Thus, tests of efficiency of the forward exchange market can be viewed as *indirect* tests of UIP - *indirect* because they rely on a maintained hypothesis of CIP.

For reasons which are not immediately obvious, *direct* tests of UIP occur relatively infrequently in the literature. Under rational expectations and risk neutrality, such a test would amount to testing the interest differential as an optimal predictor of the rate of depreciation. Such a test might, for example, involving estimating a regression relationship of the form

$$s_t = \alpha_0 s_{t-n} + \alpha_1 (i - i^*)_{t-n} + v_t \tag{6}$$

where the joint hypothesis of risk neutrality and the rationality of expectations implies that α_0 and α_1 should equal minus and plus unity respectively, and that v_t should be a stochastic process, orthogonal to past information.

Hacche and Townend (1981) test equation (6) for sterling's effective exchange rate over the period July 1972-February 1980 and find that the *a priori* constraints on α_0 and α_1 are supported by the data. The error orthogonality property was not, however, supported by the data: lagged values of Domestic Credit Expansion and the change in the exchange rate proved to be statistically significant (similar results for the sterling dollar rate, February 1973 - December 1980, are reported in Davidson (1985)). Similarly, Loopesko (1984), in testing the error orthogonality property found that it did not hold for the majority of currencies studied. Taylor (1987b) tests UIP using the bivariate vector autoregression (BVAR) approach used, for example, by Hakkio (1981) in testing forward market efficiency. He uses a data base covering spot and forward dollar exchange rates against the French franc, Italian lira, Dutch guilder, German mark, UK sterling and Japanese yen, as well as the appropriate Euro-deposit rates, for six and twelve months maturities for the period July 1979 to December 1986. UIP is easily rejected in both maturities for all exchange rates with the exception of dollar mark. Similar results are obtained using German mark and UK sterling bilateral rates (constructed assuming triangular arbritrage conditions), except that UIP cannot be rejected for sterling-lire in either maturity.

Cumby and Obstfeld (1981) estimate whether the error term v_t in equation (6) is in fact white noise when $n=1$ by using Box-Pierce and likelihood ratio tests on $[s_t - s_{t-1} - (i - i^*)_{t-1}]$ for six bilateral-dollar exchange rates (weekly data for the period 5 July 1974 to 27 June 1980). For only one exchange market, the UK pound-US dollar, is it demonstrated that the residuals are white. Cumby and Obstfeld rationalise these deviations from UIP by suggesting the existence of a variable risk premium (a further rejection of UIP is given in Cumby and Obstfeld (1984)). However, as is discussed in Chapter 1, when the joint hypothesis of efficiency is rejected, it is generally impossible to discern whether it is due to the irrationality of market participants, to the existence of a risk premium or to some other factor such as the limited information set available to agents. The way round this problem would be to utilise survey data as suggested for the tests of forward market efficiency (see Chapter 1). Thus, deviations of α_1 from unity in (6) may be decomposed into a component due to risk aversion and that due to irrationality. MacDonald and Torrance (1988d) utilise this decomposition and find, using four bilateral dollar currencies (the British pound, the German mark, the Swiss franc and the Japanese yen) that deviations of α_1 from unity for the early 1980's are explained in terms of both risk and 'irrationality'.

In an attempt to extract the risk premium for the serially correlated errors reported by Cumby and Obstfeld a number of researchers have conducted their UIP tests in an alternative way. For example, in MacDonald and Taylor

(1988) it was noted that if capital is less than perfectly mobile, due perhaps to the imperfect substitutability of non-money assets, then UIP would not hold continuously and equation (6) should be replaced with an equation such as

$$A = \beta(i - i^* - \Delta s^e) \tag{7}$$

where A is the proportion of domestic assets, B, to the domestic value of foreign assets, SF, held by domestic residents. Thus, in the PBM, the investor is assumed to balance his portfolio among the assets of different countries as a function of their expected relative return. If the supply of, say, home country assets increases, either the domestic rate of interest will have to rise or the currency must be expected to appreciate, for the asset to be willingly held. Thus, if assets are imperfect substitutes, relative demand should be systematically related to expected returns. If, however, assets are perfect substitutes then we are back in a world in which UIP holds continuously. Empirical tests of whether assets are imperfect substitutes is clearly interesting since it enables discrimination between the portfolio balance and monetary approaches to exchange rate determination (see MacDonald Taylor (1988)). In order to test the substitutability of home and foreign assets the hypothesised portfolio balance relationship is inverted to yield, for country j:

$$i - i^* - \Delta s^e = \beta^{-1}(B_j / SF_j) \tag{8}$$

and, further, by assuming expectations are formed rationally we may substiture $\Delta s + u$ for Δs^e (where u is the forecast error) and obtain

$$(i - i^* - \Delta s) = \beta^{-1}(B_j / SF_j) + u \tag{9}$$

A further assumption needs to be made before (9) can be empirically implemented: namely, the identity of the investors whose portfolios we are examining. Frankel (1983) lists three possible assumptions concerning portfolio preferences. First, if residents of each country in the world have the same portfolio preferences, and if the market under consideration is the whole world, then the B and F are simply net domestic government indebtedness and net foreign government indebtedness, respectively. Such a view of portfolio choice, classified in the literature as uniform preference, implies that the indebtedness of residents of one country to residents of another has no effect. A second assumption concerning preferences, used in the studies by Branson *et al.* (1977) is that the domestic country is small, foreign residents do not hold domestic bonds, and thus the risk premium is determined only by home residents. Finally, it is presumably more realistic to allow residents in both countries to hold assets issued by both countries. Such models are usually classed as 'preferred habitat' models because domestic residents in each country are assumed to hold a greater proportion of their wealth in domestic assets. For example, if the j's in (9) consist of residents in the UK, US and the rest of the world (ROW), if $\beta = \mathrm{a} + b$ and if the UK is the home country, we have

$$B_{UK} / SF_{UK} = \mathrm{a}_{UK} + b(i - i^* - \Delta s^e) \tag{10}$$

$$B_{US} / SF_{US} = \mathrm{a}_{US} + b(i - i^* - \Delta s^e) \tag{11}$$

$$B_{ROW} / SF_{ROW} = \mathrm{a}_{ROW} + b(i - i^* - \Delta s^e) \tag{12}$$

Unfortunately, the lack of available data at a sufficiently disaggregated level precludes the estimation of (10)-(12) separately. A specification suitable for estimation can however, be obtained by aggregating the equations in (10)-(12) and multiplying through by W_j / W (the share of world wealth held by residents of country j):

$$\begin{aligned}(B_{UK} + B_{US} + B_{ROW}) / W = {} & \mathrm{a}_{ROW} + (\mathrm{a}_{UK} - \mathrm{a}_{ROW})(W_{UK} / W) \\ & + (\mathrm{a}_{US} - \mathrm{a}_{ROW})(W_{US} / W) + b(i - i^* - \Delta s^e)\end{aligned} \tag{13}$$

assuming rational expectations, by inversion of (13) we get

$$\begin{aligned}(i - i^* - \Delta s) = {} & \mathrm{a}_{ROW} / b + 1 / b\,[(B_{UK} + B_{US} + B_{ROW}) / W] \\ & - [(\mathrm{a}_{UK} - \mathrm{a}_{ROW}) / b]\,(W_{UK} / W) + [(\mathrm{a}_{ROW} - \mathrm{a}_{US}) / b](W_{US} / W) + u\end{aligned} \tag{14}$$

where: the coefficient, $1/b$, is positive, reflecting the presumption that an increase in the relative supply of UK bonds requires, on portfolio balance grounds, either an increase in the home interest rate or an expected exchange rate appreciation; the coefficient on UK wealth is expected to be negative, because an increase in W_{UK} increases the relative demand for home assets (the preferred habitat assumption) necessitating a lower expected return on pounds if the outstanding stock of bonds is to be willingly held; the coefficient on W_{US} is expected to be positive because an increase in US wealth leads to a decreased net demand for UK bonds (preferred habitat assumption) necessitating a higher expected return on UK bonds if the supply is to be willingly held.

Notice that the uniform preference version of the portfolio balance model is captured in (14) by setting $\alpha_{UK} - \alpha_{ROW} = \alpha_{US}$. Versions of (14) have been estimated by a number of researchers for the recent floating experience. For example, Dooley and Isard (1982) test the uniform preference version of equation (14) for the German mark-US dollar over the period 1973-78 (quarterly data) and report insignificant coefficients and that only a small part of the discrepancy between $i - i^*$ and Δs can be explained by risk factors (as defined in (14)). In a further paper, Dooley and Isard (1982) relax the uniform preference assumption and (14) is tested again for the mark-dollar rate, but the resulting estimates of the risk premium are still capable of explaining only a small part of observed changes in exchange rates. Frankel (1982) also estimates the uniform preference and preferred habitat versions of equation (14) for the German mark-US dollar January 1974-October 1978 and reports that 'Many regressions were run... [but] no coefficients appeared significantly different from zero'.

A representative estimate of equation (14) from Frankel (1982) is reported here as equation (15):

$$\underset{}{i_G - i_{US} - \Delta s} = \underset{(0.15)}{0.152} - \underset{(0.91)}{0.744}\, B/W + \underset{(0.35)}{0.152}\, W_G/W - \underset{(0.09)}{0.064}\, W_{US}/W \tag{15}$$

$R^2 = 0.05 \qquad DW = 1.82$

where standard errors are in parentheses, and G subscript denotes Germany. Notice that all the coefficients in this equation are 'incorrectly' signed and insignificant. Frankel (1982, 1983) develops equation (14) further by using an insight from finance theory-namely that the parameters in asset demand functions such as (14) depend not only on the degree of risk-aversion but also on the conditional covariance matrix of returns. For example, in terms of equation (7), β should equal $[\rho\Omega]^{-1}$ (see Frankel (1985) for a deviation) and thus

$$A = [\rho\Omega]^{-1}\,(i - i^* - \Delta s^e) \tag{16}$$

where ρ is the Arrow-Pratt measure of relative risk aversion and Ω is the (conditional) covariance matrix of relative rates of return. Failure to account for this factor in estimates of (14) will give results which are biased against the PBM. But the incorporation of the variance term into equation (7) did not lead to a rejection of the null hypothesis of perfect substitutability by Frankel. Rogoff (1984) replicates Frankel's study, using weekly data for the Canadian dollar-US dollar, but also reports a statistically insignificant relationship.

It is worth noting that equation (16) has an important implication for the magnitude of the risk premium. The coefficient ρ has been estimated to be around 2 in size and Ω around 0.001 for a single asset (see Frankel (1985)). On inverting (16) it is clear that an one percent increase in the relative supply of bonds requires a 0.002 percent rise in the risk premium. Thus, with monthly data, this implies a rise in the risk premium of only 0.024 on a per annum basis (i.e. 2.4 basis points), which is clearly insignificant in magnitude compared to per annum interest rate differentials.

Although studies testing for the existence of a risk premium generally fail to reject the null hypothesis of perfect asset substitutability, it is important to note, following Frankel (1982), the obvious point that failure to reject a hypothesis is not the same as acceptance. Indeed, tests of equation (14) are likely to have very low power to reject a false null hypothesis because of the variability of the error term, representing unexpected exchange rate changes or 'news'. News is an important feature of foreign exchange markets (and has indeed been an empirical regularity of the recent floating experience – see Mussa (1979)) and thus perhaps the risk premium and news should be modelled jointly. Although the error term in equation (14) reflects expectational errors, the actual regression errors may consist of expectational errors *plus* measurement or specification error if there have been errors in the measurement of the right hand side variables, or if the asset demand equations have not been correctly specified. Further, the error term may be correlated with the right hand side variables if simultaneity is an issue (if the asset equations have been correctly specified and expectations are rational then even if the regressors are endogenous they should be uncorrelated with the error term because they are known at the time expectations are formed). To the extent that there are simultaneity and errors in variables problems, least squares estimates of (14) are likely to be biased and inconsistent.

IV. REAL INTEREST RATE PARITY

Although in much of our discussion hitherto, nominal intesert rates have been the focus of attention, it is perhaps real interest rates which are of most relevance for policy purposes. For example, savings and investment in an open economy depend crucially upon the real interest rate. If policy makers use monetary policy to influence economic activity it is the real rate they must affect. But can they? Consider the familiar Fisher closed conditions, *ex ante* purchasing power parity and UIP–equations (17) - (20):

$$r_t = i_t - \Delta p^e_{t+1} \tag{17}$$

$$r^*_t = i^*_t - \Delta p^{e*}_{t+1} \tag{18}$$

$$\Delta s^e_{t+1} = \Delta p^e_{t+1} - \Delta p^{e*}_{t+1} \tag{19}$$

$$\Delta s^e_{t+1} = i_t - i^*_t \tag{20}$$

where r denotes the real interest rate, p the logarithm of the price level and an asterisk denotes a foreign variable.

Equations (17) and (18) simply *define* the real interest rate as equal to the nominal rate payable for money lent now for a certain period less the expected erosion in the value of money (i.e. the expected inflation rate) over the same period. Equation (19) is the *ex ante* version of purchasing power parity–that the expected exchange rate depreciation over a period should be equal to expected inflation differential over the same period (see e.g. Huang (1987)). Equation (20) is, of course, the simple UIP condition.

By combining (17)-(20) we obtain

$$r_t = r^*_t \tag{21}$$

Thus, given these assumptions, real interest rates must be equalised across countries and the scope for the policy maker to alter real economic activity by changing the real interest rate is limited (of course this conclusion is crucially dependent on the restrictive underlying assumptions). Is condition (21) supported empirically? The real interest parity condition (RIP) (21) has been tested by a number of researchers for the US against other OECD countries (see e.g. Mishkin (1981, 1984), Friedman and Schwartz (1982), Von Furstenberg (1983), Cumby and Obstfeld (1984) and Cumby and Mishkin (1984)) and the results indicate a resounding rejection of real interest rate parity. For example, Cumby and Obstfeld (1984) empirically implement (21) by running the following regression

$$\Delta p_{t+1} - \Delta p^*_{t+1} = \mathrm{a} + b(i - i^*)_t + v_{t+1} \tag{21}$$

which is obtained by using (17) and (18) in (21) and by assuming expected inflation rates are formed rationally (i.e. $\Delta p_{t+1} - \Delta p^e_{t+1} = u_{t+1}$ and $\Delta p_{t+1} = \Delta p^e_{t+1} + u_{t+1}$). A test of $a = 0$, $b = 1$ (the null hypothesis) is a test of the equality of expected real interest rates. A sample of Cumby and Obstfeld's results are reported here as (22) and (23):

$$\Delta p_{t+1} - \Delta p^*_{t+1} = \underset{(0.01)}{0.028} + \underset{(0.23)}{0.503}(i - i^*)_t : \text{US-Germany Jan. 1976-Sept. 1981} \quad (22)$$

$$\Delta p_{t+1} - \Delta p^*_{t+1} = \underset{(0.01)}{0.035} + \underset{(0.19)}{0.371}(i - i^*)_t : \text{US-Switz. Jan. 1975-Sept. 1981} \quad (23)$$

where standard errors are in parentheses, the price terms are consumer price indices and the interest rates are Euro rates. For both estimated equations, the null hypothesis is rejected at the 5 per cent level or better. Cumby and Obstfeld (1984) summarise their battery of tests thus: 'The tests demonstrate that *ex ante* real interest rate quality is often rejected decisively over the recent floating exchange rate period'.

IV.1 *Some Additional Evidence on Real Interest Rate Parity*

In this section we present some additional evidence on real interest parity by an application of the bivariate vector autoregression (BVAR) approach which has been used by Hakkio (1981) and others to test efficiency in the forward foreign exchange market. The insight in using this approach is to note that, under RIP, the nominal interest differential should act as an optimal predictor of the differential rate of inflation over the relevant period (given rationality of expectations). Thus, if i_t and i_t^* denote the domestic and foreign nominal interest rates on Euro-deposits for maturity n periods ahead, then under rational expectations, RIP implies

$$E(\Delta_n p_{t+n} - \Delta_n p^*_{t+n} / \Omega_t) = i_t - i^*_t \quad (24)$$

where p and p^* denote the logarithms of the domestic and foreign price levels, Ω_t is the information set available to agents at time t, i and i^* are n-period (as opposed to annualised) nominal interest rates and Δ_n is defined as

$$\Delta_n = (1 - L^n),$$

where the lag operator, L, is implicitly defined by

$$L^n x_t = x_{t-n}\,.$$

In order to apply the BVAR methodology to testing (24) we begin by assuming that the current inflation differential, $\Delta_1(p - p^*)_t$ and the current nominal interest differential $(i - i^*)_t$, together form a jointly determined, linearly indeterministic, covariance stationary process. According to the multivariate form of a standard statistical theorem – Wald's decomposition (Hannan (1970)) – this bivariate process then has a unique, infinite-order moving average representation which can be approximated in finite samples by a j-th order bivariate vector autoregression, for suitably chosen j:

$$\begin{aligned} \Delta_1(p - p^*)_t &= \sum_{i=1}^{j} \alpha_i \Delta_1 (p - p^*)_{t-i} + \sum_{i=1}^{j} \beta_i (i - i^*)_{t-i} + \eta_t \\ (i - i^*)_t &= \sum_{i=1}^{j} \gamma_i \Delta_1 (p - p^*)_{t-i} + \sum_{i=1}^{j} \delta_i (i - i^*)_{t-i} + \varepsilon_t \end{aligned} \tag{25}$$

where $(\eta_t \;\; \varepsilon_t)'$ is a vector white noise process. Under the further assumption that the disturbance vector has a multivariate normal distribution, asymptotically efficient estimates can be obtained by individual application of ordinary least squares.

The system (25) can be expressed in companion form as

$$\begin{bmatrix} \Delta_1(p - p^*)_t \\ \Delta_1(p - p^*)_{t-1} \\ \cdot \\ \cdot \\ \cdot \\ \Delta_1(p - p^*)_{t-j+1} \\ (i - i^*)_t \\ (i - i^*)_{t-1} \\ \cdot \\ \cdot \\ \cdot \\ (i - i^*)_{t-j+1} \end{bmatrix} = \begin{bmatrix} \alpha_1\alpha_2 \;\; \alpha_{j-1} & \alpha_j & \beta_1\beta_2 \;\; \beta_{j-1} & \beta_j \\ & & & \\ I_{n-1} & 0 & 0 & 0 \\ & & & \\ \gamma_1\gamma_2 \;\; \gamma_{j-1} & \gamma_j & \delta_1\delta_2 \;\; \delta_{n-1} & \delta_j \\ & & & \\ 0 & 0 & I_{n-1} & 0 \\ & & & \end{bmatrix} \begin{bmatrix} \Delta_1(p - p^*)_{t-1} \\ \Delta_1(p - p^*)_{t-2} \\ \cdot \\ \cdot \\ \cdot \\ \Delta_1(p - p^*)_{t-j} \\ (i - i^*)_{t-1} \\ (i - i^*)_{t-2} \\ \cdot \\ \cdot \\ \cdot \\ (i - i^*)_{t-j} \end{bmatrix} + \begin{bmatrix} \eta_t \\ \\ 0 \\ \\ \varepsilon_t \\ \\ 0 \\ \\ \end{bmatrix} \tag{26}$$

TABLE 1 (a)

Arbitrage Opportunities

		One Month		Two months		Three months		Six months		Twelve months	
		(£ → $)	($ → £)	(£ → $)	($ → £)	(£ → $)	($ → £)	(£ → $)	($ → £)	(£ → $)	($ → £)
T17/9/85	7.30 am	−0.07280	−0.08351	−0.09329	−0.07030	−0.12182	−0.04153	−0.16116	−0.01677	−0.20885	0.01548
	12 noon	−0.05319	−0.06771	−0.07936	−0.04622	−0.10841	−0.02437	−0.13427	−0.02690	−0.28618	0.109396*
	4 pm	−0.06884	−0.08164	−0.08562	−0.05471	−0.12579	−0.02948	−0.14587	−0.00907	−0.23064	−0.038609*
W18/9/85	7.30 am	−0.06915	−0.08279	−0.07065	−0.08620	−0.08783	−0.07642	−0.13328	−0.04632	−0.27126	0.060409*
	12 noon	−0.07407	−0.08339	−0.09836	−0.05887	−0.11792	−0.02361	−0.15413	−0.02565	−0.13413	−0.06595*
	4 pm	−0.07552	−0.07563	−0.09135	−0.06208	−0.12292	−0.01749	−0.15649	0.032108*	−0.21706	0.033627*
T19/9/85	7.30 am	−0.09134	−0.06419	−0.07802	−0.07435	−0.11799	−0.04458	−0.13849	−0.03883	−0.26293	0.063755*
	12 noon	−0.08723	−0.06464	−0.09940	−0.05476	−0.15041	−0.00627	−0.14944	−0.02940	−0.60762	0.371954*
	4 pm	−0.07709	−0.07443	−0.07935	−0.07445	−0.11256	−0.03579	−0.11974	−0.04224	−0.26709	0.075403*
F20/9/85	7.30 am	−0.08413	−0.07115	−0.09387	−0.03761	−0.11901	−0.02782	−0.17910	0.001948*	− 0.28610	−3.95466*
	12 noon	−0.39297	−0.35136	−0.39933	−0.35266	−0.44899	−0.30327	−0.48157	−0.31747	−0.60872	−0.20760
	4 pm	−0.10220	−0.05857	−0.09221	−0.05048	−0.16654	−0.00149	−0.24282	0.058736*	−0.33650	0.198946*

TABLE 1(a) Continued

M23/9/85	7.30 am	−0.24574	−0.19057	−0.27443	−0.16134	−0.22375	−0.23256	−0.38785	−0.06098	−0.57343	0.040005*
	12 noon	−0.15680	−0.13062	−0.15937	−0.13638	−0.18668	−0.09555	−0.15531	−0.04330	−0.33936	−0.03177
	4 pm	−0.17808	−0.13018	−0.17023	−1.92244	−0.17160	−0.17166	−0.19702	−0.11955	−0.33477	0.024809*
T24/9/85	7.30 am	−0.13603	−0.14536	−0.16043	−0.13450	−0.15074	−0.12386	−0.23720	−0.08624	−0.33618	−0.03286
	12 noon	−0.05629	−0.08472	−0.08073	−0.07263	−0.08620	−0.07446	−0.09360	−0.05103	−0.17624	0.023583*
	4 pm	−0.05335	−0.09340	−0.07154	−0.08243	−0.08413	−0.06982	−0.09752	−0.04097	−0.17371	0.020738*
W25/9/85	7.30 am	−0.07154	−0.07498	−0.08318	−0.07028	−0.07892	−0.08174	−0.11035	−0.06643	−0.34723	0.127798*
	12 noon	−0.06371	−0.07807	−0.05701	−0.08659	−0.07783	−0.06086	−0.09128	−0.05504	−0.26124	0.127034*
	4 pm	−0.03355	−0.03737	−0.02767	−0.05458	−0.05022	−0.02343	−0.02569	−0.03851	−0.22900	0.120690*
T26/9/85	7.30 am	−0.09764	−0.15777	−0.07215	−0.12965	−0.10273	−0.12854	−0.16326	−0.07837	−0.27687	−0.01615
	12 noon	−0.03437	−0.05005	−0.05705	−0.03912	−0.07560	−0.02734	−0.04807	−0.03779	−0.24634	0.089198*
	4 pm	−0.07136	−0.06902	−0.08935	−0.06322	−0.11173	−0.04117	−0.15537	−0.08406	−0.29063	0.097562*
AVERAGE:		−0.10196	−0.09838	−0.11100	−0.16566	−0.13335	−0.07346	−0.16495	−0.05066	−0.30425	−0.11254

(a): An asterisk denotes a profitable arbitrage opportunity.

TABLE 2(a)

Arbitrage Opportunities (including costs)

		One month		Two months		Three months		Six months		Twelve months	
		(£ → $)	($ → £)	(£ → $)	($ → £)	(£ → $)	($ → £)	(£ → $)	($ → £)	(£ → $)	($ → £)
T17/9/85	7.30 am	−0.07704	−0.08775	−0.10177	−0.07876	−0.13455	−0.05421	−0.18670	−0.04204	−0.26007	−0.06579
	12 noon	−0.05743	−0.07195	−0.08784	−0.05469	−0.12115	−0.03705	−0.15980	−0.04596	−0.33739	0.059073*
	4 pm	−0.07308	−0.08588	−0.09411	−0.06317	−0.13853	−0.04216	−0.17140	−0.03434	−0.28185	−0.01171
W18/9/85	7.30 am	−0.07339	−0.08703	−0.07913	−0.09467	−0.10057	−0.08909	−0.15882	−0.07159	−0.32248	0.010100*
	12 noon	−0.07830	−0.08763	−0.10685	−0.06734	−0.13066	−0.03629	−0.17966	−0.05092	−0.18534	−0.11626
	4 pm	−0.07975	−0.07987	−0.09983	−0.07054	−0.13566	−0.03017	−0.18202	0.006832*	−0.26827	−0.01670
T19/9/85	7.30 am	−0.09558	−0.06843	−0.08650	−0.08281	−0.13073	−0.05726	−0.06402	−0.06410	−0.31413	0.013428*
	12 noon	−0.09147	−0.06888	−0.10788	−0.06322	−0.16315	−0.01895	−0.17498	−0.05467	−0.65880	0.321609*
	4 pm	−0.08133	−0.07867	−0.08783	−0.08291	−0.12530	−0.04847	−0.14527	−0.06752	−0.31829	0.025055*
F20/9/85	7.30 am	−0.08837	−0.07539	−0.10236	−0.04607	−0.13175	−0.04050	−0.20463	−0.02332	−0.33729	−4.00502
	12 noon	−0.39720	−0.35559	−0.40781	−0.36111	−0.46171	−0.31592	−0.50707	−0.34270	−0.65985	−0.25786
	4 pm	−0.10643	−0.06281	−0.10070	−0.05894	−0.17928	−0.01417	−0.26835	0.033461*	−0.38769	0.148598*

TABLE 2([a]) Continued

M23/9/85	7.30 am	−0.24997	−0.19480	−0.28291	−0.16980	−0.23648	−0.24523	−0.41336	−0.08624	−0.62458	−0.01031
	12 noon	−0.16104	−0.13485	−0.16786	−0.14485	−0.19941	−0.10823	−0.18083	−0.06858	−0.39054	−0.08209
	4 pm	−0.18231	−0.13442	−0.17871	−1.93090	−0.18433	−0.18434	−0.22254	−0.14483	−0.38594	−0.02552
T24/9/85	7.30 am	−0.14027	−0.14960	−0.16891	−0.14296	−0.16348	−0.13653	−0.26272	−0.11152	−0.38735	−0.08319
	12 noon	−0.06053	−0.08896	−0.08921	−0.08109	−0.09894	−0.08714	−0.11913	−0.07631	−0.22744	−0.02674
	4 pm	−0.05759	−0.09764	−0.08003	−0.09089	−0.09687	−0.08250	−0.12305	−0.06624	−0.22493	−0.02957
W25/9/85	7.30 am	−0.07578	−0.07922	−0.09167	−0.07874	−0.09166	−0.09442	−0.13588	−0.09170	−0.39844	0.077488*
	12 noon	−0.06795	−0.08231	−0.06550	−0.09505	−0.09057	−0.07353	−0.11682	−0.08031	−0.31247	0.076741*
	4 pm	−0.03779	−0.04161	−0.03616	−0.06305	−0.06296	−0.03611	−0.05124	−0.06377	−0.28024	0.070382*
T26/9/85	7.30 am	−0.10187	−0.12200	−0.08063	−0.13811	−0.11547	−0.14121	−0.18880	−0.10362	−0.32812	−0.06639
	12 noon	−0.03861	−0.05429	−0.06554	−0.4758	−0.08835	−0.04001	−0.07362	−0.06305	−0.29760	0.038934*
	4 pm	−0.07560	−0.07326	−0.09783	−0.07169	−0.12447	−0.05384	−0.18091	−0.10932	−0.34188	0.047295*
AVERAGE:		−0.10620	−0.10262	−0.11948	−0.17412	−0.14609	−0.08614	−0.19048	−0.07593	−0.35546	−0.16285

(a): An asterisk denotes a profitable arbitrage opportunity.

or, in an obvious notation:

$$Z_t = \Phi Z_{t-1} + v_t \tag{27}$$

Using the first-order formulation (27) it is then easily shown by recursive substitution that

$$E(\Delta_n p_{t+n} - \Delta_n p^*_{t+n} | \Lambda_t) = e' \sum_{K=1}^{n+1} \Phi^K Z_{t-1} \tag{28}$$

and

$$E(i_t - i^*_t \,|\, \Lambda_t) = g' \Phi Z_{t-1} \tag{29}$$

where Λ_t is a restricted information set consisting of only lagged $\Delta_1(p - p^*)_t$ and $(i - i^*)_t$:

$$\Lambda_t = \{\Delta_1(p - p^*)_{t-1}, \Delta_1(p - p^*)_{t-2}, \ldots, (i - i^*)_{t-1}, (i - i^*)_{t-2}, \ldots\}$$

$$\Lambda_t \subseteq \Omega_t$$

and e and g are $1 \times 2j$ selection vectors with unity in the first and $(j + 1)$th elements respectively and zeros elsewhere.

If we take expectations of the RIP condition (24) with respect to Λ_t and apply the law of iterated mathematical expectations, we can see, however, that (28) and (29) should be identically equal under RIP. Equating coefficients in (28) and (29) then yields the rational expectations – RIP restrictions on the BVAR:

$$g'\Phi - e' \sum_{K=1}^{n+1} \Phi^K = 0 \tag{30}$$

The $2j$ non-linear restrictions defined in (30) can then be tested by standard non-linear test procedures – i.e. Wald, likelihood ratio or Lagrange multiplier tests (see Taylor (1987b) for details of the exact form of these tests in this context). The BVAR approach should provide a more efficient test of RIP than has previously been carried out because it exploits the time series properties of the data.

We carried out tests of (30) for three country pairs – US-UK, US-Germany and US-Japan – using monthly (unadjusted) data on consumer price indices and Euro-deposit interest rates for two maturities – six and twelve months – for the period July 1979 to October 1986. We used the method outlined in Taylor (1987b) to determine the orders of the BVARs (i.e. j) – this basically involves testing down from a specification involving thirteen lags by likelihood ratio tests.

The results of the tests for the rational expectations – RIP restrictions are given in Tables 3 and 4. The results are qualitatively identical for each country pair and maturity considered – the restrictions are overwhelmingly rejected.

How may the rejection of real interest parity be rationalised? Perhaps the simplest explanation lies in the fact that underlying the derivation of (21) are a number of other parity conditions which are themselves questionable. Thus, a number of researchers in both the US and UK have indicated that closed interest parity (the so-called Fisher condition) does not hold for the sample periods utilised by the researchers noted in this section. Also, as we saw in the last section, UIP has received somewhat mixed support for the recent float. But what of the final parity condition underlying (21), namely *ex ante* purchasing power parity (equation (19))? We consider this relationship in some detail in the next section.

V. PURCHASING POWER PARITY

Tests of purchasing power parity (PPP) have been conducted in broadly four ways. The first has been to compute PPP for highly disaggregated price indices in an attempt to test the commodity arbitrage component of PPP. The second approach is to note that if PPP holds continuously, then the real exchange rate should be constant over time and independent of the nomimal exchange rate. The third empirical approach has been to test the relative and absolute versions of PPP using regression analysis. The fourth approach analyses the time series properties of the PPP relationship. Let us consider each of these approaches in turn.

Consider first whether commodity arbitrage ensures that the law of one price is maintained for internationally traded commodities. Isard (1977) for example, takes the most disaggregated groupings of manufactured goods for which US, German and Japanese prices are readily available (wholesale and export prices) and finds that for the period 1970-75 the law of one price fails to hold : changes in exchange rates are shown to result in *relative* price changes. A similar study, although at a more disaggregated level, has been conducted by Kravis and Lipsey (1978) and they reach similar conclusions.

A second set of tests of PPP rely on the observation that if PPP holds

TABLE 3

Tests of the Rational Expectations-Real Interest Parity Restrictions
Six Months Eurodeposit Rate(a)

Country Pair	n	R_1	R_2	Q_1	Q_2	$L(n-1)$	$L(n+1)$	Wald Statistic	Likelihood Ratio Statistic
US-UK	12	0.70	0.87	19.37	15.96	25.62	7.71	865.46	167.32
				(0.08)	(0.19)	(0.38E-4)	(0.10)	(0.00)	(0.00)
US-Germany	8	0.45	0.80	19.11	20.93	11.03	5.58	567.49	217.00
				(0.26)	(0.18)	(0.03)	(0.23)	(0.00)	(0.00)
US-Japan	3	0.24	0.89	28.37	27.09	23.14	4.04	729.83	191.97
				(0.13)	(0.17)	(0.12E-3)	(0.40)	(0.00)	(0.00)

(a): Period of estimation is July 1979 to October 1986, truncated as necessary due to lags, with monthly data. R_1 and R_2 are the coefficients of determination and Q_1 and Q_2 the Ljung-Box statistics from the inflation differential and interest differential regressions respectively; under the null of white noise residuals, Q_1 and Q_2 are asymptotically distributed as central chi-square with (24-n) degrees of freedom; $L(n-1)$ is a likelihood ratio statistic for a VAR of order $(n-1)$ ($VAR(n-1)$) against the alternative $VAR(n)$, whilst $L(n+1)$ tests $VAR(n)$ against $VAR(n+1)$: each is an asymptotically central chi-square variate under the appropriate null with low degrees of freedom, and was constructed with a finite-sample degrees of freedom correction as suggested in Sims (1980); the Wald and likelihood ratio statistics for the rational expectations-real interest parity restrictions are each asymptotically central chi-square under the null with $2n$ degrees of freedom: figures in parentheses are marginal significance levels in all cases.

TABLE 4

Tests of the Rational Expectations-Real Interest Parity Restrictions
Twelve Months Eurodeposit Rates(a)

Country Pair	n	R_1	R_2	Q_1	Q_2	$L(n-1)$	$L(n+1)$	Wald Statistic	Likelihood Ratio Statistic
US-UK	12	0.69	0.88	19.64	15.58	25.00	4.13	872.71	211.35
				(0.07)	(0.21)	(0.50E-4)	(0.38)	(0.00)	(0.00)
US-Germany	2	0.40	0.71	20.79	21.29	10.35	2.33	112.08	71.07
				(0.53)	(0.50)	(0.04)	(0.67)	(0.00)	(0.00)
US-Japan	3	0.23	0.89	30.27	25.00	17.98	2.97	662.52	177.76
				(0.09)	(0.25)	(0.12E-2)	(0.56)	(0.00)	(0 00)

(a): See note to Table 3.

continuously, then the real exchange rate should be independent of the nominal exchange rate. If, however, there are factors other than relative prices driving exchange rates, and if prices are relatively inflexible, then we would not expect to observe an independence between nominal and real exchange rates. Which view does the evidence support? In Figures 1 and 2 the logarithm of the UK

FIGURE 1

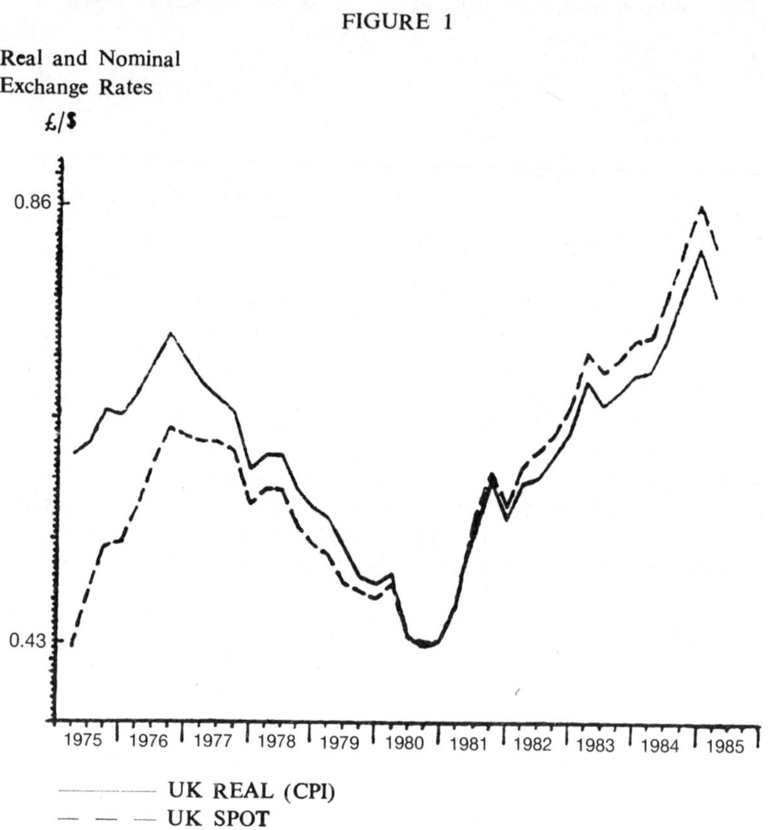

pound-US dollar and German mark-US dollar nominal and real exchange rates are presented, where the latter has been calculated using consumer price indices. It is clear that for the period considered, nominal and real exchange rates move closely together. Thus, the nominal appreciation of the sterling rate from mid-1976 to the end of the 1970s is seen also to be a real appreciation and the nominal depreciation of the exchange rate thereafter is seen to be also a real depreciation. Figures 1 and 2 are also supportive of the empirical evidence presented in Dornbusch and Krugman (1978), and in Dornbusch

(1979), where it is demonstrated that, for a variety of currencies, nominal and real exchange rates are not independent.

FIGURE 2

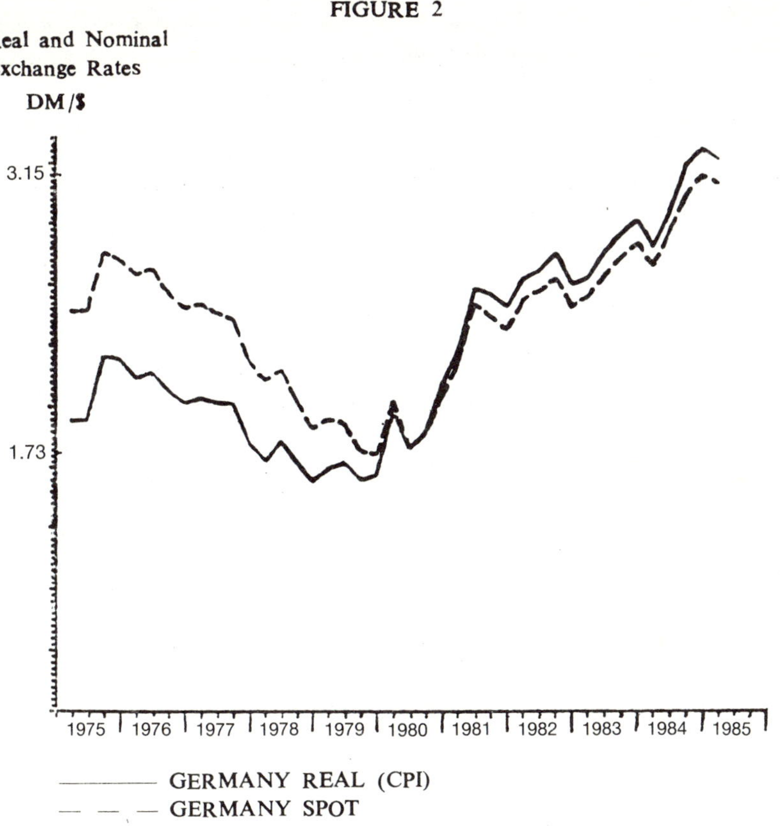

The third category of tests of PPP utilises regression analysis. For example, the absolute and relative versions of PPP may be tested by econometrically estimating equations such as (31) and (32), where it is expected that if PPP holds, then $\beta = \beta^* = 1$ and the intercept term should equal zero.

$$s_t = \alpha + \beta p_t - \beta^* p_t^* + v_t \qquad \text{(ABSOLUTE PPP)} \qquad (31)$$

$$s_t = \alpha + \beta \Delta p_t - \beta^* \Delta p_t^* + v_t \qquad \text{(RELATIVE PPP)} \qquad (32)$$

In Frenkel (1978), estimates of equations (31) and (32) are presented for the inter-war experience with floating rates and in Frenkel (1981), for the recent floating experience. Frenkel's inter-war estimates of (31) and (32) for the dollar-pound, franc-dollar and franc-pound exchange rates, using a variety of price indices for the period February 1921 - May 1925, are highly supportive of the PPP hypothesis in its absolute and relative forms. However, Frenkel's results for a variety of currencies for the recent floating experience are unsatisfactory : PPP in both its relative and absolute versions is resoundingly rejected by the data. In further tests of PPP for the inter-war and recent floating period, Krugman (1978), reports estimates of (31) and (32) which are largely unfavourable to PPP (he uses a longer sample for the inter-war period than Frenkel (1978)). Krugman concludes : 'There is some evidence then that there is more to exchange rates than PPP. This evidence is that the deviations of exchange rates from PPP are large, fairly persistent, and seem to be larger in countries with unstable monetary policy'.

These tests of equations (31) and (32), however, fail to capture the interrelatedness of bilateral foreign exchange rates, which have been such a feature of the recent and inter-war floating periods (see Edwards (1983), and MacDonald (1983), for further discussion). Hakkio (1984), therefore estimates equation (31) using a systems estimator (non-linear three stage least squares) to account for the correlation of the error term across countries and also for serial correlations within countries. The price index used by Hakkio is the CPI and the currencies studied are the British pound, Canadian dollar, French franc and Japanese yen (all against the US dollar), over the period 1973 quarter 3 to 1982 quarter 4. Interestingly, when the system is estimated in an unconstrained form the estimates of b are statistically insignificant, but when the b coefficient is constrained to be equal across countries (a restriction not rejected by the data) it proves to be statistically significant and have a value close to unity. Hakkio's estimation method does, however, adjust for first-order serial correlation within each equation estimated. Although PPP appears to be supported by the constrained results, all of the estimated first-order autocorrelation coefficients are close to unity, thereby suggesting the presence of unit roots in the *real* exchange rate series – itself evidence *against* PPP. We discuss the unit root hypothesis further below. MacDonald (1988), finds some evidence supportive of PPP for the recent float in his estimates of equations (31) and (32). MacDonald uses average annual data (which may be more appropriate for a long-run concept such as PPP, since higher frequency data tends to have a very low signal-to-noise ratio) on a wholesale and consumer price index for the same currencies as Hakkio, with the addition of the Swiss franc-US dollar. In order to improve the efficiency of the estimates, a time wise autoregressive /cross-sectionally heteroscedastic model is utilised: the hypothesis that the exchange rate is homogeneous of degree one was generally supported by the data, regardless of the definitions of prices used.

However, notwithstanding this result, the fact that a time wise autoregressive model was utilised indicates that PPP deviations are important.

A fourth way of testing for PPP involves examining the time series properties of the real exchange rate. From the Fisher equations, (17) and (13), and the UIP condition, (20), we have

$$r_t - r_t^* = \Delta p_{t+1}^{e*} - \Delta p_{t+1}^e + \Delta s_{t+1}^e \tag{33}$$

and by assuming the expected values in (33) are formed rationally we obtain

$$r_t - r_t^* = \Delta p_{t+1}^* - \Delta p_{t+1} + \Delta s_{t+1} + a_t \tag{34}$$

which we christen the efficient markets view of PPP (EMPP), and where a_t is the rational expectations forecast error. From (34), we see that if the real interest differential is constant over time then the logarithmic change in the real exchange rate should follow a random walk. If the time series properties of the real interest rate are non-constant but instead, say, follow a moving average process then it is clear that the time series properties of the real exchange rate may be more complex than a simple random walk (see Adler and Lehmann (1983) for further discussion). If the change in the real exchange rate does follow a random walk then it has important implications for the traditional view of PPP. Thus, few proponents of PPP (see Officer (1976) for a discussion) would deny that in the short term there may be shocks which push the exchange rate away from its PPP value. But this phenomenon should only be temporary, over time the real exchange rate should revert to its equilibrium value and therefore the change in the real exchange rate should be serially correlated. If, then, the random walk model of the real exchange rate is supported by the data, it must call into question the traditional view of PPP.

The majority of the evidence does in fact find in favour of the EMPP: the change in the real exchange rate follows a random walk. Thus Roll (1979), Frenkel (1981), Darby (1980), Mishkin (1984) and MacDonald (1985a, b) find in favour of EMPP whilst Cumby and Obstfeld (1984), Frankel (1985) and Frankel and Froot (1985) are able to reject the hypothesis (although these latter studies also present evidence which is supportive of the EMPP).

In a sense, testing for *ex ante* PPP is a way of testing for *long-run* PPP. If we denote the real exchange rate c_t

$$c_t = s_t - p_t + p_t^*$$

then the efficient markets version of PPP suggests that the c_t should follow a random walk – it does not display mean reversion. If this is the case, then the difference between the nominal exchange rate and relative prices, will tend to get larger and larger over time rather than converging to zero or indeed any stable value. Thus, if c_t follows a random walk or, more generally, is non-stationary, then PPP cannot, it seems, be valid even as a long-run phenomenon.

Taylor (1988b) tests for long-run purchasing power parity using cointegration techniques (see Engle and Granger (1987)). The essence of cointegration is as follows. If two time series, x and y say, are each non-stationary but stationary in, for example, first differences then they are said to be 'integrated of order one', I(1). Any linear combination of x and y will generally also be I(1), but if there *does* exist some linear combination which is I(0) – i.e. stationary, then the pair are said to be cointegrated. If the nominal exchange rate and relative prices are each I(1) (as generally turns out to be the case) then at least a *necessary* condition for PPP to hold, in a long-run sense, is that they be cointegrated.

This approach is more general than testing for EMPP for the following reasons. First, testing for cointegration of the nominal exchange rate and relative prices involves testing for stationarity of a series such as g defined in (35) :

$$g_t = \delta + s_t - \alpha(p_t - p_t^*) \tag{35}$$

where the constants δ and α are estimated in some appropriate fashion, rather than imposing $\alpha = 1$ (and perhaps $\delta = 0$), as in EMPP tests. Taylor (1988b) develops simple models involving measurement errors and transport costs which may give rise to values of α other than unity even when long-run PPP holds. Secondly, this approach tests for general (borderline) non-stationarity of the short-run deviations from PPP, rather than the more restrictive random walk hypothesis.

Taylor (1988b) tests for cointegration between relative wholesale price indices and nominal exchange rates against the US dollar for the UK, West Germany, France, Canada and Japan over the period June 1973 to December 1985, using monthly data. He concludes, '...rather than finding evidence of stable, long-run proportionality between exchange rates and prices, we were unable to reject the hypothesis that they tend to drift apart without bound'. In a comparison study of the 1920s float, however, Taylor and McMahon (1988), *do* find substantial evidence supportive of long-run PPP. They apply the cointegration methodology to a test for long-run PPP using all possible bilateral rates between the US dollar, the UK pound, the French franc and the German mark. Using monthly data for the period February 1921 through to May 1925 (to August 1923 for the mark), they are generally able easily to reject the hypothesis of non-cointegration of relative prices and nominal exchange rates, with the single exception of dollar-sterling. They suggest, however, that this exchange rate may have been subject to non-stationary non-fundamental factors during the last twelve months before Britain returned to the Gold Standard in 1925. When the last twelve months are sampled, cointegration cannot be rejected. Taylor and McMahon also present corroborative empirical evidence using other econometric techniques such as overdifferencing tests and dynamic specification tests.

The evidence on PPP may be summed up as follows. It is now quite clear that *continuous* PPP has certainly not held during the recent float, and probably did not hold during the interwar period. Further, although there is some evidence that real exchange rates during the interwar period had a strong mean-reverting component, the same cannot be said of the 1970s and 1980s. A possible rationalisation of this finding is that industrialised economies have been subject to a large number of real shocks during the last ten to twenty years – such as natural resource discoveries, technological shocks and productivity shifts. Branson (1981), for example, argues that during the 1970s the US was becoming less efficient in the production of tradeables in relation to competitors such as Japan and Germany. Further work on long-run PPP might usefully explore this avenue – for example by looking for cointegration between nominal exchange rates, relative prices and relative productivity.

VI. CONCLUDING COMMENTS

Since all recent models of exchange rate determination are built on simple parity conditions (MacDonald and Taylor (1988)) and given that such models have largely failed to track exchange rate movements, it seems of interest to ascertain whether such failure can be traced to the underlying parity conditions. This has been the purpose of the present paper and the conclusions to emerge from our discussion may be summarised in the following way.

First, the concept of covered interest parity seems to receive fairly strong support from the data, especially when the condition is implemented with appropriate interest rates and data which properly reflected the trading opportunities open to arbitragers. However, a less sanguine conclusion must emerge from our discussion of tests of uncovered interest parity: UIP seems to be resoundingly rejected for the recent experience with floating exchange rates. This conclusion clearly has important implications for exchange rate models which rely on UIP for their derivation (see, for example, Dornbusch (1976) and Frankel (1979)). The main challenge, though, facing researchers is try to determine whether the failure is due to a violation of risk neutrality to or risk aversion. Studies which have attempted to capture a risk premium, by regressing the UIP relation on determinants of risk, have not been successful and this perhaps suggests that it is the rational expectations (RE) leg of the joint hypothesis which is at fault. Indeed, single hypothesis tests of the UIP relationship by MacDonald and Torrance (1988b) do tend to indicate that it is the RE component that is failing.

Our summary of the battery of empirical tests that have been applied to PPP failing, convincingly supports the view that *continuous* PPP has not held for the recent floating periods (and indeed there is also doubt about whether it held for the inter-war period), although Taylor and McMahon (1988) do produce some evidence which strongly suggests that a form of *long-run* PPP may have held for the interwar period. The only version of PPP to derive any support from the data for the recent period is that derived from certain efficient market conditions. Thus, there is now a large body of evidence to suggest that the real exchange rate follows a random walk process. This finding is particularly damaging to the traditional view of PPP (as expounded by, for example, Cassel (1922) where the real exchange rate would be mean reverting). The random walk finding indicates that real exchange rate changes are permanent. Thus, modellers who build exchange rate models which rely on PPP (particularly in continuous form) are building their model on extremely shaky foundations. On the basis of the PPP evidence one would not expect real interest parity to hold for the recent float and, indeed, this conclusion is borne out by the evidence reported in section IV.

The findings of this paper are important since they suggest that at least three types of international parity conditions used by a number of researchers to build exchange rate models are not validated by the data. Future modelling should therefore take account of this and, at the very least, take proper account of the time series properties of UIP and PPP. Proper recognition on the limitations of certain parity conditions should help to improve our understanding of how foreign exchange rates are determined.

University of Dundee, U.K.

City University Business School, Bank of England and C.E.P.R., U.K.

REFERENCES

Adler, M. and Lehman, B. (1983) 'Deviations from Purchasing Power Parity in the Long Run', *The Journal of Finance*, 38 (5) : 1471-1487.

Aliber, R. Z. (1973) 'The Interest Parity Theorem : A Reinterpretation', *Journal of Political Economy*, 81 : 1451-1459.

Branson, W. H. (1969) 'The Minimum Covered Interest Differential Needed for International Arbitrage Activity', *Journal of Political Economy*, 77 : 1028-35.

—— (1981) 'Comment T', *European Economic Review*, 16 : 167-171.

——, Halttunnen, H. and Masson, P. (1977) 'Exchange Rates in the Short Run', *European Economic Review*, 10 : 395-402.

Cornell, B. (1983) 'Money Supply Announcements and Interest-Rates : Another View', *Journal of Business*, 56 : 1-23.

Cosander, P.A. and Laing, B.R. (1981) 'Interest Rate Parity Tests : Switzerland and Some Major Western Countries', *Journal of Banking and Finance*, 5 : 187-200.

Cumby, R. E. and Obstfeld, M. (1981) 'Exchange Rate Expectations and Nominal Interest Rates : A Test of the Fisher Hypothesis', *Journal of Finance*, 36 : 697-703.

—— (1984) 'International Interest Rate and Price Level Exchanges under Flexible Exchange Rates : A Review of Recent Evidence', in J.F.O. Bilson and R.C. Marston (eds.), *Exchange Rate Theory and Practice*, (Chicago : University of Chicago Press).

Cumby, R.E. and Mishkin, F. (1981) 'The International Linkage of Real Interest Rates : The European-US- Connection', NBER *Working Paper*, No. 1423.

Darby, M. (1980) 'Does Purchasing Power Parity Work', NBER, *Working Paper*, No. 607.

Davidson, J. (1985) 'Econometric Modelling of the Sterling Effective Exchange Rate', *Review of Economic Studies*, 52 : 231-240.

Dooley, M.P. and Isard, P. (1982) 'A Portfolio Balance Rational Expectations Model of the Dollar Mark Exchange Rate', *Journal of International Economics*, 12 : 257-276.

Dornbusch, R. (1976) 'Expectations and Exchange Rate Dynamics', *Journal of Political Economy*, 84 : 1161-1176.

—— (1979) 'Monetary Policy Under Exchange Rate Flexibility' in *The Recent Experience*, Federal Reserve Bank of Boston.

—— and Krugman, P. (1978) 'Flexible Exchange Rates in the Short Run', *Brookings Papers on Economic Activity*, 3 : 537-584.

Edwards, S. (1983) 'Exchange Rates and 'News': A Multi-Currency Approach', *Journal of International Money and Finance*, 1 (3) : 211-224.

Engel, L. and Frankel, J. (1982) 'Why Interest Rates React to Money Announcements : An Explanation from the Foreign Exchange Market', *Journal of Money and Economics*, 13 (1) : 31-40.

Frankel, J. A. (1982) 'A Test of Perfect Substitutability in the Foreign Exchange Market', *Southern Economic Journal*, 49(2) : 406-416.

—— (1983) 'Monetary and Portfolio Balance Models of Exchange Rate Determination', in J. S. Bhandari and B. H. Putnam (eds.), *Economic Interdependence and Flexible Exchange Rates*, (Cambridge, Mass.: The MIT Press).

—— (1985) 'Six Possible Meanings of 'Overvaluation' : The 1981-85 Dollar', *Essays in International Finance*, No. 159.

—— and Froot, K. (1986) 'Interpreting Tests of Forward Discount Bias Using Survey Data on Exchange Rate Expectations', NBER *Working Paper*, No 1963.

Fratianni, M. and Wakeman, L.M. (1982) 'The Law of the Price in the Eurocurrency Market', *Journal of International Money and Finance*, 1 : 307-323.

Frenkel, J. A. (1978) 'Purchasing Power Parity Doctrinal Perspective and Evidence from the 1920's', *Journal of International Economics*, 8 : 169-191.

—— (1981) 'Flexible Exchange Rates, Prices, and the Role of 'News' : Lessons for the 1970s', *Journal of Political Economy*, 89(4) : 665-705.

—— and Levich, R. M. (1975) 'Covered Interest Arbitrage : Unsupported Profits?', *Journal of Political Economy*, 83(2) : 325-338.

—— (1977) 'Transaction Costs and Interest Arbitrage : Tranquil Versus Turbulent Periods', *Journal of Political Economy*, 85(6) : 1207-1224.

Friedman, M. and Schwartz, A. (1982) *Money, Interest Rates and Prices in the United States and United Kingdom* : 1867-1975, (Chicago : University of Chicago Press).

Hacche, G. and Townend, J. (1981) 'Exchange Rates and Monetary Policy Modelling Sterling's Effective Exchange Rate, 1972-80', in W.A. Eltis and P.J.N. Sinclair (eds.), *The Money Supply and the Exchange Rate*, (Oxford: Oxford University Press), pp. 201-247.

Hakkio, G.S. (1981) 'The Term Structure of the Forward Premium', *Journal of Monetary Economics*, 8 : 41-58.

—— (1984) 'A Re-examination of Purchasing Power Parity : A Multi-Country and Multi-Period Study', *Journal of International Economics*, 17 : 265-277.

Husted, S. and Kitchen, J. (1985) 'Some Evidence on the International

Transmission of US Money Supply Announcement Effects', *Journal of Money, Credit and Banking*, 17 : 456-466.

Isard, P. (1977) 'How Far Can we Push the Law of One Price?', *American Economic Review*, 67(5) : 942-948.

Kravis, I. and Lipsey, R. (1978) 'Price Behaviour in the Light of Balance of Payments Theory', *Journal of International Economics*, 8 (2) : 193-246.

Krugman, P. (1978) 'Purchasing Power Parity and Exchange Rates: Another Look at the Evidence', *Journal of International Economics*, pp. 397-407.

Loopesko, B. (1984) 'Relationships among Exchange Rates, Intervention and Interest Rates: An Empirical Investigation', *Journal of International Money and Finance*, 3 : 257-278.

MacDonald, R. (1985a) 'Do Deviations of the Real Effective Exchange Rate Follow a Random Walk?', *Economic Notes*, 14(1) : 63-69.

—— (1985b) 'Are Deviations from Purchasing Power Parity Efficient?: Some Further Answers', *Weltwirtschaftliches Archiv*, 121(4) : 638-645.

—— (1988) 'Purchasing Power Parity : Some 'Long Run' Evidence for the Recent Float', *De Economist*, (forthcoming).

—— and Taylor, M.P. (1988) 'Economic Analysis of Foreign Exchange Markets: An Expository Survey', in R. MacDonald and M.P. Taylor (eds.), *Exchange Rates and Open Economy Macroeconomics*, (Oxford: Basil Blackwell).

MacDonald, R. and Torrance, T. S. (1987) 'Sterling M3 Surprises and Asset Prices', *Economica*, 54 : 505-515.

—— (1988a) 'On Risk, Rationality and Excessive Speculation in the Deutschemark-US Dollar Exchange Market: Some Evidence Using Survey Data', *Oxford Bulletin of Economics and Statistics*, (May).

—— (1988b) 'Expectations Formation and Risk in Four Foreign Exchange Markets', University of Aberdeen Discussion Paper, pp. 88-101.

—— (1988c) 'Covered Interest Parity and UK Monetary 'News'', *Economics Letters*, (forthcoming).

—— (1988d) 'Some Survey Based Tests of Uncovered Interest Parity', in MacDonald, R. and Taylor, M.P. (eds.), *Exchange Rates and Open Economy Macroeconomics*, (Oxford : Basil Blackwell).

McCormick, F. (1971) 'Covered Interest Arbitrage : Unexpected Profits?: Comment', *Journal of Political Economy*, (79) : 418-422.

Marston, R.C. (1976) 'Interest Arbitrage in the Euro Currency Markets', *European Economic Review*, 7 : 1-13.

Mishkin, F.S. (1981) 'The Real Interest Rate : A Multi-Country Empirical Study', *Canadian Journal of Economics*, 17 : 283-311.

—— (1984) 'Are Real Interest Rates Equal Across Countries? An Empirical Investigation of International Parity Conditions', *Journal of Finance*, pp. 1345-1358.

Mussa, M. (1979) 'Our Recent Experience with Fixed and Flexible Exchange Rates', *Carnegie Rochester Supplement*, 3 : 1-50.

Officer, L.H. (1976) 'The Purchasing-Power-Parity Theory of Exchange Rates : A Review Article', International Monetary Fund, *Staff Papers*, 23 : 1-60.

Rogoff, K. (1984) 'On the Effects of Sterilised Intervention : An Analysis of Weekly Data', *Journal of Monetary Economics*, 14 : 133-150.

Roll, R. (1979) 'Violations of Purchasing Power Parity and Their Implications for Efficient International Commodity Markets' in M. Sargent and G.P. Szego (eds.), *International Finance and Trade*, Vol. 1, pp. 133-176.

Taylor, M.P. (1987a) 'Covered Interest Parity : A High-Frequency, High-Quality Data', *Economica*, 54 : 429-438.

—— (1987b) 'Risk Premia and Foreign Exchange : A Multiple Time Series Approach to Testing Uncovered Interest Parity', *Weltwirtschaftliches Archiv*, 123 : 579-591.

—— (1988a) 'Covered Interest Parity and Market Turbulence : An Empirical Analysis', mimeo, Bank of England and *Economic Journal* (forthcoming).

—— (1988b) 'An Empirical Examination of Long Run Purchasing Power Parity Using Cointegration Techniques', mimeo, Bank of England and *Applied Economics* (forthcoming).

—— (1988c) 'A DYMIMIC Model of Forward Foreign Exchange Risk, with Estimates for Three Major Exchange Rates', *The Manchester School*, 56 : 55-68.

—— (1988d) 'Expectations, Risk and Uncertainty in the Foreign Exchange Market : Some Evidence Based on Survey Data', Bank of England Discussion Paper and *The Manchester School* (forthcoming).

—— and McMahon, P.C. (1988) 'Long Run Purchasing Power Parity in the 1920s', *European Economic Review*, 32 : 179-197.

Von Furstenberg, G. (1983) 'Changes in US Interest Rates and Their Exchange Rates', in D. Bigman and T. Taya (eds.), *Exchange Rate and Trade Instability : Causes, Consequences and Remedies*, (Cambridge, Mass.: Ballinger).

Varian, H.R. (1978) *Microeconomic Analysis*, (New York : Norton).

ASSESSING THE EFFECTS OF MONETARY SHOCKS ON EXCHANGE RATE VARIABILITY WITH A STYLISED ECONOMETRIC MODEL OF THE UK

By P. N. Smith and M. R. Wickens*

I. INTRODUCTION

In the two year period 1979-1980 the nominal effective sterling exchange rate appreciated by 27.3% (14.5% in 1979 and 12.8% in 1980), while the real effective exchange rate, measured in manufacturing output price terms, appreciated by 54.3%. Empirical models of the exchange rate available at the time were unable to explain this behaviour. A possible solution to the problem is offered by the 'overshooting' model of Dornbusch (1976) as modified by Buiter and Miller (1981). This emphasises the effects of forward-looking behaviour in foreign exchange markets in response to domestic monetary shocks and adaptive behaviour in domestic goods markets. It has the implication that variation in the real exchange rate is dominated by variation in the nominal rate. In this paper we use an estimated structural exchange rate model which contains many of the features of the 'overshooting' model to assess the extent to which domestic monetary shocks in the 1979/80 period can explain the appreciation in the exchange rate.

A number of tests of empirical models of the determination of flexible exchange rates have come to the same conclusion that none are satisfactory and some indeed are outperformed by a simple random walk model.[1] As a result it is widely held that there is no satisfactory fundamentals explanation of the behaviour of exchange rates available. This has prompted both the search for new theory and the favourable consideration of non-rational theories such as speculative bubbles explanations.[2]

* The authors would like to thank Sean Holly and Paul Levine for helpful comments and Jessica Caines for assistance. The research was supported by the ESRC.

1. Meese and Rogoff (1983a, b) demonstrate this both within and outside sample for the models of Frenkel, Frankel and Hooper and Morten. Backus (1984) and earlier Hacche and Townend (1981) reject all the models they analyse. Smith and Wickens (1986) discuss the relative importance of each of the possible causes of the failure of the rational expectations version of the monetary model.

2. Meese (1986) finds evidence in favour of bubbles in a simple monetary model of

It is our contention that few, if any, of these empirical models do sufficient justice to the economic models that underlie them. Many of the tests made to date have been carried out on the unrestricted reduced form exchange rate equations rather than the restricted reduced form or, even better, on structural equations.[3] The theoretical restrictions are commonly rejected and there is evidence of dynamic misspecification. The estimates are often inconsistent because the estimation method has failed to take account of the presence of endogenous variables on the right hand side of many of the equations.[4] The models suffer from inadequate dynamic specification both of the structural equations and of the processes generating the exogenous variables which are used to form expectations: often the structural equations are assumed to be static, while a number of studies impose untested and unlikely exogeneity restrictions.[5] Most restrict the number of exogenous variables to those which are to be used for policy simulation (e.g. money supplies) and ignore other potentially important exogenous shocks on the behaviour of the exchange rate over the period considered. This can have important implications for the form of solution implied by the estimates. In view of these shortcomings it is not surprising that there has been little support for the economic theories that these studies purport to test.

The intention behind the model presented in section II below is to produce a representation of the structural equations of a widely used theoretical model of the exchange rate which is data acceptable. Should this prove impossible, the theoretical model must be rejected. We find, however, that such a representation is feasible and is accepted by the data. In section II we describe the specification and estimation of the model together with tests of the conditioning assumptions made. In section III we describe the calculation of monetary shocks and the predicted effects on the exchange rate for the 1979/80 period.

the exchange rate, Smith and Wickens (1989) show how different conclusions to Meese can be arrived at.

3. Examples of a single equation unrestricted reduced form estimates of the monetary model are Frenkel (1976), Mussa (1976, 1979) and of the sticky-price or Dornbusch model are Driskill (1981), Frankel (1979, 1983). These are compared by Backus (1984).

4. Restricted reduced form estimates have been obtained by Demery (1984), Hartley (1983), Driskill and Sheffrin (1981), Woo (1985), Barr (1984). All these examples take explicit account of the implications for estimation of the presence of forward-looking rational expectations.

5. Frankel (1983) corrects the procedure in his 1979 paper but still fails to take account of the implications for the error process of expectational errors.

II. THE ECONOMETRIC MODEL

The structure is, with a few amendments, a discrete time version of that in Buiter and Miller (1981). We assume that the UK is a small open economy, i.e. it takes the rest of the world as given and produces one composite good for which it faces a downward sloping demand curve in world markets. These exogeneity assumptions are tested below. A stylised version of the model which reveals its underlying structure is given by (1) - (5).

$$m_t - p_t = ky_t - \lambda r_t \tag{1}$$

$$y_t = \gamma(r_t - \Delta p^e_{t+1}) + \delta(e_t + p^*_t - p_t) + \mu z_t \tag{2}$$

$$p_t = ap^y_t + (1 - a)(p^*_t + e_t) \tag{3}$$

$$\Delta p^y_t = \beta \Delta p^{ye}_{t+1} + \rho \Delta p^y_{t-1} + \varphi(y_t - \bar{y}_t) \tag{4}$$

$$\Delta e^e_{t+1} = r_t - r^*_t \tag{5}$$

where m : nominal narrow money stock, p : aggregate domestic price level, y : real domestic output, r : short-run nominal interest rate, e : exchange rate (domestic price of foreign currency), $\bar{y}$: capacity output, p^y : price of domestic production, $\Delta x_t = x_t - x_{t-1}$, x^e_{t+1} : expectation of x_{t+1} made at t using information available up to period t, x^*_t : foreign equivalent of domestic variable. All variables are logarithms except for interest rates which are annual percentage rates. Equation (1) is the domestic demand for real balances and represents portfolio balance. Equation (2) is the aggregate demand function, the variable z_t represents other exogenous variables we may introduce in estimation. Equation (3) is the domestic production price equation. Equation (4) is an expectations augmented Phillips curve where we allow for both forward-looking expectations and sluggishness in price adjustment due to contracts or other costs of adjustment. Equation (5) is the uncovered interest parity condition reflecting perfect substitutability of domestic and foreign capital and perfect capital mobility.

Estimates of the model are presented in Table 1 for the UK for the period 1973Q2-1981Q2. The exchange rate we consider is an effective rate against a composite foreign country. This is created as a trade-weighted average of the UKs five main trading partners. The data which is quarterly and seasonally unadjusted is described in detail in the Data Appendix. In the estimation all rationally expected variables are replaced by realisations and all estimates

TABLE 1

Estimates of the Econometric Model

(a) Money Demand Equation

$$
\begin{aligned}
m_t - p_t = & -\underset{(4.71)}{0.8790}\, r_t + \underset{(12.6)}{0.2316}\,(m_{t-1} - p_{t-1}) \\
& + \underset{(3.50)}{0.6372}\,(m_{t-2} - p_{t-2}) + \underset{(2.50)}{0.5747}\, y_{t-2} \\
& - \underset{(1.99)}{0.4235}\, y_{t-3} - \underset{(3.66)}{0.9525}\, \Delta p_{t-1} \\
& - \underset{(6.58)}{0.06823}\, Q1 - \underset{(3.86)}{0.06596}\, Q2 - \underset{(0.19)}{0.003338}\, Q3 \\
& + \underset{(0.55)}{0.7275}
\end{aligned}
$$

		Long-run elasticities
R^2	$= 0.947$	
$S.E.$	$= 1.82\%$	
DW	$= 2.04$	$y = 1.15$
$LM(5)$	$= 5.01$	$r = -6.70$
$Z(13)$	$= 6.06$	$\Delta p = -7.26$

(b) Aggregate Demand Equation

$$
\begin{aligned}
y_t = & -\underset{(1.79)}{0.3963}\,[(r_t/4) - E_t p_{t+1}] - \underset{(1.66)}{0.2237}\, y_{t-2} \\
& - \underset{(2.95)}{0.02591}\,(e_t + p_t^q - p_t) + \underset{(4.92)}{0.2827}\, y_t^* \\
& + \underset{(2.81)}{0.1158}\,(e_{t-4} + p_{t-4}^* - p_{t-4}) + \underset{(3.54)}{0.4395}\, g_t \\
& + \underset{(5.81)}{0.002305}\,(q_{t-4} + e_{t-4} + p_{t-4}^q - p_{t-4}) \\
& + \underset{(7.16)}{0.05085}\, Q1 - \underset{(4.33)}{0.04431}\, Q2 - \underset{(0.75)}{0.005132}\, Q3 + \underset{(6.43)}{6.792}
\end{aligned}
$$

		Long-run elasticities	
$\bar{R}^2$	$= 0.953$	$(r/4) - E_t p_{t+1} + p_t = -0.324$	$e + p^* - p = 0.0946$
$S.E.$	$= 0.935\%$	$e + p^q - p = 0.0212$	$q + e + p^q - p = 0.00188$
DW	$= 1.87$	$y^* = 0.231$	$g = 0.359$
$LM(5)$	$= 4.63$		
$Z(18)$	$= 11.08$		

TABLE 1 (continued)

(c) Aggregate Domestic Price Equation

$$\Delta p_t = \underset{(2.13)}{0.5857}\,\Delta p_t^y + \underset{(3.43)}{0.5689}\,\Delta p_{t-2} - \underset{(1.56)}{0.2969}\,\Delta p_{t-2}^y$$

$$- \underset{(1.67)}{0.1158}\,(p_{t-1} - p_{t-1}^y) - \underset{(2.94)}{0.04562}\,\Delta p_{t-1}^q + \underset{(4.44)}{0.06431}\,\Delta p_{t-2}^q$$

$$- \underset{(2.13)}{0.1576}\,\Delta e_{t-2} + \underset{(1.80)}{0.02910}\,(e_{t-1} + p_{t-1}^* - p_{t-1}) - \underset{(0.84)}{0.006272}\,Q1$$

$$- \underset{(2.65)}{0.01548}\,Q2 - \underset{(2.59)}{0.01706}\,Q3 - \underset{(1.86)}{0.1352}$$

R^2 = 0.661		Long-run elasticities
$S.E.$ = 1.05%		
DW = 2.06		p^y = 0.790
$LM(1)$ = 0.141		$e + p^*$ = 0.201
$LM(4)$ = 4.015		
$Z(14)$ = 2.094		p^q = 0

(d) Domestic Production Price Equation

$$\Delta p_t^y = \underset{(3.10)}{0.4143}\,\Delta p_{t+1}^{ye} + \underset{(5.02)}{0.5580}\,\Delta p_{t-1}^y + \underset{(2.52)}{0.2382}\,(y_{t-3} - \bar{y}_{t-3})$$

$$- \underset{(1.83)}{0.1883}\,(y_{t-4} - \bar{y}_{t-4}) + \underset{(0.69)}{0.005621}\,Q1 - \underset{(1.03)}{0.01022}\,Q2$$

$$- \underset{(1.49)}{0.01551}\,Q3 + \underset{(0.16)}{0.00077}$$

$\bar{R}^2$ = 0.761	DW = 2.83
$S.E.$ = 0.798%	$LM(1)$ = 6.40

(e) Uncovered Interest Parity

$$e_{t+1} - e_t = (r_t - r_t^*)/4 + \zeta_t$$

Estimation period = 1973Q2 — 1981Q2
Method of estimation = 2SLS
t-statistics in parentheses
$LM(n)$ = Lagrange Multiplier test for up to nth order autocorrelation
$Z(m)$ = Chi-squared test for instrument validity (m instruments)
Data described in data appendix.

TABLE 1(a)

Tests of Weak Exogeneity

p^* :	1.855	g :	0.456
y^* :	2.082	m :	2.929
r^* :	0.655	p^9 :	2.756
$\bar{y}$:	0.900	q :	0.445

Critical values for F-test: 2.57 (95%), 3.28 (99%).

TABLE 1(b)

Test of Granger-causality

	r	y	e	p^y	p
m	0.932	1.085	0.824	0.378	0.671
r^*	0.453	0.391	1.010	0.804	0.980
y^*	0.550	0.180	0.584	0.781	0.849
p^*	0.253	0.479	0.428	0.731	1.020
g	2.840	0.830	2.660	5.370*	1.700
p^q	0.675	0.419	0.650	0.793	0.805
q	0.973	0.815	0.718	0.741	0.156
$\bar{y}$	0	0	0	0	0

*: Significant at 95% level

are obtained using single equation instrumental variable methods.[6] This approach does not require the processes generating expectations of the future values of the exogenous variables to be estimated jointly with the structural equations. We therefore trade efficiency in estimation for robustness to specification error.

The demand for money function presented in Table 1 is for the narrow definition ($M1$) of real money balances. We find that the flexible dynamic structure employed produces estimates which are superior to both the static and partial adjustment forms of the equation used in most other studies.[7] The restriction that the equation determines real money balances is accepted by the data ($F(1,22) = 4.15$). The aggregate demand equation, (b) in Table 1, contains a number of shift variables in addition to the endogenous variables suggested by the theoretical form. The experience of the UK economy over the estimation period makes the inclusion of oil related variables essential. The formulation shows beneficial effects of oil price increases when North

6. These are described in Wickens (1982, 1986) and McCallum (1980).
7. Frankel (1983) and Woo (1985) are examples.

Sea oil production was positive and expenditure reducing effects before that time. The response of aggregate demand to exchange rates (*ceteris paribus*) demonstrates the operation of a *J*-curve effect. In the model we distinguish between the price of domestic production (p^y) and the general domestic price level (p). We find that the long-run level of the general domestic price level is a weighted average of the price of domestic production and the price of foreign output in domestic currency.[8] The short-run behaviour of the general price level is also affected by the domestic oil price. The change in the price of domestic output is generated by the expectations augmented Phillips curve shown as (d) in Table 1. The form of equation (4) admits two extreme possible outcomes: $\beta \neq 0$, $\rho = 0$ makes inflation entirely forward-looking; $\beta = 0$, $\rho \neq 0$ makes it entirely backward-looking. We find that both of these alternatives are rejected by the data and that a composite hypothesis is preferred. The theoretical justification for such a model is discussed in Smith and Wickens (1987). Overlapping wage contracts of the form discussed by Taylor (1980) or constrained forward-looking price setting by firms as discussed by Giovannini and Rotemberg (1983) are two possible forms of behaviour covered by the equation. An additional problem for equation (4) is the estimation of capacity or long-run trend output by $\bar{y}_t$. In the theoretical models this can be ignored by renormalisation of variables. We assume that in the long run output is determined by the use of the capital stock. In our essentially short-run analysis we take it to be exogenous.[9] The replacement of expected future inflation by its realisation creates an expectational error. This creates a serially correlated error where one had not previously existed. This requires an adjustment to the usual instrumental variable standard errors (see Hansen and Hodrick (1980), Wickens (1986)).[10] In the estimates at (d) in Table 1 we find that excess demand has a positive, if lagged, effect on inflation, whilst both expected future and past inflation have significant effects,

8. This restriction is not rejected at the 95% level ($F(1,21) = 3.88$).

9. The fitted values of the following regression are used as measure $\bar{y}_t$:

$$y_t = 0.429\,k_t + 4.039 \qquad \bar{R}^2 : 0.516 \qquad SE : 3.71\% \qquad DW : 1.38$$

The literature on cointegration (Granger and Engle (1985)) supports our assertion that this long-run relationship holds. The autocorrelation in the regression is unsurprising as the residuals are our measure of excess demand.

10. More efficient estimates can be obtained using the 2S2SLS estimator proposed by Cumby, Huizinga and Obstfeld (1983), for example.

thus ruling out both extreme models outlined above. The error process has an MA (1) structure as expected.

Finally we use uncovered interest parity at line (e) in Table 1. In Smith and Wickens (1986, 1987) we provide evidence for the hypothesis that the error ζ_t follows a white noise process given appropriate treatment of the expectational error created by replacing the expectation of the exchange rate in period $t + 1$ by its realisation. This result for quarterly data seems quite robust although estimates on more finely sampled data using more efficient estimation techniques have suggested otherwise.[11] Furthermore it can be shown that the error ζ_t is independent of information available up to time period t. That is, we cannot reject the joint hypothesis that the coefficients on lagged values of the endogenous and exogenous variables in the model are not zero in a regression of ζ_t on this information set. This test result, along with that for serial independence, is sufficient for the version of the efficient markets hypothesis implied by uncovered interest parity.

The final issue of specification is the validity of the instruments and the independence of the exogenous variables from the structural errors. The consistency of the estimates in Table 1 requires that the instruments used are uncorrelated with the error term. The $z(n)$ statistics confirm that valid instruments have been used in each case. These are the exogenous variables and lagged values of the endogenous variables. The solution, as distinct from the estimation, of the model requires that the exogenous variables are both weakly exogenous to, and not Granger-caused by, the endogenous variables in the model. This is the definition of strict exogeneity made by Engle *et al.* (1983) and implied by Hansen and Sargent (1980). In Table 1(a), (b) we provide evidence that both of these criteria are met. The results in Table 1(a) are of tests of weak exogeneity using the Lagrange Multiplier test of Engle (1984). They show that in no case are the exogenous variables correlated with the structural disturbances which confirms the instrument validity tests. In Table 1(b) we test Granger causality. At the 95% confidence level we can reject the hypothesis that the exogenous variables are Granger-caused by any of the endogenous variables. This then allows us to use the Weiner-Kolmogarov prediction formulae for expected future values of the exogenous variables independently of the structural equations.[12]

11. See Baillie, Lippens and McMahon (1983), Hansen and Hodrick (1980).

12. In Smith and Wickens (1987) we provide estimates of autoregressive processes for the exogenous variables which can be used to produce a close-form solution of the model for the estimation period. We also present a tracking exercise.

Two comments may be made concerning these results. Firstly, the result that the money supply and government expenditure can be treated as exogenous might be thought surprising. However, we have at least provided evidence for our hypothesis rather proceed by assumption. Secondly, the exogeneity tests provide support for the hypothesis that the UK can be treated as a small open economy. This is with respect to the composite foreign economy that we use here, rather than any individual country.

The long-run predictions of the model can be obtained by finding the long-run restricted reduced form equation for each of the five endogenous variables. This is the static equilibrium solution of the model given that the dynamic solution has the appropriate saddlepoint property.[13]

$$e = m + 7.776\, r^* + 12.13\, \bar{y} - 3.068\, y^* - 4.768\, g - 0.025q + 0.257p^q - 1.256\, p^* - 68.16 \quad (6)$$

$$p^y = m + 6.429\, r^* - 4.497\, \bar{y} + 0.772\, y^* + 1.202\, g + 0.0063q + 0.0645\, p^* - 0.0648\, p^q + 25.287 \quad (7)$$

$$p = m + 6.70\, r^* - 1.15\, \bar{y} + 5.545 \quad (8)$$

$$r = r^* \quad (9)$$

$$y = \bar{y} \quad (10)$$

This solution demonstrates the model's neutrality to monetary shocks and complete crowding out of fiscal changes. Real shocks drive a wedge between the price of domestic production and the general price level equivalent to the change in the real exchange rate adjusted for the share of domestic production in output. In Smith and Wickens (1989) we discuss econometric tests of the existence of the long-run solution shown in (6) - (10). These suggest in particular that the solution for the exchange rate in equation (6) is data acceptable, and one which restricts the number of exogenous variables to the money supply and capacity output, as is implied by the models of Driskill, Frankel et al, is not. In this sense too, the generality of our model produces more acceptable econometric properties.

13. It can be shown that the model, when written in state-space form, has two eigenvalues greater than one and thirteen less than one (in absolute value). This fulfils the stability condition for the existence of a saddlepoint solution. We are grateful to Paul Levine and Jessica Gaines for their help in making these calculations with his PRISM programs; described in Gaines, al-Nowaihi and Levine (1987).

III. THE IMPACT OF MONETARY SHOCKS

The model presented in section II has the same basic structure as that suggested by Buiter and Miller (1981) which was originally designed to analyse the period of exchange rate instability in 1979/80. Over that period substantial appreciation of the nominal and real exchange rate was followed by further depreciation, repeating the pattern of the mid 1970s. It would seem natural then to attempt to analyse that period using the model described above. The model has a number of exogenous variables which might be capable of explaining a large part of the appreciation in 1979 and 1980. Domestic and foreign monetary policy and fiscal policy are the most likely variables. The effect of North Sea oil production and the revaluation of reserves by increases in oil prices are further candidates but these play a rather minor role in this model. Here we concentrate on quantifying the effects of domestic monetary shocks on the exchange rate. This method of assessing the effects of monetary shocks could be applied to the other variables in the model.

The crucial factor in the analysis of the short-run dynamic behaviour of the exchange rate is the modelling of expectations of future values of the exogenous variables. The structural equations in Table 1 show how endogenous variables and their expected values are generated. Closed-form predictions require in addition the specification of processes for generating expectations of the driving variables. Incorrect specification of these processes appears to contribute substantially to the failure of many exchange rate models. The assumption of a random walk in which all changes in the values of the exogenous variables are unexpected, is common but an alternative time series representation may explain past data more accurately. It is also important that these processes are stable across time and that they are independent of expected future regime changes. The stability or otherwise of these processes has, however, no consequence for the estimates of the structural coefficients as we have established both weak and strong exogeneity of the various exogenous variables including the money supply.

We consider three possible choices of expectational process for the money supply, all of which imply non-stationary behaviour in the money supply. They are:

(a) Random walk with drift

(b) Autoregression in first differences

(c) Autoregression about a linear time trend.

The first two processes assume a difference stationary money supply while the third assumes trend stationary behaviour. The results are discussed at length in Smith and Wickens (1989). The tests are sufficiently marginal to permit each to be considered as a serious possibility. The performance of these processes in explaining the behaviour of the money supply over the estimation period can be judged by the summary statistics shown with the estimates in Table 2. In each case we have presented the most parsimonious version of the general autoregression. It is clear that none of these equations shows evidence of autocorrelation or other forms of misspecification as judged by the usual criteria. In deciding which process to select additional information from the tests of non-stationarity referred to above can be used.

Since we are examining a period that many would regard as containing a regime change in the behaviour of the money supply it is useful to carry out stability tests. In Table 2 the two tests of predictive failure and parameter stability discussed in Pesaran, Smith and Yeo (1986) are presented. There is no evidence from these that the three processes, when estimated up to the end of 1978, cannot predict the following 10 quarters values, or that the parameters of the processes are unstable over the additional observations. These results have some power as the coefficients are estimated quite precisely and the standard error of each equation is low. These results imply that we can treat all error terms from these equations's as unanticipated or unpredictable shocks. In a sense this is a counter-intuitive result. Whilst we might view shocks as unanticipated, there might be a presumption that the change in government in 1979, and the consequent announcement of monetary restraint was a change in regime. In practice the difficulty is that ex-post behaviour of the chosen monetary aggregate (£M3) was at variance to the policy plan. The narrow definition of the money supply used in the current model might be thought to be a better indicator of money market conditions as it contains little of an interest bearing nature.

The innovations ε_t in each of the three processes are shown in Table 3. The predicted behaviour of the exchange rate as a result of these shocks is computed by a period by period solution of the model. We use the standard Blanchard-Kahn technique as modified for unit roots in the state transition matrix by Gaines, Al-Nowaihi and Levine (1987). We compute the one-step ahead forecasts. (A full explanation of the closed form one-step ahead predictions of the model is made in Smith (1987).) We assume that the model holds in each period and that the only shock is the innovation in the money supply process. A full stochastic solution to the model would require that shocks to the structural equations and to the exogenous variables be considered. Here we restrict ourselves to considering the impact of domestic monetary shocks.

TABLE 2

Forecasting Processes for the Money Supply

(a) Random Walk with Drift

$$m_t = m_{t-1} + \underset{(5.65)}{0.0480} - \underset{(4.15)}{0.0498}\,Q1 - \underset{(1.38)}{0.0161}\,Q2 - \underset{(1.15)}{0.0138}\,Q3 + \varepsilon_t$$

$\bar{R}^2$: 0.328		Chow (10) :	4.09
$S.E.$: 2.40%		Stab (4) :	1.74
DW : 1.84		LM (4) :	5.25

(b) Autoregression in First Difference

$$\Delta m_t = \underset{(3.62)}{0.394}\,\Delta m_{t-2} - \underset{(1.49)}{0.247}\,\Delta m_{t-3} + \underset{(3.62)}{0.0340}$$

$$- \underset{(3.28)}{0.0415}\,Q1 - \underset{(1.05)}{0.0135}\,Q2 + \underset{(0.97)}{0.0151}\,Q3 + \varepsilon_t$$

$\bar{R}^2$: 0.443		Chow (10) :	5.39
$S.E.$: 2.19%		Stab (4) :	2.29
DW : 1.61		$LM(4)$:	9.84

(c) Autoregression about Linear Trend

$$m_t = \underset{(4.46)}{0.911}\,m_{t-1} + \underset{(1.54)}{0.374}\,m_{t-2} + \underset{(2.64)}{0.629}\,m_{t-3}$$

$$+ \underset{(0.53)}{0.105}\,m_{t-4} + \underset{(2.13)}{0.00746}\,\text{time} + \underset{(2.16)}{2.243}$$

$$- \underset{(3.67)}{0.0453}\,Q1 - \underset{(1.08)}{0.0179}\,Q2 + \underset{(0.73)}{0.0118}\,Q3 + \varepsilon_t$$

$\bar{R}^2$: 0.995		Chow (10) :	7.58
$S.E.$: 2.11%		Stab (4) :	6.61
DW : 1.80		$LM(4)$:	8.84

TABLE 3

Innovations in the Expectational Processes

	(a)	(b)	(c)
1979 Q1	0.000336	−0.00892	0.00447
Q2	−0.0175	−0.0155	−0.00574
Q3	0.00331	0.00271	0.0117
Q4	−0.0111	−0.00305	0.00671
1980 Q1	−0.0277	−0.0332	−0.0234
Q2	−0.0125	−0.00635	−0.00373
Q3	−0.0326	−0.0267	−0.0266
Q4	−0.000825	−0.00170	−0.00625

These figures are logarithmic deviations and consequently are approximately percentages.

The initial conditions or starting values for each of the predetermined variables are important when assessing the effects of monetary developments over the period in question. In setting the initial conditions we assume that with respect to monetary shocks all variables were at their steady-state values in the fourth quarter of 1978. In each of these cases these are steady-state growth paths which implies that the model will predict purely anticipated changes in the exchange rate during the 1979-80 period in addition to the unanticipated effects described above. As an example we find that process (a) generates an unanticipated decrease in the money supply of 1.75% in the second quarter of 1979. The model predicts that this will have caused an appreciation of the nominal exchange rate of 2.41%. The process generating the money supply predicts also that there was a fully anticipated change in the money supply of 2.80%. By the assumption of structural constancy this is assumed to generate an underlying perfectly anticipated depreciation in the exchange rate of the same amount. The first and second panel in Table 4 summarise these two results for each period under examination.

In each case we assume that the innovation ε_t is transitory and expected to last only one quarter. For processes (a) and (b) the shock is permanent on the level of the money supply and temporary on the rate of growth of the money supply. For process (c) it is temporary on the level and hence zero in the long run. In the table we present both the nominal and real exchange rate outcomes. From the steady-state conditions (6) - (10) above we can observe that the purely anticipated effect of domestic monetary changes is unity in the case of the nominal and zero in the case of the real exchange rate. Since the model exhibits the property of sluggish price adjustment to monetary

TABLE 4

Nominal Exchange Rate Changes

Predicted Changes: Unanticipated Monetary Shocks	(a)	(b)	(c)
1979 Q1	0.000463	−0.0143	0.00718
Q2	−0.0241	−0.0249	−0.00922
Q3	0.00456	0.00436	0.0188
Q4	−0.00153	−0.00490	0.0108
1980 Q1	−0.0381	−0.0534	−0.0376
Q2	−0.0172	−0.0102	−0.00599
Q3	−0.0449	−0.04290	−0.0427
Q4	−0.00114	−0.00273	−0.0100

Predicted Changes: Total Anticipated and Unanticipated Monetary Shocks	(a)	(b)	(c)
1979 Q1	0.0285	0.0138	0.0353
Q2	0.00398	0.00322	0.01899
Q3	0.0326	0.0325	0.0469
Q4	0.0129	0.0232	0.0389
1980 Q1	−0.0100	−0.0253	−0.00948
Q2	0.0109	0.0179	−0.0221
Q3	−0.0168	−0.0148	−0.0146
Q4	0.0269	0.0254	0.00181

Predicted Real Exchange Rate Changes: Total Monetary Shocks	(a)	(b)	(c)
1979 Q1	0.000460	−0.0143	0.00714
Q2	−0.02395	−0.0248	−0.00917
Q3	0.00453	0.00433	0.0187
Q4	−0.0152	−0.00487	0.0107
1980 Q1	−0.0373	−0.0530	−0.0374
Q2	−0.0170	−0.01010	−0.00596
Q3	−0.0446	−0.0426	−0.0425
Q4	−0.00113	−0.00272	−0.00998

Actual Changes	Nominal Exchange Rate	Real Exchange Rate
1979 Q1	−0.0376	−0.0646
Q2	−0.0606	−0.0995
Q3	−0.0502	−0.0989
Q4	0.00285	−0.0273
1980 Q1	−0.0557	−0.1071
Q2	−0.0182	−0.0572
Q3	−0.0155	−0.0383
Q4	−0.0381	−0.0503

shocks virtually all of the immediate effect on the real exchange rate is due to nominal exchange rate changes. In case (a) where all changes in the money supply are unanticipated up to a drift term the predicted appreciation of the nominal exchange rate relative to trend totals 12.5% over the two year period. The actual appreciation was 27.3%. Treating shocks as purely transitory deviations in the rate of growth in the money supply explains about half of the observed appreciation in the nominal exchange rate. The predicted changes in the real rate are not subject to the trend effect. For process (A) there is a predicted real appreciation of 13.4% compared with an actual real appreciation of 41.5%. Thus it appears from these results that money supply shocks explain about half of the appreciation in the nominal exchange rate over the two year period and a third of the real appreciation.

An alternative assumption for the exogenous money supply process is that agents may have regarded any of the shocks in the above processes as permanent rather than temporary. Given that there may have been some confusion about whether there had been a change in regime in the period in question, this may be a plausible explanation of expectational behaviour. In Table 5 we present the predicted effects of this assumption. Cases (a) and

TABLE 5

	Nominal Exchange Rate Changes: Unanticipated		
	(a)	(b)	(c)
1979 Q1	0.0147	0.229	−0.0495
Q2	−0.767	−0.294	−0.0861
Q3	0.145	0.690	0.0150
Q4	−0.487	0.344	−0.0169
1980 Q1	−1.215	−1.199	−0.1843
Q2	−0.548	−0.191	−0.0353
Q3	−1.430	−1.363	−0.1482
Q4	−0.0362	−0.320	−0.00944
	Real Exchange Rate Changes		
	(a)	(b)	(c)
1979 Q1	0.0147	0.229	−0.0493
Q2	−0.767	−0.294	−0.0857
Q3	0.145	0.600	0.0150
Q4	−0.487	0.344	−0.0169
1980 Q1	−1.215	−1.199	−0.1836
Q2	−0.0548	−0.191	−0.0351
Q3	−1.430	−1.363	−0.1477
Q4	−0.0362	−0.320	−0.0094

(b) now imply a permanent change in the rate of growth of the money supply, whereas (c) implies a permanent change in the level. It can be shown that the purely anticipated change in the real exchange rate is again zero.

The sizes of some of the figures in columns (a) and (b) appear rather implausible in that they imply an appreciation greater than 100% in 1980*Q*1 and 1980*Q*3. However, it should be recalled that they assume a permanent change in the rate of growth of the money supply and hence should not be cumulated. It is interesting that the average size of the predicted appreciation is of the order of 54% in case (a), 27.4% in case (b) and 6.4% in case (c). This may suggest that the contribution of the domestic monetary shocks in the two year period was somewhat larger than the figures in Table 4 show. Between the assumption of permanent and purely temporary shocks lies a degree of persistence which we might think is plausible. The differences between the results serve to illustrate the difficulty in assessing the informational content of exogenous shocks to a model of this type.

IV. CONCLUSIONS

The main aim of this paper has been to examine to what extent the volatility of the sterling effective exchange rate over the period 1979-1980 can be attributed to domestic monetary shocks. We have constructed a small rational expectations structural model of the UK economy based on the Buiter-Miller model which we have simulated for alternative money supply processes. Three possible money supply processes were estimated together with their one-step ahead forecast errors. From these we constructed anticipated and unanticipated monetary changes (monetary shocks) over the period 1979-1980. We considered three types of shocks : temporary (money is generated by an autoregressive process in levels), permanent in the level of the money supply (temporary in terms of the rate of growth of the money supply) and permanent in the rate of growth of the money supply. Our results suggest that around half of the nominal appreciation and a quarter of the real appreciation can be attributed to unanticipated temporary shocks to the rate of growth of the money supply and that these proportions might be increased if the shocks are assumed to be, in part, permanent.

London Business School, U.K.
University of Southampton, U.K.

APPENDIX

Data Definitions and Sources

r = annual interest rate = 3-month interbank (Annual Percentage Points). Financial Statistics (line AMIJ).

y = GDP (expenditure measure) at factor cost (£m) at 1975 prices. Economic Trends Annual Supplement.

p = GDP (expenditure measure) deflator at factor cost (index 1975=100). Economic Trends Annual Supplement.

g = general government final consumption (£m) at 1975 prices. Economic Trends Annual Supplement.

m = Money supply $M1$= Data smoothed over breaks in 1971 and 1975 (£m). Financial Statistics and Bank of England.

q = U.K. crude oil production (1,000 tonnes volume). BP Oil supplied.

k = gross capital stock series at 1975 replacement cost (1,000m). Annual observations from National Income and Expenditure were interpolated using quarterly Fixed Capital Formation data and an estimated mean depreciation rate δ=1.2297% per annum. National Income and Expenditure. Economic Trends Annual Supplement.

All foreign variables created as weighted averages of the variables for the following countries which are the U.K. 's main international competitors:

U.S.A.	0.3522
W. Germany	0.2013
Japan	0.1954
France	0.1484
Italy	0.1026

weights based upon IMF MERM model and rescaled to sum to unity.

p^* = Consumer Price Index (Index 1975 = 100). International Financial Statistics (line 64).

y^* = Industrial Production Index (Index 1975 = 100). OECD Main Economic Indicators.

r^* = annual interest rate = 3-month money market (Annual percentage points).

U.S.A.	90-day commercial paper rate
W. Germany	3-month loans
Japan	3-month repurchase agreement, Gensaki rate
France	3-month interbank deposits
Italy	interbank sight deposits, 3-month rate

(period average) rates. Bank for International Settlements.

REFERENCES

Backus, D. (1984) 'Empirical Models of the Exchange; Separating the Wheat from the Chaff', *Canadian Journal of Economics*, 17 : 824-846.

Baillie, R. T., Lippens, R. and McMahon, P. C. (1983) 'Testing Rational Expectations and Efficiency in the Foreign Exchange Market', *Econometrica*, 51 : 553-563.

Barr, D. G. (1984) 'Exchange Rate Dynamics : an Empirical Analysis', Centre for Labour Economics, London School of Economics, Discussion Paper No. 200.

Buiter, W. H. and Miller, M. H. (1981) 'Monetary Policy and International Competitiveness : The Problems of Adjustment', in W. A. Eltis and P. J. N. Sinclair (eds.), *The Money Supply and Exchange Rate*, (Oxford: Oxford University Press).

Cumby, R. E., Huizinga, J. and Obstfeld, M. (1983) 'Two-Step Two-Stage Least Squares Estimation in Models with Rational Expectations', *Journal of Econometrics*, 21 : 335 - 355.

Demery, D. (1984) 'Exchange Rate Dynamics – The Swiss / US Case', *European Economic Review*, 24 : 151-159.

Dornbusch, R. (1976) 'Expectations and Exchange Rate Dynamics', *Journal of Political Economy*, 84 (6) : 1161-1176.

Driskill, R. A. (1981) 'Exchange Rate Dynamics: An Empirical Investigation', *Journal of Political Economy*, 89 (2) : 357-371.

—— and Sheffrin, S. M. (1981) 'On the Mark : Comment', *American Economic Review*, 71 : 1068-1074.

Engle, R. F. (1984) 'Wald, Likelihood Ratio and Lagrange Multiplier Tests in Econometrics', in Z. Griliches and M. D. Intriligator (eds.), *Handbook of Econometrics*, (Amsterdam: North Holland).

Engle, R. F., Hendry, D. F. and Richard, J.-F. (1983) 'Exogeneity', *Econometrica*, 51 (2) : 277-304.

Engle, R. F. and Grandel, C. W. J. (1987) 'Co-Integration and Error Correction: Representation, Estimation and Testing', *Econometrica*, 55 (2) : 251-276.

Fisher, P. G., Holly, S. and Hughes-Hallett, A. J. (1986) 'Efficient Solution Technique for Dynamic Non-Linear Rational Expectations Models' *Journal of Economic Dynamics and Control*, 10 : 139-145.

Frankel, J. (1979) 'On the Mark : A Theory of Floating Exchange Rates Based on Interest Differentials', *American Economic Review*, 68 : 610-622.

—— (1983) 'Monetary and Portfolio Balance Models of Exchange Rate Determination', in J. S. Bhardari and B. H. Putnam (eds.), *Economic*

Independence and Flexible Exchange Rates, (Cambridge Mass. The MIT Press).

Frenkel, J. (1976) 'A Monetary Approach to the Exchange Rate: Doctrinal Aspects and Empirical Evidence', *Scandinavian Journal of Economics*, 78.

Gaines, J., al-Nowaihi, N. and Levine, P. (1987) 'An Optimal Control Package for Rational Expectations Models', London Business School, Centre for Economic Forecasting Discussion Paper No. 18-87.

Giovannini, A. and Rotemberg, J. J. (1984) 'Exchange Rate Dynamics with Sticky Prices: The Deutschemark 1974-1982', Massachusetts Institute of Technology, Working Paper No. 1522-84.

Hacche, G. and Townend, J. (1981) 'Exchange Rates and Monetary Policy: Modelling Sterling's Effective Exchange Rate 1972-80', *Oxford Economic Papers*.

Hansen, L. P. and Hodrick, R. J. (1980) 'Forward Exchange Rates as Optimal Predictors of Future Spot Rates: An Econometric Analysis', *Journal of Political Economy*, 88 (5): 829-853.

Hansen, L. P. and Sargent, T. J. (1980) 'Formulating and Estimation Dynamic Linear Rational Expectations Models', *Journal of Economic Dynamics and Control*, 7-46.

Hartley, P. R. (1983) 'Rational Expectations and the Foreign Exchange Market', in J. A. Frenkel (ed.), *Exchange Rates and International Macroeconomics*, (Chicago: University of Chicago Press).

Isard, P. (1987) 'Alternative Approaches to the Empirical Modelling of Exchange Rates: Where is the Profession Now?', IMF Staff Papers.

Levich, R. M. (1985) 'Empirical Studies of Exchange Rates: Price Behaviour, Rate Determination and Market Efficiency', in R. W. Jones and P. B. Kenen (eds.), *International Economics*, (Amsterdam: North Holland), pp. 979-1040.

McCallum, B. T. (1976) 'Rational Expectations and the Estimation of Econometric Models; An Alternative Procedure', *Econometrica*, 17: 484-490.

Meese, R. A. (1986) 'Testing for Bubbles in Exchange Markets: A Case of Sparkling Rates?', *Journal of Political Economy*, 94 (2).

—— and Rogoff, K. (1983a) 'Empirical Exchange Rate Models of the Seventies: Do they Fit out of Sample?', *Journal of International Economics*, 14: 3-24.

—— (1983b) 'The Out-of-Sample Failure of Empirical Exchange Rate Models; Sampling in Error or Misspecification', in J. A. Frenkel (ed.), *Exchange Rates and International Macroeconomics*, (Chicago: University of Chicago Press).

Mussa, M. L. (1976) 'The Exchange Rate, the Balance of Payments and Monetary and Fiscal Policy under a Regime of Controlled Floating', *Scandinavian Journal of Economics*, 78: 229-248.

—— (1979) 'Empirical Regularities in the Behaviour of Exchange Rates and Theories of the Foreign Exchange Market', in K. Brunner and A.H. Meltzer (eds.), *Policies for Employment, Prices and Exchange Rates*, Carnegie - Rochester Conference Series, Vol. 11 (Amsterdam : North Holland).

Pesaran, M. H., Smith, R. and Yeo, S. (1986) 'Tests of Preditive Failure and Parameter Stability', Manchester School.

Smith, P. N. (1987) 'Structural Models of the Exchange Rate : Theory and Evidence', Unpublished Ph. D. Thesis, University of Southampton.

Smith, P. N. and Wickens, M. R. (1986) 'An Empirical Investigation Into the Causes of the Failure of the Monetary Model of the Exchange Rate', *Journal of Applied Econometrics*.

—— (1987) 'A Stylised Econometric Model of an Open Economy : UK 1973-1981', London Business School, Centre for Economic Forecasting Discussion Paper No. 13-87.

—— (1989) 'Testing for Speculative Bubbles in Exchange Rates', London Business School, Centre for Economic Forecasting Discussion Paper No. 20-87 (forthcoming).

Taylor, J. S. (1980) 'Aggregate Dynamics and Staggered Contracts', *Journal of Political Economy*, 88 : 1-23.

Wickens, M. R. (1982) 'The Efficient Estimation of Econometric Models with Rational Expectations', *Review of Economic Studies*, 49 : 55-67.

—— (1986) 'The Estimation of Linear Models with Future Rational Expectations by Efficient and Instrumental Variable Methods', CEPR Working Paper.

—— and Thomas, S. H. (1989) 'Non-Parametric Estimates of the Equity and Exchange Risk Premia', University of Southampton, Discussion Paper (forthcoming).

Woo, W. T. (1985) 'The Monetary Approach to Exchange Rate Determination Under Rational Expectations', *Journal of International Economics*, 18: 1-16.

CHARTISTS, FUNDAMENTALISTS AND THE DEMAND FOR DOLLARS

By Jeffrey A. Frankel and Kenneth A. Froot*

The careening path of the dollar in recent years has shattered more than historical records and the financial health of some speculators. It has also helped to shatter faith in economists' models of the determination of exchange rates.

We have understood for some time that under conditions of high international capital mobility, currency values will move sharply and unexpectedly in response to new information. Even so, actual movements of exchange rates have been puzzling in two major respects. First, the proportion of exchange rate changes that we are able to predict seems to be, not just low, but zero. According to rational expectations theory we should be able to use our models to predict that proportion of exchange rate changes that is correctly predicted by exchange market participants. Yet neither models based on economic fundamentals, nor simple time series models, nor the forecasts of market participants as reflected in the forward discount or in survey data, seem able to predict better than the lagged spot rate. Second the proportion of exchange rate movements that can be explained even *after* the fact, using contemporaneous macroeconomic variables, is disturbingly low.

I. FUNDAMENTALS, BUBBLES, AND TESTS OF RATIONAL EXPECTATIONS

Most of the models of exchange rate determination that were developed after 1973 are driven by countries' supplies of assets: supplies of money alone in the case of the monetary models, and supplies of bonds and other assets as well in the case of the portfolio-balance models.[1] But observed supplies of

* This paper draws on an earlier study being published in *Macroeconomics, Agriculture and Exchange Rates* edited by P. Paarlberg and R. Chambers (Westview Press: Boulder CO). The first version was written in October 1985. Part 3 of the paper draws heavily on another paper published in the *Economic Record*, December 1986, pp. 24-38. The authors would like to thank the Sloan Foundation for support.

1. Two surveys of standard asset-market models of exchange rates are Frankel (1983) and Shafer and Loopesko (1983).

dollar assets versus other currencies are no help in explaining the 1981-85 appreciation of the dollar. The supply of U.S. assets was increasing rapidly, as measured by the federal government deficit (or the money supply). At the same time, the stock of net claims against foreigners was decreasing rapidly, as measured by the current account deficit.

There is general agreement that the 1981-85 appreciation of the dollar was attributable to an increase in the *demand* for dollars on the part of investors worldwide. There is much less agreement as to the cause of that change in demand. Four hypotheses have been commonly proposed as to why investors found U.S. assets more attractive in the early 1980s. The first, which might be termed "monetarist", is that there was a decline in the rate of expected inflation and depreciation after 1980 because of a reduced rate of money growth.[2] The second is that there was an increase in the interest differential relative to the expected inflation differential; this is the "overshooting" explanation.[3] The third is that there was a self-confirming increase in the expected rate of dollar appreciation, or fall in the expected rate of depreciation; this is the "speculative bubble" hypothesis. Each of these three attributes the increase in demand for assets to an increase in the expected rate of return, variously defined. The fourth, the "safe haven hypothesis" is different; it attributes the shift in demand to an increase in the perceived safety of U.S. assets relative to other countries' assets.

In the first half of the paper we consider briefly each of these four explanations by means of the data on expected returns for the period reported in Table 1. Of the three that depend on economic fundamentals – the monetarist, overshooting and safe haven hypotheses – we argue that only the second is capable of explaining the large real appreciation of the dollar from 1981 to 1985, and its subsequent depreciation. But even the overshooting model seems unable to explain entirely the path taken by the dollar, in particular the last 20 percent of appreciation preceding the February 1985 peak and subsequent rapid decline.

In the second half of this paper we propose the outlines of a model of a speculative bubble that is not constrained by the assumption of rational expectations. The model features three classes of actors: fundamentalists,

2. To the extent that the monetarist model attributes the decrease in expected inflation to correct perceptions of a decreased rate of money supply growth, it could be considered as one of those mentioned above that are driven by the asset supply process. The same is true of the overshooting model. The point about asset demand versus asset supply is that rates of return are a more promising set of data with which to explain recent developments than are observed asset supplies.

3. The overshooting model was developed by Dornbusch (1976).

TABLE 1

Rate of Return Differentials on US Assets Relative to Trading Partners (% per annum)

	Years				
Expected Inflation Differential	1976–78	1979–80	1981–82	1983–84	1985–86
1 One-year lag	—0.01	3.54	0.88	—0.35	0.06
2 Three-year distributed lag	—1.96	2.7	1.89	—0.18	—0.16
3 DRI three-year forecast **	NA	2.20	0.96	0.23	0.15
4 OECD two-year forecast ***	1.42	2.24	0.62	0.61	0.78
5 American Express survey #	NA	NA	4.11	2.68	—0.16
Nominal Interest Differential					
6 One-year interest differential *	—0.48	2.29	3.00	1.73	1.15
7 One-year forward discount ****	0.18	2.57	3.34	1.85	0.21
8 Ten-year interest differential	—0.50	0.56	1.91	2.47	2.92
Real Interest Differential					
9 One-year (6-1)	0.53	—1.24	2.12	2.09	1.08
10 Ten-year w/distributed lag (8-2)	1.47	—2.15	0.02	2.64	3.08
11 Ten-year w/ DRI forecast (8-3)	NA	—1.64	0.95	2.24	2.77
12 Ten-year w/OECD forecast (8-4)	—1.92	—1.68	1.29	1.86	3.12
Expected Depreciation from Surveys ##					
14 Economist three-month	NA	NA	12.99	10.10	1.50
15 Economist six-month	NA	NA	10.62	10.78	4.99
16 Amex six-month ###	2.08	NA	9.54	7.21	1.39
17 Economist twelve-month	NA	NA	8.57	8.60	5.41
18 Amex twelve-month ###	0.61	NA	6.67	6.99	3.72
19 (7/15)	NA	NA	0.31	0.17	0.04

* Calculated as ln(1 + i), 1985 contains data through June, rates for Japan not available 1976-77. ** Averages of various forecast dates, through early 1985. *** OECD forecasts available during 1976-78 only for 12/78, during 1985 for June 1985. **** Includes data through February 1986. # Available at 11 survey dates only for US, UK, WG, and at 4 survey dates (76-78) for France. ## See Frankel and Froot (1987) for an explanation of the survey data. Expected depreciation uses GNP weights for UK, FR, WG and JA. ### Available at 11 survey dates.

Sources: IMF International Financial Statistics, DRI, FACS Financial data base and forecasts, OECD Economic Outlook, Capital International Perspective, AMEX Bank Review, and Economist Financial Review.

Note: Differential calculated as US - foreign, where foreign is a GNP-weighted average of UK, FR, WG, and JA unless otherwise specified.

chartists and portfolio managers. None of the three acts utterly irrationally, in the sense that each performs the specific task assigned him in a reasonable, realistic way. Fundamentalists think of the exchange rate according to a model – the overshooting model for the sake of concreteness – that would be exactly correct if *there were no chartists in the world.* Chartists do not have fundamentals such as the long-run equilibrium rate in their information set; instead they use autoregressive models – simple extrapolation for the sake of concreteness – that have only the time series of the exchange rate itself in the information set. Finally portfolio managers, the actors who actually buy and sell foreign assets, form their expectations as a weighted average of the predictions of the fundamentalists and chartists. The portfolio managers update the weights over time in a rational Bayesian manner, according to whether the fundamentalists or the chartists have recently been doing a better job of forecasting. Thus each of the three is acting rationally subject to certain constraints. Yet the model departs from the reigning orthodoxy in that the agents could do better, in expected value terms, if they knew the complete model. When the bubble takes off, agents violate rational expectations in the sense that the model is changing as fast as they learn about it.

After we establish in Part 1 the shortcomings of the conventional approaches, including the assumption of rational expectations, to accord fully with simple empirical facts of the 1981-85 period, in Part 2 we elaborate on the importance in the marketplace of chartists or – more properly – technical analysts and we offer some evidence from expectations survey data that respondents seem to form very short-term expectations like chartists and more long-term expectations like fundamentalists. Part 3 presents the model in more detail and shows how it can work to explain the 1980-87 path of the dollar.

1.1 *Standard Explanations of the* 1981-85 *Appreciation of the Dollar Based on Rates of Return*

We begin with the simplest view of how the demand for dollars depends on rates of return, the model associated with the monetarists. In this model there are three equivalent ways of defining the rate at which the value of the dollar is expected to change in the future relative to foreign currencies : the expected inflation differential, the expected rate of depreciation, and the nominal interest differential. The first two variables are equal if purchasing power parity holds: the goods of different countries are essentially perfect substitutes in consumers' utility functions, and barriers to instantaneous adjustment in goods markets are low. The second and third variables are equal if uncovered interest parity holds: the assets of different countries are essentially perfect substitutes in investors' portfolios, and barriers to instantaneous adjustment in asset markets are low.

At any point in the late 1970s, the U.S. dollar was expected to lose value against foreign currencies, the mark and the yen in particular, whether the expected rate of change was thought of as the expected inflation differential, the expected rate of nominal depreciation, or the nominal interest differential. In response, investors, seeking to protect themselves against expected capital losses, had a relatively low demand for dollars and high demand for marks and yen. When a firm anti-inflationary U.S. monetary policy began to take hold in 1980, investors' expectations that the dollar would lose value began to diminish rapidly. This would account for an increase in the demand for dollars and for the large appreciation of the dollar in the early 1980s.

There is no single accepted way of measuring inflation expectations. The first five rows of Table 1 report five measures of expected inflation that are available for the United States as well as four trading partners (France, Japan, the United Kingdom, and West Germany). The five measures are the actual inflation rate over the preceding years, a distributed lag over the preceding three years, forecasts by Data Resources, Inc. at a three-year horizon, forecasts by the OECD at a two-year horizon and results of a survey conducted by American Express of active participants in foreign exchange markets at a one-year horizon. By the available measures, expected inflation in the U.S. by 1979-80 had climbed to a level 2-3 points above the weighted average of trading partners. The differential declined rapidly thereafter, reaching approximately zero by 1985. Thus the expected inflation numbers appear to support the first of the three explanations of the dollar appreciation listed above.

The problem is that the decline in the expected inflation differential was not at all matched by movements in other concepts of the expected rate of change of relative currency values. Directly measuring expected changes in the exchange rate is more difficult than measuring expected changes in the price level, because the former is much more volatile than the latter. A new data set is applied to this task in sections 1.2 and 2.1 below. But first we look at interest rate differentials.

Row 6 in Table 1 reports the differential in one-year nominal interest rates between the United States and the weighted average of four trading partners. Row 7 reports the one-year forward discount; the two series should be identical if covered interest parity holds. The numbers show that by 1981-82 the short-term interest differential had reached a level of 3 percent. Thus the real interest differential, reported in row 9, rose from -1 percent in 1979-80 to $+2$ percent in 1981-82. The short-term interest differential, nominal or real, peaked in 1982. However, the long-term real interest differential, which rose by 2-3 points from 1979-80 to 1981-82, depending on the measure of expected inflation used, continued to rise over the next three years. In early 1985 it stood at about 3 points by any of the three measures (up from about −2 points in 1979-80).

The increase in the real interest differential offers the explanation needed for an increase in the *real* value of the dollar. An increase in the nominal interest differential, if it were not offset by an increase in expected inflation or expected depreciation of the currency, would make domestic assets more attractive than foreign assets. The increased demand for domestic assets causes the dollar to appreciate until investors are happy with their holdings. If the dollar is perceived as having appreciated above its long-run equilibrium, there will be an expectation of future depreciation. The short-run equilibrium will occur where the expected future depreciation is sufficient in investors' minds to offset the interest differential.

This much is familiar from the Dornbusch (1976) overshooting model. One reason for looking at the long-term differential, rather than the short-term differential that he used, is as follows.[4] The return of the exchange rate to its long-run equilibrium value could be slow and irregular. If we want to choose a length of time long enough to be confident of having reached long-run equilibrium, 10 years might be necessary. Assume that the 10-year nominal interest differential measures the 10-year expected rate of change of the nominal exchange rate. Then the 10-year real interest differential measures the 10-year expected rate of change of the real exchange rate. With our argument that 10 years is long enough for the real exchange rate to be at its equilibrium value, it follows that the currently measured 10-year (per annum) real interest differential (multiplied by ten) tells us how far from long-run equilibrium investors consider the current real exchange rate to be. Following this logic, as of early 1985 the long-term real interest differential could "explain" a real "overvaluation" of the dollar of about 30 percent relative to its perceived long-run equilibrium, and could explain a real appreciation of about 50 percent relative to 1979-80.

The foregoing calculations are rather crude, and in particular are very sensitive to the term of maturity chosen. Several points can be made in defense of the approach. First, it is supported by several regression studies.[5]

4. The use of the long-term real interest differential originated with Isard (1983). Other early references include Shafer and Loopesko (1983) and Council of Economic Advisers (1984).

5. Sachs (1985), Hooper (1985), Hutchison and Throop (1985) and Feldstein (1986).

Furthermore, the increases in the real interest differential and in the real value of the dollar are the results that the standard macroeconomic theory of high international capital mobility predicts will result from a fiscal expansion such as that undertaken in the United States between 1981 and 1985, that is, a fiscal expansion not accommodated by either a monetary expansion or an offsetting increase in private saving. Finally, the large depreciation of the dollar in 1985-87, as the U.S. Congress finally took some steps to bring the fiscal deficit under control and the Federal Reserve allowed real interest rates to fall, fits the theory well. However, as always with exchange rate theories, there are problems if one tries to fit the data on as finely as a monthly basis. In particular, the long-term real interest differential was already declining during the second half of 1984, even though the dollar continued to appreciate rapidly until February 1985. The fiscal contraction did not begin until the Gramm-Rudman budget reduction bill was passed in December 1985, or at the earliest when the Congress voted to slow the future rate of growth of military spending in mid-1985. The 20 percent spike in the dollar's value centered on February 1985 appears unexplained.

An alternative fundamentals explanation sometimes given for the 1981-85 appreciation of the dollar is the safe-haven hypothesis : a worldwide increase in investors' demand for U.S. assets in response to a perceived decrease in the risk of assets held in the United States relative to those held elsewhere. Such a portfolio shift by itself would be inconsistent with the increase in the interest rate differential observed in Table 1. But the argument runs that a common set of developments – the improved treatment of investment in the 1981 tax bill and the generally improved climate for business under the Reagan Administration – is responsible for both the 1983-84 investment boom (after the investment slump of 1981-82) and the safe-haven portfolio shift, and that the former had an upward effect on real interest rates that dominated any downward effect of the latter. We will be offering some evidence against the safe-haven hypothesis in section 1.3 below. We will then turn from theories based on fundamentals to theories based on bubbles.

As early as 1982, Dornbusch applied the notion of stochastic rational bubbles to the case of the strong dollar. According to this theory, there is a probability at any point in time that the bubble will burst during the subsequent period and the value of the currency will return to the equilibrium level determined by fundamentals. The differential in interest rates fully reflects and compensates for the possibility of the bubble bursting.

More recently it has been suggested that the dollar may in fact have been on an *irrational* bubble path. Two influential papers written when the dollar was still near its peak – Marris (1985) and Krugman (1985) – argued that the mounting U.S. indebtedness to foreigners represented by record current account deficits would eventually force the dollar down sharply, and that this prospective depreciation was not correctly reflected in the small forward discount or interest differential (either short-term or long-term). "It appears that the market has simply not done its arithmetic and has failed to realise that its expectations about continued dollar strenght are not feasible" (Krugman, 1985, p. 40).[6] As late as January 1987, Krugman's calculations still gave the clear verdict that a path in which the dollar declined no faster than investors were expecting (as reflected in the forward discount) was not sustainable (Krugman, 1988, p. 82).

I.2 *Rational Expectations and the Forward Discount*

Meanwhile, evidence has continued to accumulate that the forward discount is a biased predictor of the future spot rate. A favorite way of explaining away such apparent statistical rejections of rational expectations is to appeal to the sort of "peso problem" that might arise in a speculative bubble. But, as explained in the following subsection, one of the present authors has presented calculations that tend to undermine the hypothesis that the dollar could have been on a single rational bubble from 1981 to 1985.[7] The expected probability of collapse that investors built in to the observed interest differential was high enough that it is very unlikely the dollar would have made it through four years without the bubble bursting, if that expectation was rational. This leaves the possibility of a bubble where the true probability of collapse may be different from the expected probability that investors build in to the forward discount.

Both Krugman and Marris have mentioned as partial support for their claim that the foreign exchange market may not be rational the large econometric literature that statistically rejects the hypothesis that the forward discount (or equivalently, by covered interest parity, the interest differential) is an unbiased predictor of the future spot rate. The most common test in this literature is a regression of the ex post change in the spot exchange rate against the forward discount at the beginning of the period. Under the null hypothesis the coefficient should be unity. But most authors have rejected the null hy-

6. Kling (1985) also argued that the value of the dollar rested on market expectations that did not embody a return to steady state. [Ten years earlier, McKinnon (1976) attributed exchange rate volatility to a "deficiency of stabilizing speculation" that is, an unwillingness of investors to take open positions based on fundamental equilibrium, rather than to "high capital mobility with rational expectations" as the orthodoxy has it.]

7. Frankel (1985).

pothesis, finding that the coefficient is much closer to zero, and some even finding that the coefficient is of the incorrect sign. The implication is that one could expect to make money by betting against the forward discount whenever it is non-zero.[8] Bilson (1981) interprets this finding as "excessive speculation :" investors would do better if they would routinely reduce toward zero the magnitude of their expectations of exchange rate changes.

This forward market finding poses a puzzle in the context of the Krugman-Marris characterization of the dollar. It implies that as of 1985 (or for that matter at any time over the period 1981-1987) the rationally expected rate of future dollar depreciation was less than the 3 percent a year implied in the forward discount. The Krugman-Marris argument was that the rationally expected rate of future dollar depreciation would be much *greater* than the 3 percent a year implicit in the market (against the mark or yen).[9] If we are to allow expectations to fail to be rational, we must somehow reconcile the two conflicting kinds of failure.

More discussion of the alleged bias in the forward exchange market is required. Most of the literature (for example the papers cited in footnote 8) does not interpret the finding as necessarily rejecting the hypothesis of rational expectations. Two other possible explanations are routinely offered: the existence of a risk premium, and the "peso problem". We believe that, while both factors can be very important in other contexts, neither explains the systematic prediction errors made by the forward market during the strong-dollar period. We consider the risk premium briefly here, and the peso problem in the next subsection.

The first possible explanation is that the systematic component of the apparent prediction errors is really a risk premium separating the forward rate from investors' true expectations. It is a difficult argument either to re-

8. Studies regressing against the forward discount include Tryon (1979), Levich (1980), Bilson (1981), Longworth (1981), Longworth, Boothe and Clinton (1983), Fama (1984) and Huang (1984). Cumby and Obstfeld (1984) regressed against the interest differential and again found that for most exchange rates the coefficient was significantly less than 1.0 and even less than zero. These findings are also consistent with those of Meese and Rogoff (1983) that the random walk predicts not only better than other models, but better than the forward rate as well.

9. Krugman and Marris did not say that there was any reason to think that the dollar plunge would necessarily come in the next year; the focus was on the market's expected long-term rate of depreciation implicit in the long-term interest differential. We have no tests of unbiasedness going out a year or more. The problem is not the absence of a forward market going out more than a year; we can always use the long-term interest differential. The problem is rather that twelve years of floating-rate data would not offer enough independent observations.

fute or confirm, because expectations are not directly observable. Of the countless risk-premium studies that infer expected depreciation from ex post exchange rates, most do not note explicitly that this technique implies that the expected rate of return was ten to fifteen percent per annum higher on dollars than on other currencies in the early 1980s. Two of those that do, and are ready to believe that dollar assets paid an ex ante risk premium of this magnitude, are Cumby (1987) and Canova and Ito (1987). Borensztein (1986) considers other possible explanations for this persistent difference in expected returns.

If we are not willing to impose the assumption that ex ante expectations can be inferred from what happened ex post in a given sample period, there are few sources of information to help isolate the risk premium out of the prediction errors made by the forward discount. One promising possibility is the surveys of market participants' exchange rate expectations conducted by the Economist's *Financial Report* and the *American Express Bank Review*.[10] The surveys allow us to measure expectations without the interference of the risk premium. In Frankel and Froot (1987) and Froot and Frankel (1989), we showed that those data for the 1981-85 period reflect a considerably greater expectation of dollar depreciation than do the forward discount or interest differential. (The biyearly averages are reported in rows 13-18 of Table 1.) We repeated standard tests of unbiasedness in expected depreciation and found even more significant rejections when the survey data, which must be free from any risk premium, are used than when the forward discount is used. First, we found unconditional bias : one would have persistently made money over the period June 1981-March 1985 by following the rule "buy and hold dollars". A related finding was that expectations were formed regressively – that is, the expected future spot rate puts some weight on a long-run equilibrium rate – but that the actual spot process did not bear out this expectation. Investors overestimated the speed of regression to a statistically significant degree.

An updating of the sample period to include data through December 1985 shows a dramatic shift in the nature of the bias: now it appears that investors on average *underestimated* the speed of regression toward long-run equilibrium, to a statistically significant degree (Frankel and Froot (1987)). But the most robust finding, even with investors' expectations measured by the survey

10. The Economist survey covers 13 leading international banks and has been conducted every six weeks since 1981 . The American Express survey covers 250 to 300 central bankers, private bankers, corporate treasurers and economists, and has been conducted more irregularly since 1976.

data instead of the forward discount, is excessive speculation in the sense of Bilson (1981) : investors would have done better during the 1981-85 period if they had routinely reduced their expectations of exchange rate changes. The rejection of rational expectations holds up even if one allows for measurement error in the survey data (provided it is random) : one can reject the hypothesis that expectations are rational and that the apparent bias in the survey numbers is entirely attributable to measurement error. In addition, Froot and Frankel (1989) test the hypothesis that *no* information about the risk premium is revealed in regressions of the ex post change in the spot rate on the forward discount. This hypothesis cannot be rejected, suggesting that the risk premium does not help explain why changes in the forward discount mispredict future changes in the spot rate. The rational expectations hypothesis appears in trouble.

I.3 *An Evaluation of the Safe-Haven and Rational Bubble Hypotheses*

If the survey numbers are taken seriously as measuring investors' rate of expected depreciation, they imply a large *negative* risk premium paid on dollar assets during the 1981-85 period (a sharp decline from the near-zero risk premium in the 1970s). This is very different from the positive risk premium implied by standard tests of bias in the forward discount. Is a negative risk premium plausible nevertheless? Standard portfolio considerations would suggest not. The exchange risk premium in theory should depend on such variables as asset supplies and on return variances and covariances. The large U.S. government budget deficit and current account deficits mean that asset supplies should recently have been driving the dollar risk premium *up*, not down. One could posit an increase in the perceived riskiness of European currencies relative to the dollar, attributable for example to an increase in uncertainly regarding European monetary policy relative to U.S. monetary policy. But in that case it would be difficult to explain the increase in the U.S. interest differential after 1980; by itself a shift in demand toward U.S. assets due to uncertainty should have driven U.S. interest rates down.[11]

There is one explanation that has been seriously proposed for the dollar appreciation that is consistent with both a fall in the risk premium on dollars and an increase in the interest differential, in other words, consistent with the expected rate of depreciation increasing even more than the interest dif-

11. Similarly an increase in U.S. monetary uncertainty could explain higher U.S. interest rates, but not the appreciation of the dollar. On these points, see Branson (1985) and The Council of Economic Advisers (1984, pp. 54-55).

ferential. That is the "safe haven" explanation mentioned above : an exogenous shift in demand toward U.S. assets due to perceptions of reduced country risk in the United States relative to abroad. According to this theory, risk has declined in the United States because of an improved business climate, in particular improved tax treatment for investment after 1981, which also explains the increase in U.S. real interest rates via an alleged investment boom.[12] Risk has increased in the rest of the world, not just because of debt problems in Latin America (which would alone not be relevant for the exchange rate or return differentials between the United States and Europe) but also because of political or country risk in Europe. Dooley and Isard (1985), for example, speak of a perceived threat of penalties on capital in Europe, "where the term 'penalty' is loosely defined to include formal taxation, the postponement of interest and principal payments, confiscation, destruction of property, and so forth".

We here propose a simple test be used to evaluate the safe haven hypothesis : a comparison of interest rates paid on securities that are physically located offshore, but that are denominated in dollars or otherwise covered on the forward exchange market to get around the problem of exchange risk with interest rates paid on securities in the United States. That is, we are testing international closed, or covered, interest parity, not uncovered interest parity.

Tests of the offshore-onshore differential have been frequently employed to illustrate a number of points about the existence of capital controls or country risk: a negative differential for Germany until 1974 showed that capital controls discouraged capital inflow (Dooley and Isard (1980)); a positive differential for the United Kingdom until 1979 showed that capital controls discouraged outflow; positive differentials for France and Italy show that controls still discourage outflow (e.g., Giavazzi and Pagano (1985), Claassen and Wyplosz (1982)); a negative differential for Japan until 1979 showed that controls discouraged inflow (Otani and Tiwari (1981), Ito (1986) and Frankel (1984)); and, but for the foregoing exceptions, the generally small magnitude

12. One widely cited piece of evidence against the safe haven hypothesis is that the increase in U.S. real interest rates was accompanied by a lower investment rate averaged over the 1981-85 period, not a higher one. See, for example, Friedman (1985) or Frankel (1985). However others dispute this calculation; see Blanchard and Summers (1984). Another piece of evidence against the safe haven hypothesis is that the correlation between U.S. stock market price changes and those abroad (Germany or Japan) has been positive; Obstfeld (1985) argues that if portfolio demands had exogenously shifted from foreign assets to U.S. stock market boom should have been accompanied by a stock market decline abroad. See also Feldstein (1986, 7-8).

of differentials shows that capital mobility is very high among the major industrialized countries (e.g., Frenkel and Levich (1975), McCormick (1979), Boothe et al. (1985)).[13]

Table 2 reports mean daily differentials between offshore interest rates (covered) and domestic U.S. interest rates, for seven different pairs of securities. Remarkably, there was a relatively substantial positive differential in almost all cases, until recently, regardless whether one observes the offshore interest rate in the Euromarket, in the domestic U.K. market, or in the domestic German market.[14] From 1979 to 1982, the Euromarket rates exceeded

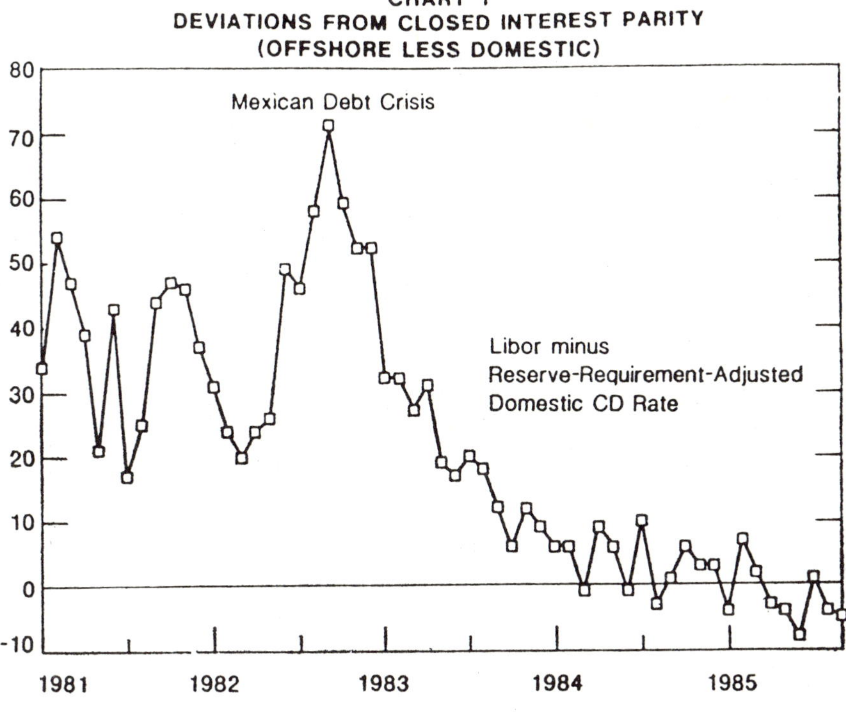

13. "Small" might be defined as less than 50 basis points, to allow for differences in default risk and tax treatment attaching to the particular security, as well as inevitable minor differences in timing.

14. In 1978 the differential between the domestic U.K. and domestic U.S. interest rate is negative (columns 4 or 5 in Table 2). This is because of the above-mentioned U.K.-capital controls that were removed in 1979, as is evident from the differential between the Europound interest rate and domestic U.K. rates (column 2 or 3 in Table 2a).

TABLE 2

Deviations from Closed Interest Parity : Offshore Interest Rate (covered for exchange risk) Minus the United States Interest Rate
(Three-month interest rates in percentage per annum)

Offshore rate U.S. rate	Euro-$ T-Bill	Euro-$ Interbank	Euro £ + fd Interbank	U.K. ib + fd Interbank	U.K. T-Bill + fd T-Bill	Euro-DM+fd Interbank	Ger. ib + fd Interbank
Means							
Year							
1978	1.573	0.564	0.618	−0.840	−0.301	0.738	1.075
1979	1.894	0.786	0.886	0.622	1.656	1.047	1.491
1980	2.581	1.016	1.145	0.989	2.070	1.384	1.931
1981	2.190	0.923	1.080	1.085	2.105	1.242	1.778
1982	2.091	0.900	1.074	1.082	2.066	1.208	1.640
1983	0.660	0.546	0.676	0.691	0.577	0.784	1.127
1984	0.878	0.408	0.566	0.558	0.583	0.709	1.008
1985	0.571	0.295	0.414	0.414	0.410	0.305	0.622
Standard Deviations							
Year							
1978	0.666	0.262	0.390	0.846	0.975	0.477	0.484
1979	0.690	0.272	0.376	0.498	0.751	0.410	0.549
1980	1.027	0.371	0.785	0.795	1.233	0.526	0.565
1981	0.578	0.280	0.353	0.316	0.742	0.344	0.455
1982	0.736	0.205	0.242	0.223	0.746	0.308	0.357
1983	0.156	0.116	0.201	0.222	0.282	0.140	0.186
1984	0.401	0.078	0.143	0.134	0.418	0.194	0.234
1985	0.176	0.109	0.301	0.275	0.498	0.552	0.555

Note : ib ≡ interbank rate.
fd ≡ adjustment for the forward exchange discount.

the U.S. interbank rate by an average of about 100 basis points. A number of studies have noted that the Eurodollar rate does not move perfectly with the U.S. interbank or CD rate (Hartman (1984), Kreicher (1982)). They attribute the differential primarily to the fact that U.S. banks face reserve requirements against domestic deposits but not against Eurodeposits, so they are willing to pay a higher interest rate to depositors offshore. But the differential has been mostly swept under the rug in more general studies of covered interest parity.

Even those who have studied the Eurodollar-U.S. interbank differential treat it as a peculiarity of the banking system alone. This would make sense only if, on the one hand, the U.S. interbank rate were depressed below other U.S. interest rates (by U.S. reserve requirements) or if, on the other hand, Eurocurrency interest rates were raised above domestic European interest rates (either by analogous reserve requirements in European countries or by perceived default risk in the Euromarket). But neither of these effects seems to hold. Table 2a shows small spreads between the Eurodollar rate and the

TABLE 2a

Deviations from Interest Parity Within Jurisdictions
(Three-month interest rates in percentages per annum)

	Euro \$ — fd Euro £	Euro £ U.S. interbank	Euro £ U.K. T-bill	Euro \$ — fd Euro DM	Euro DM Ger. interbank
Means					
Year					
1978	—0.066	1.432	1.895	—0.187	—0.335
1979	—0.103	0.289	0.363	—0.220	—0.444
1980	—0.123	0.156	0.658	—0.373	—0.549
1981	—0.161	—0.004	0.228	—0.319	—0.525
1982	—0.179	0.003	0.207	—0.311	—0.431
1983	—0.131	—0.010	0.217	—0.239	—0.341
1984	—0.158	0.009	0.451	—0.300	—0.296
1985	—0.121	0.008	0.393	—0.100	—0.222
Standard Deviations					
Year					
1978	0.280	0.866	0.822	0.350	0.175
1979	0.272	0.288	0.466	0.408	0.253
1980	0.719	0.335	0.605	0.376	0.292
1981	0.286	0.250	0.470	0.250	0.317
1982	0.214	0.188	0.300	0.270	0.168
1983	0.179	0.143	0.240	0.088	0.113
1984	0.143	0.125	0.233	0.173	0.100
1985	0.285	0.119	0.418	0.552	0.094

Europound or Euromark rates (covered) or between them and the domestic U.K. and German interest rates. Indeed, Table 2 shows that the spread between covered pound or mark interest rates and domestic U.S. rates is even higher, and comes down even more after 1982, when Treasury bill rates are used than when banking rates are used. This finding contradicts the hypothesis that U.S. reserve requirements are the only factor driving a wedge between the Euromarket and the U.S. interbank market and that more direct arbitrage through other means works to reduce that wedge.

Why were foreigners and U.S. residents buying U.S. Treasury bills in 1979-1982 when they paid about 2 percent less than U.K. Treasury bills? The obvious response is that U.S. securities were preferred for safe-haven reasons. But since the differential predates the appreciation of the dollar, there is some difficulty in associating the two. This is particularly true after 1982, when the differential declines sharply. By 1985, when the dollar had appreciated much further, the Eurodollar rate was only 30 basis points above the domestic U.S. interbank interest rate, in the same range as the differentials for the pound, mark, yen, Canadian dollar, and Swiss franc. Chart 1 shows a comparison of the London Interbank Offer Rate (LIBOR) with a domestic U.S. CD rate, adjusted for reserve requirements. The differential, which was clearly positive in the early 1980s, peaked during the Mexican debt crisis in August 1982 and declined steadily afterward, reaching zero in early 1985, about the time when the dollar's value peaked. The evidence thus suggests that the United States was perceived as *increasingly* risky after 1982, not less risky as the safe-haven hypothesis would claim.

It should be noted that in 1980-82 there also existed a differential in long-term interest rates, and that it went the opposite direction. U.S. corporations were able to borrow more cheaply by issuing Eurodollar bonds than by issuing bonds domestically. The differential reached 3.3 percent in July 1981.[15] It is not clear why U.S. borrowers did not take greater advantage of the cheaper offshore rates than they did. The differential fell sharply in mid-1982, at the same time that the short-term differential began approaching zero from the opposite direction. The mid-1982 decline in the long-term U.S. interest rate relative to the Eurobond rate is consistent with the hypothesis of a safe-haven shift into U.S. assets at that one point in time. But it is also consistent with another hypothesis.

15. The data are from Morgan Guaranty. See Frankel (1987, 9.5.1). Kim and Stulz (1987) show that U.S. corporations could indeed profit by borrowing more cheaply in the Euromarket than domestically from 1979 to the beginning of 1984. They find that the differential fell in 1982, and fell further in 1984, so that it is now zero.

As late as 1982 there remained some frictions that prevented perfect arbitrage between the U.S. and Euromarkets. After U.S. corporate bond rates rose to post-war record levels in 1980 and 1981, and after the debt crisis that began in August 1982 undermined confidence in the banking system, U.S. corporations found they had a keener interest in issuing bonds directly in the Euromarket. Such innovations as currency swaps, interest rate swaps, note issuance facilities and Eurocommercial paper developed rapidly in 1983 and 1984, making it easier for U.S. corporations to use the Euromarket without the intermediation of banks. This was the well-known trend of "securitization". Securities-market facilities (as opposed to bank loans) rose from 26 percent of total new lending facilities arranged in international financial markets in 1981, to 59 percent in 1983 and 91 percent in 1985.[16] Foreign net purchases of U.S. corporate securities rose from $ 15 billion in 1982 to $ 48 billion in 1985, most of it through the Euromarket (U.S. *Federal Reserve Bulletin*, May 1985, May 1986). Thus the hypothesis is that it simply took several years to arbitrage away the interest differential that opened up in 1980-82. This might be regarded as a relatively rapid response of the financial markets rather than a puzzlingly slow one, when viewed in the light of the institutional innovations needed and the large shift in the quantity of Eurobond issues involved. The hypothesis that the last barriers to perfect international financial integration were broken down around 1982 has the advantage that it can explain, not only the sharp fall in the positive Euro-U.S. differential at the long end of the maturity spectrum, but the sharp fall in the reverse differential at the short end of the spectrum as well.

Even if one instead interprets the mid-1982 fall in the long-term interest differential as evidence of a safe-haven shift into U.S. assets at that time, this factor cannot explain the continued increase in the demand for dollars through February 1985. The differential was steady, or if anything rose a little, in 1983 and 1984. The story based on safe-haven fundamentals does not explain the final stages of the dollar appreciation any better than the story based on real interest fundamentals. There is in any case little left of the safe-haven hypothesis after the 1985-87 depreciation. The field would appear to be open to bubble theories to explain the rise and fall of the dollar.

The possibility of speculative bubbles leads to the second explanation, besides the risk premium, that is often given for the econometric findings of biasedness in the forward exchange market : the peso problem. The standard tests presume that the error term, the difference between expected depreciation and the ex post realization, is distributed normally and independently

16. The source is Bryant (1987), p. 56.

over time. But if there is a small probability of a big decline in the value of the currency, the distributional assumption will not be met, the estimated standard errors will be incorrect, and unbiasedness may be spuriously rejected.[17] This problem is thought to be relevant for pegged currencies like the Mexican peso up until 1976, and generally less relevant for floating currencies. But if the dollar has been on a single speculative bubble path for four years, there could well be a small probability of a large decline in the form of a bursting of the bubble. It has been suggested that the forward discount may properly reflect that possibility, and that tests find a bias only because the event happens not to have occurred in the sample.

Calculations in Frankel (1985) tend to undermine the hypothesis that the forward discount during the period 1981-85 reflected rational expectations of a small probability of a large decline in the value of the dollar. Under the hypothesis that the bursting of the bubble would reverse half of the real appreciation of the dollar against the mark that has taken place since the 1970s, a 3 percent forward discount in March 1985 implied a 2.8 percent perceived probability of collapse during that month. One can multiply out the implied probabilities of non-collapse since January 1981, with no distributional assumptions needed, to find that the chance that such a bubble would have persisted for four years without bursting is only 3 percent. Thus the peso problem does not "get the forward exchange market off the hook". The period during which the forward discount was positive with no realized depreciation simply went on too long for the rational expectations hypothesis to emerge intact.

II. FUNDAMENTALISTS AND CHARTISTS

We can gather the conclusions reached so far into four propositions, each with elements of paradox.

(1) The dollar continued to rise even after all fundamentals (the interest differential, current account, country risk premium, etc.) apparently began moving the wrong way. The only explanation left would seem to be, almost tautologically, that investors were responding to a rising expected rate of change in the value of the dollar. In other words, the dollar was on a bubble path.

(2) Evidence suggests that the investor-expected rate of depreciation reflected in the forward discount is not equal to the rationally-expected rate

17. Evans (1986) avoids this problem by employing a nonparametric sign test of the forward rate prediction errors. Possible failure of the assumption that the error term is independently distributed, however, would remain a problem.

of depreciation. The failure of a fall in the dollar to materialize in four years implies that the rationally-expected rate of depreciation was *less* than the forward discount.

(3) On the other hand, Krugman-Marris current account calculations suggested that the rational-expected rate of depreciation was *greater* than the current forward discount.

(4) The survey data show that the respondents have since 1981 indeed held an expected rate of depreciation substantially greater than the forward discount. But interpreting their responses as true investor expectations raises a problem. If investors seriously expected the dollar to depreciate so fast, why did they buy dollars?

The model of fundamentalists and chartists that we are proposing has been designed to reconcile these conflicting conclusions. To begin with, we hypothesize that the views represented in the American Express and Economist long-term surveys are primarily fundamentalist, like the views of Krugman and Marris (and most other economists). But it may be wrong to assume that investors' expected rate of depreciation is necessarily the one reported in the long-term surveys or that there even is such a thing as "the" expected rate of depreciation (as most of our models do). Expectations are heterogeneous. Our model suggests that the market gives heavy weight to the chartists, whose expected rate of change in the value of the dollar has been on average much closer to zero, perhaps even positive. Paradox (4) is answered if fundamentalists' expectations are not the only ones determining positions that investors take in the market.

The increasing dollar overvaluation after the interest differential peaked in 1982 (measured short-term) or 1984 (measured long-term) would be explained by a falling market-expected rate of future depreciation (or rising expected rate of appreciation), with no necessary basis in fundamentals. The market-expected rate of depreciation declined over time, not necessarily because of any change in the expectations held by chartists or fundamentalists, but rather because of a shift in the weights assigned to the two by the portfolio managers, the agents who take positions in the market and determine the exchange rate. They gradually put less and less weight on the big-depreciation forecasts of the fundamentalists, as these forecasts continue to be proven false, and more and more weight on the chartists.

There is direct evidence that by 1985 most market participants were paying scant attention to fundamentals. By then, most of the forecasting services that appear in an annual survey by *Euromoney* were described as using technical analysis. "In the early 1980s, the surveys appeared to have convinced many readers that forecasts could be used profitably and that the most profitable forex forecasters were technical rather than those who focused on economic fundamentals". (August, 1987, p. 121). The 1987 survey of services reported that none offered pure fundamentals forecasts, 5 offered fundamentals forecasts at longer horizons and technical analysis at shorter horizons, 3 offered forecasts combining the two techniques, 13 offered only technical analysis, and 4 did not specify a technique (these last firms often show their clients how to hedge risk, rather than trying to outguess the market). Despite its widespread use in the markets, only a handful of economists have studied the phenomenon of technical analysis. Schulmeister (1987) offers a useful description of the various rules of technical analysis that are in widest use and calculates that all the rules would have made money over the period 1973-86 (his Table 9) as a whole, as well as over each of the nine 18-month subperiods. He cites a 1985 statistic from the Group of 30 that 97 percent of banks and 87 percent of securities houses report the belief that "the use of technical models has had an increasingly significant impact on the market" (p. 14), and expresses disapproval that economists have not seriously studied such rules that are actually used by traders. Reszat (1987) also reports that technical analysis is in widespread use. Goodman (1979) finds that the forecasts of technical analysis perform relatively well (for example, beating the forward rate), though Blake, Beenstock and Brasse (1986) find that forecasting services do *not* beat the forward rate.

II.1 *The Volume of Trading in the Market*

In this section we look at the volume of trading in the foreign exchange market. Mainstream finance theory has very little to say about the volume of trading, and concentrates rather on asset-pricing. When a new piece of information becomes available, if all investors process the information in the same way and are otherwise identical, no trading needs take place. The price of the asset should simply jump to its new value. To explain the volume of trading, some heterogeneity of investors is required.

Trading volume in foreign exchange markets has become enormous. In March 1986, transactions in the U.S. foreign exchange market (eliminating doublecounting) averaged \$50 billion a day among banks (up 92% from 1983), and \$34.4 billion a day among brokers and other financial institutions. Most importantly, only 11.5 percent of the trading reported by banks was with non-bank customers (of which 4.6 percent was with nonfinancial customers), only 14.3 percent of brokers' transactions involved a non-bank, and only 19.2 percent of trading reported by other financial institutions was with customers (of which 7.7 percent were nonfinancial institutions).[18] In London the total was $90 billion a day. Only 9 percent of the banks' transactions were directly with customers.[19] Tokyo was counted at $48 billion. The rest of the Pacific has been estimated at $29 to 37 billion, and Zurich and Frankfurt together have been estimated as big as New York. Thus worldwide trading exceeds $300 billion a day. These totals are not only many times greater than the volume of international trade in goods and services. They are also many times greater than the volume of international trade in long-term capital, 59 times greater, for the case of Germany, according to an estimate by Schulmeister (1987, p. 8).

Clearly, trading among themselves is a major economic activity for banks and other financial institutions. Schulmeister (1987, p. 24) has found that in 1985, twelve large U.S. banks earned a foreign exchange trading income of $1,165 million. Every single bank reported a profit from its foreign exchange business in every single year that he examined. Goodhart (1988, p. 449 and Appendix D) has surveyed banks that specialize in the London foreign exchange market: "Traders, so it is claimed, consistently make profits from their position-taking (and those who do not, get fired), over and above their return from straight dealing, owing to the bid/ask spread" (p. 456). The banks report that their speculation (that is, taking an open position) does not take place in the forward market [and only 4-5 percent of their large corporate customers were prepared to take open positions in the forward market]. Rather the banks take very short-term open positions in the spot market. Apparently they consider the taking of long-term positions based on fundamentals, or of any sort of position in the forward exchange market, as too "speculative" and risky. But the banks are willing to trust their spot exchange traders to take large open positions, provided they close most of them out by the end of the day, because these operations are profitable in the aggregate.[20] In the description of Goodhart, and others as well, a typical spot trader does not buy and sell on the basis of any fundamentals model, but rather trades on the basis of knowledge as to which other traders are offering what deals at a given time, and a feel for what their behavior is likely to be later in the day.

The reported profits are not so large that, when divided by the volume of "real" transactions for customers, they need necessarily lie outside the normal (relatively small) band on the bid-ask spread. In other words, the profits

18. The source is Federal Reserve Bank of New York (1986).

19. The source is Bank of England (1986). See also Goodhart (1988, p. 456).

20. Reportedly, a minority of traders are allowed to hold open positions overnight, at the discretion of superiors.

represent the transactions cost for the outside customers. One might expect that this large volume of trading therefore cannot be relevant from a larger macroeconomic perspective, i.e., for understanding the movement of the exchange rate (except perhaps on an intra-daily basis). But this look at the mechanics of trading does offer some important implications.

In the first place, the large volume of trading in itself suggests that market participants are not identical agents who share the same, rational, expectation. Participants are heterogeneous, with respect to both the portfolios they hold and the expectations they hold. In the *Economist* six-month expectations survey data, the high-low range of responses averages 15.2 percent.

In the second place, most trading is motivated by a very short-term horizon.[21] According to *Euromoney*, August 1987, p. 113, one forecasting service makes forecasts every 15 minutes. Another gives its customers beepers so they can be contacted at short notice. Many of the services refused to give *Euromoney* forecasts at a horizon as long as six months saying their systems "were orientated [sic] towards a shorter-term horizon" (p. 119). There were few investors, as of 1984, anxious to buy and hold long-term mark or yen securities merely because the dollar was overvalued according to the fundamentals. This is what McKinnon (1976) refers to as "an absence of stabilizing speculation".

There is for some reason a breakdown of the economists' rule of rationality that the long run is the sum of a series of expected short runs. Even though the market is not taking adequate account of the fact that the exchange rate must return to equilibrium eventually, there is no easy way for an investor to make expected profits from this mistake, unless he has sufficient patience, and sufficiently low risk-aversion, to wait through the short-term volatility. Summers (1986) argues that, because variability is so great, neither the econometrician nor the investor can tell if there are expected excess profits to be made from selling an asset whose market price appears to exceed its fundamental price due to a slow-disappearing "fad". Arrow (1982) argues similarly. Both cite the work of Tversky and Kahneman (1981) that individuals overreact to current, visible information, which in this context means putting too much weight on the current spot rate in forming their expectations, and not enough weight on long-term fundamentals. The result is that economic fundamentals do not enter into most traders' behavior, even if fundamentals must win out in the long run. Indeed, most traders are so young, and have been at their current job so short a time, that they may not even remember

21. DeLong et al (1987) call the oft-heard proposition that the markets' perspective is too short-term the "Wojnilower problem".

the preceding major upswing or downswing four years earlier! This short-term perspective need not be irrational from the viewpoint of the individual bank. Allowing its traders to take a sequence of many short-term open positions in the spot market may be the bank's only way of learning which traders can make money at it and which cannot.

II.2 *Empirical Results on Short-term versus Long-term Expectations*

Before we proceed to show how our model works, we offer further evidence from the survey data that there is not a single homogeneous expected rate of depreciation : The very short-term expectations (one-week and two-week) reported in a third survey of market participants, by Money Market Services, Inc., behave very differently from the medium-term expectations (3, 6, or 12 month) reported in any of the three surveys.[22]

One way of distinguishing empirically between the shorter- and longer-term expectations is to examine the weight survey respondents place on variables other than the contemporaneous spot rate in forming their expectations at different time horizons. Suppose, for example, that investors assign a weight of g to the lagged spot rate and a weight of $1-g$ to the current spot rate in forming their expectation of the future spot rate :

$$s^m_{t+1} = (1-g)s_t + gs_{t-1} \tag{1}$$

where s_t is the logarithm of the current spot rate, and s^m_{t+1} is the market's expected future spot rate at time t. Subtracting s from both sides we have that expected depreciation is proportional to the current change in the spot rate:

$$\Delta s^m_{t+1} = - g\Delta s_t. \tag{2}$$

We term the model in equation (2) extrapolative expectations. If investors place positive weight on the lagged spot rate, so that g is positive, then equation (1) says that investors' expected future spot rate is a simple distributed lag. On the other hand, if investors tend to extrapolate the most recent change in the spot rate, so that g is negative, then equation (2) may be termed "bandwagon" expectations. We might, for instance, associate the fundamentalist

22. The Money Market Services Survey has been conducted weekly or biweekly since 1983. For more extensive analyses of this survey data set, see Dominguez (1986), Frankel and Froot (1987), and Froot and Frankel (1989).

viewpoint with a tendency to expect a currency which has recently appreciated to depreciate in the future ($g > 0$), and the chartist viewpoint with a tendency to expect on average some continuation of the past trend ($g < 0$).

Table 3 reports regression estimates of equation (2), using the survey expected depreciation as the lefthand-side variable.[23] The findings are ordered by the forecast horizon, from the shortest-term 1 and 2 week expectations, to the longer-term 12 month expectations. It is immediately evident that the shorter term expectations – 1 week, 2 weeks and 1 month – all exhibit significant bandwagon tendencies: that $g < 0$. On the 1 week expectations, for example, an appreciation of 10 percent over the past week by itself generates the expectation that the spot rate will appreciate another 1.35 percent in the next seven days. This result is characteristic of destabilizing expectations, in which a current appreciation generates self-sustaining expectations of future appreciation.

In contrast with the shorter-term expectations, the longer-term results all point toward stabilizing distributed lag expectations. Each of the regressions at the 6 and 12 month forecast horizons estimates g to be significantly greater than zero.[24] The Economist 12 month data, for example, imply that a current 10 percent appreciation by itself generates an expectation of a 2.02 percent *depreciation* over the coming 12 months. Thus longer-term expectations feature a strongly positive weight on the lagged spot rate rather than complete weight on the contemporaneous spot rate, and in this sense they are stabilizing.

A second popular specification for the expected future spot rate is that it is a weighted average of the current spot rate and the (log) long-run equilibrium spot rate, $\bar{s}_t$:

$$s^m_{t+1} = (1 - \theta)s_t + \theta\bar{s}_t \tag{3}$$

or in terms of expected depreciation:

$$\Delta s^m_{t+1} = \theta(\bar{s}_t - s_t) \tag{4}$$

23. In the regressions reported in Tables 3, 4, and 5, we use Seemingly Unrelated Squares (SUR) to exploit efficiently the contemporaneous correlation across currencies. Each currency was given its own constant term, but the constants are not reported here. See Frankel and Froot (1987) for more detail on the behavior of the survey numbers in terms of standard models of expected depreciation.

24. In Frankel and Foot (1987), we correct for the low Durbin-Watson statistics in these regressions (and those in Tables 4 and 5) using a three stages least squares estimation technique which allows for first order serial correlation in the residuals. The results are not repeated here since they are very similar to the SUR estimates already reported in Tables 3-5.

TABLE 3

Extrapolative Expectations

Independent variables : $s_{t-1} - s_t$

SUR Regressions (1) of Survey Expected Depreciation : $s^e_{t+1} - s_t = a + g(s_{t-1} - s_t)$

Data Set	Dates	Coefficient $\hat{g}$	$t: g=0$	DW(2)	DF	R^2
MMS 1 Week	10/84– 2/86	–0.1345 (0.0254)	–5.30***	1.89	239	0.76
MMS 2 Week	1/83–10/84	–0.0565 (0.0267)	–2.12**	1.76	179	0.33
MMS 1 Month	10/84– 2/86	–0.0536 (0.0217)	–2.47**	1.48	171	0.40
MMS 3 Month	1/83–10/84	–0.0391 (0.0168)	–2.32**	1.49	179	0.37
Economist 3 Month	6/81–12/86	0.0416 (0.0210)	1.98*	1.81	184	0.30
Economist 6 Month	6/81–12/85	0.0730 (0.0225)	3.25***	1.36	184	0.54
Amex 6 Month	1/76– 8/85	0.2994 (0.0487)	6.15***	1.89	45	0.81
Economist 12 Month	6/81–12/85	0.2018 (0.0296)	6.82***	1.47	184	0.84
Amex 12 Month	1/76– 8/85	0.3796 (0.0798)	4.76***	0.94	45	0.72

(1) Amex 6 and 12 month regressions use OLS due to the small number of degrees of freedom.

(2) The DW statistic is the average of the equation-by-equation OLS Durbin-Watson statistics for each data set. * Represents significance at the 10 percent level. ** Represents significance at the 5 percent level. *** Represents significance at the 1 percent level. R^2 corresponds to an F test on all nonintercept parameters. Some of the above results are reported in Frankel and Froot (1987). Constant terms for each currency were included in the regressions, but not reported above.

If θ is positive, as, for example, in the Dornbusch overshooting model, the spot rate is expected to move in the direction of $\bar{s}_t$. Expectations are therefore regressive. This formulation for expectations is perhaps closest to the fundamentalists' view, because the long-run equilibrium to which investors expect the spot rate to return, $\bar{s}_t$, is determined by (fundamental) factors in the real economy. Alternatively, a finding of $\theta < 0$ implies that investors expect the spot rate to move away from the long-run equilibrium.

Table 4 presents tests of equation (4). Once again, there is strong evidence that shorter-term expectations are formed in a different manner than longer-term expectations. The shorter forecast horizons all yield estimates of θ that are negative, additional evidence that shorter term speculation may be destabilizing. Indeed, the 1 week data suggests that the contemporaneous deviation from the long-run equilibrium is expected on average to *grow* by 3 percent over the subsequent seven days. In other words, short-term expectations are explosive. The significantly positive estimates of θ in the longer-term data sets suggest by contrast that longer-term expectations are strongly regressive. In the Economist 12 month data, for example, respondents expect any current deviation from the long-run equilibrium to decay by 17.5 percent over the following 12 months.

The final specification we consider is adaptive expectations. In this case, agents are hypothesized to form their expectation of the future spot rate as a weighted average of the current spot rate and the lagged expected spot rate :

$$s^m_{t+1} = (1 - \gamma)s_t + \gamma s^m_t \tag{5}$$

Expected depreciation is now proportional to the contemporaneous prediction error :

$$\Delta s^m_{t+1} = \gamma(s^m_t - s_t). \tag{6}$$

Table 5 reports estimates of equation (6). The R^2 statistics are generally lower than in Tables 3 and 4, suggesting that the surveys are not characterized as well by adaptive expectations as they are by regressive and extrapolative expectations. Nevertheless, the results are qualitatively comparable with those of the previous two tables. The shorter-term expectations place significantly negative weight on the lagged expectation. At the same time there is evidence that the longer-term data place positive weight on the lagged expectation, that longer-term expectations are adaptive.

The results of Tables 3, 4 and 5 suggest that in all three of our standard models of expectations – extrapolative, regressive and adaptive – short-term and long-term expectations behave very differently from one another. In

TABLE 4

Regressive Expectations

Independent variable : $\bar{s}_t - s_t$

Long Run Equilibrium PPP

SUR Regressions (1) of Survey Expected Depreciation : $s_{t+1}^e - s_t = a + \theta(\bar{s}_t - s_t)$

Data Set	Dates	Coefficient $\hat{\theta}$	$t : \theta = 0$	DW(2)	DF	R^2
MMS 1 Week	10/84–2/86	—0.0283 (0.0080)	—3.53***	21.0	219	0.58
MMS 2 Week	1/83–10/84	—0.0299 (0.0079)	—3.78***	2.15	179	0.61
MMS 1 Month	10/84–2/86	—0.0782 (0.0134)	—5.84***	1.40	151	0.79
MMS 3 Month	1/83–10/84	—0.0270 (0.0146)	—1.41	1.55	179	0.18
Economist 3 Month	6/81–12/85	0.0223 (0.0126)	1.78*	1.66	184	0.26
Economist 6 Month	6/81–12/85	0.0600 (0.0159)	3.77***	1.32	184	0.61
Amex 6 Month	1/76–8/85	0.0315 (0.0202)	1.56	1.22	45	0.21
Economist 12 Month	6/81–12/85	0.1750 (0.0216)	8.10***	1.25	184	0.88
Amex 12 Month	1/76–8/85	0.1236 (0.0276)	4.48***	0.60	45	0.69

(1) Amex 6 and 12 month regressions use OLS due to the small number of degrees of freedom.

(2) The DW statistic is the average of the equation-by-equation OLS Durbin-Watson statistics for each data set. * Represents significance at the 10 percent level. ** Represents significance at the 5 percent level. *** Represents significance at the 1 percent level. R^2 corresponds to an F test on all nonintercept parameters. Some of the above results are reported in Frankel and Froot (1987). Constant terms for each currency were included in the regressions, but not reported above.

TABLE 5

Adaptive Expectations

Independent variable : $s_t^e - s_t$

SUR Regressions (1) of Survey Expected Depreciation : $s_{t+1}^e - s_t = a + \gamma(s_t^e - s_t)$

Data Set	Dates	Coefficient $\hat{\gamma}$	$t:\gamma = 0$	DW(2)	DF	R^2
MMS 1 Week	10/84- 2/86	—0.1047 (0.0256)	—4.09***	1.69	211	0.65
MMS 2 Week	1/83-10/84	—0.0296 (0.0255)	—1.16	1.68	175	0.13
MMS 1 Month	10/84- 2/86	0.0121 (0.0235)	0.52	1.313	135	0.03
MMS 3 Month	1/83-10/84	—0.0272 (0.0215)	—1.27	1.29	159	0.15
Economist 3 Month	6/81-12/85	0.0798 (0.0203)	3.93***	2.01	169	0.63
Economist 6 Month	6/81-12/85	0.0516 (0.0161)	3.20***	1.12	159	0.53
Amex 6 Month	1/76- 8/85	—0.0702 (0.1200)	—0.59	2.10	15	0.04
Economist 12 Month	6/81-12/85	—0.0093 (0.0244)	—0.38	1.10	139	0.02
Amex 12 Month	1/76- 8/85	0.0946 (0.0212)	4.46***	0.55	31	0.69

(1) Amex 6 and 12 month regressions use OLS due to the small number of degrees of freedom.

(2) The DW statistic is the equation-by-equation OLS Durbin-Watson statistics for each data set. * Represents significance at the 10 percent level. ** Represents significance at the 5 percent level. *** Represents significance at the 1 percent level. R^2 corresponds to an F test on all nonintercept parameters. Some of the above results are reported in Frankel and Froot (1987). Constant terms for each currency were included in the regressions, but not reported above.

terms of the distinction between fundamentalists and chartists views, we associate the longer-term expectations, which are consistently stabilizing, with the the fundamentalists, and the shorter-term forecasts, which seem to have a destabilizing nature, with the chartist expectations. Within each of the above tables, it is as if there are actually two models of expectations operating, one at each end of the spectrum of forecast horizons, and a blend in between. Under this view, respondents use some weighted average of the chartist and fundamentalist forecasts in formulating their expectations for the value of the dollar at a given future date, with weights depending on how far off that date is.

These results suggest an alternative interpretation of how chartist and fundamentalist views are aggregated in the marketplace, an aggregation that takes place without the benefit of portfolio managers. It is possible that the chartists are simply people who tend to think short-term and the fundamentalists are people who tend to think long term. For example, the former may by profession be "traders", people who buy and sell foreign exchange on a short-term basis and have evolved different ways of thinking than the latter, who may by profession buy and hold longer-term securities.[25]

In any case, one could interpret the two groups as taking positions in the market directly, rather than merely issuing forecasts for the portfolio managers to read. The market price of foreign exchange would then be determined by demand coming from both groups. But the weights that the market gives to the two change over time, according to the groups' respective wealths.[26] If the fundamentalists sell the dollar short and keep losing money, while the chartists go long and keep gaining, in the long run the fundamentalists will go bankrupt and there will only be chartists in the marketplace. The model that we develop in the next section pursues the portfolio manager's decision-making problem instead of the marketplace-aggregation idea, but the two are similar in spirit.

Yet another possible interpretation of the survey data is that the two ways of thinking represent conflicting forces within the mind of a single representative agent. When respondents answer the longer-term surveys they give the views that their economic reason tells them are correct. When they get into the trading room they give greater weight to their instincts, especially if past bets based on their economic reason have been followed by ruinous

25. It sounds strange to describe 6 to 12 months as "long-term". But such descriptions are common in the foreign exchange markets.

26. Figlewski (1978, 1982) considers an economy in which private information, weighted by traders' relative wealths, is revealed in the market price.

"negative reinforcement". A respondent may think that when the dollar begins its plunge, he or she will be able to get out before everyone else does. This opposing instinctual force comes out in the survey only when the question pertains to the very short term – one or two weeks; it would be too big a contradiction for his conscience if a respondent were to report a one-week expectation of dollar depreciation that was (proportionately) just as big as the answer to the 6-month question, at the same time that he or she was taking a long position in dollars. Again, we prefer the interpretation where the survey reflects the true expectations of the respondent, and the market trading is done by some higher authority; but others may prefer the more complex psychological interpretation.

The fragments of empirical evidence in Tables 3, 4, and 5 are the only ones we will offer by way of testing our approach. The aim in what follows is to construct a model that reconciles the apparent contradictions discussed in Part 1. There will be no further hypothesis testing.

II.3 *An Estimate of the Weights*

We think of the value of the dollar as being driven by the decisions of portfolio managers who use a weighted average of the expectations of fundamentalists and chartists. Specifically,

$$\Delta s^{m}_{t+1} = \omega_t \Delta s^{f}_{t+1} + (1 - \omega_t)\Delta s^{c}_{t+1} \tag{7}$$

where Δs^{m}_{t+1} is the rate of change in the spot rate expected by the portfolio managers, Δs^{f}_{t+1} and Δs^{c}_{t+1} are defined similarly for the fundamentalists and chartists, and ω_t is the weight given to fundamentalist views. For simplicity we assume $\Delta s^{c}_{t+1} = 0$. Thus equation (7) becomes

$$\Delta s^{m}_{t+1} = \omega_t \Delta s^{f}_{t+1} \tag{8}$$

or

$$\omega_t = \frac{\Delta s^{m}_{t+1}}{\Delta s^{f}_{t+1}}.$$

If we take the 6-month forward discount to be representative of portfolio managers' expectations and the 6-month survey to be representative of fundamentalists' expectations, we can get a rough idea of how the weight, ω, varies over time.

Table 6 contains estimates of ω from the late 1970s to 1985. (There are unfortunately, no survey data for 1980.) The table indicates a preponderance of fundamentalism in the late seventies; portfolio managers gave almost complete weight to this view. But beginning in 1981, as the dollar began to rise, the forward discount increased less rapidly than fundamentalists' expected depreciation, indicating that the market (the porfolio managers in our story) was beginning to pay less attention to the fundamentalists' view. By 1985, the market's expected depreciation had fallen to about zero. According to these computations, fundamentalists were being completely ignored.

TABLE 6

Estimated Weights Given to Fundamentalists by Portfolio Managers

	Year					
	1976–79	1981	1982	1983	1984	1985
(1) Forward discount fd	1.06	3.74	3.01	1.10	3.07	−0.16
(2) Survey expected depreciation $[s_{t+6} - s_t]^m$	1.20	8.90	10.31	10.42	11.66	4.00
(1)/(2) $\omega_t \equiv (fd/[s_{t+6} - s_t]^m)$	0.88	0.42	0.29	0.11	0.26	−0.04

Notes: Forward discount, 1976-85, is at 6 months and includes data through September 1985 for the average of five currencies, the pound, French franc, mark, Swiss franc and yen. Survey expected depreciation 1981-85 is from the Economist 6 month survey data, and for 1976-79 is from the AMEX survey data for the same five currencies.

While the above scenario solves the paradox posed in proposition (4), it leaves unanswered the question of how the weight ω_t, which appears to have fallen dramatically since the late 1970s, is determined by porfolio managers. Furthermore, if portfolio managers have small risk premia, and thus expect depreciation at a rate close to that predicted by the forward discount, we still must account for the spectacular rise of the dollar (proposition (1)), and resolve how the *rationally* expected depreciation differs from the forward discount (propositions (2) and (3)).

III. PORTFOLIO MANAGERS AND EXCHANGE RATE DYNAMICS

Up to this point we have characterized the chartist and fundamentalist views of the world, and hinted at the approximate mix that portfolio managers would need to use if the market risk premium is to be near zero. We now turn to an examination of the behavior of portfolio managers, and to the determination of the equilibrium spot rate. In particular, we first focus exclusively on the dynamics of the spot rate which are generated by the changing expectations of portfolio managers. We then extend the framework to include the evolution of fundamentals which eventually must bring the dollar back down.

III.1 *Determination of the Exchange Rate*

A general model of exchange rate determination can be written

$$s_t = c\Delta s^m_{t+1} + z_t \tag{9}$$

where s_t is the log of the spot rate, Δs^m_{t+1} is the rate of depreciation expected by "the market" (portfolio managers) and z_t represents other contemporaneous determinants. This very general formulation, in which the first term can be thought of as speculative factors and the second as fundamentals, has been used by Mussa (1976), Kohlhagen (1978), and Frenkel and Mussa (1980). An easy way to interpret equation (9) is in terms of the monetary model of Mussa (1976), Frenkel (1976) and Bilson (1978). Then c would be interpreted as the semi-elasticity of money demand with respect to the alternative rate of return (which could be the interest differential, expected depreciation or expected inflation differential; as noted in section 1.1, the three are equal if uncovered interest parity and purchasing power parity hold), and z_t would be interpreted as the log of the domestic money supply relative to the foreign (minus the log of relative income, or any other determinants of real money demand). An interpretation of equation (9) in terms of the portfolio-balance approach is slightly more awkward because of nonlinearity. But we could define

$$z_t = d_t - f_t - c\,(i_t - i^*_t) \tag{10}$$

where d_t is the log of the supply of domestic assets including not only money but also bonds and other assets, f_t is the log of the supply of foreign assets, and $i_t - i^*_t$ is the nominal interest differential. Then equation (9) can be derived as a linear approximation to the solution for the spot rate in a system where the share of the portfolio allocated to foreign assets depends on the expected return differential or risk premium, $i_t - i^*_t - \Delta s^m_{t+1}$. If investors diversify their portfolios optimally, c can be seen to depend inversely on the variance of the exchange rate and the coefficient of relative risk-aversion.[27] In any case, the key point behind equation (9), common throughout the asset-market view of exchange rates, is that an increase in the expected rate of fu-

27. See, for example, Frankel (1985).

ture depreciation will reduce demand for the currency today, and therefore will cause it to depreciate today.

The present paper imbeds in the otherwise standard asset pricing model given by equation (9) form of market expectations that follows equation (7). That is, we assume that portfolio managers' expectations are a weighted average of the expectations of fundamentalists, who think the spot rate regresses to long-run equilibrium, and the expectations of chartists who use time series methods :

$$\Delta s^{m}_{t+1} = \omega_t \Delta s^{f}_{t+1} + (1 - \omega_t)\Delta s^{c}_{t+1} \tag{11}$$

We define s to be the logarithm of the long-run equilibrium rate and θ to be the speed of regression of s_t to $\bar{s}$. In the view of fundamentalists :

$$\Delta s^{f}_{t+1} = \theta(\bar{s} - s_t) \tag{12}$$

In the context of some standard versions of equation (9) – the monetary model of Dornbusch (1976) in which goods prices adjust slowly over time or the portfolio-balance models in which the stock of foreign assets adjusts slowly over time – it can be shown that equation (12) might be precisely the rational form for expectations to take if there were no chartists in the market, $\omega_t = 1$. Unfortunately for the fundamentalists, the distinction ("if") is crucial; equation (12) will not be rational given the complete model.

For example, if we define z_t in equation (9) as the interest differential we have

$$s_t = a + c\theta(\bar{s} - s_t) - b(i_t - i^*_t) \tag{13}$$

Uncovered interest parity, $i(t) - i^* = \theta(\bar{s} - s(t))$, implies that $\theta = 1/(\beta - c)$ and $a = \bar{s}$. It is then straightforward to show that b can be rational within the Dornbusch (1976) overshooting model.[28]

In the second group of models (Kouri (1976) and Rodriguez (1980) are references), overshooting occurs because the stock of net foreign assets

28. Assume that prices evolve slowly according to $\dot{p} = \pi(\lambda(s\text{-}p) - \sigma(i - i^*))$ (where λ and σ are the elasticities of goods demand with respect to the real exchange rate and the interest rate, respectively); that the interest rate differential is proportional to the gap between the current and long-run price levels, $\lambda(i - i^*) = p - \bar{p}$ (where λ is the semi-elasticity of money demand with respect to the interest rate); and that the long-run equilibrium exchange rate is given by long-run purchasing power parity, $\bar{s} = \bar{p}$. Then it can be shown that rationality implies :

$$\theta = \frac{1}{b - c} = \frac{\pi}{2\lambda}[\gamma\lambda + \sigma + (\gamma^2\lambda^2 + 2\lambda\gamma\sigma + \sigma^2 + 4)^{1/2}]$$

adjusts slowly through current account surpluses or deficits. A monetary expansion creates an imbalance in investors' portfolios which can be resolved only by an initial increase in the value of net foreign assets. This sudden depreciation of the domestic currency sets in motion an adjustment process in which the level of net foreign assets increases and the currency appreciates to its new steady-state level. In such a model (which is similar to the simulation model below), the rate of adjustment of the spot rate, θ may also be rational, if there are no chartists. Repeating equation (13) but using the log of the stock of net foreign assets instead of the interest differential as the important fundamental, we have in continuous time :

$$s(t) = a + c\theta(\bar{s} - s(t)) - df(t) \tag{14}$$

Suppose the actual rate of depreciation is $s(t) = \upsilon(\bar{s} - s(t))$. Equation (14) then can be rewritten in terms of deviations from the steady-state levels of the exchange rate and net foreign assets, $\bar{s}$ and $\bar{f}$.

$$\dot{s}(t) = \frac{-\upsilon}{c\theta}(\bar{s} - s(t)) - \frac{d\upsilon}{c\theta}(\bar{f} - f(t)) \tag{15}$$

where rationality implies that $\upsilon = \theta$. Following Rodriguez (1980), the normalized current account surplus may also be expressed in deviations from steady-state equilibrium :

$$\dot{f} = -q(\bar{s} - s(t)) + \gamma(\bar{f} - f(t)) \tag{16}$$

where q and γ are the elasticities of the current account with respect to the exchange rate and the level of net foreign assets, respectively. The system of equations (15) and (16) then has the rational expectations solution :

$$\theta = \frac{c\gamma - 1 + [(1 - c\gamma)^2 + 4c(\gamma + dq)]^{1/2}}{2c}. \tag{17}$$

III.2 *The Model with Exogenous Fundamentals*

We now turn to describe the complete model, assuming for the time being that important fundamentals remain fixed. Regardless of which specification we use for the fundamentals, the existence of chartists whose views are given time-varying weights by the portfolio managers complicates the model. For simplicity, we study the case in which the chartists believe the exchange rate follows a random walk, $\Delta s^{m}_{t+1} = 0$. Thus equation (7) becomes

$$\Delta s^{m}_{t+1} = \omega_t \, \theta(\bar{s} - s_t) \tag{7a}$$

Since the changing weights by themselves generate self-sustaining dynamics, the expectations of fundamentalists will no longer be rational, except for the trivial case in which fundamentalist and chartist expectations are the same, $\theta = 0$.

The "bubble" path of the exchange rate will be driven by the dynamics of portfolio managers' expected depreciation. We assume that the weight given to fundamentalist views by portfolio managers, ω_t, evolves according to :

$$\Delta \omega_t = \delta(\hat{\omega}_{t-1} - \omega_{t-1}) \tag{18}$$

$\hat{\omega}_{t-1}$ is in turn defined as the weight, computed ex post, that would have accurately predicted the contemporaneous change in the spot rate, defined by the equation :

$$\Delta s_t = \hat{\omega}_{t-1} \, \theta(\bar{s} - s_{t-1}) \tag{19}$$

Equations (18) and (19) give us :

$$\Delta \omega_t = \delta \frac{\Delta s_t}{\theta(\bar{s} - s_{t-1})} - \delta \, \omega_{t-1} \tag{20}$$

The coefficient δ in equation (20) controls the adaptiveness of ω_t.

One interpretation for δ is that it is chosen by portfolio managers who use the principles of Bayesian inference to combine prior information with actual realizations of the spot process. This leads to an expression for δ which changes over time. To simplify the following analysis we assume that δ is constant; in the first appendix we explore more precisely the problem that portfolio managers face in choosing δ. The results that emerge there are qualitatively similar to those that follow here.

Taking the limit to continuous time, we can rewrite equation (20) as

$$\dot{\omega}(t) = \delta \left(\frac{\dot{s}(t)}{\theta(\bar{s} - s(t))} - \omega(t) \right) \quad \text{if } 0 < \omega(t) < 1 \tag{21}$$

$$\text{if } \omega(t) = 0 \text{ then } \begin{cases} \dot{\omega}(t) = 0 & \text{if } \dot{s}(t) \leqslant 0 \\ \dot{\omega}(t) = \dfrac{\delta \dot{s}(t)}{\theta(\bar{s} - s)} & \text{if } \dot{s}(t) > 0 \end{cases} \tag{21a}$$

$$\text{if } \omega(t) = 1 \text{ then } \begin{cases} \dot{\omega}(t) = 0 & \text{if } \dot{s}(t) < \theta(\bar{s} - s(t)) \\ \dot{\omega}(t) = \dfrac{\delta \dot{\bar{s}}(t)}{\theta(\bar{s} - s(t))} - \delta & \text{if } \dot{s}(t) \geqslant \theta(\bar{s} - s(t)) \end{cases} \tag{21b}$$

where a dot over a variable indicates the total derivative with respect to time. The restrictions that are imposed when $\omega(t) = 0$ and $\omega(t) = 1$ are to keep $\omega(t)$ from moving outside the interval [0,1]. These restrictions are in the spirit of the portfolio managers choice set: the portfolio manager can at most take one view or the other exclusively.

The evolution of the spot rate can be expressed by taking the derivative of equation (9) (for now holding z and the long-run equilibrium, $\bar{s}$, constant)

$$\dot{s}(t) = \left(\frac{\dot{\omega}(t) c\theta}{1 + c\theta\omega(t)} \right) (\bar{s} - s(t)) \tag{22}$$

Equations (21) and (22) can be solved simultaneously and rewritten, for interior values of ω, as

$$\dot{\omega}(t) = \frac{-\delta\omega(t)(1 + c\theta\omega(t))}{1 + c\theta\omega(t) - \delta c} \quad \text{if } 0 < \omega(t) < 1 \tag{23}$$

$$\dot{s}(t) = \left(\frac{-\delta\omega(t) c\theta}{1 + c\theta\omega(t) - \delta c} \right) (\bar{s} - s(t)) \tag{24}$$

In principle, an analytic solution to the differential equation (23) could be substituted into (24), and then (24) could be integrated directly.[29] For our purposes it is more desirable to use a finite difference method to simulate the motion of the system. In doing so we must pick values for the coefficients, c, θ and δ, and starting values for $\omega(t)$ and $s(t)$.

To exclude any unreasonable time paths implied by equations (23) and (24), we impose the obvious sign restrictions on the coefficients. The parame-

29. In this case, however, $\omega(t)$ does not have a closed analytic form.

ter θ must be positive and less than one if expectations are to be regressive, that is, if they are to predict a return to the long-run equilibrium at a finite rate. By definition, δ and $\omega(t)$ lie in the interval [0,1] since they are weights. The coefficient c measures the responsiveness of the spot rate to changes in expected depreciation and must be positive to be sensible.

These restrictions, however, are not enough to determine unambiguously the sign of the denominator of equations (23) and (24). The three possibilities are that: $1 + c\theta\omega(t) - \delta c < 0$ for all ω; $1 + c\theta\omega(t) > 0$ for all ω; and $1 + c\theta\omega(t) \lesseqgtr 0$ as $\omega(t) \lesseqgtr \omega^*$, where $0 < \omega^* < 1$. If $1 + c\theta\omega(t) - \delta c < 0$, the system will be stable and will tend to return to the long-run equilibrium from any initial level of the spot rate. This might be the case if portfolio managers use only the most recent realization of the spot rate to choose $\omega(t)$, that is, if $\delta = 1$. If, on the other hand portfolio managers give substantial weight to prior information so that δ is small, the expression $1 + c\theta\omega(t) - \delta c$ will be positive. In this case the spot rate will tend to move away from the long-run equilibrium if it is perturbed.[30]

Let us assume that portfolio managers are slow learners.[31] What does this assumption imply about the path of the dollar? If we take as a starting point the late 1970s, when $s(t) = \bar{s}$ and when $\omega_t = 1$ (as the calculations presented in Table 6 suggest), equation (24) says that the spot rate is in equilibrium, that $\dot{s}(t) = 0$. From equation (21b), we see that $\dot{\omega}(t) = 0$ as well. Thus the system is in a steady-state equilibrium, with market expectations exclusively reflecting the views of fundamentalists.

30. We do not consider the third case, because equations (23) and (24) are not defined at $1 + c\theta\omega(t) - \delta c = 0$.

31. The following intuition may help see why the system is stable when portfolio managers are "fast" learners and unstable when they are "slow" learners. Suppose the value of the dollar is above $\bar{s}$, so that portfolio managers are predicting depreciation at the rate $\omega\theta\,(\bar{s} - s(t))$. If the spot rate were to start depreciating at a rate slightly faster than this, portfolio managers would then shift $\omega(t)$ upwards, in favor of the fundamentalists. Under what circumstances would these hypothesized dynamics be an equilibrium? Recall from equations (21) and (22) that if δ is big, portfolio managers place substantial weight on new information. The larger is δ, the more quickly the spot rate changes. It is easy to show that if portfolio managers are fast learners (i.e., if $\delta < 1/c + \theta\omega$), they update ω so rapidly that the resulting rate of depreciation must in fact be greater than $\theta\omega(s - s(t))$. Thus the system is stable. Alternatively, if portfolio managers are "slow" learners, $\delta < 1/c + \theta\omega$, they heavily discount new information and therefore change (t) too slowly to generate a rate of depreciation greater than $\omega\theta(\bar{s} - s(t))$. If we instead hypothesize an initial rate of depreciation which is less than $\omega\theta(\bar{s} - s(t))$, portfolio managers would tend to shift ω downwards, more towards the chartists. From equation (22), a negative $\dot{\omega}(t)$ causes the spot rate to appreciate. Thus slow learning will tend to drive the spot rate further away from the long-run equilibrium (given $0 < \omega < 1$), making the system unstable.

But given that $1 + c\theta\omega(t) - \delta c > 0$, this equilibrium is unstable, and any shock starts things in motion. Suppose that there is an unanticipated appreciation (the unexpected persistence of high long-term US interest rates in the early 1980s, for example). The sign restrictions imply $\omega(t)$ is unambiguously falling over time. Equation (23) says that the chartists are gaining prominence, since $\dot{\omega}(t) < 0$. The exchange rate begins to trace out a bubble path, moving away from long-run equilibrium; equation (24) shows that $\dot{s}(t) < 0$ when $\bar{s} > s(t)$. This process cannot, however, go on forever, because market expectations are eventually determined only by chartist views. At this point the bubble dynamics die out since both $\omega(t)$ and $\dot{\omega}(t)$ fall to zero. From equation (24), the spot rate then stops moving away from long-run equilibrium, as it approaches a new, higher equilibrium level where $\dot{s}(t) = 0$. In the words of Dornbusch (1983), the exchange rate is both high and stuck.

Figures 1 and 2 trace out a "base-case" simulation of the time profile of the spot rate and ω. They are intended only to suggest that the model can potentially account for a large and sustained dollar appreciation. The figures assume that the dollar is perturbed out of a steady state equilibrium where $\bar{s} = s(t)$ and $\omega(0) = 1$ in October 1980. The dollar rises at a decreasing rate until sometime in 1985, when, as can be seen in Figure 2, the simulated weight placed on fundamentalist expectations becomes negligible. A steady state obtains at a new higher level, about 31 percent above the long-run equilibrium implied by purchasing power parity. Although we tried to choose reasonable values for the parameters used in this example, the precise level of the plateau and the rate at which the currency approaches it are sensitive to different choices of parameters. In a second appendix, available on request, we give more detail on values used in the simulation.

It is worth emphasizing that the demand for dollars increases and the currency appreciates along its bubble path even though *none* of the actors expects appreciation. This result is due to the implicit stock adjustment taking place. As portfolio managers reject their fundamentalist roots, they reshuffle their portfolios to hold a greater share in dollar assets. For fixed relative asset supplies, a greater dollar share can be obtained in equilibrium only by additional appreciation. This unexpected appreciation, in turn, further convinces portfolio managers to embrace chartism. The rising dollar becomes self-sustaining. In the end, when the spiral finally levels off at $\omega(t) = 0$, the level at which the currency becomes stuck represents a fully rational equilibrium; portfolio managers expect zero depreciation and the rate of change of the exchange rate is indeed zero.

The sense in which the model violates rational expectations can be seen by inspecting equation (24). Recall that market-expected depreciation, that of

FIGURE 1

SIMULATED VALUE OF THE DOLLAR ABOVE ITS LONG RUN EQUILIBRIUM

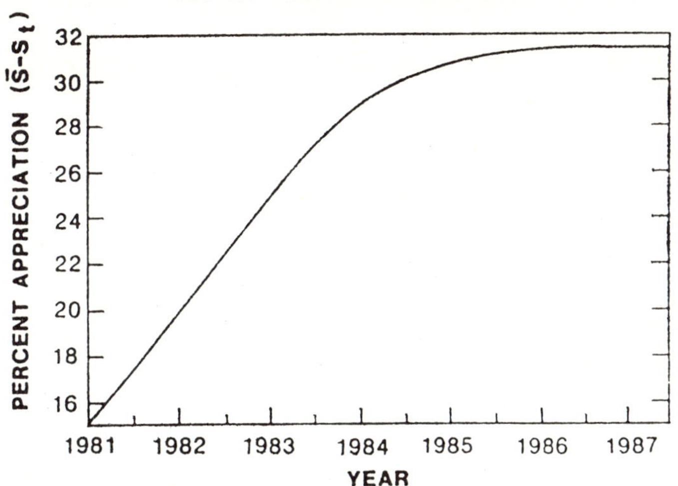

FIGURE 2

SIMULATED WEIGHT PLACED ON FUNDAMENTALIST EXPECTATIONS BY PORTFOLIO MANAGERS

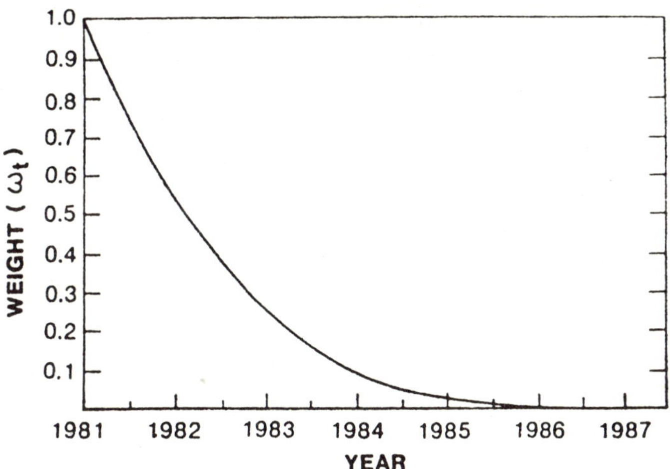

portfolio managers, is a weighted average of chartist and fundamentalist expectations, $\omega(t)\theta(\bar{s} - s(t))$. But the actual or rational, expected rate of depreciation is given by $\left(\frac{-\delta c}{1 + c\theta\omega(t) - \theta c}\right)\omega(t)\theta(\bar{s} - s(t))$. The two are not equal, unless $\omega = 0$.[32] The problem we gave portfolio managers was to pick $\omega(t)$ in a way that best describes the spot process they observe (given the prior confidence they had in fundamentalist predictions). But theirs is a thankless task, since the spot process is more complicated.

III.3 *The Model with Endogenous Fundamentals*

The results so far offer an explanation for the paradox of proposition (1), that sustained dollar appreciation occurs even though all agents expect depreciation. But a spot rate that is stuck at a disequilibrium level is an unlikely end for any reasonable story. The next step is to specify the mechanism by which the unsustainability of the dollar is manifest in the model.

The most obvious fundamental which must eventually force the dollar down is the stock of net foreign assets. Reductions in this stock, through large current account deficits, cannot take place indefinitely. Sustained borrowing would, in the long run, raise the level of debt above the present discounted value of income. But long before this point of insolvency is reached, the gains from a U.S. policy aimed at reducing the outstanding liabilities (either through direct taxes or penalties on capital, or through monetization) would increase in comparison to the costs. If foreigners associate large current account deficits with the potential for moral hazard, they would treat U.S. securities as increasingly risky and would force a decline in the level of the dollar.

To incorporate the effects of current account imbalances , we consider the model, similar to Rodriguez (1980), given in equation (14) :

$$s_t = a + c\Delta s^m_{t+1} - df \tag{25}$$

where Δs^m_{t+1} is defined in equation (7a) and where f represents the log of cumulated US current account balances. The coefficient, d, is the semi-elasticity of the spot rate with respect to transfers of wealth, and must be positive to be sensible. The differential equations (23) and (24) now become :

$$\dot{\omega}(t) = \left(\frac{\delta}{1 + c\theta\omega(t) - \delta c}\right)\left(-w(t)\,(1 + c\theta\omega(t)) - \frac{d\dot{f}}{\theta(\bar{s} - s(t))}\right) \text{ if } 0 < \omega(t) < 1 \tag{26}$$

32. There is a second root, $\omega = -1/(\theta\, c)$, which we rule out since it is less than zero.

$$\dot{s}(t) = \frac{-\ \delta\omega(t)\, c\theta(\bar{s} - s(t)) + d\dot{f}}{1 + c\omega(t)\theta - \delta c} \tag{27}$$

If we were to follow the route of trying to solve analytically the system of differential equations, we would add a third equation giving the "normalized" current account, $\dot{f}$, as a function of $s(t)$. (See, for example, equation (16) above.) But we here instead pursue the simulation approach.

In the simulation we use actual current account data for $\dot{f}$, the change in the stock of net foreign assets. Figures 3 and 4 trace out paths for the differential equations (26) and (27). During the initial phases of the dollar appreciation, the current account, which is thought to respond to the appreciation with a lag, does not noticeably affect the rise of the dollar. But as ω becomes small, the spot rate becomes more sensitive to changes in the level of the current account, and the external deficits of 1983-1985 quickly turn the trend. When ω is small and portfolio managers observe an incipient depreciation of the dollar, they begin to place more weight on the forecasts of fundamentalists, thus accelerating the depreciation initiated by the current account deficits. There is a "fundamentalist revival". Ironically, fundamentalists are initially driven out of the market as the dollar appreciates, *even though they are ultimately right about its return to* $\bar{s}$.

FIGURE 3

SIMULATED VALUE OF THE DOLLAR ABOVE ITS LONG RUN EQUILIBRIUM

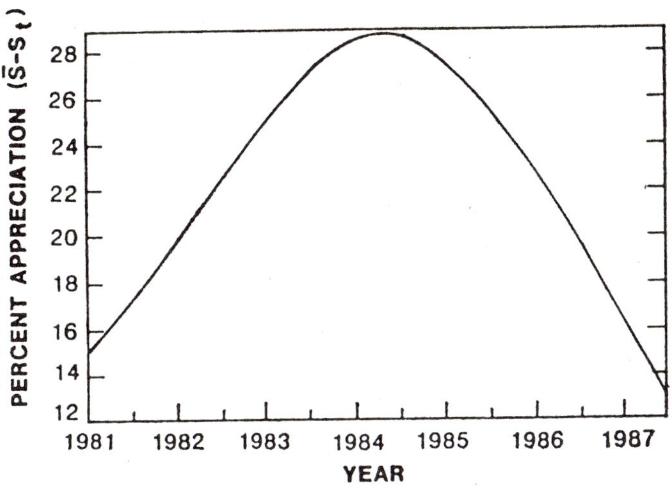

PERCENT APPRECIATION $(\bar{S}-S_t)$
28
26
24
22
20
18
16
14
12
1981 1982 1983 1984 1985 1986 1987
YEAR

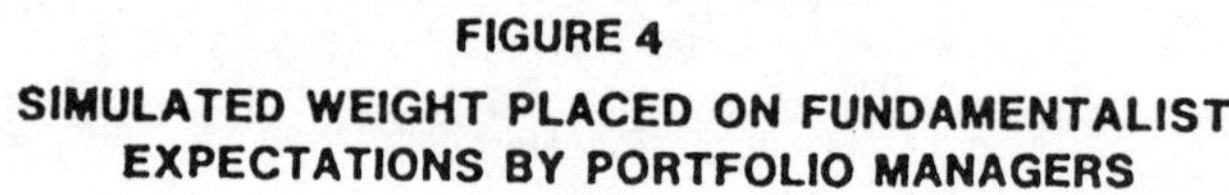

FIGURE 4
SIMULATED WEIGHT PLACED ON FUNDAMENTALIST EXPECTATIONS BY PORTFOLIO MANAGERS

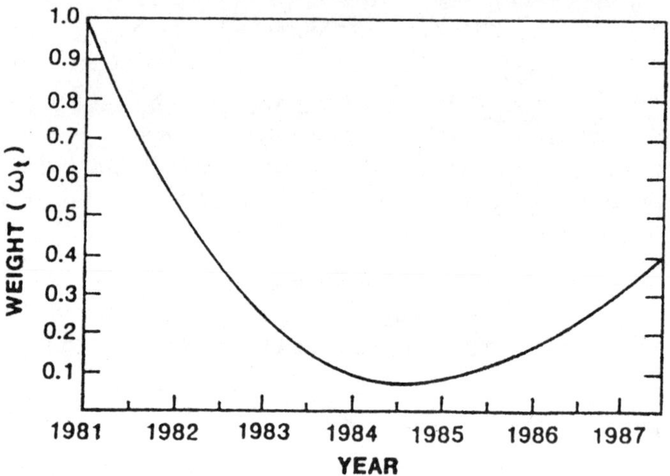

Naturally, all of our results are sensitive to the precise parameters chosen. To gain an idea of the various sensitivities, we report in Table 7 results using alternative sets of parameter values in the simulation of Figure 3 (or equation (27)). While there is some variation, the qualitative pattern of bubble appreciation, followed by a slow turnaround and depreciation, remains evident in all cases.

Recall that one of the main aims of the model is to account for the two seemingly contradictory facts given by propositions (2) and (3): first that market efficiency test results imply that the rationally expected rate of dollar depreciation has been less than the forward discount, and second that the calculations based on fundamentals, such as those by Krugman and Marris, imply that the rationally expected rate of depreciation, by 1985, became greater than the forward discount.

Table 8 clarifies how the model resolves this paradox. The first two lines show the expectations of our two forecasters, the chartists and fundamentalists. The third line repeats the six-month survey expectations to demonstrate that they may in fact be fairly well described by the simple regressive formuation we use to represent fundamentalist expectations in line two. The fourth line contains the expected depreciation of the portfolio managers. Note that these expectations are close to the forward discount in line six, even though the forecasts of the fundamentalists and of the chartists are not. Since only the portfolio managers are hypothesized to take positions in the market, we

TABLE 7

Sensitivity Analysis for the Simulation of the Dollar

Parameter				Maximum appreciation of the dollar above initial shock	Number of months until peak
delta	*c*	theta	*d*	(in percent)	
0.04	25	0.045	—0.005	11.4	41
0.06	25	0.045	—0.005	26.9	27
0.02	25	0.045	—0.005	5.8	44
0.04	15	0.045	—0.005	6.4	38
0.04	35	0.045	—0.005	18.1	40
0.04	25	0.03	—0.005	8.8	36
0.04	25	0.06	—0.005	13.5	44
0.04	25	0.045	0	16.4	80
0.04	25	0.045	—0.0025	11.6	45
0.04	25	0.045	—0.0075	11.4	38

Notes : These estimates correspond to the simulation depicted in Figure 8. The parameter delta falls over time according to equation (19).

TABLE 8

Alternative Measures of Expected Depreciation
(in percent per annum)

Expectation from :	Line	Year 1981	1982	1983	1984	1985	1986
Chartists	(1)	0	0	0	0	0	0
Fundamentalists in the Simulation	(2)	7.63	9.82	11.68	11.98	10.33	7.66
Economist 6 Month Survey	(3)	8.90	10.31	10.42	11.66	4.00	NA
Weighted Average Expected Depreciation in the Simulation	(4)	5.29	3.31	1.59	0.99	1.49	2.08
Perfect Foresight Depreciation in the Simulation	(5)	—2.97	—5.16	—4.38	—0.72	3.89	6.22
Actual Forward Discount	(6)	3.74	3.01	1.10	3.07	—0.16	NA

Notes : Fundamentalists in the simulation use regressivity parameter of .045, implying that about 70% of the contemporaneous overvaluation is expected to remain after one year. The Economist 6 month survey includes data through April 1985. Weighted average expected depreciation in the simulation is a weighted average of chartists and fundamentalists, where the weights are those of portfolio managers. Rationally expected depreciation is the perfect foresight solution given by equations (19) and (20). The actual 6 month forward discount includes data through September 1985.

can say that the magnitude of the market risk premium is small (as mean-variance optimization would predict). Finally, line five shows the actual depreciation in the simulation, which is equivalent to the rationally expected depreciation given the model above. (Of course, none of the agents has the entire model in his information set.) Notice that during the 1981-1984 period, the rationally expected depreciation is not only significantly less than the forward discount, but less than zero. This pattern agrees with the results of market efficiency tests discussed earlier. But the rationally expected depreciation is increasing over time. Sometime in late 1984 or early 1985, the rationally expected rate of depreciation becomes positive and crosses the forward discount. As calculations of the Krugman-Marris type would indicate, rationally expected depreciation in 1986 was *greater* than the forward discount. The paradox of propositions (2) and (3) is thus resolved within the model.

All this comes at what might seem a high cost: portfolio managers behave "irrationally" in that they do not use the entire model in formulating their exchange rate forecasts. But another interpretation of this behavior is possible, in that portfolio managers are actually doing the best they can in a confusing world. Within this framework they cannot have been more rational; abandoning fundamentalism more quickly would not solve the problem in the sense that their expectations would not be validated by the resulting spot process in the long run. In trying to learn about the world after a regime change, our portfolio managers use convex combinations of models which are already available to them and which have worked in the past. In this context, rationality is the rather strong presumption that one of the prior models is correct. It is hard to imagine how agents, after a regime change, would know the correct model.

IV. CONCLUSIONS AND EXTENSIONS

This paper has posed an unorthodox explanation for the recent aerobatics of the dollar. The model we use assumes less than fully rational behavior in the sense that none of the three classes of actors (chartists, fundamentalists and portfolio managers) conditions its forecasts on the full information set of the model. In effect, the bubble is the outcome of portfolio managers' attempt to learn the model. When the bubble takes off (and when it collapses), they are learning more slowly about the model than they are changing it by revising the linear combination of chartist and fundamentalist views they incorporate in their own forecasts. But as the weight given to fundamentalists approaches zero or one, portfolio managers' estimation of the true force changing the dollar comes closer to the true one. These revisions in weights become smaller until the approximation is perfect: portfolio managers have "caught up", by changing the model more slowly than they learn. In this sense the inability of agents with prior information to bring about immediate convergence to a rational expectations equilibrium may provide a framework in which to view "bubbles" in a variety of asset markets.

Several extensions of the model in this paper would be worthwhile. First, it would be desirable to allow chartists to use a class of predictors richer than a simple random walk. They might form their forecasts of future depreciation by using ARIMA models, for example. Simple bandwagon or distributed lag expectations for chartists would be the most plausible since they capture a wide range of effects and are relatively simple analytically. Second, we might want to consider extensions which give the model local stability in the neighborhood of $\omega = 1$. Small perturbations from equilibrium would then not instantly cause portfolio managers to begin losing faith in fundamentalist counsel. Only sufficiently large or prolonged perturbations, would upset portfolio managers' views enough to cause the exchange rate to break free of its fundamental equilibrium.

University of California, Berkeley, CA, U.S.A.
Massachusetts Institute of Technology, MA, U.S.A.

APPENDIX

In this appendix we consider the problem which portfolio managers face: how much weight should they give to new information concerning the "true" level of $\omega(t)$. After we obtain an explicit formulation for these optimal Bayesian weights, we report their effects on the simulated path of the dollar.

Even though in the model of the spot rate given by equation (9) the value of the currency is fully deterministic, individual portfolio managers who are unable to predict accurately ex ante changes in the spot rate may view the future spot rate as random. They would then form predictions of future depreciation on the basis of observed exchange rate changes and their prior beliefs. At each point in time, portfolio managers therefore view future depreciation as the sum of their current optimal predictor and a random term,

$$\Delta s_{t+1} = \omega_t \theta(\bar{s} - s_t) + \varepsilon_{t+1} \tag{A1}$$

where ε_{t+1} is a serially uncorrelated normal random variable with mean 0 and variance $\theta(\bar{s} - s_{t+1}) / \tau$.[33] Using Bayes' rule, the coefficient ω_t may be written as a weighted average of the previous period's estimate, ω_{t-1}, and information obtained from the contemporaneous realization of the spot rate,

$$\omega_t = \frac{T_t}{T_t + \tau}\,\omega_{t-1} + \frac{\tau}{T_t + \tau}\left(\frac{\Delta s_t}{\theta(\bar{s} - s_{t-1})}\right) \tag{A2}$$

where $T_t = T_{t-1} + \tau$. Thus, if portfolio managers use Bayesian techniques, the weight they would give to the current period's information may be expressed as

$$\delta_t = \tau / (\tau t + T_0) \tag{A3}$$

where T_0 is the precision of portfolio managers' prior information.[34] Equation (A3) shows that the weight which portfolio managers give to new information would fall over time as decision makers gain more confidence in their prior distribution, or as the prior distribution for the future change in the spot rate converges to the actual posterior distribution. If, however, portfolio managers suspect that the spot rate is nonstationary, past information would be discounted relative to more recent observations. Instead of combining prior information in the form of an OLS regression of actual depreciation on fundamentalist expectations (as they do above), portfolio managers might use a varying parameter technique to take into account the nonstationarity. In this case, the weight they put on new information might not decline over time to zero.

Computing δ_t using equation (A3) does not change substantially the results of the simulations presented in the text. Nevertheless the following pages contain the outcome of simulations using Bayesian δ's. Figures 5 and 6 give $s(t)$ and $\omega(t)$ holding fundamentals constant (note that the spot rate approaches the higher equilibrium more slowly than in the comparable figures in the text, Figures 1 and 2). Figures 7 and 8 add to this changing fundamentals according to equations (26) and (27) in the text. Table 9 reports the simulated expectations of our three sets of agents as well as the rationally expected depreciation, comparable to Table 8 in the text.

33. The assumption that ε_{t+1} exhibits such conditional heteroscedasticity results in a particularly convenient expression for δ_t (equation (A2) below). Under the assumption that ε_{t+1} is distributed normally $(0,\sigma^2)$, δ_t depends on all past values of the spot rate,

$$\delta_t = \tau / [\tau\theta \sum_{i=1} (\bar{s} - s_{t-1}) + T_0].$$

34. If the prior distribution is normal, the precision is equal to the reciprocal of the variance.

FIGURE 5

SIMULATED VALUE OF THE DOLLAR ABOVE ITS LONG RUN EQUILIBRIUM

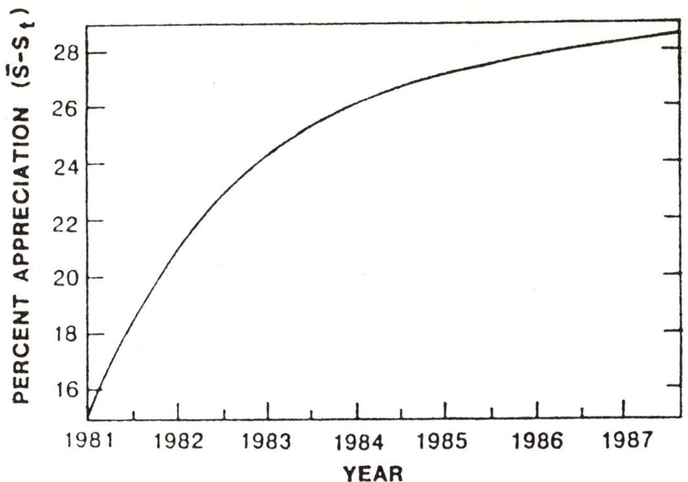

FIGURE 6

SIMULATED WEIGHT PLACED ON FUNDAMENTALIST EXPECTATIONS BY PORTFOLIO MANAGERS

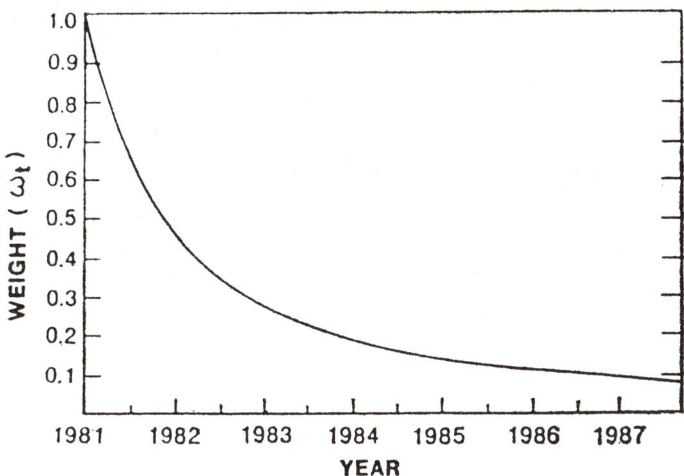

FIGURE 7

SIMULATED VALUE OF THE DOLLAR ABOVE ITS LONG RUN EQUILIBRIUM

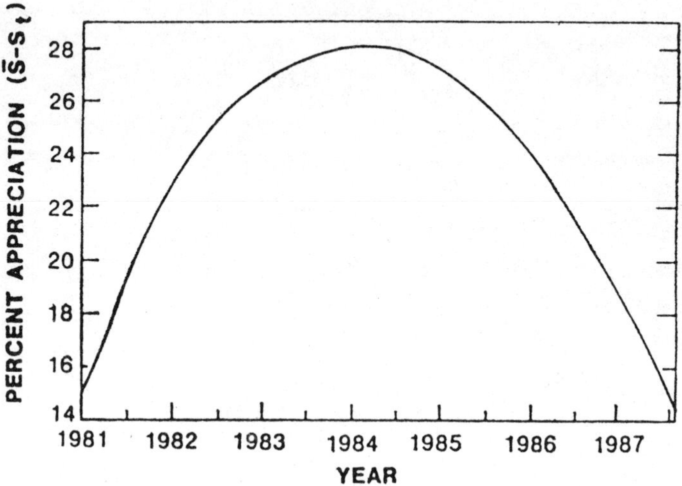

FIGURE 8

SIMULATED WEIGHT PLACED ON FUNDAMENTALIST EXPECTATIONS BY PORTFOLIO MANAGERS

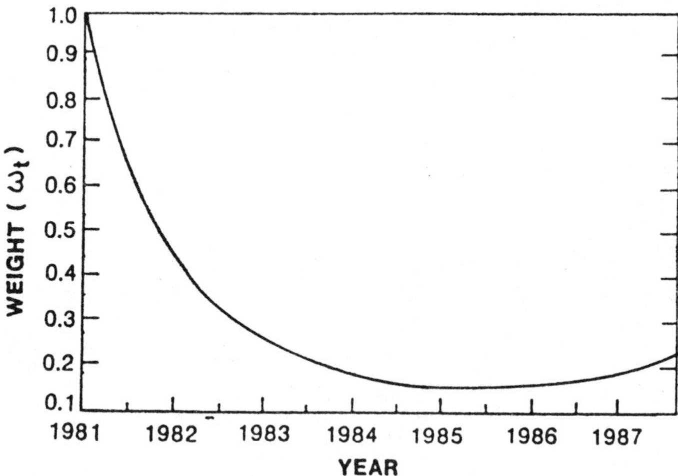

TABLE 9

Alternative Measures of Expected Depreciation With Bayesian Determination of ω (in percent per annum)

Expectations from :	Line	1981	1982	1983	1984	1985	1986
				Year			
Chartists in the Simulation	(1)	0	0	0	0	0	0
Fundamentalists in the Simulation	(2)	8.12	10.01	10.97	11.10	10.17	8.27
Economist 6 Month Survey	(3)	8.90	10.31	10.42	11.66	4.00	NA
Weighted Average Expected Depreciation in the Simulation	(4)	4.83	3.08	2.20	1.77	1.62	1.56
Perfect Foresight Depreciation in the Simulation	(5)	—4.13	—4.45	—2.27	—0.30	2.18	4.48
Actual Forward Discount	(6)	3.74	3.01	1.10	3.07	—0.16	NA

Notes : Fundamentalists in the simulation use regressivity parameter of .045, implying that about 70% of the contemporaneous overvaluation is expected to remain after one year. The Economist 6 month survey includes data through April 1985. Weighted average expected depreciation in the simulation is a weighted average of chartists and fundamentalists, where the weights are those of portfolio managers. Rationally expected depreciation is the perfect foresight solution given by equations (19) and (20). The actual 6 month forward discount includes data through September 1985.

REFERENCES

Bilson, John (1978) 'The Monetary Approach to the Exchange Rate – Some Empirical Evidence', *Staff Papers*, International Monetary Fund 25, (March).

— (1981) 'The Speculative Efficiency Hypothesis', *Journal of Business* 54: 435-51, (July).

— (1985) 'Macroeconomic Stability and Flexible Exchange Rates', *American Economic Review*, Papers and Proceedings 75 (2) : 62-67, (May).

Blake, David, Beenstock, Michael and Brasse, Valerie (1986) 'The Performance of U.K. Exchange Forecasters', *The Economic Journal*, pp. 986-999, (December).

Blanchard, Olivier and Summers, Lawrence (1984) 'Perspective on High World Real Interest Rates', *Brookings Papers on Economic Activity* 2 : 273-324.

Boothe, P., Clinton, K., Cote, A. and Longworth, D. (1985) *International Asset Substitutability : Theory and Evidence for Canada*, (Ottawa Bank of Canada), (February).

Borensztein, Eduardo (1986) 'Alternative Hypotheses on the Excess Return on Dollar Assets, 1980-84', International Monetary Fund.

Branson, William, H. (1985) 'Causes of Appreciation and Volatility of the Dollar', in *The U.S. Dollar – Recent Developments and Policy Options*, a symposium sponsored by the Federal Reserve Bank of Kansas City at Jackson Hole, Wyoming, (August 21-23). pp. 33-52.

Bryant, Ralph (1987) *International Financial Intermediation*, (Washington, D.C. : Brookings Institution).

Canova, Fabio and Takatoshi Ito, (1987) 'On the Time Varying Risk Premiums in the Yen/Dollar Exchange Market', University of Minnesota, Department of Economics Working Paper No. 244, (November).

Claassen, Emil and Wyplosz, Charles (1982) 'Capital Controls : Some Principles and the French Experience', *Annales de I'INSEE* 47-48 : 237-67, (June-December).

Council of Economic Advisers (1984) *The Economic Report of the President*, Washington, D.C.

Cumby, Robert (1987) 'Is It Risk? Explaining Deviations from Uncovered Interest Parity', National Bureau of Economic Research Working Papar No. 2380, (September).

Cumpy, Robert and Obstfeld, Maurice (1984) 'International Interest Rate and Price Level Linkages under Flexible Exchange Rates : A Review of Recent Evidence', in J. Bilson and R. Marston (eds.), *Exchange rate Theory and Practice*, (Chicago : University of Chicago Press).

DeLong, J.B., Shleifer, A., Summers, L. and Waldman, R. (1987) 'The Economic Consequences of Noise Traders', NBER Working Paper No. 2395, (October).

Dooley, Michael and Isard, Peter (1980) 'Capital Controls, Political Risk and Deviations from Interest-Rate Parity', *Journal of Political Economy* 88 (2) : 370-384, (April).

—— (1985) 'The Appreciation of the Dollar : An Analysis of the Safe-Haven Phenomenon', International Monetary Fund, DM/85/20 (April).

Dominguez, Kathryn (1986) 'Are Foreign Exchange Forecasts Rational : New Evidence from Survey Data', *Economic Letters*.

Dornbusch, Rudiger (1976) 'Expectations and Exchange Rate Dynamics', *Journal of Political Economy* 84 : 1161-76, (December).

—— (1982) 'Equilibrium and Disequilibrium Exchange Rates', *Zeitschrift fur Wirtschafts und Sozialwissenschaften* 102 (6) : 573-99.

—— (1983) 'Comment on Loopesko and Shafer', *Brookings Papers on Economic Activity* 1, pp. 78-84.

Evans, George (1986) 'A Test for Speculative Bubbles and the Sterling-Dollar Exchange Rate : 1981-84', *American Economic Review* 76 : 621-36, (September).

Fama, Eugene (1984) 'Forward and Spot Exchange Rates', *Journal of Monetary Economics.*

Feldstein, Martin (1986) 'The Budget Deficit and the Dollar', *NBER Macroeconomics Annual 1986*, (September).

Figlewski, Stephen (1978) 'Market 'Efficiency' in a Market with Heterogeneous Information', *Journal of Political Economy*, 86 (4) : 581-597.

—— (1982) 'Information Diversity and Market Behaviour', *Journal of Finance*, pp. 87-102, (March).

Frankel, Jeffrey (1983) 'Monetary and Portfolio Balance Models of Exchange Rate Determination', in J. Bhandari (ed.), *Economic Interdependence and Flexible Exchange Rates*, (Cambridge : M.I.T. Press). To be reprinted, with Epilogue (U.C. Berkeley Working Paper No. 8752, September 1987), in J. Letiche, (ed.), *International Economic Policies and Their Theoretical Foundations*, (London : Academic Press), second edition.

—— (1984) *The Yen/Dollar Agreement : Liberalizing Japanese Capital Markets*, Policy Analyses in International Economics.

—— (1985) 'The Dazzling Dollar', *Brookings Papers on Economic Activity* 1: 199-217.

—— (1987) 'International Capital Flows and Domestic Economic Policies', in M. Feldstein (ed.), *The United States in the World Economy*, (Chicago : University of Chicago Press).

Frankel, Jeffrey and Froot, Kenneth (1987) 'Using Survey Data to Test Standard Proportions Regarding Exchange Rate Expectations', *American Economic Review* 77 (1) : 133-153, (March).

Frenkel, Jacob (1976) 'A Monetary Approach to the Exchange Rate : Doctrinal Aspects and Empirical Evidence', *Scandinavian Journal of Economics* 78 : 200-24, (May).

Frenkel, Jacob and Levich, Richard (1975) 'Covered Interest Arbitrage : Unexploited Profits?' *Journal of Political Economy* 83 (2) : 325-38, (April).

—— (1977) 'Transaction Costs and Interest Arbitrage : Tranquil versus

Turbulent Periods', *Journal of Political Economy* 85 (6) : 1209-26, (December).

Frenkel, Jacob and Mussa, Michael (1980) 'The Efficiency of Foreign Exchange Markets and Measures of Turbulence', *American Economic Review*, 70 (2) : 374-38, Papers and Proceedings (May).

Friedman, Benjamin (1985) 'Implications of the U.S. Net Capital Inflow', *How Open is the U.S. Economy?*, Conference at the Federal Reserve Bank of St. Louis, (October 11-12).

Froot, Kenneth and Frankel, Jeffrey (1989) 'Forward Discount Bias: Is it an Exchange Risk Premium?', University of California, Berkeley (June), *Quarterly Journal of Economics*, (Forthcoming).

Giavazzi, Francesco and Pagano, Marco (1985) 'Capital Controls and the European Monetary System', in *Capital Controls and Foreign Exchange Legislation*, Occasional Paper, Euromobiliare, Milano (June).

Goodhart, Charles (1988) 'The Foreign Exchange Market : A Random Walk with a Dragging Anchor', (London School of Economics), *Economica* 55 : 437-480, (November).

Goodman, S. (1979) 'Foreign Exchange Forecasting Techniques : Implications for Business and Policy', *Journal of Finance*, 34 : 415-27, (May).

Hartman, David (1984) 'The International Financial Market and U.S. Interest Rates', *Journal of International Money and Finance* 3 (April).

Hooper, Peter (1985) 'International Repercussions of the U.S. Budget Deficit', Brookings Discussion Papers, No. 27, (February).

Hutchison, Michael and Throop, Adrian (1985) 'U.S. Budget Deficits and the Real Value of the Dollar', *Economic Review*, Federal Reserve Bank of San Francisco, pp. 26-43, (Fall).

Isard, Peter (1983) 'An Accounting Framework and Some Issues for Modeling How Exchange Rates Respond to the News', in Jacob Frenkel (ed.), *Exchange Rates and International Macroeconomics*, (Chicago : University of Chicago Press), pp. 19-66.

Ito, Takatoshi (1986) 'Capital Controls and Covered Interest Parity', NBER Working Paper No. 1187. *Economic Studies Quarterly*, 37 : 223-241.

Kim, Yong Cheol and Rene, Stulz (1987) 'The Eurobond Market and Corporate Financial Policy : A Test of the Clientele Supply Hypothesis', College of Business, Ohio State University (October).

Kling, Arnold (1985) 'Anticipatory Capital Flows and the Behavior of the Dollar', *International Finance Discussion Paper No.* 261, Federal Reserve Board (August).

Kohlhagen, Steven (1978) 'The Behavior of Foreign Exchange Markets

– A Critical Survey of the Empirical Literature', N.Y.U. Monograph, Series in Finance and Economics.

Kouri, Pentti, J.K. (1976) 'The Exchange Rate and the Balance of Payments in the Short Run and the Long Run: A Monetary Approach', *Scandinavian Journal of Economics*, pp. 280-304.

Kreicher, Lawrence (1982) 'Eurodollar Arbitrage', *Federal Reserve Bank of New York Quarterly Review* 7 (2): 10-12, (Summer).

Krugman, Paul (1985) 'Is the Strong Dollar Sustainable?' in *The U.S. Dollar-Recent Developments, Outlook, and Policy Options*, (Kansas City: Federal Reserve Bank of Kansas City), pp. 103-133.

—— (1988) 'Sustainability and the Decline of the Dollar' In *External Deficits and the Dollar*, (Washington, D.C.: The Brookings Institution,) pp. 82-99.

Longworth, David (1981) 'Testing the Efficiency of the Canadian-U.S. Exchange Market under the Assumption of No Risk Premium', *Journal of Finance* 36: 43-49, (March).

Marris, Stephen (1985) *Deficits and the Dollar: The World Economy at Risk*, Policy Analyses in International Economics, (Washington: Institute for International Economics).

McCormick, Frank (1979) 'Covered Interest Arbitrage: Unexploited Profits? Comment', *Journal of Political Economy*.

McKinnon, Ronald (1976) 'Floating Exchange Rates 1973-74: The Emperor's New Clothes', *Carnegie-Rochester Conference Series on Public Policy* 3: 79-114.

Meese, Richard and Rogoff, Kenneth (1983) 'Empirical Exchange Rate Models of the Seventies: Do They Fit Out of Sample?', *Journal of International Economics* 14: 3-24 (February).

Mussa, Michael (1976) 'The Exchange Rate, the Balance of Payments and Monetary and Fiscal Policy under a Regime of Controlled Floating', *Scandinavian Journal of Economics* 78: 229-48 (May).

Obstfeld, Maurice (1985) 'Floating Exchange Rates: Experience and Prospects', *Brookings Papers on Economic Activity* 2.

Otani, Ichiro and Siddarth, Tiwari (1981) 'Capital Controls and Interest Rate Parity: The Japanese Experience 1978-81', *Staff Papers*, International Monetary Fund (Washington, December).

Reszat, B. (1987) 'Technical Analysis and Computer Trading', *Intereconomics*, 107-11 (Man/June).

Rodriguez, Carlos Alfredo (1980) 'The Role of Trade Flows in Exchange Rate Determination: A Rational Expectations Approach', *Journal of Political Economy* 88: 1148-58.

Sachs, Jeffrey (1985) 'The Dollar and the Policy Mix: 1985', *Brookings Papers on Economic Activity* 1 : 117-185.

Schulmeister, S. (1987) *An Essay on Exchange Rate Dynamics*, Research Unit Labor Market and Employment Discussion Paper 87-8, Wissenschaftzentrum Berlin für Sozialforschung, Berlin.

Shafer, Jeffrey and Loopesko, Bonnie (1983) 'Floating Exchange Rates after Ten Years', *Brookings Papers on Economic Activity* 1 : 1-70.

Shiller, Robert (1984) 'Stock Prices and Social Dynamics', *Brookings 'Papers on Economic Activity* 2 : 457-510.

Tryon, Ralph (1979) 'Testing for Rational Expectations in Foreign Exchange Markets', *International Finance Discussion Paper No.* 139, Federal Reserve Board.

PART II

CAPITAL CONTROLS AND THE EUROPEAN MONETARY SYSTEM

ABOLISHING EXCHANGE CONTROL: THE UK EXPERIENCE

By Michael J. Artis and Mark P. Taylor*

I. INTRODUCTION

In 1979 the freshly-elected conservative government abolished exchange control in the UK, thus ending a continuous period of over fifty years of restricted capital movements between the UK and the international economy. The impact of this action on both inward and outward flows of capital (variously defined) was marked. The main aim of this paper is to analyse the effects of these changes on the UK economy.

It might be hoped that the abolition of exchange controls in the UK would provide some clear lessons for the effects to be expected of abolition elsewhere; yet considering the magnitude of the step involved, there has been extraordinarily little analysis of the consequences of the abolition of the controls. There is in fact a major obstacle to the precise identification of the contribution of the abolition of the controls to the exchange rate, interest rates, equity prices or to the development of balance of payments flows, due to the coincidence in timing of the abolition of the controls with two other major shocks to the British economy – the second OPEC shock (itself accompanied by the transition of the UK from oil importing to oil exporting status) and the advent of the Thatcher government and a new 'regime' of economic policy. But whilst the violation of the *ceteris paribus* conditions seems to rule out recourse to sophisticated modelling and readily explains the lack of well-quantified estimates, some effects are nonetheless clear enough and in this paper we seek to document them. Above all, it seems clear that the removal of exchange control, in removing protection for domestic banking activity, forced the reform of monetary regulation to take place on a very liberal basis; whilst a move in this direction might have taken place in any event, the abolition of exchange controls provided a ruthless logic for it. It is also now possible to see that a development of currency substitution has taken place that would have been impossible in the continued presence of these controls and that the con-

* Any views expressed in this paper are those of the authors and should in no way be construed as representing the views or policies of the Bank of England.

trols on outward portfolio investment and on the currency of financing of both portfolio and direct investment were substantially effective.

The remainder of the paper is set out as follows. In Section II we rehearse and discuss some of the main arguments which have been put forward in support of the maintenance of exchange control, whilst Section III contains a sketch of the controls as they existed before 1979. Section IV contains the main body of the analysis, and discusses the UK experience with exchange control abolition. In particular, we discuss the impact on direct and portfolio investment, the results of the lifting of monetary controls, and the implications for monetary policy and for asset prices. A final section concludes.

II. ARGUMENTS FOR EXCHANGE CONTROLS

A number of arguments have variously been put forward in favour of the maintenance of exchange controls. Amongst these, it is possible to distinguish four broad strands of thought – 'second best' arguments, 'monetary-autonomy' arguments, 'counter-speculation' arguments, arguments relating to the distribution of ownership of productive assets and finallly 'home investment' arguments.[1]

II.1 *The 'Second Best' Argument*

A general argument against the market solution and in favour of restriction of some kind may be said to flow from the 'second-best' principle of welfare economics. Specifically, if distortions remain in some set of markets, it does not follow that liberalizing others will lead to an overall improvement. The application of this principle to the regulation of trade and capital movements might be said to have governed the wisdom of the founders of BrettonWoods, for whom the creation of a stable system of exchange rates and freedom from controls on current account was coupled directly with the perceived gains from liberalization of trade and the continued restriction of capital movements. The erosion of controls over capital movements in the post war world occurred in spite of, not because of, the acceptance of the principles of Bretton Woods. More recently, the analysis of exchange rate overshooting (e.g. Dornbusch, 1976) has provided a forceful analytical example whilst the experience of, first, sterling and then the dollar, supplies ample practical evidence that unregulated markets may produce untoward exchange rate behaviour.

1. See also Cairncross (1973).

These examples are less than conclusive evidence in favour of exchange controls, however. In particular, some observers have drawn the conclusion that exchange rate behaviour can be rendered more stable without the need for exchange control, by writing rules for the conduct of policy in a world of exchange rate target zones (e.g. Williamson, 1985; Edison, Miller and Williamson, 1987).

It must be said, moreover, that the case for the market solution is now understood to involve much more than 'welfare triangles' and to extend to considerations of x-efficiency and innovation in the operations of markets, here involving the global capital and credit markets. As such, the potential gains from the generalized liberalization could be large, leading to a significantly improved allocation of resources and, through time, a higher rate of innovation and efficiency increase. It is impossible to comment in detail on the likely distribution of benefits from such a process, though it is probable that there will remain significant economies of scale in the provision of financial services. But whilst this would suggest that the provision of (though not the benefit derived from) such services might tend to be concentrated in a few centres, the persistence of distinctive national currencies provides an offsetting force.[2]

II.2 *The 'Monetary Autonomy' Argument*

Exchange controls confer monetary autonomy on those countries which deploy them in two distinct ways. First, in an adjustable peg system, interest rates would otherwise be determined by those prevailing in the other countries in the system, or in the leading country, plus or minus the expected depreciation or appreciation permitted by the bandwidth and the position of the currency within the band. With a very narrow band, interest rates are thus in effect determined directly by the leading country. The presence of effective controls breaks this interest parity link and permits some discretion for domestic interest rates to depart from the levels otherwise dictated by it. Second, in the absence of exchange controls, the type of control exercised by the Central Bank over its commercial banks is firmly disciplined by the presence, or potential presence, of off-shore banks. Any control which is onerous relative to the added cost of transacting offshore will result in a migration of business to the off-shore banks and make the control itself cosmetic in effect. Exchange controls break

2. The logic of the market solution may in the long run, however, lead to the displacement of national currencies even for the conduct of substantial amounts of domestic business — a further erosion of monetary autonomy and sovereignty. Thus exchange control may be seen as a form of protection both for banking and for the national currency of denomination.

this link and provide greater room for discretion in the design and implementation of monetary controls and regulations.

Monetary autonomy of the first type may be recovered by widening the hand: although the interest parity condition will still prevail with the wider band, increasing the band width will allow more of the effect of a change in interest rates in the leading country to be accepted in a change in the exchange rate and so require less of a parallel change in interest rates in the other country. The appearance of a slavish dependence can be so avoided. Autonomy of the second type cannot be secured by increasing the width of the exchange rate band, but it is questionable how far such autonomy is desirable. At any rate, if deregulation and liberalization of domestic monetary systems is desired, no more powerful ally than the liberalization of exchange controls can be imagined.

II.3 *The 'Productive Assets' Argument*

Exchange controls have been seen as helping to correct distortions which arise as the calculus of private rates of return yields systematically biased solutions compared to the calculus of social rates of return. The classic example here turns on the fact that private investors will rationally arbitrage aftertax rates of return; from the point of view of the capital exporting country, however, the fact that the government will absorb tax revenues arising from the returns to investment in its economy implies that the social rate of return on foreign investment falls below that on domestic investment. A developing country might also argue that exchange controls will help correct for the distortion that would otherwise arise as the exceptional external economies of investment in a developing economy will not be reflected in *ex ante* private returns. Moreover, relatively primitive capital markets may not offer investors instruments which are as attractive as those available in developed country capital markets, and the added liquidity cost of domestic investment will tip the balance in favour of investment overseas even if the social rate of return on domestic investment is higher. Arguments like these may lend some support to exchange controls; but administrative (direct) controls do not often seem the best way of securing the objectives in question, where fiscal arrangements and tax-and-subsidy policies appear to provide superior solutions. It is certainly questionable how far exchange controls will succeed in raising total investment in the protected economy for, if they are successful in creating a captive market, domestic private rates of return will be reduced and as a consequence inward capital flow will be diminished. A similar point is made by Hemmings (1981), in relation to portfolio investment and by Beenstock (1977), in relation to direct investment. In this event, the controls might have to be appraised on the different grounds that they create a redistribution of asset ownership: a larger fraction of domestic assets will be owned by domestic residents and a smaller fraction of overseas assets will be owned by domestic residents than would otherwise be the case.

II.4 *The 'Counter-Speculation' Argument*

Arguments of the kind spelt out above apply most obviously to the control of portfolio and direct investment. Often, however, more attention is focussed on the effects of what might be described, for want of a better term, 'monetary exchange controls': by this we mean to refer to the controls over the holding by residents of foreign currency denominated bank deposits and other short-term assets and controls over the lending by domestic residents and banks of domestic currency to foreign residents. These provisions are the key to the counter-speculative role of exchange controls for they limit the amount of domestic currency which can be quickly sold in anticipation of devaluation.

III. A SKETCH OF THE PRE-1979 UK CONTROLS

The principal controls abolished in 1979 pertained, separately, to direct and portfolio investment, to the holding by residents of foreign currency deposits and to sterling lending by UK residents and banks to non-residents.

In regard to *direct investment*, the controls provided for the restriction of all sterling-financed foreign investment (i.e. investment paid for with foreign exchange bought at the official rate) except where it could be shown to have advantages to the balance of payments; but direct investment financed by foreign borrowing or by foreign exchange bought from the investment currency market (see below) was freely allowed (at least, during the 1970s). In order to prevent leakage through the use of unremitted profits, the controls also normally required that at least two thirds of after-tax profits should be repatriated.

In regard to *portfolio* investment, the controls provided that purchase by residents of foreign exchange for the purpose of investment overseas should only be made from the sale of existing foreign securities or from foreign currency borrowing. This created an 'investment currency' market in which there was an implied premium over the official exchange rate (since non-residents were free to purchase securities at the official exchange rate, there would never be a discount). In addition, for a period up to the end of 1977, sales of securities were subject to a 'surrender' penalty in that 25 per cent of the proceeds of sale had to be exchanged at the official rate.

Finally, the controls required that the holding, by residents, of foreign currency deposits should be limited to 'working balances' whilst sterling lending by banks and others overseas was similarly restricted to trade-related purposes.[3]

IV. THE UK EXPERIENCE

With the adoption by the United Kingdom of a floating exchange rate regime from 1972 onward, the original declared unifying rationale for the controls (to conserve foreign exchange) was lost and there is a dearth of official explanations for their continuation. Cairncross (1973) has remarked that the continuation of the controls may have been due, as much as anything else, to a perception that they might again be needed, for the old reasons, in the future and that to abolish them would effectively prevent their future use. This suggestion is given credence by the evident belief, at the inception of the new regime, that floating was a temporary expedient.

However this may be, the controls were finally removed in three stages in 1979. On June 12, it was announced, effective from the following day, that interest charges on foreign currency borrowing for portfolio investment could be financed at the official rate and the requirement of 115% cover for such borrowing was removed; then, on July 18 it was announced that, henceforth, repayment of foreign currency borrowing outstanding for a year or more could be made with currency purchased at the official rate, whilst purchase of EEC securities was exempted from all the restrictions. At the same time, all the remaining restrictions on direct investment and the payment of foreign currency borrowing incurred to finance it were removed. The rest of the restrictions (with the exception of some which were involved in the economic sanctions against Rhodesia, themselves removed in December) were lifted as from 24 October.

With the removal of the restrictions and the reporting system associated with them, some of the information useful in assessing their effectiveness (in particular, that pertaining to the currency of finance of investment flows) was lost – a further hindrance to effective estimation of the impact of abolition.

Four attempts to quantify the effects of exchange control abolition are readily available: these are those by the Bank of England (1981), Artis (1988), Chrystal (1985) and Taylor and Tonks (1988); their assessment is combined with additional evidence in what follows.

3. All of the controls are described in detail in the Bank of England's (1977) Manual.

IV.1 *Direct Investment*

The general opinion, before the abolition of the controls on direct investment, was that the regulatory regime of the 1970s was not intended to, and did not in fact, impinge significantly on the direct investment flows themselves (cf. e.g. Cairncross, 1973; Tew, 1978), but upon the financing of these flows. Foreign currency borrowing to finance direct investment abroad had been freely allowed, and the effect of the control was described for this reason in the Bank of England's *Quarterly Bulletin* for December 1979 (p. 371) as primarily one of deferred access to official exchange (in the sense, presumably, that the profits on the investment, which would otherwise be repatriated at the official rate, could be used to repay the foreign currency loan incurred to finance it).

Certainly, it had always seemed doubtful to what extent the two thirds rule for repatriation of foreign earnings was effective for the companies covered by the balance of payments statistics, where the figures showed that the proportion repatriated (though variable) was often closer to two fifths than to two thirds (see e.g. Tew, 1978, p. 333); among other differences, the exchange control provisions extended only to companies where the voting control lay within the UK, whereas the balance of payments statistics embrace the earnings of companies in which the UK interest is in a minority. This explanation, whilst consistent with the nominal effectiveness of exchange control over direct investment suggests that the penetration of foreign investment activities by multinational companies will significantly dilute the overall impact of such restrictions.

As the outstanding foreign currency borrowing associated with portfolio investment was comparatively small, most of the refinancing which appeared to occur during the third and final quarters of 1979, could be attributed to the relaxation of the controls over direct investment: a comparison of net borrowing for overseas investment in these quarters with its average in the previous two years prompted the Bank of England to suggest an effect of the order of £1bn in each quarter (*Quarterly Bulletin*, December 1979, p. 372; March 1980, pp. 13-14). This assessment, though, is somewhat bigger than the figures adduced in the Bank's subsequent analysis of the effects of abolition (Bank of England, 1981), would readily support. These figures (see Table 1) give the amount of direct investment and its financing in the period before the relaxation of controls in June and July, and in the third and fourth quarters of 1979, after which the foreign currency financing data are no longer available. These figures suggest a turnround in identified foreign currency borrowing from £260m to a repayment of £378m, a total effect of £638m a quarter, total direct investment itself remaining more or less the same.

The direct investment data for subsequent and earlier years, together with their (end-of-year) stock counterparts are shown in Table 2. These reveal some important implied revisions to the earlier data used in Table 1; for example the revised outflow figures corresponding to the quarterly averages shown in Table 1 and with the addition of the last period shown are, in £m: 1978Q1-1979Q2: 1047; 1979Q3-1979Q4: 1563; 1980Q1-1981Q2: 1305; 1981Q3-1986Q2: 1412. But it is not clear that these revisions significantly alter the provisional verdict of the earlier studies that the controls did little to affect outward direct investment in total.

TABLE 1

Direct Investment and Refinancing

	£m: quarterly average		
	1978Q1-1979Q2	1979Q3-1979Q4	1980Q1-1981Q2
Outward direct investment	707	643	724
Financed by: Retained earnings	325	473	341
Identified foreign currency borrowing	260	−378	..
Unidentified finance	122	548	383

.. = not available

Source: Bank of England (1981), p. 371.

Table 2 indicates an increase in inward as well as in outward direct investment after abolition, consistent with some effect of the controls in reducing domestic rates of return; and whilst the net outward flow has risen over the period it is clearly an erratic series, much influenced in the last two years shown by disinvestment by overseas oil companies. Tentatively removing the oil-related component flattens the upward trend in net investment almost completely.[4] Table 2 also reports stock data for direct investment held abroad by UK residents and those held by foreign residents in the UK.

4. The data only allow this to be done up to 1983 after which oil companies' investment, which was previously located in the category 'other UK residents' (which it might be assumed to dominate) can no longer be even approximately identified. Assuming that the investment shown for "other UK residents" excluding oil companies after 1984 is representa-

The net asset position has clearly improved, but trends here are additionally complicated by valuation changes, including those due to exchange rate changes, and cannot be said to cast any light on the effect of removing exchange controls.

TABLE 2

Direct Investment 1975-1985

£000m

	Flows			Stocks		
	Outward	Inward	Net Outward	External Assets of UK	UK Liabilities to Overseas Residents	Net UK
1975	1.3	1.5	0.2	18.6	12.1	6.5
1976	2.4	1.7	0.7	23.5	13.7	9.8
1977	2.4	2.5	-0.1	24.4	15.7	8.7
1978	3.5	2.0	1.5	28.1	17.9	10.2
1979	5.9	3.0	2.9	31.4	22.0	9.4
1980	4.9	4.4	0.5	33.3	26.4	7.9
1981	6.1	2.9	3.2	45.2	30.0	.15.2
1982	4.3	3.0	1.3	53.3	31.8	21.5
1983	5.3	3.4	1.9	60.3	36.3	14.0
1984	6.0	0.4	5.6	81.5	38.0	43.5
1985	7.3	3.4	4.0	76.7	40.5	36.2

By convention these figures are shown with sign reversed in the balance of payments tables.

Source: CSO, Balance of Payments Pink Book, 1986.

What seems to emerge, then, is this: whereas the controls were not (not in their latter years) intended to reduce overseas direct investment significantly they were aimed at the financing of this investment. There is evidence that the controls had some effect in this sense, though their abolition also removed the data source needed to track this over a reasonable period of time. General considerations suggest that where there was an effect on outward investment it may have been purchased at the expense of some reduction in the incentive for inward investment to occur and this would further reduce the impact of the controls on the net flow and the net foreign exchange position. There is no strong evidence in the relevant figures for any net effect.

tive of earlier figures, the net balance of direct investment, aproximately excluding that of oil companies, beginning in 1975, emerges as, in £bn: 0.7; 1.5; 0.8; 1.6; 1.5; 1.3; 3.9; 1.4 and, in 1983, 1.5.

IV.2 *Portfolio Investment*

The effectiveness of the controls over portfolio investment was always evident in the height of the investment currency premium created by them. As Chart 1 shows, this premium was not infrequently in the range 30-50%, and on some occasions was even higher than this. Variations in the premium were frequently discussed in the pages of the Bank of England's *Quarterly Bulletin* and attributed to speculation on the exchange rate or on the stock markets in New York or London. The decline in the premium before abolition owed much to the circulation of rumours about the impending abolition of the controls.

CHART 1. UK: The Investment Currency Premium

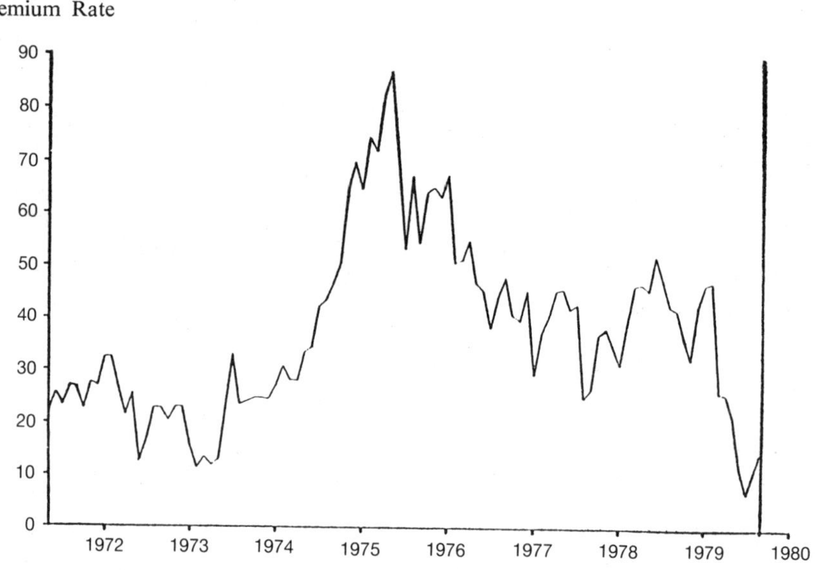

Effective Dollar Premium Rate; Exchange controls abolished October 1979.

Recourse to foreign currency borrowing to support portfolio investment was less significant than for direct investment: the Bank (1981) quoted an estimate of £1.6-£1.7bn outstanding associated foreign currency borrowing at the end of 1978. Accordingly, refinancing of the existing stock of such borrowing was less significant (and in any case indistinguishable from the refinancing of borrowing connected with direct investment); but the removal of the controls clearly allowed outward investment to increase (see Table 3) and

TABLE 3
Portfolio Investment 1975-1985[a]
£000m

	Flows			Stocks		
	Outward	Inward	Net Outward	External Assets of UK	UK Liabilities to Overseas Residents	Net UK
1975	0.1	0.2	-0.1	6.9	6.1	0.8
1976	-0.1	1.0	-1.1	8.7	7.8	0.9
1977	—	1.9	-1.9	8.7	10.6	-1.9
1978	1.1	-1.0	1.1	10.3	9.7	0.6
1979	0.9	1.5	0.6	12.3	10.4	1.9
1980	3.2	1.5	1.7	18.7	12.1	6.6
1981	4.3	0.3	4.0	25.4	12.7	12.7
1982	6.7	0.2	6.5	40.3	15.7	24.6
1983	6.5	1.9	4.6	60.0	19.3	40.7
1984	9.6	1.4	8.1	84.3	23.5	60.8
1985	18.2	7.1	11.2	100.6	32.1	68.5
1986[b]	12.0	2.3	9.7	..	..	..

By convention these figures are shown with sign reversed in the balance of payments tables.
(a) end of year; (b) first half-year; .. = not available.
Source: CSO, Balance of Payments Pink Book, 1986.

raised the net outflow sharply, despite some concurrent increase in 'inward' investment.

Strict enforcement of the controls would have implied no outward portfolio investment net of foreign currency borrowing, and in 1975-1978, the average gross outward flow was very small. Assuming that this is what would have been enforced by the continued presence of the controls, virtually the whole outward flow from 1980 on might be put down as the 'effect' of abolishing the control – an amount in excess of £45bn; granting that the controls deterred some inward investment, cumulating the increase in net outflow over the period might seem more appropriate – something of the order of £30bn. A somewhat similar order of magnitude is suggested by crude calculations based on the increase in the share of overseas assets in financial institutions' portfolios, as portrayed in Table 4. Comparing the share in 1985 with either the average for 1975-1978 or for 1978 alone suggests an increase of the order of 6-9 basis points, worth £30-40bn on 1985's total portfolio.

TABLE 4

Financial Assets and Liabilities of Other Financial (Non-Bank) Institutions: Overseas Components

£000m

	Overseas Assets	Overseas Liabilities	Net Overseas	Gross Financial Wealth (total assets)	Per Cent Portfolio Net Overseas	Per Cent Shares Gross Overseas
1975	7.0	1.4	5.6	77.3	7.3	9.1
1976	9.0	1.6	7.4	88.4	8.3	10.2
1977	8.6	1.8	6.8	117.1	5.8	7.3
1978	10.4	1.5	8.9	132.8	6.7	7.8
1979	11.0	2.2	8.9	150.1	5.9	7.3
1980	16.2	2.0	14.2	185.5	7.7	8.7
1981	22.5	2.3	20.2	210.3	9.6	10.7
1982	38.2	5.3	32.9	263.3	12.5	14.5
1983	54.9	7.6	47.3	326.7	14.5	17.7
1984	75.7	9.0	66.7	401.2	16.6	18.9
1985	77.3	9.9	67.5	472.9	14.3	16.4

Source: CSO, Financial Statistics, November 1986.

All such calculations are exceptionally crude and can only be treated as broadly indicative of what has been agreed in previous analyses (Bank of England, 1981; Chrystal, 1985), viz. that there was a large effect on portfolio investment from the removal of the controls.

IV.3 *The Monetary Controls*

The lifting of the monetary restrictions on bank lending in sterling to overseas residents and on the holding by residents of foreign currency denominated deposits has had some clear and sizeable effects. In addition, a particularly striking impact is noticeable from the removal of controls on the onshore/off-shore differential and consequently on departures from covered interest parity. These in turn have implied significant changes in the scope and form of monetary policy.

The restriction of sterling lending overseas was an important component in the system of exchange control; such lending had broadly to be associated with UK trade. The statistics collected on bank lending give a straightforward picture of the consequences of removing this control: Table 5 shows

TABLE 5

Bank Lending (in Sterling) Abroad[a]

£000m

	1975	1976	1977	1978	1979	1980	1981	1982	1983	1984	1985
Identified long-term export credit	0.2	0.2	0.5	0.6	0.1	0.2	0.2	1.0	0.9	0.3	—
Other identified export credit	—	0.1	—	0.1	0.1	0.1	–0.1	–0.2	—	–0.1	–0.1
Other sterling lending	–0.1	0.4	0.1	0.1	–0.2	2.5	3.0	3.3	1.3	4.7	1.7

By convention these figures are shown with sign reversed in the balance of payments tables.
(a)— =less than £50 millions;
Source: CSO, Balance of Payments Pink Book, 1986, Table 8.4.

bank lending in three categories – for identified long-term export credit, for other identified export credit and for 'other' purposes. Lending in the last category increases significantly after 1979, a good part of it going to the offices of unrelated banks abroad (which banks have also in this period increased their holdings of sterling deposits with UK banks as part of the growth in Eurocurrency business).

The lifting of the restriction on the holding of foreign currency bank deposits has been followed by a large increase in such deposits. M3, the broad monetary magnitude which includes foreign currency deposits, has grown faster than £M3 which excludes them. The ratio of £M3 to M3 has consequently fallen, as illustrated in the graph (Chart 2), from pre-abolition levels in the late '70s of the order of 91% to 85-87% in the mid-80s. This would not have been possible without the removal of the controls; Chart 3 illustrates the relationship of the difference £M3-M3 to trade (exports) before 1979, and the shift in this relationship in the post-abolition period.

The removal of the controls has had a dramatic effect on the on-shore/off-shore interest differential. In the presence of the controls full arbitrage is inhibited and in consequence the on-shore/off-shore differential can exhibit significant departures from zero and significant variability. A predicted effect of removing the controls is that these distortions will be removed.[5] The calculations reported in Table 6 and the graphical displays in Charts 4A and 4B

5. Phylaktis and Wood (1986) have noted such findings in Johnston (1979) for Germany and in Otani and Tiwari (1981) for Japan in similar instances.

CHART 2. Foreign Currency Deposit Holdings and Exchange Control Abolition

Ratio

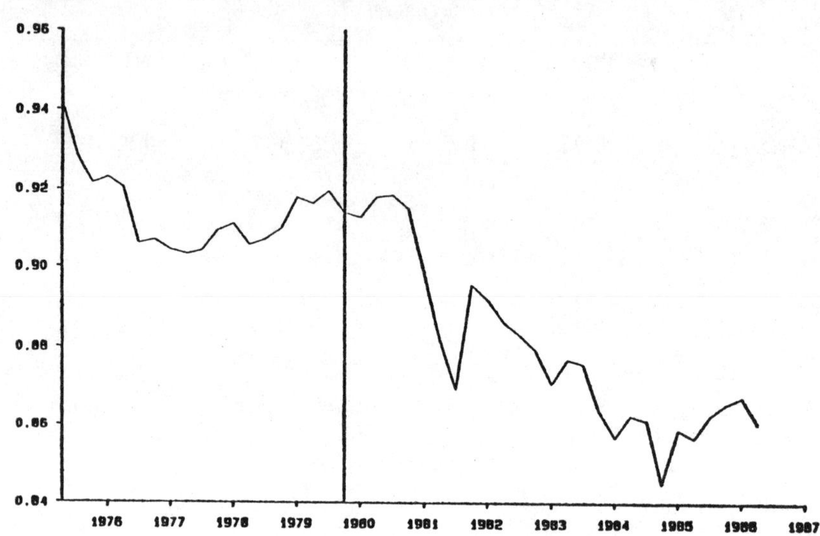

Ratio £ M3/M3; Exchange controls abolished October 1979

CHART 3. Foreign Currency Deposits, Trade and the Removal of Exchange Controls

M3 − £ M3,

Exports

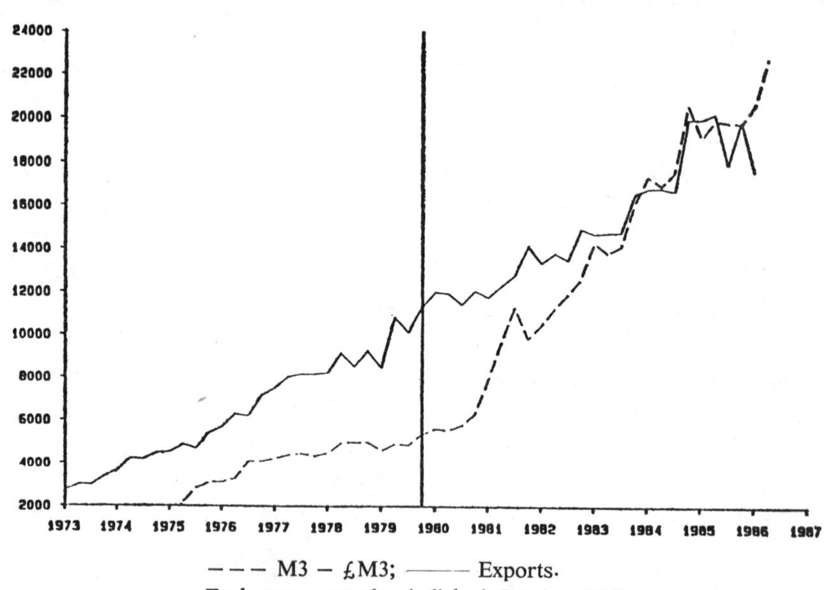

– – – M3 − £M3; ——— Exports.

Exchange controls abolished October 1979.

CHART 4a. UK: The Off-shore/on-shore Differential (Local Authority Loans)

Percentage

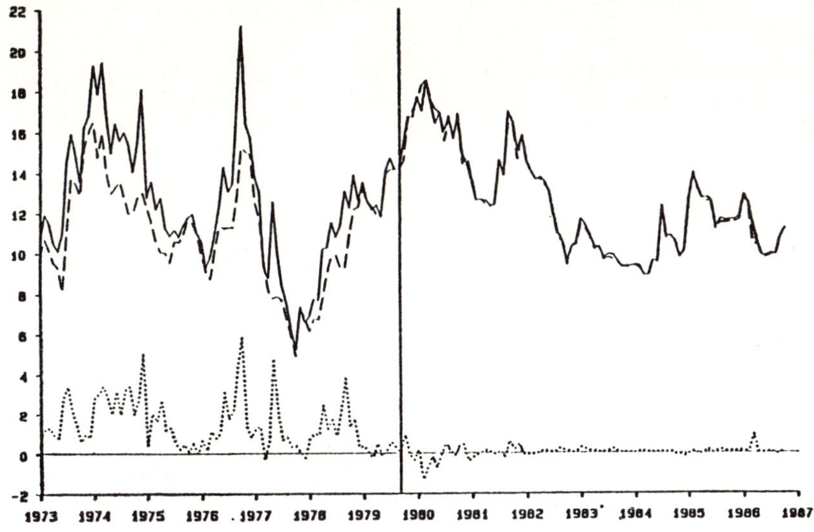

——— 3 month Euro-sterling; – – – 3 month Local Authority Temporary Loans;
.... Differential (Euro £ - LATL).
Exchange controls abolished October 1979.

CHART 4b. UK: The Off-shore/on-shore Differential (Interbank Rate)

Percentage

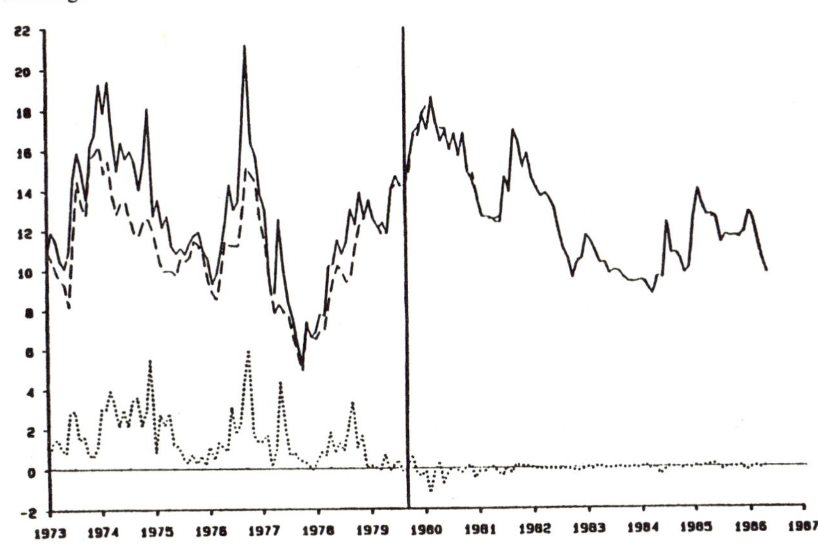

——— 3 month Euro-sterling; – – – 3 month Interbank £ market rates;
.... Differential (Euro £ - Interbank).
Exchange controls abolished October 1979.

show the 3-month Euro-sterling rate and the 3-month Local Authority Temporary Loan rate and the differential between them, whilst Chart 4B displays the Euro-sterling rate against interbank rate. In the table is given information on the mean, variance and range of each of these differentials before and after October 1979.

TABLE 6

On-shore /Off-shore Interest Differentials per cent per annum (end of month data)

	Euro-£ minus Local Authority Rate	Euro-£ minus Interbank Rate
Jan. 1973 - Sept. 1979		
Mean	1.476	1.510
Variance	1.731	1.735
Range	–0.250 to 5.940	–0.160 to 6.000
Oct. 1979 - Oct. 1986		
Mean	0.075	–0.040
Variance	0.069	0.045
Range	–1.280 to 0.940	–1.220 to 0.690

In order to assess scientifically the contribution of exchange control in this respect, one should perhaps use inferential rather than purely descriptive statistics. Accordingly, we decided to test for a downward shift in the UK on-shore /off-shore interest differential (difference between three month local authority and Euro-sterling rates) after October 1979. Because of the uncertainty concerning the statistical distributions of asset prices, we used non-parametric tests for a variety of distributional assumptions. The statistical methods are described in the appendix; the results are reported in Table 7. In each case, the test statistic is distributed as standard normal N(0,1), under the null hypothesis of no shift in volatility; a significantly positive (negative) statistic implies a reduction (increase) in volatility. The results show an unequivocal volatility reduction in the on-shore /off-shore interest differential as a result of the relaxation of exchange controls.

It is known that interest rates in Euro markets closely reproduce covered interest parity (Taylor 1987a, b); the interest rate on Euro-X deposits may actually be set directly by adjusting the corresponding \$ rate for the cost of forward cover in the \$/X market. This being so, deviations from covered interest parity between on-shore rates will primarily reflect the wedge between on-shore and Euro-rates and will tend to vanish as the wedge is re-

TABLE 7

Non-Parametric Tests for a Shift in the Volatility of the UK Off-shore/On-shore Interest Differential after October 1979[a]

Assumed underlying distribution:	Normal	Logistic	Double Exponential	Cauchy
Test Statistic:	5.74	4.92	4.85	4.98

(a) All statistics are standard normal variates under the null hypothesis of no shift in volatility (see Appendix). Significantly positive statistics indicate a reduction in volatility post-October 1979.

moved. Since we have already found the abolition of exchange controls to be effective in this respect, it must be expected that deviations from covered interest parity between on-shore rates will tend to zero after abolition of exchange control. Once again the graphical evidence (Charts 5A and 5B) strongly confirms this. It will be seen that both the on-shore/off-shore differential and the covered interest differentials after abolition have non-zero means, however much reduced they are from pre-abolition levels. *Inter alia*, these are likely to be explicable in terms of observation error and systematic differences in perceived risk and transactions costs. In their study of this question Frenkel and Levich (1977) argued that the presence of transactions costs meant that there was a band within which such deviations from interest parity could fall consistently with perfect arbitrage and they argued that a large proportion of observed deviations from covered parity between US and UK interest rates actually fell within this band. McCormick (1979) subsequently showed, however, that Frenkel and Levich had estimated too wide a band and calculated that the proportion of observed deviations from parity of on-shore rates which fell within the band was less than 30 percent, not 96 per cent as implied by Frenkel and Levich. (For off-shore rates, the recalculation sustained the contention that virtually all deviations fell within the neutral band.) These observations serve to strengthen the suggestion here that exchange controls did inhibit full arbitrage and that the decline in observed deviations from parity ensuing upon their abolition does indicate a real change in this respect.[6]

6. Some recent work by Chrystal (1986), however, might provide a possible qualification. Using daily data on Euro-sterling and Interbank rates Chrystal finds evidence of a move to integration before the abolition of the controls, especially in the period September

CHART 5a. UK: Departures from Covered Interest Parity (Local Authority Loan)

% Differential

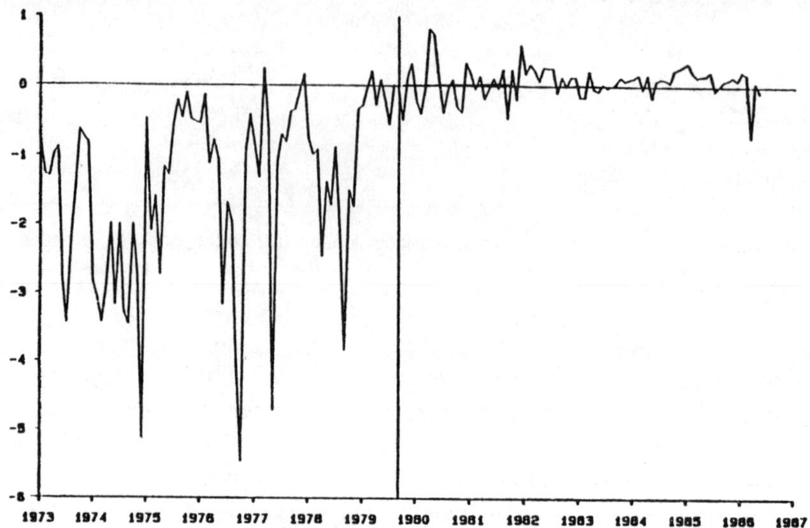

Covered Interest Rate Differentials (Local authority temporary loans – Euro market rate). Exchange controls abolished October 1979.

CHART 5b. UK: Departures from Covered Interest Parity (Interbank Rate)

% Differential

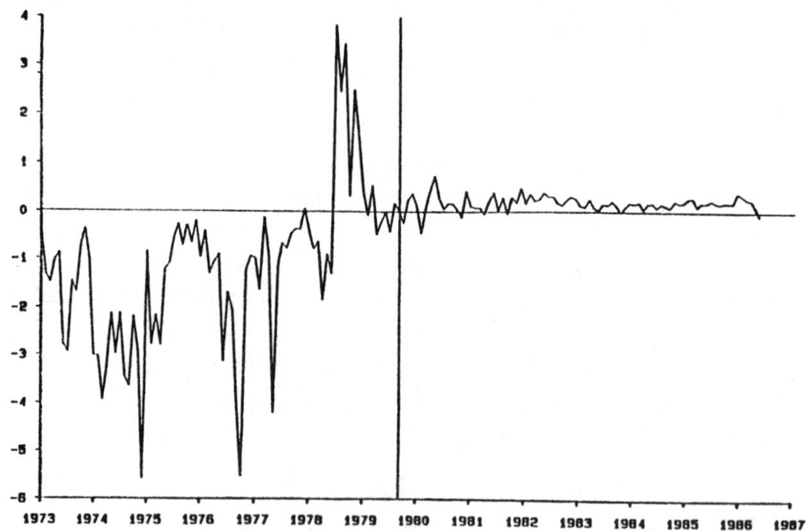

Covered Interest Rate Differentials (3 month Interbank market rate – 3 month Euro rate). Exchange controls abolished October 1979.

IV.4 *Implications for Monetary Policy*

The abolition of the monetary exchange controls in principle poses several problems for monetary control and in practice has disciplined the system of monetary regulation and control employed in the United Kingdom.

Three aspects of this may be singled out for discussion: the scope for intervention in the foreign exchange markets; the nature of monetary regulation; and, finally, the consequences of currency substitution.

Considered as part of a trend towards greater integration, and more efficient financial markets, abolition of exchange control can be considered to reduce the scope for sterilized intervention and for manoeuvres in the forward markets. As an example of the latter, a traditional Bank of England tactic to exploit the forward markets to exert a bear squeeze on speculators may be mentioned. This tactic consisted of selling sterling forward, thus raising Euro-sterling interest rates but not on-shore rates of interest, discouraging spot sales and reducing the profit from selling sterling short. This manoeuvre cannot take place in the absence of exchange control, because the possibility of raising off-shore rates without also raising on-shore rates no longer exists.[7] Kearney and MacDonald (1986), more generally, have found some evidence that sterilized intervention was an effective instrument of policy in the 1970s for the UK, in contrast to Obstfeld's (1984) findings for Germany. Since the finding for the UK implies that capital mobility was less than perfect, they tentatively suggest that exchange control may have been responsible.

That the liberalization of exchange controls has had implications for the nature of monetary control and regulation is not in doubt. In a liberal regime, quantitative credit restrictions, or similar instruments, are subject to added leakage as frustrated business moves off-shore: this was forcefully illustrated in the British case (as noted in Artis and Lewis, 1981) when the Governor of the Bank of England requested the domestic banks in 1979 not to participate in or encourage the use of off-shore facilities to frustrate the impact of the then existing Special Supplementary Deposit scheme (popularly known as the 'corset'). The corset control specified a steeply rising rate of call to zero-interest account at the Bank of England on interest bearing deposits received by banks in excess of pre-specified allowable rates of growth. The banks reacted to this by rationing borrowers for credit and reducing their competition

1978 — February 1979. What is unknown of course is whether this movement would have proved irreversible in the absence of a lifting of the controls or would, on the contrary, have been shown to be a temporary and accidental phase. On our view of the matter, the latter is more likely.

7. This is discussed in Llewellyn (1980).

for deposits. In the presence of freely available off-shore banking facilities, frustrated borrowers could tap off-shore banking facilities, whilst lenders would find it profitable to divert deposits from on-shore to off-shore banks. The lifting of the exchange restrictions thus rendered the use of this control otiose and it was subsequently dropped in June 1980. Aside from its implications for the use of quantitative controls, or controls with a rationing, effect, the lifting of exchange restrictions also implies that monetary regulations of the classical balance sheet ratio type may be redundant too. The ready availability of off-shore banking services, undertaken on the basis of complete freedom from imposed balance sheet ratios, implies that the scope for imposing such ratios on competing on-shore banks must be strictly limited. Ratios which are onerous will result in a migration of banking services to off-shore locations. In this light, the reform of the regulations governing the British banking system in 1981, which placed the system on a very liberal and essentially ratio-free basis was inevitable; though there would probably have been a movement in this direction in any case, the absence of exchange control was compelling.

In the long haul, these trends inevitably raise questions about the extent to which currency substitution will grow. The market solution draws its legitimacy from the efficiency gains of locating production in the lowest cost location; since banking services are highly mobile there is no guarantee that these services will not in future be purchased more efficiently from off-shore locations, perhaps involving non-sterling currencies as transactions media. Alternatively, as there are economies of scale in production, a UK location may prove efficient for global services performed for other economies. In either event, widespread currency substitution would have radical consequences for monetary policy, as has been spelt out in a number of recent papers by McKinnon.[8]

IV.5 *Consequences for Asset Prices*

It is particularly difficult to draw inferences from the removal of exchange control for its consequences for the exchange rate, interest rates and other financial asset prices such as equity prices. The coincidence of other major shocks at this time is especially awkward in this respect.

The Bank of England's (1981) study cautiously concluded that the abolition of controls must have had some depreciating effect on the exchange rate, considered in itself, and may have had some effect in keeping interest rates

8. See e.g. McKinnon (1984).

down. The two effects are to some degree alternatives; if the controls succeeded in holding down the rate of return on British assets, investment in them would have been correspondingly less attractive for foreign investors and the impact on the net demand for sterling and therefore the exchange rate consequently diminished.

It seems plausible, in view of our discussion of the probable impact of abolition on balance of payments flows, that the controls did contain the net demand for foreign currency: removing them should have depreciated the exchange rate. The evidence of the change in on-shore/off-shore interest differentials might be thought to indicate that domestic rates were reduced by the controls, since positive pre-abolition differentials in favour of off-shore rates fall or become negative after abolition. But the off-shore rate is in covered interest parity with the US domestic rate, and would only be itself unaffected by abolition if abolition made no difference to the exchange rate and expectations of its future value. Raw data processing on a pre-and post-abolition basis has no chance of revealing effects on either the exchange rate or on interest rates; as is well known, the sterling exchange rate continued to appreciate strongly through 1980 and 1981 whilst nominal interest rates also rose through 1980. Chrystal (1985) has also looked at real interest rates, but arrived at no firm conclusion that abolition had definite effects on either nominal or real interest rates. There were strong coincidental forces making for an effect in the direction opposite to that which might have been associated with abolition *per se* both on the exchange rate and on interest rates.

Concerning the effects on equity prices, there exists quite a large literature which examines more general questions of stock market internationalisation and segmentation. One group of studies[9] has examined the question of gains from international portfolio diversification, whilst a second strand in the literature[10] has examined stock market segmentation. In a segmented market, assets are priced according to factors particular to that market, whilst in an integrated market domestic assets are priced according to international factors.

Given the marked impact of UK exchange control abolition on portfolio investment, noted above, one might conjecture that this may have led to a closer integration of UK and overseas stock markets post 1979. In order to test this proposition, we carried out two kinds of procedures. Firstly, we

9. See e.g. Grubel (1968), Levy and Sarnat (1970), Grubel and Fadner (1971), Ripley (1973), Panton, Lessig and Joy (1976).

10. See e.g. Agmon (1972, 1973), Lessard (1974), Stehle (1977), Errunza and Losq (1985) and Jorion and Schwartz (1986). All of these studies find significant national factors in the pricing of assets.

tested for closer *short-run* integration of stock markets by testing for a significant shift in the correlation of monthly stock market returns post October 1979; and secondly, we tested for *long-run* stock market integration post 1979 by testing for cointegration of stock market prices (Engle and Granger, 1987).

Monthly data were collected for five major stock market indices, United Kingdom, West Germany, Netherlands, Japan and the United States, for the period January 1973 to June 1986.[11,12] Tests were carried out with respect to two sub-periods : October 1979 to June 1986 and April 1973 to September 1979.

Table 8 reports correlation coefficients of UK stock market returns (first difference in the log-level) with those of four other countries examined, for each of the sub-periods. In no case does there appear to be a marked increase in the correlation during the second sub-period, and a test statistic for equality of correlation coefficients across the two sub-periods is in each case highly insignificant.[13] These results suggest that there has been no signi-

11. All data are from Datastream and are monthly (closing reading, last working day), unadjusted. The precise indices used are : UK, FTA All Share Index; US, Standard and Poor's Composite Index; Japan, Tokyo New Stock Exchange Index; West Germany, Commerzbank Index; Netherlands, Datastream Total Market Index. All data were deflated by the sterling exchange rate and converted to natural logarithms.

12. Some justification should perhaps be given for converting the indices into common currency (sterling) terms, apart from the fact that this is standard practice in the literature. The point is that we are implictly examining the short- and long-run gains available to a *British* investor by diversifying his or her portfolio into foreign stock markets. Clearly, this requires the conversion of all returns into sterling terms. It might be argued that this procedure begs a question concerning exchange rate risk, and that separate exchange rate equations should be included in the analysis. However, we are mainly concerned with *ex post* rather than *ex ante* phenomena: was there a significant increase in the degree of correlation of *ex post* British and overseas stock market returns after 1979?

13. The test statistic for the equality of the correlation coefficient (column 3, Table 8) was constructed as follows. If r is the sample correlation coefficient, then the statistic

$$\delta = \frac{1}{2}\, ln\, \frac{1+r}{1-r}$$

is approximately normally distributed with approximate mean and variance of $1/2\, ln\, \{(1+\rho)/(1-\rho)\}$ and $1/(T-3)$ respectively, where T is the sample size and ρ is the population correlation coefficient. Moreover, these approximations will be close in sample sizes greater than fifty (Kendall and Stuart, 1967, pp. 292-293). Hence, denoting two subsamples by subscripts 1 and 2, under the null hypothesis $H_0: \rho_1 = \rho_2$ the statistic

$$\pi = \frac{ln\, \{(1+r_1)/(1-r_1)\} - ln\, \{(1+r_2)/(1-r_2)\}}{2/\{1/(T_1-3)+1/(T_2-3)\}}$$

will be distributed approximately standard normal.

ficant increase in the correlation of *short-run* stock market returns as a result of the abolition of exchange control.

TABLE 8

Correlation of Stock Market Returns[a]

Correlation of UK with	(1) 73(4) - 79(9)	(2) 79(10) - 86(6)	(3) Test (1) = (2)
West Germany	0.211	0.220	0.058
Netherlands	0.439	0.445	0.348
Japan	0.157	0.303	0.955
United States	0.418	0.289	0.914

(a) Under the hypothesis that the population correlation coefficients are the same over both sub-periods, the test statistic listed in column 3 has a standard normal distribution.

Table 9 reports the results of unit root tests. For the stock market indices, the null hypothesis of a unit root can in no case be rejected at even the ten per cent level. For stock market returns, however, the null hypothesis is strongly rejected with significance levels much less than one per cent. Thus, there appears to be a unit root in each of the stock market index series which cancels out on first differencing – i.e. they appear to be integrated of order one, I(1), during each sub-period (Engle and Granger, 1987).

TABLE 9

Unit Root Test for Stock Market Indices and Returns[a]

	Stock Market Indices		Stock Market Returns	
	73(4) - 79(9)	79(10) - 86(6)	73(4) - 79(9)	79(10) - 86(6)
United Kingdom	–0.940	0.141	–6.920	–10.290
West Germany	–0.932	1.251	–8.738	–8.673
Netherlands	–0.841	0.868	–8.996	–9.574
Japan	–0.331	1.072	–7.534	–8.669
United States	–1.247	–0.250	–9.447	–8.695

(a) All test statistics are (non-augmented) Dickey-Fuller statistics. Approximate critical value at the 5% level is —2.89, with rejection region ($\theta/\theta < -2.89$).

Table 10 contains results of estimating the cointegrating regressions and of testing for a unit root in the cointegrating residuals. Although non-cointegration can in no case be rejected for the first sub-period, the test statistics (except for the US) become significant at the 5% level for the post-

TABLE 10

Cointegrating Regressions and Tests for a Unit Root in the Cointegrating Residuals[a]

$S_{UK} = a + \beta\, S_{country} + e$

	73(4) - 79(9)				79(10) - 86(6)			
Country	$\hat{a}$	$\hat{\beta}$	R^2	ADF	$\hat{a}$	$\hat{\beta}$	R^2	ADF
West Germany	14.86	0.71	0.45	–2.21	137.41	1.17	0.85	–3.43
Netherlands	14.11	0.97	0.58	–2.35	90.51	1.085	0.96	–3.73
Japan	59.79	1.62	0.63	–2.64	149.54	1.43	0.97	–3.50
United States	50.17	2.62	0.23	–1.70	57.86	3.97	0.92	–2.36

(a) Coefficient estimates were obtained by ordinary least squares. Standard errors are not reported as they may be misleading in this context (Granger and Newbold, 1974). R^2 is the coefficient of determination. ADF is the augmented Dickey-Fuller statistic for the null hypothesis of non-cointegration; approximate critical value for ADF at the 5% level is –3.17, with rejection region ($\theta/\theta < -3.17$), (Engle and Granger, 1987).

abolition of exchange control period. These results imply that the UK and foreign (non-US) stock market indices were cointegrated post-1979, but not before.[14,15] Since the stock market indices were found to be non-stationary, (more particularly I(1)), the coefficient estimates where cointegration was *not* found (pre-1979 for all countries and post-1979 for the US) are of little interest, since they are from 'spurious regressions' (Granger and Newbold, 1974). Although Stock (1988) shows that coefficient estimates of cointegrating parameters may have desirable asymptotic properties, he does suggest that there may be substantial finite-sample bias, and this is borne out in the Monte Carlo study of Banerjee et al (1986). Since, moreover, we currently have no way of estimating the standard errors in cointegrating regressions, we cannot infer that the estimated slope coefficients for Germany, the Netherlands and Japan post-1979 are significantly different from unity. This in no way affects our inferences concerning cointegration, however.

Note also that we cannot infer from these results that the UK market is *perfectly* correlated with the German, Dutch and Japanese markets in the long run post-1979. We can infer, however, that these markets will be *highly*

14. Note that it is unnecessary to test for cointegration amongst other stock market pairs in the system because of the transitivity property of cointegration. That is to say, if we have three I(1) variables, x, y and z, and x and y, and x and z are cointegrated then, for some b and c we have $-x + by \sim$ I(0) and $x - cz \sim$ I(0), hence adding and rearranging, $y - (c/b)\, z \sim$ I(0) – i.e. y and z are cointegrated. The UK market may act as a 'clearing house' in this sense.

15. In each case, the 'reverse regressions' were also used to test cointegration, e.g. regressing the German index on the UK index, etc. This yielded qualitatively identical results.

correlated in the long run, so the long-run gains from diversification across them will be slight.[16] Thus, it seems that the abolition of exchange control has very probably contributed to the internationalisation of the UK stock market.

V. CONCLUSION

Several conclusions can be drawn from the British experience in removing exchange controls. First, the removal of those controls does appear to have contributed towards eliminating deviations from covered interest parity and reveals their presence to have been more of a hindrance to financial integration than was perhaps fully realized at the time. The integration which abolition has accomplished has in turn posed a felt discipline on the type of monetary policy available; it creates a presumption of a strong decline in the effectiveness of sterilized intervention, a presumption against quantitative controls on credit (or controls producting this effect) and a presumption in favour of a very liberal regime of monetary regulation such as the UK now enjoys. Further into the future, the potential for currency substitution has still to be revealed. Second, various effects on the balance of payments flows can be discerned; in particular, a market outflow of portfolio investment is to be found, and the balance of payments flows (on both sides of the balance sheet) bear witness to a greater degree of financial integration. This is also evidenced by our finding that the UK stock market appears to be cointegrated with certain overseas stock markets post-1979. Third, whilst there is a presumption from the apparent balance of payments effects that abolition produced a depreciation impact on the exchange rate and some presumption that interest rates may have been raised *ceteris paribus*, neither effect is evident from the data. At the time when the restrictions were lifted the UK balance of payments was also affected by other important shocks: the new monetary regime of the Thatcher Government, the second oil price shock and the move from oil deficit to self-sufficiency in production. These factors serve to obscure any effects abolition may have had on asset prices and hinder quantitative assessment of the effects on balance of payments flows. They also qualify the value of the British experiment as a guide to the likely experience of other countries taking the same route; among the findings, those pertaining to the impetus to financial integration are perhaps the most robust to this qualification.

University of Manchester and C.E.P.R., London.
City University Business School, Bank of England and C.E.P.R., London.

16. The presence of cointegration in this context also has some interesting implications for market efficiency — see Taylor and Tonks, 1989.

APPENDIX

Non-Parametric Tests

This appendix describes the non-parametric method used to test for a shift in the on-shore/off-shore interest differential post-October 1979 as reported in Section IV.

Let di_t be the on-shore/off-shore interest differential at time t, then the maintained hypothesis is:

$$\begin{aligned} di_t &= \mu + \sigma_t \varepsilon_t \\ \sigma_t &= exp\,(a + \beta z_t) \end{aligned} \tag{1}$$

where μ, a and β are unknown, constant scalars, ε_t is independently and identically distributed with distribution function F and density function f, and z_t is a binary variable reflecting the hypothesised change in volatility, i.e.:

$$z_t = \begin{cases} 1, & t < \text{October 1979} \\ 0, & \text{otherwise} \end{cases}$$

Given (1), the null hypothesis of no shift in volatility is then:

$$H_o : \beta = 0 \tag{2}$$

Hajek and Sidak (1967) (henceforth HS) develop a number of non-parametric rank tests for dealing with problems involving this kind of framework, which, under appropriate regularity conditions, are locally most powerful (HS pp. 70-71).

The test statistics take the form

$$\delta = \sum_{t=1}^{T} (z_t - \bar{z})\, a(u_t) \tag{3}$$

where $\bar{z}$ is the arithmetic mean of the z_t sequence of T observations ($\bar{z} = \mathrm{T}^{-1} \sum_{t=1}^{\mathrm{T}} z_t$), and u_t is defined as follows. Let $r(di_t)$ be the rank of di_t – i.e. di_t is the $r(di_t)$-th smallest change in the total sequence of length T considered; then

$$u_t = r(di_t) / (T + 1).$$

Clearly, u_t must lie in the closed interval $[1/(T + 1),\ T/(T + 1)]$ (for no ties in rank). The function $a(.)$ in (3) is a score function defined in HS (p. 70), depending upon the assumed density of ε_t, i.e., f. HS define a class of functions which can be used in place of the score function in large samples, since $a(.)$ may in practice be difficult to evaluate. If F is the assumed distribution function of ε_t:

$$F(x) = \int_{-\infty}^{x} (y)dy$$

and $F^{-1}(u)$ is the inverse of F:

$$F^{-1}(u) = inf\{ x / F(x) \geqslant u \}$$

then the asymptotic score function, $\varnothing(.)$ is defined (HS p. 19):

$$\varnothing : (0, 1) \rightarrow IR$$

$$\varnothing(u) = - F^{-1}(u) \left[\frac{f'\{F^{-1}(u)\}}{f\{F^{-1}(u)\}} \right]^{-1} \qquad (4)$$

Under the maintained hypothesis (1), the statistic

$$\pi = \sum_{t=1}^{T} (z_t - \bar{z}) \varnothing(u_t) \qquad (5)$$

(i.e. as in (3) with $a(.)$ replaced by $\varnothing(.)$). will by asymptotically normally distributed. Under the null hypothesis (2), π will have mean zero and variance ρ^2 given by (HS pp. 159-160):

$$\rho^2 = \sum_{t=1}^{T} (z_t - \bar{z})^2 \int_0^1 \{ \varnothing(u) - \bar{\varnothing} \}^2 \ du \qquad (6)$$

where

$$\bar{\varnothing} = \int_0^1 \varnothing(u) \ du.$$

The test is now as follows. For a given choice of f, π can be calculated as in (5) and referred to the normal distribution, to construct a test of any given nominal size, of the null hypothesis (2) (no change in volatility). Significantly negative values of π reflect a negative value for β in (1) – ie an increase in volatility post-October 1979. The statistic π in (5) provides the locally most powerful test among the class of all possible tests (HS p. 249). The statistic π/ϱ (as reported in Section IV) will be standard normally distributed under the null hypothesis (no shift in volatility).

Note that although the test procedure just outlined is non-parametric in the sense that no volatility measures are actually estimated, in implementing the procedure we cannot avoid choosing an appropriate distribution for changes in the interest differential. In order to try and minimise the damage due to choosing an inappropriate distribution we selected four well-known ones – hopefully, the true distribution of exchange rate changes is close to one of them. The densities used correspond to the normal, logistic, double exponential and Cauchy distributions. All of the chosen distributions are symmetric and both the double exponential and Cauchy distributions have fat tails.

REFERENCES

Agmon, T. (1972) 'The Relationship Among Equity Markets: A Study of Share Price Co-Movements in the United States, United Kingdom, Germany and Japan', *Journal of Finance*, pp. 839-855.

— (1973) 'Country Risk: The Significance of the Country Factor for Share Price Movements in the United Kingdom, Germany and Japan', *Journal of Business*, (January), pp. 24-32.

Artis, M. J. (1988) 'Exchange Controls and the ECUs', *European Economy*, (May).

Artis, M. J. and Lewis, M. K. (1981) *Monetary Control in the United Kingdom*, (London: Philip Allan).

Banerjee, A., Dolado, J.J., Hendry, D. F. and Smith, G. W. (1986) 'Exploring Equilibrium Relationships in Econometrics Through Static Models: Some Monte Carlo Evidence', *Oxford Bulletin of Economics and Statistics*, 48: 253-277.

Bank of England (1977) *A Guide to United Kingdom Exchange Control.*

— (1981) 'The Effects of Exchange Control Abolition on Capital Flows', *Quarterly Bulletin of the Bank of England*, (September).

Beenstock, M. (1977) 'Policies Towards International Direct Investment: A Neoclassical Reappraisal', *Economic Journal*, (September).

Cairncross, Sir Alec (1973) *Control of Long Term International Capital Movements*, (New York: Brookings).

Chrystal, K. A. (1985) 'The Abolition of Exchange Controls in the UK: Are There Any Lessons for Other Countries?', *Capital Controls and Foreign Exchange Legislation*, Euromobiliare, Milano, (June).

— (1986) 'Financial Integration and Exchange Controls: the UK before and after 1979', (mimeo), University of Sheffield.

Edison, H., Miller, M. H. and Williamson, J. (1987) 'On Evaluating and

Extending the Target Zone Proposal', *Journal of Policy Modelling*, 9: 199-224.

Engle, R. E. and Granger, C. W. J. (1987) 'Cointegration and Error Correction: Representation, Estimation and Testing', *Econometrica*, 55: 251-276.

Errunza, V. and Losq, E. (1985) 'International Asset Pricing Under Mild Segmentation: Theory and Tests', *Journal of Finance*, 40: 105-124.

Frenkel, J. A. and Levich, R. M. (1977) 'Transactions Costs and Interest Arbitrage', *Journal of Political Economy* (2).

Granger, C. W. J. and Newbold, P. (1974) 'Spurious Regressions in Econometrics', *Journal of Econometrics*, 2: 111-120.

Granger, C. W. J. (1983) 'Cointegrated Variables and Error Correcting Models', (mimeo), University of California, San Diego.

Grubel, H. G. (1968) 'Internationally Diversified Portfolios: Welfare Gains and Capital Flows', *American Economic Review*, 58: 1299-1314, (December).

Grubel, H. G. and Fadner, K. (1971) 'The Interdependence of International Equity Markets', *Journal of Finance*, (March), pp. 89-94.

Hajek, J. and Sidak, Z. (1967) *Theory of Rank Tests*, (New York and Prague: Academic Press).

Hemmings, D. B. (1981) 'Exchange Controls, Security Prices and Exchange Rates', *Bulletin of Economic Research*.

Johnston, R. B. (1979) 'Some Aspects of the Determination of Euro-Currency Interest Rates', *Quarterly Bulletin of the Bank of England*, (March).

Jorion, P. and Schwartz, E. (1986) 'Integration and Segmentation in the Canadian Stock Market', *Journal of Finance*, 41: 603-614.

Kearney, C. and MacDonald, R. (1986) 'Intervention and Sterilization Under Floating Exchange Rates: the UK 1973-1983', *European Economic Review*, 30: 245-364.

Kendall, M.G. and Stuart, A. (1967) *The Advanced Theory of Statistics*, 2, (London: Charles Griffen).

Lessard, D. (1974) 'World, National and Industry Factors in Equity Returns', *Journal of Finance*, 29: 379-391 (May).

Levy, H. and Sarnat, M. (1970) 'International Diversification of Investment Portfolios', *American Economic Review*, Vol. LX, (September).

Llewellyn, D. T. (1980) *International Financial Integration*, (London: Macmillan Press).

McCormick, F. (1979) 'Covered Interest Arbitrage: Unexploited Profits?: Comment', *Journal of Political Economy*, 87(2): 411-417.

McKinnon, R.I. (1984) 'Why Floating Exchange Rates Fail', Temi di discussione, Banca d'Italia.

Obstfeld, M. (1983) 'Exchange Rates, Inflation and the Sterilization Problem : Germany 1975-1981', *European Economic Review*, 21 : 161-189.

Otani, I. and Tiwari, S. (1981) 'Capital Controls and Interest Parity : the Japanese Experience, 1978-1981', *International Monetary Fund Staff Papers*, (December).

Panton, D. B., Lessig, V. P. and Joy, O.M. (1976) 'Co-Movement of International Equity Markets : A Taxonomic Approach', *Journal of Financial and Quantitative Analysis*, 11 : 415-432 (September).

Phylaktis, K. and Wood, G. E. (1986) 'An Analytic and Taxonomic Framework for the Study of Exchange Controls', in Black, J. and G. S. Dorrance (eds.), *Problems of International Finance*, papers of the Seventh Annual Conference of the International Economics Study Group, 1984.

Ripley, D. M. (1973) 'Systematic Elements in the Linkage of National Stock Market Indices', *Review of Economics and Statistics*, 55 : 356-361 (August).

Stehle, R. (1977) 'An Empirical Test of the Alternative Hypotheses of National and International Pricing of Risky Assets', *Journal of Finance*, 32 : 493-502 (May).

Stock, J. H. (1984) 'Asymptotic Properties of a Least Squares Estimator of Cointegrating Vectors', (mimeo), Harvard University.

(1987a) 'Covered Interest Parity : A High-Frequency, High-Quality Data Study', *Economica*, 54, (November).

(1987b) 'Covered Interest Arbitrage and Market Turbulence : An Empirical Analysis', (mimeo), University of Dundee.

Taylor, M. P. and Tonks, I. (1989) 'The Internationalization of Stock Markets and the Abolition of UK Exchange Control', *Review of Economics and Statistics*.

Tew, J. H. B. (1978) 'Policies Aimed at Improving the Balance of Payments', Chap. 7 in F. T. Blackaby (ed.), *British Economic Policy* 1960-74, (Cambridge : Cambridge University Press).

Williamson, J. (1985) : *The Exchange Rate System*, (Washington : Institute for International Economics).

EMS STABILITY, CAPITAL CONTROLS, AND FOREIGN EXCHANGE MARKET INTERVENTION

By Giorgio Radaelli*

I. INTRODUCTION

Quite a few papers have been written recently focusing on two major aspects of the EMS. The first concerns the extent to which the system has actually produced welfare gains to date. Here, particular issues at stake are those related with the concepts of exchange rate *volatility* and *misalignments*. Therefore, it has been important to assess empirically to what degree the EMS has actually favoured greater exchange rate stability, both in nominal and real terms. *Nominal* exchange rate stability can be seen as a value in itself (to be prepared to pay for it) as long as it favours international trade and investment. An IMF study (1984) found no evidence of effects from *nominal* exchange rate volatility to world trade volumes. On the other hand, Cushman (1983) did find evidence of a negative effect from *real* exchange rate volatility to trade flows. Moreover, it is clear that exchange rate misalignments link in an undesirable way (via *real* exchange rate instability) one country's monetary policy with its international competitiveness, hence output and employment (Buiter and Miller (1981)). In sum, it seems that what is needed is real – not just nominal – exchange rate stability.

Whilst it can be shown that the EMS has actually fostered a higher degree of *real* exchange rate stability, it is unclear what are the "costs" at which this has been achieved. This constitutes the second major aspect of the EMS debate to-date.

In particular, have the costs been in terms of lost monetary policy independence, capital controls, or foreign exchange market intervention, or a combination of the three? To date, it appears to be commonly held that costs have been in the form of capital controls only. In fact, some claim that the EMS has stood together only thanks to administrative measures which distort

* I wish to thank Niso Abuaf, Mike Artis, David Begg, Gregory Hoelscher, Nick Robinson, Lakis Vouyoukas and Sykes Wilford for useful comments on an earlier draft, presented at the Sixteenth Money Study Group Conference, Brasenose College, Oxford, September 1987. Any remaining errors are, of course, my responsibility only. The views expressed do not necessarily reflect those of the Chase Manhattan Bank.

the efficient allocation of resources.[1] Monetary integration is not credited to have played any role, let alone foreign exchange intervention. The main scope of this paper is to reassess the relative importance of foreign exchange intervention as determinant of the EMS stability.

In the second section, we start discussing empirical evidence pertaining to the EMS performance to date, particularly in terms of exchange rate stability. Then, we move to analysing the likely determinants of that performance. We present some results on monetary convergence in the EMS area after 1979, and we put forward some arguments to weaken the relative importance of capital controls in determining the EMS stability.

In the third section, we discuss some empirical evidence supporting the view that the relative importance of EMS foreign exchange intervention has been unduly neglected. Our evidence concerns a portfolio balance-channel affecting the risk premium on the major EMS currency markets and the compatibility of actual exchange rates behaviour with a posited (EMS) central banks' intervention rule of thumb.

The final section summarizes our results and conclusions.

II. THE EMS PERFORMANCE AND ITS DETERMINANTS

It is widely held that the major (if not only) achievement of the EMS to date is to have favoured an unexperienced degree of exchange rate stability. The latter might be seen as a value in itself, particularly as long as dampened misalignments soften undesirable *real* exchange rate effects from domestic policy to international competitiveness. It seems still to be proved that nominal exchange rate "volatility" per se has negative repercussions on international trade. Therefore, the main merit of the EMS to date is likely to be its contribution to greater *real* exchange rate stability.

Table 1 presents coefficients of variation for some major nominal and real exchange rates, both before and during the EMS period. Although analogous evidence has already been presented elsewhere, we think that a few further qualifications are not superfluous.

The picture emerging from Table 1 is one of higher nominal and real stability among EMS currencies during the EMS period. On the other hand, both nominal and real volatility have increased, after 1979, for the major non-EMS rates. In particular, "average" real exchange rate volatility after 1979 has decreased by more than 40% within the EMS, whilst it has increased by nearly 80% among non-EMS rates.

1. The view that the EMS has stood together only thanks to capital controls is shared, for instance, by Rogoff (1985) and Goodhart (1986).

Qualitatively similar results are reported e.g. by Padoa Schioppa (1985), Wood (1986), Ungerer et alii (1986), and Rogoff (1985). Rogoff's results are of particular interest in that they refer to conditional variances (variances of forecasting errors) as opposed to unconditional variances, thus interpreting the concept of volatility in terms of forecastability.[2]

TABLE 1

Exchange Rate Volatility (coefficients of variation)[1]

	Nominal Exchange Rates		Real Exchange Rates	
	1973 : 1–1979 : 3	1979 : 4–1986 : 6	1973 : 1–1979 : 3	1979 : 4–1985 : 12
L/FF	0.0167	0.0039	0.0069	0.0047
L/DM	0.0284	0.0144	0.0059	0.0035
FF/DM	0.0132	0.0129	0.0093	0.0045
Y/$	0.0149	0.0096	0.0095	0.0099
Y/ DM	0.0087	0.0189	0.0062	0.0129
£/$	0.0157	0.0237	0.0086	0.0182
£/DM	0.0238	0.0092	0.0062	0.0078
DM/$	0.0132	0.0189	0.0075	0.0189
EMS[2]	0.0194	0.0104	0.0074	0.0042
Non-EMS[3]	0.0153	0.0161	0.0076	0.0135

1. Data are monthly averages. WPI*s* used to compute real exchange rates.
2. Average across: L/FF, L/DM, FF/DM.
3. Average across: Y/$, Y/DM, £/$, £/DM, DM/$.

Source: International Financial Statistics.

It has been argued (e.g. Artis (1986)) that assessing volatility with respect to bilateral rates – as opposed to effective ones – is not appropriate in this context. The argument is that a member of the EMS could gain more stability for its currency vis a vis EMS members at the cost of increased volatility vis a vis non-EMS currencies. However, we would argue that a trade-off between intra-EMS and EMS-non EMS stability is implied by the very fact that the System's original task was to achieve greater *internal* stability.

2. Volatility interpreted as 'forecastability' may be more relevant to micro agents than to national economies. Micro agents are interested in forecastability of exchange rates since unpredictability can be offset through hedging instruments. National economies are more interested in (real) volatility because the latter affects competitiveness, hence output and employment.

This would naturally imply lower 'external' stability as long as the EMS stands up as a single currency area facing other major ones. Greater 'external' stability is out of the EMS reach, and might be a task for a more general programme of international monetary reform (which could or could not contemplate with the existence of the EMS).

Therefore we would restate the conclusion that the EMS has led to greater exchange rate stability. Although this can be seen as a value in itself, it is important to identify the means by which such a performance has been achieved. This in turn may allow one to gain a better perspective on how the system will (should) develop.

One major criticism against the EMS as it stands now is that exchange rate stability has been warranted by capital controls, rather than by convergence in economic policies. There is less consensus on whether (monetary) policies have been more convergent between member countries after 1979 than on the issue of relative exchange rate stability.

An unambiguous criterion to measure policy convergence (let alone cooperation) does not seem to be available yet. Therefore, in what follows we provide a rough idea of the extent to which the degree of convergence between EMS monetary policies has varied over the last decade.

Tables 2 and 3 contain correlation coefficients (referring to Germany, France and Italy) between those variables which are most likely to be affected by monetary policy : monetary aggregates, interest rates, and inflation rates. It turns out that the degree of correlation between all these variables has been higher during the EMS period than before.

However, these results should not lead one to claim that greater exchange rate stability has been unambiguously due to higher monetary convergence. First, as Artis (1986) notices, there is analogous evidence of increased monetary convergence also outside the EMS area, yet in the latter case this is not mirrored by greater exchange rate stability. Second, convergence may simply result from a process by which everyone "puts his own house in order"; it need not result from adaptations of national monetary policies in recognition of international interdependence.[3] Third, alternative attempts to detect an increased degree of monetary convergence between Germany, France and Italy after 1979 failed. For instance, Rogoff (1985) cannot find evidence of a reduction in the conditional

3. For instance, the McKinnon (1982) proposal of controlling world money supply also aims at stabilizing exchange rates. Yet such a form of cooperation would not necessarily show up in higher correlations between national money supplies. This is because the latter should be targeted just to accommodate money demand shifts from one currency to another.

TABLE 2

Correlation Between Money Supply[1] in EMS Countries

	FRANCE before EMS[2]	FRANCE after EMS[3]	ITALY before EMS[2]	ITALY after EMS[3]	GERMANY before EMS[2]	GERMANY after EMS[3]
			M1			
FRANCE	—	—	–0.174	0.769	0.341	0.893
ITALY	—	—	—	—	–0.457	0.637
			M2			
FRANCE	—	—	–0.078	0.80	0.33	0.371
ITALY	—	—	—	—	–0.534	0.735

1. Annual Growth Rates.
2. Monthly data, 1974 : 1–1979 : 3
3. Monthly data, 1979 : 4–1986 : 6

Source : *OECD*, "Main Economic Indicators", not seasonally adjusted data.

TABLE 3

Correlation Between Interest Rates and Inflation[1] in EMS Countries

	FRANCE before EMS[2]	FRANCE after EMS[3]	ITALY before EMS[2]	ITALY after EMS[3]	GERMANY before EMS[2]	GERMANY after EMS[3]
			Interest rates			
FRANCE	—	—	0.464	0.750	0.856	0.873
ITALY	—	—	—	—	0.203	0.513
			Inflation rates			
FRANCE	—	—	0.997	0.999	0.574	0.995
ITALY	—	—	—	—	0.574	0.993

1. Consumer Price Index rate of inflation (annual), and three month interest rates.
2. Monthly data, 1974 : 1–1979 : 3.
3. Monthly data, 1979 : 4–1986 : 6.

Source : "International Financial Statistics", and "Intline" data bank, Chase Econometrics.

variance of real interest rate differentials between those three countries over the EMS period. Moreover, casual observation would point out periods in which the policy mix in these three countries has been set to a large extent independently.[4] Fourth, taking a broader perspective, Bini Smaghi and Vona (1987) stressed that the real threat to EMS stability comes from a pronounced divergence in *fiscal* policy stance – thus leading to mounting trade imbalances – among Germany, France and Italy.

Therefore, we cannot conclude that there is clear cut evidence supporting the claim that economic policy coordination has been the only determinant of the EMS stability. There is, however, some evidence indicating that intra-EMS monetary policies have been more convergent in the 1980s than during the 1970s.

As a consequence, some alternative determinants of the EMS stability should be looked for. Up to now the literature has commonly held that the main (only?) determinant of the EMS stability has been capital controls.[5] The presumption here is that exchange rate variability can be reduced only by either coordinated policies, capital controls, or a combination of the two.

With reference to the EMS, the picture would be one in which (a) the lack of policy coordination shifts the burden of stabilizing exchange rates onto domestic interest rates, (b) domestic authorities counter the consequent (and undesired) interest rate volatility by setting up capital controls which (c) shift the burden of the absorbing ('jump') variable onto euromarket interest rates. Such a strategy would thus allow domestic authorities to maintain policy independence and exchange rate stability without paying the costs of greater interest rates volatility.

That such a scheme diverts volatility from domestic to euro-interest rates is shown by graphs 1 and 2, referring to French and Italian interest rates.

In particular, in the proximity of an EMS realignment (whose dates are indicated by the Rs on the X – axis) the eurolira and eurofranc interest rates typically carry the whole burden of compensating the holders of lira and franc denominated assets for expected exchange rate losses. Domestic rates are almost unaffected. Whilst these divergencies are, to a certain extent, a sign of the stringency of capital controls, such a kind of evidence should not be overstated due to the relatively small number of agents operating in the euromarkets concerned.

4. One could contrast the German monetary discipline throughout the period either with the French abrupt change in monetary policy which accompanied the advent of the socialist government, or with the repeated overshooting of intermediate monetary policy targets (chiefly total domestic credit) in Italy.

5. See, e.g., Rogoff (1985) and Goodhart (1986).

GRAPH 1
Domestic Rate vs. Eurofranc Rate
one month maturity, Feb. 81 - Apr. 86

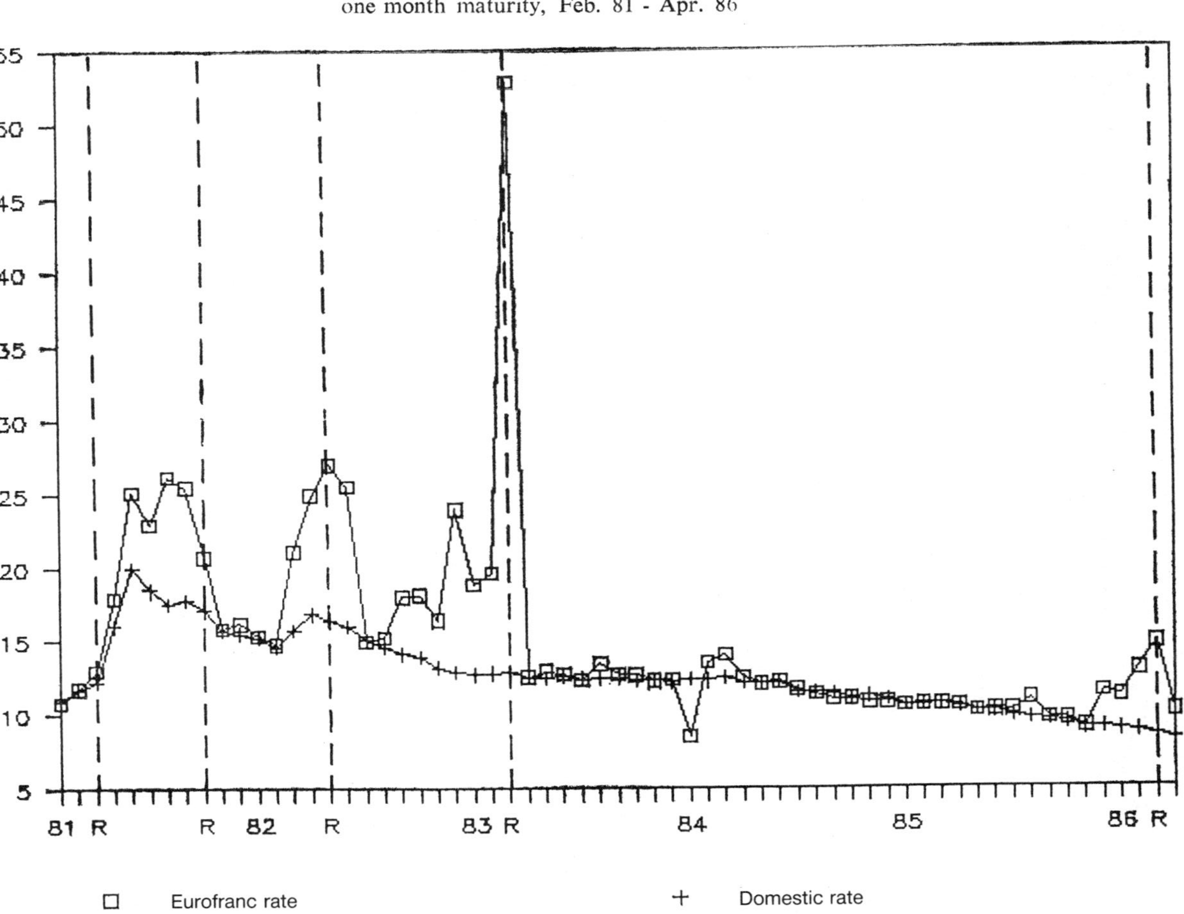

GRAPH 2
Domestic Rate vs. Eurolira Rate
one month maturity, Feb. 81 - Apr. 86

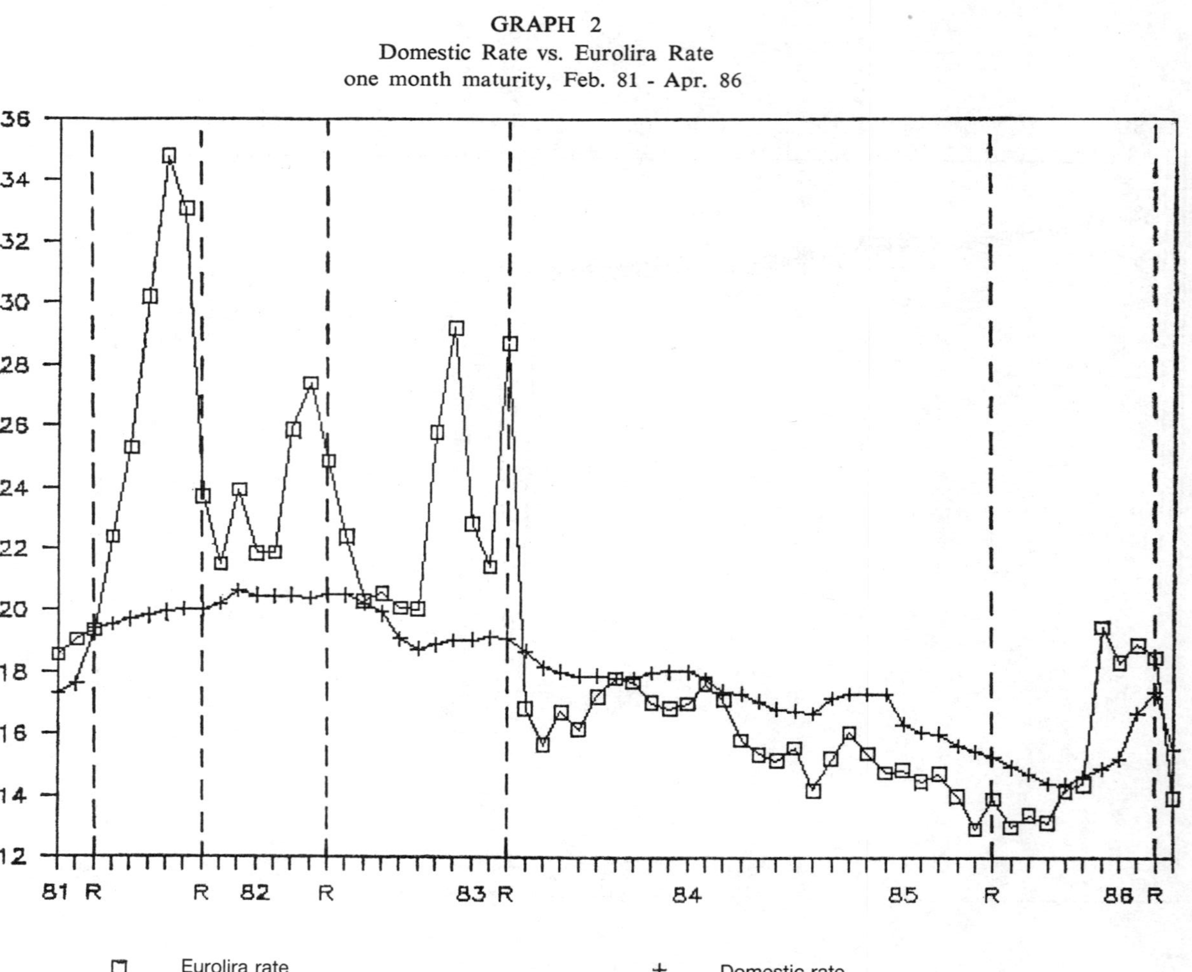

Be as it may, we think that the relative role of capital controls has been, up to date, overestimated.[6] During the 1970's, european monetary-fiscal mixes were nearly as uncooperative as they are now, and capital controls were – in Italy and France – no less biting than they are now. However, exchange rate volatility between Germany, France and Italy was far greater than it has been during the EMS period. It is difficult to reconcile this with the presumption that capital controls are the only determinant of exchange rate stability in the presence of independent policies. We would thus suspect that the importance of capital controls has been – in this respect – overstated.

Morever, Van Wijnbergen (1985) highlighted that capital controls are just interventions in intertemporal trade. Coeteris paribus they are unlikely to affect the real exchange rate, if expenditure patterns at home and abroad are identical. Given that the latter is a plausible assumption for the three major EMS countries, capital controls should not affect their bilateral real exchange rates. If reality turned out to be different it was probably because real exchange rates were held in check by means different from capital controls. In particular, we would argue that foreign exchange market intervention (coupled with more convergent monetary policies) contributed to foster the experienced EMS stability, especially with reference to *nominal* exchange rates. On the other hand, timely realignments can be seen as the 'safety valve' that guaranteed *real* exchange rate stability.

It is somehow surprising that the debate on the likely determinants of the EMS stability has neglected the role of intervention. Abstracting from theoretical considerations, one reason for such a neglect might be due to the fact that the size of the typical intervention operation is negligible relative to the existing stocks of assets. However, such an argument is weakened, in the present context, by the presence of EMS institutional arrangements explicitly aiming at providing the member central banks with more funds to intervene.

The agreement of 13/3/1979 among EEC central banks laying down the EMS procedures specifies that "interventions will be unlimited at the compulsory intervention rates" and that "other interventions (those not at the margins) will be conducted in accordance with the ... guidelines adopted by the committee of governors ... or will be subject to concertations among all the participating central banks". Moreover, "... when a currency crosses its threshold of divergence, this results in the presumption that the authorities concerned will correct this situation by adequate measures, including diver-

6. A consequence of this is the common presumption that the EMS would collapse were capital controls removed.

sified intervention". Thus (also) intramarginal intervention appears to have a role in the management of the system.

The financing of EMS intervention is ensured by the Very Short Term Financing Facility (VSTFF). This consists of mutual loans enabling each system's central bank to make its own currency available to others. The operations are in the form of spot sales /purchases of EMS currencies against the crediting/debiting of ECU accounts held with the European Monetary Cooperation Fund. Such operations are automatically renewable (at the debtors request), being thus possible to postpone the final settlement. Moreover, in the spring of 1985 a new scheme has been set up for mobilizing ECU holdings whereby participating central banks can obtain dollars or EMS currencies through three month swaps, without restrictions on the type of intervention involved. Thus it is now possible to obtain currency for intramarginal intervention too.[7] Furthermore, the divergence threshold (vis-a-vis the ECU) mechanism has ensured that the burden of intervention is typically more evenly distributed than in a Bretton-Woods like setting. This, of course, can be thought of as further boosting the role of intervention within the EMS framework. Finally, the very fact that the participating countries are fairly homogeneous and commercially integrated ensures that they share real disturbances – particularly supply shocks. This should contribute to minimize the number of times in which it is optimal to realign,[8] and should also allow one to recognize promptly when exchange rate adjustments are called for. Therefore, the reserves losses typical of strenuous attempts to defend parities in the presence of fundamental changes should be minimized as well. As a consequence, there would be relatively more resources left available – especially to weak currency central banks – to intervene in a more routine fashion.

In the next section, we discuss some empirical evidence pertaining to the role of foreign exchange intervention within the EMS.

III. FOREIGN EXCHANGE MARKET INTERVENTION WITHIN THE EMS

As pointed out by Masera (1986), two types of intervention can be envisaged within the System :

i) Symmetric – monetary base interventions, i.e. those entailing simulta-

7. For further details on this point, see Micossi (1985).

8. For example, when real as opposed to nominal shocks impinge on the system. See Henderson (1984).

neously opposite effects on the monetary base of both the country causing the intervention and the country whose currency is used.[9]

ii) Asymmetric – monetary base interventions, carried out by one central bank through eurocurrency or domestic private banking assets in the other currency. Only the monetary base of the country which originated the intervention is affected in this case, unless domestic authorities "sterilize".

Given that intramarginal intervention has, as we show below, been widely used, ii) has probably been the most used scheme despite i) would theoretically warrant a stronger impact on the exchange rate.

Some evidence of an increased role for intervention after 1979 is already available. Galy (1984) estimates an exchange rate – interest rate – net foreign assets model for major EMS countries. He finds that parameters stability – before and after the EMS inception – cannot be rejected for the exchange rate equations only. In particular, the statistical significance of the parameters in the net foreign assets equation generally increases after 1979. The proposed explanation for such a structural break is that after 1979 EMS central banks intervened more aggressively in the foreign exchange market.

Some additional evidence is reported in Table 4. From our viewpoint the most important implication of the reported data is that less than 15% of total EMS interventions were carried out at the compulsory intervention limits.[10] The rest of intervention was intramarginal, in constrast with the ex-ante perception of a modest role for intramarginal intervention (see Micossi (1985)). Such an empirical regularity is consonant with our previous arguments supporting the role of this type of intervention.

However, one thing is to know that central banks have regularly intervened to an unexpected degree, and another is to maintain that these interventions did affect EMS exchange rates.

Generally speaking, a necessary condition for *sterilized* intervention being effective is one of the following:

i) that agents regard domestic and foreign securities as imperfect substitu-

9. Interventions relying on the VSTFF have such property. The perceived effectiveness of preventive intra-marginal intervention has prompted some central banks to advocate extending the use of the VSTFF to finance this kind of intervention too. However, such a move has been resisted by the Bundesbank, presumably due to the desire to maintain control over its monetary base.

10. Interventions in dollars (and other currencies) have probably been intramarginal given the impossibility, until September 1987, of drawing on the VSTFF (to obtain EMS currencies) to finance intramarginal intervention. Further evidence supporting the role of intramarginal interventions can be found in the Report of the Deutsche Bundesbank for the year 1987, p. 68.

tes and they do not treat the securities held by authorities as being implicitly part of their own portfolio;

ii) that intervention affects expectations about the future course of monetary policy.[11]

TABLE 4

Foreign Exchange Intervention by EMS Countries[1]

	1979[2]	1980	1981	1982	1983	1984	1985[3]
US Dollars (plus others)	23.6	27.5	42.6	39.3	32.5	23.2	12.8
EMS Currencies							
— at the limits	2.5	3.9	11.1	3.0	13.3	1.9	—
— intramarginal	5.4	4.5	9.4	9.9	13.1	13.7	7.1
Recourse to VSTFF	3.3	2.5	9.0	2.3	5.4	1.8	—

1. In US Dollars billions. Figures are the sum of purchases and sales.
2. March to December.
3. First semester only.
Source: European Monetary Cooperation Fund (Via Micossi (1985)).

(i) is the most commonly tested of the two hypotheses, and implies that a portfolio balance model of exchange rate determination holds. The currency composition of assets would be a key determinant of both the exchange rate and its risk premium. Although the latter might in principle be affected also by default risk, we would rule out such a possibility, at least within the EMS context. Of course, the presence of capital controls makes domestic and foreign assets more likely to be imperfect substitutes. Therefore, only detection of a systematic risk premium component *independent* from capital controls would support effective EMS intervention carried out in the absence of controls.

It is customary to associate the idea of perfect assets substitutability with the monetary model of exchange rate determination. Such a model maintains, as one of its distinguishing assumptions, that ex-post uncovered interest parity (UIP) holds on average.

Broadly speaking there are two possible reasons for (ex-post) UIP not holding:

i) agents may not be rational;

11. In what follows, we assume that central banks sterilize domestically.

ii) agents, whilst being rational, may be risk–averse thus requiring a risk premium in the presence of imperfectly substitutable domestic and foreign assets.

Up to now, two empirical strategies have been employed in trying to detect a portfolio – balance channel capable of explaining the risk premium: a) estimation of inverted bond demand (risk premium) equations, b) estimation of exchange rate quasi–reduced forms derived from the general portfolio balance model.[12]

In our empirical analysis we follow a), considering the risk premium as systematic deviations from UIP. Our tests will involve – not unusually – testing of a joint hypothesis concerning expectations formation and the presence of (portfolio-balance-related) risk premium.

Typically, this kind of empirical work finds it difficult to explain systematic deviations from UIP. However, maintaining the risk premium interpretation seems to be the only way to continue to believe that agents are rational in the face of deviations from UIP.

When domestic and foreign assets are perfect substitutes, i.e. there is no risk premium, expectations are rational, and interest rates movements are not dampened by capital controls, the following holds :

$$(1 + i_t) / (1 + i_t^*) = \underset{t}{E} S_{t+1} / S_t \qquad (1)$$

where : i = domestic interest rate
i^* = foreign interest rate
S = units of domestic currency per unit of foreign currency
E = mathematical expectation (conditional on information available at time t) operator

Within the monetary model of exchange rate determination, domestic and foreign assets are perfect substitutes, i.e., there is no systematic risk premium so that (1) holds on average. On the other hand, the portfolio-balance model emphasises imperfect assets substitutability and systematic deviations from (1).

Within a portfolio-balance model framework it is possible to derive (see Appendix 1) the following relative assets demand function :

$$(A / SA^*)_t = a + b(i_t - i_t^* - ln \underset{t}{E} S_{t+1} + ln S_t) + v_t \qquad (2)$$

12. Some researchers also tried to allow for the existence of ex-post bias in the forward exchange rate without requiring the presence of outside assets. However, testing for risk premium along these lines requires one to consider models not easily amenable to conventional estimation. On this point, see Boothe and Longworth (1986).

where : A = domestic bonds
A^* = foreign bonds
v = disturbance $\rightarrow N(0, \sigma_v^2)$.

Notice that, because of the way (2) is derived, no wealth variable appears in the equation. Therefore, there should be no need to proxy "wealth" (as done in Rogoff (1984)) if one wants to estimate a model derived from (2). By the same token, v need not be autocorrelated due to the "omission of wealth" from the equation. Following Frankel (1982), inversion of (2) yields:

$$(i_t - i_t^* - ln \underset{t}{E} S_{t+1} + ln S_t) = \alpha + \beta(A / SA^*)_t + \theta_t \quad (3)$$

where : $\alpha = -a / b < 0$
$\beta = 1 / b > 0$
$\theta = v / b \rightarrow N(0, \sigma_v^2 / b^2)$.

Then, thanks to the (weak form) hypothesis of rational expectations :

$$\begin{aligned} & ln S_{+t1} = \underset{t}{E} S_{t+1} + \varepsilon_{t+1} \\ & \varepsilon \rightarrow N(0, \sigma_\varepsilon^2), \quad E(\varepsilon_t, \varepsilon_{t+i}) = 0 \quad i = \pm 1 \end{aligned} \quad (4)$$

Finally, combining (3) with (4) :

$$(i_t - i_t^* - ln S_{t+1} + ln S_t) = \alpha + \beta(A / SA^*)_t + \mu_t \quad (5)$$

where $\mu_t = \theta_t - \varepsilon_{t+1}$.

Estimation of (5) allows to test the null hypothesis (H_0) of perfect assets substitutability. Under H_0, $b \rightarrow \infty$ (see Appendix 1) and both α and β equal zero. Under $H_1 : \alpha < 0, \beta > 0$. Rejection of H_0 would thus support the existence of a portfolio-balance link affecting the risk premium. Such a link in turn allows sterilized intervention – which changes relative assets supply – to affect the spot rate. The latter is, in fact, the "jump" variable which typically bears the major burden of risk premium changes.

However, (5) presents some empirical problems. First, (A / SA^*) is correlated with the structural component of the error term via equation (2). Moreover, the right hand side variable of the equation will be endogenous, as long as S is endogenous. Therefore, an instrumental variable (IV) technique is required to avoid simultaneity bias. The bias is expected to be negative. In fact, an examination of equations (2) and (5) reveals that plim $[(A\,/\,SA^*)_t,\mu_t] < 0$. Second, the error term in (5) is likely to be autocorrelated. In fact, there is no way to rule out correlation between the forecast error ε_t revealed at time t and the innovation θ_t, also occuring at t. Therefore, $E\ (\mu_t,\mu_{t-1}) = \rho_{\theta\varepsilon} \neq 0$, and IV estimation will lack efficiency. Use of standard GLS corrections in the present context would yield inconsistent estimates (see, eg: Begg (1982), p. 112). Cumby, Huizinga and Obstfeld (1983) propose a two-step two-stage least squares estimator to cope with both simultaneity and autocorrelation in a rational expectations context. However, we found computationally easier to cope with autocorrelation as explained below.

We ran regressions of (5) over the EMS sample employing monthly data on France (considered to be the domestic country) and Germany. Data sources are reported in Appendix 2. We used end of month observations to avoid overlapping forecast periods. Lack of end of month data on Italian assets prevented us from testing H_0 in the Italy-Germany case too.[13] As proxies for A and A^* we used public bonds held by privates only, i.e. outside assets as opposed to *all* bonds. The point is that the latter include also those assets which net out within the private sector (inside assets). These assets will carry different degrees of risk even among the same country's investors, because some of these investors are issuers of some "inside" bonds. On the other hand, outside assets do not net out within the private sector, hence they are homogeneous (from a risk view point) in the eyes of private investors. In sum, consideration of outside assets should reduce aggregation problems. It should also be noted that use of public bonds *only* as opposed to bonds plus monetary base implies the least severe test for accepting H_0 (see Frankel, 1982).

Due to the presence of capital controls in France, one-month *eurointerest* rates have been used as opposed to domestic ones. Therefore, the dependent variable in (5) should capture risk premium independent from the presence of capital controls. Our main empirical results are reported in Table 5.

The major result is that both $\hat{\alpha}$ and $\hat{\beta}$ almost always turn out to be significantly different from zero and "correctly" signed – under H_1. This would point out a systematic portfolio-balance effect on the FF-DM risk premium.

The OLS estimate in Table 5 is downward biased. Moreover, it is inefficient due – not surprisingly – to autocorrelation problems. The OLS-AR (1) estimates cope with autocorrelation only. The DW and BP statistics on

13. Preliminary estimates on (5) using monthly averages data on Italy-Germany yielded 'significant' $\hat{\alpha} < 0$, $\hat{\beta} > 0$, thus rejecting the null hypothesis.

OLS-AR (1) coupled with the rho estimate suggest that the OLS residuals follow an AR (1) process. The IV-1 estimates should take care of simultaneity. In fact, both $\hat{\alpha}$ and $\hat{\beta}$ change in magnitude (not in sign) with respect to their OLS estimates, still remaining "significant". With the IV-2 regression we attempted to cope with *both* simultaneity and autocorrelation.[14] An examination of the IV-1 residuals revealed that prior to French Franc (FF) devaluations the fitted values systematically underpredicted the actual ones. The implied discrete jumps in the risk premium may be due to the thinness of the euroFF market and consequent variability of the aggregate degree of risk aversion. Therefore, we introduced a dummy variable taking value one in the few observations preceding each of the mentioned realignments. The IV-2

TABLE 5

Risk Premium Equations, France-Germany (1981 : 3–1986 : 8)[1]

	Const.	$(A/SA^*)_t$	μ_{t-1}	DUMMY	$\bar{R}^2$	SER	DW	BP(12)[2]
OLS	—0.086 (0.037)	0.284 (0.065)			0.219	0.038	1.249	31.52*
OLS-AR(1)	—0.063 (0.051)	0.246 (0.091)	0.363 (0.117)		0.308	0.035	1.986	12.9
IV-1	—0.148 (0.076)	0.393 (0.134)			0.184	0.039	1.217	25.53*
IV-2	—0.099 (0.05)	0.284 (0.088)		0.0711 (0.008)	0.637	0.026	1.872	17.09

1. Autocorrelation correction on OLS-AR(1) carried out through the Cochrane-Orcutt procedure. Dependent variable lagged two periods used as instrument for $(A/SA^*)_t$ in IV regressions. Data observations refer to the last working day in each month. Standard errors in parentheses.

2. Box-Pierce statistics with twelve degrees of freedom. Critical value at 5% level is 21.03. An asterisk indicates rejection of the null hypothesis of residuals serial independence.

14. Attempts with alternative dynamic specifications proved to be unsuccessful. The residuals' correlogram showed mainly a first order autocorrelation problem. Therefore, we tried to cope by including among the regressors also the dependent variable at (t-1) and/or first (and second) lag on the explanatory variable, thus assuming in turn partial adjustment, geometric lag on (A/SA^*) and AR(1) residuals. In any event, assuming adjustment lags on the euromarkets would have been theoretically implausible.

estimates show that thanks to the dummy – admittedly not the best way to cope with something which has been 'left out' – we could cope with simultaneity and autocorrelation at the same time. Therefore, the IV-2 estimates should be consistent and more efficient than IV-1. An estimate of β equal to 0.28 would imply that – coeteris paribus – sterilized intervention which increased $(A/SA^*)_t$ by 10% would, on average, favour a *FF/DM* depreciation by 1.6%.[15] Graph 3 shows that the IV-2 fitted values track fairly well the turning points in the risk premium. The graph also shows that the risk premium actually jumped prior to the *FF* devaluations (whose dates are indicated by vertical dotted lines labelled *D*).

In summary, we would argue that the evidence presented in Table 5 supports the effectiveness of sterilized intervention on the main EMS foreign exchange market.

Up to this stage, we have shown that day to day (intramarginal) EMS intervention has been unexpectedly relevant, and that the necessary condition for the latter being effective – i.e., a portfolio-balance effect on the risk premium – is plausibly satisfied. This might suffice to restore a "balance" between the relative importance of capital controls and foreign exchange intervention in keeping the EMS together.

Although more direct estimates on the extent to which intervention affects the exchange rate would be desirable, we are limited in this by the lack of data on actual intervention.

However, additional indirect evidence may be provided if one starts by assuming that EMS central banks did intervene, and then tries to detect empirical compatibility between a plausible intervention rule and actual exchange rates' behaviour.

Much of the theoretical literature on intervention assumes that, given a structural model of the economy, the central bank may then intervene in order to minimise a loss function dependent on some ultimate policy goals.

However, such an approach is difficult to implement empirically, especially if one considers different countries simultaneously.[16] Moreover, as long as capital controls are set up to maintain a certain degree of policy independence, it seems plausible to think that domestic monetary variables are maneouvred to achieve the ultimate goals, whilst sterilized intervention is used merely to respect the EMS stability requirement.

15. Assuming — as customary — that the spot rate is the 'jump' variable which accommodates changes in the risk premium.

16. Different monetary authorities are likely to rely on different models of the economy and to have different macroeconomic goals.

GRAPH 3
France - Germany Regression
actual vs. fitted values 1981 : 3–1986 : 8

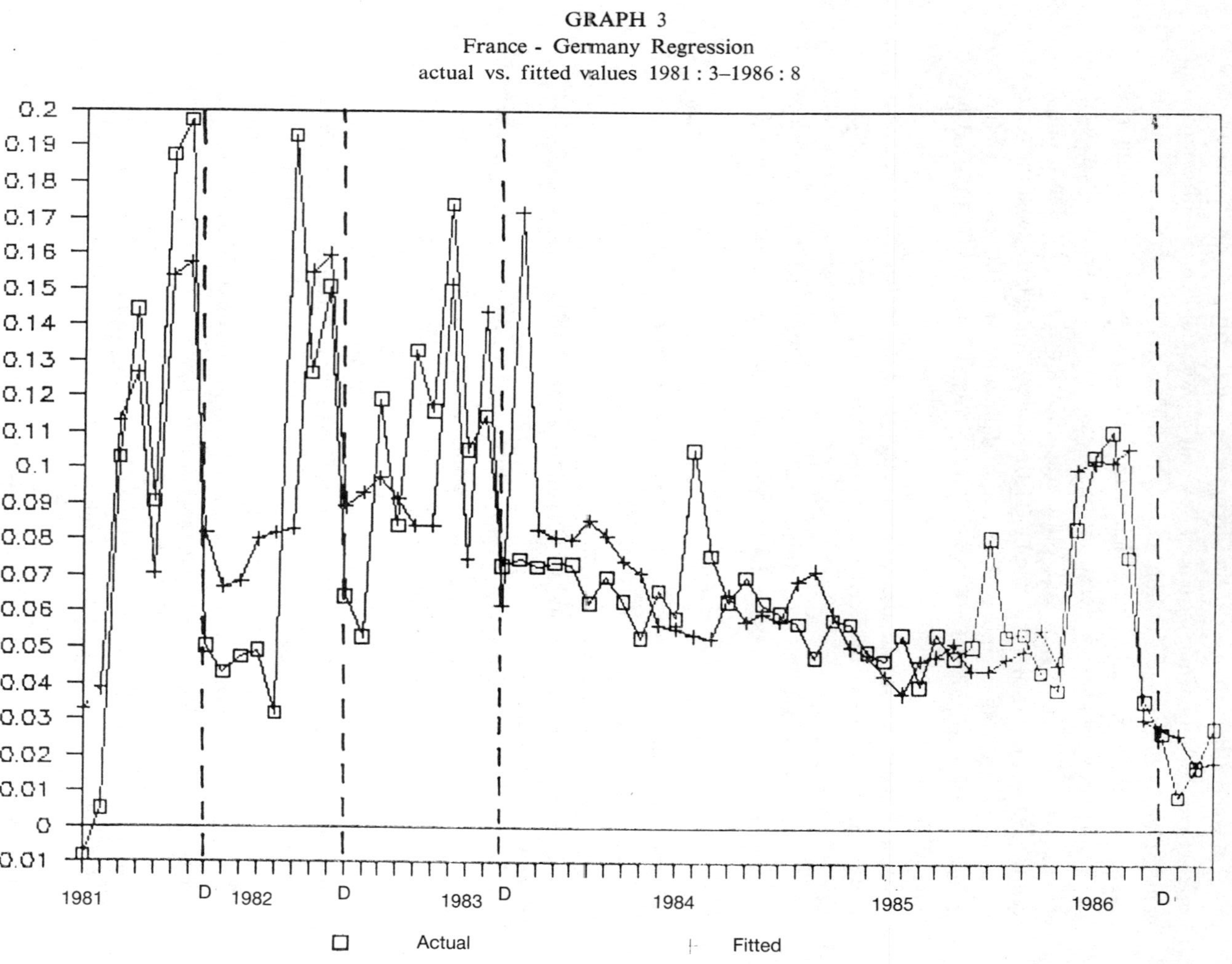

Therefore, we assume that the typical central bank tries to smooth its *effective* exchange rate by stabilizing its two key bilateral rates: vis a vis the DM and vis a vis the Dollar. In particular, we expect an EMS central bank to have given a relatively higher weight to the Dollar before 1979, and to the DM thereafter. Although such an assumption may be oversimplifying, consideration of very simple intervention rules is not novel in the literature. For example, Black (1976) argues that a country faced with a combination of real shocks and differential inflation rates should adopt a crawling-peg vis a vis a basket of currencies, in order to stabilize the real exchange rate.

Such an intervention rule of thumb would see a central bank trying to affect its currency effective exchange rate as follows :[17]

$$S_{i,t} = aS(i/DM)_t + (1 - a)S(i/\$)_t + \varepsilon_t \tag{6}$$

where : S_i = effective exchange rate of currency i,

$S(i/j)$ = units of i per one unit of j; $j = DM, \$$,

$0 \leqslant a \leqslant 1$,

ε = white noise normally distributed shock.

The disturbance should capture those random factors, beyond systematic intervention, which affect the external value of i. (6) can be manipulated to obtain

$$S_{i,t} = S(i/\$)_t - aS(DM/\$)_t + \varepsilon_t. \tag{7}$$

Let us now define the steady state for S_i :

$$S_i = \overline{S}_i \tag{8}$$

In practice, the steady state is never attained due to the continuous impinging of shocks, news, etc. on the market, but also due to the fact that (especially EMS) intervention does not necessasrily stabilize S_i. Therefore, we assume that between any two periods the steady state is only approached by a factor λ :

$$S_{i,t} - S_{i,t-1} = \lambda(\overline{S}_i - S_{i,t-1}) \tag{9}$$

with $0 \leqslant \lambda \leqslant 1$ if the process is convergent.

17. All variables are in logarithms.

Letting (7) into (9) and after a few manipulations we obtain :

$$\Delta S(i/\$)_t = \alpha_0 + \alpha_1 \Delta S(DM/\$)_t + \alpha_2\ S(i/\$)_{t-1} + \alpha_3\ S(DM/\$)_{t-1} - \varepsilon_t + \varphi\varepsilon_{t-1} \quad (10)$$

where : $\alpha_0 = \lambda \bar{S}_i \geqslant 0$

$0 \leqslant \alpha_1 = a \leqslant 1$

$\alpha_2 = -\lambda < 0$

$\alpha_3 = -\alpha_1\alpha_2 = a\lambda \geqslant 0$

$\varphi = 1 - \lambda$

(10) is an estimating equation which allows us to estimate a ($= \alpha_1$), i.e. the parameter is identified. Equation (6) tells us that the parameter a is the weight given to the DM by our intervention rule of thumb. Hence, we would expect estimation of (10) for System's currencies to yield the following results :

i) $0 \leqslant \alpha_1 \leqslant 0.5$ before the EMS period,

ii) $0.5 \leqslant \alpha_1 \leqslant 1$ during the EMS period.

We have estimated (10) for the following currencies vis a vis the Dollar : Sterling, Swiss Franc, French Franc, Lira and Yen. Data are monthly averages over the samples 1974 : 2 – 1979 : 3 and 1979 : 4 – 1986 : 6. All the equations have been estimated by OLS allowing for AR (1) residuals as the derivation of (10) would suggest. SUR estimation did not provide qualitatively different results. The results are presented in Tables 6 and 7.

First of all we notice that – having allowed for AR(1) residuals – the obtained estimates are substantially free from autocorrelation. The φ estimate is always 'significant' and positive as the derivation of (10) would suggest. The remaining parameters' estimates are almost always 'correctly' signed, though $\hat{\alpha}_2$ and $\hat{\alpha}_3$ are rarely 'significant' during the pre-EMS period. The equations' explanatory power is satisfactory, and it increases over the EMS period. The non linear restriction is rejected only in one case out of ten. All in all, the results are consistent with the view that central banks – particularly after 1979 – may have had effective exchange rate targets to be achieved through interventions carried out in dollars and DMs.

Moreover, the estimates of $\alpha_1 \equiv$ a confirm our expectations. $\hat{\alpha}_1$ is always within its expected range and significantly different from zero. The F stability tests and the size of $\hat{\alpha}_1$ in the two sub-periods indicate that up to 1979 the DM was never unambiguously the reference currency for foreign exchange market

TABLE 6

Pre-EMS Regressions, 1974:2–1979:3[1]

	α_0	α_1	α_2	α_3	φ	$\bar{R}^2$	SER	DW	W_1^2
ΔS ($/£)	—0.013 (0.042)	0.394 (0.1)	—0.036 (0.073)	0.037 (0.027)	0.438 (0.123)	0.41	0.016	1.778	0.259
ΔS (SF/$)	—0.017 (0.039)	0.969 (0.098)	—0.067 (0.055)	0.083 (0.097)	0.553 (0.115)	0.664	0.016	1.865	0.137
ΔS (FF/$)	0.017 (0.065)	0.576 (0.095)	—0.024 (0.046)	0.024 (0.025)	0.34 (0.127)	0.409	0.014	1.981	0.135
ΔS (L/$)	0.01 (0.192)	0.387 (0.113)	—0.005 (0.026)	0.038 (0.033)	0.366 (0.125)	0.287	0.018	1.733	0.84
ΔS (Y/$)	0.344 (0.29)	0.61 (0.12)	—0.078 (0.064)	0.103 (0.089)	0.478 (0.124)	0.361	0.018	1.832	0.259

1. Standard errors in parentheses.

2. Wald statistic on the restriction $\alpha_3 = -\alpha_1\alpha_2$. The statistic follows a chi squared distribution, whose 5% level value is 3.84. An asterisk indicates rejection of the null hypothesis.

TABLE 7

Post-EMS Inception Regressions, 1979 : 4–1986 : 6

	α_0	α_1	α_2	α_3	φ	$\bar{R}^2$	SER	DW	F (1,82)[1]	W_1
ΔS ($/£)	0.012	0.633	—0.391	0.147	0.538	0.598	0.018	2.039	13.87*	1.488
	(0.018)	(0.064)	(0.097)	(0.044)	(0.095)					
ΔS (SF/$)	0.002	1.016	—0.357	0.125	0.567	0.886	0.011	1.953	1.43	3.836
	(0.009)	(0.039)	(0.062)	(0.05)	(0.096)					
ΔS (FF/$)	0.011	0.982	—0.351	0.024	0.482	0.917	0.009	1.998	151.04*	0.46
	(0.011)	(0.033)	(0.118)	(0.031)	(0.107)					
ΔS (L/$)	0.217	0.862	—0.371	0.064	0.32	0.918	0.008	2.0	266.5*	6.913*
	(0.081)	(0.029)	(0.14)	(0.023)	(0.106)					
ΔS (Y/$)	0.155	0.653	—0.291	—0.03	0.536	0.501	0.022	2.066	0.291	0.462
	(0.022)	(0.079)	(0.043)	(0.022)	(0.096)					

1. F test for α_1 not being significantly different from its estimated value over the pre-EMS period. An asterisk indicates rejection of the null hypothesis at the 5% level (critical value = 3.95).

intervention, with the only (unsurprising) exception of Switzerland. However, things do change during the EMS period. The DM importance unambiguously grows, overcoming that of the Dollar, both for France and Italy, and quite surprisingly, for the UK too.[18] Such results would point out, in the present context, that the DM has gradually assumed the role of major stabilization target. This is quite understandable as far as Italy and France are concerned, implying that imperfect asset substitutability has been exploited to intervene in order to influence the FF/DM and L/DM rates. However, the fact that a similar result holds for the UK as well is somewhat surprising. On the other hand, such a result may imply that – either thanks to sterilized intervention or to explicit monetary policy[19] – Sterling by now tends to behave like an EMS currency. This would support the view that the UK authorities have been 'shadowing' the EMS for some time. Was it so, one of the main arguments against Sterling joining the System full-status – i.e.: the unwillingness to give up monetary policy independence – would be much softened.

Our main conclusions, however, remain those of (a) evidence that day to day EMS intervention has been more substantial than expected, (b) evidence that the necessary condition for EMS sterilized intervention being effective is satisfied, (c) evidence that (b) may have been exploited through EMS central banks intervening by following a simple stabilizing rule of thumb. In our view, such evidence coupled with the arguments presented in the second section supports the claim that the EMS stability has not depended solely on capital controls but also on foreign exchange market intervention. In turn, the latter would have been facilitated by some of the EMS institutional features. Of course, it is also possible that national policies have actually been more convergent – as the evidence of section II would suggest – than it has been commonly assumed. However, was it so the case for capital controls as only determinants of the EMS stability would be further weakened.

IV. CONCLUSIONS

The major scope of this paper has been to put into a more balanced perspective the relative importance of capital controls, foreign exchange market intervention, and monetary convergence as determinants of the EMS

18. The F test for $\hat{\alpha}_1$ stability tells us that the null hypothesis cannot be rejected for Japan only.

19. It is difficult to say which of the two, in the absence of any risk premium test for the DM/£ rate. Such test is of difficult implementation due to the lack of readily available data on UK outside assets.

stability. The evidence provided in section II seems to point out that monetary policies have been more convergent during the EMS period than before. However, 'convergence' does not imply 'cooperation' (see Artis, 1986) and many would argue that the latter is what is needed to gear domestic monetary *and* fiscal policies towards an exchange rate stability goal. In the second section we also discussed empirical evidence supporting the fairly accepted view that the EMS has indeed secured an unexperienced degree of exchange rate stability among member countries. Then, we have discussed the commonly held argument that such stability has been obtained only thanks to capital controls. We did not deny the role of capital controls, particularly as long as they have been actually "biting". Prima facie evidence on this is provided by the divergent behaviour of domestic and euro-interest rate in the vicinity of an (expected) EMS realignment. Analogous evidence has already been provided by Giavazzi and Giovannini (1986).

We have, however, stressed our belief that the importance of capital controls has been overstated. First, during the 1970's capital controls (in France and Italy) were no less stringent than in the 1980's yet exchange rate volatility among Germany, France and Italy was far greater than experienced during the EMS period. Second, the Van Wijnbergen (1985) argument that capital controls are generally unlikely to stabilize real exchange rates coupled with the evidence of greater EMS real exchange rates stability implies that such stability must have been achieved through means different from capital controls. We thus argued that such means may have been foreign exchange market intervention (coupled with greater monetary convergence). Such claim is also supported by the fact that some of the EMS institutional features are explicitly geared towards making intervention more effective.

In the third section we discussed some stylized facts supporting the role of EMS intervention. In particular, we presented empirical evidence consistent with the presence, on the major EMS currency markets, of risk premium whose main determinant is the relative supply of outside assets. Such portfolio balance channel (independent from the presence of controls on capital flows) satisfies the necessary condition for sterilized intervention being effective. Then, we also presented empirical evidence showing that actual exchange rates behaviour has been consistent with the assumption that central banks have intervened relying on a simple rule of thumb. In particular, the results are consonant with the presumption that after 1979 the EMS central banks' behaviour has structurally changed, taking into account explicitly the new exchange rate constraints.

Our major conclusion is, therefore, that capital controls cannot *alone* have secured greater EMS exchange rate stability. It is likely that EMS intervention has played a role in that sense, though a neglected one to-date. Was it so it would be possible to argue that a gradual removal of capital controls should not necessarily jeopardize the EMS stability. Day to day intervention could partially take care of the strains thus induced, the rest of the burden being borne by *short term* domestic interest rates becoming more volatile. Such volatility should not harm investment and would gradually decline as (both monetary and fiscal) policy coordination grows. In a sense our claim parallels that of Giavazzi-Pagano (1986), who too advocate the removal of controls within the EMS area, on the grounds that this would not disrupt the System.

The Chase Manhattan Bank, London.

APPENDIX I

Equation (2) in the text can be derived as follows. Consider a two country portfolio-balance model aggregating across domestic and foreign agents with four assets traded. If agents are wealth mean-variance optimizers, bond demands are functions of the risk premium only (Frankel (1983)). All the parameters are positive.

$$\left(\frac{M}{W}\right)_t = f(.) \tag{A.1}$$

$$\left(\frac{A}{W}\right)_t = \beta_0 + \beta_1\left(\frac{1+i_t}{1+i_t^*} - \frac{\underset{t}{E}\, S_{t+1}}{S_t}\right) \tag{A.2}$$

$$\left(\frac{SA^*}{W}\right)_t = \gamma_0 - \gamma_1\left(\frac{1+i_t}{1+i_t^*} - \frac{\underset{t}{E}\, S_{t+1}}{S_t}\right) \tag{A.3}$$

$$\left(\frac{SM^*}{W}\right)_t = g(.) \tag{A.4}$$

$$W_t = M_t + A_t + SA_t^* + SM_t^* \tag{A.5}$$

M = domestic money supply
A = domestic bonds supply
SA^* = foreign bonds supply, in domestic currency
SM^* = foreign money supply, in domestic currency
W = financial wealth

Notice that in the case of perfect substitutability between A and A^*: $\beta_1 = \gamma_1 \rightarrow \infty$.

Thanks to the Walras's Law we can drop (A.4). Then let us subtract (A.3) from (A.2):

$$\left(\frac{A}{W}\right)_t - \left(\frac{SA^*}{W}\right)_t = \varphi_0 + \varphi_1 \left(\frac{1+i_t}{1+i_t^*} - \frac{\underset{t}{E}S_{t+1}}{S_t}\right) \tag{A.6}$$

$\varphi_1 = \beta_1 + \gamma_1$ ($\rightarrow \infty$ in the case of perfect substitutability)
$\varphi_0 = \beta_0 - \gamma_0 > 0.$[20]

Now we can solve (A.1) for M and substitute for the latter into (A.5). Then, we substitute for the resulting W_t expression into (A.6) and take logarithms, thus obtaining:

$$ln\left(\frac{A}{SA^*}\right)_t = ln\ \varphi_0 + \varphi_1(RP) \tag{A.7}$$

$$RP = i_t - i_t^* - ln\underset{t}{E}S_{t+1} + lnS_t \tag{A.8}$$

Taking anti-logarithms (A.7) becomes:

$$\left(\frac{A}{SA^*}\right)_t = exp[ln\varphi_0 + \varphi_1(RP)] \tag{A.9}$$

We can now linearise (A.9) taking its first-order expansion around $RP = 0$.

$$\begin{aligned}\left(\frac{A}{SA^*}\right)_t &= exp\,(ln\varphi_0) + \varphi_1[exp(ln\varphi_0)](RP - 0) \\ &= exp\,(ln\varphi_0) + \varphi_1[exp\,(ln\varphi_0)]RP \end{aligned} \tag{A.10}$$

Recalling (A.8), (A.10) can be rewritten as:

$$\left(\frac{A}{SA^*}\right)_t = a + b(i_t - i_t^* - ln\underset{t}{E}S_{t+1} + lnS_t) \tag{A.11}$$

20. Frankel (1983) shows that given an asset share demand function of the type $a + b$ (RP) (where RP = risk premium) a = $\alpha\,[f(\varrho)]$. Moreover, α is the weight of foreign goods in the consumers' utility function, whilst ϱ is the coefficient of relative risk aversion. Therefore, assuming equal risk aversion at home and abroad, $\varphi_0 < 0$ (in (A.6)) as long as the weight of foreign goods in the consumers' utility function is greater at home than abroad.

where: $a = exp\,(ln\varphi_0) > 0$, for $\beta_0 > \gamma_0$

$b = \varphi_1 [exp\,(ln\varphi_0)] \rightarrow \infty$, if A and A^* are perfect substitutes.

(A.11) is equation (2) reported in the text, apart from the error term.

APPENDIX II

DATA SOURCES

– All exchange rates:	End of month and monthly averages from "International Financial Statistics".
– Eurointerest rates:	End of month (monthly averages for graphs 1, 2), one month maturity, from "Analystics" data base, Chase Econometrics.
– German outside assets:	Public bonds in circulation (minus public holdings), end of month, from "Monthly Report of the Bundesbank".
– French outside assets:	Public bonds in circulation (minus public holdings), end of month, from INSEE, "Bulletin Mensuel de Statistique".

REFERENCES

Artis, M. J. (1986) 'External Aspects of the EMS', paper presented at the S.U.E.R.F. Colloquium, Luxembourg, (October).

Begg, D. K. H. (1982) *The Rational Expectations Revolution in Macroeconomics. Theories and Evidence*, (Oxford: Philip Allan).

Bini Smaghi, L. and Vona, S. (1987) 'The Effects of Economic Convergence and Competitiveness on Trade Among the EMS Countries', in Hodgman, D. Woods, J. (eds.), *Macroeconomic Policy and Economic Interdependence*, (London: Macmillan Press).

Black, S. W. (1976) 'Comment on J. Williamson, 'Exchange Rate Flexibility and Reserves Use', *Scandinavian Journal of Economics*, pp. 340-345.

Boothe, P. and Longworth, D. (1986) 'Foreign Exchange Market Efficiency Tests: Implications of Recent Empirical Findings', *Journal of International Money and Finance*, (June), pp. 135-152.

Buiter, W. H. and Miller, M. (1981) 'Monetary Policy and International Competitiveness: The Problems of Adjustment', *Oxford Economic Papers*, (September), pp. 143-175.

Cumby, R. E., Huizinga, J. and Obstfeld, M. (1983) 'Two-step, Two-stage Least Squares Estimation in Models with Rational Expectations', *Journal of Econometrics*, (March), pp. 333-355.

Cusham, D. B. (1983) 'The Effects of Exchange Rate Risk on International Trade', *Journal of International Economics*, (December), pp. 403-429.

Frankel, J. (1982) 'A Test of Perfect Substitutability in the Foreign Exchange Market', *Southern Economic Journal*, (October), pp. 406-416.

—— (1983) 'Estimation of Portfolio-balance Functions that are Mean-Variance Optimising: the Mark and the Dollar', *European Economic Review*, pp. 315-327.

Galy, M. (1984) 'An Empirical Evaluation of the Monetary Integration Process within EMS Members', presented at the Conference: 'The EMS: Policy Coordination and Exchange Rate Systems', Manchester, (September).

Giavazzi, F. and Giovannini, A. (1986) 'The EMS and the Dollar', *Economic Policy*, (April), pp. 456-485.

Giavazzi, F. and Pagano, M. (1986) 'Capital Controls and the EMS', paper presented at the S.U.E.R.F. Colloquium, Luxembourg, (October).

Goodhart, C. (1986) 'Has the Time Come for the UK to join the EMS?' *The Banker*, (February), pp. 26-28.

Henderson, D. W. (1984) 'Exchange Market Intervention Operations: their Role in Financial Policy and their Effects', in Bilson - Marston, (eds.). *Exchange Rate Theory and Practice*, (Chicago: University of Chicago Press), pp. 359-406.

IMF, (1984) 'Exchange Rate Volatility and World Trade', Occasional Paper, n. 28.

Masera, S. (1986) 'An Increasing Role for the ECU: a Character in Search of a Script', Banca d'Italia, Temi di Discussione, (June).

McKinnon, I. (1982) 'Currency Substitution and Instability in the World Dollar Standard', *American Economic Review*, (June), pp. 321-333.

Micossi, S. (1985) 'The Intervention and Financing Mechanisms of the EMS and their Role for the ECU', Banca Nazionale del Lavoro Quarterly Review, (December), pp. 327-345.

Padoa Schioppa, T. (1985) 'Policy Cooperation and the EMS Experience' in Buiter - Marston, (eds.), *International Economic Policy Cooperation*, (Cambridge: Cambridge University Press), pp. 331-355.

Rogoff, K. (1984) 'On the Effects of Sterilized Intervention: an Analysis of Weekly Data', *Journal of Monetary Economics*, (September), pp. 133-150.

—— (1985) 'Can Exchange Rate Predictability be Achieved without Monetary Convergence? Evidence from the EMS', *European Economic Review*, (September), pp. 93-115.

Van Wijnbergen, S. (1985) 'Capital Controls and the Real Exchange Rate', C.E.P.R. Discussion Paper, n. 89, (December).

Wood, G. E. (1986) 'EMS Arrangements: Their Functioning and their Future', City University, Centre for Banking and International Finance, Discussion Paper, n. 40, (April).

MODELLING ASYMMETRIC EXCHANGE RATE UNIONS: A STYLIZED MODEL OF THE EMS

By Michael J. Artis and S. Gazioglu*

I. INTRODUCTION

This paper presents simulations on a two-country model which can be read, albeit in a highly-stylized way, as a representation of some key features of the European Monetary System (EMS). In particular, the model focusses on an asymmetry in the wage-price sectors of the two constituent economies: this parallels empirical findings of asymmetry in this respect between Germany on the one hand, and other member countries on the other. In all other respects the economies are assumed identical. The authorities are assumed to intervene in the foreign exchange market to stabilise competitiveness (the real rate of exchange), and to be able to deploy measures ('exchange controls') which slow down the free flow of capital between the two economies.

The impacts of the wage-price asymmetries and the putative effect of exchange controls in offsetting them, are assessed by way of evaluating the response of the system to a set of pre-specified shocks, the degree of asymmetry and the severity of the controls being manipulated by appropriate changes in parameter values. The simulation results, being derived from quite a large system, are numerical rather than analytical.

The rest of the paper proceeds as follows. In the next section there is a description of the basic model employed; this is followed by a discussion of results of simulations designed to highlight the effects of exchange market intervention; following this there is an account of the asymmetry in wage behaviour which it is desired to characterize; then come the simulations on the asymmetric model. In the final section a few conclusions are presented.

II. THE MODEL

The basic model, which is in continuous time, is defined for a two-country set-up, described by the following thirty equations (with dashed equations referring to the second country and the prefix I denoting an identity). Foreign

* The authors gratefully acknowledge the financial support of the Leverhulme Foundation, administered through the Centre for Economic Policy Research.

or second country variables are indicated by an asterisk and all variables are measured in logarithms unless otherwise stated. A glossary of terms appears in an Appendix. For convenience, we discuss these equations in blocks, the first being represented by equations (1) – (4') below.

$$\dot{\Pi} = h_1 (q - \Pi) \tag{1}$$

$$\dot{\Pi}^* = h_1^* (q^* - \Pi^*) \tag{1'}$$

$$\dot{q} = [h_2 (q - \Pi) - h_0 h_2 (y - \bar{y})] \tag{2}$$

$$\dot{q}^* = [h_2^* (q^* - \Pi^*) - h_0^* h_2^* (y^* - \bar{y}^*)] \tag{2'}$$

$$\dot{p}_d = h_0 (y - \bar{y}) + \Pi + u_4 \tag{3}$$

$$\dot{p}_d^* = h_0^* (y^* - \bar{y}^*) + \Pi^* + u_4^* \tag{3'}$$

$$P = d_0 P_d + (1 - d_0)(E + P_d^*) = P_d + (1 - d_0) e \tag{4}$$

$$P^* = d_0^* P_d^* - (1 - d_0^*)(E - P_d) = P_d^* - (1 - d_0^*) e \tag{4'}$$

Equations (1) – (4) represent the wage - price sector of the model. Wage inflation and core inflation are determined in (1), (1') and (2), (2'). (3) and (3') give GDP deflator inflation ($\dot{p}$, $\dot{p}^*$) as a Phillips Curve function of deviations from natural rate output ($y - \bar{y}, y^* - \bar{y}^*$), and of 'core' inflation (Π, Π^*). Taking account of (3), (3'), wage inflation depends partly on a backward looking expectations generator, partly on a forward looking component and on deviations from the natural rate of output. The set-up follows an over-lapping contracts formulation of a type made familiar by Taylor (1979, 1980) and Calvo (1980, 1985). (4) and (4') represent consumer prices (P, P^*) as Cobb-Douglas functions of GDP deflator or domestic value added prices (P_d, P_d^*) and foreign prices, where E is the nominal and e the real, exchange rate, defined as the domestic price of foreign currency. u_4 is a shock parameter.

The equations listed as I (5) to I (10') below are all identities. I (5) identifies the current account surplus of one country as the deficit of the other, φ being a parameter representing relative size whilst I (10, 10') define the budget deficit of each country (in ratio to GDP), g representing government expenditure, s an income tax parameter while I (6, 6') define the private sector's wealth identity in terms of the government deficit and current account surplus. The intervening equations pertain to the issue and distribution of debt. The debt in question is a non-interest-bearing government liability ('money'); I (7, 7′) show that debt is issued to cover the budget deficit, net of any reduction in the government's holding of overseas debt – the domestic government's debt is denoted H, that of the foreign government L, subscripts g and p pertaining to the sector (government, private) holding the debt. I (8, 8′) describe the distribution of outstanding debt at any time – which is held by the private sectors of each of the two countries and by the government of the opposing country; I (9, 9′) exhausts the net acquisition of foreign debt between the various components. The μ parameters have the interpretation of being ratios to output.

$$cab^* = -\varphi cab \qquad \text{I (5)}$$

$$\mu_2 \dot{H}_p + \mu_3 \dot{L}_p = (def + cab) \qquad \text{I (6)}$$

$$\mu_2^* \dot{L}_p^* + \mu_3^* \dot{H}_p = (def^* + cab^*) \qquad \text{I (6′)}$$

$$\mu_1 \dot{H} - \mu_4 \dot{L}_g = def \qquad \text{I (7)}$$

$$\mu_1^* \dot{L}^* - \mu_4^* \dot{H}_g^* = def^* \qquad \text{I (7′)}$$

$$\mu_1 H = \mu_2 H_p + \mu_3^* \varphi^{-1} H_p + \mu_4 \varphi^{-1} H_g^* \qquad \text{I (8)}$$

$$\mu_1^* L^* = \mu_2^* L_p + \mu_3 \varphi L_p^* + \mu_4 \varphi L_g \qquad \text{I (8′)}$$

$$\mu_3 \dot{L}_p + \mu_4 \dot{L}_g - \varphi^{-1} (\mu_3^* \dot{H}_p^* + \mu_4^* \dot{H}_g^*) = cab \qquad \text{I (9)}$$

$$\mu_3^* \dot{H}_p^* + \mu_4 \dot{H}_h^* - \varphi^* (\mu_3 \dot{L}_p + \mu_4 \dot{L}_g) = cab^* \qquad \text{I (9′)}$$

$$def = g - sy \qquad \text{I (10)}$$

$$def^* = g^* - sy^* \qquad \text{I (10′)}$$

The next block of equations is predominantly behavioural. Equations (11, 11′) describe the determination of the current account surplus as dependent upon incomes in the two countries, and the real exchange rate. u_1 is a shock parameter. (12, 12′) and (14, 14′) are asset demand functions, dependent on real wealth ($W - P$, $W^* - P^*$), income and expected exchange rate depreciation ($\dot{E}^e$), u_1 being another shock parameter. I (13, 13′) are identities which ensure that exchange rate revaluations are captured in the wealth terms. Finally (15, 15′) below describe the formation of aggregate demand in the two countries; this depends on government spending, the current account surplus (determined in (11, 11′)), real wealth, expected inflation and expected depreciation.

$$cab = -k_1 y + k_1^* \varphi^{-1} y^* + k_2(E + P_d - P_d^*) + u_1 \tag{11}$$

$$cab^* = -k_1 y^* + k_1 \varphi y - k_2 \varphi(E + P_d - P_d^*) - \varphi u_1 \tag{11'}$$

$$(H_p - P) = (a_1(W - P) + a_2 y) - a_3 \dot{E}^e + u_2 \tag{12}$$

$$(L_p^* - p^*) = (a_1^*(W^* - P^*) + a_2^* y^*) + a_3^* \dot{E}^e + u_2^* \tag{12'}$$

$$(\mu_2 + \mu_3)W = \mu_2 H_p + \mu_3(L_p + E) \qquad \text{I (13)}$$

$$(\mu_2^* + \mu_3^*) W^* = \mu_2^* L_p + \mu_3^*(H_p^* - E) \qquad \text{I (13')}$$

$$(L_p + E - P) = [(1 + \mu_3 \mu_3^{-1} (1 - a_1)(W - P) - \mu_3^{-1} \mu_2 a_2 y] + \mu_3^{-1} \mu_2 a_3 \dot{E}^e - \mu_3^{-1} \mu_2 u_2 \tag{14}$$

$$(H_p^* - E - P^*) = [1 - \mu_3^{-1} \mu_2^*(1 - a_1^*) \ (W^* - P^*) - \mu_3^{-1*} \mu_2^* a_2^* y^*]$$

$$+ \mu_3^{-1*} \mu_2^* a_3^* \dot{E}^e - \mu_3^{-1*} \mu_2^* u_2^* \tag{14'}$$

$$y = d_1(g + cab) + d_2(W - P) + d_3 \dot{P}^e + d_4 \dot{E}^e + u_3 \tag{15}$$

$$y^* = d_1^* (g^* + cab^*) + d_2^* (W^* - P^*) + d_3^* \dot{P}^{e*} - d_4^* E^e + u_3^* \tag{15'}$$

The option of intervention to stabilize or dampen the exchange rate is expressed in (16, 16′), where L_g, H_g^* are respectively the domestic and foreign country's foreign exchange reserves and E^{**} is a target exchange rate.

$$\dot{L}_q = f_1(-f_2 (E - E^{**}) - L_g) \tag{16}$$

$$\dot{H}_g^* = f_1(f_2^* (E - E^{**}) - H_g^*) \tag{16'}$$

Given a value for f_1, setting f_2 to zero eliminates intervention and allows the model to solve under the assumption of flexible exchange rates.

No explicit equations are listed for the determination of expectations since these are assumed to be rational and the model is solved under this assumption, using the PRISM package (Al - Nowaihi, et al. (1984)). For this purpose, the exchange rate and the rate of wage inflation (q) are treated as jump variables. To ensure non - explosive solutions, it was found convenient to work with price - deflated variables throughout; this implies *inter alia* that when intervention is switched in ($f_2 \neq 0$), the target is a real exchange rate. Basic case parameter values are listed in the Appendix.

III. SIMULATION PROPERTIES AND THE EFFECT OF INTERVENTION

We leave on one side a discussion of the long run properties of the model (those are reviewed in Artis and Gazioglu (1986a)) and proceed to examine the effects of foreign exchange market intervention. At this stage the economies are assumed to be identical. The asymmetry is introduced later. The effects of intervention are identified with the difference in response of output variables of interest, as prespecified shocks occur with, or without, intervention by the authorities. These results are shown in Table 1, where the left hand column under each shock pertains to the floating rate regime, the right hand one to a regime in which foreign exchange market intervention takes place. Five types of disturbances are considered; a government spending shock, a capacity shock, a net export shock (u_1), an asset demand shock (u_2) and an aggregate demand shock (u_3). The results are then shown as the impact and (in parentheses) the long run effect, computed as the deviation from base. In order to generate the results shown for the intervention case, the f_2 parameter in the intervention equation was chosen so as to minimize the short run impact on the real exchange rate of the u_2 (asset demand) disturbance. Clearly, a different choice criterion could have been chosen; this one was appealing because exchange rate targeting has been advocated as especially suitable for cases where the predominant disturbances are in asset demands (see e.g. McKinnon (1983)), and indeed it seemed interesting to enquire what consequences would follow from having chosen to intervene on such grounds when the shocks turn out to be of a different nature. We now turn to each of the shocks in turn.

A Government Spending Shock (g). The long run effects of the spending shocks are not significantly altered by intervention, but it is evident that the short run impact is substantially changed. The real exchange rate appreciates

TABLE 1

Short (and Long-run) Effects on Selected Variables of Specified Shocks: Basic Case Parameter Values *, Under Free Float (FF) and Intervention (I)

Shock	g		$\bar{y}$		u_1		u_2		u_3	
Regime	FF	I	FF	I	FF	I	FF	I	FF	I
Real Exchange Rate	—0.139	—0.034	0.198	0.049	—0.312	—0.076	—0.146	—0.043	—0.046	—0.016
	(—0.091)	(—0.078)	(0.170)	(0.141)	(—0.333)	(—0.274)	(0.000)	(—0.001)	(0.000)	(—0.001)
Output:										
Domestic	0.879	1.105	0.486	0.161	0.044	0.557	—0.295	—0.071	0.517	0.620
	(0.000)	(—0.001)	(1.000)	(1.002)	(0.000)	(0.005)	(0.000)	(0.000)	(0.000)	(0.000)
Foreign	0.758	—0.531	—0.395	—0.071	—0.044	—0.557	0.295	0.071	0.392	0.289
	(0.000)	(0.001)	(0.000)	(—0.002)	(0.000)	(—0.005)	(0.000)	(0.000)	(0.000)	(0.004)
Inflation:										
Domestic	0.176	0.221	—0.103	—0.103	0.009	0.111	—0.059	—0.014	0.103	0.124
	(1.009)	(1.090)	(—0.404)	(—0.576)	(0.000)	(0.355)	(0.000)	(—0.008)	(0.001)	(—0.007)
Foreign	0.152	0.106	—0.079	—0.014	—0.009	—0.111	0.059	0.014	0.078	0.058
	(0.103)	(0.021)	(—0.041)	(0.131)	(0.000)	(—0.355)	(0.000)	(0.008)	(—0.001)	(0.007)
Budget Deficit:										
Domestic	0.649	0.538	—0.194	—0.065	—0.018	—0.223	0.118	0.029	—0.207	—0.248
	(1.000)	(1.000)	(—0.400)	(—0.401)	(0.000)	(0.002)	(—0.000)	(0.000)	(0.000)	(0.000)
Foreign	—0.303	—0.213	0.158	0.028	0.018	0.223	—0.118	—0.029	—0.157	—0.115
	(0.000)	(0.000)	(0.000)	(0.001)	(0.000)	(—0.002)	(0.000)	(0.000)	(0.000)	(0.000)
Balance of Payments on	—0.464	—0.333	0.242	0.053	0.028	0.325	—0.202	—0.073	—0.241	—0.181
Current Account	(—0.274)	(—0.232)	(0.109)	(0.020)	(0.000)	(0.183)	(0.000)	(—0.004)	(0.000)	(—0.04)

* Listed in the Appendix. In the basic case domestic and foreign parameter values are maintained identical to each other.

less[1] and partly in consequence there is a more pronounced expansionary impact on domestic output and a less pronounced deflationary one on foreign output, whilst inflation is increased more in the home country and less in the foreign country. The budget deficit accordingly rises less in the home country and falls more in the foreign country.

A Capacity Shock ($\bar{y}$). The capacity shock requires a long run depreciation of the real exchange rate (essentially to stimulate the additional demand required to meet the added supply); the extent of this, however, is less in the case where the exchange rate is smoothed through intervention. There is a bigger fall in inflation, which helps to create additional private sector demand in this case, foreign inflation now rising, not falling. Short run differences in impact are quite pronounced, the much smaller real depreciation leading to a more modest increase in domestic output and a smaller fall in foreign output, and to a larger decline in inflation at home, but a smaller one overseas.

A Net Exports Shock (u_1). The exchange rate intervention makes a considerable difference to the impact effect of the net export shock; with a much reduced appreciation under intervention the net export shock is transmitted into considerably higher output, more inflation and a lower budget deficit in the short run with opposing impacts on the foreign country. Indeed these effects spill over into the model's 'long run' solution.[2]

An Asset Demand Shock (u_2). The asset demand shock causes the real exchange rate to appreciate on impact, resulting in some decline in domestic output and inflation and a consequential rise in the budget deficit and deterioration in the balance of payments. In the long run, the shock washes out and leaves no trace. The intervention regime simply dampens all the short run responses as the initial departure of the exchange rate is reduced.

An Aggregate Demand Shock (u_3). The aggregate demand shock under free floating raises domestic output and inflation, reduces the budget deficit and leads to a deterioration in the current account of the balance of payments.

1. There is a long run appreciation in the real exchange rate following fiscal expansion as discussed in detail in Artis and Gazioglu (1986). In brief, with output tied in the long run to the natural rate this 'Reaganomics' result comes about as a rise in government demand requires an accommodating fall in net exports, and this in turn is achieved through an appreciation of the real exchange rate.

2. This is arbitrarily fixed at 30 'periods' but the analytical properties of the model require output deviations to go to zero in the long run (inflation surprises cannot be indefinitely maintained under rational expectations).

Nonetheless, the exchange rate appreciates, as the domestic inflation differential makes foreign assets more attractive unless there is a compensating exchange rate gain in prospect. The rise in the exchange rate helps to damp out the expansion and in the long run the output and inflation effects tend towards zero. Intervention tends to dampen the initial departure of the exchange rate, raising the domestic output and inflation effects in the short run with compensating reductions in the overseas impacts and consequential effects on the budget deficit at home and overseas as well as on the current acount deficit.

Overall, intervention has a marked effect on the model, uniformly reducing (real) exchange volatility, but thereby increasing output and inflation impacts in those cases where an induced appreciation is serving to dampen these impacts, whilst reducing the output and inflation declines which would otherwise be associated, through exchange rate appreciation, with an asset demand shock.

IV. ASYMMETRIES IN WAGE BEHAVIOUR

In the simulation model used in this paper the key parameters of wage behaviour are those which pertain to the sensitivity of wage inflation to the pressure of demand (h_0, h_0^*) and those which pertain to the responsiveness of wages to prices (h_1, h_2, h_1^*, h_2^*). Available empirical evidence suggests that asymmetries in wage behaviour, as between Germany on the one hand and other members of the EMS on the other, can conveniently – if loosely – be stylized as the possession by Germany of a high degree of responsiveness to labour market excess demand (Phillips Curve slope) and a relatively low degree of responsiveness of wages to prices. In Artis et al. (1984, 1986) this emerges in a particularly stark form since the estimation procedure submits to test at an early stage of the work the propriety of assuming long run dynamic homogeneity of wages in prices in a generously specified model of the wage process and this restriction is decisively rejected for Germany, though accepted for each of the other countries examined (viz Italy, France, Netherlands, U.K. and Belgium);[3] indeed, no significant role at all is found for inflation expectations (however modelled – and the 1984 study tests four alternative models) in the German wage equation, though static homogeneity is confirmed. As to the presence of a demand effect, in the 1984 study it was only in the German case that the level of unemployment was found to exert a sig-

3. In the case of Belgium the data accept the imposition of short run homogeneity.

nificant negative effect on wage inflation, though for France the level of vacancies and for the UK a combined set of unemployment and vacancy terms also were found significant. In the 1986 paper an extension of the earlier model broadly confirmed these results.

Further support for the view that the parameters of the German wage inflation process mark it off from the processes to be encountered in other EMS countries can be found in the work of Coe & Gagliardi (1985) who study the determinants of wage inflation in the OECD countries. They note that in a wage equation of the form $\dot{w} = a_0 + a_1\dot{p} + a_2u + a_3\dot{q}$ where $\dot{w}$ is the rate of wage growth, $\dot{p}$ is the price inflation and $\dot{q}$ is productivity growth, a general expression for 'real wage rigidity' or the sacrifice of unemployment required to dampen out an inflation shock can be found by setting the differential to zero, yielding

$$du = \frac{a_1 d\dot{p} + a_3 d\dot{q}}{a_3}.$$

Given that they find estimates of a_3 significant only in the case of Germany, the resultant values for this expression for a unit inflation shock are derived by them as:

real wage rigidity (%):	France	3.03
	UK	5.82
	Italy	1.62
	Netherlands	4.09 – 5.87[4]
	Germany	0.61.

The differing approaches to the measurement of the wage inflation process in the different studies preclude a more definite comparison and the empirical questions undoubtedly deserve more attention. For the present purpose it is sufficient that there is some presumption of asymmetries between the wage processes of members of the EMS.

V. SIMULATING THE EFFECTS OF PHILLIPS CURVE ASYMMETRIES

Within the framework of the present model, these asymmetries can be mimicked by suitable variations in the parameters h_0, h_1 and h_2 (and /or their

4. The former figure in the case of the Netherlands is derived assuming mean levels of unemployment in the estimation period and the latter figure, as well as that for Germany, by assuming the unemployment levels of the first half of 1984.

TABLE 2A

Financial Integration with Asymmetry in the Phillips Curve Slopes: Short and (Long-run) Effects on the Real Exchange Rate and Output of Specified Shocks*

Shock	I: $h_0 = 0.15$			II: $h_0 = 0.25$			III: $h_0 = 0.275$		
	Real Exchange Rate	Output Domestic	Output Foreign	Real Exchange Rate	Output Domestic	Output Foreign	Real Exchange Rate	Output Domestic	Output Foreign
g	0.001	1.200	0.465	—0.085	0.982	0.632	—0.164	0.807	—0.801
	(0.108)	(1.176)	(—0.000)	(0.055)	(0.869)	(—0.000)	(—0.043)	(0.292)	(—0.001)
g^*	0.278	1.074	0.586	0.202	0.882	0.734	0.129	0.721	0.891
	(0.115)	(0.131)	(0.000)	(0.109)	(0.097)	(0.000)	(0.099)	(0.033)	(10.001)
$\bar{y}$	0.128	0.323	—0.248	0.175	0.442	—0.339	0.215	0.531	—0.424
	(0.090)	(0.528)	(0.000)	(0.111)	(0.651)	(0.000)	(0.151)	(0.883)	(0.000)
$\bar{y}^*$	—0.269	—0.556	0.634	—0.230	—0.458	0.560	—0.193	—0.376	0.479
	(—0.179)	(—0.052)	(1.000)	(—0.177)	(—0.039)	(1.000)	(—0.173)	(—0.013)	(1.000)
u_1	—0.313	0.045	—0.044	—0.315	0.038	—0.039	—0.315	0.038	—0.039
	(—0.333)	(0.001)	(0.000)	(—0.333)	(0.001)	(0.000)	(—0.333)	(0.000)	(0.000)

TABLE 2A Continued

u_2	—0.104 (—0.001)	—0.214 (—0.002)	0.209 (—0.000)	—0.093 (—0.001)	—0.184 (—0.002)	0.188 (—0.000)	—0.092 (—0.000)	—0.182 (—0.001)	0.188 (—0.000)
u_2^*	0.104 (0.001)	0.214 (0.002)	—0.209 (0.000)	0.093 (0.001)	0.184 (0.002)	—0.188 (0.000)	0.092 (0.000)	0.182 (0.001)	—0.188 (0.000)
u_3	—0.012 (0.000)	0.639 (0.003)	0.285 (0.000)	—0.052 (0.000)	0.535 (0.002)	0.362 (0.000)	—0.082 (0.000)	0.467 (10.001)	0.426 (10.000)
u_3^*	0.118 (—0.000)	—0.516 (0.001)	0.405 (0.000)	0.085 (—0.000)	0.432 (—0.001)	0.468 (—0.000)	0.055 (—0.000)	0.366 (—0.000)	0.531 (—0.000)
u_4	0.246 (—0.006)	0.540 (—3.351)	—0.528 (—3.333)	0.218 (0.146)	0.466 (—2.477)	—0.476 (—3.333)	0.113 (0.238)	0.241 (—3.151)	—0.249 (—4.545)

* Notes:

1. a_3 is the substitution parameter in the asset demand functions (cf. equations (12), (12)′), with a value of 2.0 in the basic case (Table 1), and of 3.0 here, representing a high degree of financial integration.

2. h_0 is the slope of the Phillips curve (cf. equations (3), (3)′), with a value of 0.2 in the basic run (Table 1). Here the Phillips Curve slope of the domestic country is varied, while that of the foreign country is held at the basic case value.

foreign counterparts). The slope of the Phillips Curve is represented by h_0, set at 0.2 in the basic case where both countries are treated as identical.

As a first step, therefore, we ask how the behaviour of the model is affected by an asymmetry in h_0. Specifically, in Tables 2A and 2B, we report the simulation results of the model as h_0 is varied from 0.15 through 0.25 to 0.275. In contrast to later results to be discussed, the degree of financial integration is taken to be high, this being represented by a value of 3.0 for the parameter a_3 in the asset demand function which determines the substi-

TABLE 2B

Financial Integration with Asymmetry in the Phillips Curve Slopes: Short and (Long-run Effects on Inflation of Specified Shocks*

	I: $h_0 = 0{,}15$		II: $h_0 = 0.25$		III: $h_0 = 0.275$	
	Inflation		Inflation		Inflation	
Shock	Domestic	Foreign	Domestic	Foreign	Domestic	Foreign
g	0.180 (0.529)	0.093 (0.059)	0.245 (0.651)	0.126 (0.073)	0.260 (0.609)	0.132 (0.134)
g^*	0.096 (0.001)	0.057 (—0.000)	0.220 (0.074)	0.147 (0.998)	0.234 (0.179)	0.151 (0.900)
$\bar{y}$	—0.102 (—0.212)	—0.050 (—0.023)	—0.139 (—0.261)	—0.068 (—0.029)	—0.148 (—0.251)	—0.071 (—0.063)
$\bar{y}^*$	—0.083 (—0.023)	—0.073 (—0.400)	—0.115 (—0.029)	—0.088 (—0.400)	—0.122 (—0.064)	—0.090 (—0.373)
u_1	0.007 (0.000)	—0.009 (—0.001)	0.010 (0.000)	—0.008 (—0.001)	0.010 (0.007)	—0.008 (—0.009)
u_2	—0.032 (—0.001)	0.042 (0.002)	—0.046 (—0.001)	0.038 (0.002)	—0.049 (—0.019)	0.031 (0.024)
u_2^*	0.032 (0.001)	—0.042 (—0.002)	0.046 (0.001)	—0.038 (—0.002)	0.049 (0.019)	—0.037 (—0.024)
u_3	0.096 (0.001)	0.057 (—0.000)	0.134 (0.002)	0.072 (—0.000)	0.142 (0.016)	0.075 (—0.012)
u_3^*	0.077 (—0.001)	0.001 (0.003)	0.108 (—0.001)	0.094 (0.003)	0.115 (—0.016)	0.095 (0.032)
u_4	0.081 (1.491)	—0.106 (1.490)	0.116 (1.142)	—0.095 (1.451)	0.124 (1.126)	—0.093 (1.508)

* For table notes, see Table 2A.

tutability of the foreign and domestic assets. Because only h_0 is varied, h_0^* being kept at the 'basic case' value of 0.2; the three cases show what happens as the 'domestic' country's Phillips Curve is (Case I) slightly flatter, (Case II) slightly steeper or (Case III) much steeper than that of the foreign country. Because of the asymmetry which is now introduced, certain shocks are no longer symmetrical in their effects and the list of disturbances to be considered is increased in consequence. To ease the expositional burden the number of endogenous variables considered has been reduced to five – the real exchange rate, domestic and foreign output and domestic and foreign inflation. We now turn to consider how the response of these variables to the various shocks varies according to the slope of the Phillips Curve.

Effects on the Real Exchange Rate. The relative slope of the Phillips Curve is clearly of considerable consequence to the behaviour of the real exchange rate. The case of the domestic government spending shock is particularly notable in this respect. As the Phillips Curve slope is increased the real exchange rate impact of this shock is changed from one of depreciation to one of appreciation; elsewhere the real exchange rate impact varies monotically with h_0, except in the case of the u_1 (net exports) shock where the real exchange rate effect seems to be inelastic with respect to the Phillips Curve slope. For the asset demand (u_2) shock, the effects are symmetrical between foreign and domestic shocks; for the u_3, aggregate demand, shock however the effects are only qualitatively symmetrical. The inflation shock (u_4) has a smaller (depreciation) impact on the real exchange rate the bigger the Philips Curve slope. The effects of the capacity shocks on the real exchange rate, whilst qualitatively symmetrical, now depend heavily on their source. A domestic capacity shock creates a depreciation impact on the real exchange rate which is smaller than the appreciation impact of a foreign capacity shock: but the differences appear to diminish as the relative slope of the domestic country's Philips Curve is increased.

Output Effects. The effects of Phillips Curve asymmetry on output are similarly marked. A domestic fiscal expansion (g – shock) has smaller impact on domestic output (and larger impact on foreign output) the larger the Phillips Curve slope of the domestic country. A foreign fiscal shock, similarly, has less effect on domestic output the larger is the domestic country's relative Phillips Curve slope. (As might be expected, the higher the Phillips Curve slope, the greater the inflation response – see Table 2B – to fiscal stimulus and the more the appreciation of the real exchange rate. Thus, the Phillips

Curve slope plays an important role in the crowding out of fiscal policy.)[5]

The Phillips Curve slope also plays an important role in mediating the effects of the capacity shock, where a higher slope is favourable to a larger rise in domestic output and a bigger fall in foreign output in the short run.[6] Foreign capacity shocks have less expansionary effects on foreign output and less contractionary effects on domestic output as the domestic Phillips Curve is steepened.

The effect of the net export shock on the two countries is only very mildly sensitive to the Phillips Curve slope, with the expansionary impact on domestic output rising slightly as the slope increases, and the contractionary impact on foreign output diminishing; but these effects are only visible as the slope is raised from 0.15 to 0.25 and vanish at the higher value.

The symmetry of the asset demand (u_2) shock is wholly unaffected by the variations in the Phillips Curve slope examined in Table 2, which affect the output impacts only in a mild way.

For the aggregate demand (u_3) shock, however, there is some evidence of asymmetry, though surprisingly it does not appear to be the case that the country with the relatively lower Phillips Curve slope necessarily evinces a stronger expansionary effect on output from an aggregate demand shock – compare Cases I and III where this is so, with Case II where it is not.[7] Evidently, the absolute, as well as the relative levels of the parameter are important.

Effects on Inflation. Table 2B reports the effects on domestic and foreign inflation of the same shocks, when the asymmetry in the Phillips Curve slope is introduced. Not surprisingly, the domestic inflation impact of domestic demand shocks (g, u_1, u_3^*) rises as the Phillips Curve slope is increased: only a little less obviously, perhaps, the same is true also of the foreign inflation impact of these same shocks except, naturally, where the shock is distributive as in the case of a shock to net exports. As the countries are intervening on

5. It will be seen that the 'long-run' domestic output effects of this shock are quoted as non-zero values, so that the model has not fully converged after 30 'periods'. The natural rate property of the model ensures analytically that the long run effect of a demand shock is zero.

6. Once again, as with the domestic output effects of a domestic fiscal shock, it is evident that the 'long run' domestic capacity shock effects are not as analytically they should be (identically unity in this case). Note that the discrepancy appears to be confined to the 'domestic' country effects of the capacity shocks.

7. Recall that h_0* is maintained at 0.2, the basic case value.

the real exchange rate a degree of accommodation of inflation shocks is implied. The capacity shocks ($\bar{y}$, $\bar{y}^*$) *mutatis mutandis*, are similarly affected by an increase in the domestic country's Phillips Curve slope: the resultant *deflationary* impact is thereby increased, in both countries. The asset demand (u_2) shock, which again has a distributive character, is associated with an increasingly deflationary *domestic* but increasingly inflationary *foreign* impact as the Phillips Curve slope is increased (and vice versa for u_2^*). The inflation shock per se (u_4) produces an increasingly inflationary impact at home, and an increasingly deflationary impact abroad as the Phillips Curve slope is raised.

VI. SIMULATING THE EFFECTS OF EXCHANGE CONTROLS

A practical means of limiting exchange rate variation without intervention is exemplified by the use of exchange controls. Whilst these may take many forms and can be analysed from different points of view accordingly, it is common to regard them as reducing the degree of financial integration (see Johnston (1979), Otani and Tiwari (1981) for examples). In the framework of the present model this can be mimicked by reducing the value of a_3, the parameter on the expected exchange rate, in the asset demand function.

Thus in Tables 3A and 3B we present results for the case where a_3 has been reduced to a value of 0.2 from the value of 3.0 it held in Tables 2A and 2B. Two variants for values of h_0 are presented, 0.25 and 0.275, corresponding to Cases II and III of Tables 2A and 2B with which the results shown in Table 3 may be compared.

Upon doing so, we see that the values of a_3 and h_0 are in fact highly interactive in a number of cases. Comparing the results first for the real exchange rate in Cases II (Table 2A) and II′ (Table 3A), it can be seen that the impacts are dampened by lower financial integration in every case except that of the asset demand shock. This seems to be, broadly, what we might expect. The imposition of a lower degree of financial integration generally serves to make the exchange market more sluggish, but the effect of a shock in the asset market itself is an inversion of this sluggish behaviour and actually makes for a more disruptive response. Comparing Cases III and III′ however, for a higher value of h_0, reveals four additional cases in which the real exchange rate impact effect is increased by reducing the degree of financial integration. Whilst entirely possible in principle, the extent of this interaction effect is somewhat surprising, producing the result in this instance that $g^*, \bar{y}^*$, u_3^* and u_4 shocks are all more disruptive in their real exchange rate impacts under a low degree of financial integration than under a high degree. These results suggest caution in appealing to the 'second best' theorem to justify the use of exchange controls in a world of sticky wages and prices.

Inspection of the results for output, again comparing Cases II and II′, III and III′ between Tables 2A and 3A reinforces this impression. In the former case there are several instances in which the output deviation is greater

TABLE 3A

Asymmetry in the Phillips Curve Slopes with Reduced Financial Integration: Short & (Long-run) Effects on the Real Exchange Rate and Output of Specified Shocks*

Shock	II′: $h_0 = 0.25$ Real exchange rate	Output Domestic	Output Foreign	III′: $h_0 = 0.275$ Real exchange rate	Output Domestic	Output Foreign
g	—0.078 (0.059)	0.997 (0.874)	0.617 (0.000)	—0.094 (0.048)	0.955 (0.820)	0.649 (—0.000)
g^*	0.186 (0.107)	0.850 (0.091)	0.768 (0.000)	0.172 (0.106)	0.815 (0.086)	0.794 (0.000)
$\bar{y}$	0.168 (0.110)	0.428 (0.650)	—0.324 (0.000)	0.177 (0.114)	0.452 (0.671)	—0.342 (0.000)
$\bar{y}^*$	—0.220 (—0.176)	—0.436 (—0.036)	0.537 (1.000)	—0.213 (—0.176)	—0.418 (—0.034)	0.523 (1.000)
u_1	—0.307 (—0.333)	0.054 (0.000)	—0.056 (0.000)	—0.308 (—0.333)	0.052 (0.000)	—0.054 (0.000)
u_2	—0.133 (—0.000)	—0.263 (—0.001)	0.269 (—0.000)	—0.130 (0.000)	—0.254 (—0.001)	0.263 (0.000)
u_2^*	0.133 (0.000)	0.263 (0.001)	—0.269 (0.000)	0.130 (0.000)	0.254 (0.001)	—0.263 (0.000)
u_3	—0.050 (0.000)	0.540 (0.002)	0.357 (0.000)	—0.057 (0.000)	0.520 (0.002)	0.372 (0.000)
u_3^*	0.079 (0.000)	0.420 (0.000)	0.479 (—0.000)	0.172 (0.106)	0.815 (0.086)	0.794 (—0.000)
u_4	0.204 (0.145)	0.438 (—2.478)	—0.448 (—3.333)	0.199 (0.171)	0.424 (—2.327)	—0.439 (3.333)

* Notes: Parameter a_3 set at 0.2 to characterize low financial integration (cf. Table 2); parameter h_0, the Phillips Curve slope in the domestic country is varied from 0.25 to 0.275 (cf. Table 2 for a more extended variation).

under a lower degree of financial integration; in the latter case, this is true for the majority of shocks considered.

The difference in inflation impacts can be studied by comparing Tables 2B and 3B. Here, it appears that a lowering of the degree of financial integration has the effect of bottling up inflationary impacts domestically – thus, the inflationary response to the g, u_1 and u_3 shocks is increased, as is the deflationary impact of domestic capacity shocks. On the other hand, the re-

TABLE 3B

Asymmetry in the Phillips Curve Slope with Reduced Financial Integration: Short and (Long-run) Effects on Inflation of Specified Shocks*

Shock	II′ : $h_0 = 0.25$ Inflation		III′ : $h_0 = 0.275$ Inflation	
	Domestic	Foreign	Domestic	Foreign
g	0.249 (0.655)	0.123 (0.069)	0.263 (0.677)	0.130 (0.071)
g^*	0.212 (0.069)	0.154 (1.005)	0.224 (0.071)	0.159 (1.005)
$\bar{y}$	—0.143 (—0.263)	—0.065 (—0.027)	—0.151 (—0.271)	—0.068 (—0.028)
$\bar{y}^*$	—0.109 (—0.027)	—0.093 (—0.403)	—0.115 (0.028)	—0.095 (—0.403)
u_1	0.014 (0.000)	—0.011 (—0.000)	0.014 (0.000)	—0.011 (—0.000)
u_2	—0.066 (—0.001)	0.054 (0.001)	—0.070 (—0.001)	0.053 (0.001)
u_2^*	0.066 (0.001)	—0.054 (—0.001)	0.070 (0.001)	—0.053 (—0.001)
u_3	0.135 (0.001)	0.071 (0.000)	0.143 (0.001)	0.074 (0.000)
u_3^*	0.105 (∓0.000)	0.096 (0.000)	0.111 (∓0.000)	0.098 (0.002)
u_4	0.109 (1.141)	—0.090 (1.451)	0.117 (1.080)	—0.088 (1.445)

* For notes, see Table 3A.

sponse of domestic inflation to foreign shocks (g^*, u_3^*, $\bar{y}^*$) is diminished. Reciprocally, where the impact on domestic inflation is increased, that on foreign inflation is reduced.

VII. THE PRICE RESPONSIVENESS OF WAGES

Tables 4A – 4C introduce an additional source of asymmetry in wage behaviour, this time in respect of the response of wages to prices. In the model this is represented by the parameters h_1, h_2. In the earlier discussion, we found that the distinctive character of the German wage inflation process appeared to reside in its comparative lack of response to the labour market. Thus, in terms of our present model set - up to mimic this requires endowing the country with the relatively high h_0 parameter value with comparatively low values of the h_1, h_2 parameters – or equivalently, to endow the 'other' country with relatively high h_1^*, h_2^* values. This latter is what is done in Tables 4A – 4C.

In these tables we report the impacts on the real exchange rate, domestic and foreign output, as the parameter sets h_0, h_1^*, h_2^* and a_3 are varied for a single (domestic fiscal) shock. The choice of shock is illustrative.

As might be expected, for this shock, the two parameter variations have broadly opposing impacts. As the relative slope of the domestic country's Phillips Curve is increased (h_0 rising), the real exchange rate appreciation impact is increased, and as the relative price - response parameters are reduced (h_1^*, h_2^* rising) the appreciation impact is reduced. In a similar way, the output impacts are also opposing.

For given values of h_1^*, h_2^* and $h_0 = 0.3$, it seems clear that the lower the degree of financial integration the lower the amount of exchange rate overshooting, though the sensitivity of overshooting to the degree of financial integration as the h_1^*, h_2^* parameters are raised tends to decline the higher the degree of financial integration. Variations in the h_0 parameter, however, are capable of overturning this picture; with a low value (0.15), for this parameter, for example, overshooting appears to *decrease* with the degree of financial integration whilst for the next two higher variations of this parameter ($h_0 = 0.2, 0.251$), the largest degree of overshooting is to be found in the 'middle' range of financial integration.

The output impacts seem more straightforward; the broad picture is, as might be expected for this shock, that a higher domestic Phillips Curve slope reduces the domestic output impact and raises the foreign output impact, for all degrees of financial integration. At the same time, a reduction in the relative degree of wage indexation raises the domestic output and reduces the

TABLE 4A

Asymmetries in Phillips Curve Slopes (h_0) and Price Responsiveness (h_1^*, h_2^*) with Variation in the Degree (a_3) of Financial Integration Short and (Long-run) Effects on the Real Exchange Rate of a Domestic Fiscal (g) Shock*

	Higher Financial Integration ($a_3 = 0.3$)				Lower Financial Integration ($a_3 = 0.2$)				Minimal Financial Integration ($a_3 = 0.1$)			
$h_1^* = h_2^*$	1.5	1.25	1.15	1.10	1.5	1.25	1.15	1.10	1.5	1.25	1.15	1.10
$h_0 = 0.3$	+	−0.149 (−0.003)	−0.167 (−0.030)	−0.178 (−0.047)	−0.109 (0.040)	−0.139 (−0.020)	−0.156 (0.028)	−0.167 −(0.045)	−0.089 (0.040)	−0.114 (0.001)	−0.128 (−0.028)	−0.137 (−0.045)
$h_0 = 0.275$	+				−0.094 (0.048)				−0.074 (0.048)			
$h_0 = 0.251$	0.085 (0.055)				−0.078 (0.186)				−0.059 (0.057)			
$h_0 = 0.2$	−0.046 (0.078)				−0.040 (0.079)				−0.024 (0.080)			
$h_0 = 0.15$	0.001 (0.108)				−0.040 (0.079)				0.018 (0.110)			

* Notes : h_0^* and h_1, h_2 are maintained at their base values (viz: 0.2, 1.0, 1.0).
+ System does not solve.

TABLE 4B

Asymmetries in Phillips Curve Slopes (h_0) and Price Responsiveness (h_1*, h_2*) with Variation in the Degree of Financial Integration (a_3): Short and (Long-run) Effects on Domestic Output of a Domestic Fiscal (g) Shock*

	Higher Financial Integration ($a_3 = 0.3$)				Lower Financial Integration ($a_3 = 0.2$)				Minimal Financial Integration ($a_3 = 0.1$)			
$h_1^* = h_2^*$	1.5	1.25	1.15	1.10	1.5	1.25	1.15	1.10	1.5	1.25	1.15	1.10
$h_0 = 0.3$	+	0.833 (0.526)	0.795 (0.371)	0.772 (0.271)	0.916 (0.773)	0.854 (0.530)	0.818 (0.373)	0.795 (0.272)	0.959 (0.774)	0.906 (0.531)	0.876 (0.374)	0.85 (0.27)
$h_0 = 0.275$	+		0.807 (0.292)		0.955 (0.820)				0.996 (0.822)			
$h_0 = 0.25$	0.980 (0.869)				0.997 (0.874)				1.037 (0.875)			
$h_0 = 0.20$	1.080 (1.000)				1.093 (1.004)				1.128 (1.006)			
$h_0 = 0.15$	1.199 (1.176)								1.237 (1.182)			

* Notes: h_0* and h_1, h_2 are maintained at their base values (viz 0.2, 1.0, 1.0).
+ System does not solve.

TABLE 4C

Asymmetries in Phillips Curve Slopes (h_0) and Price Responsiveness (h_1*, h_2*) with Variation in the Degree of Financial Integration (a_3): Short and (Long-run) Effects on Foreign Output of a Domestic Fiscal (g) Shock*

	Higher Financial Integration ($a_3 = 0.3$)				Lower Financial Integration ($a_3 = 0.2$)				Minimal Financial Integration ($a_3 = 0.1$)			
	1.5	1.25	1.15	1.10	1.5	1.25	1.15	1.1	1.5	1.5	1.15	1.10
$h_0 = 0.3$	+	0.765 (–0.000)	0.805 (–0.001)	0.829 (–0.001)	0.678 (0.000)	0.744 (–0.000)	0.782 (–0.000)	0.805 (–0.000)	0.634 (–0.000)	0.689 (–0.000)	0.721 (–0.000)	0.74 (–0.000)
$h_0 = 0.275$	+		0.801 (–0.001)		0.649 (–0.000)				0.606 (–0.000)			
$h_0 = 0.25$	0.632 (–0.000)				0.617 (–0.000)				0.576 (–0.000)			
$h_0 = 0.20$	–0.557 (–0.000)				0.543 (–0.000)				0.508 (–0.000)			
$h_0 = 0.15$	0.465 (–0.000)								0.428 (–0.000)			

* Notes: h_0* and h_1, h_2 are maintained at their base values (viz: 0.2, 1.0, 1.0).
\+ System does not solve.

foreign output impacts. An increase in the degree of financial integration, broadly, reduces the domestic output impacts and raises the foreign output impact.

VIII. CONCLUSIONS

The motivation for this paper was provided by evidence that marked asymmetries in wage-price behaviour characterize the European Monetary System. Particularly now that a programme for the removal of exchange controls is under way in Europe the problems that these asymmetries may pose for the stability of the System require examination.

Two relevant issues in this connection which are not dealt with in this paper should be mentioned at this point. The first is that the Lucas critique may apply to the observed asymmetries in wage-price behaviour: that is to say, with liberalization of capital flows wage-price behaviour may itself be modified. The maintained hypothesis of the paper is of course, that it will not; the parameters of the model are 'deep structure' parameters. In this sense the paper denies a potential source of flexibility. On the other hand, the second point to make is that we assume that the object of intervention is the real rather than the nominal exchange rate. EMS practice to date has been to 'under-index' nominal exchange rates for inflation in order to maintain discipline thus approximating a grudging crawling peg. More recently and for the further future the intention seems to be target nominal rates of exchange more closely. In comparison with this, our assumption of real pegging obviously represents a more flexible regime.

It is clear from our results that 'Phillips Curve' asymmetries are very important, making for quite marked changes in the response of the economies as we model them, to the range of disturbances considered. Moreover, it does appear from our results that the 'second best' argument for exchange controls is limited. Thus, whilst it is commonly argued that 'overshooting' occurs as a result of the coexistence of sluggish goods and labour markets with fast-moving foreign exchange markets (and thus that there is a case for exchange controls) our results show that liberalizing the foreign exchange market does not invariably lead to, or exacerbate, overshooting. Whether it does so or not, is shock-specific. A further general result obtained is that the two sources of asymmetry in wage-price behaviour are to some extent offsetting: whilst the steeper sloped short run Phillips Curve typical of 'Germany' increases the short run inflation response (for a given change in unemployment), the lower degree of wage response to prices, also typical of 'Germany' tends to reduce it.

The extent to which generalization is possible is, however, limited. The results show a considerable degree of interaction between parameter variations, so that it is often not possible to predict accurately the effect of a joint change in parameters from knowledge of the effect of individual changes in parameter values, and correspondingly difficult to present useful generalizations. But there is a moral here, too. Whilst the limited generality of the conclusions appears to be an expositional disadvantage it should be recalled that the point of building the more complicated kind of model presented here for which analytical solutions are generally very difficult or impossible to obtain, is precisely to represent a more complicated view of the world than analytically tractable methods alone can handle.

University of Manchester and C.E.P.R., London.
University of Stirling, U.K.

APPENDIX

Notation

Foreign counterparts are indicated by *; lower case counterparts to upper case variables represent deflated (real) values.

P, P^*	domestic (foreign) consumer price index
P_d, P_d^*	domestic (foreign) value added deflator
E, E^{**}	nominal exchange rate and 'target' nominal exchange rate defined in units of domestic currency per unit of foreign currency.
π, π^*	core inflation
q, q^*	contract (forward looking) inflation
p_d, p_d^*	domestic, foreign price (value added) inflation
y, y^*	output
$\bar{y}, \bar{y}^*$	natural rate of output
H, h	total stock of domestic money (deflated by domestic prices)
L^*, l^*	total stock of foreign money (deflated by foreign prices)
H_p, h_p	part of H held by domestic private sector (deflated by foreign prices)
L_p^*, l_p^*	part of L^* held by foreign private sector (deflated by foreign CPI)

H_g^*, h_g^*	part of H held by foreign government (deflated by domestic CPI)
L_g, l_g	part of L^* held by domestic government (deflated by domestic CPI)
def, def^*	government deficit as proportion of mean domestic/foreign output
s, s^*	proportional rate of income tax
cab, cab^*	current account surplus as proportion of mean domestic/foreign output
g, g^*	government spending as proportion of average domestic/foreign output
W, W^*; w, w^*	domestic/foreign private sector financial wealth deflated by domestic/foreign consumer prices
e^{**}	real exchange rate target
e	real exchange rate (defined with respect to producer prices) i.e. $e = E - Pd + Pd^*$ and a real devaluation causes a rise in e
u_i, u_i^*	shock variables

Parameters

μ_1	ratio of domestic money stock to domestic output
μ_1^*	ratio of foreign money stock to foreign income
μ_2	ratio of domestic private sector holdings of domestic money to domestic output
μ_2^*	ratio of foreign private sector holdings of foreign money to foreign output
μ_3	ratio of domestic private sector holdings foreign money to domestic output
μ_3^*	ratio of foreign private sector holdings of domestic money to foreign output
φ	ratio of domestic income to foreign income
μ_4	ratio of foreign money stock held by domestic government to foreign output
μ_4^*	ratio of domestic money stock held by foreign government to domestic output

$$\mu_1 = \mu_2 + \mu_3^* \varphi + \mu_4^* \varphi$$
$$\mu_1^* = \mu_2^* + \mu_3 \varphi^{-1} + \mu_4 \varphi^{-1}$$

Basic Case Parameter Values

In the 'basic case' runs of the model, the following parameter values are assigned, identical values being assumed for the foreign country.

$\varphi = 1$	$k_1 = 0.4$	$d_1 = 0.5$
$\mu_1 = 1$	$k_2 = 3$	$d_2 = 0.5$
$\mu_2 = 0.7$	$d_0 = 0.75$	$d_3 = 0.5$
$\mu_3 = 0.2$	$a_1 = 1\ (1, 10)$	$d_4 = 0.1$
$\mu_4 = \mu_1 - \mu_2 - \mu_3 = 0.1$	$a_2 = 0$	$f_1 = 0$
$s = 0.4$	$a_3 = 2\ (1, 10)$	$f_2 = 0$
$h_1 = 1.0$	$h_0 = 0.2$	$h_2 = 1$

REFERENCES

Artis, M.J., Farmelo, C., Murfin, A. and Ormerod, P. (1984) 'Price Expectations and Wage Inflation in Western Europe', Manchester University Discussion Papers No. 42.

Artis, M.J., Farmelo, C. and Ormerod, P. (1986) 'Asymmetries in the Inflation Response to Shocks Among Western European Economies', *Mimeo.*

Artis, M.J. and Gazioglu, S. (1986). 'Currency Substitution in a Two-Asset-Two-Country Model: A Simulation Approach', CEPR Discussion Paper No. 107, London.

Calvo, G. (1982) 'Real Exchange Rate Dynamics with Fixed Nominal Parities: On the Economics of Overshooting and in Interest Rate Management with National Price Setting', International Economic Reasearch Center, Paper No. 5, Discussion Paper Series, No. 162.

—— (1985) 'Macroeconomic Implications of the Government Budget: Some Basic Considerations', *Journal of Monetary Economics*, 15: 95–112.

Coe, D.T. and Gagliardi, O.F. (1985) 'Nominal Wage Determination in Ten OECD Economies', OECD Economies and Statistics Department, *Working Papers* No. 19.

Giavazzi, F. and Giovannini, A. (1984) 'Monetary Policy Interactions Under Managed Exchange Rates', CEPR Discussion Paper Series, No. 123, London.

Johnston, R. B. (1979) 'Some Aspects of the Determination of Eurocurrency Interest Rates', *Quarterly Bulletin of the Bank of England*, 19: 35–44, (March).

McKinnon, R. I. (1984) 'An International Standard for Monetary Stabilization', *Policy Analyses in International Economies*, Institute for International Economics, Washington, D.C.

Otani, I. and Tiwari, S. (1981) 'Capital Controls and Interest Parity: The Japanese Experience, 1978–1981', *International Monetary Fund Staff Papers*, 28 : 793–815, (December).

Taylor, J. (1979) 'Staggered Wage Setting in a Macro-model', Papers and Proceedings, American Economic Association, 91 : 108–113.

—— (1980) 'Aggregated Dynamics and Staggered Contracts', *Journal of Political Economy*, 88 : 1–23, (February).

DEFLATIONARY CONSEQUENCES OF A HARD CURRENCY PEG

By Michael J. Moore*

I. INTRODUCTION

It is well known that disinflation policies can lead to output and welfare losses. Standard theoretical treatments of this topic include papers by Buiter and Miller (1981, 1982, 1983). They argue that in an open economy with a floating exchange rate, a decline in the rate of monetary growth can cause overshooting of the real exchange rate and give rise to temporary output losses. However, policy debate often forgets the generality of this result. For example, it is frequently argued that an easy formula for a high-inflation country to obtain and sustain a low inflation rate is to form a fixed exchange rate with a hard currency area. This was one of the motivations behind the formation of the European Monetary System in 1979. Some of the smaller members of the EMS have instead suffered from overvalued real exchange rates and prolonged recession.

A number of European countries such as Great Britain, Portugal, Spain[1] and Greece are currently considering joining the EMS, at least partly with a view to securing lower rates of inflation. The present paper details a theoretical structure in which the experience of some of the original EMS members can be evaluated and the outlook for some prospective new members can be examined. The decision to join the EMS is characterised as a movement from a fixed exchange rate with a *high* inflation country to a fixed exchange rate with a *low* inflation country.

Three models with different institutional assumptions are constructed to examine the circumstances under which changing to a hard currency peg is contractionary. The first of these is a benchmark by which the other two can be evaluated. It is a two-period distortion-free model of a small open economy where there are two goods—traded and non-traded. It thus builds

* I am indebted to Charles Goodhart for his encouragement. My thanks also to Tony Courakis and Mark Taylor and to an anonymous referee. My colleagues Tom O'Connell, Frank Browne and Gabriel Fagan have given generously with their time in discussing this paper with me. All errors are, of course, my own. The views expressed are not necessarily those of the Central Bank of Ireland.

1. Spain joined the Exchange Rate Mechanism of the EMS on 19 June, 1 989.

on Bruno (1976), Dornbusch (1983) and Moore (1986). The comparative dynamics of a fall in the expected rate of foreign inflation on the real interest rate, the real exchange rate, and other key variables is shown to follow the 'conventional wisdom'.

The second model is a development of the first in that it differs only by the inclusion of exchange controls. The analysis closely follows the exchange controls literature of Adams and Greenwood (1985) and Obstfeld (1986).The comparative dynamics results are critically changed: it appears that many of the essential 'deflationary consequences of a hard currency peg' emerge only when capital controls are in place. However, even with capital controls, instantaneous market clearing ensures that a policy change in favour of a hard currency peg is welfare enhancing.

The third and final model combines capital controls and nominal price stickiness. From this, we can see that the deflationary effects of the policy change are amplified and lead to multiplier losses of income in the traditional Keynesian sense. This introduces the possibility that the policy change may give rise to perverse welfare losses.

II. MICROFOUNDATIONS

The full technical details are given in Appendix 1. At this point it is sufficient to outline the main features which are common to the three models.

There are two goods, traded and non-traded, and two periods, the present and the future. There is a single aggregate household that chooses its demands according to a two stage budgeting process. Firstly, it decides how much to consume overall in the present and how much to save. Then it determines the division of its consumption in each period between traded and non-traded goods. The consumption/savings decision depends on the real interest rate and wealth. The within-period choice between traded and non-traded goods depends on the current real exchange rate and, of course, the overall level of consumption in the period in question.

Savings take the form of a riskless internationally traded bond which can be held or issued by both the private sector and the public sector. Money is modelled as a medium of exchange: the household has the choice of either foregoing real income in order to conduct transactions or of holding money. The latter is also costly because it involves foregoing interest income. The demand for money emerges as the optimal tradeoff between the two. In this respect the monetary aspect of the models is more flexible than cash-in-advance theory and follows the lead set by Dornbusch and Frenkel (1973), Greenwood (1983, 1984), Adams and Greenwood (1985) and Moore (1987). It makes the demand for money depend only on the nominal interest rate and *current* real income: it does not depend on relative prices or wealth.

Real income is composed of both traded and non-traded goods in each period. Income in the form of traded goods is a non-produced endowment in both periods. The output of non-traded goods is limited by a fixed labour supply which is the only factor of production. The *full employment* level of overall real income is fixed in each period in terms of the basket of consumption goods. Thus we abstract from valuation changes in real income caused by within-period relative price changes.

III. THE DISTORTION-FREE MODEL

Without any loss of generality, it is assumed that there are no Government purchases. The purpose of Government is to maintain the exchange rate at a fixed level. The Central Bank's first-period budget constraint is:

$$m^1 = \mu^1 + b, \tag{3.1}$$

where b is the real value of foreign reserves in domestic currency. μ^1 has the interpretation 'domestic credit' and takes the form of lump-sun transfers to the household. The sum of the two is, of course, the current real money stock, m^1.

The first equilibrium condition of the model is that the demand and supply of domestic money must be instantaneously equated by changes in the reserves.

$$m^1(i^*)\, y_1 = \mu^1 + b \tag{3.2}$$

The left hand side of (3.2) is the current demand for money function and is developed in Appendix 1. The asterisk superscript indicates that in the absence of exchange controls, the nominal interest rate is determined abroad.

The second equilibrium condition model relates current and future consumption behaviour. Its substantive content is that the only way the private sector can transfer purchasing power intertemporally on aggregate is by external capital accumulation. This simplification comes from the way the production sector is treated which is discussed in section VI.

$$z^1(r, w) = [1 - V(1)]\, y_1 - a - b \tag{3.3}$$

z^1 is current consumption which is shown in Appendix 1 to depend on the real interest rate, r, and welfare, w. $V(1)$ is the fraction of current income which is used up in transactions costs. Finally 'a' is private sector savings.

The final equilibrium condition states that the domestic real interest rate is derived from essentially two sources. These are the foreign real rate of interest and the own real rate of interest in the sheltered sector.

$$r = f\,[\,r^*, \theta^1\,(Z^1), \theta^2\,(Z^2)\,] \tag{3.4}$$

θ^1 and θ^2 are the relative prices of non-traded goods in each period: they also have the interpretation 'real exchange rate'. Because of the two stage budgeting specification of the model and the assumptions about production, these only depend on the overall level of consumption in each period. For further details, consult Appendix 1.

The three equilibrium conditions (3.2), (3.3) and (3.4) can be solved for the endogenous variables, a, b and r, in terms of a range of exogenous variables. However, the only two exogenous variables of relevance in this context, are the foreign nominal and real rates of interest, i^* and r^*, respectively. Movements in the foreign nominal rate of interest, i, for a given foreign real rate of interest r^*, means variations in the expected rate of foreign inflation on traded goods.

As stated in the introduction, the change of policy to a hard currency peg is stylised as a fall in the rate of inflation on traded goods.

The effect of a fall in inflation in a distortion free world is well known. A fall in foreign inflation leads to a higher demand for money and thus to a reserve inflow, i.e. $-\,db\,/\,di^* > 0$. Since lower foreign inflation brings money holdings closer to Friedman's optimum quantity, welfare improves, i.e., $-\,dw\,/\,di^* > 0$. Because of the welfare improvement, permanent consumption rises, i.e. $-\,dz^1\,/\,di^* = -\,dz^2\,/\,di^* > 0$. There are no intertemporal real effects. In particular, there is no change in either the real rate of interest nor the rate of change of the real exchange rate (π^θ).

IV. THE MODEL WITH CAPITAL CONTROLS AND MARKET CLEARING

The main criticism of the benchmark case of section III is that it applies to an undistorted economy only. An important possible distortion is the presence of capital controls. This is particularly relevant because countries which change their exchange rate policy often take additional measures with the putative objective of preventing speculative attacks. It is to this we now turn.

We use the result that an administrative system of capital controls is equivalent in every respect to a dual exchange rate system. In the latter case, a floating exchange rate for financial transactions exists side by side with a fixed exchange rate for trade-related transactions. In the case of administered capital controls, the analogue of the financial exchange rate is the virtual price of foreign exchange which tracks the extent to which the capital controls are endogenously binding. This is the approach of Adams and Greenwood (1985), Obstfeld (1986) and Moore (1987) who also introduce the harmless fiction that capital controls are administered by a second branch of Government – the financial exchange rate authority. This agency is responsible for intervening in the capital market. It can approach its task in two ways. Either it imposes direct capital controls to secure a capital account target of $\overline{ca}$, allowing the financial exchange rate to find its rate of appreciation f, or it sets the rate of appreciation of the financial exchange rate to achieve a target level for the capital account.

If $\bar{e}$ is the commercial rate of exchange and S_i, $i = 1, 2$ is the financial rate where $(1+f) = S_1 / S_2$, f is the forward premium on the financial rate. The financial exchange rate authority's first period budget constraint is:

$$T_1 = a\left[1 - \frac{\bar{e}}{S^1}\right] \tag{4.1}$$

where $$a = [1 - V(1)]\, y_1 + t_1 - z^1 - m^1$$

T_i, $i = 1, 2$ is lump-sum transfers by the financial exchange rate authority to the household.

There are again three equilibrium conditions for this model by analogy with (3.2), (3.3) and (3.4) in the previous section. The main difference is that private capital flows and thus private saving are exogenous under the assumption of capital controls. Thus the endogenous variables are now r and b as before, with 'a' replaced by its virtual price, f.

The money market equilibrium condition (3.2) is replaced by a revised condition which has the domestic nominal interest rate endogenous:

$$m^1(i)\, y_1 = \mu_1 + b \tag{4.2}$$

The intertemporal budget constraint (3.3) becomes:

$$z^1(r, w) = [1 - V(1)]\, y_1 + \overline{ca} - b \tag{4.3}$$

where $\overline{ca}$ is the Government imposed constraint on the capital account. In effect (4.3) states that the only way purchasing power can be transferred intertemporally is by the accumulation or decumulation of reserves by the Central Bank.

The real interest rate determination equation (3.4) must now take account of the forward premium or discount, f. The revised equation is:

$$r = g[r^*, f, \theta^1(Z^1), \theta^2(Z^2)] \tag{4.4}$$

We are now in a position to compare the effect of changing to a hard currency peg when capital controls are in place as distinct from the distortion free world of the last section. Although the technical details are presented in Appendix 3 rather than here, the main intuitions are easy to outline.

A fall in the foreign nominal rate of interest is only partially reflected in the domestic nominal rate of interest due to the insulation effects of exchange controls. Nevertheless, it induces an increase in the demand for money through a reserve inflow, i. e. $-db/di^* > 0$, as before. However, this effect operates exclusively through the current account since the impact of capital controls is to block off adjustment through the capital account. The only way in which the demand for money can increase is by a reduction in private consumption in the short-run, i.e. $-dz^1/di^* < 0$. This contrasts sharply with the distortion free model of the previous section. Since the market for non-traded goods clears, the current real exchange rate, θ^1, must fall to offset the fall in overall consumption.

In the earlier model, a fall in foreign inflation had no effect on the domestic real interest rate. The neutrality result no longer holds because the insulation effect of capital controls ensures that the domestic nominal rate of interest does not fall as much as the domestic rate of inflation. Hence the real interest rate rises, i.e. $-dr/di^* > 0$. Despite the distortion of capital controls, a fall in foreign inflation still improves welfare because of closer-to-optimum use of money. Since both welfare and the real rate of interest increases, it is clear from the optimisation problem in Appendix 1 that future private consumption Z^2 also increases. To ensure market clearing for non-traded goods in the second period, the future real exchange rate, θ^2, must rise. It has already been observed that θ^1 falls. Thus, over time, the real exchange rate rises, i.e. $-d\pi^0/di^* > 0$. In contrast to the neutral effect in the first model, the impact of the hard currency policy is to drive up the real exchange rate.

To summarise: A fall in foreign inflation in the presence of exchange controls leads to a rise in the real interest rate and the real exchange rate and to a fall in consumption. Of course, these have very limited implications for output, employment and welfare in a market-clearing model.

V. CAPITAL CONTROLS WITH KEYNESIAN UNEMPLOYMENT

In sections III and IV, it was assumed that all markets clear instantaneously. This section completes the model by allowing for the likelihood that the market for non-traded goods (and implicitly labour) may not clear in the short run. This occurs because the *nominal* price of non-traded goods P_1^N is sticky due to explicit contacts. Since the nominal exchange rate is fixed, this means that the *real* exchange rate θ^1 is also sticky. The present analysis follows Moore (1987) which is in the tradition of the intertemporal disequilibrium literature.[2] It assumes that the stickiness only persists in the short run, i.e. for the first period in our model. This could lead to either excess demand or supply in the non-traded goods market: however, it is suggested that only the latter is empirically relevant in western economies. Thus output of non-traded goods is demand-determined in the first period:

$$dy_1 = dy_1^N = \frac{\delta C_1^N}{\delta z^1}\, dz^1 \qquad (5.1)^3$$

In the second period, there is no price stickiness so that $y^2 = \bar{y}^2$.

There are *four* equilibrium conditions for the model. Two of these have already been given in section IV, as equations (4.2) and (4.3). The real interest rate determination equation (4.4) can be simplified because of the assumption of price stickiness:

$$r = h\,[\,r^*, f, \theta^2(z^2)\,] \qquad (5.2)$$

In effect, (5.2) includes the assumption that in the long run, non-traded goods prices flex-up and the market clears. The fourth equilibrium condition has already been stated in equation (5.1).

It is easy to show that the main results of section IV carry over into the disequilibrium context. Thus a fall in the foreign rate of inflation leads to a *rise* in the real interest rate, a *rise* in the rate of change of the real exchange rate and a *fall* in consumption in the short run. In a market-clearing world, these have limited output or employment consequences but with demand deficiency this is no longer the case. The fall in consumption causes a fall in the demand and thus output of non-traded goods. With traded goods output

2. Key references are Persson and Svennson (1983), Van Wijnbergen (1985) and Moore and Neary (1986). See Moore (1987) for additional references.

3. The first equality in (5.1) follows from the discussion on real income in section II.

fixed at its natural level, this implies that overall output falls in the short run as a consequence of the fall in the foreign rate of inflation,

In the market-clearing worlds of sections III and IV, the effect of a fall in foreign inflation was to increase domestic welfare. Because of the demand-induced fall in output, this may no longer be the case. There are two conflicting effects on welfare. It tends to rise following a fall in the foreign nominal rates of interest and inflation. This is the conventional benefit of closer-to-optimum use of money. However, the induced fall in output which is specific to sticky price models works in the opposite direction, i.e. towards a fall in welfare. This ambiguity cannot be resolved *a priori*. However the policy change to a hard currency peg is more likely to decrease welfare, the higher the marginal propensity to consume non-traded goods. For further technical details, see Appendix 4.

VI. LIMITATIONS OF THE MODELS

There are a number of unsatisfactory features which are common to the three models in the present study.

All of the behavioural implications flow from the choices of households: there is no production sector to speak of: thus there are no inventories and no capital accumulation. The neglect of firm behaviour also means that supply-side channels through a variable labour supply or through imported intermediate goods are ignored. However much of the literature on open economy intertemporal models suffers from this limitation. For example, Adams and Greenwood (1985), various papers by Obstfeld (1981, 1982, 1986) and Svennson and Razin (1983). For an exception, see Moore (1988). As it stands, the models are not designed to address supply-side issues. However a tractably designed model for the supply side might well be unable to handle the issues which are discussed here.

It has been assumed that the Government runs balanced budgets. However, the countries mentioned in the introduction have typically done nothing of the sort. In a perfect foresight world such as is considered here, budgets must be balanced intertemporally. The difficulties of drawing results from models where transversality conditions do not hold are well known. Nevertheless, it is possible that governments could be obliged, for political reasons, to monetise the current fiscal deficit. In terms of the three models in this study, the government would be restricted in the setting of μ, domestic credit expansion.

This latter effect can easily give to credibility problems for a hard currency peg. In this way, an additional wedge could be driven between the foreign and domestic nominal interest rate. This would be particularly important if the private sector believed that the Government had a policy rule whereby 'excessive' rises in the real exchange rate would be reversed by nominal devaluations. In terms of the second and third models presented here, such expected devaluations would diminish the insulation effects of capital controls and thus make the results less relevant.

VII. CONCLUSION

This paper has examined the consequences for a small open economy of adopting a hard currency exchange rate regime. This was stylised as an exogenous fall in the foreign rate of inflation. An intertemporal version of the dependent economy model was used to analyse the consequences of such a change for, *inter alia*, the real interest rate, the real exchange rate, output and welfare. It was shown that the key source of non-neutrality for this type of disinflation policy was the presence of capital controls. When the capital market distortion is confounded by short-run demand deficiency, output and possibly welfare losses will arise.

Central Bank of Ireland.

APPENDIX 1

More on Microfoundation

A single aggregate household derives utility from two goods – traded and non-traded goods – over two periods.

$$U[C_1^N, C_1^T, C_2^N, C_2^T] \tag{A1.1}$$

where C_i^N, $i = 1, 2$ is consumption of non-traded goods in each period.

C_i^T, $i = 1, 2$ is consumption of traded goods in each period.

Following Svennson and Razin (1983) and Moore (1986), we assume that (A1.1) is intertemporally homogeneously separable, i.e.

$$U\,[z^1\,(C_1^N C_1^T),\quad z^2\,(C_2^N C_2^T)] \tag{A1.2}$$

The subutility functions z^1 and z^2 are linearly homogenous: z^1 and z^2 can also be interpreted as real consumption in each period.

$$P_i\,z^i\,(C_i^N\,C_i^T) = P_i^N\,C_i^N + P_i^T\,C_i^T \qquad i = 1, 2 \tag{A1.3}$$

where P_i^N and P_i^T, $i = 1, 2$ are the nominal prices of non-traded and traded goods, respectively. P_i is a price index for period i: it is related to the observed prices P_i^N and P_i^T as follows:

$$P_i = E[P_i^N\,P_i^T\,z^i] \qquad \text{with} \quad z^i = 1 \tag{A1.4}$$

(A1.4) is a unit utility expenditure function: when z^i is also interpreted as real consumption, P_i is the minimum cost of one unit of period i goods.

Transactions are costly to conduct: part of the household's income is directly used up in this way. However, the household has the option of economising on the direct transactions cost of holding money.

The fraction of income, V_i, which is used in direct transactions costs depends on the ratio of real balances held in each period m^i to real income y_i, .i.e

$$V_i = V_i\left(\frac{m^i}{y_i}\right) = V(i)\,; \qquad 0 < V' < 1 \qquad i = 1, 2 \tag{A1.5}$$

V_i is a decreasing convex function of m^i/y_i, *i.e.* $V_i' < 0$ and $V_i'' > 0$.[4,5]

The household can also save in the form of internationally tradeable bonds paying a domestic nominal rate of interest, i, which is identical to the foreign nominal rate of interest, i^*. This equivalence follows from the

4. It is useful to note that an increase in gross income always leads to an increase in income net of transactions costs, i.e. $Q = \dfrac{\delta y_1(1-V)}{\delta y_1} = 1 - V + (m^1/y_1)\,(V') > 0.$

5. This type of monetary specification is in fact no different from assigning a non-pecuniary utility to real balances. See Feenstra (1986). It is easy to show that it is in fact equivalent to a restrictive form of money-in-the-utility function.

assumption of a permanently fixed credible nominal exchange rate and the absence of exchange controls.[6]

Since the rate of exchange is fixed and since instantaneous purchasing power parity is assumed for traded goods, we can normalise $P_i^T = (P_i^T)^*$ for $i = 1, 2$, where $(P_i^T)^*$ is the foreign price of traded goods. The rates of inflation for non-traded goods and traded goods, Π^j, $j = n, T$ are defined by $1 + \Pi^j = P_2^j / P_1^j$. The overall rate of inflation is equal to $a\Pi^n + (1 - a)\,\Pi^T$ where a is the consumption share of non-traded goods.[7] The domestic real rate of interest, r, is defined through:

$$1 + r = \frac{1+i}{1+I} = \frac{1+i^*}{1+\Pi} = \frac{(1+r^*)(1+\Pi^T)}{1+\Pi} \qquad \text{(A1.6)}$$

where r^* is the foreign real rate of interest.

Thus the household's optimisation problem can be written as a two-stage process:

$$\underset{z^1\ z^2}{Max} \quad U\,[z^1\ \ z^2]$$

Subject to

$$z^1 + m^1 + \frac{z^2}{1+r} + \frac{m^2 - m^1[P_1/P_2]}{1+r} = y_1\left[1 - V\left(\frac{m^1}{y_1}\right)\right] + t_1 + \frac{y_2\left[1 - V\left(\frac{m^2}{Y^2}\right)\right] + t_2}{1+r} \qquad \text{(A1.7)}^8$$

where t_i $i = 1, 2$ are lump-sum transfers from the authorities.

The second stage of the process is to allocate expenditure between traded and non-traded goods in each period:

$$\underset{C_i^N\, C_i^T}{\text{Max}} \quad z^i\,(C_i^N\ \ C_i^T)$$

6. This assumption is relaxed in section IV. The credibility issue is discussed in section VI.

7. This Lespeyres-type of relation is shown in Svennson and Razin (1983). Π is also equal to $P_2 / P_1 - 1$.

8. The solution to a problem similar to (A1.7) is discussed in detail in Adams and Greenwood (1985).

Subject to

$$P_i z^i (C_i^N C_i^T) = P_i^N C_i^N + P_i^T C_i^T \qquad i = 1, 2 \tag{A1.8}$$ [9]

(A1.7) and (A1.8) together yield the behavioural functions of the firm which are summarised in (A1.9) to (A1.14).

$$C_1^N = C_1^N \underset{-\quad\;\; +\quad\; -\;+}{[\theta_1, \; z^1 (r \;\; w)]} \tag{A1.9}$$

$$C_1^T = C_1^T \underset{-\quad\;\; +\quad\; -\;+}{[\theta_1, \; z^1 (r \;\; w)]} \tag{A1.10}$$

$$C_2^N = C_2^N \underset{-\quad\;\; +\quad\; +\;+}{[\theta_2, \; z^2 (r \;\; w)]} \tag{A1.11}$$

$$C_2^T = C_2^T \underset{+\quad\;\; +\quad\; +\;+}{[\theta_2, \; z^2 (r \;\; w)]} \tag{A1.12}$$

where w is normalised utility and is defined by $dw = du \div \dfrac{\delta U}{\delta z} z^1$. θ_i is the real exchange rate and is defined as the internal terms of trade P_i^N / P_i^T, i=1,2.

In addition,

$$m_1 = m_1 \, [\underset{-}{i}] \, y_1 \tag{A1.13}$$

$$m_2 = k \, y_2 \tag{A1.14}$$

where k is constant.

The rate of change of the real exchange rate Π^θ is defined as $\theta_2 / \theta_1 - 1$. It is easy to show that

$$1 + a\Pi^\theta = \frac{1 + \Pi}{1 + \Pi^T} \tag{A1.15}$$

9. (A1.7) and (A1.8) assume perfect foresight with respect to prices and exchange rates.

Thus the wedge between the domestic and foreign real interest rates can be derived from (A1.6) and (A1.15):

$$1 + r = \frac{1 + r^*}{1 + a\Pi^\theta} \tag{A1.16}$$

(A1.16) is the discrete time version of the relationship shown in Moore (1986) which states that the gap between foreign and domestic real interest rates is proportionate to the expected rate of change of the real exchange rate where the factor of proportionality is the share of non-traded goods in consumption. See also Bruno (1976) and Dornbusch (1983).

APPENDIX 2

Model I: Distortion-Free Equilibrium

1. The second-period budget constraint of the Central Bank is:

$$m^2 - \frac{m^1}{1 + \Pi} = \mu^2 - b(1 + r) \tag{A2.1}$$

where all the variables in (A2.1) are measured in terms of second-period prices.

2. The second equilibrium condition of section III equation (3.3) is the aggregate intertemporal budget constraint. It is obtained by combining the household budget constraint (A1.7) and the Central Bank's first-period budget constraint (3.1).

3. The intertemporal budget constraint can also be cast in terms of second period variables using (A2.1).

$$y_2\,[1 - V(k)] - z^2 = -(b + a)(1 + r) \tag{A2.2}$$

4. Changes in welfare are defined using a first order condition for the problem in (A1.7):

$$dw = \frac{\mathrm{d}U}{\partial U / \partial z^1} = dz^1 + \frac{dz^2}{1 + r} \tag{A2.3}$$

5. The real interest rate determination equation is derived from the real interest rate parity condition (A1.16) and from the requirement that the market for non-traded goods should instantaneously clear in each period.

$$y_i = C_i^N(\theta^i, z^i) \qquad i = 1, 2 \tag{A2.4}$$

6. Finally, the equilibrium conditions (3.2), (3.3) and (3.4) can be expressed in differentiated form evaluated at $(a + b) = 0$ as follows:

$$db = \frac{\delta m^1}{\delta i} y_1 \, di^* \tag{A2.5}$$

$$\frac{\delta z^1}{\delta r} dr + da + [1 + V^1(1)] df = V^1(1) \frac{\delta z^1}{\delta w} \frac{\delta m^1}{\delta i} y_1 \, di^* \tag{A2.6}$$

$$dr - [q_2(1 + r) - q_1] da - [q_2(1 + r) - q_1[1 + V^1(1)]] db =$$

$$\frac{(1 + r)}{(1 + r^*)} dr^* \tag{A2.7}$$

where $$q = \frac{a(1 + r)}{\theta_i} \frac{\delta C_i^N / \delta z^i}{\delta C_i^N / \delta \theta_i}, \qquad i = 1, 2.$$

Note that if the utility function in (A2.7) is additively separable and the sub-utility functions are identical, $q_1 = -q_2$.

APPENDIX 3

Model II: Capital Controls with Market Clearing

1. The primary consequence of capital controls is that they drive a wedge between the domestic and foreign nominal rates of interest. The relationship is now given by:

$$1 + i = \frac{1 + i^*}{1 + f} \tag{A3.1}$$

Similarly the domestic real rate of interest is no longer given by (A1.6), but instead:

$$1 + r = \frac{1+i}{1+\Pi} = \frac{1+i^*}{(1+f)(1+\Pi)} = \frac{1+r^*}{1+f}\,\frac{1+\Pi^T}{1+\Pi} \qquad \text{(A3.2)}$$

Finally, (A3.2) can be combined with (A1.15) to yield:

$$1 + r = \frac{1+r^*}{(1+f)(1+a\Pi^0)} \qquad \text{(A3.3)}$$

(A3.3) replaces (A1.16).

2. The second period budget constraint of the financial exchange rate authority is:

$$T_2 = \left[\left(\frac{\bar{e} - S_2}{S_1}\right)\left(\frac{1+i^*}{1+\Pi}\right)\right] a = \left[\left(\frac{\bar{e} - S_2}{S_1}\right)(1+r)(1+f)\right] a \qquad \text{(A3.4)}$$

3. The complete system (4.2) to (4.4) is rewritten in differentiated form, evaluated at $(\overline{ca} - b) = 0$ as follows:

$$\frac{\delta m^1}{\delta i} y_1 \frac{(1+i)}{(1+f)} df + db = \frac{\delta m^1}{\delta i} y_1 \frac{1+i}{1+i^*} di^* \qquad \text{(A3.5)}$$

$$\frac{\delta z^1}{\delta r} dr + \left[\frac{\delta z^1}{\delta w}(1+f) + [1 + V^1(1)]\left(1 - \frac{\delta z^1}{\delta w}\right)\right] db = 0 \qquad \text{(A3.6)}$$

$$dr + \frac{(1+r)}{(1+f)} df - [q_2(1+r)(1+f) - q_1[1 + V^1(1)]]\, db =$$

$$\frac{(1+r)}{(1+r^*)} dr^* \qquad \text{(A3.7)}$$

APPENDIX 4

Model III: Capital Controls with Keynesian Unemployment

The four equilibrium conditions (4.2), (4.3), (5.1) and (5.2) in differentiated form are:

$$\frac{\delta m^1}{\delta i} y_1 \frac{(1+i)}{(1+f)} df + db - \frac{m^1}{y_1} dy_1 = \frac{\delta m^1}{\delta i} y_1 \frac{(1+i)}{(1+i^*)} di^* \qquad \text{(A4.1)}$$

$$\frac{\delta z^1}{\delta r} dr + \left[\frac{\delta z^1}{\delta w}(1+f) + [1+V^1(1)]\left[1 - \frac{\delta z_1}{\delta w}\right]\right] db -$$

$$Q\left[1 - \frac{\delta z_1}{\delta w}\right] dy_1 = 0 \qquad \text{(A4.2)}$$

$$[1+V^1(1)] \frac{\delta C^N}{\delta z} db + [1 - \frac{\delta C^N}{\delta z} Q]\, dy_1 = 0 \qquad \text{(A4.3)}$$

$$dr + \frac{(1+r)}{(1+f)} df - [q_2(1+r)(1+f)]\, db = \frac{(1+r)}{(1+r^*)} dr^* \qquad \text{(A4.4)}$$

For a definition of $Q > 0$ see Appendix 1.

2. The effect of a fall in the nominal interest on output is:

$$-\frac{\partial y_1}{\partial i^*} = \frac{\partial C_1^N}{\partial z^1}\left[-\frac{\partial z}{\partial i^*}\right] < 0 \qquad \text{(A4.5)}$$

The absolute value of this effect is proportional to $\partial C^N/\partial z$. The marginal propensity to consume non-traded goods is $\frac{P_1^N}{P_1} \cdot \frac{\partial C_1^N}{\partial z^1}$

3. The effect of a fall in i^* on welfare is :

$$-\frac{\partial w}{\partial i^*} = Q\left[-\frac{dy}{di^*}\right] + [f - V^1 + (1)]\left[-\frac{db}{di^*}\right] \qquad \text{(A4.6)}$$

It is easy to show that $[f - V^1(1)] = \frac{i^*}{1+i} > 0$ (See Adams and Greenwood (1985)). Thus the two components of (A4.6) have opposite signs.

REFERENCES

Adams, Charles and Greenwood, Jeremy (1985) 'Dual Exchange Rates and Capital Controls: An Investigation', *Journal of International Economics*, 18: 43–63.

Bruno, M. (1976) 'The Two-Sector Open Economy and the Real Exchange Rate', *American Economic Review*, 66: 566–577.

Buiter, W.H. and Miller, M. (1981) 'Monetary Policy and International Competitiveness: The Problems of Adjustment', *Oxford Economic Papers*, 33: 143–175.

—— (1982) 'Real Exchange Rate Overshooting and the Output Cost of Bringing Down Inflation', *European Economic Review*, 18: 83–123.

—— (1983) 'Real Exchange Rate Overshooting and the Output Cost of Bringing Down Inflation: Some Further Results', in J.A. Frenkel (ed.), *Exchange Rates and International Macroeconomics*, (Chicago: University of Chicago Press).

Dornbusch, R. (1983) 'Real Interest Rates, Home Goods and Optimal External Borrowing', *Journal of Political Economy*, 91: 141–153.

Dornbusch, Rudiger and Frenkel, Jacob (1973) 'Inflation and Growth: Alternative Approaches', *Journal of Money, Credit and Banking*, 5(1): 141–156.

Feenstra, Robert, C. (1986) 'Functional Equivalence between Liquidity Costs and the Utility of Money', *Journal of Monetary Economics*, 17 (2): 251–270.

Greenwood, Jeremy (1983) 'Expectations, the Exchange Rate and the Current Account', *Journal of Monetary Economics*, 12: 543–569.

—— (1984) 'Non-Traded Goods, the Trade Balance and the Balance of Payments', *Canadian Journal of Economics*, 17: 806–823.

Moore, Michael, J. (1986) 'Exchange Rate Dynamics, Relative Price Stickiness and Wealth Effects in an Optimising Model', Central Bank of Ireland Technical Paper 9/RT/86.

—— (1987) 'Dual Exchange Rates, Capital Controls and Sticky Prices', Central Bank of Ireland Technical Paper 6/RT/87.

—— (1988) 'Inventories in the Open Economy Macro Model: A Disequilibrium Analysis', *Review of Economic Studies*, (Forthcoming).

Moore, M.J. and Neary, J.P. (1986) 'Disequilibre Intertemporal dans une Economie Ouverte', in P.Y. Henin *et al*, 'Disequilibres en Economie Ouverte', (Paris: *Economica*). An earlier version was available (in English) in June 1984, (University College Dublin, Centre for Economic Research, Working Paper No. 23).

Obstfeld, Maurice (1981) 'Macroeconomic Policy, Exchange Rate Dynamics and Optimal Asset Accumulation', *Journal of Political Economy*, 89 : 1142-1161, (December).

—— (1982) 'Aggregate Spending and the Terms of Trade: Is there a Laursen-Metzler Effect? ', *Quarterly Journal of Economics*, 97 : 251-270.

—— (1986) 'Capital Controls, the Dual Exchange Rate and Devaluation', *Journal of International Economics*, 20 : 1-20.

Persson, T. and Svennson, L.E.O. (1983) 'Is Optimism Good in a Keynesian Economy? ', *Economica*, 50 : 291-300.

Svennson, L.E.O. and Razin, A. (1983) 'The Terms of Trade and the Current Account: the Harberger-Laursen-Metzler Effect', *Journal of Political Economy*, 91 : 97-125.

Van Wijnbergen, S. (1985) 'Oil Price Shocks, Unemployment, Investment and the Current Account: An Intertemporal Disequilibrium Analysis', *Review of Economic Studies*, 52 : 627-645.

PART III

THE NATURE OF ECONOMIC INTERDEPENDENCE

MACROECONOMIC INTERDEPENDENCE, FLOATING EXCHANGE RATES, AND PRODUCT SUBSTITUTABILITY

By Neil Rankin*

I. INTRODUCTION

The "standard" results on macroeconomic interdependence are those originally derived in a two-country, IS-LM-based model of the world economy by Mundell (1968). Under perfect capital mobility and floating exchange rates, Mundell found that a fiscal expansion in one country had an expansionary effect abroad, while a monetary expansion had a contractionary foreign effect. Under fixed exchange rates, these effects were reversed. In this paper, we re-examine Mundell's results for floating exchange rates in an intertemporal, disequilibrium version of this original two-country model. As a preliminary to this, we also start by looking at a "small open" version of the same model, which is the counterpart of the Mundell-Fleming model of textbook fame. Our approach thus derives from recent applications of "disequilibrium" model-building technology to open economies, originated by Dixit (1978) and Neary (1980), and further exemplified in the collections of papers by Cuddington *et al.* (1984), and Henin *et al.* (1985). The thrust of this work is to obtain new insights by imposing more microeconomic structure on macroeconomic models, but without thereby restricting them to be of a neoclassical or Walrasian nature.

The particular feature of the present model is its two-period, intertemporal structure in which nominal rigidities generate disequilibrium and unemployment in period one (the "short run"), while perfect flexibility, guaranteeing full employment, is restored in period two (the "long run"). Such a framework for analysis of open economies has notably been employed by van Wijnbergen (1985, 1986). Within it, a number of major possibilities for the structure of a two-country model exist to be explored, including differences with

* Financial support through the CEPR "International Macroeconomics" programme from the Rockefeller Foundation for the project on "The Conduct of Macroeconomic Policy by Interdependent Countries and Blocs" (GA-IR-8603) is gratefully acknowledged. Thanks, but no responsibility, go to David Currie and Marco Vannini for helpful conversations.

regard to, first, the number and substitutability of the products of the two countries, and, second, the presence or absence of price rigidities in particular markets. A companion paper to this one (Rankin (1989)) considers one extreme in which the countries' outputs are perfect substitutes, and the only nominal rigidities are in wages. Here, we take outputs to be imperfect substitutes, and consider both the price and wage to be rigid. The resulting model is much closer to Mundell's, since it does not constrain the real exchange rate to equal unity, and since it incorporates product as well as labour market disequilibrium.

The key finding is that the degree of substitutability between the countries' products is critical to the nature of macroeconomic interdependence. When the products are gross substitutes, both monetary and fiscal policy have contractionary effects abroad. When they are gross complements, these effects are both expansionary. In the intermediate case, there are no foreign effects at all. This is a significant modification of Mundell's (1968) results, in which the exact degree of substitutability did not appear to be of any importance. The results for the gross substitutes case are similar to those in the companion paper, where, however, the possibility of positive foreign fiscal effects remained open.

The structure of the paper is as follows. Section II details the underlying assumptions and derives individual behaviour. In section III, these elements are combined to obtain a small open economy model. The two-country model, permitting the study of interdependence, is constructed in section IV. Conclusions, both specific and more general, are drawn in section V.

II. THE STRUCTURE OF AN INDIVIDUAL ECONOMY

The world lasts for two periods, and the individual country each consists of three agents : a representative household, a representative firm, and the government. The model is non-stochastic, and all agents have perfect foresight. In any period, three real commodities are traded : labour, which is internationally immobile and the only input to production; the domestic output; and the foreign output. Both the latter are consumed in each country. Two assets are issued by each government: money, and interest-bearing bonds. Perfect international mobility of capital is assumed, so that both governments' bonds are perfect substitutes.

In the first period, the money wage and output price are rigid, at levels such as to cause excess supply in both markets. This distinguishes the model from that in Rankin(1989), where the goods price was assumed to be flexible, allowing the goods market to clear. Thus, in the present model, changes in demand give rise to pure quantity spillovers from the goods to the labour market and back again: the disequilibrium regime is truly one of "Keynesian unemployment", in the sense of Malinvaud (1977). In the previous treatment, by contrast, demand only affects output through raising the goods price and depressing the real wage, so stimulating firms' notional demand for labour. In the second period, both the wage and the price level are flexible. Labour supply is taken to be exogenous, so that the clearing of the labour market then fixes output at some exogenous level. In both periods bond prices, and hence interest rates, are also flexible, moving to equate demand and supply for money. The model is thus intentionally as similar as possible to the IS-LM framework employed by Mundell.

Turning to the optimisation problems of individual agents, that of the household is to maximise utility from the consumption of the two outputs in each of the two periods, and from real money balances held at the end of each period. The presence of the latter represents the implicit "liquidity services", in terms of facilitating transactions, which money is assumed to provide. Such a derivation of the demand for money, while a short cut, is no more simplistic than the device of imposing a "cash-in-advance" constraint used in a number of recent open-economy monetary models, and avoids the severe restriction on the velocity of circulation which this alternative imposes.[1]

The household's choice problem may then be expressed as :

$$\max \quad u\left(h_1, f_1, \frac{M_1}{p_2}; \ h_2, f_2, \frac{M_2}{p_2}\right)$$

$$\text{s.t.} \qquad a = h_1 + e_1 f_1 + id\frac{P_2}{p_2}\frac{M_1}{P_2} + dh_2 + de_2 f_2 + d\frac{P_2}{p_2}\frac{M_2}{P_2} \tag{1}$$

where

a = lifetime real assets (see below)
h_t, f_t = consumption of home and foreign goods (respectively)
p_t, p_t^* = (exogenous) own-currency prices of the above
e_t $\equiv E_t p_t / p_t^*$ = real exchange rate
E_t = nominal exchange rate (the home-currency price of foreign currency)
M_t = end-of-period nominal money holdings
i_t = nominal interest rate
d = real discount factor ($= 1/[1 + r]$, where r is the real interest rate)

1. The cash-in-advance constraint is used, for example, in a small open economy by Cuddington and Vinals (1986), and in a two-country model by Persson (1982). The latter acknowledges that it is responsible for his special result that monetary policy has no foreign effects.

The symbol * will be used generally to indicate variables pertaining to the foreign country. P_2, used to deflate M_1 and M_2, is an index of p_2 and $E_2 p_2^*$: since M_1 is presumably held mainly to buy goods in period two, this is the relevant deflator for both periods. The lifetime budget constraint (1) may be derived from the household's single-period budget constraints by combining them to eliminate bond holdings in the usual way. Lifetime real assets or wealth are exogenous to the household and defined by:

$$a = \frac{M_0}{p_1} + y_1 - \tau_t + d\,[y_2 - \tau_2] \tag{2}$$

where M_0 = initial money holdings, y_t = real domestic output and income, τ_t = a lump-sum tax. The inclusion of y_t reflects the assumption that both wage and profit income are immediately distributed.

From the way the choice problem is expressed, it is clear that the general set of arguments of the demand functions which result from solving it is $(a, e_1, e_2, i, d, P_2/p_2)$. To make the model tractable, some restriction on these functions, and thus on the form of the utility function, is necessary. For present purposes, we adopt a nested Cobb-Douglas / CES form, which permits variation of the degree of substitutability between the countries' products, but also enables an important simplification of the model's structure:

$$u = c_1^{\alpha}\left(\frac{M_1}{p_2}\right)^{\gamma} c_2^{\delta}\left(\frac{M_2}{p_2}\right)^{\zeta} \tag{3}$$

with $$c_t = [\beta h_t^{\rho} + [1 - \beta] f_t^{\rho}]^{1/\rho} \qquad t = 1, 2$$

and $$\alpha, \gamma, \delta, \zeta > 0, \quad \alpha + \gamma + \delta + \zeta = 1, \quad 0 < \beta < 1, \quad \rho < 1.$$

The elasticity of substitution between home and foreign goods is given by $1/[1 - \rho]$, whence an elasticity greater than one is implied by $\rho > 0$ and an elasticity less than one by $\rho < 0$. The special case $\rho = 0$ yields the fully Cobb-Douglas function, with a substitution elasticity of unity.

The resulting demand functions are listed below. In order to assist the understanding, they are written first in a schematic notation and then explicitly:

$$h_1 = \underset{+\ \ ?}{h_1(a, e_1)} = \alpha a \frac{1}{1 + \varphi(e_1)} \tag{4a}$$

$$f_1 = \underset{+\ \ -}{f_1(a, e_1)} = \frac{\alpha a}{e_1} \frac{\varphi(e_1)}{1 + \varphi(e_1)} \tag{4b}$$

$$M_1/P_2 = \underset{+\ -\ -\quad -}{m_1(a, i, d, P_2/p_2)} = \frac{\gamma a}{i d P_2/p_2} \tag{4c}$$

$$h_2 = \underset{+\ -\ ?}{h_2(a, d, e_2)} = \frac{\delta a}{d}\frac{1}{1+\varphi(e_2)} \tag{4d}$$

$$f_2 = \underset{+\ -\ -}{f_2(a, d, e_2)} = \frac{\delta a}{d e_2}\frac{\varphi(e_2)}{1+\varphi(e_2)} \tag{4e}$$

$$M_2/P_2 = \underset{+\quad -\quad -}{m_2(a, d, P_2/p_2)} = \frac{\zeta a}{d P_2/p_2} \tag{4f}$$

where

$$\varphi(e_t) \equiv \left(\frac{1-\beta}{\beta}\right)^{\frac{1}{1-\rho}} e_t^{\frac{\rho}{\rho-1}} \qquad t = 1, 2. \tag{5}$$

Signs under variables are those of the respective partial derivatives. Note that $h_1 + e_1 f_1 = \alpha a$, $h_2 + e_2 f_2 = \delta a/d$, i.e. the demands for total consumption expenditure in any period have simple Cobb-Douglas forms, with the exchange rate only affecting the division between domestic and imported goods.

Consider now the microeconomic behaviour of the representative firm. In the first period, facing a quantity constraint on its output, the firm simply demands whatever labour is necessary to produce this. Since profits as well as wages are immediately distributed to the household, goods demand is unaffected by the division of income. The shape of the production function thus plays no part in the determination of output. In the second period, the firm fully employs the exogenous labour supply, so that output is fixed by this in combination with the production function.

We turn thirdly to the government, whose policy choice is subject to the intertemporal budget constraint:

$$g_1 + d g_2 - \tau_1 - d\tau_2 = \frac{1}{1+i}\frac{M_2}{p_1} + \frac{i}{1+i}\frac{M_1}{p_1} - \frac{M_0}{p_1}. \tag{6}$$

In both periods, the government makes purchases of domestic output g_t, and imposes a lump-sum tax on the household, τ_t. In period one, any deficit is financed by issuing money or bonds. In period two, when the world ends, all bonds must be redeemed, so that only money is available to finance any deficit. We assume no initial outstanding debt. Like that for the household, the intertemporal budget constraint may be derived by combining the government's single-period constraints to eliminate bond issues. Clearly only five of the six policy instruments $(g_1, g_2, \tau_1, \tau_2, M_1, M_2)$ can be independent. The results of any comparative static exercise will depend on which one responds passively when another is changed. We choose τ_2 as the passive instrument, since this allows (g_1, g_2, M_1, M_2) to be chosen independently, so keeping monetary and fiscal changes separate. τ_2 is then endogenous, and it is convenient to substitute it out of (2) using (6), which yields :

$$a = y_1 - g_1 + d[y_2 - g_2] + \frac{i}{1+i}\frac{M_1}{p_1} + \frac{1}{1+i}\frac{M_2}{p_1} \tag{7}$$

A consequence of having a single household whose life is co-extensive with that of the economy, is that government bonds will not be part of the household's "net wealth". That is, a bond issue brought about by a cut in τ_1 will result in a rise in τ_2 of equal present value, exactly offsetting the value of the bonds in the household's lifetime wealth. This can already be seen indirectly from the fact that τ_1 has been eliminated from (7). Cuts in τ_1 are thus neutral, and, for the same reason, all changes in government spending are effectively "balanced-budget" changes: bond-financing is equivalent to tax-financing.

III. A SMALL OPEN ECONOMY

The small open economy is interesting both for its own sake and because it assists the understanding of the more complex, two-country model. In this case it is assumed that the country is a price-taker in the international markets for the imported good and for capital. Thus the foreign real interest rate or discount factor, d^*, and foreign lifetime real assets, a^*, are exogenous; while the equilibrium values of (y_1, d, i, e_1, e_2) are determined by the conditions:

$$y_1 = h_1(a, e_1) + g_1 + f_1^*\left(a^*, \frac{1}{e_1}\right) \tag{8a}$$

$$\bar{y}_2 = h_2(a, d, e_2) + g_2 + f_2^*\left(a^*, d^*, \frac{1}{e_2}\right) \tag{8b}$$

$$\frac{M_1}{P_2} = m_1\left(a, i, d, \frac{P_2}{p_2}\right) \tag{8c}$$

$$f_1^*\left(a^*, \frac{1}{e_1}\right) - e_1 f_1(a, e_1) = -d\left[f_2^*\left(a^*, d^*, \frac{1}{e_2}\right) - e_2 f_2(a, d, e_2)\right] \tag{8d}$$

$$e_1 d^* = e_2 d \tag{8e}$$

where

$$a = y_1 - g_1 + d[\bar{y}_2 - g_2] + \frac{i}{1+i}\frac{M_1}{p_1} + \frac{1}{1+i}\frac{M_2}{p_1}. \tag{9}$$

(8a) states that output in period one is demand-determined, while (8b) equates goods demand in period two to its exogenous supply, $\bar{y}_2$; (8c) imposes money market equilibrium; (8d) is an intertemporal balance of payments equilibrium condition, requiring that any first-period surplus on the current account should be matched by a second-period deficit of equal present value. This is the same as saying that the economy as a whole must satisfy its intertemporal budget constraint (see (11) below). (8e) is the uncovered interest parity condition which follows from perfect capital mobility; (9) was previously derived as (7).

Since it consists of five simultaneous equations, even this small open version of the model is potentially rather complex. However, a number of major simplifications are possible. First, we shall in general analyse its properties assuming an initial position where $M_1 = M_2$. From (9), this eliminates the dependence of a on i. Given this, the system (8a-e) is block-recursive, in that i then only appears in (8c), allowing the remaining equations to be solved independently for (y_1, d, e_1, e_2). This already brings out a notable difference in the structure of the present model from that of Mundell-Fleming. In the latter, the LM equation is central, since it is this alone which determines output. Here, the LM equation is solved last, and plays no role in determining output. It may be noted that (8c) appears to contain two extra unknowns, P_2 and p_2. However, using the explicit form of the money demand function from (4c), P_2 cancels; while p_2 may be substituted out as $p_1[1+i]d$, so that (8c) reduces to:

$$\frac{M_1}{p_1[1+i]} = \frac{\gamma a}{i}. \tag{10}$$

We next show how the sub-system consisting of (8a,b,d,e) may be reduced to two relationships in (e_1, e_2), enabling the model to be drawn in two dimensions. Substituting the expression for a given by (7) into the household's intertemporal budget constraint (1), gives the following budget constraint for the country as a whole:

$$y_1 + dy_2 = h_1 + g_1 + e_1 f_1 + d[h_2 + g_2 + e_2 f_2]. \tag{11}$$

(11) simply states that the lifetime value of the country's production must equal the lifetime value of consumption plus government spending. Inserting into the R.H.S. the explicit forms of the demand functions (4a-e) yields:

$$y_1 + dy_2 = \alpha a + g_1 + \delta a + dg_2$$

Hence

$$\begin{aligned} y_1 - g_1 + d[y_2 - g_2] &= [\alpha + \delta]\, a \\ &= [\alpha + \delta]\left[y_1 - g_1 + d[y_2 - g_2] + \frac{i}{1+i}\frac{M_1}{p_1} + \frac{1}{1+i}\frac{M_2}{p_1}\right] \end{aligned}$$

using (7). Noting $\alpha + \gamma + \delta + \zeta = 1$,

$$y_1 - g_1 + d[y_2 - g_2] = \frac{\alpha + \delta}{\gamma + \zeta}\left[\frac{i}{1+i}\frac{M_1}{p_1} + \frac{1}{1+i}\frac{M_2}{p_1}\right]$$

Therefore

$$\begin{aligned} a &= y_1 - g_1 + d[y_2 - g_2] + \frac{i}{1+i}\frac{M_1}{p_1} + \frac{1}{1+i}\frac{M_2}{p_1} \\ &= \frac{1}{\gamma + \zeta}\left[\frac{i}{1+i}\frac{M_1}{p_1} + \frac{1}{1+i}\frac{M_2}{p_1}\right] \end{aligned} \tag{12}$$

(12) shows that when the model is solved choosing $M_1 = M_2 = M$, a becomes the exogenous quantity $\frac{1}{\gamma+\zeta}\frac{M}{p_1}$. Since we adopt this assumption in what follows, a may now be regarded as an exogenous monetary policy variable.

With the dependence of a on y_1, removed, it can now be seen that (8b,d,e) can be solved independently for (d, e_1, e_2). Further, if (8e) is used to substitute out d as $e_1 d^* / e_2$, this system can be reduced to two relationships in (e_1, e_2). Equations (13) and (14) are obtained by these means (also introducing the explicit functional forms from (4) and slightly rearranging):

$$d^*[y_2 - g_2] = \frac{e_2}{e_1}\frac{\delta a}{1 + \varphi(e_2)} + e_2 \delta^* a^* \frac{\varphi^*(1/e_2)}{1 + \varphi^*(1/e_2)} \tag{13}$$

$$e_1 = \frac{a^*}{a}\,\frac{\alpha \dfrac{\varphi(e_1)}{1 + \varphi(e_1)} + \delta \dfrac{\varphi(e_2)}{1 + \varphi(e_2)}}{\alpha^* \dfrac{\varphi^*(1/e_1)}{1 + \varphi^*(1/e_1)} + \delta^* \dfrac{\varphi^*(1/e_2)}{1 + \varphi^*(1/e_2)}} \tag{14}$$

The comparative statics may thus be studied by graphing these two relationships and considering how they are affected by various shocks. From this the changes in (e_1, e_2) may be found, which information can then be used in (8a) to determine the impact on y_1. (8a) re-written with the explicit forms of the demand functions becomes :

$$y_1 = \alpha a \frac{1}{1 + \varphi(e_1)} + g_1 + \alpha^* a^* e_1 \frac{\varphi^*(1/e_1)}{1 + \varphi^*(1/e_1)} \tag{15}$$

We first consider the case where $\rho, \rho^* > 0$, i.e. where households' elasticity of substitution between home and foreign goods is greater than one, both at home and abroad. Note from (5) that $\varphi(.)$ is then a strictly decreasing function, and from (4a) and (4d) that home and foreign goods are gross substitutes, i.e. $\partial h_t/\partial e_t > 0$. When $\rho < 0$, conversely, $\varphi(.)$ is strictly increasing, and home and foreign goods are gross complements, i.e. $\partial h_t/\partial e_t < 0$. In the intermediate, "Cobb-Douglas" case in which $\rho = 0$, φ is a constant and there are no cross-price effects. This is a useful reference point, since the model's properties are then drastically simplified. Figure 1 depicts the relationships (13) and (14).

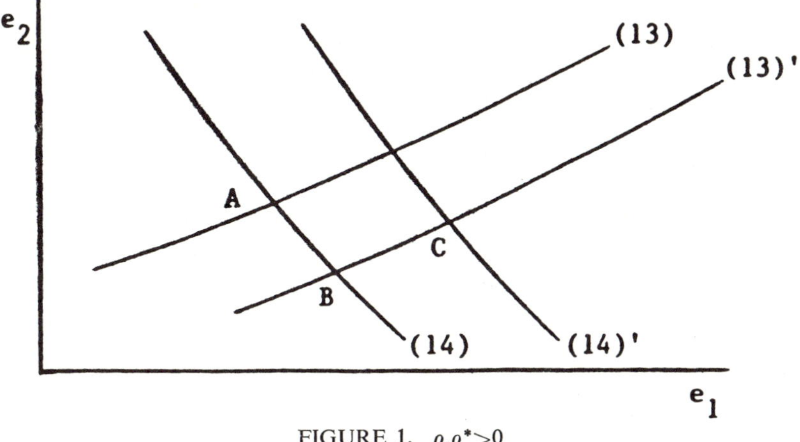

FIGURE 1. $\varrho, \varrho^* > 0$

Inspection of (13) confirms that it is positively-sloped in the gross substitutes case, since the R.H.S. is unambiguously decreasing in e_1 and increasing in e_2. Similarly, (14) must be negatively-sloped, since the R.H.S. is unambiguously decreasing in e_2, while e_1 unambiguously raises the L.H.S. and lowers the R.H.S.

Fiscal Policy

Fiscal policy in the present model consists of changes in g_1 or g_2. As observed earlier, all such changes are effectively "balanced-budget" ones, since government debt is neutral in the model. This fact should especially be borne in mind when considering the effect of a rise in g_1. It can be seen that g_1 does not enter (13) or (14), either directly or indirectly. Thus it has no effect on the real exchange rates in the two periods. Referring to (15), it follows that $dy_1/dg_1 = 1$. There is a clear difference here from the Mundell-Fleming model, where the exchange rate appreciates and output is unchanged (under either deficit-financing or tax-financing). A simple explanation for this difference may be found in the fact that, here, where all demands are derived from household optimisation, the demands for imports and money depend on (the present value of) disposable rather than gross income. This is clear from (2), the original definition of a. If such a specification were employed in the traditional Mundell-Fleming model, we would have, in an obvious notation:

$$Y = C(Y - T) + G + B(Y - T, e) \qquad \text{IS}$$

$$M = L(Y - T, \bar{r}) \qquad \text{LM}$$

Under balanced-budget conditions in which $T = G$, it is clear that the LM equation determines $Y - G$ rather than Y, which guarantees a multiplier of one. At the same time the IS equation uniquely links e to $Y - G$, explaining why e is unaffected by G. Thus, by overlooking the possible dependence of the import and money demand functions on taxation, the traditional model obtains unduly pessimistic results for fiscal policy. By deriving behaviour from individual optimisation, such an oversight is automatically avoided.[2]

Looking at g_2, it can be seen that this does enter (13), though not (14). Higher g_2 clearly requires higher e_1 at any level of e_2, so shifting the curve of (13) to the right in Figure 1. In the new equilibrium at B, e_1 is higher and e_2 lower. An anticipated future increase in government spending thus appreciates the future real exchange rate, but depreciates the current one. Referring to (15), it can be seen that y_1 is positively related to e_1, whence current output expands. This again contributes to the view that the Mundell-Fleming outlook on fiscal

2. An early analysis of the consequences of the demand for money depending on disposable income in a closed-economy, IS-LM, context, is by Holmes and Smyth (1972). It is easily shown that the balanced-budget multiplier is unity here too, and that there is no effect on the interest rate. Identical behaviour was obtained in Rankin (1985), for a disequilibrium version of the closed-economy IS-LM model. Some empirical evidence bearing on the question is discussed in Marselli and Vannini (1987).

policy is excessively gloomy. A permanent increase in spending, i.e. an equal rise in g_1 and g_2, would have a still greater impact.

The picture is altered somewhat if home and foreign goods are gross complements, i.e. $\rho,\rho^* < 0$. To analyse this case, it is useful to consider also the intermediate situation where $\rho = \rho^* = 0$. Since φ is then a constant, (13) remains positively-sloped, while (14) becomes a vertical line, determining e_1 by itself. A rise in g_2, shifting (13) right, now leaves e_1 unaffected, and thus, by (15), it has no effect on y_1 either. For $\rho,\rho^* < 0$, $\varphi(.)$ is an increasing function. This makes the slopes of both curves *prima facie* ambiguous. However, note from (5) that φ increases less than proportionately to e_t. It can then be seen

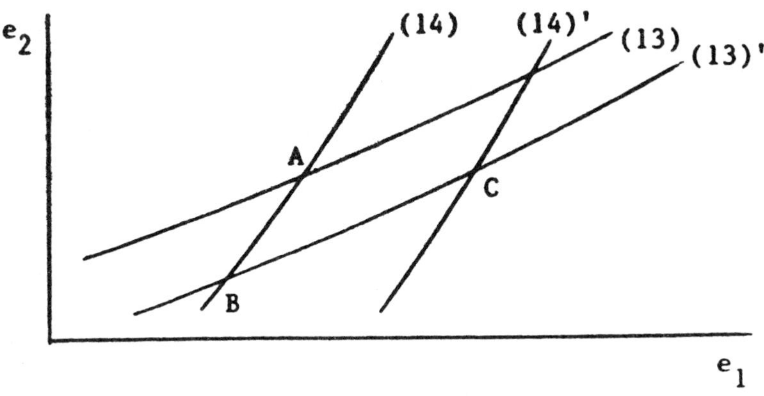

FIGURE 2. $\varrho,\varrho^* < 0$

that the R.H.S. of (13) is still increasing in e_2, so the positive slope is retained. The R.H.S. of (14) is now increasing, rather than decreasing, in (e_1,e_2), creating an uncertainty as to whether a rise in e_1 still causes the L.H.S. to exceed the R.H.S. Note that the R.H.S. rises less than proportionately to φ/φ^*. When $\rho = \rho^*$, $\varphi/\varphi^* = \left(\frac{[1-\beta]\beta^*}{\beta[1-\beta^*]}\right)^{1/[1-\rho]} e_1^{2\rho/[\rho-1]}$, which increases less than proportionately to e_1 if $\rho > -1$. This is therefore a sufficient, though not necessary, condition for (14) now to have a positive slope. For ρ,ρ^* sufficiently close to zero, (14) will be close to the vertical, and thus steeper than (13). A rise in g_2, shifting (13) right, now lowers rather than raises e_1. The effect of this on y_1, from (15), is at first glance ambiguous. However greater reflection shows that it is negative for ρ,ρ^* sufficiently close to zero, when the positive dependence of φ on e_t is weak. Gross complementarity thus reverses the impact of g_2. The impact of g_1 is clearly unaltered, so that the net effect of a permanent increase in g would still be positive for small absolute values of ρ,ρ^*, though possibly negative for larger ones.

These and other comparative static results are summarised in Table 1. The effect of fiscal policy on d is easily deduced from the effects on e_1 and e_2, given that $d = d^* e_1/e_2$. The effect on the current account surplus, b, may be seen by examining :

$$b \equiv f_1^* - e_1 f_1 = \alpha^* a^* e_1 \frac{\varphi^*(1/e_1)}{1 + \varphi^*(1/e_1)} - \alpha a \frac{\varphi(e_1)}{1 + \varphi(e_1)} \tag{16}$$

b is clearly increasing in e_1 (i.e. the Marshall-Lerner condition holds) for $\rho \geqslant 0$, and also, by extension, for small, negative ρ. Table 1 also gives the

TABLE 1

Policy Effects in the Small Open Economy

	y_1	e_1, E_1	$d, \frac{e_1}{e_2}$	$i, \frac{E_2}{E_1}$	b
g_1	+ (=1)	0	0	0	0
g_2	+ / −	+ / −	+	0	+ / −
g	+	+ / −	+	0	+ / −
M_1	+	+	+ [1]	−	+ / − [2]
M_2	+	+	+ [1]	+	+ / − [2]
M	+	+	+	0	+ / −

Notes :

(i) Signs are those of the multipliers of variables in the left-hand column on variables in the first row.

(ii) Multipliers with respect to g and M represent permanent changes, i.e. the summation of the effects in the two cells vertically above.

(iii) Where a cell is diagonally divided, the top left-hand entry is for the gross substitutes case where $\varrho,\varrho^* > 0$; the bottom right-hand entry is for the gross complements case where $\varrho,\varrho^* < 0$. In undivided cells, the sign is the same for both positive and negative values of ϱ,ϱ^*.

(iv) All results can be obtained without the need for differentiation except those marked (1) and (2). Those marked (2) are derived in the appendices.

effects on the nominal interest rate, and thus (using $E_2/E_1 = [1+i]/[1+i^*]$, the uncovered interest parity condition in nominal terms) also on the nominal exchange rate "overshooting" variable, E_2/E_1. The fact that fiscal policy has no effect on the nominal interest rate may appear surprising. Substituting (12) into (10) gives:

$$\frac{M_1}{p_1[1+i]} = \frac{\gamma}{\gamma+\zeta}\frac{1}{i}\left[\frac{i}{1+i}\frac{M_1}{p_1} + \frac{1}{1+i}\frac{M_2}{p_1}\right].$$

This may be rearranged as:

$$i = \frac{\gamma}{\zeta}\frac{M_2}{M_1}. \qquad (17)$$

(17) shows that the equilibrium interest rate depends only on the ratio of the two periods' money supplies. To understand this, it should be remembered that bonds are not net wealth, so that there is no influence on the interest rate from this source.[3]

Monetary Policy

Monetary policy consists of changes in M_1 or M_2. All such changes are effectively "helicopter drops", in the sense that their financing counterparts are subsidies or tax cuts. This is because bonds are not net wealth, so that an increase in M_1 brought about by an open market purchase of bonds is equivalent to the same increase through a reduction in taxation. Continuing our assumption of an initial situation in which $M_1 = M_2$, it is clear that nearly all the effects of monetary policy come through the then exogenous variable a, as given by (12), and so are independent of whether it is M_1 or M_2 which is changed. Consider first the gross substitutes case where $\rho, \rho^* > 0$. A rise in a unambiguously shifts both (13) and (14) to the right in Figure 1, moving the equilibrium from A to C. e_1 clearly rises (depreciates), while the change in e_2 is uncertain. From (15), y_1 rises, both on account of the rise in a itself, and of the rise in e_1. These effects are much the same when ρ, ρ^* are zero or negative. In Figure 2, both loci shift right, generating a new equilibrium at C. It is not hard to satisfy

3. This is the major part of the story, but admittedly not all of it, since balanced- budget fiscal policy might be expected to affect the interest rate as well. The remainder has partly to do with the specification of money demand (see footnote 2), and partly with the exact form of the utility function.

oneself, following the lines of previous reasoning, that e_1 and y_1 definitely rise for values of ρ, ρ^* sufficiently close to zero.

The basic conclusions of Mundell-Fleming as regards output and the current exchange rate are thus not upset. However, as Table 1 indicates, there may be a difference concerning the trade balance. Under gross complementarity, the trade balance deteriorates rather than improves. From (16), the increase in a and that in e_1 pull in opposite directions – this is a conflict between the simple "absorption" and "elasticities" approaches to the balance of payments. A resort to differentiation (see Appendix A) is necessary to show that the exchange rate effect dominates if and only if the elasticity of substitution is greater than one. The effects of monetary policy on the nominal interest rate are ones which clearly do depend on whether M_1 or M_2 is increased, as is apparent from (17) : an increase in M_1 lowers the interest rate, and an anticipated future increase in M_2 raises it.

The results from the small open version of our model may be compared with those of two similar papers, by Cuddington and Vinals (1986), and by Fender (1986). Both these employ the intertemporal disequilibrium approach, and – unlike van Wijnbergen (1985, 1986) – include money in the analysis. Both allow a tradeables and a non-tradeables sector. The country is a price-taker in the flex-price world tradeables market, while there is excess supply in the non-tradeables sector due to a rigid price. Such a specification provides an alternative way of combining Keynesian unemployment with a flexible real exchange rate to the one chosen here. Cuddington and Vinals also assume Walrasian equilibrium in period two, as here, while Fender postulates disequilibrium in both. On the other hand, the first authors obtain the demand for money by a cash-in-advance constraint, while Fender shares our assumption that real balances provide utility. The present results are most directly comparable with those of Cuddington and Vinals, who find that a balanced-budget increase in government spending in the first period worsens the trade balance, rather than leaves it unaffected. This difference appears to stem directly from the different treatment of money demand, since they further find that under an accommodating monetary policy the balance is unchanged.

IV. A TWO-COUNTRY MODEL

The two-country world is taken to consist of two countries with the same general structure as already described. To simplify the analysis it will often be assumed that there is an exact symmetry between the two, though approximate symmetry is all that is in general necessary. The endogenous variables (y_1,d, i,e_1,e_2) from the small open economy model are now extended to include

(y_1^*, d^*, i^*). To determine these we have the three extra equations, the foreign equivalents of (8a-c) :

$$y_1^* = h_1^*\left(a^*, \frac{1}{e_1}\right) + g_1^* + f_1(a, e_1) \tag{18a}$$

$$\bar{y}_2^* = h_2^*\left(a^*, d^*, \frac{1}{e_2}\right) + g_2^* + f_2(a, d, e_2) \tag{18b}$$

$$\frac{M_1^*}{P_2^*} = m_1^*\left(a^*, i^*, d^*, \frac{P_2^*}{p_2^*}\right) \tag{18c}$$

where

$$a^* = y_1^* - g_1^* + d^*[\bar{y}_2^* - g_2^*] + \frac{i^*}{1+i^*}\frac{M_1^*}{p_1^*} + \frac{1}{1+i^*}\frac{M^*}{p_2^*}.$$

The same simplifications as applied to the small open economy can be appealed to here. When evaluated at $M_1 = M_2$, $M_1^* = M_2^*$, a and a^* can be interpreted as exogenous monetary policy variables, given by (12). The core of the model then consists of the four equations (8b,d,e) and (18b), defining the equilibrium values of (e_1, e_2, d, d^*). As before, substituting (8e) into (8b,d) and using the explicit forms of the demand functions yields the system (13) and (14). However, d^*, which this contains, is now endogenous. To eliminate it, we make use of the explicit form of (18b) which, after substituting out d using (8e), may be arranged as :

$$d^*[\bar{y}_2^* - g_2^*] = \frac{\delta^* a^*}{1 + \varphi^*(1/e_2)} + \delta a \frac{1}{e_1}\frac{\varphi(e_2)}{1+\varphi(e_2)} \tag{19}$$

Combining this with (13) to eliminate d^* gives (20). The old system (13) and (14) is thus replaced by :

$$[\bar{y}_2 - g_2]\left[\frac{\delta^* a^*}{1+\varphi^*(1/e_2)} + \delta a \frac{1}{e_1}\frac{\varphi(e_2)}{1+\varphi(e_2)}\right]$$

$$= [\bar{y}_2^* - g_2^*]\left[\frac{e_2}{e_1}\cdot\frac{\delta a}{1+\varphi(e_2)} + \delta^* a^* e_2 \frac{\varphi^*(1/e_2)}{1+\varphi^*(1/e_2)}\right] \tag{20}$$

$$e_1 = \frac{a}{a^*}\,\frac{\alpha\dfrac{\varphi(e_1)}{1+\varphi(e_1)} + \delta\dfrac{\varphi(e_2)}{1+\varphi(e_2)}}{\alpha^*\dfrac{\varphi^*(1/e_1)}{1+\varphi^*(1/e_1)} + \delta^*\dfrac{(1/e_2)}{1+\varphi^*(1/e_2)}} \tag{14}$$

As found in section III , (14) is negatively-sloped when $\rho,\rho^* > 0$, vertical when $\rho = \rho^* = 0$, and positively-sloped when $\rho,\rho^* < 0$. Consider the slope of (20). The R.H. term [.] is identical to the R.H.S. of (13), and so decreasing in e_1 and increasing in e_2 for all ρ,ρ^*, as found earlier. The L.H. term [.] is also decreasing in e_1, and decreasing or increasing in e_2 according as ρ,ρ^* are positive or negative, respectively. If an initial state of symmetry between the two countries is assumed (implying, *inter alia*, $e_1 = e_2 = 1$), then a rise in e_1 will depress the R.H.S. more than the L.H.S. if and only if $\varphi(1) = \left(\frac{1-\beta}{\beta}\right)^{\frac{1}{1-\rho}} < 1$. This holds if and only if $\beta > 0.5$, i.e. if each country's preferences are weighted towards its own output (see (3)). On this assumption, when $\rho,\rho^* > 0$, a rise in e_2 is needed to restore the equality, so that (20) slopes upwards. The same is true when $\rho = \rho^* = 0$ (whence φ,φ^* are constants), and thus also for small, negative values.

Fiscal Policy

A rise in g_1 or in g_1^*, since neither enter (20) or (14), leaves the exchange rates unchanged. The effects on y_1 are once more deducible from (15). Since e_1 is unaffected, we must have $dy_1/dg_1 = 1$, as in the small open economy. It is also apparent that $dy_1/dg_1^* = 0$, i.e. a foreign first-period expansion has no effect on home output. These results are a generalisation of the quasi-neutrality found in section III, and derive from the dependence of all demands on disposable incomes, as found there.

A rise in g_2 does not affect (14), but depresses the L.H.S. of (20). With the assumption made previously that $\varphi(1) < 1$, this necessitates a rise in e_1 to restore the equality, so that (20) shifts right. In Figure 3, the equilibrium moves from A to B, so that e_1 rises and e_2 falls. From (15), recalling the negative dependence of φ on e_t for this case where $\rho,\rho^* > 0$, y_1 then rises. These results are qualitatively identical to those in the small open economy. Next consider the effect of a rise in g_2^*. This lowers the R.H.S. rather than the L.H.S. of (20), so reversing the shift of the curve. In Figure 3, the equilibrium can be envisaged as moving from B to A. Since e_1 then falls it is clear from (15) that y_1 does likewise. The foreign effect of an anticipated fiscal expansion when the countries' products are gross substitutes is thus negative, and since the effect of a first-period expansion is zero, the net foreign effect of a permanent fiscal expansion must also be negative. This is at odds with Mundell's (1968) finding that the foreign effect is unambiguously expansionary.

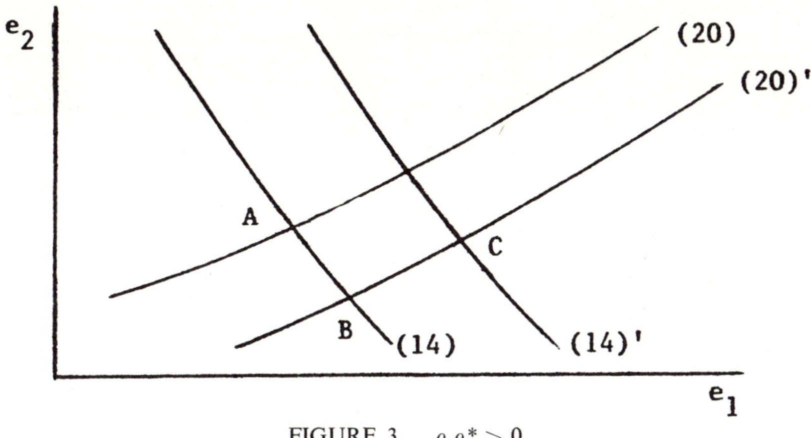

FIGURE 3. $\varrho,\varrho^* > 0$

Figure 4 depicts the case where $\rho,\rho^* < 0$. For values not too far distant from zero, (14) is close to the vertical and so steeper than (20). The effects of a rise in g_2 are once more the same as in the small open economy: (20) shifts right, e_1 falls, and thus so does y_1. The effects of a rise in g_2^* are again to reverse such a shift. This time e_1 rises, and so y_1 rises as well. Thus gross complementarity restores the positive transmission of fiscal policy found by Mundell.

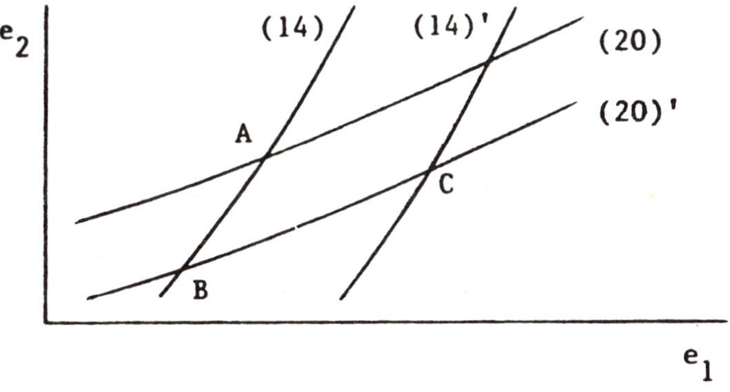

FIGURE 4. $\varrho,\varrho^* < 0$

Table 2 provides a complete picture of the effects for the two-country case. Most of these are obtained by the methods already described, without recourse to differentiation; however, in a few cases this proves necessary, and some of the relevant calculations are given in Appendix B. Note that all own-country effects, and effects on variables linking the two countries (e_1,e_2,b), are

TABLE 2

Policy Effects in the Two-country Model

	y_1	y_1^*	e_1, E_1	d	d^*	i	i^*	$\frac{e_2}{e_1}$	$\frac{E_2}{E_1}$	b
g_1	+ (=1)	0	0	0	0	0	0	0	0	0
g_2	+ / −	− / +	+ / −	+[1]	+ / −[1]	0	0	−	0	+ / −
g	+	− / +	+ / −	+	+ / −	0	0	−	0	+ / −
M_1	+	− / +[2]	+	+[1]	+ / −[1]	−	0	−[1]	−	+ / −[2]
M_2	+	− / +[2]	+	+[1]	+ / −[1]	+	0	−[1]	+	+ / −[2]
M	+	− / +	+	+	+ / −	0	0	−	0	+ / −

Notes: see Table 1.

qualitatively identical to those in the small open economy. The interest of the two-country model is therefore mainly in its implications for interdependence between the countries.

Monetary Policy

We proceed as before by considering monetary policy as changes in a. A rise in a shifts (14) to the right, as in section III. Its effect on (20) is at first sight ambiguous, but can be seen to turn on the already-encountered condition of whether $\varphi(1) \gtrless 1$. Continuing to assume $\varphi(1) < 1$, inspection of (20) shows, it must also move to the right. In Figures 3 and 4, the equilibrium then moves from A to C. Thus, as in the small open economy, e_1 rises and, from (15), this contributes, along with the rise in a itself, to a rise in y_1. An increase in a^* predictably, reverses these shifts, causing e_1 to fall. This creates an apparent ambiguity for the effect on y_1, for, as can be seen from (15), the rise in a^* and the fall in e_1 counteract each other. Differentiation (see Appendix B) shows that the fall in e_1 dominates when and only when $\rho,\rho^* > 0$. Thus, as with fiscal policy, monetary policy has a contractionary foreign effect when products are gross substitutes, and an expansionary one when they are gross complements.

The effects of monetary policy on other variables may be traced through using similar techniques. Table 2 shows that, as for fiscal policy, extending the model to two countries does not upset the conclusions as regards the internal consequences of policy or those for the exchange rate and trade balance variables.

V. CONCLUSIONS

Our aim has been to construct an analytical model of macroeconomic interdependence under floating exchange rates which incorporates individual optimisation and the intertemporal dimension, while remaining faithful to most of the features of Mundell's (1968) seminal study. The results point to the importance of the degree of substitutability in consumers' preferences of the products of the two countries as a factor in determining the direction of the foreign effects of macroeconomic policies. For the forms of policy studied here, both fiscal and monetary expansions in one country have a negative impact on output in the other when their products are gross substitutes, and a positive one when they are gross complements. This differs from Mundell's findings in that the foreign effects of the two policy types are always in the same, rather than in conflicting, directions; and in that the degree of substitutability was not a consideration in Mundell's work. On the other hand the results for the substitutes case are in line with those in a companion paper (Rankin (1989)), in which the countries' products are treated as perfect substitutes sold in a flex-price world market.[4]

The more general conclusion which this suggests is that there are important aspects of macroeconomic interdependence which are not captured by simple, static, IS-LM-based analysis. That the standard results can be turned round so completely, and made to depend on aspects of microeconomic structure, such as product substitutability, for which there is no room in the traditional analysis, is surely a warning of this. It would be wrong to see the present results, based on a model which still omits many important factors, as competing to replace the general propositions about interdependence associated with Mundell; rather they are an indication that much more remains to be learnt about interdependence, and that any general propositions may have to give way to more complex statements.

Queen Mary College and C.E.P.R., London.

APPENDIX A

From (16),

$$\frac{db}{da} = \Bigg[\frac{\alpha^* a^* \varphi_1^*}{1+\varphi_1^*} + \underset{(+)}{\frac{e_1 \alpha^* a^*}{[1+\varphi_1^*]^2} \frac{\rho^*}{1-\rho^*}} \frac{\varphi_1^*}{e_1}$$

$$- \frac{a\alpha}{[1+\varphi_1]^2} \frac{\rho}{\rho - 1} \frac{\varphi_1}{e_1} \Bigg] \underset{(+)}{\frac{de_1}{da}} - \underset{(+)}{\frac{\alpha\varphi_1}{1+\varphi_1}} = ?$$

where φ_1 is used as shorthand for $\varphi(e_1)$, etc. This uses $d\varphi(e_t)/de_t = \frac{\rho}{\rho-1}\frac{\varphi}{e_t}$ etc., from (5). de_1/da is found totally differentiating the system (13) and (14). The resulting expression for db/da may then be simplified: we omit the

4. After this paper was written, I became aware of a recent article by Svensson (1987), which contains some similar results as regards the two-country case. Svensson uses a considerably more complicated framework, incorporating an infinite time horizon and stochastic disturbances, with monopolistic firms who set prices one period in advance. A cash-in-advance constraint is used to derive money demand. Whereas a temporary fiscal expansion in our model has identical (i.e. zero) foreign effects to a fiscal expansion in Svensson's, a permanent expansion has non-zero effects: this appears to arise from the existence of full employment, rather than excess capacity, in the long run in our model.

space-consuming details. When it is evaluated at $b = 0$, implying $\alpha^* a^* \varphi_1^* / [1 + \varphi_1^*] = [\alpha a / e_1] \varphi_1 / [1 + \varphi_1]$, we obtain :

$$\frac{db}{da} = \frac{z_5 z_4 - z_6 z_2}{z_1 z_4 - z_3 z_2}$$

where

$$z_1 = \frac{\alpha^* \varphi_1^*}{1+\varphi_1^*} + \frac{\delta^* \varphi_2^*}{1+\varphi_2^*} + \frac{e_1 \alpha^*}{[1+\varphi_2^*]^2} \frac{\rho^*}{1-\rho^*} \varphi_1^* e_1 - \frac{a}{a^*} \alpha \frac{1}{[1+\varphi_1]^2} \frac{\rho}{\rho - 1} \frac{\varphi_1}{e_1} > 0$$

$$z_2 = \frac{e_1 \delta^*}{[1+\varphi_2^*]^2} \frac{\rho^*}{1-\rho^*} \varphi_2^* e_2 - \frac{a}{a^*} \frac{\delta}{[1+\varphi_2]^2} \frac{\rho}{\rho-1} \frac{\varphi_2}{e_2}$$

$$z_3 = \frac{e_2}{e_1} \frac{\delta a}{1+\varphi_2} > 0$$

$$z_4 = -\frac{\delta a}{1+\varphi_2} - \frac{e_1 \delta^* a^* \varphi_2^*}{1+\varphi_2^*} + \frac{e_2 \delta a}{[1+\varphi_2]^2} \frac{\rho}{\rho-1} \frac{\varphi_2}{e_2} - \frac{e_2 e_1 \delta^* a^*}{[1+\varphi_2^*]^2} \frac{\rho^*}{1-\rho^*} \varphi_2^* e_2 < 0$$

$$z_5 = \left[\frac{e_1 \alpha^* a^*}{[1+\varphi_1^*]^2} \frac{\rho^*}{1-\rho^*} \varphi_1^* e_1 - \frac{\alpha a}{[1+\varphi_1]^2} \frac{\rho}{\rho-1} \frac{\varphi_1}{e_1} \right] \frac{1}{a^*} \frac{\delta \varphi_2}{1+\varphi_2}$$

$$z_6 = \left[\frac{e_1 \alpha^* a^*}{[1+\varphi_1^*]^2} \frac{\rho^*}{1-\rho^*} \varphi_1^* e_1 - \frac{\alpha a}{[1+\varphi_1]^2} \frac{\rho}{\rho-1} \frac{\varphi_1}{e_1} \right] \frac{e_2 \delta}{1+\varphi_2}.$$

Where signs are given they apply both for positive and for small negative values of ρ, ρ^* . z_1, z_3 and z_4 are unambiguous; z_2, z_5 and z_6 are positive or negative according as ρ, ρ^* are positive or negative, respectively. The denominator of db/da is thus negative both for positive and for small negative values of ρ, ρ^*; while the numerator is negative for positive ρ, ρ^* and positive for small negative ρ, ρ^*. Hence db/da is respectively positive or negative for these ranges.

APPENDIX B

From (15),

$$\frac{dy_1}{da^*} = \frac{\alpha a \varphi}{1+\varphi} \left[1 + 2 \underset{(+)}{\frac{1}{1+\varphi} \frac{\rho}{1-\rho}} \right] \underset{(-)}{\frac{de_1}{da^*}} + \underset{(+)}{\frac{\alpha \varphi}{1+\varphi}} = ?$$

and from (16),

$$\frac{db}{da} = \frac{\alpha a\varphi}{1+\varphi}\left[1 + 2\frac{1}{1+\varphi}\frac{\rho}{1-\rho}\right]\frac{de_1}{da} - \frac{\alpha\varphi}{1+\varphi} = ?$$
$$\qquad\qquad (+) \qquad\qquad (+) \qquad (+)$$

This assumes initial complete symmetry between the two countries; hence all asterisks may be dropped and the expressions simplified. de_1/da^* and de_1/da are found by totally differentiating the system (20) and (14). Since it must be true that $de_1/da^* = -de_1/da$ under symmetry, the resulting expressions have the common form :

$$\frac{dy_1}{da^*} = -\frac{db}{da} = -2\frac{\alpha\varphi}{[1+\varphi]^2}\frac{\rho}{1-\rho}\left[\delta[(1+\varphi) + 4\frac{\rho}{1-\rho}\frac{\varphi}{1+\varphi}]\right.$$
$$\left. + 2\delta\frac{1-\varphi}{1+\varphi}\frac{\rho}{1-\rho}\right]\Delta^{-1}$$

where

$$\Delta = \left[(\alpha+\delta) + \frac{2\alpha}{1+\varphi}\frac{\rho}{1-\rho}\right]\left[(1+\varphi) + 4\frac{\rho}{1-\rho}\frac{\varphi}{1+\varphi}\right] + 2\delta\frac{1-\varphi}{1+\varphi}\frac{\rho}{1-\rho}.$$

For $\varphi < 1$, Δ is positive for all positive and for small negative ρ. Hence dy_1/da^* is negative for positive ρ and positive for negative ρ, while db/da is respectively positive and negative.

REFERENCES

Cuddington, J.T., Johansson, P.-O. and Lofgren K.-G. (1984) *Disequilibrium Macroeconomics in Open Economies*, (Oxford: Basil Blackwell).

—— and Vinals, J. M. (1986) 'Budget Deficits and the Current Account: An Intertemporal Disequilibrium Approach', *Journal of International Economics*, 21 : 1-24.

Dixit, A. K. (1978) 'The Balance of Trade in a Model of Temporary Equilibrium with Rationing', *Review of Economic Studies*, 45 : 393-404.

Fender, J. (1986) 'Monetary and Exchange Rate Policies in an Open Macroeconomic Model with Unemployment and Rational Expectations', *Oxford Economic Papers*, 38 : 501-515.

Henin, P.-Y., Marois, W. and Michel, P. (1985) *Desequilibres en Economie Ouverte*, Paris, Economica.

Holmes, J. M. and Smyth, D. J. (1972) 'The Specification of the Demand for Money and the Tax Multiplier', *Journal of Political Economy*, 80 : 179-185.

Malinvaud, E. (1977) *The Theory of Unemployment Reconsidered*, (Oxford : Basil Blackwell).

Marselli, R. and Vannini, M. (1987) 'The Holmes-Smyth Effect : Some Preliminary Exercises with the U.K. Demand for Narrow Money', *Applied Economics.*

Mundell, R. A. (1968) *International Economics*, (New York : Macmillan Press).

Neary, J. P. (1980) 'Non-Traded Goods and the Balance of Trade in a Neo-Keynesian Temporary Equilibrium', *Quarterly Journal of Economics*, 95 : 403-430.

Persson, T. (1982) 'Global Effects of National Stabilisation Policies under Fixed and Floating Exchange Rates', *Scandinavian Journal of Economics*, 64 : 165-192.

Rankin, N. (1985) 'Debt Neutrality in Disequilibrium', in Currie, D. (ed.), *Advances in Monetary Economics*, (London : Croom Helm).

—— (1989) 'Monetary, Fiscal and Exchange Intervention Policy in a Two-Country Intertemporal Disequilibrium Model', *European Economic Review*, (forthcoming).

Svensson, L. E. O. (1987) 'International Fiscal Policy Transmission', *Scandinavian Journal of Economics*, 89 : 305-334.

Van Wijnbergen, S. (1985) 'Oil Price Shocks, Private Investment, Employment and the Current Account : An Intertemporal Disequilibrium Analysis', *Review of Economic Studies*, 52 : 627-645.

—— (1986) 'Government Deficits, Private Investment and the Current Account: An Intertemporal Disequilibrium Analysis', *Economic Journal*, 97 : 596-615.

INFLATION AND MACROECONOMIC ADJUSTMENTS IN A NORTH-SOUTH MODEL

By S. Mansoob Murshed and Somnath Sen*

I. INTRODUCTION

The economic relationships between North and South have usually been described to exhibit 'asymmetric interdependence' or 'non-reciprocal dependence' – a structuralist tradition, harking back to Prebisch (1950), and more recently discussed in Taylor (1983). The clear implication of these terms is that the North wields greater economic power over the South than the latter does upon the former. The first major asymmetry arises from the structuralist notion that in the short run at least the North exhibits Keynesian features while the South is classical (Walrasian) in nature. This means that demand determines *output* in the North and *prices or the terms of trade* in the South. When we combine this feature with the fact that in the South supply in the short run is usually invariant, the terms of trade for the South can be entirely determined by Northern demand. The South, however, has no influence over Northern prices, which are determined by Northern cost considerations. Another major asymmetry in North - South relations is the fact that the North being Keynesian, benefits from an export multiplier effect in the short run, whereas the South does not benefit from any such effect.

In the setting of these asymmetries in North-South economic interactions, we will focus, in this paper, upon one particular aspect where North-South relations are of considerable interest in the North, i.e. inflation control in the North. The fact that commodity prices feed into the Northern inflationary process is not a new idea (see Kanbur and Vines (1986)). The manner in which Southern prices influence the Northern inflation rate is through the growing phenomenon of real wage resistance in the North. Real wage resistance implies a target level of the real wage (standard of living) aimed at by Northern workers. If the Northern consumption basket includes Southern commodities, excess demand for them will lead to rising commodity prices, and cause Northern inflation to rise via wage costs, given the invariant real

* We are grateful to A. Courakis, D. Currie, C. Goodhart and E. Karakitsos for their comments on an earlier draft.

wage aspirations in the North. This was definitely the case in the early 1970s. More recently (the 1980s), empirical evidence suggests (see Beckerman and Jenkinson (1986)), that the deflationary policies employed in the North to combat inflation, by reducing Northern demand, have lowered both the Southern terms of trade and Northern inflation rates, in the setting of real wage resistance, which they found was not weakened in the short run. In what follows we will outline a model which generates steady state inflation, similar to Cardoso (1981), in the short to medium run in both regions. We will then demonstrate that the cost of controlling inflation will be substantial for the global economy, but the output cost of doing so would be *higher* in the North, if not for the presence of the South.

In the medium term we also analyse changes in Northern and Southern productivity, as well as the effects of protectionism in the North against Southerngoods. We hope to show that unlike the CEPG position of authors such as Cripps and Godley (1978), protectionism is not a successful macroeconomic devise to raise output given the presence of real wage resistance. There has been a growing protectionist tendency in the North towards Southern goods (see Page (1987)), which is greater than in the intra-Northern case. The inability of the South to effectively retaliate and the loss of competitiveness in (Southern) import competing industries in the North, all point to this increasing phenomenon.

We make a fundamental distinction, following the classification proposed by Hicks, between fix-price and flex-price markets. In the context of North-South models, the basic structuralist assumption is that the North obeys a Keynesian quantity adjustment process whereby excess effective demand is met by increased output. Aggregate price level in the North responds to cost push factors, in particular the strength of workers resistance to real wage cuts. On the other hand, the South operates within an auction market system and increases the price of its product when there is excess demand. The nature of the goods produced in each region, the form in which specialisation has taken place historically, the cost of holding inventories, the competitiveness or monopolistic nature of the markets-all dictate the choice of flex/fix price structures for the two agents.

Another important feature of the dynamic adjustment mechanism, *for the South*, is the use of the Marshallian distinction between the short-run and the the long-run. In the short or medium run, output supply is relatively inelastic and price movements must bear all the burden of adjustment under disequilibrium. However, in the long run, output supplied by the South on world markets can and does change; thus some supply adjustments are possible when demand parameters shift. The long run version of our model leads to a complete decoupling of the South from the world system, as far as the determination of the terms of trade are concerned. More importantly, the long-term expansion of the government sector or autonomous demand in the North is at the cost of *falling* Southern terms of trade. This is supported by the fact that Southern terms of trade have tended to decline secularly, whereas the Northern government sector has grown in the *overall* post-war period.

II. THE MODEL

The equilibrium relation for the South is modelled, following Kanbur and Vines (1986) by postulating a linear expenditure system. In other words, total consumption and its division between home and Northern goods are fixed proportions of income or the value of output. Thus:

$$P_A \overline{Q}_A = c_S P_A \overline{Q}_A + P_A M(Q_I, \sigma) - c_S(1 - v_S) P_A \overline{Q}_A + P_A R \qquad (1)$$

where $\overline{Q}_A$ is Southern output, assumed exogenous for the sake of tractability (otherwise it can be made a positive function of its own price or terms of trade); P_A is the price of the Southern good ('agriculture'); M is the quantity of Southern exports (Northern imports) and R denotes some form of residual expenditure or spending on basic (subsistence) needs, carried out by the Southern government say. The terms c_S, v_S and $1 - v_S$ are the fixed consumption propensities, share of home goods and Northern goods respectively in the South. The rationale behind the assumption of fixed propensities are the low levels of income in the South which makes for fixed expenditure patterns in the short run, proportional to income but invariant to relative price changes. Normalising (1) by P_A and cancelling terms give us the equilibrium relation for the South:

$$\overline{Q}_A = c_S v_S \overline{Q}_A + M(Q_I, \sigma) + R \qquad (2)$$

For the North we assume a Keynesian economy where output or aggregate demand, Q_I, is composed of absorption, A, autonomous expenditure G, and the trade balance (exports, $c_S (1 - v_S) \overline{Q}_A$ minus imports, M). Thus:

$$P_I Q_I = P_I A(Q_I, \sigma) + P_I G + P_A c_S (1 - v_S) Q_A - P_A M(Q_I, \sigma) \qquad (3)$$

where P_I is the price of the Northern good and $\sigma = P_A/P_I$ is the terms of trade. Normalising (3) by P_I gives:

$$Q_I = A(Q_I, \sigma) + G + \sigma c_S (1 - v_S) \overline{Q}_A - \sigma M(Q_I, \sigma) \qquad (4)$$

Northern absorption is assumed to be increasing in both its arguments – income, Q_I and the terms of trade, σ. The latter is usually referred to in the literature as the Laursen – Metzler effect (see Laursen and Metzler (1950) and Dornbusch (1980) for a detailed derivation). The intuition behind this notion is based upon a concept of real income and expenditure which is obtained by deflating nominal income by a composite price level, which is a weighted product of the domestic and foreign price levels. Thus if the terms of trade improve (import prices fall relative to home goods prices) then there is an increase in real income and consequently absorption. However, since the marginal propensity to absorb (consume) is less than unity only a part of the increased income is absorbed. Nominal absorption (in terms of home prices) will decline. This will operate as an adverse aggregate demand effect.

But it is worthwhile observing that in most of the literature on North-South interaction, attention on the terms of trade is focussed almost exclusively on the South. We bring it more firmly into the centre of things by giving it due emphasis in the *Northern* model. This constitutes our major argument for employing the Laursen-Metzler effect. Furthermore, in a Keynesian economy, as in the case of the North, the fixity of prices during the period of analysis in question, justifies the standard convention of making absorption or expenditure a function of income, but not of the price level. But, when expenditure is divided up between domestic and imported goods, the price of the former being fixed in the short run and the latter variable, we have a strong case for adding the terms of trade as an argument in the absorption function.

The partial derivatives of the various functions are the following:

$1 > A_1 > 0$, $A_2 = M(1-\epsilon) > 0$, where ϵ = the elasticity of absorption with respect to real income,

$$M_1 > 0, \quad A_1 > \sigma M_1, \quad M_2 < 0.$$

In addition we assume that the Marshall – Lerner condition holds and

$$c_S\,(1-v_S)\,\overline{Q}_A - M - \sigma M_2 > 0.$$

Another major feature of the Northern economy is the phenomenon of of real wage resistance. This is seen to imply that workers are concerned with a particular standard of living or *level* of real wages which is defined in terms of a consumption basket, containing both domestic and foreign (Southern) goods. The cost of purchasing this basket will be given by a price index, P, where $P = P_I^{\delta} P_A^{1-\delta}$ (δ and $1-\delta$ are the expenditure shares of Northern and Southern goods, respectively). Northern firms follow a mark-up pricing rule:

$$P_I = \frac{W(1+g)}{\alpha} \tag{5}$$

The price of the Northern good is a mark-up on nominal wage costs W, given the productivity of labour, (output-labour ratio, α) and the desired profit margins or mark-up rate, g, of firms. A detailed description of the process can be found in Dornbusch (1980).

The Northern worker will have a targeted real wage, $\bar{w}$, which is related to the cost of living index, P. Therefore given that workers do obtain their desired level of real wage, their money wage will be given by

$$W = \bar{w}\ P.$$

Thus given $\bar{w}$, any rise in P will lead to a rise in W, which is passed on by firms in the form of higher prices of the Northern good, P_I. Related to $\bar{w}$ there will also be an associated level of the terms of trade $\bar{\sigma}$, which can be construed as the required terms of trade from the point of view of Northern workers and firms. Consequently, for price *equilibrium* in the North,

$$\sigma = \bar{\sigma} \tag{6}$$

If $\sigma > \bar{\sigma}$, P_I would be rising due to the mounting pressure of higher money wages.

This completes the short-run description of the model with equations (2), (4) and (6) as the fundamental equations of the model which define equilibrium.

III. MEDIUM TERM DYNAMICS

We assume the North is Keynesian in the sense of quantities adjusting to clear the goods market in the short (medium) run. In other words, excess demand will lead to greater output being supplied and vice versa.

$$\dot{Q}_I = \alpha\ [A(Q_I, \sigma) + G + \sigma\ c_S\ (1-v_S)\ \bar{Q}_A - \sigma M\ (Q_I, \sigma) - Q_I] \tag{7}$$

Furthermore, we assume that when the actual terms of trade, σ exceeds the required terms of trade, $\bar{\sigma}$ in (6), consistent with workers' desired standard of living, Northern workers obtain higher money wages, which via (5) leads to higher P_I as costs to firms increase:

$$\frac{\dot{P}_I}{P_I} = \frac{\dot{W}}{W} = \gamma\,[\sigma - \bar{\sigma}] \tag{8}$$

In the South we assume that excess demand or supply leads to price adjustments. Hence the Southern goods market can be said to have a Walrasian flex-price structure in contrast to the North which exhibits fix-price characteristics:

$$\frac{\dot{P}_A}{P_A} = \beta\,[c_s v_s\,\bar{Q}_A + M\,(Q_I, \sigma) + R - \bar{Q}_A] \tag{9}$$

What of the terms of trade? We have defined it as $\sigma = P_A/P_I$. Thus changes in the terms of trade would be given by $\dot{P}_A/P_A$ minus $\dot{P}_I/P_I$ or (9) – (8). Thus:

$$\dot{\sigma}/\sigma = \beta[c_s v_s \bar{Q}_A + M(Q_I, \sigma) + R - \bar{Q}_A] - \gamma\,[\sigma - \bar{\sigma}] \tag{10}$$

Given that Q_I, σ are the variables of most interest, (10) implies the possibility of steady state inflation. This could occur if there was excess demand for the Southern good in the North, say. This would mean rising Southern prices i.e. $\dot{P}_A/P_A > 0$ in (9). But rising costs of the Southern good, would lower the Northern workers standard of living, leading to higher money wage demands. Firms will pass these increased wage costs in the form of higher prices. Thus $\dot{P}_I/P_I > 0$ in (8). But an inspection of (10) indicates that $\dot{\sigma}/\sigma = 0$, i.e. the terms of trade are constant if $\dot{P}_I/P_I = \dot{P}_A/P_A$. In other words we could have a steady state with $\dot{Q}_I = 0$ and $\dot{\sigma}/\sigma = 0$, but positive inflation rates in both regions as $\dot{P}_I/P_I$ and $\dot{P}_A/P_A$ were both positive.

These ideas can be depicted diagrammatically in Q_I, σ space. We begin by obtaining a curve along which the Northern goods market is in equilibrium (zero excess demand) – the *NN* curve from (7). Its slope is given by:

$$\frac{d\sigma}{dQ_I / NN,\ \dot{Q}_I = 0} = \frac{1 - A_1 + \sigma M_1}{A_2 + c_s\,(1 - v_s)\,\bar{Q}_A - M - \sigma M_2} \tag{11}$$

It will be positively sloped as long as the Marshall-Lerner conditions hold.

In other words, a deterioration of the Northern terms of trade, rise in σ, causes the Northern trade balance to improve. *NN* is upward sloping as higher values of Q_I are associated with higher demand for Southern goods, hence higher P_A and σ.

Next we obtain the curve along which $\dot{P}_I/P_I = 0$ from (8), indicating that the actual real wage in the North is equal to its desired level, thus W and P_I are constant over time $\sigma = \bar{\sigma}$. The *RWR* curve will be infinitely elastic at the required $\bar{\sigma}$, consistent with workers and firms objectives in the North.

We then obtain the *SS* curve along which excess demand in the South is zero, hence $\dot{P}_A/P_A = 0$ in (9):

$$\frac{d\sigma}{dQ_I/SS, \dot{P}_A/P_A = 0} = -\frac{M_1}{M_2} > 0 \tag{12}$$

Its positive slope implies that higher values of Q_I are associated with excess demand for Southern goods, raising P_A and σ for given P_I, and also increasing the value of any given output, Q_A in the South.

Finally, the slope of the relationship giving constant terms of trade over time (10):

$$\frac{d\sigma}{dQ_I/\dot{\sigma}/\sigma = 0} = \frac{-\beta M_1}{\beta M_2 - \gamma} \tag{13}$$

This is positive as well.

Comparing the slopes of the *NN* and *SS* curves, consider a point like *F* in Figure 1. There $\dot{P}_A = 0$ but $\dot{P}_I > 0$, since $\sigma > \bar{\sigma}$. Then the terms of trade, σ decline over time and σ falls. In a hypothetical experiment, with Q_I constant, σ declines along *FG*. This increases demand for the Southern good, which in turn makes inflation in the South positive. For points near *F*, where excess demand is low, P_I inflation outstrips the growth in P_A, thus σ continues to fall. However, as excess demand increases, and the gap between σ and $\bar{\sigma}$ is reduced with the fall in σ, we have situation where $\dot{P}_I/P_I = 0$ curve is less than that of $NN(\dot{Q}_I = 0)$. It is clear from comparing (12) and (13), that the slope of *SS* is greater than the $\dot{\sigma}/\sigma = 0$ curve. As mentioned above, we could have a steady state at such a point as E_1^* in Figure 1 with positive inflation in *both* North and South. At E_1^* there is no excess demand in the Northern goods market and there is no change in the terms of trade, $\dot{\sigma}/\sigma$, although $\dot{P}_A/P_A > 0$ (excess demand for Southern goods) and $\dot{P}_I/P_I > 0$

FIGURE 1

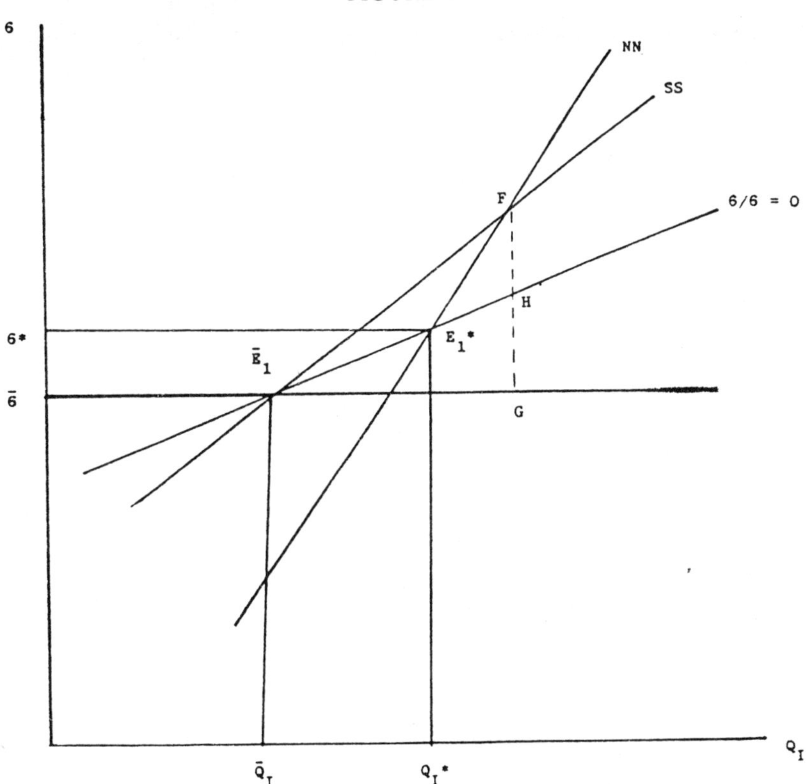

(actual term of trade above the desired level). A non-inflationary equilibrium would obtain at a point like $\overline{E}_1$, with zero inflation and no excess demand in both regions. However, that would require a reduction in Northern output.

The steady state equilibrium at E_1^* with positive inflation is defined by:

$$A(Q_I, \sigma) + G + \sigma c_S (1 - v_s) \; \overline{Q}_A - \sigma M(Q_I, \sigma) - Q_I = 0 \qquad (7')$$

(setting $\alpha = 1$ by choice of units) and

$$\beta \; [c_S \; v_S \; \overline{Q}_A + M \; (Q_I, \sigma) + R - \overline{Q}_A] - \gamma \, (\sigma - \bar{\sigma}) = 0 \qquad (10')$$

This will give steady state values of Q_I^* and σ^*.

It is interesting at this stage to consider variations in parameters such as $\bar{\sigma}$, $\overline{Q}_A$ and consider the effects of a tariff imposed by the North on

Southern goods, in this medium–term scenario. In order to proceed we totally differentiate (7′) and (10′) and arrange them in matrix form:

$$\begin{bmatrix} a_{11} & a_{12} \\ a_{21} & a_{22} \end{bmatrix} \begin{bmatrix} dQ_I^* \\ d\sigma^* \end{bmatrix} = \begin{bmatrix} b_{11} & b_{12} & b_{13} \\ b_{21} & b_{22} & b_{23} \end{bmatrix} \begin{bmatrix} dG \\ d\bar{\sigma} \\ d\bar{Q}_A \end{bmatrix}$$

where:

$$a_{11} = A_1 - 1 - \sigma M_1$$

$$a_{21} = \beta M_1$$

$$a_{12} = A_2 + c_s(1 - v_s)\,\bar{Q}_A - M - \sigma M_2, \text{ where } A_2 = M(1 - \epsilon)$$

$$a_{22} = \beta M_2 - \gamma$$

$$b_{11} = -1$$

$$b_{21} = 0$$

$$b_{12} = 0$$

$$b_{22} = -\gamma$$

$$b_{13} = -\sigma\, c_s(1 - v_s)$$

$$b_{23} = \beta(1 - c_s\, v_s)$$

The trace of the Jacobian will be found to be negative and the determinant positive by stability.

An Improvement in Northern Labour Productivity

From equation (5) above, an improvement in Northern labour productivity, α, will lower P_1 for given W, as production costs decline for firms. Given any target level of real wages, $\bar{w}$, desired by workers, the implication is that the associated (required) terms of trade $\bar{\sigma}$ will rise, as the cost o living declines. Thus a productivity improvement in the North implies a higher required terms of trade, $\bar{\sigma}$.

$$\frac{dQ_I^*}{d\bar{\sigma}} = \frac{\gamma[A_2 + c_s(1 - v_s)\,\bar{Q}_A - M - \sigma M_2]}{|J|} > 0$$

and $$\frac{d\sigma^*}{d\bar{\sigma}} = \frac{\gamma(1 - A_1 + \sigma M_1)}{|\mathcal{J}|} > 0$$

Not surprisingly, Northern output rises. In terms of Figure 2,[1] the $\dot{\sigma}/\sigma = 0$ curve moves up to $\dot{\sigma}/\sigma' = 0$. The new equilibrium is at E_2^*, with higher Q_I and σ. As pointed out by Prebisch (1950), productivity improvements in the North benefit the South via improved terms of trade.

FIGURE 2

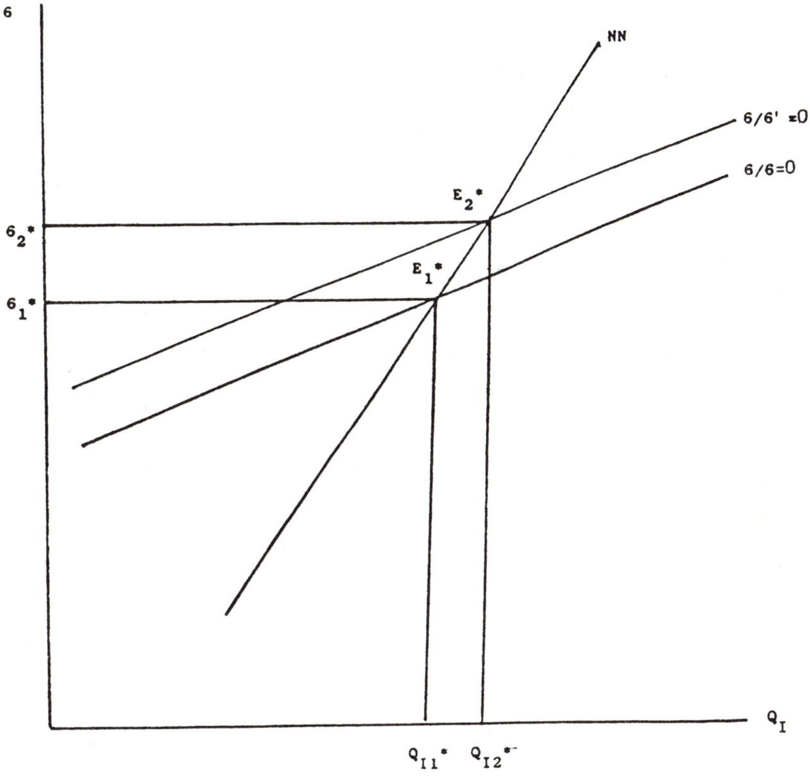

An improvement in Southern Productivity.

In our model, productivity improvements or technical progress in the

1. We omit the RWR and SS curves for the sake of clarity, as medium run equilibrium is given by the NN and $\dot{\sigma}/\sigma$ curves.

South will take the form of an increase in the exogenous output level of the South, $\bar{Q}_A$.

$$dQ_I^*/d\bar{Q}_A = \beta M\Omega (1 - c_s) + \beta \in M (1 - c_s v_s) + c_s (1 - v_s) [\gamma\sigma - \beta(1 - c_s v_s)\bar{Q}_A]$$

and

$$d\sigma^* /d\bar{Q}_A = (A_1 - 1)(1 - c_s v_s)\beta - \sigma M_1 \beta (1 - c_s),$$

both divided by $|J| > 0$; Ω is the price elasticity of demand of Northern imports where $\Omega = \sigma M_2/M$ and $\Omega < 0$; and $\in$ is the elasticity of Northern absorption with respect to real income, the Laursen-Metzler effect.

Since $|1 - c_s v_s| > |1 - c_s|$, as $v_s < 1$ even if $c_s > 1$, the sufficient condition for $d\sigma^*/d\bar{Q}_A < 0$ is that $|1 - A_1| > |\sigma M_1|$. The necessary condition for $dQ_I^* /d\bar{Q}_A > 0$ is that $|\in| > |\Omega|$. The former condition ensures that imports from the South are moderated after output rises there. The latter condition, $|\in| > |\Omega|$ concerns effects on Northern aggregate demand. As the terms of trade, σ fall, improve for the North, there is an adverse Laursen-Metzler effect on her absorption. This effect is moderated the higher the magnitude of $\in$ (*N.B.* $\in < 1$). Also if $|\in| > |\Omega|$, since $\in < 1$, it implies $|\Omega| < 1$, imports are inelastic plugging the leakage on Northern aggregate demand of increased imports.

In Figure 3, increased Southern output implies lower σ and P_A for any level of Q_I to clear the market (or higher Q_I for any σ). The $\dot{\sigma} /\sigma = 0$ curve moves down also to $\dot{\sigma} / \sigma' = 0$. The *NN* curve moves rightwards if aggregate demand rises in the North. The new equilibrium is likely to be at a point as E_2^*, with higher Q_I and lower σ. The new steady state is still associated with excess demand for Southern goods, but it is reduced, and consequently the (positive) inflation rates are lower in both regions. As Prebisch (1950) indicated productivity improvements in the South, injure her via lower terms of trade but benefit the North as aggregate demand and income rise there due to increased Southern demand. The South has no export multiplier effect unlike the Keynesian North. The North additionally gains in our model through reduced inflation.

FIGURE 3

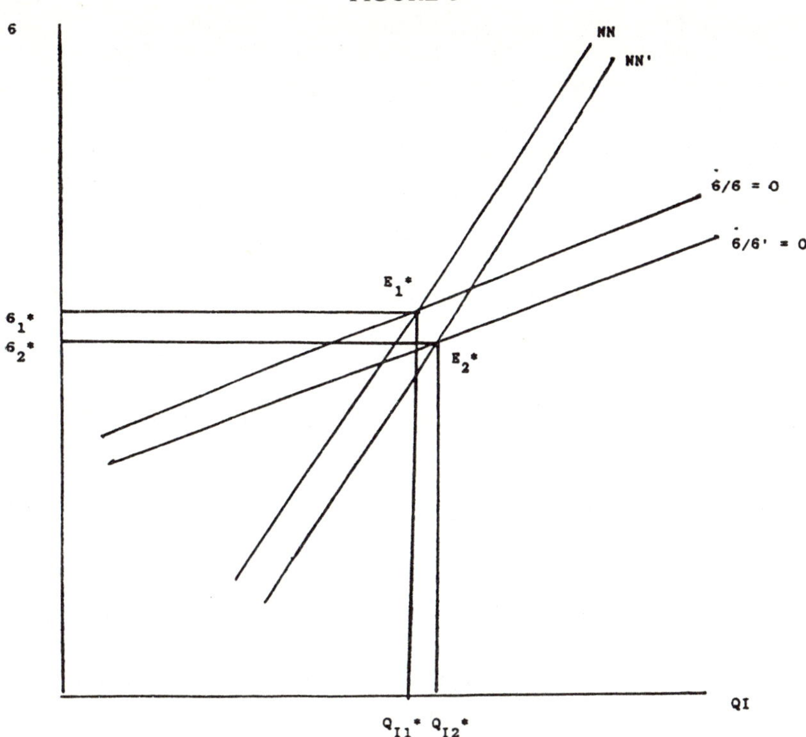

Effects of Northern Protectionism

The protection will take the form of an ad-valorem tariff on Southern goods, τ. We have to modify (7′) and (10′):

$$A(Q_I;\ \sigma(1+\tau)) + c_s(1-v_s)\sigma\overline{Q}_A - \sigma M(Q_I;\ \sigma(1+\tau))\,(1+\tau) + G - Q_I = 0$$

If the government spends the tariff revenue itself,

$$A(Q_I;\ \sigma(1+\tau)) + c_s\,(1-v_s)\sigma\overline{Q}_A - \sigma M(Q_I;\ \sigma(1+\tau)) - Q_I = 0 \qquad (7'')$$

Similarly

$$\beta[c_s v_s\overline{Q}_A - M(Q_I;\sigma(1+\tau)) + R - \overline{Q}_A] - \gamma\,[\sigma(1+\tau) - \overline{\sigma}] = 0 \quad (10'')$$

Following the usual custom of setting the initial $\tau = 0$ (but $d\tau \neq 0$), we will obtain the same matrix as above, except,

$$b_{14} = \sigma M(\epsilon - 1 + \Omega)$$

$$b_{24} = -\beta M + \gamma\sigma.$$

This gives:

$$dQ_I^*/d\tau = \frac{[c_s(1 - v_s)\bar{Q}_A - M]\ \sigma[\beta M_2 - \gamma M]}{|J|}$$

and
$$d\sigma^*/d\tau = \frac{\beta\sigma(MM_1 + M_2) - \beta\sigma A_1(M_2 + MM_1 Q_I/A)}{|J|}$$

The sufficient condition for $dQ_I^*/d\tau < 0$ is that the North runs a trade surplus, i.e. $c_s(1 - v_s)\bar{Q}_A > M$ and vice versa for $dQ_I^*/d\tau > 0$. As far as $d\sigma^*/d\tau$ is concerned, the sufficient condition for it be negative is $MM_1Q_I/A > M_2$. Given that $MM_1 + M_2 < 0$ by the Slutsky equation this can only occur if $Q_I > A$ i.e., income exceeds private absorption in the North, pointing to a trade balance surplus. The contractionary case is depicted in Figure 4, where the tariff shifts the NN curve rightwards and $\dot{\sigma}/\sigma = 0$ curve downwards. Final equilibrium is at E_2^* with lower output, Q_I and lower terms of trade, σ.

It is more plausible that the North runs a surplus with the South (see World Tables (1983)). In this case the tariff is contractionary for the North. When there is a trade surplus, one of the outlets for Northern savings is to finance the Southern deficit. After the imposition of the tariff, the terms of trade are likely to fall, reducing the value of Southern income and hence its imports, $c_s(1 - v_s)\sigma\bar{Q}_A$ from the North. The North will experience a negative export multiplier effect. This is in addition to the fact that Northern costs of production will rise; as the domestic cost of the importable, $P_A(1+\tau)$ increases so will the demand for money wages by Northern workers, resulting in an adverse supply effect. In all, the imposition of a tariff by the North, can have a deleterious effect upon both North and South, as the former suffers from a lower Q_I and the latter from reduced terms of trade. Our results do not lend a great deal of support to the CEPG position (Cripps and Godley (1978)), who advocate macro-commercial policy, as an expansionary device, precisely because of the presence of real wage resistance in the North.

FIGURE 4

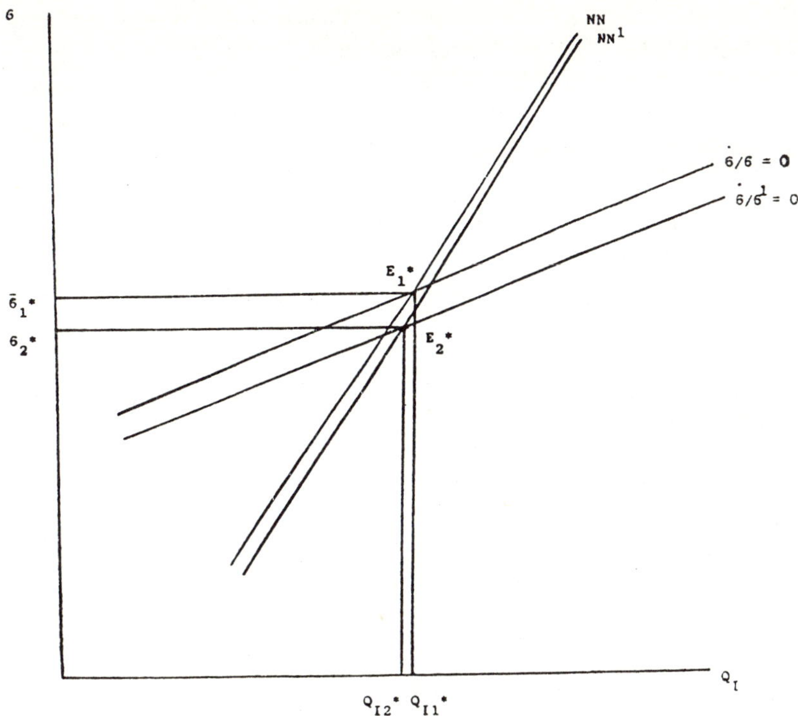

IV. COST OF CONTROLLING GLOBAL INFLATION

Before looking at policies, such as a reduction in autonomous expenditure, G, pursued to combat Northern inflation, it is worthwhile looking at the impact of changes in G, on Northern output, Q_I and the terms of trade σ.

$$dQ_I^*/dG = \frac{\gamma - \beta M_2}{|J|} > 0$$

$$d\sigma^*/dG = \frac{\beta M_1}{|J|} > 0$$

The expressions above are for an increase in G. It is clear that a rise in G raises aggregate demand in the North, raising output Q_I. It also intensifies excess demand for the Southern good, raising P_A; then W (given real wage resistance) and P_I; increasing the steady state inflation rates (which are equal) in both regions. Thus a reduction in G will decrease excess demand for Southern goods in the North and bring down the equilibrium terms of trade and the inflation rates, but at the expense of output Q_I (and employment) in the North. It is worthwhile noting that we do not have a monetary policy instrument available to the North in our model. But a reduction in G, fits the bill as an instrument of contractionary policy in the North, and as such reductions in G have been an OECD wide policy objective to combat inflation in the 1980s.

Suppose the target rate of Northern inflation is zero; then we need to have $\dot{P}_I = 0$. However, this is consistent with medium term steady state inflation provided $\dot{\sigma} = 0$. We therefore, also need $\dot{P}_A = 0$. For a 'proper' steady state to exist, inflation in the North and South must proceed at the same rate (here assumed to be zero). In Figure 5.1 this is given by the point E_2. The level of Northern output, Q_I in the figure, is determined by (8) and (10) to set

$$(1 - c_S v_S)\overline{Q}_A = R + M(\overline{Q}_I, \overline{\sigma}) \tag{14}$$

The 'required' or target government expenditure which will make this output feasible is one which makes output equal to aggregate demand. Hence, from (7),

$$G = \overline{Q}_I - A(\overline{Q}_I, \overline{\sigma}) - \overline{\sigma}\, c_S(1 - v_S)\, \overline{Q}_A + \overline{\sigma} M(\overline{Q}_I, \overline{\sigma}) \tag{15}$$

It is clear from Figure 5.1 that both the North and South have to bear the burden of adjustment of disinflation. If the initial equilibrium is at E_1, (with positive inflation) and the new equilibrium is at E_2 (with zero inflation) then output in the North falls from Q_I^* to $\overline{Q}_I$. The rise in unemployment is the obvious price that the North pays for inflation control. On the other hand the terms of trade decline thus reducing the relative price of the Southern good in the world market. National income of the South, in terms of the Northern good, σQ_A falls. Hence the South suffers in the medium term.

Up until now the analysis was conducted on the basis of a comparison between two equilibrium points, giving two steady state inflation rates. A more instructive point of view can be taken by considering the time path of adjustment. Consider a situation where output supply adjusts quickly, in the short run, to aggregate demand. Thus during the period of analysis $Q_I = AD$. The terms of trade σ, on the other hand, moves slowly over time. Thus the phase lines are given by the arrowed paths $Q_I = AD$.

The time path of adjustment is now E_1 to F and then F to E_2. For a given terms of trade, contractionary fiscal policy reduces Northern out-

FIGURE 5.1

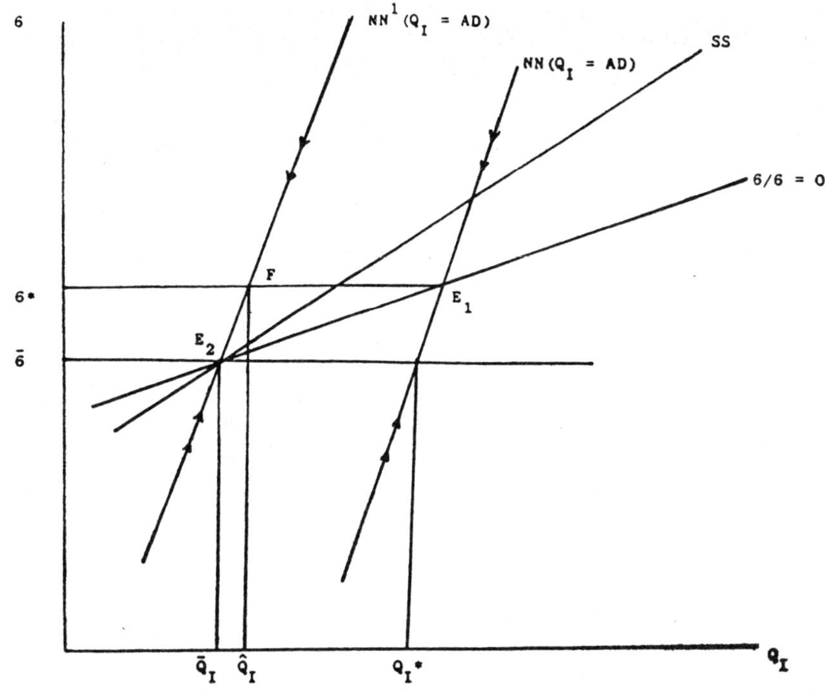

FIGURE 5.2

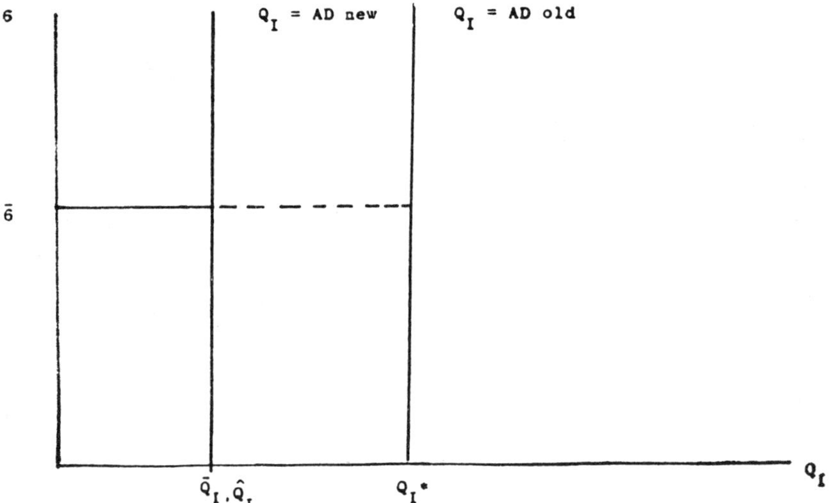

put from Q_I^* to $\hat{Q}_I$. At this stage, there is an excess supply of Southern goods (F is above $\dot{P}_A = 0$). This drives the price of Southern goods down, thus reducing the cost of living index in the North. A cheaper consumption basket reduces nominal wage growth thus contributing to a lower inflation rate. Since inflation is a product of real wage resistance in the North, it can be curtailed by a two pronged attack: a rise in unemployment following domestic deflation and a fall in imported inflation leading to a lower consumer price index.

The presence of the South, and the concomitant trading links, makes the North an 'open' economy. It is now well known that the costs of disinflation is *lower* in an open economy relative to a closed economy (Miller (1985)). A similar phenomenon can be observed here by comparing the standard North South model (as depicted in Figure 5.1) and a hypothetical 'closed' Northern economy, for example if trade was decoupled (as shown in Figure 5.2). The adjustment in the latter case calls for a much sharper initial fall in output, straightaway from Q_I^* to $\bar{Q}_I$. Thus the amount of fiscal contraction, for the hypothetical situation of Figure 5.2, is more severe. The whole burden of adjustment must fall on domestic deflation. In the usual North-South case of Figure 5.1, the absolute level of the fall in G is less since part of the burden of adjustment falls on σ. Thus there will be an initial shallow deflation, from Q_I^* to $\hat{Q}_I$; then the fall in σ will reduce exports of the North, as Southern income σQ_A and with it imports from the North decline, causing a further fall in output from $\hat{Q}_I$ to $\bar{Q}_I$. Essentially, the initial size of the recession is *lower* since part of the adjustment is transferred to the South. The fall in σ is therefore the price that the South will have to pay for the global recession initiated by the North.

A formal derivation is not given here due to intractabilities induced by the essential non–linearities of the system. But the reasoning follows from the formal results in Miller (1985). Essentially the North has a loss function:

$$L = \int_0^\infty [Q_I(s) - Q_F]^2 + [\pi(s) - 0]^2 ds \qquad (16)$$

where Q_F is full employment output and the targeted inflation rate is zero. Minimising the loss function subject to constraints will give us the optimal policy that the North can pursue. The value of the integral, L, is expected to be less in the North-South case (à la Miller) compared to the situation where the North goes it alone.

V. THE LONG RUN

The history of the post-war period, viewed in the very long-run, presents a different picture. In general, over this long cycle, governments in the North have usually pursued expansionary fiscal policies to boost output in the Keynesian fashion.[2] Growth, and output expansion, have generally been high in the North with cyclical fluctations smoothed out by Keynesian demand management policies. However, as the adherents of the Prebisch-Singer hypothesis take pains to point out, the terms of trade between the North and South (price of 'agriculture' to 'industry') have witnessed a secular decline. Thus global Keynesianism does not seem to have helped the South in general, even though there are localised exceptions (such as the Gang of Four).

Another major feature of the Northern economy is the power of trade unions which strengthens the phenomenon of real wage resistance discussed earlier. Over the long-run workers' awareness and resistance to real wage cuts have increased considerably. Thus their ability to attain their target real wage, related to the cost of living index, increases with time; hence the speed of adjustment, of nominal wages to achieve the desired target, also becomes large. Inflationary pressures in the North are heightened by workers attitudes. Industrial price inflation in turn plays a dominant role in the determination of the international terms of trade.

However, it would be unrealistic to suppose that increased militancy of Northern workers, will be unconnected to the degree of unemployment prevailing in the economy. In particular it is expected that the target wage would be scaled down during periods of unemployment and increased when there is a boom in the economy. This procyclical movement can be captured by assuming that the desired target level of real wages, $\bar{w}$, is an increasing function of Northern output, Q_I. We have

$$\bar{w} = \bar{w}(Q_I) \tag{17}$$

with $w_1 > 0$

where $\bar{w} = W/P$

and $P_I = (1+g)\, W/a.$

2. Government expenditure in the Keynesian North wil' still be expansionary even if it is met by increased taxation via the balanced budget multiplier.

Thus, we have

$$\bar{\sigma} = \left[\frac{(1+g)}{\alpha}\bar{w}(Q_I)\right]^{\frac{1}{\delta-1}} = \bar{\sigma}(Q_I) \tag{18}$$

δ is once more the share of the Northern good in the Northern worker's expenditure basket.

Equation (18) gives a *negative* relation between Northern output, Q_I, and the required terms of trade, $\bar{\sigma}$. We believe that this portrays the relation between wage behaviour and the terms of trade, for the North, over the business cycles which is itself embedded in the long-term secular dynamics of the system.

Another interpretation of (18) can be given from the point of view of the Northern firm. Any rise in output in the North, Q_I has to be associated with a higher P_I relative to W (a lower real product wage). The only manner in which a lower real product wage to firms can be reconciled with the objectives of workers desired living standards is for P_A to fall. This is because a decline in the price of the Southern good, P_A compensates workers for the rise in P_I relative to money wages, W, maintaining a constant standard of living. Thus, a higher Q_I will be associated with lower equilibrium terms of trade, $\sigma = P_A/P_I$. In other words, given the goals of firms and workers a higher Q_I has to be associated with a lower $\bar{\sigma}$.

We now turn to the dynamic behaviour of the terms of trade in this long run model. In the previous section we have seen that the differential equation governing the time path of σ was given by equation (10):

$$\frac{\dot{\sigma}}{\sigma} = \beta\ [c_S\, v_S\, \bar{Q}_A + M(Q_I, \sigma) + R - \bar{Q}_A] - \gamma\,(\sigma - \bar{\sigma})$$

which can be written as

$$\frac{\dot{\sigma}}{\sigma} = \gamma\ \{(\beta/\gamma)\ [c_S v_S \bar{Q}_A + M\,(Q_I, \sigma) + R - \bar{Q}_A] - (\sigma - \bar{\sigma})\} \tag{19}$$

The coefficient γ gives the speed of adjustment by which Northern workers respond to the discrepancy between the actual and desired terms of trade. Alternatively, it shows how workers will react to a cut in their real wage, from its targeted level, by trying to increase their nominal wage. Our earlier discussion suggests that in the long run this coefficient has increased considerably over time. Coupled with this is the fact that the South has found it increasingly difficult to increase the price of its own good, 'agriculture', in the face of excess demand. Technical substitution, growth of European food surpluses, increased competition, and other such factors have made it more and more difficult for Southern price to respond fast to market conditions (in the long run). Thus it is thought that the coefficient β in (equation (10) and (19)) has become smaller over time.

If γ is high and β low then $(\beta/\gamma) \rightarrow 0$ and equation (19) degenerates to

$$\frac{\dot{\sigma}}{\sigma} = \gamma\,[\bar{\sigma} - \sigma] \tag{20}$$

The implications of (20) should be carefully noted. The dynamic behaviour of the international terms of trade are now being determined, exclusively, by domestic economic behaviour of the North. If the actual real wage is below the desired level (alternately, $\sigma > \bar{\sigma}$), Northern workers will push up their nominal wage sufficiently high to cause the terms of trade $\sigma = P_A/P_I$ to decline (remember P_I is proportional to the nominal wage). In a sense the South is now impotent to influence relative prices.

Since it cannot influence σ in the long run, it will try to accommodate to excess demand (supply) for "agriculture" by trying to change the *effective* quantity of goods put on the market. One way of doing this would be to vary the constant proportions, c_S, v_S of the Southern expenditure basket. But this has not been a viable option for most *LDCs* due to various historical and cultural reasons, not least being the resistance of the elite to any changes in consumption patterns. Most Southern nations have gone for the 'soft' option i.e. to change residual consumption and make R an accommodating variable. In effect, when there is excess demand for the Southern product then R falls so that this additional demand can be met. We therefore have

$$\dot{R} = \Phi[\bar{Q}_A - c_S v_S \bar{Q}_A - R - M(Q_I, \sigma)] \tag{21}$$

Adding on the dynamic equation (7) for the North completes the long run model.

One of the most interesting features of the long run dynamic model is that the South becomes effectively 'decoupled' from the international system although it fully participates in world trade. Although the South must be crucially interested in the equilibrium value of σ, it finds it cannot influence it in any meaningful way. *Both* Q_I and σ are determined by Northern actions and behaviour, the South only accommodates through its residual expenditure, R.

Figure 6 gives the diagrammatics of the situation. It represents *long-run equilibrium* in Q_I, σ space and is constructed on the basis of the following equations (setting $\dot{Q}_I = \dot{\sigma} = \dot{R} = 0$):

$$Q_I^* = A(Q_I^*, \sigma^*) + \sigma^* c_s (1 - v_s) \overline{Q}_A - \sigma^* M (Q_I^*, \sigma^*) + G \tag{22}$$

$$\sigma^* = \overline{\sigma}(Q_I^*) \tag{23}$$

$$R^* = (1 - c_s v_s) \overline{Q}_A - M(Q_I^*, \sigma^*) \tag{24}$$

FIGURE 6

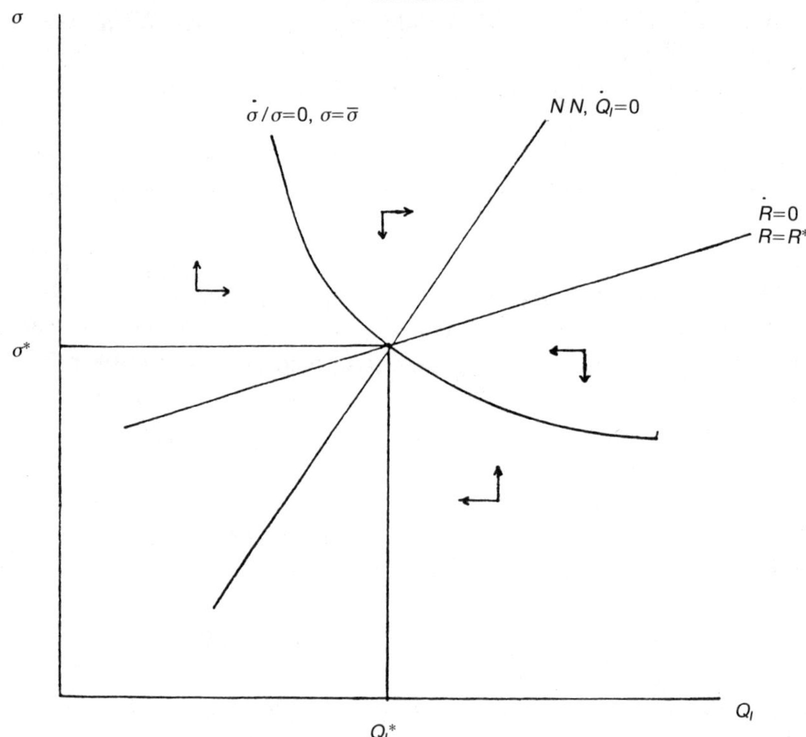

The curve $\dot{\sigma}/\sigma = 0$ or $\sigma = \overline{\sigma}(Q_I)$ is negatively sloping given that $\overline{\sigma}_1 < 0$. The curve NN, ($\dot{Q}_I = 0$) is upward rising as in our earlier discussion. The line $\dot{R}=0$ is drawn on the basis of a given R^* which is the equilibrium residual consumption in the South (see equation (24)).

It is clear by observing equations (22) and (23) that Q_I and σ are derived, in long run equilibrium, from the economic behaviour of the North alone. The system is decomposable in the sense that (22) and (23) determine Q_I and σ without reference to the Southern equilibrium relation (24). This is the formal counterpart of the concept of "decoupling" mentioned earlier. The only thing that remains for the South to determine is its own consumption, specifically the value of residual expenditure, R^*.

FIGURE 7

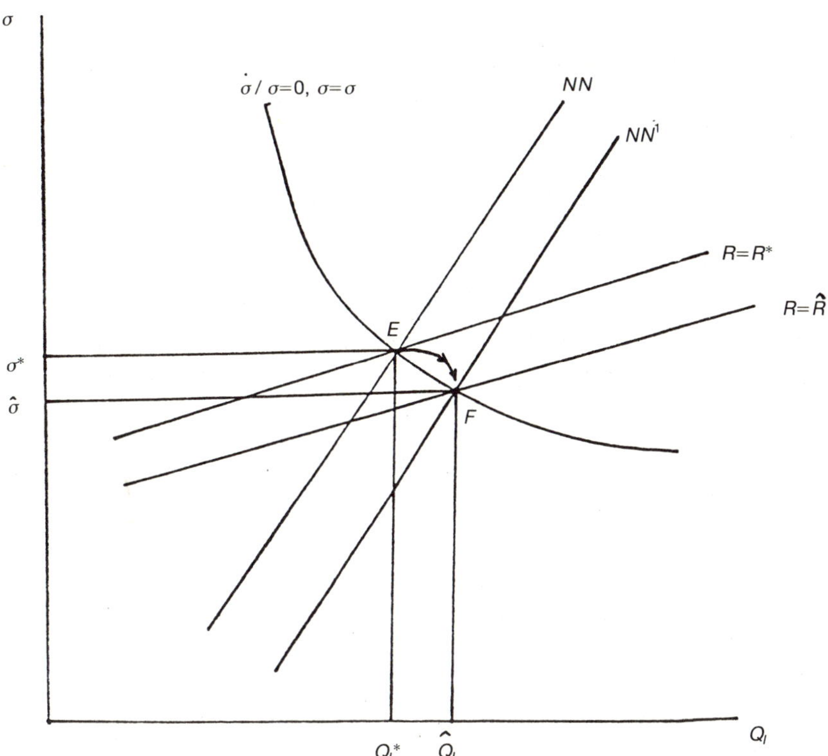

The new equilibrium values are denoted by a hat ^ in Figure 7. An expansionary Northern policy raises aggregate demand; hence Q_I should rise. But this calls for an increase in nominal wage which in turn leads to a decline in the terms of trade, σ, wage costs are passed on to a higher Northern price level; given the inability of the South to effectively counteract, the relative price of "agriculture" falls. We get a movement from E to F. Both the rise in Q_I and the fall in σ increases the North's import of the South's product. Since Q_A is inelastic (or may even fall in the face of a decline in σ), residual consumption in the South must fall to accommodate this additional export demand. Thus R declines. This causes the $R^* = R$ line to float downwards. In the final analysis R becomes equal to $\hat{R} < R^*$ and its actual level can be derived from an equation like (24) given the values of $Q_I = \hat{Q}_I$ and $\sigma = \hat{\sigma}$.

Our analysis, in this section, suggests that over the very long run (say during the last four decades), Northern governments have generally followed expansionary fiscal policies. This has benefitted the North whose long term output, in spite of some ironing out, is at unprecedented high levels by historical standards. This could have increased Southern prices, through additional exports, and benefitted their terms of trade. However, Northern workers increased strength has caused nominal and hence real wages to increase. Cost increases in the North, passed on to 'industrial' prices have in fact reduced the terms of trade. The twin effects of higher Northern output and lower Southern (relative) prices have increased imports from the South. Faced with inelastic output, the South has accommodated this higher demand by reducing its own residual consumption and supplying more on the world market. In effect, the long-term decline in R has caused entitlement losses, reductions in the provision of basic needs and probably a higher incidence of malnutrition and famines. Effectively, as the South continues in its traditional role of 'the hewers of raw materials and drawers of oil'[3] for the North, en-route it may also suffer losses in basic consumption needs.

VI. CONCLUDING IMPLICATIONS

In the medium-run version of our model, increases in Northern autonomous expenditure raises both Northern output and Southern terms of trade This squares in with the facts of the major post-war booms, such as the periods associated .with the Korean and Vietnam wars. Global Keynesianism of the Brandtian variety works; but given the presence of real wage resistance in the North, it has inflationary consequences. These booms are followed by policy induced recessions, aimed at reducing inflation. This can shift some of the costs of disinflation to the South, in the form of lower Southern terms of trade. Thus, in the medium-term, it is in Southern interests to moderate the extent of Northern recessions, as far as possible.

The long-run variant of our model attempts to explain the secular decline in the Southern terms of trade. This could be because Northern real wage resistance gradually stiffened as Northern output grew in the post-war period. It seems that as Northern demand for Southern goods increased, the

3. Quoted from Taylor (1983).

South met this by reductions in the quantities of basic needs consumption, instead of substantially lowering its propensity to import from the North. The clear implication for the South in the long-run is to reduce its dependence on the North, in favour of more South-South trade. The alternative is technological progress in the North, which could mitigate the adverse effects of real wage resistance by lowering Northern price inflation. However, technological progress in the South by lowering its terms of trade, has immiserising effects in that region.

University of Birmingham, U.K.

REFERENCES

Beckerman, W. and Jenkinson, T. (1986) 'What stopped the Inflation? Unemployment or Commodity Prices?', *Economic Journal*, 96 : 39 – 54.

Cardoso, E.A. (1981) 'Food Supply and Inflation', *Journal of Development Economics*, 8 : 269–284.

Cripps, F. and Godley, W. (1978) 'Control of Imports as Means to Full Employment and the Expansion of World Trade: The U.K.'s Case', *Cambridge Journal of Economics*, 2 : 327–334.

Dornbusch, R. (1980) *Open Economy Macroeconomics*, (New York: Basic Books).

Kanbur, R. and Vines, D. (1986) 'North – South Interaction and Commod Control', *Journal of Development Economics*, 23 : 371 - 387.

Laursen, S. and Metzler, L.A. (1950) 'Flexible Exchange Rates and the Theory of Employment', *Review of Economics and Statistics*, 32 : 281 - 299.

Miller, M.H. (1985) 'Monetary Stabilization Policy in an Open Economy', *International Finance Discussion Papers*, 262.

Page, S. (1987) 'The Rise in Protection since 1974', *Oxford Review of Economic Policy*, 3 /1 : 37 – 51.

Prebisch, R. (1950) *The Economic Development of Latin America and its Principal Problems*, (New York : U.N.).

Taylor, L. (1983) *Structuralist Macroeconomics*, (New York : Basic Books).

World Bank (1983) 3rd edition 'World Tables', (Baltimore : Johns Hopkins University Press).

ECONOMIC INTERACTIONS AND THE FISCAL POLICIES OF MAJOR INDUSTRIAL COUNTRIES: 1980 — 1988

By Paul R. Masson and Malcolm Knight*

Throughout much of the period since 1980, economic interactions among the major industrial countries have been characterized by three stylized facts. First, long-term interest rates adjusted for inflation – real interest rates – have generally remained at levels that are high by historical standards. Second, as regards international payments positions, the external current account deficit of the United States and the surpluses of Japan and the Federal Republic of Germany rose sharply after 1982, and this pattern of large imbalances has persisted since then. Third, the real value of the U.S. dollar – the dollar's nominal exchange rate adjusted for movements in U.S. unit labor costs relative to those in a weighted average of trading partners – experienced an enormous swing. From the third quarter of 1980 to the first quarter of 1985 the real value of the dollar rose by nearly 60 percent. Thereafter, over the three-year period to the first quarter of 1988, it depreciated by almost the same percentage.

It is widely recognized that a number of factors contributed to these major features of recent economic experience (Frenkel (1985)). This paper emphasizes one such factor; namely, the role of shifts in the fiscal positions of the three largest industrial countries. The paper elaborates the theoretical and empirical aspects of this linkage (see also Knight and Masson (1988)). Using a simple heuristic model as well as simulation experiments on a more sophisticated econometric system, we attempt to get both a qualitative and a quantitative impression of the importance of fiscal developments as causes of these stylized facts.

A first version of this analysis[1] published in 1986, emphasized the role

* International Monetary Fund. This chapter reflects views of the authors which are not necessarily those of the IMF.

1. An earlier version of this study, entitled "International Transmission of Fiscal Policies in Major Industrial Countries" was published in IMF Staff Papers Vol. 33 no. 3 (September 1986), pp.387-438. For the present version, the material has been updated to end-1987 (in some cases, early 1988), a new Section IV, describing the results of a further simulation experiment has been added, and the conclusions (Section V) incorporate the inferences drawn from the updated simulation work.

of fiscal developments in the appreciation phase of the swing in the dollar's exchange rate from 1980 to 1985. However, our model also serves to show how the actual and announced shifts in the fiscal positions of the three largest industrial economies during the past three years have contributed to the substantial real depreciation of the U.S. dollar that has taken place since early 1985. To emphasize this aspect of the model, we have updated our 1986 study by including the results of a new simulation experiment. The broad conclusion emphasized by the new simulation experiment is that while the impact effect of the increased U.S. fiscal deficits on saving and investment flows tended to raise the U.S. dollar in the early 1980s, the prospective shift to a more restrained fiscal stance in the United States after 1985 has been a major reason for the dollar's decline from 1985 to 1988. The simulation experiment also suggests that a second factor contributing to the depreciation phase in the dollar's swing has been the gradual buildup of U.S. external liabilities resulting from the large U.S. fiscal deficits of the early 1980s. The rising external debt service obligations of the United States have necessitated a gradual improvement in the U.S. merchandise trade balance in order to maintain a sustainable external current account position. Other things equal, the international competitiveness of the U.S. economy must be enhanced via a real exchange rate depreciation in order for the reduction in the trade deficit to occur.

Table 1 summarizes macroeconomic developments in the three largest industrial economies during the period from 1980 to the first quarter of 1988. It shows that from 1980 through 1985 a simple measure of the U.S. real long-term interest rate rose by over six percentage points. During the same period the U.S. current account shifted from a balanced position to an annual deficit of over $ 116 billion, while those of Japan and Germany moved from substantial deficits to surpluses of $ 49 billion and $ 15 billion, respectively. Finally, the annual average level of the dollar's real effective exchange rate was some 46 percent higher in 1985 than it had been in 1980, while the yen's real value remained roughly unchanged and that of the deutschemark declined by about 10 percent.

After 1985 the dollar depreciated sharply in real effective terms, by some 36 percent from its average level in 1985 to the first quarter of 1988. Nevertheless, both high real interest rates and the pattern of current account imbalances among the three largest industrial countries that had been established in 1980-85 remained little changed : The U.S. current account deficit was $ 152 billion in 1987 (3.4 percent of GNP) while the surplus of Japan was $ 85 billion (3.6 percent of GNP) and that of Germany was $ 41 billion (3.6 percent of GNP).

The fiscal developments emphasized in this paper are : first, the sustained

TABLE 1

Selected Variables for the United States, the Federal Republic of Germany, and Japan, 1980-1988

Variable	1980	1983	1985	1986	1987	1988	Cumulative Fiscal Impulse[a] 1980–1986	Cumulative Fiscal Impulse[a] 1987–1988
Real effective exchange rate[b]								
United States	100	130	146	117	102	93[f]	—	—
Germany	100	93	90	89	104	106[f]	—	—
Japan	100	101	100	120	123	132[f]	—	—
Current account balance[c]								
United States	+2	—46	—116	—141	—152	—141[g]		
Germany	—16	+4	+15	+37	+41	+33[g]		
Japan	—11	+21	+49	+86	+85	+83[g]		
Real long-term interest rate[d]								
United States	1.3	7.8	7.9	4.6	4.7	4.4[f]	—	—
Germany	2.6	4.8	6.3	5.7	3.8	4.3[f]	—	—
Japan	3.9	6.6	5.9	6.2	4.7	4.3[f]	—	—
General Government fiscal balance[e]								
United States	—1.3	—3.8	—3.3	—3.5	—2.3	—2.4[g]	+2.9	—1.2[g]
Germany	—2.9	—2.5	—1.1	—1.2	—1.5	—2.0[g]	—2.8	+0.5[g]
Japan	—4.4	—3.7	—0.8	—0.6	—1.2	—1.6[g]	—4.8	+0.7[g]

Sources: International Monetary Fund, International Financial Statistics (Washington, various issues), and World Economic Outlook (Washington, October 1987, Tables A17 and A31).

a. Simple sum of annual fiscal impulses. A net expansionary impulse (discretionary increase in the fiscal deficit) is indicated by a plus, a contractionary impulse (movement toward surplus) by a minus.

b. Foreign currency per unit of domestic currency (index : 1980 = 100); annual averages as measured by relarive normalized unit labor costs.

c. In billions of U.S. dollars; includes official transfers.

d. In percent; annual average yields on long-term government bonds, adjusted by change in gross national product (GNP) deflator.

e. Actual values measured as percentage of GNP; a fiscal deficit is indicated by a minus, a surplus by a plus.

f. Average values during first three months.

g. Projected.

shift in the pattern of fiscal positions that resulted from the strong expansion of the U.S. fiscal deficit at a time of fiscal consolidation in Germany and Japan (roughly over 1982-85); second, the tax incentives for investment spending that were implemented during this period in the United States; and third the actual and projected move to a more restrained fiscal stance in the United States since 1986, together with modest stimulus in Japan and Germany.

Table 1 presents data on the shifts from 1980 to 1988, as measured by actual fiscal positions and by actual and projected cumulative fiscal impulses, which attempt to gauge the short-term discretionary thrust of fiscal policy in each country. Although there is considerable dispute about the best way of measuring the fiscal stance from the point of view of the variables that are of interest here (see International Monetary Fund (1986, Supplementary Note 1, pp. 109-23)), there can be little doubt that, over the period 1980-85 taken as a whole, the broad stance of U.S. fiscal policy was very expansionary at a time when Germany and Japan were moving vigorously toward restraint.

By contrast, since 1986 the pattern of fiscal positions in the three major countries has changed significantly. The last column of Table 1 is the simple sum of the estimated fiscal impulse for each country in 1987 and the projected impulse for 1988 (as given in the October 1987 IMF, *World Economic Outlook*, Table A17). These estimates suggest that in 1987-88 the actual and projected fiscal stance in the United States has shifted from the strong expansionary impulse of the earlier years to a strong contractionary impulse. At the same time the cumulative fiscal impulses in Japan and the Federal Republic of Germany have shifted from sharp contraction to modest expansion.

Because our purpose is to analyze the relationship between the stance of fiscal policies and the pattern of current account positions and exchange rates that can be sustained over the medium term, we abstract from short-run portfolio-allocation decisions about stocks of domestic and foreign assets – see Kouri and Porter (1974); Dornbusch (1975); Girton and Henderson (1977); Branson, Halttunen, and Masson (1977); and Knight and Mathieson (1983) – and concentrate instead on the intertemporal decisions that determine flows of domestic saving and capital accumulation.[2] Although such an approach cannot provide much insight into the causes of day-to-day or month-to-month fluctuations in market exchange rates, which in any case approximate a random walk (see Frenkel (1985)), it may serve to highlight how shifts in fiscal policy in the largest industrial economies influence private saving

2. Obviously, a complete model would derive the determinants of both portfolio allocation and saving-investment decisions from a general maximizing framework. However, the role of intertemporal choice in the determination of exchange rates has, until recently, received less attention in the literature.

and investment behavior both at home and abroad, leading to changes in the level of world interest rates and in the pattern of real exchange rates and current account positions that is sustainable over the medium term. Such an approach seems particularly relevant, given the developments of recent years that are summarized in Table 1.

The basic point that is emphasized by our analysis is that both the actual fiscal changes in the United States, Germany, and Japan since the early 1980s and the large prospective shifts that would occur if a comprehensive fiscal deficit reduction program were fully implemented in the United States constitute major exogenous disturbances to total saving and investment flows in the largest industrial countries. Thus, we model the determinants of the overall current account not in standard terms of import demand and export supply, but in terms of intertemporal decisions about saving and investment. Such an approach has a long history in the literature, dating back to the work of Laursen and Metzler (1950) and Mundell (1963). More recent contributions include Dornbusch (1975), Dornbusch and Fischer (1980), Sachs (1981), Svensson and Razin (1983), Sachs and Wyplosz (1984), Frenkel and Razin (1984, 1985a, 1985b), Branson (1985), and Feldstein (1986).

The rest of the paper is organized as follows. Section I describes a simple theoretical model of the international transmission of fiscal policies. Section II briefly sets out the specification and estimates of a more complete empirical model that shares the basic features of the model of the preceding section but also allows for a number of crucial, real-world complications : the effects of shifts in the general level of economic activity on private saving and investment, and the consequences of the gradual accumulations of productive capital and wealth for the behavior of the major world variables in which we are interested – interest rates, exchange rates, and current account positions – in both the short and the long run. Section III describes four sets of simulation experiments designed to analyze the effects of several exogenous shocks, including shifts in fiscal deficits of the broad order of magnitude experienced in the three largest industrial countries in 1982-85 and the investment incentives introduced in the United States during that period. Section IV presents an update and extension of the simulation work on the international transmission of fiscal policies that was described in our original paper. Finally, Section V summarizes the main conclusions.

I. A SIMPLE MODEL OF INTERNATIONAL TRANSMISSION OF FISCAL POLICIES

Our model is "classical" in the sense that it emphasizes capital transfers and the saving-investment balance and is consistent with all three of the stylized facts of the international economy that were noted in the introduction to this paper. It starts from the proposition that if there is an autonomous rise in a country's fiscal deficit or in intended private investment, that country will have to rely more heavily on saving from abroad (or on a reduction in the amount of domestic saving it provides to the rest of the world). For the increased saving from abroad to enter through the capital account, the current account must be pushed into deficit via an appreciation of the real effective exchange rate and a loss of international competitiveness. In addition, if the home country is large enough to affect the aggregate demand for saving in the world market, the general level of real interest rates in international credit markets may be expected to rise.[3]

This process can be described by a model that does not depend on an elaborate specification of the effects of fiscal policy on the level of real income[4] and that avoids the complex issue of the effect of international interest rate differentials on exchange rates and capital flows. Consider a world of two large countries : the home country and the rest of the world, *ROW* (with variables for the rest of the world indicated by an asterisk). All variables, including the exchange rate and the interest rate, are defined in real terms, taking units of domestic output as the numeraire.

The notation of the model is

ε = the exchange rate (relative price of *ROW* output in terms of home-country output),

R = the world real interest rate,

S, S^* = flows of private sector saving in the home country and the rest of the world, respectively,

I, I^* = private sector fixed-capital formation in the home country and the rest of the world,

N, N^* = the current account balance of the home country and the rest of the world (with a surplus indicated by a plus),

D, D^* = the public sector fiscal deficit in the home country and the rest of the world,

where for any function $F(x)$, $F_x = \partial F / \partial x$.

3. Our analysis refers specifically to the largest industrial economies. It also excludes cases in which a country's initial fiscal position is viewed as unsustainable, either because it implies a continuously rising ratio of government debt to national income (Masson (1985)) or because the initial outstanding stock of official foreign debt poses significant problems of "sovereign credit risk".

4. This is so even though, as Buiter (1983) has rightly emphasized, both the time path and the steady-state effects of shifts in fiscal policy depend crucially on the specific types of public sector spending and tax changes by which they are implemented.

Because we are here taking simplicity to be a virtue, we initially make a number of highly restrictive assumptions. In particular, we suppose that there is perfect flexibility of goods prices (thus allowing us to ignore the effects of changes in money stocks on real magnitudes). Both private investment and government spending are financed by the issue of one-period bonds, and all bonds, wherever issued, are viewed as perfect substitutes for one another. Finally, we suppose that market participants expect the real exchange rate to persist at its current level in the future. The assumptions about substitutability and expectations ensure that there is a fully integrated world credit market with a single world interest rate. These assumptions are all made so that we can highlight the implications of the model with the greatest possible clarity; the assumptions will be relaxed when we proceed to the empirical analysis of Section III.

Ex ante saving and investment are both assumed to depend on the real interest rate. Because of adjustment costs, real private net investment exhibits lagged adjustment to an optimal capital stock, which in turn depends on the user cost of capital (Gould (1968)). At a given level of the real interest rate R, changes in the tax treatment of investment will also affect firms' incentives to undertake fixed-capital formation. We specify a simple investment function of the form

$$I = I(R) \tag{1}$$

where $I(\ )$ is also affected (in a way to be specified later) by changes in tax legislation.

Private saving is taken as the outcome of individuals' intertemporal optimization of the utility from consumption (Mussa (1976)). For a given rate of time preference and expected future wage income, higher real interest rates will decrease consumption. A rise in the real interest rate, however, may either raise or lower real private saving, since current income is increased for households holding positive net claims; hence the sign of the partial derivative of saving with respect to R is ambiguous. Here we impose the weaker restriction that if intended saving declines when the interest rate rises, such saving falls by less than intended investment.

Because private sector saving decisions are likely to depend on the perceived level of household net wealth, any analysis of the international transmission of fiscal policies must confront the issue of debt neutrality (Barro (1974)). The Barro-Ricardo hypothesis of debt neutrality asserts that if individuals and firms expect that the government will raise taxes in the future to finance the debt service on the bonds, and that they or their descendants will have to pay those taxes eventually, then there may be little difference between financing government spending through tax increases or through bond issues (Barro (1974) and Carmichael (1982)). Under the extreme assumptions that individuals are fully rational, can borrow and lend in perfect capital markets, and value their descendants' consumption as highly as their own, bonds issued by the home government are not properly treated as a component of the private sector's net wealth, which will consist only of the capital stock and net claims on foreign residents. In this case a rise in the fiscal deficit (that is, an increase in public sector dissaving) would be exactly offset by a higher flow of saving by the private sector. Holdings of bonds issued by foreign governments would still be part of wealth because the taxes to service them are levied on foreign residents.[5]

Although most economists would now concede that changes in public sector saving are likely to be offset at least partially by alterations in private saving behavior, there are several reasons for expecting that, in practice, households would not make a full offset of any change in their holdings of bonds to take account of future taxes. In particular, they face significant capital market imperfections, and they may not value their descendants' welfare equally with their own (Buiter and Tobin (1979)).

If taxes and real interest rates are expected to remain constant in the future, then a simple model of aggregate consumption behavior implies that the proportion of government bond holdings that is considered net wealth by the private sector will be unity minus the ratio of the government's discount rate to that of the private sector (Blanchard (1985), Knight and Masson (1988)). We call this proportion φ; it should lie between zero and unity. A value of φ that is less than unity implies that the private sector treats only a corresponding fraction of government debt as part of its net worth, with the rest reflecting the present discounted value of future tax liabilities.

Measured private saving equals the private sector's total net asset accumulation, including its acquisition of government debt. Thus, total private saving S equals the change in private net wealth plus $(1 - \varphi)$ times the government deficit D (that is, the increase in the outstanding stock of government debt):

$$S = S(R) + (1 - \varphi)D, \qquad (2)$$

where $S(R)$ is the component of private saving that corresponds to net wealth accumulation and $(1 - \varphi)D$ is the "Barro-Ricardo component" reflecting the private sector's induced response to public sector dissaving.

5. It is assumed that governments levy taxes on their own residents only, and that taxes are levied in lump-sum, so that they modify neither the return to labor nor that to capital.

Because net exports of goods and services N (the current account surplus) respond to the price of the home good relative to the foreign good, we assume that the home country's real current account in terms of domestic output tends toward deficit when its currency appreciates in real terms (that is ε, falls), and vice versa when the home currency depreciates.[6]

Macroeconomic equilibrium in the home country occurs when ex ante private saving minus private domestic investment and the government's fiscal deficit equals the current account surplus :

$$S - I(R) - D = N(\varepsilon). \tag{3}$$

Substituting equation (2) into equation (3) yields the following modification of the equilibrium condition :

$$S(R) - I(R) - \varphi D = N(\varepsilon). \tag{4}$$

The restrictions on the partial derivatives of the behavioral functions of equation (4) are

$$N_\varepsilon > 0, \quad I_R < 0, \quad (S_R - I_R) > 0, \quad 1 \geqslant \varphi \geqslant 0.$$

The analogous saving-investment equilibrium for the rest of the world is

$$S^*(R) - I^*(R) - \varphi^* D^* = N^*(\varepsilon), \tag{5}$$

with the restrictions

$$I_R^* < 0, \quad (S_R^* - I_R^*) > 0, \quad 1 \geqslant \varphi^* \geqslant 0.$$

Equations (4) and (5) do not constitute two independent conditions for macroeconomic equilibrium because, in a two-country world, the home country's current account surplus must equal the deficit of the rest of the world :

$$N^*(\varepsilon) = - N(\varepsilon). \tag{6}$$

This identity serves to emphasize the fact that the partial derivative N_ε embodies the effects of expenditure switching by both home and foreign residents : a fall in the relative price of home-country output (an improvement in inter-

6. Because a change in the real exchange rate (the price of foreign output in terms of domestic output) has a valuation effect as well as a volume effect on N, our assumption that $N < 0$ requires that the Marshall-Lerner condition be fulfilled.

national competitiveness) leads to higher demand for home goods by both domestic residents and foreigners. Finally, assuming a "pure" float, real private capital transfers from the rest of the world to the home country (that is, the use of foreign saving by the home country) must always equal N^*.

The model of equations (4)-(6) determines three endogenous variables: the world real interest rate, R; the real exchange rate, ε; and the current account balance, $N = -N^*$, prevailing between the home country and the rest of the world. The exogenous variables are the public sector fiscal deficits at home and abroad, D and D^*, and the (unspecified) factors that may shift saving, investment, and net export schedules.

The total differential of the system represented by equations (4)-(6) is

$$\begin{bmatrix} (S_R - I_R) & -N_\varepsilon \\ (S_R^* - I_R^*) & N_\varepsilon \end{bmatrix} \begin{bmatrix} dR \\ d\varepsilon \end{bmatrix} = \begin{bmatrix} \varphi dD \\ \varphi^* dD^* \end{bmatrix}. \tag{7}$$

The determinant of the coefficient matrix, Δ, is

$$\Delta = N_\varepsilon(S_R - I_R) + N_\varepsilon(S_R^* - I_R^*), \tag{8}$$

which, given our assumptions about the partial derivatives, is unambiguously positive.

Suppose that, starting from a balanced current account position, either the government of the home country increases its fiscal deficit by some amount dD or the foreign country raises its fiscal deficit by dD^*. The system of equation (7) gives the following effects on the endogenous variables:

$$\begin{aligned} \frac{dR}{dD} &= \frac{\varphi N_\varepsilon}{\Delta} > 0 & \frac{dR}{dD^*} &= \frac{\varphi^* N_\varepsilon}{\Delta} > 0 \\ \frac{d\varepsilon}{dD} &= \frac{\varphi(I_R^* - S_R^*)}{\Delta} < 0 & \frac{d\varepsilon}{dD^*} &= \frac{\varphi^*(S_R - I_R)}{\Delta} > 0 \\ \frac{dN}{dD} &= \frac{\varphi N_\varepsilon(I_R^* - S_R^*)}{\Delta} < 0 & \frac{dN}{dD^*} &= \frac{\varphi^* N_\varepsilon(S_R - I_R)}{\Delta} > 0. \end{aligned} \tag{9}$$

Consider first the case of fiscal expansion in the home country. If the private sector treats some fraction ($0 < \varphi < 1$) of domestic government bonds as a component of its net worth, an increase in the home country's fiscal deficit, dD, will raise the world interest rate, cause the domestic currency to appreciate in real terms, and induce a deterioration of the home country's current account balance that will be financed by a transfer of capital from the rest of the world. These results have a simple intuitive rationale. When an increase in the home country's public sector fiscal deficit disturbs the domestic saving-investment balance, the excess demand for saving must be financed by an inflow of capital from the rest of the world. For this capital transfer to be effected, the home country's current account must move into deficit, and this movement is accomplished by a real appreciation of the domestic currency in the foreign exchange market. However, other things being equal, an increase in public sector dissaving by the home country creates an imbalance between global saving and investment, necessitating a rise in the *world* real interest rate to restore equilibrium.[7] Finally, the results in equations (9) make it clear that the deterioration in both the home country's international competitiveness and its current account position will be greater the larger is the interest sensitivity of private investment minus private saving in the *foreign* country.

Analogous results hold for the case of an increase of the public sector fiscal deficit, dD^*, in the rest of the world : provided that $\varphi^* > 0$, a more expansionary fiscal policy in the rest of the world will also raise the world interest rate but will cause the home currency to depreciate and will induce a current account movement in the opposite direction to that referred to above.[8]

Note once more that these results hold for deficit shifts in each country only if the relevant value of φ does not equal zero, implying that full Barro-Ricardo equivalence does not hold. In general, the value of φ depends, among other things, on the life expectancies of households (Blanchard (1985)) and on private sector expectations about the specific types of future tax and spending measures that the government will introduce to achieve its desired stance of fiscal policy. Thus the values of φ may differ significantly, not only among countries but over time, as views change about likely future fiscal policies.

It would also be possible to calculate the comparative static effects of autonomous changes in private investment expenditure or in private saving behavior, although this is not done formally here. An autonomous increase in private investment spending, for instance, would have the same effects on the world real interest rate, the home country's real exchange rate, and the current account position as a rise in the fiscal deficit, except that in this case the comparative static effects (analogous to equations (9) above) would not be premultiplied by φ and φ^*. Because both parameters lie between zero and unity,

7. If domestic and foreign securities were not perfect substitutes, domestic interest rates would also rise relative to the world interest rate. The implications of this latter mechanism for the determination of real exchange rates are considered in Branson (1985).

8. Also note that a one-unit increase in the *ROW* fiscal deficit would increase the world interest rate by the same amount as a one-unit increase in the domestic deficit only if $\varphi = \varphi^*$.

it is obvious that the effects of a given increase in private investment on interest rates, the current account, and the exchange rate are always larger than those of a rise of the same size in the fiscal deficit. Put simply, unless domestic households regard all increases in the outstanding stock of government debt as a full addition to their wealth, a dollar of investment spending will always yield more "bang per buck" than a dollar rise in the fiscal deficit, in terms of the variables discussed here. The reason for this difference is also intuitively apparent : unlike current government spending, net investment always represents an addition to the stock of private sector productive capital; hence it is an increment to private sector wealth.

To summarize, an autonomous increase in private investment in the home country will tend to raise interest rates at home and abroad and to appreciate the home currency by more than an equal increase in the fiscal deficit. Higher interest rates will tend to reduce investment in the foreign economy, which did not experience the initial autonomous investment shift. Analogous results hold for the case of an increase in investment in the rest of the world.

The implications of the preceding analysis for the world real interest rate and the real exchange rate between the two countries are illustrated in Figure 1. In the figure, the vertical axis is the real exchange rate (ε) – the relative price of the rest of the world's output in terms of home output – and the horizontal axis is the world real interest rate (R). The SI curve is the locus of combinations of the interest rate and the real exchange rate that, for given public sector fiscal positions, equates the ex ante home-country private saving-investment balance with the ex ante current account balance. This curve slopes upward because of our assumption that a rise in the interest rate causes desired investment to fall relative to intended saving, leading to an improvement in the home country's current account balance in real terms. Such an improvement requires a depreciation of the home currency (a rise in ε) to equate the ex ante current account balance to the new desired pattern of saving and investment. For analogous reasons, the rest of the world's saving-investment balance curve, SI^*, slopes downward in $\varepsilon - R$ space. The nature of the interest rate and exchange rate movements that result from an autonomous shift in one country's fiscal position or in ex ante investment will obviously depend on the responsiveness of the real interest rate and exchange rate to a disturbance in the world market for saving or to a disequilibrium in the world goods market.

We can now use the graphical apparatus to render more specific the model's conclusions about the effects of changes in fiscal policy and in investment incentives such as those described in the introduction to the paper.

We will therefore refer to the home country as "the *US*" and the foreign country as "the *ROW*". Suppose that the *US* experiences an expansionary fiscal policy, an autonomous increase in the private sector's desire to invest, or some combination of the two. The effects of these shocks are illustrated in Figure 1 by a shift of the *SI* curve from its starting position at *A* to *SI'*. The rightward shift of the *SI* curve occurs because at the initial exchange rate and current account the increased demand for private saving can only be brought about through a rise in the real interest rate that "crowds out" private investment relative to desired saving. The new equilibrium, *B*, will involve a real appreciation of the *US* currency to ε_1, a higher world interest rate R_1, and hence (directly from equation (6)) a larger *US* current account deficit.

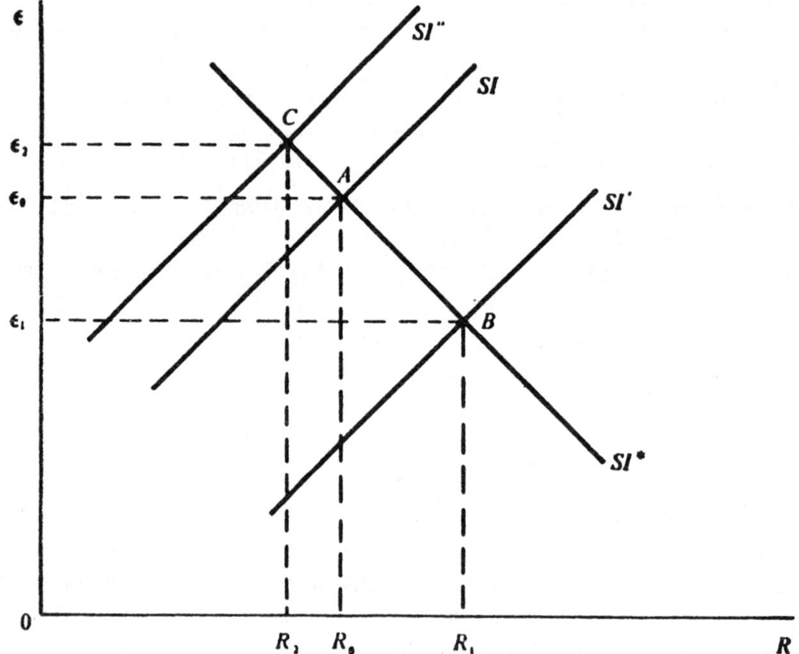

FIGURE 1. Determination of Real Exchange Rate (ε) and World Interest Rate (R).

Fiscal restraint or a weakening of private investment spending in the *ROW* would shift the *SI** locus to the left, thereby magnifying the exchange rate and current account effects just described, but moderating the upward pressure on the world interest rate. By contrast, a credible fiscal deficit reduction package in the *US* would involve an inward shift of the *SI* curve to a position such as *SI''*. Compared with the equilibrium at *B*, the new short-run equilibrium at C would involve a lower value of the US currency, ε_2, a smaller US current account deficit, and a decline in the world interest rate to R_2.

It is important to emphasize, however, that this simple model does not capture some of the long-run international transmission effects of fiscal policies and investment (or saving) shifts. Whereas the effects on the world interest rate may be expected to endure, those on exchange rates and current accounts may be altered substantially over time as the processes of asset and wealth accumulation influence saving and investment behavior and induce changes in the factor service flows of the balance of payments. These longer-run aspects of the international transmission mechanism are considered in detail in Section III.

The conclusions of the simple model of this section support the view that, provided certain assumptions hold, shifts in fiscal deficits and in private investment in the three largest industrial economies over the first half of the 1980s were consistent with the stylized facts of the period 1980-85. In addition, assuming that the Gramm-Rudman-Hollings Act[9] and subsequent fiscal deficit reduction efforts were regarded as "credible" by market participants,[10] the analysis of the model is also consistent with the partial reversal of these developments that occured in late 1985 and the first half of 1986. The assumptions required for these conclusions are those relating to the partial derivatives of the behavioral functions. Most important among these is the assumption that full Barro-Ricardo neutrality does not hold. In this case the standard model yields results that are, in qualitative terms, consistent with experience.

The empirical work in Knight and Masson (1988), which is briefly summarized in the next section of this paper, provides preliminary estimates of the values of the interest elasticities of private saving and investment and of the Barro-Ricardo parameter that are consistent with these conclusions. Nevertheless, some important empirical questions remain unanswered. First, how large are the exchange rate and interest rate effects of a change either in the public sector fiscal deficit or in private investment, taken in isolation; and how large might these effects be when combined? In particular, would their

9. The Balanced Budget and Emergency Deficit Control Act of 1985, generally referred to as the Gramm-Rudman-Hollings legislation, was signed by the President of the United States on December 12, 1985. It required that the federal budget deficit, which stood at approximately $ 210 billion in the fiscal year 1985, must be reduced according to a fixed schedule that would attain a balanced budget in the fiscal year 1991.

10. We do not attempt to define the word "credible" here, and in any case our model does not distinguish between the announcement of a change in fiscal policy and its implementation. For a model in which such a distinction is made, see Masson and Blundell-Wignall (1985).

combined impact be strong enough to account for a large proportion of the net movements that actually occurred over the 1980-87 period? Do these simple conclusions hold in the longer run, when the effects of saving on wealth and of investment on the stock of productive capital are fully accounted for? To address these questions, even in a rudimentary way, we need a dynamic empirical model. Such a model is considered in the next section.

II. EMPIRICAL ANALYSIS FOR THE UNITED STATES, GERMANY AND JAPAN

This section briefly describes the specification and estimation of the empirical model that is used to perform the simulations discussed later, in Section III. In the spirit of the theoretical model of the preceding section, the empirical model includes equations for private saving, private investment, and non-oil merchandise exports and imports. The two-country theoretical framework, however, is now extended to include the three largest industrial economies : the United States, Germany, and Japan. The rest of the world is also captured in a rudimentary way by using an aggregate function that explains total *ROW* saving minus investment. The effects of cyclical variations in output (relative to its capacity level) on private saving and investment behavior in each of the included countries are taken into account in estimation, although these "gap" variables are held constant in the simulation experiments reported in Section III.

To catch long-run as well as impact effects, the empirical model also goes beyond the comparative static analysis by explicitly allowing for the accumulation of assets that are the counterpart of the flows of saving, of investment, and of the net receipts from or payments to foreigners associated with current surpluses and deficits. Thus, for each of the three included countries there are equations that link fiscal deficits to the increase in outstanding government debt, net investment to the change in the real capital stock, and imports and exports (via an identity equating the current balance to net merchandise exports plus the balance on services) to the change in claims on foreigners. These processes of accumulation are specified such that the outstanding stock of each type of asset settles down to some stable proportion of output in the steady state.

Like the simple theoretical model, the system of this section retains the assumption of a single integrated international capital market with perfect substitutability among assets held by residents of the three countries. Thus it implicitly determines the level of the real effective exchange rate of each of the three countries as the rate that makes the supply of private saving minus the demands for saving from net private domestic investment and the government deficit, equal to net exports plus net foreign investment income. (The real effective exchange rate of the remaining countries as a group is residually determined, as are their net exports.) The world real interest rate, expressed in terms of U.S. output as numeraire, adjusts to ensure equilibrium in the world market for saving. However, we relax the assumption that real exchange rates are expected to remain unchanged in the future. In the empirical model, real interest rates in Germany and Japan will be lower (higher) than the rate in the United States by an amount equal to the expected rate of dollar depreciation (appreciation).

Specification

The structural equations of the model (equations (10)-(24)) are summarized in Table 2, and the symbols used are identified in Table 3. In Table 2 and in the discussion that follows, the subscript i is incremented over the three included countries (the United States, Germany, and Japan) unless otherwise noted. The derivation of the equations in Table 2 will only be summarized here; a fuller discussion is contained in Knight and Masson (1988).

Following Metzler (1951) and Dornbusch (1975), the empirical model assumes that the private sector adjusts its flow of saving so as to close the gap between its desired stock of wealth and its actual holdings at the beginning of each period. Desired wealth is a function of the domestic real interest rate and permanent income (here proxied by the current level of income). Because all structural equations of the model, including those for real private saving and wealth, are deflated by a measure of capacity output (see the Appendix for sources of data), the income variable appears in each equation in the form of a gap between actual and capacity output.

Because the assumptions that are required for autonomous shifts in public sector saving to be offset fully by induced movements in private saving are so stringent, our empirical model assumes that the private sector's perceived net wealth may include any proportion of government debt, with φ to be dictated by the data. Thus we can test whether Barro-Ricardo equivalence of government debt and taxes is consistent with the data for our sample.

The equation for private saving in each country, i, embodies the hypothesis that the change in private sector real wealth, as a proportion of capacity output, YC, is equal to a fraction of the gap between the private sector's end-of-period target real wealth, W, and lagged wealth,

$$\Delta(W_i/YC_i) = a_i[\hat{W}_i/YC_i - W_i(-1)/YC_i(-1)],$$

TABLE 2

Equations of the Empirical Model

Equation Number	Equation
	For i = United States (US), Germany (GE), and Japan (JA)
(10)	$S_i/YC_i = b0_i + b1_i R_i + b2_i GAP_i + b3_i W_i(-1)/YC_i(-1) + (1-\varphi_i)D_i/YC_i$
(11)	$I/_i YC_i = f0_i + f1_i R_i + f2_i GAP_i + f3_i K_i(-1)/YC_i(-1)$
(12)	$W_i = K_i + \varphi_i B_i + F_i$
(13)	$XV_i/YC_i = g0_i + g1_i T_i + g2_i GAPF_i + g3_i REEX_i + g4_i XV_i(-1)/YC_i(-1)$
(14)	$MV_i/YC_i = h0_i + h1_i T_i + h2_i GAP_i + h3_i REEX_i + h4_i MV_i(-1)/YC_i(-1)$
(15)	$K_i = K_i(-1) + I_i$
(16)	$N_i = XV_i - MV_i + R_i F_i(-1) + RES_i$
(17)	$N_i = S_i - I_i - D_i$
(18)	$B_i = B_i(-1) + D_i$
(19)	$F_i = F_i(-1) + N_i$
(20)	$\ln(YC_i) = j0_i + j1\ T_i \ .\ \ln(1_i + n_i) + (1 - j1_i)\ln(K_i)$
	For i = GE and JA
(21)	$R_i = R_{US} - ERDOT_i$
	For the rest of the world (ROW)
(22)	$N_{ROW}/YC_{ROW} = k0 + k1\ .\ R_{ROW}$
(23)	$R_{ROW} = w1\ .\ R_{US} + w2\ .\ R_{GE} + w3\ .\ R_{JA}$
(24)	$N_{ROW} = -(N_{US} + N_{GE}/e80_{GE} + N_{JA}/e80_{JA})$

Note: In the private saving equation (10), $b3_i = [n_i/(1+n_i) - a_i]$, where n_i is the growth rate of capacity output; $b0_i$, $b1_i$, and $b2_i$ depend on the W function as well as on the speed of adjustment a_i. In the private investment equation (11), $f3_i = [n_i/(1+n_i) - c_i]$.

where $\hat{W}_i = \hat{W}_i(Y_i, R_i)$; that is, target wealth is a function of domestic real income and the domestic real interest rate. Wealth is defined in identity (12) of Table 2 as the real net capital stock, K_i, plus some proportion, φ_i, of the real stock of government debt, B_i, plus real net claims on foreigners, F_i.[11]

11. It may appear that if domestic and foreign residents exchange claims on their own government for claims on the other government, net wealth of both private sectors will rise when $\varphi < 1$. This is not the case, however; B includes all government debt, whether held domestically or abroad, and φ reflects the fact that it is domestic residents alone who will be forced to service that debt. A swap of claims of the type described will neither change B nor affect net foreign claims, F. Hence net wealth (and private saving) will be unaffected.

TABLE 3

Key to Symbols of the Empirical Model

Symbol	Definition
	Endogenous variables
S	Private net saving
I	Private net investment
W	Private sector net wealth
XV	Volume of non-oil merchandise exports
MV	Volume of non-oil merchandise imports
K	Private net capital stock
N	Net exports of goods and services
$REEX$	Real effective exchange rate (foreign output per unit of domestic output)
B	Government net debt
F	Net foreign asset position
YC	Capacity output
R	Long-term interest rate
	Exogenous variables
D	General government fiscal deficit
GAP	Actual domestic output as ratio to capacity
$GAPF$	Weighted foreign output as ratio to capacity
$ERDOT_i$	Expected rate of change of real bilateral exchange rate against U.S. dollar ($i = GE, JA$).
RES	Residual current account item
YC_{ROW}	ROW capacity output

Note: All variables are in real terms — that is, in constant (1980) units of domestic currency. For more detailed definitions, see the Appendix.

The real interest rate on (private and government) bonds valued in units of U.S. output is R_{US}. Because we no longer impose the assumption of static expectations of the future real exchange rate, however, expected changes in the real value of the U.S. dollar in terms of the other two currencies over the holding period can drive a wedge between the interest rates prevailing in the three countries. Thus real interest rates in Germany and Japan, $R_i (i = GE, JA)$, satisfy equation (21) in Table 2, where $ERDOT_i$ is the market's anticipated rate of appreciation in the real exchange rate of currency i with respect to the U.S. dollar.[12]

In the national accounts, private saving is defined to equal the difference between after-tax disposable income and consumption; that is, the private

12. In the estimation work that follows, the $ERDOT_i$ are taken to be exogenous.

sector's acquisition of assets including government debt. On the basis of the arguments of Section I above, we therefore define private saving as the change in net wealth plus $(1 - \varphi)$ times the real government deficit (D, equal to ΔB):

$$S_i = \Delta W_i + (1 - \varphi_i)D_i,$$

where, again, the first term is the "wealth-accumulation component" of private sector saving, and the second is the "Barro-Ricardo component". This specification of the flow of private saving is therefore consistent with the definition of the stock of private sector wealth given by identity (12). Combining this identity with the wealth adjustment equation given above, we obtain

$$S_i / YC_i = a_i [\hat{W}_i / YC_i - W_i(-1) / YC_i(-1)] + (1 - \varphi_i)D_i / YC_i$$
$$+ [n_i / (1 + n_i)] W_i(-1) / YC_i(-1),$$

where n is the growth rate of capacity output. After substitution for $\hat{W}$ and grouping terms, the final form of the structural equation is given in equation (10) of Table 2.

The current account balance, which is the difference between total national saving $(S_i - D_i)$ and private investment, is given by

$$N_i \equiv S_i - I_i - D_i .$$

If Barro-Ricardo equivalence $(\varphi \equiv 0)$ holds, induced private saving increases one-for-one with the government deficit, and total (public plus private) net national saving does not depend on the government deficit. In this case the current account balance would also be unaffected, and changes in fiscal deficits (if unaccompanied by output changes) would not be transmitted internationally. In the other polar case, $\varphi \equiv 1$, all of the increased government debt would be considered part of private net wealth, so that there would be no automatic increase in private saving to allow for future tax liabilities. Here the current account balance would change by an amount that would depend on endogenous movements in interest rates and exchange rates. Of course, our model also admits intermediate cases $(0 < \varphi < 1)$ in which there would be a partial response of private saving to increases in government deficits.

The investment equation assumes lagged adjustment of the real (net) capital stock divided by capacity output, where the desired capital stock depends on expected output and the domestic real interest rate, and expected output is assumed to be equal to actual output:

$$\Delta(K_i / YC_i) = c_i[\hat{K}_i / YC_i - K_i(-1) / YC_i(-1)],$$

where $\hat{K}_i = \hat{K}_i(Y_i, R_i)$. The interest rate affects the desired stock through the user cost of capital, which also depends on tax considerations, discussed more fully below. The investment equation has the familiar accelerator property: an increase in output, relative to capacity output, tends to increase investment. We assume that the $\hat{K}$ function is homogeneous in Y, and we write the investment equation in terms of the output gap. After grouping terms, the structural equation takes the form of equation (11) in Table 2.

The merchandise trade equations closely follow those of the International Monetary Fund's World Trade Model (see Spencer (1984)). Non-oil merchandise export volumes, XV, are assumed to depend on foreign demand, here proxied by the foreign output gap, $GAPF = (YF/YCF) - 1$, and on the real effective exchange rate, $REEX$. In addition, the ratio of exports to the home country's capacity output, YC, may vary with a time trend, T – for instance, as a result of a gradual expansion of trade flows, relative to output, over the period since World War II. Non-oil merchandise import volumes, MV, are assumed to depend on the country's output gap and its real effective exchange rate and, again, may exhibit a time trend when divided by capacity output. In addition, we allow for slow adjustment of volumes to activity and exchange rate changes. The resultant structural equations for export and import volume are given in equations (13) and (14), respectively, of Table 2. Note that because – in contrast to the theoretical model – the real effective exchange rate $REEX$ is now defined as the ratio of normalized unit labor costs in the home country to those in foreign countries (that is, the inverse of ε in Section I), an increase in $REEX$ indicates a real *appreciation*. Thus the a priori restrictions on the price elasticities of equations (13) and (14) are $g3_i < 0$ and $h3_i > 0$.

The last estimated equation of the model is equation (22), which determines the aggregate level of saving (minus investment) of the rest of the world. In the absence of data on the fiscal positions and wealth stocks of those countries, we simply make this net saving variable (also equal to the current account position of the rest of the world, N_{ROW}) a function of their real interest rate (R_{ROW}), proxied by an average of rates prevailing in the United States, Germany, and Japan (equation (23)).

The remaining equations in Table 2 are relations that close the system. First, we include an identity (16) that equates the overall current account balance N_i to non-oil merchandise exports minus non-oil merchandise imports, plus investment income (which we proxy by the real interest rate multiplied by the stock of real net foreign assets), plus an exogenous residual (RES_i) that consists of other net exports of goods and services (oil trade, other services, and unilateral transfers). For each country i, the model solves implicitly for the values of the real interest rate, R_i, and of the real effective exchange rate,

$REEX_i$, that make this definition consistent with the other way of expressing the current balance identity – that is, private saving minus private investment minus the government fiscal deficit (equation (17)). Although the model is simultaneous, it is useful to think of the role of the real exchange rate as that of making these two definitions equal, given real interest rates and output gaps in each of the countries.

We also include a simple production function relationship (equation (20)) that relates capacity output to the capital stock. The labour force is not explicitly included ; rather, there is a trend term that captures both population growth and technical progress. On the basis of sample averages for the growth of the capital stock and output, we impose a plausible number for this growth rate, 3 percent per year, and make it common to all countries so that we can compare steady-state solutions of the model. We also arbitrarily impose a common Cobb-Douglas production function (differing, however, by a scale factor), with a share of capital equal to one third.

In the theoretical model of Section I, the world rate of interest brings about equality of world saving and world investment ; the distribution of saving and investment between countries helps determine the real exchange rate between their currencies. The equality of world saving and investment is equivalent to the condition that current account balances sum to zero globally, and in the simulation model we add the equation, equation (24) of Table 2, that enforces this condition for the United States, Germany, Japan, and the remaining countries taken as a group. In the data this condition also holds because we have calculated residually the rest-of-world current balance, expressed in real U.S. dollars; $e80_{GE}$ and $e80_{JA}$ are merely base-period (1980) dollar exchange rates of the deutschemark and the yen.

Data sources are described in the Appendix, but it is useful here to mention briefly how our data on government debt and deficits were obtained. For our estimate of the real value of government debt, a correction has been made to fiscal deficits for the portion of nominal interest payments that corresponds to compensation for inflation (see Jump (1980)). The calculation was performed in the following fashion : nominal deficits were cumulated from a benchmark stock for government debt, and this series was divided by the gross domestic product (GDP) deflator to get the real debt stock. The adjusted real fiscal deficit was then calculated as the first difference of this stock.

Estimation

The structural equations were estimated in two separate blocks on annual data by using nonlinear three-stage least squares. Joint estimation by blocks allowed appropriate restrictions, discussed below, to be imposed across equations. It also permitted gains in efficiency by allowing for correlations among the shocks affecting the same sectors in different countries. Because real interest rates, real exchange rates, and output gaps are endogenous to the full model, they were not treated as being predetermined in each block ; instruments used included the lagged asset stocks, government deficits, and capacity output. In the first block, saving and investment equations were estimated jointly for the three countries, along with the net saving function for the rest of the world, over the period 1966-83. Estimates are presented in Table 4. The second block of jointly estimated equations consisted of the import and export functions for the three countries estimated over the period 1961-83; results are reported in Table 5. Joint estimation of all the equations together was not feasible because of data and computer limitations.

The saving equation for each country embodies a nonlinear restriction on the coefficients, since φ appears in both the definition of wealth and the coefficient applied to the budget deficit. We initially estimated φ separately for each country. On the basis of the arguments of the preceding section, one would expect the value of φ to vary both among countries and over time.[13] Nevertheless, for this preliminary estimation and simulation work we chose to employ the strong simplifying assumption that φ has the same value in all three countries. This restriction is accepted by the data, on the basis of a likelihood-ratio test, at the 2.5 percent level of significance. The estimated common value of φ is significantly different from both zero and unity. The value of 0.43 yielded by our sample implies that neither Barro-Ricardo debt neutrality nor the full inclusion of government bonds in private net wealth is warranted on the basis of the data ; this result is consistent with earlier estimates based on consumption functions (see Kochin (1974), Tanner (1979), Buiter and Tobin (1979), and Seater (1982)).

Because of the well-known difficulties in isolating a statistically robust effect of the real interest rate on saving, our second simplification was to constrain this coefficient to be the same for the three countries. Our estimate implies a small negative response of saving to an increase in the interest rate, a result that accords with recent empirical research in the United States by Bernheim and Shoven (1985). The equations for net investment are similar in the three countries; in all cases, investment responds positively to the

13. When φ was estimated separately for each country, its value was significantly different from zero in all three cases, indicating that full Barro-Ricardo equivalence (and thus debt neutrality) does not hold. The unrestricted estimate yielded a lower value of φ for the United States than for Germany and Japan.

TABLE 4

Coefficient Estimates for Investment and Saving Equations. Three-Stage Least Squares, 1966-83

Country	Saving: Parameter and Associated Variable						
	*b*0 (Constant)	*b*1[1] (*R*)	*b*2 (*GAP*)	*b*3 [*W*(—1)]	φ[1] (*B*, *D*)	R^2	SEE
United States	.2181	—.0707	.257	—.0776	.4252	.629	.0076
	(8.85)	(1.68)	(16.59)	(6.00)	(10.32)		
Germany	.4274	—.0707	.157	—.1322	.4252	.806	.0071
	(13.94)	(1.68)	(5.91)	(10.40)	(10.32)		
Japan	.2678	—.0707	.202	—.0513	.4252	.153	.0127
	(8.80)	(1.68)	(5.16)	(3.67)	(10.32)		
	Investment: Parameter and Associated Variable						
Country	*f*0 (Constant)	*f*1 (*R*)	*f*2 (*GAP*)	*f*3 [*K*(—1)]	—	R^2	SEE
United States	.2838	—.1713	.327	—.1208	—	.888	.0069
	(8.41)	(2.90)	(15.84)	(6.30)			
Germany	.4647	—.2155	.342	—.1477	—	.621	.0139
	(4.58)	(1.33)	(4.94)	(3.51)			
Japan	.4045	—.1233	.338	—.1174	—	.858	.0087
	(10.97)	(2.55)	(9.09)	(6.95)			
	Saving Minus Investment: Parameter and Associated Variable						
Country	*k*0 (Constant)	*k*1 (*R*)	—	—	—	R^2	SEE
Rest of world	.0042	.0401	—	—	—	.249	.0014
	(9.77)	(3.06)					

Note: For the form of the equations, see equations (10), (11), and (22), respectively, of Table 2. All variables are expressed as decimal fractions or as ratios to capacity output, and *t*-ratios, appear in parentheses beneath the coefficient estimates. For the system as a whole, the log-likelihood is 412.6; the coefficient of determination (R^2) is .969; and the weighted standard error of estimate (SEE) is .0102. Variables are as defined in Table 3.

1. Constrained to the same value for all three countries.

TABLE 5

Coefficient Estimates for Export and Import Volume Equations. Three-Stage Least Squares, 1961-83

Country	Export Volume : Parameter and Associated Variable						
	*g*0 (Constant)	*g*1 (T)	*g*2 ($GAPF$)	*g*3 ($REEX$)	*g*4 [XV(—1)]	R^2	SEE
United States	.0825	.00055	.150	—.03548	.3988	.974	.0025
	(8.67)	(2.99)	(6.36)	(7.59)	(4.35)		
Germany	.0227	.00097	.206	—.00535[1]	.9086	.959	.0079
	(1.39)	(1.25)	(4.86)	—	(8.04)		
Japan	.0663	.00258	—.012	—.05200	.4797	.971	.0047
	(5.28)	(4.89)	(.42)	(4.35)	(11.62)		

Country	Import Volume : Parameter and Associated Variable						
	*h*0 (Constant)	*h*1 (AP)	*h*2 (GAP)	*h*3 ($REEX$)	*h*4 [(MV—1)]	R^2	SEE
United States	.0021	.00144	.058	.01015	.3940	.904	.0040
	(.20)	(4.49)	(3.98)	(1.76)	(3.23)		
Germany	—.0017	.00180	.137	.04867[2]	.5840	.955	.0068
	(2.52)	(4.13)	(3.22)	—	(4.80)		
Japan	—.0278	.00106	.085	.05271	.3384	.826	.0057
	(1.98)	(3.74)	(4.60)	(3.70)	(3.12)		

Note : For the form of the equations, see equations (13) and (14), respectively, of Table 2. All variables are expressed as decimal fractions or as ratios to capacity output except time T, which is incremented by one each year, and the real effective exchange rate $REEX$, which is an index number (1980 = 1); t-ratios appear in parentheses beneath the coefficient estimates. For the system as a whole, the log-likelihood is 520.9; the R^2 is .989; and the SEE is .0055. Variables are as defined in Table 3.

1. Long-run elasticity is constrained to equal the average of the export price elasticities cited for Germany in Helliwell and Padmore (1985, p. 1148).

2. Long-run elasticity is constrained to equal the average of the import price elasticities cited for Germany in Goldstein and Khan (1985, p. 1079).

similar, rather slow, speed of adjustment to the desired capital stock in all three countries. The effect of the real interest rate on investment is larger than that on saving; consequently, saving minus investment in each of these countries responds positively to the interest rate. Saving minus investment in the rest of the world also responds positively to an increase in the real interest rate, proxied here as a weighted average of real rates in the United States, Germany, and Japan.

As regards the trade volume equations, for the three largest industrial countries there is a positive and statistically significant trend effect in the ratios of both (non-oil) import and export volumes to capacity output that is attributable to the secular trend toward greater openness associated with trade liberalization and specialization. There are also significant cyclical effects, as measured by foreign and domestic gap variables in export and import equations, respectively. For Germany, we had difficulty in isolating the price elasticities of non-oil imports and exports on the basis of annual data. Because the values of these parameters are well established from empirical work using quarterly data, however, we imposed a long-run elasticity of imports equal to 0.28 (at sample means), which is an average of estimates for Germany presented in Helliwell and Padmore (1985, p. 1148); and a long-run elasticity of exports equal to 0.79, the average of estimates for German total exports (Goldstein and Khan (1985, p. 1079)).[14] For the United States and Japan, as expected, export volumes respond negatively and imports positively to an appreciation of the home country's real effective exchange rate (an increase in *REEX*). For both exports and imports, lags in adjustment to changes in relative prices and activity seem to be present in all three countries. Finally, it should be noted that the parameter estimates reported in this section are consistent with the a priori restrictions that are needed for the simple theoretical model of Section I to yield the three stylized facts summarized in the introduction.

III. INTERNATIONAL TRANSMISSION OF FISCAL POLICIES: SIMULATION EXPERIMENTS

This section describes four simulation experiments designed to highlight the international transmission of fiscal policies in major industrial countries: (1) a benchmark simulation involving a reduction in the fiscal deficit of 1 percent of GNP in each country taken in isolation; (2) year-by-year shifts in

14. Speeds of adjustment of exports and imports — $g4$ and $h4$, respectively — are nevertheless estimated for Germany.

the pattern of fiscal deficits of the order of magnitude that actually occurred in the United States, Germany, and Japan over the period 1982-85; (3) tax incentives for private investment in the United States starting in 1982; and (4) combined effects of simultaneous changes in both fiscal deficits and investment incentives.

Although the empirical model just described incorporates several real-world complications that were neglected in the very simple model of Section I, it is not intended to provide a comprehensive description of all the macroeconomic processes at work in the international economy. In particular, it intentionally neglects the well-known Keynesian adjustment mechanism, whereby shifts in saving and investment induce changes in output. Specifically, the *GAP* variable, which is exogenous to the model, is held constant in the simulations; thus the results of the simulation experiments implicitly relate to a time period long enough for actual output to return to its normal (or cyclically adjusted) relation to capacity output. This medium-term focus also provides the rationale for our neglect of the influence of monetary factors on real interest rates and real exchange rates. As already noted, under floating exchange rates perfect substitutability between domestic and foreign assets does not require that real interest rates be equal at home and abroad: the two real rates will differ by the expected rate of change of the real exchange rate, which we call *ERDOT*. The simulation model includes the equations that relate real interest rates in Germany and Japan to the U.S. real interest rate and to the expected real appreciation or depreciation of the deutschemark or the yen relative to the dollar. In the simulations reported below, however, these expected rates of change, $ERDOT_i$, are treated as exogenous.

The simulation model consists of the equations in Table 2 of the preceding section, together with the estimated numerical values for the structural parameters set out in Tables 4 and 5. To begin the simulations, a baseline was created with residuals added back to the equations so that the model replicated historical data through 1983. For convenience it was further assumed that from 1983 onward the values of variables were consistent with a steady state for the economy: in the baseline, ratios of real flows and stocks divided by capacity output are constant, as are real interest rates and real exchange rates. The baseline thus embodies the simplifying assumption that the secular growth in the relative importance of international trade comes to an end, so that there is no trend growth in exports and imports relative to capacity output. However, capacity output itself does grow in the baseline solution, by 3 percent a year, as do other stock and flow variables.

Benchmark Simulations: Deficit Reduction in a Single Country

The analysis of Section II suggests that, other things being equal, an increase in the fiscal deficit in a major industrial country will raise the real interest rate, appreciate its real exchange rate, and cause its current account to move into deficit. An exogenous reduction in the fiscal deficit should exert opposite effects. As a starting point for the new simulations that will be discussed later in this paper, we reproduce the first simulation from Knight and Masson (1988). In the present discussion, however, we stress the international transmission of such a policy shift. Each experiment represents a discretionary reduction in the home country's fiscal deficit equal to 1 percent of capacity output, with the stance of fiscal policy in both of the other countries held constant. We calculate the effects of these hypothetical changes on the steady state of the model, as well as on the dynamic path of the endogenous variables. Stock and flow variables are scaled by capacity output so that induced changes in them can be compared directly with the autonomous shock to the fiscal deficit, and also so that the simulation results are comparable across countries.[15]

Table 6 gives the simulation results for the United States, whereas Tables 7 and 8 present separate simulation results for isolated deficit reduction programs in Germany and Japan, respectively. The paths of real interest and exchange rates are presented in Chart 1; those of current account and investment ratios are shown in Chart 2.

First consider the simulated first-round effects of this policy on the United States economy (Table 6). Given the estimated value of φ, a fiscal program that permanently reduces public sector dissaving will be only partially offset by an induced decline in private saving, S. The first column of Table 6 shows that a permanent reduction in the fiscal deficit equal to 1 percent of capacity output will be associated with a decline of only about 0.48 percent in the U.S. private sector's propensity to save (both on impact and in the long run). Thus there is a permanent increase in total public plus private saving (not shown in Table 6) of just over 0.5 percent of capacity output. The rise in national saving exerts downward pressure on the U.S. real interest

15. In these simulations it is the *total* fiscal deficit (inclusive of real interest payments) that is being changed; thus (unless $ni = 0$) the model does not produce explosive growth in the ratio of the debt stock to capacity output, as would be the case if the *primary* deficit were increased autonomously and interest payments were allowed to grow accordingly. Our experiments should therefore be viewed as changing the steady-state stock of bonds, with offsetting changes to taxes, so that the government's intertemporal budget constraint is satisfied.

TABLE 6

Simulation of a U.S. Fiscal Deficit Reduction, Equal to 1 Percent of Capacity Output, Starting in 1985

	U.S. Variables							
Year	*S*	*I*	*N*	*K*	*F*	*W*	*REEX*	*R*
1985	—0.48	0.24	0.28	0.24	0.28	0.10	—5.57	—1.40
1986	—0.47	0.24	0.29	0.48	0.57	0.21	—3.30	—1.51
1987	—0.46	0.24	0.30	0.71	0.85	0.32	—3.26	—1.61
1988	—0.45	0.24	0.31	0.93	1.13	0.43	—3.22	—1.71
1989	—0.45	0.24	0.31	1.14	1.41	0.55	—3.18	—1.79
1990	—0.44	0.24	0.32	1.34	1.69	0.67	—3.14	—1.88
1991	—0.44	0.24	0.32	1.54	1.96	0.79	—3.10	—1.95
1995	—0.43	0.22	0.34	2.25	3.04	1.25	—2.92	—2.20
1999	—0.43	0.21	0.36	2.82	4.06	1.67	—2.72	—2.34
Long run	—0.48	0.13	0.39	4.48	12.96	3.32	0.52	—2.72

	German Variables				Japanese Variables			
Year	*S*	*I*	*K*	*W*	*S*	*I*	*K*	*W*
1985	0.10	0.30	0.30	0.10	0.10	0.18	0.18	0.10
1986	0.11	0.30	0.60	0.21	0.11	0.18	0.35	0.21
1987	0.12	0.30	0.87	0.33	0.12	0.18	0.52	0.32
1988	0.13	0.29	1.14	0.45	0.13	0.18	0.68	0.44
1989	0.13	0.29	1.40	0.57	0.13	0.18	0.84	0.56
1990	0.14	0.28	1.63	0.69	0.14	0.18	0.99	0.68
1991	0.14	0.27	1.76	0.81	0.14	0.18	1.14	0.80
1995	0.14	0.25	2.65	1.27	0.15	0.17	1.69	1.28
1999	0.14	0.23	3.28	1.67	0.16	0.16	2.14	1.74
Long run	0.09	0.15	4.87	2.87	0.12	0.11	3.54	3.89

Note: All variables are deviations from baseline (expressed as percentages of baseline capacity output) except *REEX*, which is given as percentage deviation from baseline, and *R*, which is given as percentage-point deviation from baseline. Variables are as defined in Table 3.

TABLE 7

Simulation of a German Fiscal Deficit Reduction, Equal to 1 Percent of Capacity Output, Starting in 1985

	German Variables							
Year	*S*	*I*	*N*	*K*	*F*	*W*	*REEX*	*R*
1985	—0.54	0.09	0.36	0.09	0.36	0.03	—7.90	—0.43
1986	—0.54	0.09	0.37	0.18	0.72	0.07	—2.83	—0.47
1987	—0.54	0.09	0.37	0.27	1.07	0.10	—2.67	—0.50
1988	—0.54	0.09	0.37	0.35	1.41	0.14	—2.53	—0.53
1989	—0.53	0.09	0.38	0.43	1.74	0.18	—2.40	—0.56
1990	—0.53	0.09	0.38	0.50	2.07	0.21	—2.28	—0.58
1991	—0.53	0.09	0.38	0.58	2.39	0.25	—2.17	—0.60
1995	—0.53	0.08	0.39	0.82	3.61	0.40	—1.80	—0.68
1999	—0.53	0.07	0.39	1.01	4.71	0.52	—1.53	—0.74
Long run	—0.55	0.05	0.41	1.50	13.50	0.88	0.37	—0.84

	U.S. Variables				Japanese Variables			
Year	*S*	*I*	*K*	*W*	*S*	*I*	*K*	*W*
1985	0.03	0.07	0.07	0.03	0.03	0.05	0.05	0.03
1986	0.03	0.07	0.15	0.06	0.03	0.05	0.11	0.06
1987	0.04	0.07	0.22	0.10	0.04	0.05	0.16	0.10
1988	0.04	0.07	0.29	0.13	0.04	0.06	0.21	0.14
1989	0.04	0.07	0.35	0.17	0.04	0.06	0.26	0.17
1990	0.04	0.07	0.42	0.21	0.04	0.06	0.31	0.21
1991	0.04	0.07	0.48	0.24	0.04	0.05	0.35	0.25
1995	0.04	0.07	0.69	0.39	0.05	0.05	0.52	0.40
1999	0.05	0.07	0.87	0.52	0.05	0.05	0.66	0.54
Long run	0.03	0.04	1.38	1.03	0.04	0.03	1.09	1.20

Note: All variables are deviations from baseline (expressed as percentages of baseline capacity output) except *REEX*, which is given as percentage deviation from baseline, and *R*, which is given as percentage-point deviation from baseline. Variables are as defined in Table 3.

TABLE 8

Simulation of a Japanese Fiscal Deficit Reduction, Equal to 1 Percent of Capacity Output, Starting in 1985

	Japanese Variables							
Year	*S*	*I*	*N*	*K*	*F*	*W*	*REEX*	*R*
1985	—0.54	0.07	0.40	0.07	0.40	0.04	—3.31	—0.55
1986	—0.53	0.07	0.40	0.14	0.78	0.08	—2.02	—0.59
1987	—0.53	0.07	0.40	0.20	1.16	0.13	—1.91	—0.63
1988	—0.53	0.07	0.40	0.27	1.53	0.17	—1.81	—0.67
1989	—0.52	0.07	0.41	0.33	1.89	0.22	—1.72	—0.70
1990	—0.52	0.07	0.41	0.45	2.25	0.26	—1.63	—0.73
1991	—0.52	0.07	0.41	0.50	2.59	0.31	—1.54	—0.76
1995	—0.52	0.07	0.42	0.66	3.89	0.50	—1.22	—0.86
1999	—0.51	0.06	0.42	0.83	5.07	0.68	—0.93	—0.93
Long run	—0.53	0.04	0.43	1.38	14.31	1.51	1.75	—1.06

	U.S. Variables				German Variables			
Year	*S*	*I*	*K*	*W*	*S*	*I*	*K*	*W*
1985	0.04	0.09	0.09	0.04	0.04	0.12	0.12	0.04
1986	0.04	0.09	0.19	0.08	0.04	0.12	0.23	0.08
1987	0.05	0.09	0.28	0.12	0.05	0.12	0.34	0.13
1988	0.05	0.09	0.36	0.17	0.05	0.11	0.44	0.17
1989	0.05	0.09	0.44	0.21	0.05	0.11	0.54	0.22
1990	0.05	0.09	0.53	0.26	0.05	0.11	1.64	0.27
1991	0.05	0.09	0.60	0.31	0.05	0.11	1.73	0.32
1995	0.06	0.09	0.88	0.49	0.06	0.10	1.03	0.54
1999	0.06	0.08	1.10	0.65	0.05	0.09	1.28	0.65
Long run	0.04	0.05	1.75	1.29	0.03	0.06	1.90	1.12

Note: All variables are deviations from baseline (expressed as percentages of baseline capacity output) except *REEX*, which is given as percentage deviation from baseline, and *R*, which is given as percentage-point deviation from baseline. Variables are as defined in Table 3.

Chart 1. *Simulated Changes in Real Exchange Rates and Real Interest Rates in Response to a Fiscal Deficit Reduction, Starting in 1985, Equal to 1 Percent of Capacity Output*

(Deviations from baseline)

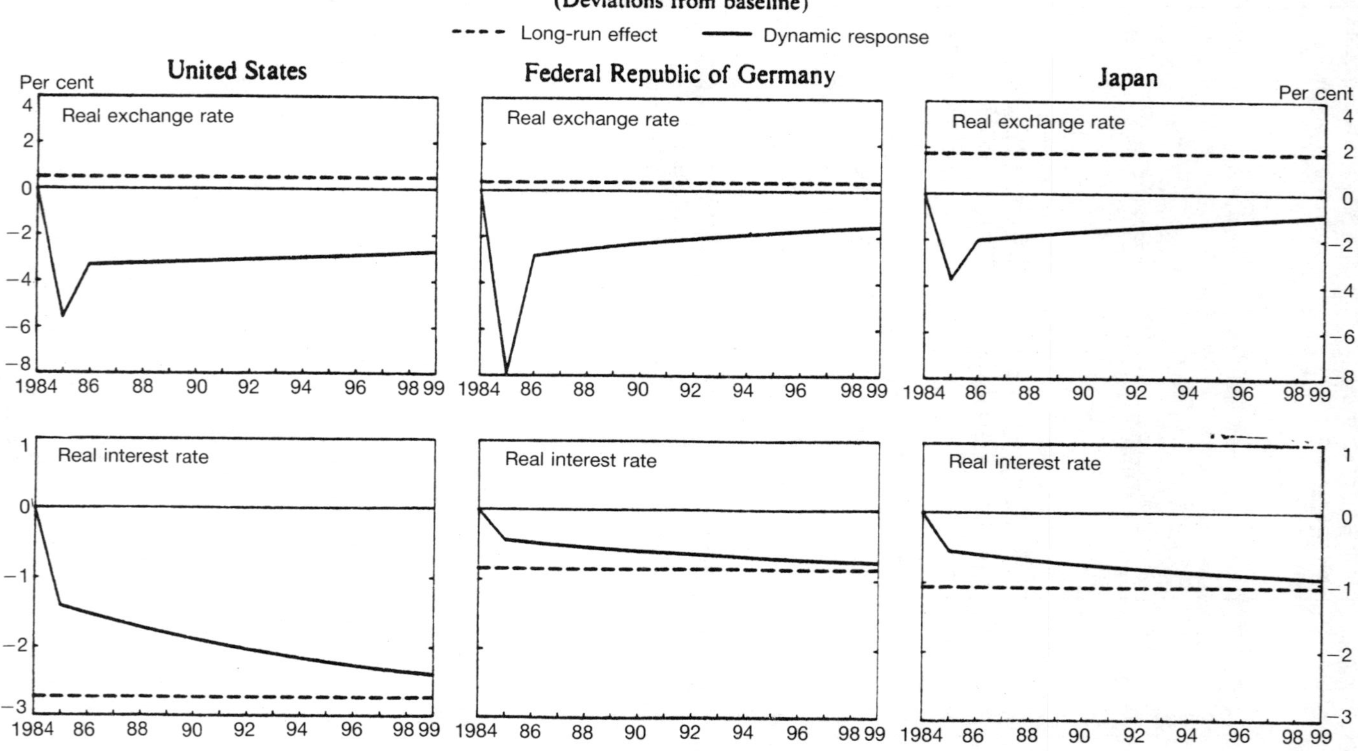

Source: Tables 6–8.

Chart 2. *Simulated Changes in Current Balances and Private Investment in Response to a Fiscal Deficit Reduction, Starting in 1985, Equal to 1 Percent of Capacity Output*

(Deviations from baseline)

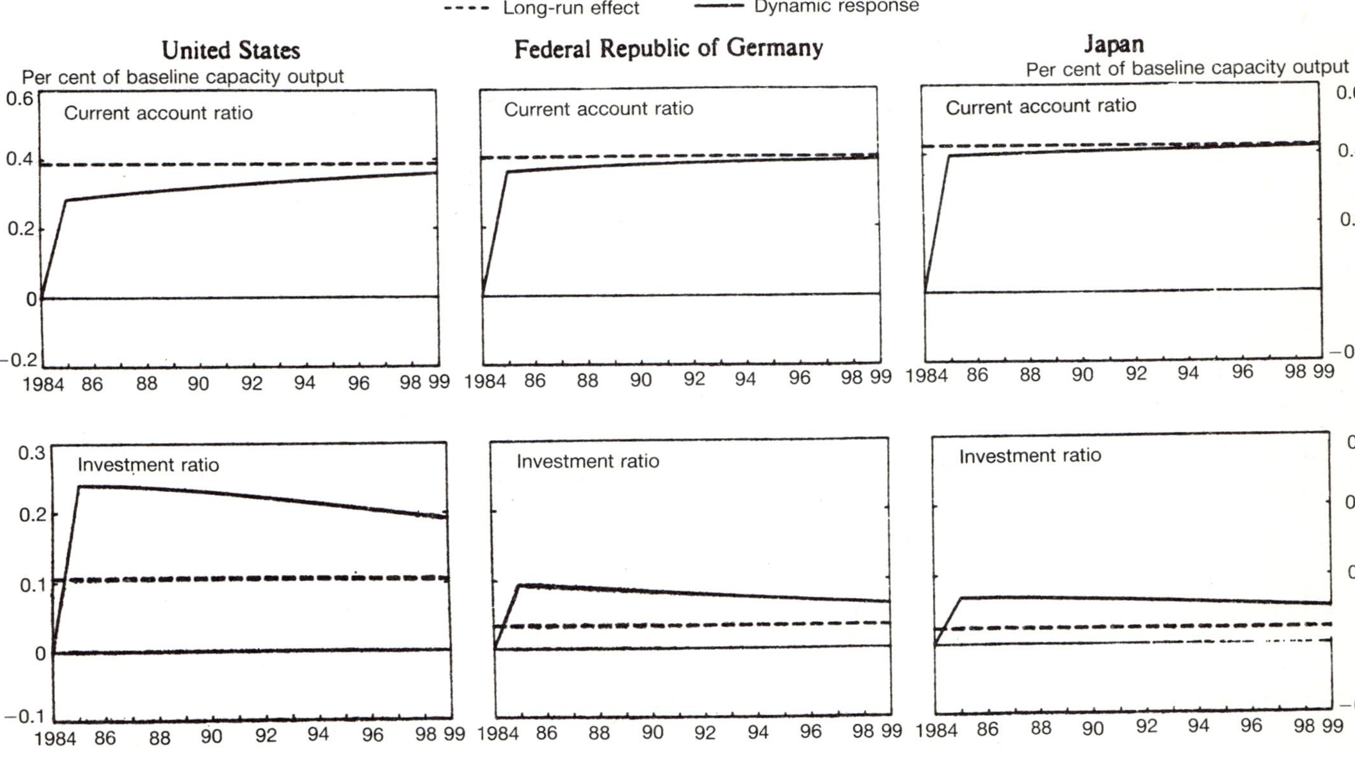

Source: Tables 6–8.

rate, R, so that private domestic investment, I, increases strongly, by about 0.25 percent of capacity output on impact (and by some 0.13 percent in the long run). This expansion in investment, however, is less than the rise in total national saving in the United States, so that there is an ex ante current account surplus. The mechanism by which this surplus appears involves a rather large (nearly 6 percent) initial depreciation of the dollar (*REEX*) that improves U.S. competitiveness and increases non-oil merchandise exports relative to imports. As a result the U.S. current account moves into a surplus that is initially 0.28 percent of capacity output (third column of Table 6) and continues to rise gradually thereafter.

The way in which these effects are transmitted internationally is also very interesting. Because interest parity holds for real interest rates in the model and expected real exchange rate changes are assumed to be exogenous, interest rates in Germany and Japan (not reported in Table 6) decline by the same amount as in the United States – 1.4 percentage points on impact, and 2.7 percentage points in the long run. Hence private investment also rises strongly in Germany and Japan. Because there has been no autonomous increase in national saving in these countries, however, their current accounts move into deficit by means of an appreciation of their currencies that is the counterpart of the move already noted for the United States. To summarize the first-round international effects of implementing the policy, the simulation results in Table 6 suggest that a U.S. fiscal deficit reduction program would lower the general level of world interest rates, depreciate the dollar, and stimulate private investment in all three countries of the model.

The effects that occur on impact are modified over time as productive capital is accumulated and the net claims on foreigners held by residents of each country rise or fall in response to current account flows. The U.S. current account surplus gradually rises to 0.4 percent of baseline capacity output, and claims of U.S. residents on foreigners eventually increase by 13 percent of capacity output. As U.S. private claims on foreigners rise, the investment income account also improves, requiring less of a surplus in non-oil merchandise trade to maintain the overall current account position that is sustainable given the new saving-investment balance. As this happens, and as lags in the response of import and export volumes work themselves out, the dollar gradually reverses its depreciation. Given the parameters of the model, the new steady-state value of the dollar is actually slightly *above* the initial level (see Table 6 and the broken line in Chart 1), since total national saving has been permanently increased relative to U.S. private investment. Because the simulation experiment shows that the steady-state change in the real exchange rate may actually be in a direction opposite to the initial effects given by the simple model of the preceding section, it illustrates the importance of taking into account the consequences of alternative policies for the rates of wealth and capital accumulation. Furthermore, it shows that real exchange rate overshooting can occur not only because of monetary stocks in economies with sticky goods prices (Dornbusch (1976)), but also as a consequence of real shocks in a system where there is slow adjustment of trade flows and where the accumulation of claims on foreigners is explicitly taken into account (Dornbusch and Fischer (1980), Frenkel and Rodriguez (1982)).

In long-run equilibrium the net wealth of the U.S. private sector is higher than it would have been in the absence of the fiscal shift, owing to the accumulation of both productive capital at home and net claims on foreigners. More surprisingly, because of the fall in world interest rates, the accumulation of capital in both Germany and Japan is greater than the rise in their net foreign liabilities, so that their wealth is higher as well. Other things being equal, the larger equilibrium levels of national capital stocks imply that the paths of per capita income would be higher in all three countries in the long run. It should again be noted that our model, being classical in nature, neglects any short-run effect of fiscal consolidation on activity levels.

The simulation results for an isolated fiscal deficit reduction of 1 percent of capacity output in either Germany or Japan, with fiscal policy in the other two countries held constant, are presented in Tables 7 and 8, respectively. Because the model assumes the same value of φ in all three countries, the simulated effects of these programs of fiscal restraint in Germany and Japan are qualitatively the same as those already described for the United States. Effects on domestic (and world) interest rates, however, are smaller in response to a fiscal deficit reduction equivalent to 1 percent of capacity output, and the current account effects in the country reducing its deficit are considerably larger in relation to its GNP. These results are due not only to the obvious fact that the levels of total output in Germany and Japan are smaller than those in the United States, but also because a given program of fiscal restraint provides less of a stimulus to private investment in these two countries. It is also interesting to note that for Germany and Japan, as well as for the United States, the long-run effect on the real exchange rate is opposite to its short-run effect. In the long run the real exchange rate appreciates in response to a shift to fiscal restraint because the resultant increase in the net foreign claims position improves the services account sufficiently that the trade balance must be pushed into deficit by an appreciation, in order for net foreign claims to settle down to a constant proportion of capacity output (or of wealth). It need not necessarily be the case, however, that appreciation is the long-run outcome. For a given positive net claim position, the services account surplus will decrease as interest rates decline. Thus it is possible that the services balance will deteriorate, and the real exchange rate depreciate, in the long run. The sign of this long-run effect obviously is dependent on several parameters, including investment and saving elasticities, the net creditor or debtor position of the country, and the country's "economic size" (see Sachs and Wyplosz (1984)).

With this set of benchmark simulations in mind, we may now assess the implications of our model for the effects of the fiscal shifts that actually occurred in the largest industrial countries over the period 1982-85. This is done in three stages, as described in the three subsections that follow. First, actual changes in overall fiscal deficits in the United States, Germany, and Japan are simulated. Next, the effects of shifts in investment resulting from changes in tax incentives in the United States are calculated by the model. Finally, the combined effects of deficit changes in the three major industrial countries and investment incentives in the United States are simulated.

Changes in Fiscal Deficits, 1982-85

It was emphasized in the introduction that during the early 1980s there were important changes in the pattern of overall fiscal positions in the United States, Germany, and Japan. Our second simulation experiment attempts to gauge the direction and rough order of magnitude of the international transmission of these fiscal shifts. This experiment is similar to that contained in Knight and Masson (1988), except that, since that paper emphasizes how wealth and expectations effects influence the time path of adjustment, it makes use of the extreme simplifying assumption that the entire net shift in fiscal positions from 1981 through 1985 took place in the first year. In the present experiment we relax this assumption slightly and use the year-by-year shifts in fiscal stance that took place during this period. Column 1 of Table 9 gives figures for each year's fiscal deficit, measured as the difference between the initial (1981) deficit and the actual inflation-corrected general government deficit, D_i, in each subsequent year. These figures, of course, indicate a large move to fiscal expansion in the United States in 1982, and to fiscal contraction in Germany and (starting in 1984) in Japan.

As can be seen from Table 9, the simulation results for the model suggest that these fiscal changes would have rapidly led to an appreciation of the U.S. dollar that would have been sustained throughout the period, to a comparable depreciation of the deutsche mark, and to a modest (and delayed) depreciation of the yen. The model simulation also implies a substantial deterioration of the U.S. current account – by some 1 percent of U.S. capacity output –

and large increases (measured in percentage of capacity output) in the surplus positions of Germany and Japan. Furthermore, this pattern of changes in fiscal deficits is simulated to produce a rise in world interest rates of 4 percentage points in 1982, a further rise in 1983, and a net decline in 1984-85.

The path of interest rates and exchange rates depends on the form that expectations of exchange rates and interest rates take, and on whether movements in those variables, by affecting the current *valuation* of wealth, are allowed to influence saving behavior. The model as it stands assumes that exchange rate expectations are exogenous; hence, given the convenient assumptions of perfect asset substitutability and flexible prices, real interest rate movements are equalized internationally. The model also values asset stocks in such a way that relative price changes are not allowed to affect the real value of wealth.

TABLE 9

Simulations of Deficit Changes in the United States, Germany, and Japan for the Period 1982–1985

Country and Year	Variable					
	D	*S*	*I*	*N*	*REEX*	*R*
United States						
1982	2.88	0.37	–0.69	–0.82	16.6	4.02
1983	3.64	1.73	–0.82	–1.10	13.6	5.05
1984	2.71	1.31	–0.48	–0.92	6.3	3.47
1985	3.38	1.68	–0.49	–1.21	12.0	3.72
Germany						
1982	–0.63	–0.65	–0.87	0.85	–15.2	4.02
1983	–1.30	–1.12	–1.01	1.19	–10.6	5.05
1984	–1.54	–1.15	–0.58	0.97	–2.1	3.47
1985	–2.20	–1.55	–0.59	1.24	–9.2	3.72
Japan						
1982	0.37	–0.08	–0.50	0.05	0.1	4.02
1983	0.33	–0.18	–0.60	0.09	0.2	5.05
1984	–0.62	–0.61	–0.36	0.37	–2.0	3.47
1985	–1.68	–1.24	–0.37	0.81	–4.7	3.72

Note: All variables are deviations from baseline (expressed as percentages of baseline capacity output) except *REEX*, which is given as percentage deviation from baseline, and *R*, which is given as percentage-point deviation from baseline.

In our other paper (Knight and Masson (1988)), however, we have shown that relaxing these assumptions does not make a great difference in either the qualitative or quantitative results of simulating the model's response to the fiscal deficit shocks that are imposed there. A version of the model in which expectations of exchange rates and interest rates are formed "rationally" (that is, in which they are consistent with the model's predictions) – with beginning-of-period stocks of real government debt revalued as a function of changes in the real interest rate, and with real net foreign claims revalued as a function of changes in the real effective exchange rate – gives quite similar results for most variables (including exchange rates), at least when the fiscal changes occur all at once and at the beginning of the simulation period. The main difference in that version is that interest rates in the three countries are uncoupled, so that a country implementing a fiscal expansion has real interest rates that are *higher* than elsewhere, with the converse obtaining for countries implementing fiscal contraction. With a path of deficit changes that grows over time, rational expectations of financial variables would likely bring forward the effects of exchange rates and interest rates but, on the basis of our previous results, would be unlikely to change greatly the magnitudes of these effects.

Tax Incentives for Private Investment

The two preceding simulations have analyzed the effects of changes in overall fiscal deficits, but they have not incorporated the impact of tax changes on investment incentives. Such an analysis is important for explaining the behavior of interest rates and the U.S. dollar over the period we are considering. In 1981 and 1982 the United States implemented substantial changes in the tax treatment of depreciation that tended to lower the user cost of capital for nonresidential investment; at the same time a reduction in personal income tax rates increased the cost of capital for residential investment. These changes are embodied in the Economic Recovery Tax Act of 1981 (ERTA) and in the Tax Equity and Fiscal Responsibility Act of 1982 (TEFRA). Hooper (1984) cites estimates that the cost of capital relevant to investment in producers' durable equipment and structures fell by 1 percentage point and 3 percentage points, respectively, as a result of these changes (see also Brayton and Clark (1985)). In contrast, the cost of capital for rental housing increased by an estimated $^1/_2$ percentage point, and by 1 percentage point for owner-occupied housing (Hooper (1984, p.14)). Averaged together using shares in 1983 investment as weights, these changes yield a decrease in the cost of capital relevant to total investment of about $1^1/_4$ percentage points.[16]

16. The Tax Reform Act of 1986 (TRA) is a far-reaching revision of U.S. tax law that both reduces the progressivity of personal income tax rates and lowers statutory corporate

For the estimates cited above, the user cost of capital was calculated in the following way (see Brayton and Clark (1985, p. 5)):

$$C = [(1 - t)R_n + \delta - \pi]\Delta, \tag{25}$$

where

t = the tax rate (corporate or personal)
R_n = the nominal interest rate
δ = the rate of economic depreciation
π = the rate of change of the price of the investment good
Δ = a factor that depends on the tax treatment of depreciation and investment tax credits (for housing, Δ is equal to unity).

ERTA and TEFRA lowered the value of Δ for business investment and lowered the value of t for individuals. To simulate the effects of these measures on investment, we first calculate the changes in the interest rate, for given rates of inflation, that would have produced the same change in the user cost of capital. From equation (25) above, these changes are approximately

$$dR_n = \frac{1}{\Delta(1 - t)} dC,$$

where $t = .46$ for corporations and $t = .19$ for individuals.[17] If we average these implied changes in the real interest rate using investment shares, the same effect as the tax changes would have been produced through a decrease of 2 percentage points in the real interest rate. Table 10 presents the result of simulating the model in such a way that this change is embodied in the equation

tax rates significantly. However, since many types of business tax credits and deductions have also been repealed or limited, the effective corporate tax burden is intended to be increased by an amount that will more than offset the negative revenue effect of the decrease in statutory corporate tax rates. Thus, TRA is projected to be broadly neutral in its overall revenue effect for the period 1987-91 taken as a whole. For a description of TRA and an empirical analysis of its effects, see Evans and Kenward (1988). These authors estimate that under the assumption of unchanged interest rates the abolition of the investment tax credit and the lengthening of depreciation schedule in TRA would be likely to reduce the incentive to invest in nonresidential structures and in machinery and equipment — by some $3\,{}^1/_2$ percent and $4\,{}^3/_4$ percent, respectively, over the period to 1992 — relative to what would otherwise have occured. When the induced decline in U.S. interest rates (estimated at roughly half a percentage point) is allowed for, the overall effect of TRA on investment is estimated to be negative but small.

17. The figures underlying the calculations in Brayton and Clark (1985) were obtained directly from Flint Brayton.

TABLE 10

Simulation of U.S. Tax Changes Affecting the Cost of Capital, Starting in 1982

	U.S. Variables							
Year	S	I	N	K	F	W	$REEX$	R
1982	—0.08	0.15	—0.23	0.15	—0.23	—0.08	5.1	1.14
1983	—0.07	0.14	—0.21	0.28	—0.42	—0.14	2.2	1.10
1984	—0.05	0.14	—0.19	0.42	—0.61	—0.19	1.9	1.06
1985	—0.04	0.14	—0.18	0.55	—0.77	—0.23	1.5	1.02
1986	—0.03	0.13	—0.17	0.66	—0.92	—0.25	1.3	0.99
1990	0.00	0.12	—0.12	1.17	—1.43	—0.26	0.4	0.83
Long run	0.02	0.08	—0.06	2.59	—2.00	0.59	—0.6	0.42

	German Variables				Japanese Variables			
Year	S	I	K	W	S	I	K	W
1982	—0.08	—0.25	—0.25	—0.08	—0.08	—0.14	—0.14	—0.08
1983	—0.08	—0.22	—0.45	—0.16	—0.08	—0.13	—0.27	—0.16
1984	—0.08	—0.19	—0.63	—0.24	—0.08	—0.11	—0.37	—0.23
1985	—0.08	—0.16	—0.78	—0.31	—0.07	—0.10	—0.46	—0.30
1986	—0.07	—0.14	—0.90	—0.37	—0.07	—0.09	—0.54	—0.36
1990	—0.05	—0.07	—1.22	—0.60	—0.06	—0.05	—0.78	—0.60
Long-run	—0.01	—0.02	—0.75	—0.44	—0.02	—0.02	—0.55	—0.60

Note: All variables are deviations from baseline (expressed as percentages of baseline capacity output) except $REEX$, which is given as percentage deviation from baseline, and R, which is given as percentage-point deviation from baseline. Variables are as defined in Table 3.

for U.S. investment; in particular, the constant term in that equation is decreased by 0.02 times the coefficient of the interest rate (with the sign reversed). However, effects on government revenue are ignored here: the deficit is assumed to remain unchanged in this simulation.

As would be expected, the simulation indicates that the decline in the user cost of capital stimulates investment in the United States and leads to a current account deficit there. In long-run equilibrium, both the U.S. capital stock and external indebtedness are permanently higher. The dynamics of adjustment produce an initial substantial rise in the real exchange rate of the dollar and an increase in world real interest rates in excess of 1 percentage point. In long-run equilibrium, real interest rates are higher than in the baseline, but the exchange value of the dollar is close to its initial equilibrium. Higher interest rates discourage capital formation in the other countries, which are assumed not to benefit from greater investment incentives. Despite increased claims on the United States, wealth in Germany and Japan is lower than in the baseline.

Combined Effects of Fiscal Deficits and Investment Incentives

In Table 11 we combine the effects of the decrease in the user cost of capital in the United States with the pattern of changes in overall fiscal deficits that was simulated in Table 9. The results indicate substantial movements in exchange rates relative to the baseline among the three countries and a rise in interest rates that reaches 6 percentage points in 1983. This increase more than offsets the effect of investment incentives in the United States, and U.S. investment declines relative to baseline.

The issue of how much of the dollar's strength can be attributed to shifts in fiscal policy – and of the extent to which such fiscal changes also explain high real interest rates in the United States and elsewhere – has been addressed in several recent papers. Blanchard and Summers (1984, p. 302) have concluded that "on balance,... we find no evidence that fiscal policy in the OECD (Organization for Economic Cooperation and Development) as a whole is responsible, through its effect on saving, for high long real rates." By contrast, simulations of a small global macroeconomic model by Sachs (1985) tend to support the view that the U.S. monetary-fiscal policy mix – even accompanied by fiscal contraction in the rest of the OECD – goes a long way toward explaining developments in financial and exchange markets in the first half of the 1980's.

Our results imply effects on the exchange rate of the dollar and on real interest rates that are similar to those of Sachs, although somewhat smaller in magnitude. When inflation-adjusted deficit changes are simulated in the three countries in combination with tax-induced changes in the user cost of capital in the United States, the peak dollar appreciation relative to the baseline yielded by our model is 21 percent in real effective terms, and the peak real interest rate increase is 6 percentage points. Because we do not take account of the tightening of U.S. monetary policy in 1980-81, we do not expect to account fully for the rise in interest rates and in the value of the dollar that

TABLE 11

Simulation of Deficit Changes in the United States, Germany, and Japan for the Period 1982-85, and of U.S. Tax Changes Affecting the Cost of Capital, Starting in 1982

Country	Variables					
and Year	*D*	*S*	*I*	*N*	*REEX*	*R*
United States						
1982	2.88	1.29	—0.54	—1.05	21.3	5.16
1983	3.64	1.66	—0.67	—1.31	15.4	6.14
1984	2.71	1.25	—0.34	—1.11	7.6	4.52
1985	3.38	1.64	—0.35	—1.39	12.9	4.73
Germany						
1982	—0.63	—0.74	—1.12	1.01	—18.0	5.16
1983	—1.30	—1.20	—1.23	1.32	—0.4	6.14
1984	—1.54	—1.23	—0.77	1.07	—1.7	4.52
1985	—2.20	—1.62	—0.75	1.32	—8.6	4.73
Japan						
1982	0.37	—0.16	—0.64	0.11	—0.3	5.16
1983	0.33	—0.26	—0.72	0.13	0.2	6.14
1984	—0.62	—0.69	—0.48	0.41	—1.8	4.52
1985	—1.68	—1.31	—0.47	0.84	—4.4	4.73

Note: All variables are deviations from baseline (expressed as percentages of baseline capacity output) except *REEX*, which is given as percentage deviation from baseline, and *R*, which is given as percentage-point deviation from baseline.

was observed in the first half of the 1980s. Our model does, however, seem to explain a substantial portion of observed movements. From its trough in 1980 to the peak of early 1985, the dollar appreciated by 57 percent, of which 37 percent was from the end of 1981; at their peak, real short-term interest rates were about 4 percentage points higher, and long term rates about 8 percentage points higher, than in 1980 (International Monetary Fund (1985, pp. 8 and 18)). To summarize, if one accepts the size of the fiscal shifts assumed in the simulation, then the view that changes in fiscal policy help to explain the direction and rough order of magnitude of the net movements in real interest rates and real exchange rates of the three largest industrial countries during the first half of the 1980s receives strong support.

IV. INTERNATIONAL TRANSMISSION OF FISCAL POLICIES: UPDATE AND EXTENSION

The simulation experiments in the preceding section, which were reported in our earlier paper (Masson and Knight (1986)), strongly support the view that the appreciation of the dollar in the first half-decade of the 1980s was due in large part to the combination of an expansionary fiscal stance in the United States and restrained fiscal stances in the Federal Republic of Germany and Japan – as evidenced by large shifts in their inflation-adjusted fiscal deficits. In the period since the mid–1980s, however, high real interest rates and the pattern of current account imbalances have persisted, while the real effective exchange rate of the U.S. dollar has depreciated by some 60 percent from its peak in the first quarter of 1985 to the first quarter of 1988. Thus it is of interest to compare the events of this more recent period with the predictions of our original model. A second purpose of this new section is to describe possible scenarios for the dollar and the U.S. current account, using the model to generate paths for endogenous variables that take into account the dynamics of the accumulation of asset stocks – in particular, government debt, physical capital, and net liabilities to foreigners.

The depreciation in the real effective exchange rate of the U.S. dollar since 1985 is documented in Column (1) of Table 12, which repeats the data from Table 1 for the index based on relative normalized unit labor costs.[18] The dollar's real appreciation relative to 1980, which reached about 50 percent on average in 1985, declined to 20 percent in 1986 (a depreciation of 20 percent from its 1985 level) and to 5 percent in 1987 (a further depreciation of 14 percent); at the end of 1987, the dollar in real terms was in fact slightly below its 1980 level.

As discussed above, a key exogenous variable in our model is the inflation-adjusted fiscal deficit of the general government sector;[19] Table 13 gives historical values for this variable in column (1). After a strong movement to

18. Since the movements in the real effective exchange rates of the yen and deutschemark have been broadly similar to each other, this note will focus on the U.S. dollar's effective rate and the fiscal deficit of the United States. Data are calculated by the IMF. Sources are given in the Appendix.

19. Including federal, state, and local governments.

declining somewhat in 1984 and 1987, but rising in 1985 and 1986. The Gramm Rudman-Hollings (GRH) Act, passed in December 1985, legislated a path for the Federal fiscal deficit that would lead to a zero figure for 1991; however, parts of the Act were ruled unconstitutional, and the initial targets were not met. Targets for later years have since been revised, and are part of a new deficit reduction act. However, the low U.S. fiscal deficit figure for 1987 is generally thought to be the result of a combination of favorable factors that are unlikely to persist, and there is now considerable uncertainty about the future stance of U.S. fiscal policy.

As described in our earlier paper, the equations of the model were estimated using data through 1983. In comparing the predictions of the model with recent data, residuals since 1983 were set to zero. Exogenous variables were updated – output gaps, government deficits, and the balancing item in the current account identity – and actual values were used for them in the model simulations. After 1987, these exogenous variables were extrapolated such that they remained unchanged as ratios to capacity output; therefore, output gap ratios (GAP and GAPF) were assumed to remain unchanged, while government deficits (D) and the balance of payments items (RES) were allowed to grow in real terms by the trend growth in capacity output, assumed to be 3 percent per year for all countries.[20]

In this new experiment, the model was simulated under the assumption that exchange rate expectations are static, so that real interest rates were equalized in the United States, Germany and Japan; the value for the exchange rate is presented in column (2) of Table 12. It can be seen that given the developments in fiscal positions described above, the model predicts that the period of U.S. dollar appreciation in the early 1980s would be followed by a depreciation. Indeed, the model predicts that the dollar decline begins in 1984, whereas it actually began in the following year. The value of the dollar's real effective exchange rate for 1985 is also higher than predicted, while the 1986 value is somewhat lower. For the last period for which actual values of exogenous variables are used, 1987, the actual value of the dollar's real effective exchange rate is fairly close to that predicted by the model.

The model projections beyond 1987 are also instructive. The simulation implies a steady, but gradual depreciation of the dollar; from its 1988 level (which is higher than 1987 because of lags in export and import equations),

20. However, trends in export and import equations were progressively made to flatten, such that they approach a constant value asymptotically; this assumption was made because these trends, which capture the secular growth in world trade, prevent the eventual attainment of a steady state in the model, where all stock and flow variables grow at a common rate.

the dollar depreciates by about 10 percent in real terms over the following 10 years. Because asset stocks do not adjust immediately, the transition to a new long-run equilibrium takes time, and interest rates and exchange rates can be expected to change over the transition period; the fact that the initial

TABLE 12

United States: Index of Real Effective Exchange Rate (1980 = 100)

	Actual	Projected, Starting in 1984	
		Static Expectations	Forward-Looking Expectations
	(1)	(2)	(3)
1980	100		
1981	111		
1982	126		
1983	130		
1984	140	119	119
1985	146	136	131
1986	117	134	131
1987	102	97	106
1988		101	101
1989		98	96
1990		96	93
1991		95	91
1992		94	90

values of asset stocks were not steady state ones makes it difficult to describe precisely the nature of the adjustment process.[21]

Given the changes that have occured in the value of the dollar and in the stance of fiscal policy in the United States, it is of interest to consider other hypotheses concerning the formation of expectations, in addition to static expectations of exchange rate changes. If investors correctly anticipated the decline in the dollar against other major currencies, then they would have put downward pressure on the dollar sooner. Knight and Masson (1988) presented simulations in which exchange rate expectations were assumed to be consistent with the model's solution for the exchange rate in subsequent periods; likewise, the developments in recent years can also be evaluated in such a framework. Investors are assumed to make predictions of future exchange rates given forecasts of the exogenous variables. Two crucial questions involved in expansion in 1982-83, the deficit moved erratically over the 1984-87 period,

21. The dynamics of adjustment to a U.S. fiscal deficit reduction are as described above in Table 6, when starting from a position of steady-state equilibrium.

such an evaluation are: 1) were the changes in fiscal policy over the period 1984-87 correctly anticipated and 2) is the U.S. federal government expected to reduce its budget deficit to zero by 1992, as mandated by the revised Gramm-Rudman-Hollings Act?

The simulations were done on the assumption that expectations changed markedly when the GRH Act was passed at the end of 1985. Before that date, investors are presumed to have anticipated that large fiscal deficits would continue; deficits for 1984-86 are assumed to have been correctly anticipated,

TABLE 13

United States: Inflation-Adjusted General Government Deficit (as Percent of Capacity GNP)

	Actual	Projected, Starting in 1984		
		Static Expectations	Forward-Looking Pre-GRH	Expectations Post-GRH
	(1)	(2)	(3)	(4)
1980	—0.8			
1981	—0.8			
1982	2.1			
1983	2.7			
1984	1.8	1.8	1.8	
1985	2.4	2.4	2.4	
1986	2.6	2.6	2.6	2.6
1987	2.1	2.1	2.6	2.1
1988		2.1	2.6	1.5
1989		2.1	2.6	1.0
1990		2.1	2.6	0.5
1991		2.1	2.6	0.0
1992		2.1	2.6	0.0

and before 1986 investors are assumed to have projected a continuation of the 1986 deficit, 2.6 percent of capacity GNP, indefinitely (column 3 of Table 13). From 1986 onward, in contrast, they are assumed to have believed that the original GRH targets for federal fiscal deficits would be achieved; consequently, the projected path for the deficit ratio involves a decline from its 1986 value of 2.6 percent to balance in 1991 (column 4).[22] Thus, investors are

22. Such a decline in fact understates the contractionary nature of the GRH Act, since our deficit variable, for the general government, includes state and local governments which currently have a surplus of about 1 percent of GNP. However given doubts about the exact implementation of the Act (which involves margins for error) as well as difficulties in forecasting the state and local position, achievement of a zero general government position would seem consistent with the spirit of the deficit reduction program.

assumed to make projections of the U.S. fiscal position that differ from subsequently realized values, and also to have different expectations relating to a particular year, pre- and post-GRH.

The path for the exchange rate that results from such a simulation, presented in column (3) of Table 12, is not very different from the static expectations simulation, though the dollar appreciates somewhat less and declines more smoothly; it ends up at a similar level.[23] The major difference is in the path for interest rates (not reported); the decline in the value of the dollar, which is assumed to be at least partly anticipated, drives a wedge between interest rates in the United States and those in Germany and Japan; U.S. rates are higher throughout the simulation. In summary, developments in fiscal policies seem to explain a good part of the decline in the value of the U.S. dollar since 1985.

V. CONCLUSIONS

In periods when international economic developments are strongly influenced by large autonomous changes in national saving and investment balances – particularly those induced by shifts in public sector fiscal positions in the largest industrial countries – such disturbances may be expected to exert an overriding influence on the pattern of real exchange rates and current account positions. The developments analyzed in this paper are clearly not the only factors that have been at work over the past few years. Nevertheless, the analysis of this paper suggests that a careful examination of national saving and investment balances, and of the shifts in fiscal positions and tax laws that influence them, may be expected to yield useful insights into the behavior of exchange rates and payments balances among the industrial countries, at least over the medium term.

More specifically, the work of the preceding sections suggests several conclusions. First, under plausible assumptions, a very simple and standard classical model will yield the result that fiscal shifts such as those that have taken place among the largest industrial countries in recent years are indeed consistent with all three of the stylized facts mentioned in the introduction to this paper : the persistently high level of real interest rates in international financial markets, shifts to a large current account deficit in the United States and to surpluses in Germany and Japan, and persistent appreciation of the U.S. dollar. Second, preliminary estimation results suggest that the assumptions

23. The similarity of results for static and rational expectations — which however is specific to this model — confirms the conclusion in Knight and Masson (1988).

needed for the model to yield these effects are themselves consistent with the data for the period. Third, although the timing of exchange rate movements depends on many factors, the effects of fiscal shifts on real interest rates and exchange rates are clearly important. In terms of direction and order of magnitude, the simulation experiments support the view that the shifts in the pattern of fiscal positions that took place among the three largest industrial economies over approximately the period 1982-85 – combined with changes in U.S. tax incentives for investment – were responsible for a substantial proportion of the net changes in interest rates and exchange rates that actually occured in the United States, Germany, and Japan during the first half of the 1980s. Movements up to the end of 1987 have also been broadly consistent with predictions of the model. In particular, the depreciation in the real exchange rate of the U.S. dollar since early 1985 is explained both by the actual and projected decline in the U.S. fiscal deficit in recent years and by the gradual buildup of service payments on external debt.

International Monetary Fund, Washington, D.C., U.S.A.

APPENDIX

Data Sources and Definitions

Except where otherwise noted, all flow data were taken from the national accounts of the country concerned. Sources were Data Resources, Inc. (DRI) for the United States and the OECD's *National Accounts* (Paris, the issues for 1960-77 and 1971-83) for Germany and Japan. Real flows and stocks were valued at 1980 local currency prices.

Variables for the United States, Germany, and Japan ($i = US, GE, JA$)

B_i is the real government net debt, calculated by cumulating general government fiscal deficits from benchmark figures, based on ratios of debt to GDP in 1982 (Muller and Price (1984)) : 13.6 percent for the United States, 23.4 percent for Japan, and 19.8 percent for Germany. The net debt series was then divided by the GDP deflator.

D_i represents the real general government deficit corrected for inflation, calculated as $B_i - B_i(-1)$.

F_i is the real net foreign assets position, calculated by cumulating N_i. Benchmark figures for the F_i were obtained by dividing nominal net claims on foreigners valued in local currency at the end of 1982 by the 1982 GDP deflator.

For the United States, net claims on foreigners at the end of 1982 were US \$ 149.5 billion (U.S. Department of Commerce, *Survey of Current Business* (Washington, June 1984, p. 75)); for Germany, DM 66.5 billion (*Monthly Report of the Deutsche Bundesbank* (Bonn, October 1984, p. 35)); and for Japan, US \$ 24.7 billion (Bank of Japan, *Economic Statistics Annual* (Tokyo, 1983., p. 248)).

GAP_i stands for the output gap, as a ratio to capacity output: the gap equals actual GDP divided by capacity output (YC_i), minus one. Given the way in which YC_i is calculated, GAP_t is the same as the output gap in manufacturing (see Artus (1977)).

$GAPF_i$ is the foreign output gap; that is, actual GDP for nine industrial countries (excluding the country concerned) divided by the corresponding potential output, minus one. The set of ten countries comprises the United States, Japan, Germany, the United Kingdom, France, Italy, Canada, Belgium, the Netherlands, and Sweden.

I_i represents real private net investment, residential plus nonresidential.

K_i is the real private net capital stock. For the United States it was calculated as the sum of the nonresidential and residential real stocks, minus the government residential stock (source: DRI). For Germany and Japan, K was calculated by cumulating I_i using a benchmark figure. This figure for Germany was the 1970 total net capital stock minus the 1970 government capital stock (OECD, *Flows and Stocks of Fixed Capital* (Paris, the issue for 1955-80)). For Japan, where a figure for the real net capital stock was not available, preliminary estimation of an investment equation chose the value of the 1960 ratio of capital to GDP (3.18) that maximized the fit of the equation.

MV_i stands for the volume of non-oil merchandise imports in real local currency terms; figures were obtained from International Monetary Fund data files.

N_i is the national account net exports of goods and services divided by the GDP deflator.

R_i represents the real long-term interest rate, calculated as the nominal long-term government bond rate (source: International Monetary Fund, *International Financial Statistics, or IFS* (Washington, various issues)) minus the percentage change in the GDP deflator. The result was divided by 100 to get an interest rate expressed as a decimal fraction.

$REEX_i$ is the real effective exchange rate index (1980 = 1; an increase indicates appreciation), calculated as the country's normalized unit labor costs (*NULC*) relative to a weighted average of its competitors' *NULC*, in a common currency (source: *IFS*).

RES_i is a residual current account item that includes the oil trade balance, the balance on services excluding investment income, and unilateral transfers. It is calculated as $N_i - XV_i + MV_i - R_i F_i(-1)$.

S_i represents real net private saving, calculated as $N_i + I_i + D_i$.

W_i is real private sector net wealth, calculated as $\varphi B_i + K_i + F_i$.

XV_i stands for the volume of non-oil merchandise exports in real local currency terms (source : International Monetary Fund data files).

YC_i is capacity GDP, calculated by applying the gap between actual and potential manufacturing output (Artus (1977)) to actual GDP.

Variables for Germany and Japan

$ERDOT_i$ represents the expected rate of change of the bilateral real exchange rate against the U.S. dollar (with a positive value indicating depreciation of the dollar), calculated as $R_{US} - R_i$.

Variables for the Rest of the World (ROW)

N_{ROW} is a proxy for the ROW real current balance calculated as $-(N_{US} + N_{GE}/1.815 + N_{JA}/225.82)$; denominators contain 1980 bilateral rates of the deutschemark and the yen against the dollar.

R_{ROW} represents the real interest rate, calculated as a GDP-weighted average of R_{US}, R_{GE}, and R_{JA}.

YC_{ROW} is capacity output in 1980 U.S. dollars, calculated by aggregating the remaining seven of our sample of ten industrial countries.

REFERENCES

Artus, Jacques, R. (1977) 'Measures of Potential Output in Manufacturing for Eight Industrial Countries, 1955-78', *IMF Staff Papers*, 24 : 1-35, (Washington : International Monetary Fund), (March).

——, and Knight, Malcolm D. (1984) *Issues in the Assessment of Exchange Rates of Industrial Countries*, IMF Occasional Paper 29, (Washington : International Monetary Fund), (July).

Barro, Robert J. (1974) 'Are Government Bonds Net Wealth?' *Journal of Political Economy*, 82 : 1095-1117 (November-December).

Bernheim, B. Douglas and Shoven, John B. (1985) 'Pension Funding and Saving', NBER Working Paper 1622, (Cambridge, Massachusetts : National Bureau of Economic Research), (May).

Blanchard, Olivier J. (1985) 'Debt, Deficits, and Finite Horizons', *Journal of Political Economy*, 93 : 223-47 (April).

—— and Summers, Lawrence H. (1984) 'Perspectives on High World Real Interest Rates,' *Brookings Papers on Economic Activity*, 2: 273-324, (Washington : The Brookings Institution).

Branson, William H. (1985) 'Causes of Appreciation and Volatility of the Dollar' NBER Working Paper 1777 (Cambridge, Massachusetts : National Bureau of Economic Research), (December).

——, Halttunen, Hannu and Masson, Paul (1977) 'Exchange Rates in the Short-Run : The Dollar-Deutschemark Rate', *European Economic Review*, 10 : 303-24 (December).

Brayton, Flint and Clark, Peter B. (1985) 'The Macroeconomic and Sectoral Effects of the Economic Recovery Tax Act : Some Simulation Results', Staff Study 148, (Washington : Board of Governors of the Federal Reserve System), (December).

Buiter, Willem H. (1983) 'Measurement of the Public Sector Deficit and Its Implications for Policy Evaluation and Design', *IMF Staff Papers*, 30: 306-49, (Washington : International Monetary Fund), (June).

—— and Tobin, James (1979) 'Debt Neutrality : A Brief Review of Doctrine and Evidence,' in *Social Security Versus Private Saving*, ed. by George M. von Furstenberg (Cambridge, Massachusetts : Ballinger), pp. 39-63.

Carmichael, Jeffrey (1982) 'On Barro's Theorem of Debt Neutrality : The Irrelevance of Net Wealth', *American Economic Review*, 72 : 202-13 (March).

Dornbusch, Rudiger (1975) 'A Portfolio Balance Model of the Open Economy', *Journal of Monetary Economics*, 1 : 3-20 (January).

—— (1976) 'Expectations and Exchange Rate Dynamics', *Journal of Political Economy*, 84 : 1161-76 (December).

—— and Fisher, Stanley (1980) 'Exchange Rates and the Current Account', *American Economic Review*, 70 : 960-71 (December).

Evans, Owen and Kenward, Lloyd (1988) 'Macroeconomic Effects of Tax Reform in the United States', *IMF Staff Papers*, 35(1): 141-165, (Washington : International Monetary Fund), (March).

Feldstein, Martin (1986) 'U.S. Budget Deficits and the European Economies : Resolving the Political Economy Puzzle', *American Economic Review, Papers and Proceedings*, 76: 342-46 (May).

Frenkel, Jacob A. (1985) Comment on William H. Branson, 'Causes of Appreciation and Volatility of the Dollar', in NBER Working Paper 1777 (Cambridge, Massachussetts : National Bureau of Economic Research), (December).

—— and Razin, Assaf (1984) 'Budget Deficit and Rates of Interest in the World Economy', NBER Working Paper 1354 (Cambridge, Massachusetts : National Bureau of Economic Research), (May).

—— (1985a) 'Government Spending, Debt, and International Economic Interdependence', *Economic Journal*, 95: 619-36 (September).

—— (1985b) 'Fiscal Expenditures and International Economic Interdependence', in *International Economic Policy Coordination*, ed. by Willem H. Buiter and Richard C. Marston, (New York: Cambridge University Press), pp. 37-73.

Frenkel, Jacob A. and Rodriguez, Carlos (1982) 'Exchange Rate Dynamics and the Overshooting Hypothesis', *IMF Staff Papers*, 29: 1-30, (Washington: International Monetary Fund), (March).

Girton, Lance and Henderson, Dale (1977) 'Central Bank Operationsin Foreign and Domestic Assets Under Fixed and Flexible Exchange Rates', in *The Effects of Exchange Rate Adjustment: Proceedings of a Conference Sponsored by the Office of the Assistant Secretary for International Affairs*, ed. by Peter B. Clark, Dennis E. Logue, and Richard J. Sweeney, Document No. T1.2: Ex 2/2 (Washington: U.S. Department of the Treasury).

Goldstein, Morris and Khan Mohsin, S. (1985) 'Income and Price Effects in Foreign Trade', in *Handbook of International Economics*, Vol. 2, ed. by Ronald W. Jones and Peter B. Kenen, (Amsterdam: North-Holland, New York: Elsevier), pp. 1041-1105.

Gould, J. P. (1968) 'Adjustment Costs and the Theory of Investment of the Firm', *Review of Economic Studies*, 35: 47-55 (January).

Helliwell, John F. and Padmore, Tim (1985) 'Empirical Studies of Macroeconomic Interdependence', in *Handbook of International Economics*, Vol. 2, ed. by Ronald W. Jones and Peter B. Kenen, (Amsterdam: North-Holland, New York: Elsevier), pp. 1107-51.

Hooper, Peter (1984) 'International Repercussions of the U.S. Budget Deficit', International Finance Discussion Paper 246 (Washington: Board of the Federal Reserve System), (September).

International Monetary Fund (1985, 1986) *World Economic Outlook: A Survey by the Staff of the International Monetary Fund*, World Economic and Financial Surveys, (Washington, October and April issues).

Jump, Gregory V. (1980) 'Interest Rates, Inflation Expectations, and Spurious Elements in Measured Real Income and Saving', *American Economic Review*, 70: 990-1004 (December).

Knight, Malcolm D, and Masson, Paul R. (1988) 'Fiscal Policies, Net Saving, and Real Exchange Rates: The United States, the Federal Republic of Germany, and Japan', in *International Aspects of Fiscal Policies*, ed. by Jacob A. Frenkel, (Chicago: University of Chicago Press for the National Bureau of Economic Research).

Knight, Malcolm D., and Mathieson, Donald J. (1983) 'Economic Change and Policy Response in Canada Under Fixed and Flexible Exchange Rates', in *Economic Interdependence and Flexible Exchange Rates*, ed. by Jagdeep S. Bhandari and Bluford H. Putnam, with Jay H. Levin, (Cambridge, Massachusetts : MIT Press), pp. 500-29.

Kochin, Lewis, A. (1974) 'Are Future Taxes Anticipated by Consumers? Comment', *Journal of Money, Credit and Banking*, 6 : 385-94 (August).

Kouri, Pentti and Porter, Michael G. (1974) 'International Capital Flows and Portfolio Equilibrium,' *Journal of Political Economy*, 82 : 443-67 (May-June).

Laursen, Svendt and Metzler, Lloyd A. (1950) 'Flexible Exchange Rates and the Theory of Employment', *Review of Economics and Statistics*, 32 : 281-99 (November).

Masson, Paul R. (1985) 'The Sustainability of Fiscal Deficits', *IMF Staff Papers*, 32 : 577-605 (Washington, International Monetary Fund), December).

—— and Blundell-Wignall, Adrian (1985) 'Fiscal Policy and the Exchange Rate in the Big Seven : Transmission of U.S. Government Spending Shocks', *European Economic Review*, 28 : 11-42 (May).

—— and Malcolm, D. Knight (1986) 'International Transmission of Fiscal Policies in Major Industrial Countries', *IMF Staff Papers*, 33(3) : 387-438 (Washington : International Monetary Fund), (September).

Masson, Paul R. and Knight, Malcolm D. (1986) : "International Transmission of Fiscal Policies in Major Industrial Countries", *IMF Staff Papers*, 33(3) : 387-438 (Washington : International Monetary Fund), (September).

Metzler, Lloyd A. (1951) 'Wealth, Saving and the Rate of Interest', *Journal of Political Economy*, 59 : 93-116 (April).

Muller, Patrice and Price, Robert W.R. (1984) 'Structural Budget Indicators and the Interpretation of Fiscal Policy Stance in OECD Countries', *OECD Economic Studies*, No. 3 Paris, pp. 27-72, (Autumn).

Mundell, Robert A. (1963) Capital Mobility and Stabilization Policy Under Fixed and Flexible Exchange Rates', *Canadian Journal of Economics and Political Science*, 29 : 303-24 (November).

Mussa, Michael, A. (1976) *Study in Macroeconomics* (Amsterdam : North-Holland, New York : Elsevier).

Sachs, Jeffrey D. (1981) 'The Current Account and Macroeconomic Adjustment in the 1970s', *Brookings Papers on Economic Activity*, 1 : 201-68 (Washington : The Brookings Institution).

—— (1985) 'The Dollar and the Policy Mix: 1985', *Brookings Papers on Economic Activity*, 1: 117-97 (Washington: The Brookings Institution).

—— and Wyplosz, Charles (1984) 'Real Exchange Rate Effects of Fiscal Policy', NBER Working Paper 1255 (Cambridge Massachusetts: National, Bureau of Economic Research, January).

Seater, John J. (1982): 'Are Future Taxes Discounted?' *Journal of Money, Credit and Banking*, 14: 376-89 (August).

Spencer, Grant H. (1984): 'The World Trade Model: Revised Estimates', *IMF Staff Papers*, 31: 469-98 (Washington: International Monetary Fund, September).

Svensson, Lars E.O. and Razin, Assaf (1983) 'The Terms of Trade and the Current Account: The Harberger-Laursen-Metzler Effect', *Journal of Political Economy*, 91: 97-125 (February).

Tanner, J. Ernest (1979): 'An Empirical Investigation of Tax Discounting: A Comment', *Journal of Money, Credit and Banking*, 11: 214-18 (May).

PART IV

THE SETTING OF POLICY IN THE OPEN ECONOMY

ULYSSES AND THE SIRENS: A POLITICAL MODEL OF CREDIBILITY IN AN OPEN ECONOMY

By Patrick Minford*

I. INTRODUCTION

Credibility of policy is a topic which is of great importance in evaluating policy particularly in an open economy context; and in the last few years a number of interesting new contributions to understanding it have been made, building on game theoretic work on reputation – Backus and Driffill (1985), Barro and Gordon (1983), Barro (1986), Canzoneri (1985). These contributions have all focussed on the surprise Phillips curve and government's temptation to exploit it to reduce unemployment by surprising the private sector with an inflationary stimulus.

However, a number of difficulties are apparent with this general approach. First, the surprise Phillips curve may not be an adequate way to describe output reactions in an open economy; estimates of the surprise inflation term vary greatly across countries and in a number (notably in those with heavy indexing) are not significant, while the real exchange rate defined as either the terms of trade or the ratio of traded to non-traded goods is an important determinant of supply. Secondly, the objective function of governments is not grounded in a rational theory of government behaviour; governments are supplied by political parties which have interests. This means that the mechanisms by which 'credibility' occurs or fails are highly contrived; for example in Backus and Driffill, and Barro, governments are of different types ('wet' and 'dry') for no apparent reason, while in Barro and Gordon, punishment periods, (i.e. periods of 'disbelief'), are arbitrary – there is an infinity of disbelief equilibria, with nothing to motivate the choice between them (an individual in the public has no power to punish a government and no opportunity to coordinate a punishment strategy with others). Thirdly, none of the

* I am grateful to Anupam Rastogi for carrying out the simulations; and for helpful discussion to seminar participants at LSE, Hull, and HM Treasury, and in particular David Begg, Tapan Biswas, Willem Buiter, Andrew Hughes - Hallett, Peter Kenen, Mervyn King and Marcus Miller, and an anonymous referee. Financial support was provided by the ESRC Consortium for Modelling and Forecasting the Economy and also by the Centre for Economic Policy Research.

work has made any empirical progress, nor does it seem suitable for estimation. Yet from a modelling viewpoint, credibility is a key factor; the rational expectations solution when a policy is incredible is generally quite different from that when it is fully believed.

What I aim to set out in this paper is an empirical model of government behaviour in an open economy setting, derived, like private sector behaviour, from maximising principles. This model is to be solved along with the model of private sector behaviour (i.e. the content of a normal open economy macro model) in the following way. Government is a Stackelberg leader; it and the private sector have rational expectations and both know the full model (including the government's preferences and constraints) – this distinguishes the set - up from Vickers' (1986) model with incomplete information, though this work strengthens the view taken here that it should be possible to gauge politicians' preferences. Governments can choose between two types of plan: discretionary or pre-committed. But rational expectations rules out time-inconsistency (it imposes 'sub-game perfect' equilibrium), because everyone knows the circumstances under which the government would find it in its interest to 'renege' and any plan containing such circumstances would not be viable. Thus, in any pre-commitment the government itself must specify precisely the punishments it will undergo and who will inflict them and monitor its performance; such punishments as would actually be carried out (because it is in the interest of the agent carrying them out to do so) are then allowed for in computing what the government will actually do in its own interest. In this way, *one* and only one (entirely credible) strategy will be optimal, chosen and of course expected.[1] The paper attempts to estimate the differences between pre-committed and discretionary strategies, and whether party affiliation matters.

II. A MODEL OF GOVERNMENT BEHAVIOUR

A starting point for such a model should be that governments are *political*. But not political in the traditional 'political business cycle' sense (e.g. Nordhaus, 1975), for any government engineering a business cycle will be acting sub-optimally by creating an unwarranted private sector fluctuation, for which it would be penalised at the election.

The Downs (1957) median voter theory implied that different parties in-

1. This point is not new; and it has recently been re-emphasised by Hughes-Hallett (1986).

dulge exclusively in competitive bidding for the median voter, so offering identical policies to the electorate. However, a party which sacrifices its 'principles' in this process will not be acting optimally as a party; for a party depends for survival on its supporters (who staff it, finance it, etc.). Minford and Peel (1982) develop this idea which implies that each party maximises a weighted average of the utilities of its supporters and of floating voters; the weights will depend on how strongly the supporters feel about their principles.

Common observation and empirical evidence suggest that conservative parties are supported by 'capitalists' and labour parties by 'workers', while floating voters are those making a transition between these two 'classes' (this is of course a simplification from a continuum of voters). Building on this, Minford and Peel emphasise the distributional effects of macro policy. If workers mainly hold human capital, capitalists mainly financial capital (equity and bonds), then Conservative policies will maximise at each period, t:

$$V_{C,t} = [\lambda_C U_C(W_t) + (1 - \lambda_C)\, U_F(W_t, H_t)] \tag{1}$$

and Labour policies will maximise

$$V_{L,t} = [\lambda_L U_L(H_t) + (1 - \lambda_L)\, U_F(W_t, H_t)] \tag{2}$$

where W = financial capital at current market prices deflated by the retail price index, H = human capital similarly valued, subscripts C, L, F denote Conservative, Labour and Floating, respectively. It is assumed that by maximising these functions the parties are achieving the best trade off between the chances of winning elections and retaining the loyalty of their supporters. Since elections are occurring regularly and supporters' work is required continuously, it seems plausible to suppose that the trade off parameters, λ_C and λ_L, are constant over time and specifically, between periods in and out of office. W_t and H_t, of course, represent expected discounted income streams, so V_C and V_L can be thought of as expected utility up to a *first* order Taylor expansion; we ignore risk in this analysis.

We shall consider a simple macroeconomic policy 'instrument', a reflationary impulse consisting of a rise in public spending (including debt interest) financed by an equiproportionate expansion in bonds and money supply; for example, a one-year rise in spending equal to 1% of the stock of 'outside money' (bonds and monetary base), would be accompanied by a 1% rise in the stock of bonds and also in the monetary base. Call this R_t. A permanent rise in spending of this size would thus raise the growth rate of the money supply by 1% p.a. and, by normal monetary logic, thus raise inflation in steady state by 1% p.a.

The relevant decision period for a party is clearly the electoral period; that is, the time from just before one election up to the run-up to the next (typically four years). Each party offers certain policies in its manifesto at election time, to be implemented in the coming Parliament. We assume that the party cannot influence policies after that Parliament. This is not quite correct; calculations can be made of how policies pursued in one Parliament will condition the chosen policies at the *next* election both of one's own party and of the other party, but such calculations are highly uncertain and will be heavily discounted in a party's choice for that reason (see Alesina and Tabellini (1986), for a different view, used to rationalise variations in public debt).

Pre-commitment will therefore mean a manifesto undertaking, suitably supported by penalties for deviation, to fix the macro instrument for four years ('permanently'); for simplicity, we take this to be a constant value of this instrument, denoted as $\bar{R}$. Discretionary policy will imply that the government will choose the macro instrument setting in each of those four years according to the circumstancees of the time.

The set-up, to summarise, is one where the public forms expectations *before* the election of what each party would do if elected. A weighted average of these expectations (weighted by the probability of electoral success) are the rational expectations in the 'base case' (where for purposes of computation we assume both parties have pre-committed). The parties then decide – *prior* to the election – on either pre-commitment or discretion; the election then is the only 'surprise' event, for once it is over the public can form a new set of expectations which will be fully validated. The public will of course fully anticipate the period-by-period optimising moves of the discretionary party.

Before considering a practical representation of V_C and V_L, it is of interest to observe how W_t and H_t react to R_t – see Figures 1-4 – in the Liverpool model of the UK (Minford et al., 1984). The Liverpool model is a rational expectations open economy model, which is the relevant description in this context: *any* rational expectations model is likely to throw up similar effects of surprise persistent inflation on financial capital (the Fisher effect on interest rates) and on human capital (the Phillips curve effect on output and the effect of shifting the tax burden from labour to bondholders).

The model exhibits strong open economy linkage with the rest of the world; through perfect capital mobility, through trade, and through terms of trade effects on supply (or the wage/price sector). The first of these three implies that real interest rates are affected by reflation only to the extent that

FIGURE 1. Effect on ΔH_t, ΔW_t as Shock to ΔR_t Increases in Size

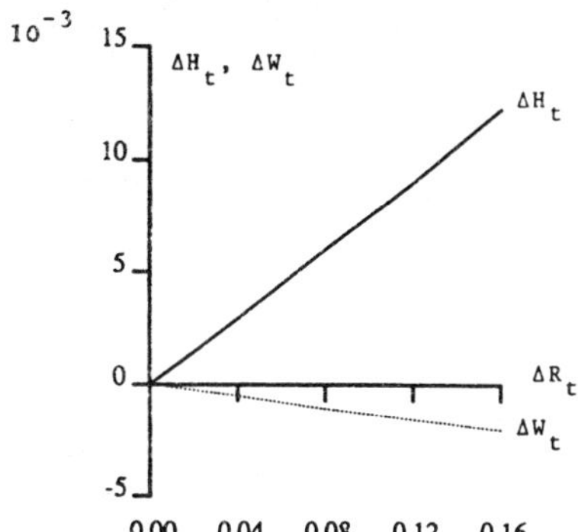

FIGURE 2. Effect on Current W of Current and Future R

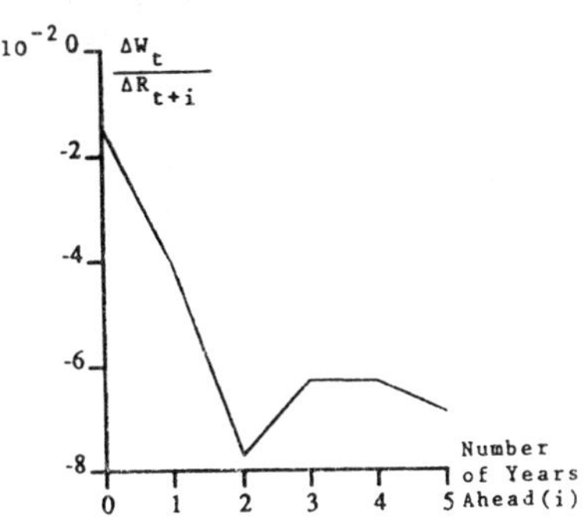

FIGURE 3. Effect of Current R on Current and Future W

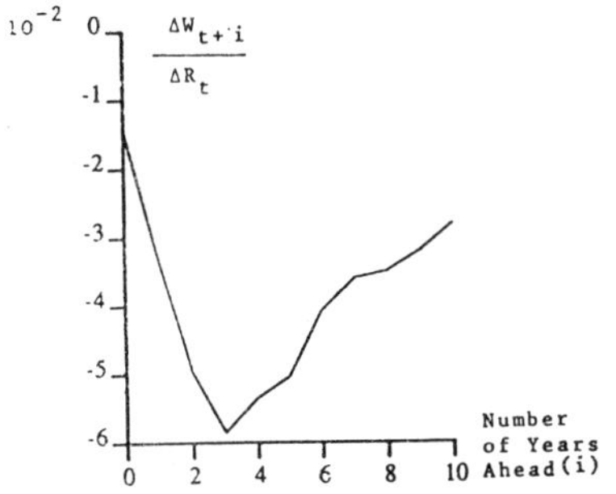

FIGURE 4. Effect on Current H of Current and Future R

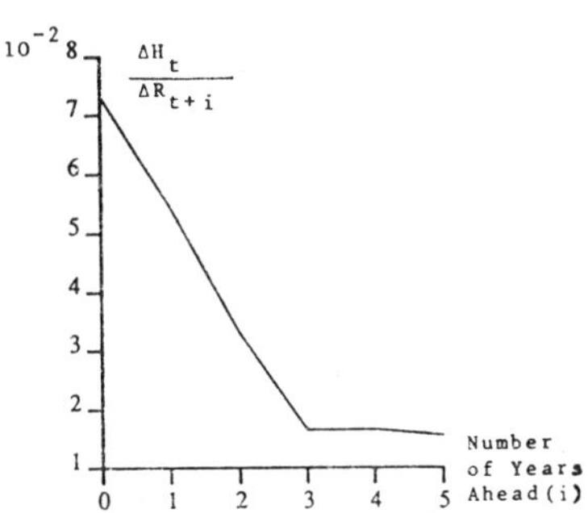

the real exchange rate moves, the second that the real depreciation brought about by reflation reinforces demand expansion; the third that real depreciation counteracts the Phillips curve effect on supply. The mechanism by which reflation raises H_t and lowers W_t is primarily that higher inflation devalues nominal government debt (in W_t), enabling higher government spending to benefit workers' living standards (in H_t) without higher taxation: an inflation tax redistribution story. (Though there may also be changes in levels of tax distortion, as tax structure changes, these are not included.) A secondary mechanism is that of the Phillips curve, augmented by the terms of trade effects, expanding output (raising H_t). H_t is represented by the discounted sum of GDP (less tax) and government spending excluding debt interest; the real discount rate is set at 5% p.a. W_t consists of the stock of goods (i.e. equity) held by the private sector plus the stock of privately held government bonds, money, and foreign assets. We measure both as fractional deviations from a base projection (made on the assumption of R_t roughly constant at .04, i.e. 4% p.a.). It turns out that W_t and H_t (measured in fractions of their base value) respond more or less linearly (within the range of interest to us) both to future and current R_t. Simulations of the full model show that for the four year horizon of interest the relevant coefficients relating W and H to R are as follows:

	R_t	R_{t+1}	R_{t+2}	R_{t+3}
W_t	−0.0144	−0.0403	−0.0717	−0.0628
W_{t+1}	−0.0330	−0.0144	−0.0403	−0.0717
W_{t+2}	−0.0496	−0.0330	−0.0144	−0.0403
W_{t+3}	−0.0584	−0.0496	−0.0330	−0.0144
H_t	0.0732	0.0546	0.0332	0.0166
H_{t+1}	–	0.0732	0.0546	0.0332
H_{t+2}	–	–	0.0732	0.0546
H_{t+3}	–	–	–	0.0732

(other elements of H matrix not required).

We adopt the following simplest (i.e. least parameterised) representations of V_C and V_L:

$$V_{C,t} = W_t - \frac{1}{2}\alpha W_t^2 + u_C H_t \tag{3}$$

$$V_{L,t} = W_t - \frac{1}{2}\alpha W_t^2 + u_L H_t \tag{4}$$

u_C and u_L reflect the weights λ_C and λ_L. As will be seen, we have just enough information to parameterise these, i.e. to set α, u_C and u_L. This set up, as we will see, implies that Conservatives, whose preferences are captured by $W_t - 1/2\,\alpha W_t^2$, would, if unconstrained, not wish to drive $\overline{R}_t$ below some level even though doing so would drive W_t higher still; we rationalise this as a desirable *minimum* price change (specifically price *stability*) because of uncertainty induced for example by falling prices. It is less easy to rationalise the *upper* limit on $\overline{R}_t$ for Labour preferences, or at any rate to specify quantitatively what that upper limit would be; so Labour preferences, H_t, are not themselves quadratic. However, Labour is seen as constrained in pushing up R_t by the effects this will have on W_t; they care about this because floating voters have financial capital.

To calculate optimal pre-committed and discretionary policies write

$$W_t = 1 + w_{00} R_t + w_{01} R_{t+1} + w_{02} R_{t+2} + w_{03} R_{t+3} \tag{5}$$

$$W_{t+1} = 1 + w_{10} R_t + w_{11} R_{t+1} + w_{12} R_{t+2} + w_{13} R_{t+3} \tag{6}$$

etc. where w_{ij} $(i, j = 0,..,3)$ are taken from the matrix above. Similarly

$$H_t = 1 + h_{00} R_t + \ldots + h_{03} R_{t+3}. \tag{7}$$

Note that a pre-committed policy is one where $R_t = \ldots = R_{t+3} = \bar{R}_t$ hence $W_t = 1 + \bar{w}_0 \bar{R}_t$ where $\bar{w}_0 = w_{00} + \ldots + w_{03}$ and $H_t = 1 + \bar{h}_0 \bar{R}_t$ where $\bar{h}_0 = h_{00} + \ldots + h_{03}$.

The precommitted policy sets $\dfrac{\partial V_t}{\partial \bar{R}_t} = 0$ so that

$$\bar{R}_{C,t} = \frac{(1-\alpha)\bar{w}_0 + u_C \bar{h}_0}{\alpha \bar{w}_0^2} \text{ (8a)}, \qquad \bar{R}_{L,t} = \frac{(1-\alpha)\bar{w}_0 + u_L \bar{h}_0}{\alpha \bar{w}_0^2}. \tag{8b}$$

In other words, each party computes the optimum at the start of the electoral period and is compelled to stick to it by some set of penalties to be discussed.

The discretionary policy is found by backward recursion, setting first $\dfrac{\partial V_{t+3}}{\partial R_{t+3}} = 0$ (taking R_t ,..., R_{t+2} as given by the past), then $\dfrac{\partial V_{t+2}}{\partial R_{t+2}} = 0$ (taking R_t, R_{t+1} as given by the past; and R_{t+3} as given by next period's decision), and so on back to the current period where $\dfrac{\partial V_t}{\partial R_t} = 0$ (which fixes R_t given R_{t+1} ,..., R_{t+3}). This is Bellman's Principle under rational expectations; it yields[2] (for the Conservatives)

$$R_C = W^{-1} k_C. \tag{9}$$

2. Under the assumption that $\alpha = 1$, to be justified below. A further (general) assumption is that the party, when setting policy for the current period, does not take into account its influence on next period's decision; clearly it could do so, and so 'bind the hands' of the party in the next period. (It has the ability to be a 'Stackelberg leader' for succeeding periods' decisions.) But this *limits* the discretion in the next period. It would introduce an element of pre-commitment; and it therefore seems to be against the spirit of (pure) discretion. It turns out, furthermore, that if it *was* allowed, the results for discretion would be highly volatile. For example, Conservative R_t (with u_C calibrated to the 1971-74

where R_C is the vector of R_{t+i}, W is the matrix of w_{ij} above, and $k_C = \dfrac{u_C h_{ii}}{w_{ii}}$; h_{ii}, w_{ii} are the contemporaneous effect of R_{t+i} on H_{t+i}, W_{t+i} (i.e. h_{00} and w_{00}, or the diagonal of the W matrix). For Labour, we have analogously

$$R_L = W^{-1} k_L \tag{10}$$

where $k_L = \dfrac{u_L h_{ii}}{w_{ii}}$.

We now estimate the parameters of the preference functions, α, and u_C, u_L.

First, α. Capitalists' preferences in (3) and (4) are implicitly given by $W_t - 1/2\, aW_t^2$. If the term $-1/2\, aW_t^2$ were not included, capitalists would benefit more from *negative* inflation than from price stability; however, this seems unlikely because price riskiness increases with price change, positive or negative (e.g. Minford and Hilliard, 1978). So α is set so that $W_t - 1/2\, aW_t^2$ is maximised at permanent price stability (i.e. $\bar{R}_t = 0$); arithmetically, (8a) is set to 0, with $u_C = 0$, giving $\alpha = 1$.

u_C can be derived if we assume that 1971 – 74 was a period of discretionary policy. During that period the average growth rate of MO was about 9% p.a. So we solve (9) for (average) R_C =0.09. This yields u_C= 0.00427.

Labour policies can be assumed to have been discretionary from 1974 to 1976 (from 1976, Labour operated until 1979 under IMF conditionality, a form of pre-commitment). We can calculate u_L from the period 1974 – 76, during which average MO growth was about 14% p.a. We therefore solve (10) for average $R_L = 0.14$. This yields $u_L = 0.00664$.

In all this, we treat third parties as aligning themselves implicitly either with Labour or Conservative preferences; thus a 'hung' Parliament could hang either way. A complete treatment would allow for a combination of parties with 'preferences' mid-way between C and L. However, we ignore it here for simplicity; it is in any case readily allowed for.

III. THE GAIN FROM PRE – COMMITMENT

Using these estimates we can calculate the optimal pre-committed policies. They turn out in *both* Conservative and Labour cases to be trivially

discretionary episode at u_C = .00718) would become 0.91, –0.72, 0.91, –0.73; alternating reflation and deflation. The gap between discretion and pre-commitment is, as one would expect, reduced; $\bar{R}_C$ =.036. (The Labour behaviour is affected in exactly the same way; the numbers for Labour are the same as for Conservatives times a factor of 1.5, reflecting their greater inflation tolerance.)

different from zero MO growth under Conservatives, $R_C = .021$, under Labour $R_L = .033$, implying near price stability.

By contrast, the discretionary policies, which of course must *average* the numbers used to fix u_C and u_L, follow a path which starts high, dips in the third year before rising again in the pre-election year (Figure 5); this pattern is dictated by the structure of the W matrix of lead-lag effects on W_{t+i}, and it is not easy to interpret intuitively. It is certainly not a 'political business cycle'. The optimal path requires W_{t+i} to be reduced from base by an equal percentage at all times; so it pays to raise inflation equally at the start and at the end and then as the effects of this on W_{t+i} cumulate backwards and forwards, the middle two years require a 'bang-bang' alteration to keep W_{t+i} on track.

FIGURE 5. Discretionary and Pre-committed Policies (MO Growth)

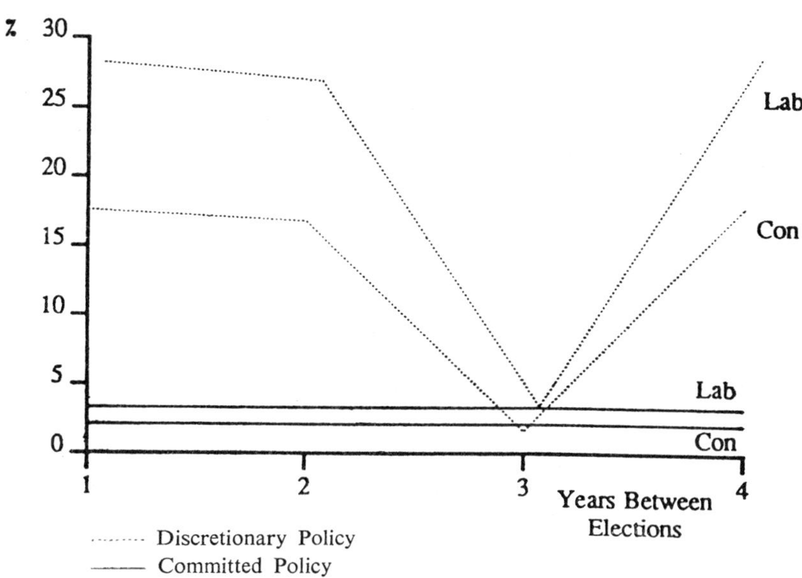

Welfare of both parties is less under discretionary than under pre-committed policies. The index differences are 'small' (for Conservatives, 0.03% on the index, for Labour, 0.12%); but this has no interpretation because the index is a weighted combination of two groups' utilities. The point is merely the *ordering* for political choice which is here unambiguous.

This is likely to be so, once the possibility of a discretionary surprise is ruled out (because agents are rational). The reason – I owe this point to David Begg – is that the optimum instrument under (time-consistent) discretion must be chosen subject to constraints on future values (namely that they be set by future decisions); whereas under pre-commitment future values of this instrument can be freely chosen simultaneously with the current value. The constraint that under pre-commitment all future values are equal at $\bar{R}$ could alter this. While it seems unlikely to do so, it does imply that the previous empirical investigation was a necessary one and of some interest.

There is accordingly a gain to pre-commitment for *both* parties, even for the Conservatives with a much lower preference for human capital (and so the gains to that made possible by higher inflation). Released from pre-commitment, Conservatives and Labour alike go for expansionary policies, nearly five times more expansionary than in this pre-committed state. Under pre-commitment, both go for near-price-stability. The results are shown in Figures 5 and 6.

The reason for this is clear. Under pre-commitment, each party finds that a decision to 'reflate' long term (a) reduces the value of outside money, and so of W_t, (b) by raising interest rates both depresses current output and lowers the government spending (excluding debt interest) that can be accommodated within the higher PSBR, so reducing by both routes the value of H_t. But under discretionary policy, the decision to reflate is taken in the light of the effects *excluding* such costs, since the past is given and the future is already determined by prior recursion; expected future inflation barely moves in response to the discretionary decision to reflate.

In this, the Liverpool model parallels the results obtained with the surprise Phillips curve mechanism by Kydland and Prescott (1977), Barro and Gordon (1983), and Canzoneri (1985) among others; the difference here is that the dominant mechanism is the devaluation of outside money (presumed to include bonds with long maturities, as well as monetary base and short dated bonds) by inflation (implicitly, in the case of bonds devalued, not anticipated at the time the bond contracts were drawn up).

Thus, our party political actors who 'choose' discretion become thereby the victims of a deterministic fate. Everyone knows what they will do and that it will turn out badly for them; yet they are compelled to do it in their own interests, subject to that initial choice of discretion.

FIGURE 6. Effects of Discretion (Difference Between Discretionary and Pre-committed)

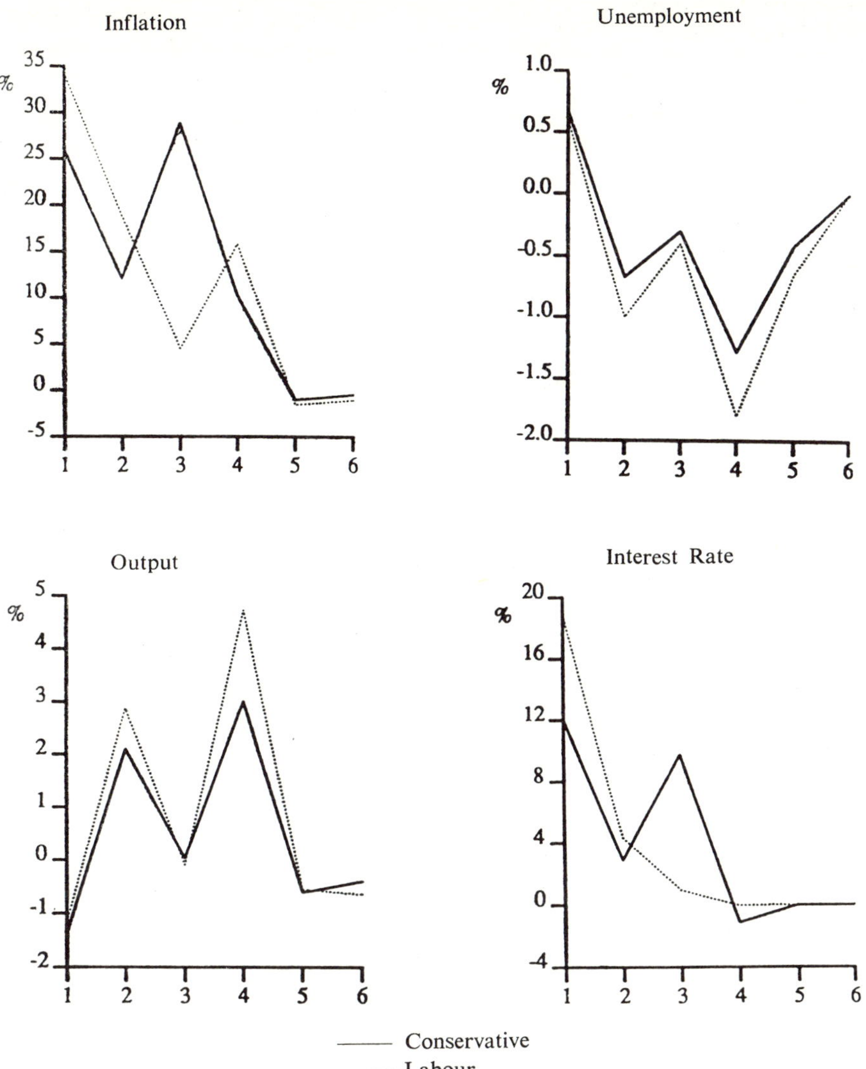

IV. WHY THEN DISCRETION?

This is a paradox indeed; and it implies on the face of it that a rational party should never choose discretion. Since parties appear to do so at least from time to time, something is clearly missing.

Yet before we assume that discretion is the rule – to be explained –

we should recall that in fact it is the exception. The Gold Standard ruled up to the first world war, and was restored in 1925 until the second world war. From 1945 to 1972, Britain was on a fixed exchange rate, a monetary rule only to be broken by the occasional devaluation (two, in 1948 and 1967). From 1976 to 1979, the UK was subject to IMF conditionality. From 1979 to date, the Medium Term Financial Strategy has imposed monetary rules. Even during the high noon of discretion from 1972-79, the need for some pre-commitment was acknowledged in the institution of incomes policies; unfortunately the incomes policies failed predictably to be binding on crucial variables because pre-commitment did not apply to fiscal and monetary policy. But it may well be that the 1972–79 episode is not so much an example of pure discretion as of a failed attempt at pre-commitment, with failure resulting from mistaken policy design and intellectual errors about the model of the economy.

To balance against the gains from pre-commitment we must set the costs of (a) monitoring and punishing (b) losing flexibility of response. Let us examine them in turn.

(a) For pre-commitment to be binding, and so a valid rational expectations equilibrium, it must be in the interest of the governing party to carry out the plan. Yet it is obvious from the discretionary reaction that, in the absence of monitoring and punishment, this is not so. To gauge appropriate penalties, we examine the gains from cheating on the pre-committed plan. The point is that though this time-inconsistent path is *not* a valid solution, because the absence of punishment makes the pre-commitment incredible, nevertheless, it gives a measure of the necessary scale of punishment that needs to be meted out by the monitor agency.[3]

Alesina and Tabellini (1986) have pointed out the time-inconsistency potential for a party elected to government; once elected it is tempted to pay off its supporters, so that λ may well rise immediately after the election. Strictly speaking if the party does not consider the effect on its chances in the *next* election, λ should go to unity. We have assumed this problem away by fixing λ, on the grounds that parties are involved in a repeated game where such behaviour would be particularly severely penalised. Nevertheless, while a party may be limited, for fear of such penalties, (in favouring its own supporters by reneging on an announced rule) merely to maximising V (λ *constant*) the *gain* to it by doing so should be measured as the utility gain of its own supporters on such a U-turn. To assess the temptation then we ask what is the percentage rise in utility of one's own supporters of moving to discretion

3. I am grateful to Andrew Hughes-Hallett for helping me to see this point clearly.

at some point after an election, having announced pre-commitment; we assume that having broken a commitment the party cannot reinstate it until the next election.

If we view temptation solely in this way, then *Conservative* governments would need no policing, since their own supportes lose from inflation. This makes them rather natural candidates for pre-commitment. They can argue, knowing that it benefits their own supporters, that pre-commitment is better for the nation than discretion; a happy situation. However, this is rather too sanguine; for Conservatives' temptation lies in the electoral appeal of inflation to floating voters. This presumably exerts its biggest attraction in the run-up to the next election. If the Conservatives break their commitment in the last year before the election, in order to maximise their (weighted-utility) welfare function, they would produce one year's monetary growth of 150%. So Conservative governments require some form of pre-election policing at least.

Labour's case is harder. Its supporters gain from the maximum inflation (at least to the point where the model's nonlinearity drives the marginal inflation response of H_t negative). Their gain from discretionary policy pursued after the election would be a substantial 4%. By deferring the break with commitment until 2 years before the election, the gain rises to 7% discounted back to the year of the election. And by deferring the break until the last year, when the discretionary maximum involves a massive one-year monetary growth of 234%, Labour supporters gain 14% discounted. These gains are consistent with those from Labour's weighted-utility welfare function. For example the largest gain to Labour supporters, the final year 14% for a 234% inflation, translates into a (weighted) welfare gain of 0.1% (the temptation to interpret this cardinally must be resisted). Thus both overall political calculus and supporters' interests create temptation for Labour.

This suggests, plausibly enough, that for the potential monitor (designer of a monetary institution or of international rules of co-operation) penalties designed to achieve the pre-commitment path will depend on the preferences of the supporters of the party in power and of the floating voter. This is not exactly news to IMF officials used to framing stabilisation programmes. It illustrates the practical difficulties of such design clearly enough.

A British Parliamentary government is sovereign. So it must make arrangements to *punish itself* if required to do so. This is not such an extraordinary idea as the myth of Ulysses and the Sirens reminds us. What is necessary is that the government does certain things at time t which, regardless of what it may wish at time $t+1$, will trigger certain events at $t+1$; it therefore effectively surrenders a measure of sovereignty over its actions at $t+1$ (in order to improve its overall situation). In this respect it is no different from a person signing a contract, e.g. to deliver certain work in return for payment in advance. The difference is that that contract is subject to the law whereas the government is able to make the law.

How the government can achieve some of the same effect, of surrendering sovereignty, can be illustrated by the Medium Term Financial Strategy. This was the announcement of a set of targets designed to reduce inflation without fail and permanently. The MTFS has survived overruns in a key specific target (£M3) and an evolving definition of another (the PSBR which deducts asset sales, not originally an important item). What it could not have survived would have been a failure to lower inflation. The opposition could have persuaded the general public with ease that the government had failed to carry out its own objectives according to its own intentions; no government could have survived such an embarrassing attack, precisely because it had handed the opposition the amunition in the MTFS itself.[4]

What the government is exploiting in setting up this self-punishment mechanism is the fact that ultimately public opinion is sovereign. It is rather as if you and I are candidates for a public post, and I say to you, 'If I do not achieve such-and-such an objective, I am the worse man for the job'; you *must* win if I fail to achieve my stated objective.

Other means available to a government are the signing of treaties as with Bretton Woods and fixed exchange rates or receipt of foreign loans under conditionality (as with the IMF in 1976). The EMS has apparently been such a device for the Italian and French governments in recent years.

It may well be that under their political systems this is an easier forum of pre-commitment than that of the MTFS in the UK (see Minford (1988) for discussion and further references). This is not the place to weigh the pros and cons of different means of surrendering sovereignty to support the pre-committed solution. The point is merely to emphasise that means exist to inflict the necessary punishment, and that they are not costly to implement in purely economic terms; their costs are essentially political, to be evaluated by the the political parties themselves.

4. As it happens the MTFS was not believed at least until late 1981; should it not have been credible if it involved such certain punishment? It was, in one sense; it was clear to all that Mrs. Thatcher and Sir Geoffrey Howe would have to *try* to achieve these targets; but most expected them to fail and be punished by losing their offices to other Tories who would be less deflationary. Hence the expectations of a 'U-turn'. Such observers regarded the MTFS as a form of political suicide. For some discussion of these years see Matthews and Minford (1987) and Walters (1985).

(b) The MTFS example also illustrates the flexibility of response possible in a pre-committed strategy. The monitor, in this case public opinion, is allowed to judge – when unexpected events turn up – whether the strategy has been deviated from. In this case, much was allowed provided that the central commitment of bringing down and keeping down inflation was honoured. This is recognised in formal games where each person adopting a pre-committed strategy is allowed to write down a complete list of contingent responses. He may even write down an 'open clause' of the type: 'if an event I have not thought of occurs, I reserve the right to take unspecified actions, the validity of which within the terms of this strategy I hope to persuade the monitor'. The limits on (useful) freedom of action implied here do not seem to be very cramping.

V. CONCLUSIONS

This paper has argued that the time-inconsistent solution is ruled out by rational expectations. Hence governments can only choose between pre-commitment and discretion. The costs of pre-commitment are those involved in designing a self-punishment mechanism and in surrendering some residual freedom of response to a monitoring agency. They do not seem, on the face of it at least, to be large, though the costs lie in the realm of politics, beyond the scope of our modelling efforts. The benefits of pre-commitment are, on the other hand, clear and measurable in economic terms. Rational governments seem likely to pre-commit, therefore, with respect to the sort of fiscal/monetary instrument considered in this paper. In this light, episodes of apparent discretion can perhaps be explained as the result of errors in the design of pre-committed policy. The general conclusion for modelling procedures with regard to government policy is (a) to evaluate how far policy is discretionary in the light of the gains/losses to political parties, as illustrated here (b) to embed the resulting permitted rule in discretionary feedback response into the model and solve normally. This can be regarded as a procedure for determining the set of credible (i.e. relevant) policies.

University of Liverpool, U.K.

APPENDIX

A NOTE ON THE LUCAS CRITIQUE[5]

Under rational expectations, economic agents maximise utility or profits subject to constraints and the exogenous processes or 'forcing variables'. The parameters of these exogenous processes enter the Euler equations for the endogenous variables; they give a current endogenous variable in terms of predetermined variables and error terms. If the parameter of the exogenous process changes, so will the Euler equations. In order to predict *how* these equations will change in those circumstances, you must have estimates the 'deep' structure parameters (agents' tastes and technology) which remain invariant; you can then reconstruct the Euler equations from them and the new exogenous parameters. That is the Lucas (1976) critique of policy evaluation.

The question this note addresses is: what is a 'policy change' and specifically is there such a thing at all? I shall take it in what follows that all non-policy exogenous processes can be regarded as stable; in this I follow the (implicit) treatment of Lucas. Though it cannot, one must admit, be correct, nevertheless, modellers will generally be forced to such an assumption. In any case it is with 'policy changes' that economists have been pre-eminently concerned; and that is the focus here.

The point I have in mind is that governments are formed by parties, and parties have well-defined preferences; their behaviour is in principle as modellable as that of private agents. In the main text of this paper, I discuss the problem for a party in choosing its best 'macro' policy. It turns out that it may pay a party to pre-commit itself to a macro stance for its term of office; if so, it will provide the relevant punishments to ensure it will be in its own interests to 'follow-through'. Alternatively, if the costs of pre-commitment in inflexibility or monitoring outweigh the benefits, then it may choose discretion. Either way, the party's macro behaviour in office can be specified, either as a fixed set of numbers for the macro instrument or as a response to the state of the economy.

It is clear that, if the parameters of participants' tastes and technology and of parties' preferences are unchanged, there will be no change in policy behaviour of each party and so no policy change to disturb our Euler equations. As the parties alternate with swings in electoral fortune, so policy be-

5. I am indebted to Marcus Miller and through him, I understand, Mark Salmon, for suggesting the question posed here and offering an answer much along the lines I sketch out here.

haviour will swing back and forth. Euler equations for *one* party's behaviour may differ from those for the other party's. But this at most means that one should split one's sample according to the different *set of players* involved – an obvious criterion, quite different from the notion that the *same* set of players can suddenly change course. Another possibility is that a party's constraints change and it becomes desirable to go discretionary instead of precommitted. In the main text I find there is a much bigger difference between discretionary and precommitted policy than there is across parties as such.

'Policy change' then amounts to change in a party's preferences or constraints (such as monitoring costs). Perhaps parties' preferences do shift around frequently and we are better off viewing policy behaviour as a time series coming from a black box. But if so then it is hard to talk of an exogenous process over some sample period. A modeller is surely forced back to assuming that party preferences are stable in order to justify a fixed exogenous policy process.

The merit of thinking about policy in this way is that :

(a) it makes it possible to identify homogeneous samples (these cut across 'fixed v. floating' which must represent an optimal *regime choice* by a party; for example, the Tory decision to float in 1972 was surely the expression of a decision to pursue discretionary policy),

(b) it avoids the necessity to estimate 'deep structure' provided these samples can be identified and estimated over,

(c) it stimulates necessary research into the public choice topic of party preferences, monitoring costs, costs of tying oneself down, etc., and

(d) it focusses policy discussion on *feasible* policies – i.e. those that parties could espouse. There is no point in simulating a policy which public choice research under (c) shows to be infeasible.

The Lucas critique under this viewpoint largely disappears. It would only arise under (d) where feasible policies *never so far pursued* are under discussion. This may not be a large or significant set. In human affairs it seems unlikely that there is much that is new under the sun, even if there is something.

If the argument in this paper is correct, it is encouraging. The programme to estimate deep structural parameters has not been very fruitful from the viewpoint of conventional modelling (nevertheless we have got all sorts of other insights – e.g. in the modelling of artificial economies in Prescott (1986)). Conventional modelling has however done quite well out of reduced forms and various forms of shallow structure equations of the Euler type. If these can be useful in forecasting when policy players alter, so much the better.

REFERENCES

Alesina, A. and Tabellini, G. (1986) 'A Positive Theory of Fiscal Deficits and Government Debt in a Democracy', mimeo, (December).

Backus, D. and Driffill, J. (1985) 'Inflation and Reputation', *American Economic Review*, 75 : 530 – 538.

Barro, R. J. (1986) 'Reputation in a Model of Monetary Policy', *Journal of Monetary Economics*, 17 : 3–20.

—— and Gordon, D. (1983) 'Rules, Discretion and Reputation in a Model of Monetary Policy', *Journal of Political Economy*, 91 : 589–610.

Canzoneri, M.B. (1985) 'Monetary Policy Games and the Role of Private Information', *American Economic Review*, 75 : 1050–1070.

Downs, A. (1957) *An Economic Theory of Democracy*, (New York : Harper and Row).

Hughes-Hallett, A. (1986) 'Is Time-inconsistent Behaviour Really Possible?' CEPR Working Paper No. 138.

Kydland, F.E. and Prescott, E.C. (1977) 'Rules Rather than Discretion: the Inconsistency of Optimal Plans', *Journal of Political Economy*, 85 : 473–91.

Nordhaus, W.D. (1975) 'The Political Business Cycle', *Review of Economic Studies*, 42 : 169–90.

Matthews, K.G.P. and Minford, A.P.L. (1987) 'Mrs. Thatcher's Economic Policies, 1974–86', *Economic Policy*, 5 : 57–101 (October).

Minford, A.P.L. (1988) 'Exchange Rate Regimes and Policy Coordination', paper for CEPR conference on International Regimes and Macroeconomic Policy, (September).

Minford, A.P.L. and Hilliard, G.W. (1978) 'The Costs of Variable Inflation', in M.J. Artis and A.R. Nobay (eds.), *Contemporary Economic Analysis*, Vol. 1, (London : Croom Helm), pp. 109-139.

Minford, A.P.L. and Peel, D.H. (1982) 'The Political Theory of the Business Cycle', *European Economic Review*, 17 : 253–70.

Minford, A.P.L., Marwaha, S., Matthews, K.G.P. and Sprague, A. (1984) 'The Liverpool Macroeconomic Model of the United Kingdom', *Economic Modelling*, 1 : 24–61.

Prescott, E.C. (1986) 'Theory ahead of Business Cycle Measurements', Federal Reserve Bank of Minneapolis, *Quarterly Review*, 9–22, (Fall).

Vickers, S. J. (1986) 'Signalling in a Model of Monetary Policy with Incomplete Information', *Oxford Economic Papers*, 38 : 443–455.

Walters, A. A. (1985) *Britain's Economic Renaissance*, (Oxford : Oxford University Press).

EFFICIENT AND CREDIBLE EXCHANGE RATE AND MONETARY POLICIES FOR STABILISING THE ECONOMY

By E. Pikoulakis

I. INTRODUCTION

With the advent of flexible exchange rates monetary policy was thought to have regained control of its principal tools of managing the economy. Freed from the obligation to support the exchange rate monetary authorities could target the money supply and its rate of growth to achieve the domestic objectives of high employment and low inflation. However it was soon realised that these objectives could only be achieved at a cost. When domestic prices are less than perfectly flexible, usually as a result of long-term wage contracts, an unanticipated reduction in the core rate of monetary growth, for instance, is associated with a loss in output and in international competitiveness. The departure of output from its natural level and the departure of international competitiveness from its 'fundamentals' can be large and protracted.

Attention was soon focused to devise measures to minimise the large and persistent departures of the real exchange rate from its fundamentals. At the policy level, the authorities of the major western economies have, on several occasions, entered into agreements to coordinate their policies with the view to stabilise the exchange rate. At the theoretical level a debate has been going on about the merits of competing proposals to manage the exchange rate within 'target zones'. In this paper I join this debate to offer two alternative policy proposals each of which succeeds in reducing the output loss associated with a policy of disinflation.

In section II of this paper I examine in some detail a version of an extended Mundell-Fleming model made popular by Dornbusch (1976) and more recently by Buiter and Miller (1981), (1982), (1983). In my version of the model the growth of high-powered money derives from the two sources it can possibly derive from in reality, namely, budget deficits and non-sterilised intervention in foreign exchange markets. I attribute the core rate of monetary growth to budget deficits and deviations from the core rate of monetary growth to non-sterilised intervention of a 'leaning-against-the-wind' type. However, in order to insulate the fiscal component of aggregate demand from variations in the rate of monetary growth I assume that the authorities continuously vary lump sum taxes with the view to maintain a target level of government spending. In line with a firmly established long tradition in monetary theory I allow for a real balance effect in aggregate demand.

Two major findings emerge from section II. At the policy level, non-sterilised intervention is shown to be an effective means of reducing the cumulative loss in output that results from a reduction in the core rate of monetary growth. At the theoretical level, the real balance effect is shown to break the link between the size of real exchange rate overshooting and the size of the initial loss in output.

As Buiter and Miller (1981) observe: 'Real-exchange rate overshooting and departures of output from its full employment level are, in the model used in this paper, due to the inability of the *real* money stock to respond promptly to changes in demand for liquidity. This reflects stickiness of both the domestic price level and of the *level* of the nominal stock'. Their proposed remedy of raising the nominal stock of money by an appropriate amount at the same time that the rate of monetary growth is reduced has raised questions about the credibility of such an action. In section III, I present a credible policy rule which succeeds in eliminating completely deviations of output from full employment and deviations of the real exchange rate from fundamentals. The policy rule, which shares McKinnon's (1984) views, is very simple. Let the authorities set the nominal exchange rate at the level which, for a given set of predetermined and exogenous variables, equates the current level of the real exchange rate to its fundamental level. One may wish to call this a policy of adjustable P.P.P. To implement this policy the authorities must be prepared to supply nominal money at the level required to equate the current level of real balances to the long run equilibrium level of these balances. This is the fundamental reason that this policy works. Allowing the money supply to be completely demand determined is the best way of insulating the economy from shocks.

Finally, the paper ends with a very brief section IV which sets the agenda for further research.

II. A MODEL OF INTERVENTION IN THE MARKET FOR FOREIGN EXCHANGE

II.a *The Structure of the Model*

$$y = -\gamma(r - Dp) + \delta(e - p) + \varepsilon(m - p) + bg, \qquad \gamma > 0, \delta > 0, \varepsilon > 0, b > 0 \quad (2.1)$$

$$m - p = ky - \lambda r, \qquad k > 0, \ \lambda > 0 \tag{2.2}$$

$$r = r^* + De \tag{2.3}$$

$$Dp = D\overline{m} + \psi(y - \overline{y}), \qquad \psi > 0 \tag{2.4}$$

$$Dm = D\overline{m} + \theta[(\overline{e} - \overline{p}) - (e - p)], \qquad \theta > 0 \tag{2.5}$$

where :

y : The logarithm of the domestic product.

$\overline{y}$: The 'natural' level of y, assumed exogenous.

m : The logarithm of the nominal stock of domestic money.

$\overline{m}$: The long-run equilibrium path of m.

p : The logarithm of the price of the domestic goods.

$\overline{p}$: The long-run equilibrium path of p.

e : The logarithm of the price of foreign currency in units of domestic currency.

$\overline{e}$: The long-run equilibrium path of e.

r : The domestic nominal interest rate.

r^* : The foreign nominal (and real) interest rate.

g : The logarithm of government expenditure on the domestic good.

D : The differential operator so that, for example,

$$Dp = \frac{dp}{dt}$$

Equation (2.1) is a version of an open economy IS relation. Output, which is demand determined, is taken to be a decreasing function of the real interest rate and an increasing function of the relative price of the foreign good, of real balances, and of government spending on the domestic good. Equation (2.2) is a standard textbook version of an LM relation. Equation (2.3) expresses an uncovered interest parity condition and the assumption that expectations about the rate of depreciation of the exchange rate follow a perfect foresight path. Equation (2.4) is a version of the Phillips curve. According to (2.4) the current rate of inflation consists of the sum of an equilibrium or 'core' component and a disequilibrium component. The core component is taken to be measured by the trend growth rate in the money supply. The disequilibrium component reflects the influence of excess demand in the goods market. In particular, the excess of the current rate of inflation over the 'core' rate is taken to be proportional to the excess of the current level of production over the 'natural' level. Equation (2.5) expresses the current rate of monetary growth as the sum of a core component and a disequilibrium component. The disequelibrium component reflects the assumption of non-sterilised intervention. The authorities, by assumption, purchase (sell) foreign exchange whenever the real price of foreign exchange is below (above) its long run equilibrium level. In particular, the excess of the current rate of monetary growth over the core rate is taken to be proportional to the excess of the long run equilibrium level of the real price of foreign exchange over its current level.

II.b *Budget Deficits: A Source for Monetary Growth*

What is left to be explained is the source for the core rate of monetary growth. The familiar helicopter is clearly a most unsatisfactory candidate. The only realistic candidates are (a) budget deficits and (b) non-sterilised foreign exchange intervention. Since I have already made an appeal for non-sterilised intervention to explain disequilibrium monetary growth, I shall be assuming that the core rate of monetary growth derives from the monetisation of budget deficits. To keep the analysis as simple as possible I shall be assuming that budget deficits are fully monetised and

$$G = T + \frac{1}{P}\frac{dL}{dt} = T + \left\{\frac{dL}{dt}\frac{1}{M}\right\}\frac{M}{P}, \tag{2.6}$$

where G is the flow of government spending on the domestic good, T is the flow of tax revenue net of transfers, L is the stock of government debt held by the monetary authorities valued at current prices and assumed to be interest free, M is the stock of nominal balances outstanding and P is the price of the domestic good in domestic currency. In what follows I shall be assuming that L constitutes the entire domestic component of the money stock and that the rate of issue of domestic credit per unit money.

$\frac{dL}{dt}\frac{1}{M}$, is kept constant and equal to μ. Accordingly

$$\frac{dL}{dt}\frac{1}{M} = \mu = D\bar{m}. \tag{2.7}$$

Letting h denote the fraction of G financed by T, I shall write

$$T = hG, \qquad 0 < h < 1 \tag{2.8}$$

Substituting (2.7) and (2.8) into (2.6) I shall write

$$G(1-h) = \mu \frac{M}{P}. \tag{2.9}$$

Taking logarithms to rewrite (2.9),

$$g = \hat{\mu} + m - p + \varphi \tag*{(2.9)$'$}$$

where $\hat{\mu}$ is the logarithm of μ and φ is minus the logarith of $1-h$.

The budget constraint expressed by (2.9)′ contains four policy instruments: g, $\hat{\mu}$, m and φ. At any time the authorities can control any three of these instruments but not all four. The remainder instrument must be endogenously determined. Having already assumed that m and $\hat{\mu}$ are policy controlled there remains for the authorities to choose whether to control government expenditures, g, and let taxes (via φ) be endogenously determined or whether to control φ letting government expenditures be endogenously determined. Notice that an attractive feature of treating φ as a policy instrument is that this allows for an analysis of 'pure' fiscal policy, a policy in which expenditures and net taxes are varied so as to achieve a 'marginally balanced budget'. A pure fiscal expansion, for instance, is captured by a rise in φ.

Whether we treat g or φ as policy controlled does not have any substantive bearing upon the issues I choose to focus upon in this paper. Treating g as exogenously controlled means that the authorities neutralise the effects on aggregate demand stemming from variations in domestic credit expansion by continuously varying taxes. Treating φ as exogenously controlled means that the authorities allow variations in domestic credit expansion to be fully reflected in aggregate demand. I shall follow the simplest and most familiar approach and treat g as exogenous.

II.c *The Stability Analysis of the Model*

Before proceeding with the analysis at hand it will be convenient to introduce new notation to define liquidity, competitiveness and the real interest rate. To this effect I shall write

$$l \equiv m - p, \qquad c \equiv e - p, \qquad i \equiv r - Dp$$

Introducing this notation in the model presented by (2.1) - (2.5) and noting that $D\bar{m} = \mu$, I shall write

$$y = \gamma i + \delta c + \varepsilon l + bg \tag{2.1$'$}$$

$$l = ky - \lambda(i + Dp) \tag{2.2$'$}$$

$$r - Dp \equiv i = r^* + De - Dp = r^* + Dc \tag{2.3$'$}$$

$$Dp = \mu + \psi(y - \bar{y}) \tag{2.4$'$}$$

$$Dm = \mu + \theta(\bar{c} - c) \tag{2.5$'$}$$

Letting a bar ($^{-}$) over an endogenous variable denote the steady-state path of that variable and taking deviations from the steady-state I shall write:

$$y - \bar{y} = -\gamma(i - \bar{i}) + \delta(c - \bar{c}) + \varepsilon(l - \bar{l}) \tag{2.1*}$$

$$l - \bar{l} = k(y - \bar{y}) - \lambda(i - \bar{i}) - \lambda(Dp - D\bar{p}) \tag{2.2*}$$

$$i - \bar{i} = Dc \tag{2.3*}$$

$$Dp - D\bar{p} = \psi(y - \bar{y}) \tag{2.4*}$$

$$Dm - D\bar{m} = -\theta(c - \bar{c}) \tag{2.5*}$$

Substituting out $y - \bar{y}$, $i - \bar{i}$, and $Dp - D\bar{p}$ and noting that $Dm - D\bar{m} - Dp + D\bar{p} = D[(m - p) - (\bar{m} - \bar{p})] = Dl$, I shall write

$$\begin{bmatrix} Dl \\ Dc \end{bmatrix} = \begin{bmatrix} a_{11} & a_{12} \\ a_{21} & a_{22} \end{bmatrix} = \begin{bmatrix} l - \bar{l} \\ c - \bar{c} \end{bmatrix} \tag{2.10}$$

where: $a_{11} = \dfrac{\psi(\lambda\varepsilon + \gamma)}{\Delta}$, $a_{12} = \dfrac{-\theta\Delta + \delta\lambda\psi}{\Delta}$

$a_{21} = \dfrac{1 + \varepsilon(\lambda\psi - k)}{\Delta}$, $a_{22} = \dfrac{\delta(\lambda\psi - k)}{\Delta}$, $\Delta = \gamma(\lambda\psi - k) - \lambda$

and $a_{11}a_{22} - a_{21}a_{12} = \dfrac{\delta\psi + \theta[1 + \varepsilon(\lambda\psi - k)]}{\Delta}$

In (2.10) above we have a system of two first order linear differential equations in the two state variables, liquidity, l, and competitiveness, c. With liquidity taken to be predetermined and competitiveness forward looking there exists a unique saddle-path provided that the coefficient matrix in (2.10) above possesses one stable characteristic root and one unstable. To put it another way, the necessary and sufficient condition for the equilibrium of the model to be a saddle-point is that the determinant of the coefficient matrix in (2.10) is negative. Following Buiter and Miller I shall take Δ to be negative. The assumption that Δ is negative corresponds to the assumption that an autonomous increase (decrease) in aggregate demand will increase (decrease) output given competitiveness. This is a perfectly sensible and appealing assumption to make. Accordingly, the requirement that the equilibrium is a saddle-point reduces to the requirement that $\delta\psi + \theta[1 + \varepsilon(\lambda\psi - k)] > 0$.

II.d *The Characteristics of the Saddle-Path*

To formally derive the saddle-path consider, first, that at $t = 0$

$$(Dl)_0 = a_{11}(l_0 - \bar{l}) + a_{12}(c_0 - \bar{c}), \quad \text{and} \quad (Dc)_0 = a_{21}(l_0 - \bar{l}) + a_{22}(c_0 - \bar{c})$$

Since there is only one stable root driving the system, call it ρ, at $t = 0$, we must have $(Dl)_0 = \rho(l_0 - \bar{l})$ and $(Dc)_0 = \rho(c_0 - \bar{c})$ which upon substitution yields the slope of the saddle-path as follows:

$$\frac{c - \bar{c}}{l - \bar{l}} = \frac{c_0 - \bar{c}}{l_0 - \bar{l}} = \frac{\rho - a_{11}}{a_{12}} = \frac{a_{21}}{\rho - a_{22}} \tag{2.11}$$

One can easily confirm that the slope of the saddle-path crucially depends on the sign of $1 + \varepsilon(\lambda\psi - k)$. Specifically,

(a) When $1 + \varepsilon(\lambda\psi - k) > 0$, $a_{21} < 0$, $\rho - a_{22} < 0$ and the saddle-path is upward sloping.

(b) When $1 + \varepsilon(\lambda\psi - k) = 0$, $a_{21} = 0$, $(\rho = a_{21})$ and the saddle-path has zero-slope.

(c) When $1 + \varepsilon(\lambda\psi - k) < 0$, $a_{21} > 0$, $\rho - a_{22} < 0$ and the saddle-path is downward sloping.

The phase diagrams below illustrate these cases.

FIGURE 1. The dynamics of adjustment of liquidity and of competitiveness and the saddle-path.

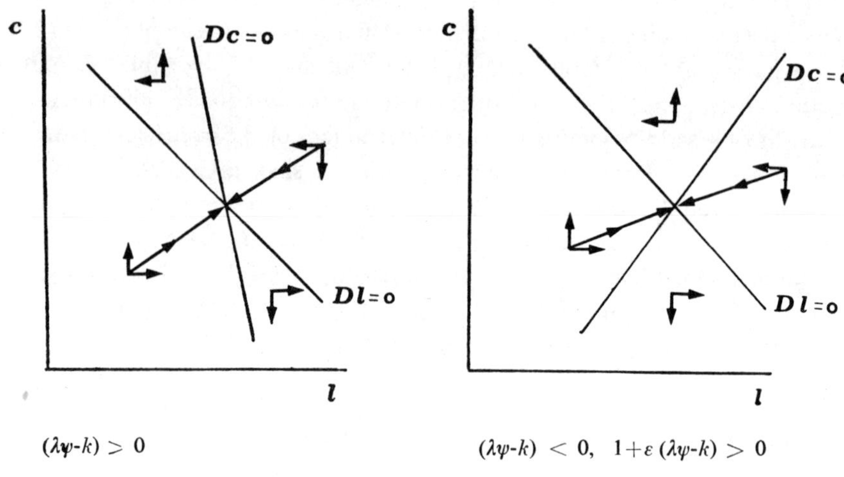

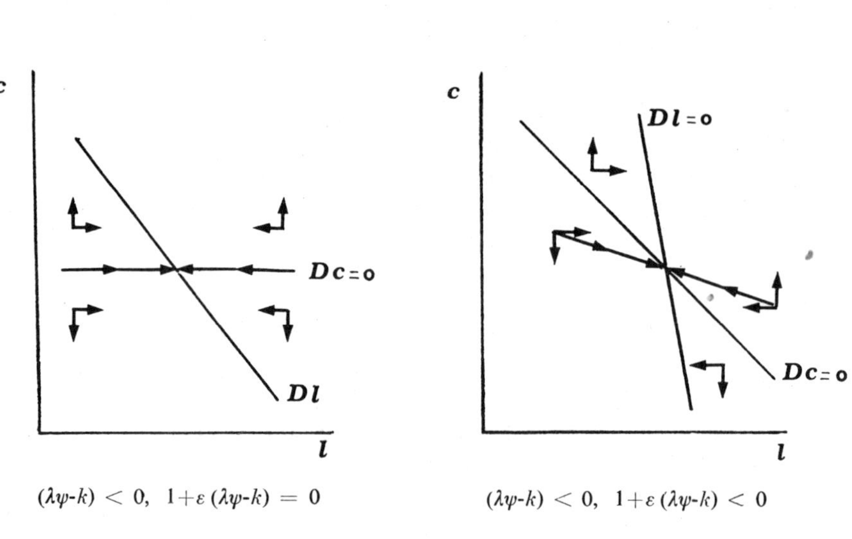

Since the sign of $1 + \varepsilon(\lambda\psi - k)$ is crucial to the characteristics of the saddle-path it is important to consider the economic significance of this expression. To this effect consider the consequences of a unit rise in liquidity. Such a rise in liquidity raises aggregate demand directly by ε units. For a given competitiveness and a given real interest rate output must also rise by ε units and inflation and the nominal interest rate must both rise by $\psi\varepsilon$ units. As a result money demand will rise by $k\varepsilon - \lambda\psi\varepsilon = \varepsilon(k - \lambda\psi)$ units and there will be an excess supply of money of $1 + \varepsilon(\lambda\psi - k)$ units. If, for instance, $1 + \varepsilon(\lambda\psi - k) < 0$ a rising liquidity along the adjustment path would be associated with an excess demand for money given competitiveness and given the real interest rate. To preserve equilibrium in the money market competitiveness must be falling and the real interest rate must be rising along the adjustment path.

What has been established is the fact that once a real balance effect is allowed for, i.e. once $\varepsilon > 0$, the characteristics of the saddle-path can no longer be determined *a priori*. Whether or not a reduction in the core rate of monetary growth is to be associated with overshooting in competitiveness is a matter to be established empirically.

II.e *The Characteristics of the Steady-State*

At the steady-state $Dp = De = Dm = \mu$. Accordingly the solution for steady-state liquidity and competitiveness can simply be determined by

$$\bar{y} = -\gamma r^* + \delta\bar{c} + \varepsilon\bar{l} + bg, \quad \text{and} \tag{2.1*}$$

$$\bar{l} = k\bar{y} - \lambda r^* - \lambda\mu \tag{2.2*}$$

In matrix form,

$$\begin{bmatrix} \bar{l} \\ \\ \bar{c} \end{bmatrix} = \begin{bmatrix} k & -\lambda & -\lambda & 0 \\ \dfrac{1-\varepsilon k}{\delta} & \dfrac{\gamma + \lambda\varepsilon}{\delta} & \dfrac{\varepsilon\lambda}{\delta} & \dfrac{-b}{\delta} \end{bmatrix} \begin{bmatrix} \bar{y} \\ r^* \\ \mu \\ g \end{bmatrix} \tag{2.11}$$

The solution for steady-state liquidity is straightforward and requires no particular comment. However the solution for steady-state competitiveness differs fundamentally from that in the Buiter-Miller model. Again the difference is explained by the inclusion of a real balance effect which is absent from the central Buiter-Miller model.

To appreciate the contribution of the real balance effect consider, first, a permanent reduction in the core rate of monetary growth. Steady-state real balances rise by $\lambda d\mu$, in absolute terms, and this contributes to a rise in aggregate demand by $\varepsilon\lambda d\mu$ units. Since output at the steady-state is given by its natural level, $\bar{y}$, competitiveness must deteriorate by $\dfrac{\varepsilon\lambda}{\delta}\, d\mu$ units to maintain aggregate demand at its natural level. In short, variations in the core rate of monetary growth are no longer neutral. Consider, next, a permanent increase in the natural level of output. This contributes to an increase in real balances by $kd\bar{y}$ which, via the real balance effect, raises aggregate demand by $\varepsilon kd\bar{y}$. If εk were to exceed unity the rise in capacity output would create an excess demand rather than an excess supply. In that case competitiveness would have to deteriorate to reduce demand sufficiently to restore equilibrium. Consider, finally, the effect of a rise in the foreign interest rate, r^*. Such an event would reduce aggregate demand directly by γdr^* and indirectly, via the real balance effect, by an additional $\varepsilon\lambda dr^*$. All in all, competitiveness would have to improve by $\left(\frac{\gamma + \lambda\varepsilon}{\delta}\right) dr^*$ to restore aggregate demand to its natural level.

II.f *The Role of the Real Balance Effect in the Process of Output Adjustment*

The simplest way to focus on the role of the real balance effect in the process of output adjustment is to assume away, for the moment, non-sterilised intervention. To this effect I shall assume, for the moment, that $\theta = 0$. In that case

$$Dl = -\psi(y - \bar{y}) = \rho(l - \bar{l}) = \rho\,(l_0 - \bar{l})e^{\rho t} \tag{2.12}$$

and, accordingly

$$(y_0 - \bar{y}) = -\frac{\rho}{\psi}\,(l_0 - \bar{l}) = -\frac{\rho\lambda d\mu}{\psi}, \tag{2.13}$$

and
$$\int_0^\infty (y - \bar{y})dt = -\frac{l}{\psi}\int_0^\infty \rho(l_0 - \bar{l})e^{\rho t} = \frac{\lambda d\mu}{\psi} \tag{2.14}$$

Whereas the cumulative loss in output is independent of the parameter ε, the speed of adjustment ρ and, thereby, the initial loss in output is not.

To investigate this relationship note that

$$\frac{\partial\rho}{\partial\varepsilon} = {}^1/_2\,\frac{\psi\lambda}{\Delta}\left[\frac{[(a_{11} + a_{22})^2 - 4D]^{1/2} - (a_{11} + a_{22})}{[(a_{11} + a_{22})^2 - 4D]^{1/2}}\right] < 0 \tag{2.15}$$

where $D = \dfrac{\psi\delta}{\Delta}$

This finding suggests that the greater is the sensitivity of aggregate demand to real balances the bigger is the initial loss in output associated with disinflation and the faster is the adjustment to the steady-state. To explain this consider that a reduction in the core rate of monetary growth raises the return provided by real balances and induces a shift in demand from consumption goods to the services provided by real balances. The reduction in the production of consumption goods associated with this demand shift induces a further reduction in demand for consumption goods via the real balance effect. Accordingly there is a multiplier effect which magnifies the initial loss in output. However, as real balances build up the real balance effect induces a faster adjustment of demand to its natural level.

One of the beliefs held by economists is that exchange rate overshooting contributes to the loss in output that results from a policy of disinflation. The discussion above suggests that this is an erroneous belief. To see this compare the initial loss in output that results from disinflation when $\varepsilon = 0$, with the loss in output which results when $\varepsilon > 0$, $1 + \varepsilon(\lambda\psi - k) = 0$ and all parameter values other than ε are the same in the two cases compared. Notice that when $\varepsilon = 0$ the saddle path is upward sloping and overshooting occurs whereas when $1 + \varepsilon(\lambda\psi - k) = 0$ the saddle path has zero slope and the real exchange rate jumps immediately onto its steady-state path. By equation (2.15) the initial loss in output associated with the overshooting case is less than the initial loss in output associated with zero overshooting.

II.g *Non-Sterilised Intervention: An Efficient aud Credible Policy for the Stabilisation of Aggregate Demand*

My aim here is to argue that non-sterilised intervention can be a credible and relatively efficient policy in stabilising aggregate demand. I shall be focusing attention to the case where the saddle-path is upward sloping. This is because a downward sloping saddle-path is a very unlikely event, on empirical grounds, and because intervention is completely ineffective when the saddle-path has zero slope.

To begin with consider the process of real monetary growth when the monetary authorities intervene in the market for foreign exchange according to the rule given by equation (2.5) that is, consider

$$Dl = -\psi(y - \bar{y}) - \theta(c - \bar{c}) = -\psi(y - \bar{y}) - \theta\frac{(c - \bar{c})}{(l - \bar{l})}(l - \bar{l}) \quad (2.16)$$

Using the solution for the saddle-path to rewrite (2.16)

$$Dl = -\psi(y - \bar{y}) - \theta\left[\frac{a_{21}}{\rho - a_{22}}\right](l - \bar{l}) \tag{2.16$'$}$$

$$= -\psi(y - \bar{y}) - \theta\left[\frac{\rho - a_{11}}{a_{12}}\right](l - \bar{l}) = \rho(l - \bar{l})$$

Accordingly,

$$y - \bar{y} = -\frac{\rho}{\psi}\left[l + \frac{\theta}{\rho}\left[\frac{a_{21}}{\rho - a_{22}}\right]\right](l - \bar{l})$$

$$= \frac{-\rho}{\psi}\left[l + \frac{\theta}{\rho}\left[\frac{\rho - a_{11}}{a_{12}}\right]\right](l - \bar{l}) \tag{2.16*}$$

With an upward sloping saddle-path the expression in brackets is positive but, necessarily, less than one. For instance,

$$l + \frac{\theta}{\rho}\left[\frac{\rho - a_{11}}{a_{12}}\right] = \frac{\rho a_{12} + \theta\rho - \theta a_{11}}{\rho a_{12}} = \frac{\rho(\theta + a_{12}) - \theta a_{11}}{\rho a_{12}} > 0$$

but necessarily less than one.

To appreciate the significance of this finding let me denote the expressions in big brackets in (2.16)* by π where $0 < \pi < 1$. Then the cumulative loss in output associated with disinflation and non-sterilised intervention is given by

$$\int_0^\infty (y - \bar{y})dt = -\frac{\rho}{\psi}\pi\int_0^\infty (l - \bar{l})dt = -\frac{\rho}{\psi}\pi\int_0^\infty \rho(l_0 - \bar{l})e^{\rho t}dt = \pi\frac{\lambda}{\psi}d\mu \tag{2.17}$$

When the authorities intervene and do not sterilise they can reduce the cumulative loss in output associated with disinflation to a fraction π of what this cost would be otherwise.

To get a better understanding of what is involved behind this result consider that $Dp - \mu = Dp - D\bar{p} = D(p - \bar{p}) = \psi(y - \bar{y})$. Accordingly,

$$\int_0^\infty (y - \bar{y})dt = \frac{l}{\psi}\int_0^\infty D(p - \bar{p})\,dt = \frac{l}{\psi}\int_0^\infty \rho(p_0 - \bar{p})e^{\rho t}dt = -\frac{(p_0 - \bar{p})}{\psi}$$

Other things equal the smaller the gap between the initial price level and its equilibrium path the smaller the cumulative change in output following some disturbance. In the extreme case of perfect price flexibility the price level jumps onto its equilibrium path instantly following a disturbance and, hence, this gap is zero. Barring discrete jumps in the price level the gap can only be narrowed by *devising policies which bring the equilibrium path closer to the initial price level.* This is precisely what happens in the intervention model. To illustrate and compare with the central Buiter-Miller we shall utilise one of their diagrams.

In Figures 2 and 3 we have assumed, for simplicity, that for $t < t_0$, $\bar{m}(t) = \bar{p}(t)$. At $t = t_0$ the steady state component of monetary growth is reduced. Accordingly steady-state real balances must rise by $-\lambda d\mu$ and this measures the vertical gap between $\bar{m}(t) - \bar{p}(t)$ for $t \geqslant t_0$. Since in both models the steady-state increase in real balances is the same and since nominal balances rise faster in the intervention model, the equilibrium path of prices, $\bar{p}(t)$, must be higher in the intervention model for all $t \geqslant t_0$.

FIGURE 2. The path of money and prices in the central Buiter-Miller model.

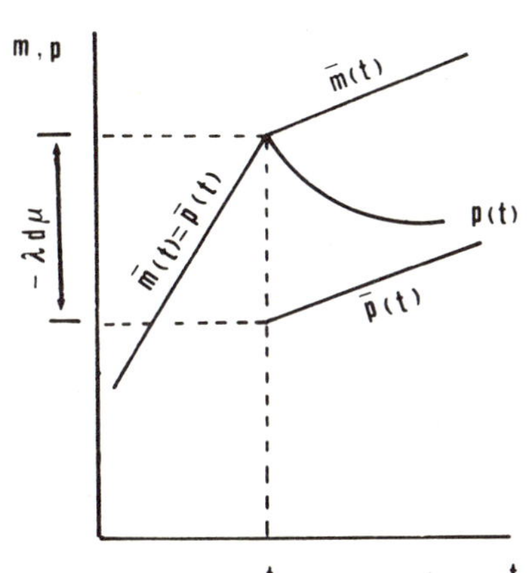

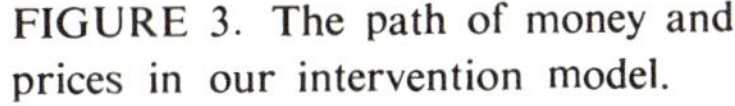
FIGURE 3. The path of money and prices in our intervention model.

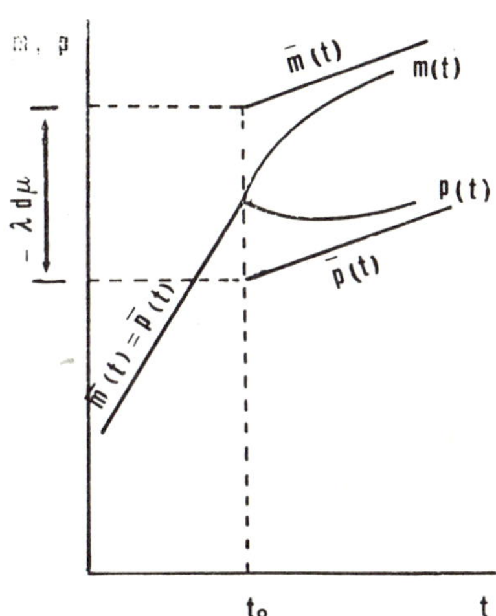

Buiter and Miller's answer to reducing the cost in output associated with disinflation is to propose a once and for all increase in the nominal stock of money by $-\lambda d\mu$ at the same time that the core rate of monetary growth is reduced by $d\mu$. However this proposal has met with criticism. Critics, and Buiter and Miller themselves, expressed doubts about the credibility of this policy. The question is, does the monetary policy rule described by equation

(2.5) suffer from the same lack of credibility? In my view the answer is clearly no. The proposed policy of non-sterilised intervention is a simple, sensible and easily understood feedback rule. More to the point, it does not involve jumps in the money supply.

III. AN ADJUSTABLE P.P.P. AND A FULLY ACCOMMODATING MONETARY POLICY: TWO EQUIVALENT AND EFFICIENT STABILISATION POLICIES

III.a *Introduction*

Deviations from P.P.P can be classified as either structural or purely transitory. Structural deviations, or deviations from fundamentals, are associated with 'real' disturbances. Transitory deviations from P.P.P. reflect differential speeds of adjustment in goods and assets markets. In any economy where goods markets adjust relatively sluggishly a real disturbance will bring about both a structural and a transitory deviation from P.P.P. Following such a disturbance the real exchange rate fails to adjust instantly to its *new* equilibrium path.

However, the monetary authorities can always devise exchange rate policies that can eliminate completely transitory deviations from P.P.P. For instance, the monetary authorities can always set the nominal exchange rate to a level which, given the predetermined price level, produces a real exchange rate whose current level equals its fundamental level. I shall call this an adjustable P.P.P. policy. Whether such an adjustable P.P.P. policy succeeds in eliminating the loss in output associated with disinflation will depend on whether the underlying monetary policy is fully accomodating.

In what follows I shall show that an adjustable P.P.P. policy is equivalent to a fully accomodating monetary policy which can be applied efficiently and credibly for stabilisation purposes.

III.b *The Model(s)*

$$y = -\gamma(r - Dp) + \delta(e - p) + \varepsilon(m - p) + bg \tag{3.1}$$

$$m - p = ky - \lambda r \tag{3.2}$$

$$r = r^* + De \tag{3.3}$$

$$Dp = \mu + \psi(y - y) \tag{3.4}$$

$$e - p = \bar{e} - \bar{p} \tag{3.5a}$$

$$m - p = \bar{m} - \bar{p} \tag{3.5b}$$

Equations (3.1) - (3.4) need no comment. Equation (3.5a) reflects what one may call an adjustable P.P.P. policy. For a given set of behavioural and policy parameters and the exogenous variables of the model there exists a unique long run equilibrium real exchange rate, $\bar{e} - \bar{p}$, known to the authorities and to private agents. At any point in time p is taken to be, as before, predetermined. Accordingly at any point in time there exists a nominal exchange rate equal to the long run equilibrium real exchange rate. I am assuming that the monetary authorities perform the task of setting the exchange rate to the level required to equate the current real exchange rate, $e - p$ with the long run equilibrium real exchange rate. Notice that the nominal exchange rate can jump but only in response to shocks that disturb the equilibrium real exchange rate. Equation (3.5b) reflects what one may call an adjustable monetary accommodation policy. Again for a given structure and exogenous variables there exists a unique long run equilibrium level of real balances, $\bar{m} - \bar{p}$, known to the authorities and to private agents. Accordingly for a given p there existes a nominal stock of money, m, which would yield a level of current real balances, $m - p$, equal to $\bar{m} - \bar{p}$. The interpretation of (3.5b) is that the authorities set m at the level required to equated $m - p$ to $\bar{m} - \bar{p}$. Notice, again, that the nominal stock of money can jump but only in response to shocks that disturb the equilibrium level of real balances. Clearly the policies described by (3.5a) and (3.5b) are not independent. What perhaps has not been sufficiently recognised, and here it will suffice to cite Dornbuch (1982) in this respect, is that in the context of the present model (3.5a) and (3.5b) are exactly equivalent. In what follows I shall describe the workings of the model under policy (3.5a) and I shall show the equivalence of policies (3.5a) and (3.5b).

Consider the model (3.1) - (3.5a) in deviation form :

$$y - \bar{y} = -\gamma(r - \bar{r}) + \gamma(Dp - D\bar{p}) + \delta[(e - p) - (\bar{e} - \bar{p})] + \varepsilon[(m - p) - (\bar{m} - \bar{p})] \tag{3.1$'$}$$

$$m - p - (\bar{m} - \bar{p}) = k(y - \bar{y}) - \lambda(r - \bar{r}) \tag{3.2$'$}$$

$$r - \bar{r} = De - D\bar{e} \tag{3.3$'$}$$

$$Dp - D\bar{p} = \psi(y - \bar{y}) \tag{3.4$'$}$$

$$e - p - (\bar{e} - \bar{p}) = 0 \tag{3.5a$'$}$$

Substituting out (3.3)′ and (3.5a)′ and noting that $De - D\bar{e} = Dp - D\bar{p}$ one obtains

$$y - \bar{y} = \varepsilon[(m - p) - (\bar{m} - \bar{p})] \tag{3.1)''}$$

$$m - p - (\bar{m} - \bar{p}) = k(y - \bar{y}) - \lambda(Dp - D\bar{p}) \tag{3.2)'}$$

$$Dp - D\bar{p} = \psi(y - \bar{y}) \tag{3.4)'}$$

which upon further substitution yield

$$y - \bar{y} = \varepsilon[(m - p) - (\bar{m} - \bar{p})] \tag{3.1)*}$$

$$m - p - (\bar{m} - \bar{p}) = (k - \lambda\psi)(y - \bar{y}) \tag{3.2)*}$$

The reader is asked to observe again that $\bar{y}$ is taken to be exogenous and that $\bar{m} - \bar{p} = k\bar{y} - \lambda(r^* + \mu)$. This implies that the current level of liquidity $m - p$, must be endogenous if the model is to have a consistent and unique solution. The intuition behind this is that the authorities cannot pursue an exchange rate target independently from a monetary target.

The remarkable finding from solving (3.1)* – (3.2)* is that $y = \bar{y}$ and $m - p = \bar{m} - \bar{p}$. The authorities can implement a previously unanticipated reduction in the core rate of monetary growth entirely without cost! All they have to do is announce and implement a reduction in the core rate of monetary growth and pursue the P.P.P. policy rule (3.5a). Private agents who know the structure of the model realise that exchange rate targetting under (3.5a) implies monetary targetting under (3.5b) which in turn requires a discrete jump in nominal money by $-\lambda d\mu$. Figure 4 decribes the adjustment in money and prices.

As before I am assuming that for $t < t_0$ the path of money and prices is given by $\bar{m}(t)$ and $\bar{p}(t)$ and that $\bar{m}(t) = \bar{p}(t)$. At t_0 the authorities reduce the core rate of monetary growth and they "activate" the P.P.P. rule described by (3.5a). To defend this rule the authorities are prepared to accomodate the increased demand for money by purchasing foreign exchange and supplying money at the new appreciated nominal and real exchange rate. In other words the supply of money is perfectly elastic at the new exchange rate target. This leads to a once and for all jump in the money supply by $-\lambda d\mu$. The money supply jumps onto its new equilibrium path given by $\bar{\bar{m}}(t)$ which is located vertically above the new equilibrium path for prices, $\bar{\bar{p}}(t)$, separated by a distance $-\lambda d\mu$. The slope of $\bar{\bar{m}}(t)$ and of $\bar{\bar{p}}(t)$ reflect the reduced core rate of monetary growth.

FIGURE 4. The path of money and prices with an adjustable P.P.P or fully accommodating monetary policy.

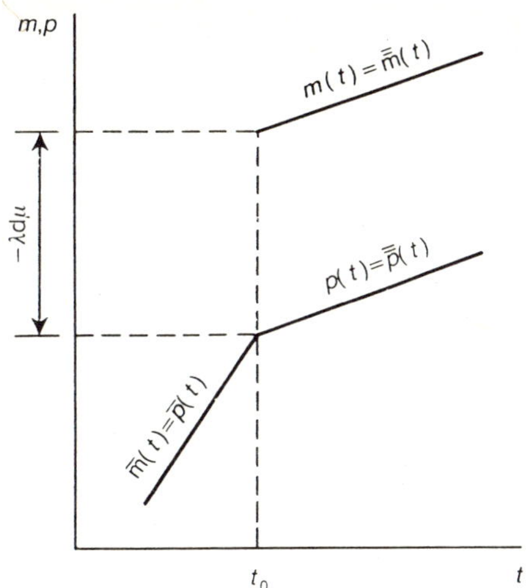

The above description of the workings of the model should make it perfectly clear that the policy pursued by the authorities is wholly credible.

IV. AN AGENDA FOR FURTHER RESEARCH

The model presented in sections II and III is very simple. It would be very interesting to examine the robustness of the policy rule proposed in section III within a richer structure. The list of desirable additions to the model is numerous. However to retain some analytic tractability I propose two worthy additions. An enlarged model should allow for a richer menu of assets to include real physical capital, or claims to capital, and model explicitly capital formation. It should also allow for the effect of variations in the level of foreign assets through the current account.

The model presented above is non-stochastic and, therefore, it only applies to a non-stochastic world. Subsequently, it does not allow any inferences to be made about behaviour in response to unanticipated stochastic shocks. But this is wholly a separate issue.

University of Hull, U.K.

REFERENCES

Buiter, W.H. and Miller, M.H. (1981) 'Monetary Policy and International Competitiveness', *Oxford Economic Papers*, 33:143-175, (Supplement).

—— (1982) 'Real Exchange Rate Over-shooting and the Output Cost of Bringing Down Inflation', *European Economic Review*, 18 (1/2): 85-123.

—— (1983) 'Real Exchange Rate Over-shooting and the Output Cost of Bringing Down Inflation: Some Further Results', in J. Frenkel (ed.), *Exchange Rates and International Macroeconomics*, (Chicago: University of Chicago Press).

Dornbusch, R. (1976) 'Expectations and Exchange Rate Dynamics', *Journal of Political Economy*, 84: 1161-1176.

—— (1982) 'P.P.P. Exchange Rate Rules and Macroeconomic Stability', *Journal of Political Economy*, 90: 158-165.

McKinnon, R. I. (1984) 'An International Standard for Monetary Stabilisation', (Washington, DC: Institute for International Economics).

FISCAL POLICY COORDINATION, INFLATION AND REPUTATION IN A NATURAL RATE WORLD

By David Currie and Ullrich Hoffmeyer

I. INTRODUCTION

In the past few years, the literature concerned with international macroeconomic policy coordination has developed and expanded very considerably. It has, in particular, developed in two important respects. First, whereas the earlier pioneering literature (see, for example, the work of Hamada, collected in Hamada (1985)) dealt with simple analytical, and usually static, models of interdependence, the recent literature has emphasised the dynamic aspects of the problem of policy coordination, and has developed techniques for their analysis in the context of empirical multi-country models. Second, the recent literature has grappled with the issues raised by rational expectations, particularly with questions of credibility and sustainability of cooperative policies.[1] The latter focus has emphasised the importance of reputation in the appraisal and design of international policy.

In this context, reputational policies are those which rely on the credibility of government announcements about future policy actions. Formally, if governments are assumed to maximise a given objective function, optimal reputational policies can be dervied using Pontryagin's maximum principle. Such policies correspond to the full optimal rule, or, in the terms of Barro and Gordon (1983), the ideal rule. They are frequently regarded as time inconsistent in that an incentive to renege may emerge with the mere elapse of time. However, if the cost of reneging is a loss of reputation for all time, then such policies may well turn out to lead to worse results than under a reputational but time inconsistent regime. This may also be true if reputation can be regained after some time. Because of this, reputational policies are of interest.

Optimal non-reputational policies are those that correspond to the backward dynamic programming solution (see Cohen and Michel (1985),

1. See, for example, certain of the papers in Buiter and Marston (1985), such as Currie and Levine (1982), Miller and Salmon (1985) and Oudiz and Sachs (1985). For recent papers that address both issues together, see Currie and Levine (1987) and Currie, Levine and Vidalis (1988).

Oudiz and Sachs (1985)), which avoids any potential problem of time inconsistency, but at the cost of a poorer performance relative to the optimal reputational policy.

In analysing cooperation between governments in a two-country world, we may therefore distinguish between reputational and non-reputational policies, as well as between cooperative and non-cooperative policies. Allowing either government to pursue either reputational or non-reputational policies, this gives rise to eight possible regimes. Of these, one half are asymmetric, in that one country pursues a reputational policy, while the other pursues a non-reputational policy. In the following, we focus only on symmetric regimes, for reasons of analytic simplicity. The resulting four regimes are summarised below.

		Relations between Governments	
		Cooperation (*C*)	*Non-Cooperation* (*NC*)
Relations between Government and Private Sector	*Reputation* (*R*)	CR	NCR
	Non-Reputation (*NR*)	CNR	NCNR

Of these four regimes, the cooperative reputational (CR) policy is necessarily the best – given that the governments do not cheat – since they can always agree not to cooperate. However, the relative ranking of the remaining three policies varies depending on the model and its disturbances. Rogoff (1985) has produced an analytical example where cooperation without reputation does not pay, i.e. NCNR dominates CNR. Levine and Currie (1987) and Currie, Levine and Vidalis (1988), using a reduced version of the OECD Interlink model, find that the ranking of these two regimes depends on the nature and the persistence of the shock to the model. More importantly, they find that the non-cooperative reputational (NCR) policy is potentially unstable, the instability arising from the attempts of governments individually to manipulate the exchange rate to anti-inflationary ends. Thus they find that, without cooperation, reputation may not pay. The gains from reputation and coordination are therefore joint, and are, moreover, found to be considerable.

In this paper, we present a simple analytical two country model with instantaneous market clearing. We adopt this natural rate model for three reasons. First, it provides a sufficiently simple, yet nonetheless interesting, context in which the issues of reputation and coordination discussed above can be analysed and illustrated. Indeed, the model is of sufficient simplicity that it could be used for pedagogic purposes, whilst our results nonetheless have interest in their own right. Second, it is interesting to examine whether and how problems of coordination may arise even in a natural rate world. Since a significant part of the profession, particularly in at least two out of the three G3 countries, seem to believe in quite rapid market-clearing, it is helpful to note that coordination failures can be important even in such a world. Third, the analysis was partly motivated by the wish to understand the long run results thrown up by our earlier analysis of an empirically based non-market clearing model (see Currie, Levine and Vidalis (1988)). Since this model embodied a long run natural rate it was of interest to see whether an analytical natural rate model with instantaneous market clearing would throw up comparable results.

The plan of the paper is as follows. The next section sets out the model, and defines the assumed behaviour of governments. Section III examines certain of the model's properties by defining equilibrium and taking a first look at monetary and fiscal policy. Section IV and V consider the determination of monetary policy and fiscal policy respectively for the reputational and non-reputational, cooperative and non-cooperative regimes. Section VI draws some conclusions. An appendix sets out the mathematical analysis underlying the text of the main paper and presents a numerical example.

II. THE MODEL

We use the following symmetric two-country natural rate model with perfectly flexible prices :

$$y_t = a_0 + a_1 e_t - a_2 r_t + a_3 g_t + a_4 y_t^* \tag{2.1}$$

$$y_t^* = a_0 - a_1 e_t - a_2 r_t^* + a_3 g_t^* + a_4 y_t \tag{2.2}$$

$$y_t = b_0 - b_1 e_t - b_2 r_t + b_3 (p_t - p_{t,t}^e) \tag{2.3}$$

$$y_t^* = b_0 + b_1 e_t - b_2 r_t^* + b_3 (p_t^* - p_{t,t}^{*e}) \tag{2.4}$$

$$m_t = p_t + c_1 y_t - c_2 (r_t + p_{t+1,t}^e - p_{t,t}^e) \tag{2.5}$$

$$m_t^* = p_t^* + c_1 y_t^* - c_2 (r_t^* + p_{t+1,t}^{*e} - p_{t,t}^{*e}) \tag{2.6}$$

$$e_t = r_t^* - r_t + e_{t+1,t}^e \tag{2.7}$$

where a '*' superscript denotes variables for the second country. All variables are measured as logarithms, with the exception of interest rates which are measured as proportions. All parameters are taken to be positive and the following notation is used:

y : output

e : real exchange rate (measured such that an increase represents a depreciation for the first country)

r : expected real rate of interest

g : government spending

p : price level

m : money supply

$p^e_{t,t}, p^e_{t+1,t}$: expectations of p_t and p_{t+1} respectively, based on information available at the start of period t.

Equations (2.1) and (2.2) represent aggregate demand, dependent on the real exchange rate, the real interest rate, government expenditure and foreign demand. Throughout the paper it is assumed that government spending is unproductive. Equations (2.3) and (2.4) represent aggregate supply, depending positively on the surprise in prices, and negatively on the real rate of interest and competitiveness as measured by the exchange rate. The influence of the surprise in prices may be rationalised in terms of Lucas's argument about confusion between local and aggregate price changes. Alternatively, it could be rationalised in terms of wages being set at the beginning of the period on the basis of information then available. The real interest rate exerts a depressing effect on supply because of its effect on the desired capital stock and hence on supply; the dynamics of this process is totally suppressed in the interests of simplicity. A gain in competitiveness exerts a negative influence on supply, since it drives a larger wedge between the consumption and producer real wage. Equations (2.5) and (2.6) are standard money demand functions, dependent on prices, income and the nominal rate of interest. Equation (2.7) is the uncovered interest parity condition.

For the first government, we assume an objective function of the form:

$$\text{Min } W_t = \frac{1}{2} \sum_{i=0}^{\infty} \rho^i [(y_{t+i} - \bar{y})^2 + d_1 (p_{t+i} - p_{t+i-1})^2 + d_2 (g_{t+i} - \bar{g})^2] \quad (2.8)$$

with a similar expression with '*' variables for the second country. This quadratic function penalises output deviations around some targer, $\bar{y}$, inflation, and deviations of government spending around some target, $\bar{g}$. The target for government spending is assumed to arise from efficiency and/or social considerations influencing the desired level of public spending. Similar considerations would arise were we to choose taxes as the fiscal instrument. No instrument costs are attached to the use of the money supply, since neither social nor efficiency arguments are obviously applicable. Throughout the following, we assume that government's output objectives are ambitious, in the sense that $\bar{y}$ is in excess of feasible output levels. As in Barro and Gordon (1983), this may impart an inflationary bias to certain of the regimes.

III. EQUILIBRIUM

The determination of the equilibrium of the real economy is illustrated in Figure 1 and 2. Let $y_t^a = {}^1/_2(y_t + y_t^*)$ and $y_t^d = {}^1/_2(y_t - y_t^*)$, with similar definitions for other variables. Thus the superscript '*a*' denotes the aggregate system, while '*d*' denotes the divergence system. Then the aggregate equilibrium for the two countries taken together is given by adding the individual demand and supply functions

$$y_t^a = a_5(a_0 - a_2 r_t^a + a_3 g_t^a) \tag{3.1}$$

$$y_t^a = b_0 - b_2 r_t^a + b_3(p_t^a - p_{t,t}^{ae}) \tag{3.2}$$

where $a_5 = (1 - a_4)^{-1}$. Equation (3.1) represents the aggregate demand relationship, depicted by D^a; while (3.2) represents the aggregate supply relationship, depicted by S^a in Figure 1. We assume throughout the following that D^a is more interest elastic than S^a (for reasons of intra-period stability i.e $a_2 a_5 > b_2$), so that an increase in government spending raises real interest rates. Furthermore, we shall assume that $b_1 > {}^1/_2 b_2$. This assumption is not crucial since its converse does not alter any conclusions of this paper. It simply facilitates comparisons among different regimes.

Figure 2 represents the equilibrium of the divergence system, obtained by subtracting country 2's demand and supply schedules from country 1's.

$$y_t^d = a_6(a_1 e_t - a_2 r_t^d + a_3 g_t^d) \tag{3.3}$$

$$y_t^d = -b_1 e_t - b_2 r_t^d + b_3(p_t^d - p_{t,t}^{de}) \tag{3.4}$$

$$e_t = -2r_t^d + e_{t+1,t}^e = -2 \sum_{i=0}^{\infty} r_{t+1,t}^{de} \tag{3.5}$$

with $a_6 = (1 + a_4)^{-1}$. In equilibrium (3.5) implies that $r_t^d = 0$. (This condition will of course also hold in the face of permanent shocks). Thus we can depict equilibrium of the difference system as in Figure 2. Equation (3.3) gives an upward sloping demand schedule, D^d, between e_t and y_t^d; while (3.4) gives downward sloping supply schedule, S^d.

We first consider the general effects of fiscal policy and monetary policy on output in both countries. A permanent shock to aggregate demand, arising from an increase in government spending in country 1, will shift both demand schedules, D^a in Figure 1 and D^d in Figure 2 to the right. From Figure 1, this raises aggregate interest rates and lowers world output $y_t^a = {}^1/_2(y_t + y_t^*)$. From Figure 2, this appreciates the real exchange rate of country 1, permitting an increase in output in country 1 relative to country 2, leading to an increase in $y_t^d = {}^1/_2(y_t - y_t^*)$. Output in country 2 therefore falls unambiguously: the depreciation of its real exchange rate and induced rise in real interest rate causes a fall in aggregate supply. However, output in country 1 may rise, if the exchange rate elasticities are sufficiently large that the rise in output in the divergence system outweighs the fall in the aggregate system.

A key feature of the model, arising from its natural rate features, is that the real equilibrium of the system is independent of monetary policy. Thus monetary policy influences the real economy only via price surprises. Such price surprises administer shocks to aggregate supply that are necessarily temporary, lasting only one period. From (3.5), the real exchange rate, e_t, and and the difference in real interest rates, r_t^d, move inversely on a one-for-one basis. Eliminating r_t^d from (3.3) and (3.4) using this relationship yields an upward sloping demand schedule, D^d, as in Figure 2. This is more elastic with respect to the exchange rate than for permanent shocks. The slope of the supply schedule, S^d, is ambiguous, being downward sloping as in Figure 2 for $b_1 > {}^1/_2 b_2$, but positively sloped for $b_1 < {}^1/_2 b_2$. A price surprise in country 1 therefore shifts both S^a and S^d to the right, raising aggregate output, lowering average real interest rates and depreciating the exchange rate, regardless of the slope of S^d. Output in country 1 rises unambiguously. Whether output rises in country 2 depends on whether the favourable effects of the appreciating exchange rate (assuming that $a_2 > b_2$) outweigh the unfavourble effect of possible higher interest rates.

IV. MONETARY POLICY

The Closed Economy Case

Having considered the influence on the real equilibrium of the system, we now fix government spending in both countries and focus on the determi-

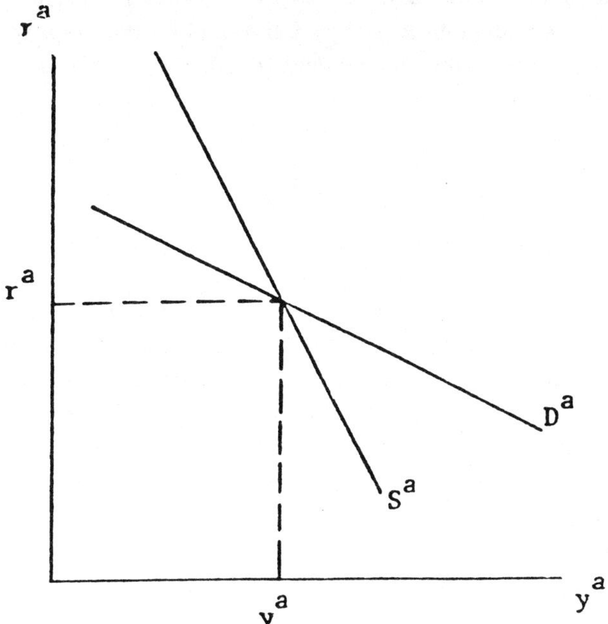

FIGURE 1. Equilibrium of the Aggregate Real Economy

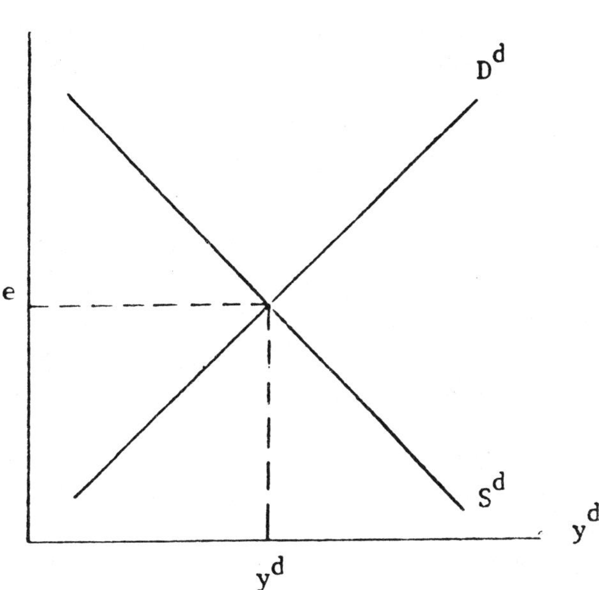

FIGURE 2. Equilibrium of the Divergence Real Economy

nation of monetary policy and prices. First, consider this problem in the closed economy context considered by Barro and Gordon (1983). Solving out for real interest rates from the demand function (2.1) and substituting into the supply function (2.3) the reduced form equation for output becomes :

$$y_t = \tilde{y} + \tilde{b}_3(p_t - p^e_{t,t}) \tag{4.1}$$

where $\tilde{b}_3 = b_3(1 - b_2 a_2^{-1})^{-1}$ and $\tilde{y}$ is equilibrium output.

The problem for the government is then to minimise (2.8) subject to (4.1).

If we assume that the government has no reputation, this optimisation problem is solved by treating private sector expectations as given or parametric. This is because a government without reputation perceives that it can have no influence on future expectations of policy actions either because it has zero credibility or it has a negligible probability of survival. The first order condition for a minimum is given by :

$$\tilde{b}_3[\tilde{y} + \tilde{b}_3(p_t - p^e_{t,t}) - \bar{y}] + d_1(p_t - p_{t-1}) = 0$$

so that

$$p_t = (d_1 + \tilde{b}_3^2)^{-1}\,[(\bar{y} - \tilde{y} + \tilde{b}_3 p^e_{t,t})\tilde{b}_3 + d_1 p_{t-1}] \tag{4.2}$$

However, the private sector can calculate that the government will choose p_t as in (4.2), and will therefore form its expectations in accordance with (4.2). Substituting in for $p^e_{t,t}$ yields :

$$\pi_t^{NR} = d_1^{-1}\tilde{b}_3\,(\bar{y} - \tilde{y}) \tag{4.3}$$

where $\pi_t = p_t - p_{t-1}$ is the inflation rate. The inflation rate is therefore related to the gap between target output $(\bar{y})$ and equilibrium output $(\tilde{y})$.

This is depicted in Figure 3. Government indifference curves describe ellipses around the point $(y_t, \pi_t) = (\bar{y}, 0)$. The zero inflation equilibrium is at $(\tilde{y}, 0)$, at a welfare loss of W_0. However, without reputation this point is not sustainable. This is because, with expectations treated as parametric, the trade-off between inflation and output appears positively sloped, so that the government is tempted to spring a monetary surprise to take the economy to y_1. Such a temptation exists for all rates of expected inflation below π_t^{NR} and at this rate of inflation the government has no temptation unexpectedly to expand the money supply at a faster rate. Clearly the welfare loss at π_t^{NR} exceed that at $\pi_t = 0$.

With reputation the government no longer treats expectations as parametric, but may instead seek to influence expectations by announcing its future policy actions. If it does so, and carries out its stated intentions, the best policy is to go for the zero inflation equilibrium with $y_t = \tilde{y}$, yielding a welfare loss of W_0:

$$\pi_t^R = 0 \tag{4.4}$$

However, there is still the question as to whether this position is sustainable, or whether the government has an incentive to renege on this policy by springing a monetary surprise on the private sector. Much here depends on the private sector's reaction when reneging takes place. It seems reasonable to suppose that the private sector will suspend belief in the government's reputation for

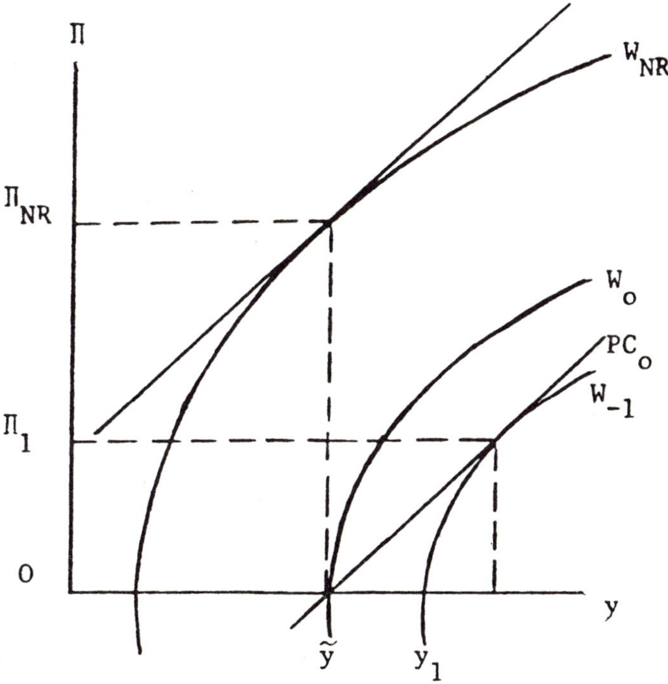

FIGURE 3. Equilibrium Inflation without Reputation

a period of time (say, n periods), so that after the period of reneging the system reverts to the non-reputational equilibrium for n periods. Then the government must weigh the gains from reneging against the subsequent costs arising from loss of reputation. In terms of the welfare losses of Figure 3, the welfare gains from the reneging strategy, $\hat{W}$, is given by :

$$\hat{W} = W_0 - W_{-1} - \sum_{i=1}^{n} \rho^i (W_{NR} - W_0)$$

$$= W_0 - W_{-1} - \left(\frac{1 - \rho^n}{1 - \rho}\right) \rho (W_{NR} - W_0) < 0.$$

We require $\hat{W}$ to be negative for the reputational policy to be sustainable. The gains from reneging fall as the period of loss of reputation rises, and as the degree of discounting falls. In general, a large value of n and a value of ρ close to 1 will easily ensure that zero inflation can be sustained as a reputational equilibrium.

The Open Economy Case

Now consider the case of two symmetric interdependent economies. We assume that fiscal policy is fixed, and focus solely for the moment on the determination of monetary policy; we relax this assumption in the next section. Because our model is a natural rate model it exhibits long-run neutrality. It follows that the real equilibrium of the system is identical irrespective of the regime, i.e. whether we are considering a cooperative or non-cooperative regime, or a reputational or a non-reputational one. All that can vary across the four regimes is the rate of inflation.

IV.1 THE CR AND CNR REGIME

We assume that governments minimise a simple weighted average, $\tilde{W}$, of the two objective functions. But

$$\tilde{W}_t = \frac{1}{2}(W_t + W_t^*) = W_t^a + W_t^d$$

where W_t^a and W_t^d are defined as in (2.8) but with y_t^a and y_t^d replacing y_t and similarly for other variables. Thus the global welfare loss can be expressed as the sum of a loss defined on the aggregate variables of the system and a loss defined on the difference variables. Hence, because of the assumption of symmetry, each economy under the cooperative regimes behaves just like the aggregate system, i.e. $W_t = W_t^a$. Accordingly, the difference system is always zero, and minimizing the joint objective function is equivalent to minimising W_t^a. But the aggregate system, defined by (3.1) and (3.2) above, behaves exactly like the closed economy case considered above with

$$\pi_t^{CNR} = d_1^{-1}\tilde{b}_3(\bar{y} - y_t^a \tag{4.5}$$

now, however, with $\tilde{b}_3 = (a_2a_5 - b_2)^{-1}a_2a_5b_3$ and

$$y_t^a = (a_2a_5 - b_2)^{-1}a_2a_5[b_0 - b_2a_2^{-1}(a_0 + a_3g_t^a)].$$

For the CR regime, inflation will certainly be lower, and may be zero, as discussed above. For the purpose of subsequent discussion, and comparison with other parts of the literature, we assume that the social optimum is sustainable, so that

$$\pi_t^{CR} = 0 \tag{4.6}$$

IV.2 THE NCNR AND NCR REGIME

What difference does the absence of cooperation make to the equilibrium inflation rate? The answer depends critically on whether a price surprise in one country raises or lowers output in the other. As noted above, this spillover may be positive or negative, depending on whether the beneficial supply side effects in the other country resulting from improved terms of trade offset or are outweighed by the deleterious effects of higher real interest rates. If this spillover is positive, some of the expansionary output effects of a price surprise in country 1 accrue to country 2. Accordingly, the short run inflation/output tradeoff is less advantageous for the single country acting alone than for joint price surprises coordinated between the two countries. But this diminishes the incentive for governments to spring surprises on the private sector, so it follows from the previous analysis that equilibrium inflation will be lower. Thus $\tilde{b}_3$ will be lower for the non-cooperative case, so that $\pi_t^{NCNR} < \pi_t^{CNR}$. Since the real equilibrium is unaffected, it follows that the welfare loss under cooperation exceeds that without cooperation. This is essentially the result of Rogoff (1985), which claims that international co-operation need not pay. As noted by Currie and Levine (1987), this result depends on the assumption that governments lack reputation.

If, however, the spillover is negative, the short run inflation/output tradeoff is more favourable for the single country than for the aggregate system. In this case, the converse argument leads to the conclusion that $\pi_t^{NCNR} > \pi_t^{CNR}$, so that cooperation is beneficial. As shown in the appendix the inflation rate under the NCNR regime is now given by

$$\pi_t^{NCNR} = d_1^{-1} \tilde{b}_3 (\bar{y} - y_t^a) \tag{4.7}$$

with

$$\tilde{b}_3 = \frac{1}{2} b_3 \{(a_2 a_5 - b_2)^{-1} a_2 a_5 + [2b_1 - b_2 + a_6(2a_1 + a_2)]^{-1} a_6 (2a_1 + a_2)\}.$$

If governments pursue reputational policies, they are constrained not to spring price surprises on their private sectors, otherwise they will lose reputation. But since anticipated monetary policy is neutral in our natural rate model, it follows that, with reputation, the equilibrium inflation rate will be zero, i.e.

$$\pi_t^{NCR} = 0 \tag{4.8}$$

To summarise, therefore, we have found that, with fiscal policy given, the optimal choice of monetary policy ensures that

$$0 = \pi_t^{CR} = \pi_t^{NCR} < \pi_t^{NCNR} < \pi_t^{CNR} \tag{4.9}$$

with positive output spillovers from price surprises, and that

$$0 = \pi_t^{CR} = \pi_t^{NCR} < \pi_t^{CNR} < \pi_t^{NCNR} \tag{4.10}$$

with negative output spillovers from price surprises. In the next section, we investigate the consequences of allowing fiscal policy to vary.

V. FISCAL POLICY

We now turn to consider the determination of fiscal policy in our four regimes. In so doing, the neutrality of anticipated money is analytically convenient, for it allows us to analyze the setting of fiscal policy independently of monetary policy. This is not to say that the setting of the two aspects of policy are independent, for as we have shown above, monetary policy depends on equilibrium output, which in turn depends on the setting of fiscal policy. However, while the setting of monetary policy is not independent of the setting of fiscal policy, the setting of fiscal policy is independent of that of monetary policy. Accordingly, we analyse the setting of fiscal policy in this section, and then go on to analyse the consequences for monetary policy. In what follows, we concentrate on the main results, whereas all derivations and calculations are given in the appendix.

V.1 THE CR AND CNR REGIME

We start by considering cooperative regimes. With reputation, governments refrain from springing price surprises on their private sectors so that equilibrium inflation will be zero. Furthermore, from (3.1) and (3.2) we have that

$$y_t^a = c_0^a - c_1^a g_t^a \tag{5.1}$$

with c_0^a and c_1^a defined in the appendix and with $c_1^a > 0$ (given our intra-period stability condition, i.e. $a_2 a_5 > b_2$). Equilibrium output depends negatively on government spending because of the adverse supply side effects of higher real interest rates. Choosing g_t to minimise $W_t^* = W_t^a$ as defined in (2.8) subject to (5.1), and, additionally (4.5) for the CNR regime, involves setting

$$g_t^a = [d_2 + c_1^{a2}(1 + \Phi_1)]^{-1}[(\bar{y} - c_0^a)(-c_1^a)(1 + \Phi_1) + d_2\bar{g}] \tag{5.2}$$

$$\text{with} \qquad \Phi_1 = \begin{cases} 0 & \text{for the CR regime} \\ d_1^{-1}(a_2 a_5 - b_2)^{-2} a_2^2 a_5^2 b_3^2 & \text{for the CNR regime.} \end{cases}$$

Since the output multiplier is negative, a more ambitious output target leads to a lower level of aggregate government spending. Thus the cooperative policy involves lowering government spending, subject to social and/or efficiency constraints, in order to lower real interest rates.

V.2 THE NCNR REGIME

For the non-cooperative setting we assume that the single government treats the policy actions of the other government as parametric. It therefore perceives that a domestic fiscal expansion will influence output as well as the exchange rate. While y_t^a remains unchanged, we have the additional requirement

$$y_t^d = c_2^d g_t^d - c_3^d e_{t+1,t}^e \tag{5.3}$$

with c_2^d and c_3^d defined in the appendix. A sufficient condition for c_2^d and c_3^d to be positive is $b_1 > {}^1/_2 b_2$, which was an assumption in the setup of the model. Choosing g_t to minimise W subject to (4.7), (5.1) and (5.3) gives

$$g_t^a = [2d_2 + c_1^{a2}(1 + \Phi_2)]^{-1}[(\bar{y} - c_0^a)(-c_1^a)(1 + \Phi_2) + 2d_2\bar{g}] \qquad (5.4)$$

with $$\Phi_2 = \frac{1}{4} d_1^{-1}\{(a_2a_5 - b_2)^{-1} a_2a_5b_3 + [2b_1 - b_2 + a_6(2a_1 + a_2)]^{-1} a_6b_3(2a_1 + a_2)\}^2 - c_2^d c_1^{a(-1)}.$$

Since it is possible that a positive output multiplier may result (for a large value of a_4 equation (5.4) collapses to the formula for the cooperative cases), we can expect aggregate government spending to be higher and equilibrium income to be lower in the non-cooperative case as opposed to the cooperative cases. A one-period fiscal expansion in country 1 appreciates the real exchange rate, giving rise to favourable supply side effects that outweigh any negative effects of a higher real interest rate.

The analysis of fiscal policy interactions therefore predicts a bias under non-cooperation towards too high a level of government spending. However, this bias is not confined to the real side of the model. The higher level of government spending under non-cooperation lowers real output. But this in turn has consequences for monetary policy. As we noted in the previous section, in the absence of reputation, the equilibrium rate of inflation is positively related to the gap between target and equilibrium output (see(4.7)). But a high level of government spending lowers equilibrium output, thereby increasing this gap. Thus the bias towards higher government spending in the NCNR regime is associated with a bias towards higher inflation.

When analysing monetary policy alone, we found that inflation was higher in the CNR regime than the NCNR regime if price surprises caused positive output spillovers on the other country, and was lower with negative spillovers. Our analysis of fiscal policy and the consequences for monetary policy modifies this result, since it increases inflation in the NCNR regime and lowers it in the CNR regime. The interaction between monetary and fiscal policy increases the possibility that inflation will be higher under non-cooperation than with cooperation.

It is of interest to contrast the policy response under the two regimes to a productivity shock, lowering equilibrium output (in our notation: c_0^a). It is equivalent to think of an increase in the output target of governments, $\bar{y}$. The CNR response is to cut government spending (see (5.2)) with a view to dampening the fall in equilibrium output (see (5.1)). At the same time monetary policy will become laxer, implying higher inflation, since the gap between target and equilibrium output has risen (see (4.5)). In contrast, the NCNR response is to raise government spending (see (5.4)), with a view to sustaining equilibrium output in the single country by a favourable terms of trade effect. The consequence is that output falls by more (see (5.1)), while inflation also rises, and very likely by more than under the CNR regime (see (4.7)).

V.3 THE NCR REGIME

In the absence of cooperation, the pursuit of reputational policies may well dampen the bias towards too high a level of government spending that arose in the NCNR regime. The reason for this is as follows. In the absence of reputation, governments must treat as parametric the expected exchange rate in the future. This limits their ability to induce an appreciation of their currency by expansionary fiscal policy, since such an appreciation can be induced only by government operating on the current interest rate, not on expected future rates. By contrast, with reputation, government can also operate on the current exchange rate through expected future interest rates, so that commitments about future fiscal action also influence the current exchange rate. Taking this into account, the single government minimizes W_t subject to (5.1) as well as subject to

$$y_t^d = -c_4^d g_t^d - c_5^d e_t \tag{5.5}$$

$$e_t = -c_6^d g_t^d + c_7^d e_{t+1,t}^e \tag{5.6}$$

with all parameters defined in the appendix. Hence, the efficacy of fiscal policy to influence the exchange rate, and thereby deliver apparent supply side benefits, is much increased by reputation. Of course, the benefits are only apparent, since they disappear when both countries seek them simultaneously. This (apparently) enhanced effectiveness of fiscal policy is used partly to enhance the effects of fiscal policy, but also to reduce the extent to which government spending deviates from its desired level. Thus the effect of reputation is to reduce the actual use of government spending to influence the exchange rate, while enhancing its apparent effect.

However, matters are not quite so simple. For the NCR regime exhibits aggregate dynamics in terms of fiscal policy, in contrast to the other regimes. This is because future expected fiscal policy actions impinge on future expected interest differentials, and hence on the current account. For the cooperative cases, given our assumption of symmetry, such influences are disregarded as being self-defeating in the aggregate. For the non-cooperative, non-reputational case, this link is ignored because future commitments about policy carry no credibility. Only for the NCR regime do such influences come into play. Given that the dynamic system described by (2.8), (5.1), (5.5) and (5.6) is stable, the government sets fiscal policy according to

$$g_t^a = \left[2d_2 - c_1^a\left(-c_4^d - c_1^a + \frac{c_5^d\, c_6^d\, \rho}{\rho - c_7^d}\right)\right]^{-1}\left[2d_2\bar{g} + (\bar{y} - c_0^a)\left(-c_4^a - c_1^a + \frac{c_5^a\, c_6^d\, \rho}{\rho - c_7^d}\right)\right] \tag{5.7}$$

Note that if the government acts without reputation, it treats the exchange rate as parametric. Thus $c_5^d = 0$ in (5.5) and therefore (5.7) eventually reduces to (5.4) but with a negative output multiplier since c_4^d is likely to be greater than zero. Under the NCR regime the output multiplier can be expected to be greater than under the NCNR regime, which means that government spending is higher (smaller) for a positive (negative) multiplier and output will raise even less than under the NCNR regime. This is exactly the case of the numerical example given in the appendix. It may also be shown that too high a degree of discounting (too low a value for ρ) generates instability because of this dynamics. In the numerical example this arises for the case of an extremely myopic government with $\rho < 0.11$. Instability arises because very short sighted governments are tempted to announce future expansions in government spending, in order to induce current favourable side effects via anticipations. The fact that government spending is thereby raised to excessive levels in the future is disregarded because of the short time horizon of governments.

VI. CONCLUSION

This paper has been concerned to analyse the consequences of policy conflicts in a two-country natural rate world for the setting of monetary and fiscal policy. Our main conclusions are as follows.

In the setting of fiscal policy, non-cooperative relations between governments with ambitious targets tends to create a bias towards too high a level of government spending. This occurs because governments acting non-cooperatively seek to obtain beneficial supply side effects from a real exchange rate appreciation, brought about by fiscal expansion. The absence of reputation exacerbates this bias : Since governments without reputation have a small influence on the real exchange rate (for a given policy change), they make greater use of their instruments at the margin. However, reputation is not necessarily desirable in the absence of cooperation, since governments that discount the future very heavily may act to destabilise the system.

These differences in fiscal stance then have consequences for inflation if governments do not have reputation. This is because, without reputation, equilibrium inflation is related to the gap between target and equilibrium output. Since unduly high levels of government spending lower equilibrium output via supply side effects (government spending in the context being assumed to be unproductive), this increases the gap between target and equilibrium output, and thereby adds to inflation. Because the non-cooperative non-reputational policy leads to an unduly high level of government spending, this policy also generates high levels of inflation. This factor tends to increase the case for cooperation even without reputation, contrary to Rogoff's (1985) result.

These results bear some similarities with those of Currie, Levine and Vidalis (1987), albeit in the context of a wholly different model. That analysis was conducted in the context of an empirical model with substantial price sluggishness though with a long run natural rate. Since the natural rate was constant, the supply side effects analysed in this paper were absent. However, the analogous effects might be argued to exist in the transitional path: an appreciated exchange rate helps output performance by making more favourable the inflation/output trade-off, so that the incentive exists to expand fiscal policy unduly in the non-cooperative cases. As in the above analysis, Currie, Levine and Vidalis found a bias towards unduly high levels of government spending in the non-cooperative cases (though larger for the reputational policy in contrast to our analysis). And inflation was highest for the non-cooperative non-reputational policy, as our analysis here tends to suggest.

This analysis has been conducted in a highly simplified analytical framework with a view to analytical clarity. However, future work might well investigate further issues. The current model neglects financing consequences of government spending. This means that the issue of the sustainability of fiscal policy is neglected. This would be an important issue, particularly for policies, such as the non-cooperative reputational one, which involve tight monetary policy in combination with lax fiscal policy.

The analysis also points to the issue of how best to cooperate in the setting of fiscal and monetary policy. In practice, we observe the greater degree of cooperation in monetary policy, and very little in fiscal policy. Yet our analysis points to the significance of fiscal policy coordination. Indeed, in the absence of reputation, it might be most advantageous to coordinate fiscal policy while setting monetary policy non-cooperatively. This could avoid the potential misalignment of real exchange rates resulting from fiscal policy; while maintaining the discipline on inflation resulting from floating nominal exchange rates. This applies especially to the case when spillovers from price surprises are positive. This is, of course, the opposite of what we observe in practice. Future work will focus on these issues of fiscal policy coordination.

Queen Mary College and C.E.P.R., London.
Queen Mary College, London.

APPENDIX

We consider the case of fiscal policy under the four regimes: Cooperation with reputation [CR], cooperation without reputation [CNR], non-cooperation without reputation [NCNR] and, finally, non-cooperation with reputation [NCR]. We use the model as outlined in equations (2.1) - (2.7) as well as the aggregate system [equations (3.1) and (3.2)] and the divergence system [equations (3.3) and (3.5)]. It is assumed that the first government minimizes a welfare loss function of the form

$$W_t = \frac{1}{2} \sum_{i=0}^{\infty} \rho^i [(y_{t+i} - \bar{y})^2 + d_1(p_{t+i} - p_{t+i-1})^2 + d_2(g_{t+i} - \bar{g})^2] \quad \text{(A.1)}$$

with a similar expression with '*' variables for the second country.

1. *Cooperative Policy with Reputation* [CR]

Assuming cooperation, we expect identical policies in both countries. Hence, by symmetry, $W^d_t = 0$ and the joint welfare loss is $^1/_2(W_t + W^*_t) = W^a_t + W^d_t = W^a_t$. Furthermore, since both governments have reputation, the optimal rate of inflation is

$$\pi^{CR}_t = p_t - p_{t-1} = 0 \quad \text{(A.2)}$$

Turning to fiscal policy we substitute (3.2) into (3.1) by eliminating r^a_t which yields

$$y^a_t = c^a_0 - c^a_1 g^a_t \quad \text{(A.3)}$$

where the term $(p^a_t - p^{ae}_{t,t})$ cancels because of correct anticipations of the price level (i.e. rational expectations) by the private sector and where

$c_0^a = \alpha a_5(a_2 b_0 - a_0 b_2)$, $c_1^a = \alpha a_3 a_5 b_2$ and $\alpha = (a_5 a_2 - b_2)^{-1}$. Substituting (A.2) and (A.3) into (A.1) we get the static welfare loss function

$$W_t = \frac{1}{2} \sum_{i=0}^{\infty} \rho^i [(c_0^a - c_1^a g_t^a - \bar{y})^2 + d_2 (g_t^a - \bar{g})^2] \qquad \text{(A.4)}$$

Differentiating with respect to g_t^a gives

$$g_t^a = (d_2 + c_1^{a2})^{-1} [- c_1^a (\bar{y} - c_0^a) + d_2 \bar{g}] \qquad \text{(A.5)}$$

Given an output target $\bar{y}$, the government chooses g_t^a according to (A.5) which in turn determines equilibrium output via (A.3) and the welfare loss via (A.1). The real rate of interest in the new equilibrium is given by setting (3.1) equal to (3.2)

$$r_t^a = \alpha (a_0 a_5 - b_0) + \alpha a_3 a_5 g_t^a \qquad \text{(A.6)}$$

2. *Cooperative Policy without Reputation* [CNR]

In the absence of reputation, the rate of inflation will be positive. The governments in both countries have to take this into account when determining their optimal setting of government expenditure. Note, that given g_t^a, y_t^a and r_t^a can be calculated via (A.3) and (A.6). The difference occurs in the treatment of inflation. Assuming that the government has no reputation, private sector expectations have to be taken into acount. Equation (A.3) now becomes

$$y_t^a = c_0^a - c_1^a g_t^a + \alpha a_2 a_5 b_3 (p_t^a - p_{t,t}^{ae}) \qquad \text{(A.3')}$$

Substituting (A.3′) into (A.1) gives the first order condition for a minimum for π_t as

$$[c_0^a - c_1^a g_t^a + \alpha a_2 a_5 b_3 (p_t^a - p_{t,t}^{ae}) - \bar{y}]\, \alpha a_2 a_5 b_3 + d_1 (p_t - p_{t-1}) = 0 \qquad \text{(A.7)}$$

Substituting $p_{t,t}^{ae} = p_t$ since the private sector will form its expectations according to (A.7) yields

$$\pi_t^{CNR} = (\bar{y} - y_t^a)\, \alpha a_2 a_5 b_3 d_1^{-1} \qquad \text{(A.8)}$$

Substituting (A.3) into (A.8) and (A.3) and (A.8) into (A.1) gives a welfare loss function which is only dependent on g^a_t. Minimization yields :

$$g^a_t = [c_1^{a2} + c_1^{a2} a^2 \alpha_2^2 a_5^2 b_3^2 d_1^{-1} + d_2]^{-1} [(\bar{y} - c_0^a)(- c_1^a - c_1^a \alpha^2 a_2^2 a_5^2 b_3^2 d_1^{-1}) + d_2 \bar{g}] \tag{A.9}$$

3. *Non Cooperative Policy without Reputation* [NCNR]

Given a non-cooperative setting we assume that for this regime the single government treats the policy actions of the other government as parametric. Moreover, it treats its future policy actions as parametric. It therefore perceives that a one period change in g_t will alter e_t and r^d_t. Substituting (3.5) in (3.3) and (3.4) of the divergence system gives

$$y^d_t = (-2a_1a_6 - a_2a_6)r^d_t + a_3a_6g^d_t + a_1a_6\, e^e_{t+1,t} \tag{A.10}$$

$$y^d_t = (2b_1 - b_2)r^d_t - b_1e^e_{t+1,t} + b_3(p^d_t - p^{de}_{t,t}) \tag{A.11}$$

Solving (A.10) - (A.11) by eliminating r^d_t gives

$$y^d_t = c^d_2\, g^d_t - c^d_3 e^e_{t+1,t} + \beta b_3a_6(2a_1 + a_2)(p^d_t - p^{de}_{t,t}) \tag{A.12}$$

with $c^d_2 = \beta a_3a_6(2b_1 - b_2)$, $c^d_3 = \beta a_6(a_1b_2 + a_2b_1)$ and $\beta = [2b_1 - b_2 + a_6(2a_1 + a_2)]^{-1}$

The total welfare loss is dependent on the inflationary bias. In the absence of reputation the government cannot enforce the ideal rule of zero inflation. Substituting (A.3′) and (A.12) into (A.1) and differentiating with respect to π_t gives then

$$(y^a_t + y^d_t - \bar{y})\left[\frac{1}{2}\alpha a_2a_5b_3 + \frac{1}{2}\beta b_3a_6(2a_1 + a_2)\right] + d_1(p_t - p_{t-1}) = 0 \tag{A.13}$$

Using the fact that an identical reaction function exists for country 2 with an opposite sign for $e^e_{t+1,t}$ simplifies (A.13) :

$$(y^a_t - \bar{y})\left[\frac{1}{2}\alpha a_2a_5b_3 + \frac{1}{2}\beta b_3a_6(2a_1 + a_2)\right] + d_1(p_t - p_{t-1}) = 0 \tag{A.14}$$

or

$$\pi^{NCNR}_t = (\bar{y} - y^a_t)\, d_1^{-1}\, \frac{1}{2}\, b_3[\alpha a_2a_5 + \beta a_6(2a_1 + a_2)] \tag{A.15}$$

A comparison with (A.8) shows that $\pi_t^{NCNR}(y_t^{a,\,NCNR}) = \pi_t^{CNR}\,(y_t^{a,\,CNR})$ plus an added component which is due to non-cooperation. A sufficient conditiou for this component to be positive is $b_1 > {}^1/_2\, b_2$.

Optimizing government expenditure country 1 minimizes its welfare loss $W_t = \frac{1}{2}\,\Sigma\rho^i\,[(y_t^a + y_t^d - \bar{y})^2 + d_1(\pi_t^{NCNR})^2 + d_2(g_t - \bar{g})^2]$ with y_t^a defined in (A.3), y_t^d defined in (A.12) (where the last term cancels due to the rational expectations assumption), and π_t^{NCNR} defined in (A.15). Note that $g_t^a = {}^1/_2\,(g_t + g_t^*)$ and $g_t^d = {}^1/_2(g_t - g_t^*)$. This defines a reaction function for country 1 as

$$\left[c_0^a - \frac{1}{2}\,c_1^a(g_t + g_t^*) + \frac{1}{2}\,c_2^d\,(g_t - g_t^*) - c_3^d e_{t+1,t}^e - \bar{y}\right]\left(-\frac{1}{2}\,c_1^a + \frac{1}{2}\,c_2^d\right)$$

$$+ d_2(g_t - \bar{g}) + d_1\left[\bar{y} - c_0^a + \frac{1}{2}\,c_1^a(g_t + g_t^*)\right]\frac{1}{2}\,c_1^a\,\Delta^2 = 0;$$

with $\Delta = \frac{1}{2}\,d_1^{-1}\,b_3\,[\alpha a_2 a_5 + \beta a_6(2a_1 + a_2)]$

By symmetry there exists an identical reaction for country 2 with $e_{t+1,t}^e$ entering with opposite sign. Spending in the aggregate is therefore given by

$$g_t^a = [2d_2 + c_1^a\,(c_1^a - c_2^d + c_1^a\,\Delta^2 d_1]^{-1}[(c_0^a - \bar{y})(c_1^a - c_2^d + c_1^a\Delta^2 d_1) + 2d_2\,\bar{g}] \quad \text{(A.16)}$$

y_t^a, r_t^a and W_t can then be determined by (A.3), (A.6) and (A.1).

4. *Non Cooperative Policy with Reputation* [NCR]

First, note that with reputation the governments policy is to go for zero inflation, which we assume can be achieved :

$$\pi_t^{NCR} = 0 \quad \text{(A.17)}$$

As in the NCNR case the government treats the policy actions of the other government as given. However, the government is now able to influence the exchange rate by its fiscal policy actions. Under the NCR regime we therefore have a new policy variable :

$$y_t^d = -\,c_4^d\,g_t^d - c_5^d\,e_t \quad \text{(A.18)}$$

$$e_t = -\,c_6^d\,g_t^d + c_7^d\,e_{t+1,t}^e \quad \text{(A.19)}$$

(A.18) is obtained by substituting (3.3) into (3.4) eliminating r_t^d. (A.19) is obtained by substituting (3.3) into (3.4) eliminating y_t^d and then inserting (3.5) eliminating r_t^d. We have $c_4^d = \gamma a_3 a_6 b_2$, $c_5^d = \gamma a_6(a_2 b_1 + a_1 b_2)$, $c_6^d = 2\beta a_3 a_6$, $c_7^d = \beta(a_2 a_6 - b_2)$, $\gamma = (a_2 a_6 - b_2)^{-1}$ and β as defined previously. The NCR problem then becomes that of minimizing

$$W_t = \frac{1}{2}\sum_{i=0}^{\infty} \rho^i[(c_0^a - c_1^a g_{t+i}^a - c_4^d g_{t+i}^d - c_5^d e_{t+i} - \bar{y})^2 + d_2(g_{t+i} - \bar{g})^2$$
$$+ \lambda_{t+i}(e_{t+i} + c_6^d g_{t+i}^d - c_7^d e_{t+i+1,\,t+i}^e)] \qquad \text{(A.20)}$$

Differentiating with respect to g_t and e_t we obtain [again using the fact that $g_t^a = {}^1/_2(g_t + g_t^*)$ and $g_t^d = {}^1/_2(g_t - g_t^*)$]

$$[c_a^0 - (c_4^d + c_1^a)\frac{1}{2} g_t + (c_4^d - c_1^a)\frac{1}{2} g_t^* - c_5^d e_t - \bar{y}](c_4^d + c_1^a)\left(-\frac{1}{2}\right)$$
$$+ d_2(g_t - \bar{g}) + \frac{1}{4} c_6^d \lambda_t = 0 \qquad \text{(A.21)}$$

$$[c_0^a - (c_4^d + c_1^a)\frac{1}{2} g_t + (c_4^d - c_1^a)\frac{1}{2} g_t^* - c_5^d e_t - \bar{y}](-c_5^d) + \frac{1}{2}\lambda_t - \frac{1}{2}\lambda_{t-1}\rho^{-1} c_7^d = 0$$
$$\text{(A.22)}$$

Recalling that there exist equivalent reaction functions for country 2 with e_t entering with opposite sign we add these together which gives

$$-2(c_0^a - c_1^a g_t^a - \bar{y})(c_4^d + c_1^a) + 4d_2(g_t^a - \bar{g}) + c_6^d \lambda_t = 0 \qquad \text{(A.23)}$$

$$-2(c_0^a - c_1^a g_t^a - \bar{y})c_5^d + \lambda_t - \rho^{-1}\lambda_{t-1} c_7^d = 0 \qquad \text{(A.24)}$$

which defines the dynamic aggregate system. Substituting (A.23) into (A.24) for λ_t and λ_{t-1} yields a single differential equation of the form

$$A + B g_{t-1}^a = C g_t^a \qquad \text{(A.25)}$$

with $A = 2d_2\bar{g}(1 - \rho^{-1} c_7^d) + (\bar{y} - c_0^a)(-c_4^d - c_1^a)(1 - \rho^{-1} c_7^d) + (\bar{y} - c_0^a) c_5^d c_6^d$;

$B = \rho^{-1} c_1^a c_7^d (c_4^d + c_1^a) + 2\rho^{-1} c_7^d d_2$ and $C = 2d_2 + c_1^a(c_4^d + c_1^a - c_5^d c_6^d)$

The solution for (A.25) for g_t^a is then $A/(C-B)$, provided that the stability condition $0 \leqslant B/C < 1$ holds. This implies setting g_t^a as

$$g_t^a = \left[2d_2 - c_1^a\left(-c_4^d - c_1^a + \frac{c_5^d c_6^d \rho}{\rho - c_7^d}\right)\right]^{-1}$$

$$\left[2d_2\bar{g} + (\bar{y} - c_0^a)\left(-c_4^d - c_1^a + \frac{c_5^d c_6^d \rho}{\rho - c_7^d}\right)\right] \qquad \text{(A.26)}$$

given that the stability condition

$$0 \leqslant \frac{c_7^d[c_1^a(c_4^d + c_1^a) + 2d_2]}{\rho\,[c_1^a(c_4^d + c_1^a - c_5^d c_6^d) + 2d_2]} < 1 \text{ holds.} \qquad \text{(A.27)}$$

Given g_t^a we can then solve for y_t^a (A.3), r_t^a (A.6) and W_t(A.1). If the government acts without reputation it treats the exchange rate as parametric. This implies setting c_5^d equal zero in (A.18). If, furthermore, the government would agree to cooperation it would disregard the divergence system and thus set c_4^d equal zero. In this case (A.26) reduces to (A.5), the equivalent equilibrium condition for the CR regime.

5. *A Numerical Example*

Table 1 gives the results for the four regimes given an ambitious output target which the government tries to achieve by fiscal means. The coefficients are chosen as :

$$a_0 = 0,\quad a_1 = 2,\quad a_2 = 1,\quad a_3 = 1,\quad a_4 = 0.5,\quad a_5 = 2,\quad a_6 = 0.667$$

$$b_0 = 0,\quad b_1 = 1,\quad b_2 = 0.5,\quad b_3 = 1,\quad \rho = 0.9,\quad \bar{y} = 0.05$$

$$d_1^{(1)} = 0.5,\quad d_1^{(2)} = 1,\quad d_2 = 0.2.$$

The first entry is the value for $d_1^{(1)} = 0.5$, the second entry is the value for $d_1^{(2)} = 1$ [See Table 1].

6. *Some Sensitivity Analysis*

The stability condition was given as

$$0 \leqslant \frac{c_7^d[c_1^a(c_4^d + c_1^a) + 2d_2]}{\rho[c_7^a(c_4^d + c_1^a - c_5^d c_6^d) + 2d_2]} < 1 \qquad \text{(A.27)}$$

TABLE 1

(All figures in %)

	g_t^a	y_t^a	r_t^a	π_t	W_t
CR	—5.17	+3.45	—6.89	0.00	+0.38
	—5.17	+3.45	—6.89	0.00	+0.38
CNR	—6.83	+4.55	—9.11	+1.20	+0.51
	—6.45	+4.30	—8.59	+0.93	+0.48
NCNR	—5.64	+3.76	—7.52	+2.51	+0.55
	—4.92	+3.28	—6.56	+1.74	+0.54
NCR	—2.87	+1.91	—3.82	0.00	+0.56
[0 ⩽ (A.27) < 1]	—2.87	+1.91	—3.82	0.00	+0.56

This is most obviously fulfilled if the stability condition takes its lower bound for $c_7^d = 0$ (or, alternatively, $a_2a_6 = b_2$). But this is hardly surprising as $c_7^d = 0$ eliminates the dynamical constraint in the optimizing function [(A.19), (A.20)]. Other, rather artificial but sufficient conditions can be constructed , as for example :

$$\begin{cases} a_3 = 0 \\ b_2 \leqslant a_2a_6 < \rho\beta^{-1} + b_2 < \rho\beta^{-1} + 2b_1 \end{cases} \tag{A.28}$$

If, furthermore, $\rho = 1$ (no rate of discounting future welfare losses) then (A.28) reduces to

$$\begin{cases} a_3 = 0 \\ b_2 \leqslant a_2a_6 \end{cases} \tag{A.29}$$

with the equality in the second condition rendering the first condition obsolete. Given the data of the numerical example above we need a $\rho > 0.1063$ in order to guarantee stability.

Working backwards for a feasible range of coefficients is somewhat more tedious. We concentrate on the demand side of the model for various rates of ρ. Table 2 gives the values. It shows that as long as the degree of discounting is not too high, stability is guaranteed for virtually every positive parameter of the model, except for a_2 (measuring the marginal contribution of the interest rate to the determination of output), which is sensitive for the lower range of ρ-values.

TABLE 2

(n.r.: no restrictions for positive values)

ρ	a_1	a_2	a_3	$a_4 = 1 - a_5^{-1}$
0.1	$a_1 > 2.191$	$0.750 < a_2 < 0.960$	$a_3 < 0.926$	$a_4 > 1.246$
0.3	$a_1 > 0.042$	$0.750 < a_2 < 3.216$	n.r.	n.r.
0.5	n.r.	$0.750 < a_2 < 7.313$	n.r.	n.r.
0.7	n.r.	$0.750 < a_2$	n.r.	n.r.
0.9	n.r.	$0.750 < a_2$	n.r.	n.r.

7. *A Closer Look at the* NCR *Regime*

It is of interest to analyse a situation where only country 1 pursues some active policies to achieve growth of output as given by an (ambitious) output target. This means that we now drop the assumption of symmetric behaviour of the two countries. Instead, we look at the case where country 1 and country 2 do not cooperate and where, furthermore, country 1 assumes (correctly) the behaviour of country 2 as being given and being static. We analyze this constellation only for the NCR regime, since it is the resulting dynamics hereby which is of interest. As in section 4 country 1 is now using government expenditure and the exchange rate as instrument variables (taking expectations about the future exchange rate by the private sector into account). The optimal setting of both policies is determined by the minimisation of the well known welfare loss function. Consequently, we cannot use the equivalent reaction functions (A.21) and (A.22) for the second country. Instead we analyze the following dynamical system [obtained by inserting (A.21) into (A.22) for λ_t and λ_{t-1}, inserting (A.22) in (A.19) and substituting for g_t from the above]:

$$\begin{bmatrix} g_t \\ e_t \\ e^e_{t+1,t} \end{bmatrix} = \begin{bmatrix} -c_7^d \mu \theta & -2c_5^d c_7^d \delta \theta & -2c_5^d \rho \varepsilon \theta \\ 0 & 0 & 1 \\ -c_7^d \mu \theta \omega & -2c_5^d c_7^d \delta \theta \omega & \beta^{-1}\gamma - 2c_5^d \rho \varepsilon \theta \omega \end{bmatrix} \begin{bmatrix} g_{t-1} \\ e_{t-1} \\ e_t \end{bmatrix}$$

$$+ \begin{bmatrix} \rho\delta^*\varepsilon\theta & c_7^d \delta\delta^*\theta & \psi \\ 0 & 0 & 0 \\ \rho\delta^*\varepsilon\theta\omega - \omega & 0 & 0 \end{bmatrix} \begin{bmatrix} g_t^* \\ g_{t-1}^* \\ x_t \end{bmatrix} \qquad \text{(A.30)}$$

with

$$\begin{aligned}
\delta &= c_4^d + c_1^a \\
\delta^* &= c_4^d - c_1^a \\
\varepsilon &= c_5^d c_6^d - \delta \\
\mu &= \delta^2 + 4d_2 \\
\theta &= [\rho(\delta\varepsilon - 4d_2)]^{-1} \\
\omega &= a_3 a_6 (a_2 a_6 - b_2)^{-1} \\
\psi &= 2\theta\{\rho c_5^d c_6^d (c_0^a - c_5^d \bar{y}) - (\rho - c_7^d)\,[\delta(c_0^a - \bar{y}) + 2d_2\, g]\}
\end{aligned}$$

To simplify the analysis we use the parametric values from section 5. In addition, we set $g_t^* = g_{t-1}^* = 0$ (i.e. government expenditure in country 2 remains on a constant level) and x_t, the dummy variable, is equal to one. (A.30) then reads

$$\begin{bmatrix} g_t \\ e_t \\ e^e_{t+1,t} \end{bmatrix} = \begin{bmatrix} 0.148 & 0.797 & -3.630 \\ 0 & 0 & 1 \\ 0.592 & 3.189 & 25.360 \end{bmatrix} \begin{bmatrix} g_{t-1} \\ e_{t-1} \\ e_t \end{bmatrix} + \begin{bmatrix} 0.744 \\ 0 \\ 0 \end{bmatrix}$$

or, for short

$$\begin{bmatrix} \underline{z}_{t+1} \\ \underline{x}^e_{t+1,t} \end{bmatrix} = A \begin{bmatrix} \underline{z}_t \\ \underline{x}_t \end{bmatrix} + \underline{u}^t \tag{A.31}$$

where $\underline{z}_{t+1} = [g_t\ e_t]'$; $\underline{z}_t = [g_{t-1}\ e_{t-1}]'$; $\underline{x}^e_{t+1,t} = [e_{t+1,t}]'$

and $\underline{x}_t = [e_t]'$.

The matrix A has eigenvalues $\lambda_1 = 0.107$; $\lambda_2 = 0.000$ and $\lambda_3 = 25.481$, two of which lie inside the unit circle whereas one lies outside the unit circle. Thus the condition for stability as introduced in Blanchard and Kahn (1980) is satisified, which we already know from section 5. We use the solution procedure for linear, rational expectation models, formulated in discrete time, as set out by Currie and Levine (1982). The general solution for $\underline{x}_t$ and $\underline{z}_{t+1}$ is then given by

$$\underline{x}_t = -M_{22}^{-1} M_{21} \underline{z}_t - M_{22}^{-1} \Lambda_2^{-1} [0 \;\vdots\; M_{22}]\, \underline{u}_t \tag{A.32}$$

$$\underline{z}_{t+1} = (A_{11} - A_{12} M_{22}^{-1} \mathrm{M}_{21}) \underline{z}_t + [I_{11} \;\vdots\; -A_{12} M_{22}^{-1} \Lambda_2^{-1} M_{22}]\, \underline{u}_t \tag{A.33}$$

where A is the matrix given in (A.31), Λ is the matrix of eigenvalues, I is the identity matrix and M is the matrix of the following (row) eigensectors to Λ:

$$M = \begin{bmatrix} 0.183 & 0.983 & -0.013 \\ 0.100 & 0.995 & -0.025 \\ 0.023 & 0.125 & 0.992 \end{bmatrix}; \quad MA = \Lambda M \tag{A.34}$$

Matrices are partitioned conformably as denoted by the subscripts. These submatrices are furthermore assumed to be non-singular. Inserting the parameter values gives as solution

$$g_t = 0.232\, g_{t-1} + 1.254\, e_{t-1} + 0.744 \tag{A.35}$$

$$e_t = -\, 0.023\, g_{t-1} - 0.126\, e_{t-1} \tag{A.36}$$

We may construct an example of instability for the NCR case by choosing $\rho = 0.1$. Recall that for the numerical example in section 5 the governments must discount future welfare losses at a rate greater than 0.1063 in order to guarantee stability. The other parameters are assumed to remain the same. The stability condition (A.27) clearly does not hold, in fact $B/C = 1.063 > 1$. Instead of obtaining the solution for g_t^a given in (A.26) we have (eg. (A.25)):

$$g_t^a = 1.063\, g_{t-1}^a + 0.0325 \tag{A.37}$$

Table 3 gives the trajectory for time periods 0 to 10 if it is assumed that the government incorrectly perceives it has reputation. Thus it assumes acting according to the NCNR regime, setting g_t^a initially at -3.25% (the optimal value), whereas it is the NCR regime which prevails. Since the system is unstable the welfare losses tend to infinity.

8. *Reneging*

In section V we have defined a reneging strategy $\hat{W}$ as follows:

$$\hat{W} = W_R - W_C - \sum_{i=1}^{n} \rho^i (W_{NR} - W_R)$$

$$= W_R - W_C - \left(\frac{(1-\rho^n}{1-\rho}\right)(W_{NR} - W_R) \tag{A.38}$$

which we require to be negative for the reputational policy to be sustainable.

TABLE 3

(All figures in %)

t	g_t^a	y_t^a	r_t^a	π_t
0	—3.25	+2.17	—4.33	0
1	—0.20	+0.13	—0.27	0
2	+3.04	—2.03	+4.05	0
3	+6.48	—4.32	+8.64	0
4	+10.14	—6.76	+13.52	0
5	+14.03	—9.35	+18.71	0
6	+18.16	—12.11	+24.21	0
7	+22.56	—15.04	+30.08	0
8	+27.23	—18.15	+36.31	0
9	+32.19	—21.46	+42.92	0
10	+37.47	—24.98	+49.96	0

W_R is the welfare loss under the reputational regime (either with cooperation or without cooperation). W_C is the welfare loss if the government cheats which we assume it can do for just one period. After that period the private sector will form its expectations in accordance with a non-reputational government. We calculate W_C by assuming that the government is succesfull in springing of a monetary surprise which leads to a higher output than that which would have prevailed under a non-surprise reputational regime. In effect, we calculate W_C by substituting $y_t^{a,NR}$ into W_R. Since $y_t^{a,NR}$, $y_t^{a,R}$ the difference between W_R and W_C is positive. This difference in welfare losses can be referred to as the gains from cheating. The loss resulting from this policy is the discounted sum of the welfare loss differences between W_{NR} which now prevails for n periods (because the private sector mistrusts any future commitment of the government) and W_R, the (lower) welfare loss of what could have been achieved if cheating would not have taken place. We thus require these losses to be greater than the gains if reputation is sustainable.

We shall calculate $\hat{W}$ for both the cooperative and the non-cooperative regime, but only for $d_1(^1) = 0.5$. Substituting the respective values from Table 1 into (A.38) we get for the cooperative regime

$$0.9^n < 0.905 \tag{A.39}$$

whereas for the non-cooperative regime (A.38) reduces to

$$0.9^n < 0.948 \tag{A.40}$$

Our numerical example speaks very much in favour of reputation. For every n (n being an integer) greater than zero, reputation is sustainable. Only for $n = 0$ (note that in this case (A.38) reduces to $W_R - W_C > 0$) should the government cheat. This latter result makes sense since the government should indeed try to renege if it faces a public which is either completely ignorant or extremely forgiving with regard to broken commitments of the government.

It is of course of interest to have a more general relationship between ρ, the discount factor, and n, the punishment period. For the cooperative and the non-cooperative regimes these conditions can be given as

$$n > \frac{\ln(1.846\,\rho - 0.846)}{\ln \rho} - 1 \tag{A.41}$$

$$n > \frac{\ln(1.465\,\rho - 0.465)}{\ln \rho} - 1 \tag{A.42}$$

Table 4 states the minimum value for ρ which guarantees sustainability of the reputational policy for various punishment periods n.

TABLE 4

	ρ_C	ρ_{CN}
$n = 1$	0.85	0.47
$n = 2$	0.54	0.35
$n = 3$	0.49	0.33
$n = \infty$	0.46	0.32

REFERENCES

Barro, R. and Gordon, D. (1983) 'Rules, Discretion and Reputation in a Model of Monetary Policy', *Journal of Monetary Economics* 12 : 101-122.

Blanchard, O. and Kahn, C. (1980) 'The Solution of Linear Models Under Rational Expectations', *Econometrica* 48 : 1305-1311.

Cohen, D. and Michel, P. (1985) 'Dynamic Consistency of Government's Behaviour : A Users Guide', CEPREMAP (mimeo).

Currie, D. and Levine, P. (1982) 'A Solution Technique for Discrete and Continuous Time Stochastic Dynamic Models Under Rational Expectations with Full and Partial Information Sets', Programme of Research into Small Macromodels, Queen Mary College (mimeo).

—— (1987) 'Credibility and Time Inconsistency in a Stochastic World', *Journal of Economics* 47 : 225-252.

Currie, D., Levine, P. and Vidalis, N. (1988) 'International Cooperation and Reputation in an Empirical Two-Bloc Model', in R. Bryart and R. Portes (eds.), *Global Macroeconomic Policy Conflict and Cooperation*, (London : Macmillan Press).

Hamada, K. (1985) *The Political Economy of International Monetary Interdependence*, (Cambridge : MIT Press).

Miller, M. and Salmon, M. (1985) 'Policy Coordination and Dynamic Games', in W. H. Buiter and R. C. Marston (eds.), *International Economic Policy Coordination*, (Cambridge : Cambridge University Press).

Oudiz, G. and Sachs, J. (1985) 'International Policy Coordination in Dynamic Macroeconomic Models', in W. H. Buiter and R. C. Marston (eds.), *International Economic Policy Coordination*, (Cambridge : Cambridge University Press).

Rogoff, K. (1985) 'Can International Monetary Cooperation be Counterproductive?', *Journal of International Economics* 18 : 199-217.

INTERNATIONAL INTERDEPENDENCE AND POLICY COORDINATION IN ECONOMIES WITH REAL AND NOMINAL WAGE RIGIDITY

By Frederick van der Ploeg*

I. INTRODUCTION

Most of the policy debate about the performance of the OECD economies in the eighties seems to be concerned with the relative tightness of Europe's fiscal policy and the relative looseness of US fiscal policy. Many commentators have urged Europe to engage in a fiscal expansion and the US to engage in a fiscal contraction (e.g., Layard et al., 1984),[1] but neither of the governments on the two sides of the Atlantic have been particularly keen to implement these recommendations. The main objectives of this paper are to understand these suggestions for economic policy, to understand why the European governments and the US government have no apparent desire to implement them, and in particular to understand why recovery in Europe seems so hard. The framework that be will used is a two-country model with asymmetries in aggregate supply, i.e., nominal wage rigidity in the US and real wage rigidity in Europe (cf., Branson and Rotemberg, 1980), and then elementary differential game theory is used to assess the potential merits of international policy coordination. Before these particular issues are addressed, it is useful to review the assumptions underlying the standard Mundell-Fleming models and the consequent effects of fiscal and monetary policy on output and employment.

In the traditional one-country Mundell-Fleming world with floating exchange rates and perfect capital mobility a monetary expansion is doubly

* Financial support from the Economic and Social Research Council, the Ford Foundation, the Alfred P. Sloan Foundation and the Centre for Economic Policy Research is gratefully acknowledged. The author is grateful to Stewart Robertson for the preparation of the graphs of the main economic indicators for the seven largest OECD economies.

1. "There is world-wide agreement, it seems, that the prospective US long-run deficits are harmful to the world economy. It is also the case, less generally agreed, that European recovery is too slow and too precarious. The natural conclusion is some intertemporal trade : more rapid European recovery through fiscal stimulus traded off for reduced long-run US deficits" (Layard et al., 1984, p. 63).

powerful, because the incipient capital outflows (induced by the downward pressure on interest rates) are choked off by a depreciation of the exchange rate and this results in a further increase is aggregate demand. A fiscal expansion leads to incipient capital inflows, which are choked off by an appreciation of the exchange rate. The contraction in net exports completely crowds out the increase in government spending, so that a fiscal expansion has no effects on output. The Mundell-Fleming model of a small open economy assumes fixed prices of goods and labour and only considers aggregate demand; it also ignores expectational dynamics. A more fully specified model also considers aggregate supply. The Mundell-Fleming model assumes nominal wage rigidity, but the policy results are reversed when there is real wage rigidity. In that case a monetary expansion has no real effects and simply leads to a one-for-one increase in prices and wages, so that a fully indexed economy is insulated from monetary shocks. However, a fiscal expansion leads to an appreciation of the real exchange rate and therefore to a reduction in the wedge between the producers' and consumers' wage. This leads to an increase in output and employment (Casas, 1975; Argy and Salop, 1977; Sachs, 1980, van de Klundert and van der Ploeg, 1989). Hence, the qualitative conclusions on the effectiveness of monetary and fiscal policies are not robust to the degree of real or nominal wage rigidity. However, employers' subsidies or cuts in employers' taxes increases output and employment in a small open economy irrespective of whether nominal or real wages are rigid (Argy and Salop, 1977). In the first case, the cut in employers' taxes reduces the price level, increases the real money supply and therefore increases aggregate demand. In the second case, the wedge between the producers' and consumers' wage is reduced and therefore aggregate supply is increased.

In the two-country Mundell-Fleming world a home monetary expansion increases net exports of the home country, so that home output increases and foreign output decreases. In other words, monetary expansion is a beggar-thy-neighbour policy. Similarly, fiscal expansion is a locomotive policy. The nature of these spill-over effects depend on the assumption of nominal wage rigidity in both countries. When both countries have real wage rigidity, monetary expansion has no real effects whilst fiscal expansion is a beggar-thy-neighbour policy (as the associated appreciation of the real exchange rate increases the foreign wedge). More interestingly, when Europe has real wage rigidity and the US has nominal wage rigidity, a European fiscal expansion and a US monetary expansion are locomotive policies whilst a US fiscal expansion is, typically, a beggar-thy-neighbour policy (e.g., Argy and Salop, 1983).[2] This

2. Similar results for the effectiveness of fiscal and monetary policy in two-country models with nominal and real wage rigidity are discussed in Oudiz and Sachs (1984).

implies that, in the absence of international policy coordination, the European fiscal stance is too tight from the US point of view and too loose from the European point of view whilst US fiscal policy is, typically, too loose (see Section 6). Some German commentators might have a world with the "law of one price" (purchasing power parity) in mind, because they argue that (European) fiscal policy has no real effects whatsoever (as it cannot affect the wedge) and therefore should be set at a level consistent with no inflation. Such an asymmetric two-country model allows one, as has been pointed out by Branson and Rotemberg (1980) before, to understand the recent suggestions for international policy coordination and at the same time to understand why recovery in Europe is so hard.

Simple differential game theory is usually used to assess the merits of international policy coordination (see Hamada (1985) for the pioneering work in this area). For example, Miller and Salmon (1985), Currie and Levine (1985), and Oudiz and Sachs (1985) use symmetric two-country real-exchange-rate overshooting models with nominal wage rigidity and the natural rate hypothesis to investigate the gains from coordination in the transient phase when countries are involved in monetary disinflation. Since reductions in monetary growth in such models are a beggar-thy-neighbour policy, the non-cooperative Nash equilibrium solution gives rise to excessively fast disinflation relative to the cooperative solution. These results assume that the Central Banks can pre-commit themselves, but when they cannot international policy coordination may be counter-productive (Rogoff, 1985; van der Ploeg, 1988). The point is that, in the absence of coordination, a surprise increase in monetary growth induces a depreciation of the exchange rate and leads to inflation costs whilst, in the presence of coordination, such a disincentive does not exist, hence coordination exacerbates the credibility problems and becomes counter-productive. It is also possible that coordination between two countries (say, France and Germany) is counter-productive, because it may provoke an adverse response from a third country (say the US) (e.g., Canzoneri and Henderson, 1986). Interesting empirical work in this area has only just started (e.g., Oudiz and Sachs, 1984; McKibbin and Sachs, 1986). The present paper builds on this work and attempts to assess the merits of coordination of fiscal and supply-side as well as monetary policies in two-country models with real as well as nominal wage rigidity.

The four main objectives of this paper are : (i) to provide new empirical evidence on real and nominal wage rigidity in the OECD economies; (ii) to develop a convenient diagrammatic exposition that can be used for teaching purposes to analyse the spill-over effects of fiscal, monetary and supply-side policies in a two-country model with floating exchange rates, perfect capital mobility and real/or nominal wage rigidity; (iii) to analyse, with the aid of simple game theory, the nature of the bias in economic policies arising from the lack of international policy coordination; and (iv) to analyse the effects of an oil shock in a two-country model with real wage rigidity at home and nominal wage rigidity abroad.

Section 2 examines the development of unemployment, inflation, competitiveness, interest rates, monetary policy, fiscal stance and supply-side policies in the seven largest OECD economies during the seventies and eighties. Section 2 also estimates annual wage equations, of the error-correction type, for these economies and tests which economies have a significant degree of nominal wage rigidity in the short run. It turns out that Canada, the UK and the US show evidence of nominal wage rigidity, but that France, Germany, Italy and Japan have real wage rigidity. Section 3 then sets up an analytical two-country model with floating exchange rates, uncovered interest parity, imperfect substitution between home and foreign goods, and sluggish labour markets. For each country two extreme cases of nominal and real wage rigidity can be considered, that is either growth in nominal wages is given by monetary growth or the real consumers' wage is constant. It follows that the only dynamics in this model then arises from the perfect-foresight dynamics of the real exchange rate, so that for unanticipated permanent shocks the transition to the new equilibrium is instantaneous. Section 4 considers a world with nominal wage rigidity at home and abroad, which is closest to the conventional Mundell-Fleming world, and develops a convenient diagrammatic apparatus to analyse the spill-over effects of various economic policies. It is shown that an expansion in monetary growth and a cut in taxes are beggar-thy-neighbour policies as they lead to a fall in the world real interest rate, an excess demand for foreign money, a downward pressure on the foreign price level, and therefore an increase in the foreign real wage and fall in foreign output. Fiscal expansion is a locomotive policy. Section 4 also assesses the merits of international policy coordination with the aid of discounted social welfare loss functions that depend on output and inflation in the consumers' price index. In the absence of international policy coordination, optimal monetary growth is too high and time-inconsistent. Section 5 considers a world with real wage rigidity at home and abroad. Now monetary growth has no real effects, fiscal expansion is a beggar-thy-neighbour policy (as the associated appreciation of the real exchange rate increases the wedge between the foreign producers' and consumers' wage), and supply-side improvements are a locomotive policy (as they lead to a depreciation of the real exchange rate and therefore to a fall in the foreign wedge). Section 5 also employs discounted social welfare loss functions, that depend on output and the public deficit, to show that in the absense of coordination fiscal policy is too loose and time-inconsistent. It also contains a brief discussion on the optimal coordination of monetary growth rates in a world with pegged exchange rates. Section 6 considers an asymmetric world with real wage rigidity at home (Europe and Japan) and nominal wage rigidity abroad (Canada and US). Now a European fiscal expansion, an increase in US monetary growth and a US tax cut are locomotive policies whilst a European tax cut and, typically, a US fiscal expansion are beggar-thy-neighbour policies. Oil price shocks typically hit European output and employment much harder than US output and employment. It follows that, in the absence of international coordination and in the aftermath of the OPEC oil shocks, the European fiscal stance is too tight from the US point of view and too loose from the European point of view whilst the US fiscal stance is, typically, too loose, and the US monetary growth rate is too low. Section 7 concludes the paper.

II. THE MAIN OECD ECONOMIES

II.1 *Economic Developments in the Seventies and Eighties*

Graph 1 shows the standardised unemployment rates for the economies of the Group of Seven during the period 1970-1984. In all economies, except the US, there has been a steady rise in the unemployment rate since 1970. The rise in the unemployment rate has been particularly dramatic for the European economies. For example, for the UK it has risen from 3 per cent in 1970 to 13.2 per cent in 1985, for Italy from 5.3 per cent to 10.5 per cent, for Germany from 0.8 per cent to 10.6 per cent and for France from 2.4 per cent to 10.1 per cent. It is well known that the rise in European unemployment is mainly due to the failure to create sufficient jobs rather than due to increases in the labour force or other demographic factors (e.g., Newell and Symons, 1987). The US economy seems to have adjusted much better to the OPEC shocks of 1973 and 1979 than the other economies, since its unemployment rate has risen from 4.8 per cent in 1970 to a peak of 8.3 per cent in 1975 and another peak of 9.5 per cent in 1982/83 and has fallen to 7.1 per cent in 1985. The recessions in the US seem to be shorter and deeper than elsewhere, which may be due to the US adjusting employment more rapidly than the wage. In contrast to the US economy, the Canadian economy has seen its unemployment rate rise fairly steadily from 5.6 per cent in 1970 to 10.4 per cent in 1985. The Japanese economy has very low unemployment rates and has seen a modest increase from 1.1 per cent in 1970 to 2.6 per cent in 1985, but these figures are probably an under-estimate (Hamada and Kurosaka, 1986). Graph 2

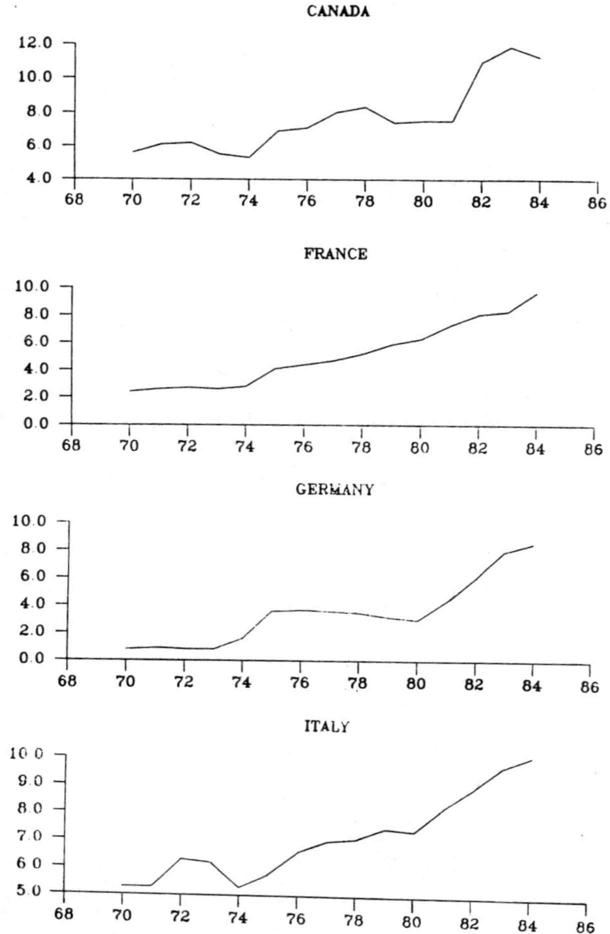

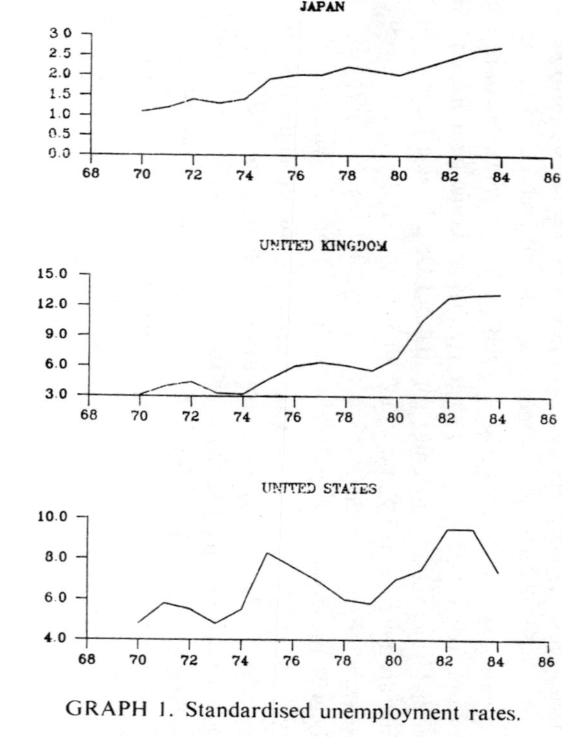

GRAPH 1. Standardised unemployment rates.

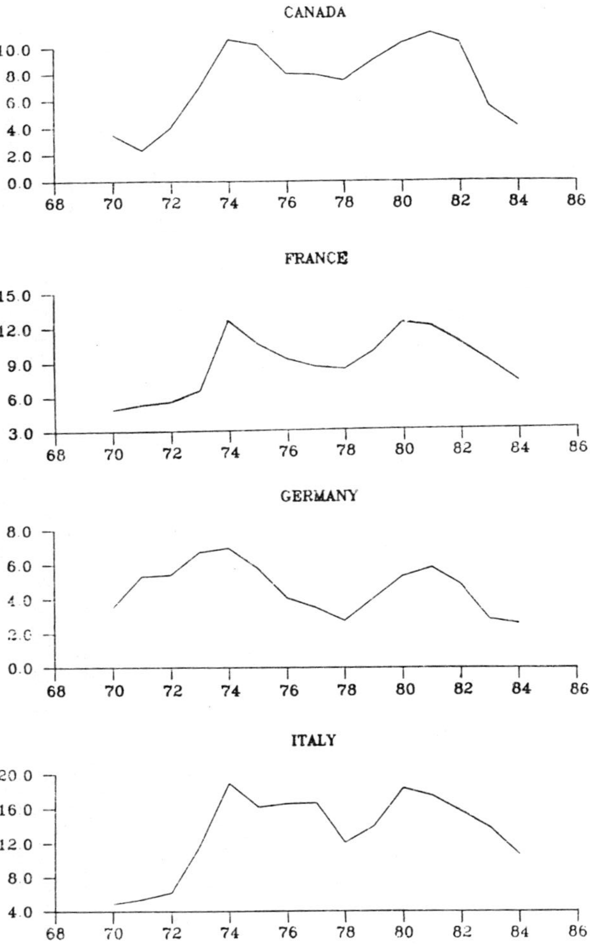

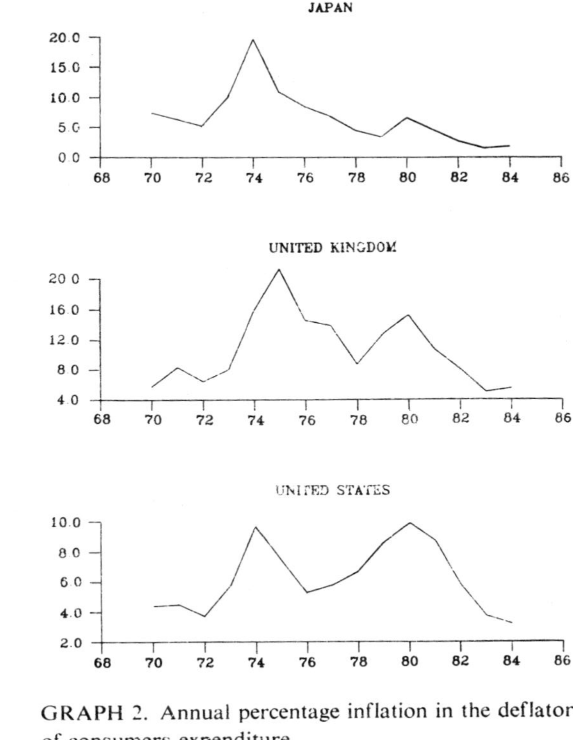

GRAPH 2. Annual percentage inflation in the deflator of consumers expenditure.

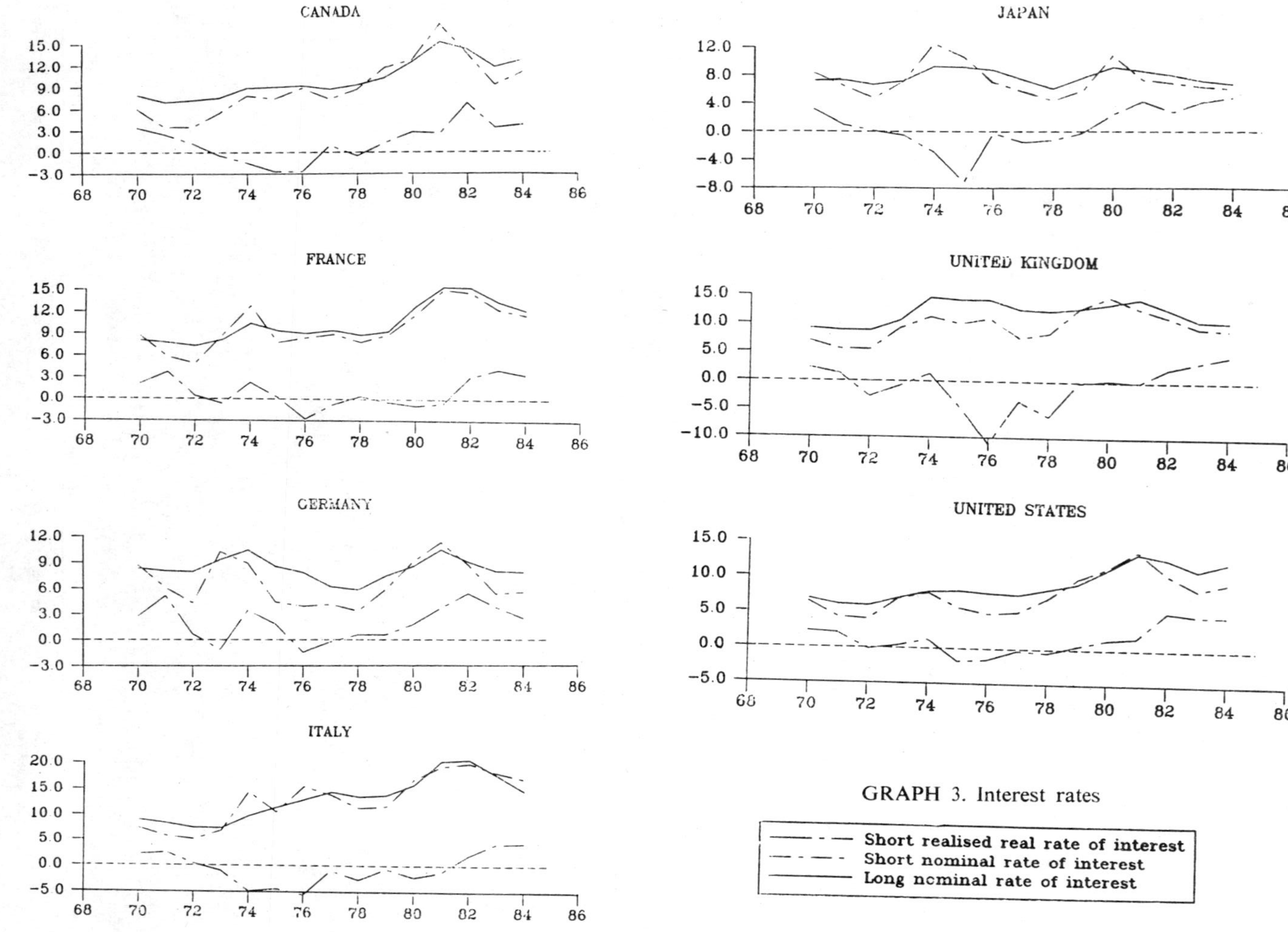

GRAPH 3. Interest rates

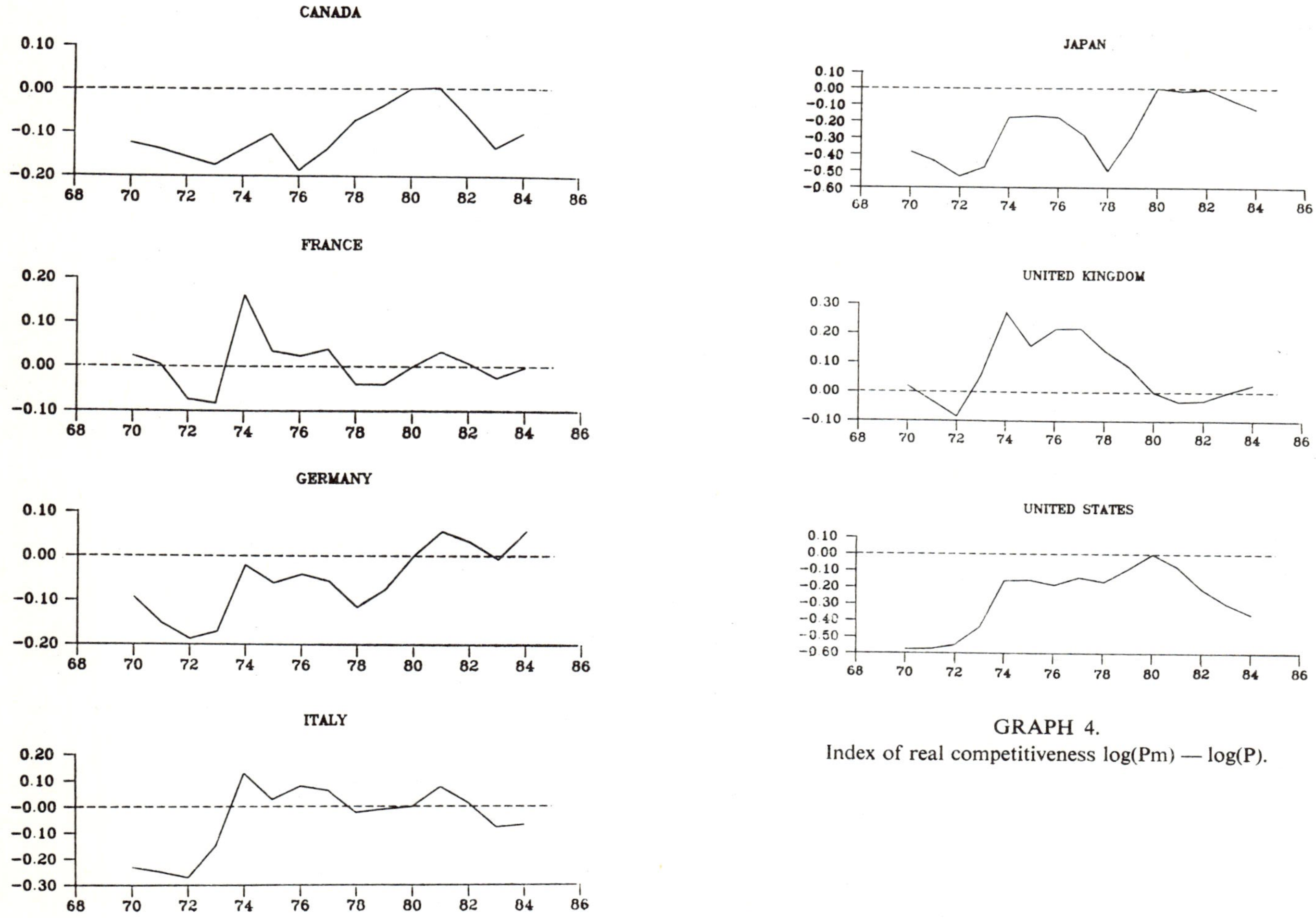

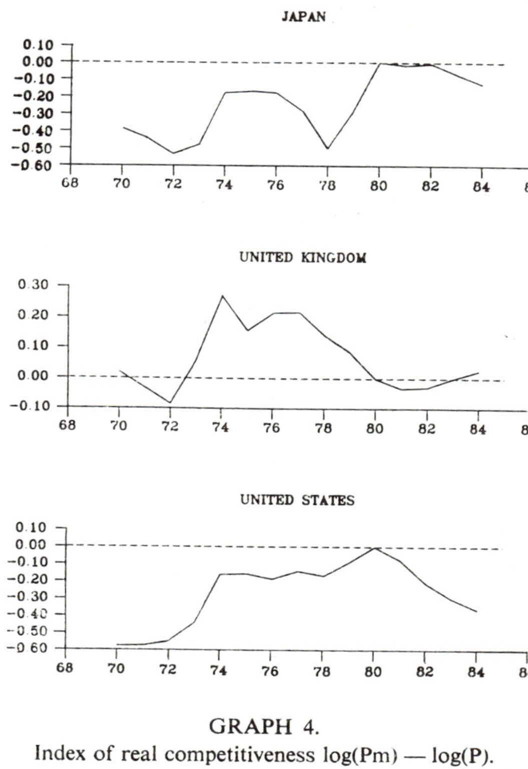

GRAPH 4.
Index of real competitiveness log(Pm) — log(P).

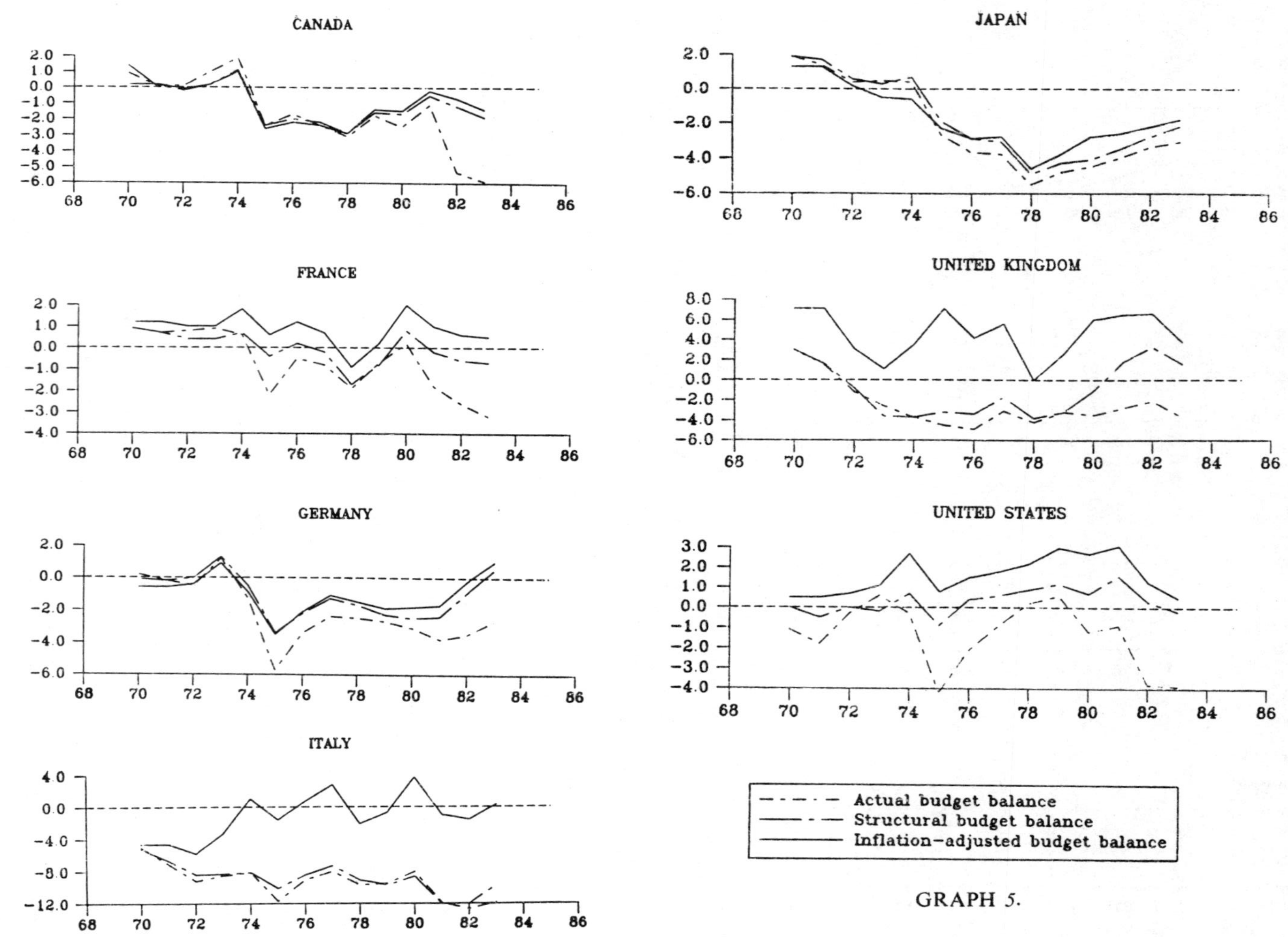
CANADA
FRANCE
GERMANY
ITALY
JAPAN
UNITED KINGDOM
UNITED STATES
Actual budget balance
Structural budget balance
Inflation-adjusted budget balance

GRAPH 5.

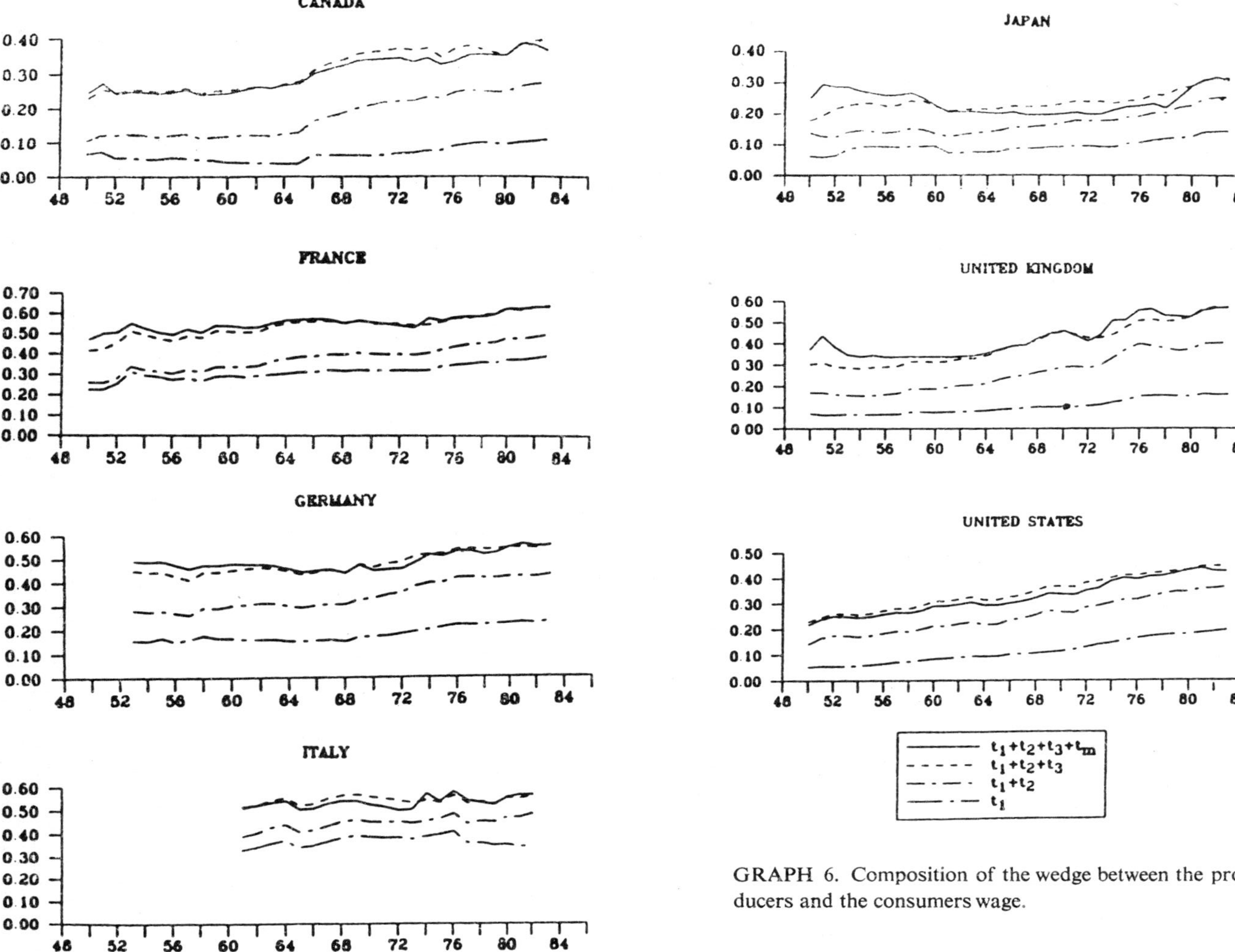

GRAPH 6. Composition of the wedge between the producers and the consumers wage.

shows the annual percentage inflation in the deflators of consumers' expenditures. Apart from Germany, the European economies have relatively high inflation rates. For all countries there are peaks in the inflation rates around 1974 and 1980 which are related to the two OPEC shocks in oil prices, and subsequently there are steady falls in inflation rates, which are related to the tightening of monetary policy in the Group of Seven during the 1980s. Graph 3 shows various interest rates. Most of the economies of the Group of Seven have very low (even negative) realised real interest rates during the 1970s and quite a large rise in real interest rates during the 1980s, which again is a result of the tightening of monetary policy in the 1980s. Graph 4 shows the indices of real competitiveness. The US (and to a lesser extent Canada) experienced a gradual increase in the real price of imports, associated with an increase in raw material prices and depreciation of the US real exchange rate, until 1980 and subsequently a gradual fall in the real price of imports, associated with appreciation of the US real exchange rate. The UK has experienced appreciation of its real exchange rate since 1974, which may be due to the advent of North Sea oil and later on due to the Thatcher experiment. However, since 1981 this trend in the UK has been reversed. Europe as a whole has seen a loss of competitiveness up to 1980, with a gain since then.

Graph 5 shows various government budget surpluses. Even when one corrects for the business cycle and for inflation, the US, Canada and France have loosened their fiscal stance whilst Germany, Italy, the UK and especially Japan have tightened their fiscal stance during the 1980s. Hence Europe (ignoring the Mitterrand experiment in France) and Japan have recently tightened their fiscal stance whilst the US and Canada have loosened their fiscal stance. One of the main objectives of this paper is to explain these differences in fiscal stance (see Section 6). It will be argued that a European or Japanese fiscal expansion is a locomotive policy, so that in the absence of coordination their fiscal expansion is too tight from the US point of view. However, a US or Canadian fiscal expansion is, typically, a beggar-thy-neighbour policy and therefore their fiscal stance is, typically, too loose. This insight helps to understand why during the 1980s European unemployment has risen so much, world interest rates have risen, and the European (US) real exchange rate has depreciated (appreciated) (see Graphs 1, 3, 4 and 5). Graph 6 shows the composition of the wedge between the producers' wage and the consumers' wage. The wedge is the sum of the employers' tax rate (τ_1), the employees' tax rate (τ_2), the indirect tax rate (τ_3), and the share of imports in total expenditures times the wedge between the import price and the output price (τ_m). The wedge is one of the indicators of supply-side policy. In most countries the wedge has risen steadily throughout the post-war period. For the US the wedge has increased from 24.8 per cent in 1953 to 42.2 per cent in 1983, for Canada from 24.7 per cent to 36.6 per cent, for France from 54.9 per cent to 63.6 per cent, for Germany from 48.9 per cent to 55.1 per cent, and for the UK from 34.6 per cent to 57.0 per cent. Hence, the rise in the wedge has been particularly spectacular for the UK and the US. For Italy the rise in the wedge has been modest, from 51.4 per cent in 1961 to 56.5 per cent in 1983. The trend increase in the wedge is due to the steadily rising burden of taxation in the OECD economies, which no doubt has had an adverse effect on the NAIRU's of these economies. However, fluctuations of the wedge around trend have been mainly due to fluctuations in the import price wedge and the real exchange rate (also see Graph 4). For example, during the eighties, the tightening of the European fiscal stance and the loosening of the US fiscal stance might have contributed to the depreciation of the European real exchange and consequently to the increase in the European wedge, the worsening of European supply and the increase in the European unemployment rate (see Graphs 1, 4, 5 and 6 and the discussion in Section 6).

II.2 *Empirical Evidence for Real and Nominal Wage Rigidity*[3]

It has been argued that the US economy has stickiness of nominal wages (money illusion) and that the European and Japanese economies have real wage rigidity (Branson and Rotemberg, 1980; and Bruno and Sachs, 1985). This section employs annual, time-series data for the 7 largest economies of the OECD to test whether the above hypothesis is valid. The sample period is 1955-83, except for Italy and Japan for which it is 1962-83. The following regression model has been estimated for each of these countries (see Attanasio, Manasse and van der Ploeg, 1987) :

$$\Delta w = \alpha_0 + \alpha_1 \Delta p_c + (1 - \alpha_1)\Delta w_{-1} - \alpha_2 u - \alpha_3 \Delta u + \alpha_4 PROD + \alpha_5 NC - \alpha_6 (w - \tau_2 - p_c) + \varepsilon, \tag{2.1}$$

where w, p_c, τ_2, u, $PROD$, NC and ε denote the logarithm of the nominal wage, the logarithm of the consumers' price index, the employees' (direct) tax rate, the unemployment rate (except for Japan for which it is the ratio of jobs wanted to jobs offered), the trend (three-year moving average) of the logarithm

3. The regression results in this Section have been obtained by Orazio Attanasio and are part of the London School of Economics Econometric Model of the Group of Seven (Attanasio, Manasse and van der Ploeg, 1987).

of the output-employment ratio, a measure of industrial conflicts (except for the UK for which it is an incomes policy dummy), and a white-noise error term, respectively.

Equation (2.1) is an error-correction mechanism (Sargan, 1964), which ensures that the (post-tax real) consumers' wage, $w - \tau_2 - p_c$, always returns to its long-run equilibrium value $(\alpha_0 - \alpha_1 \rho - \alpha_2 u + \alpha_4 PROD + \alpha_5 NC)/\alpha_6$ $(\alpha_6 > 0)$ where ρ denotes the feasible growth in real wages (trend growth in labour productivity). The long-run consumers' wage increases when the bargaining strength of workers or "wage push" increases, i.e., when unemployment falls $(\alpha_2 > 0)$ and labour productivity, increases $(\alpha_4 > 0)$, and when the firms' ability to pay, i.e., the feasible growth in real wages decreases $(\alpha_1 > 0)$. There may also be hysteresis effects (Blanchard and Summers, 1987), so that changes in (rather than the levels of) the unemployment rate determine the bargaining strength of workers $(\alpha_3 > 0)$. One reason for hysteresis is that the long-term unemployed do not actively seek for a job and therefore do not exercise a downward pressure on wages. An alternative explanation is based on an analysis of insiders versus outsiders.

To allow for some nominal inertia in the short run, the growth in nominal wages is assumed to depend on a weighted average of inflation in the consumers' price index and past growth in nominal wages $(0 < \alpha_1 \leqslant 1)$. When wages are instantaneously indexed to the consumers' price level $(\alpha_1 = 1)$, there is no nominal inertia or money illusion and therefore one has *real wage rigidity*. When there are lags in the process of wage indexation $(\alpha_1 < 1)$, one has *nominal wage rigidity*.[4] Note that the homogeneity of (2.1) ensures that in the long run, the growth in nominal wages is fully indexed to inflation in the consumers' price index and therefore in the long run real wage rigidity always prevails. An alternative interpretation is that core inflation influences wage inflation one-for-one and that core inflation equals current inflation in the consumers' price index under "rational expectations" (real wage rigidity) and is a weighted average of past rates of inflation in the consumers' price index under "adaptive expectations" (nominal wage rigidity). However, the interpretation of α_1 as an adjustment coefficient in the indexation process seems preferable.

Table 1 presents the regression results for Canada (CA), France (FR) Germany (GE), Italy (IT), Japan (JA), UK and US. All the equations appear, to be well determined, the reported diagnostics show no signs of misspecifi-

4. When lags in price formation are ignored, (α_1/α_3) is a measure of real wage rigidity and $(1-\alpha_1)/\alpha_3$ is a measure of nominal wage rigidity (see Grubb, Jackman and Layard, 1983, but strictly speaking these measures are derived for the case $\alpha_6 = 0$).

TABLE 1

Econometric Estimates of Wage Equations for the Main OECD Economies

Δw	CA	FR	GE	IT	JA	UK	US
Constant	–0.785	–0.569	–2.235	–1.310	–0.014	–0.810	–0.306
t-ratio	2.09	3.26	3.52	3.48	0.05	2.73	1.65
Δp_c^a	0.632	0.913	0.808	0.992	0.895	0.717	0.641
t-ratio	5.81	7.28	4.63	7.26	7.90	5.65	4.40
Δw_{-1}^a	0.368	0.087	0.192	0.008	0.105	0.283	0.359
t-ratio	3.38	0.69	1.10	0.06	0.93	2.23	2.47
u^b	–0.444	–0.164	–1.458	–1.367	–0.083	–0.350	
t-ratio	2.22	6.56	5.02	1.62	3.02	1.77	—
Δu	—	–1.750	—	—	—	—	–0.514
t-ratio		1.85					2.90
PROD	0.202	0.069	0.561	0.282	0.062	0.366	0.071
t-ratio	1.85	2.30	3.58	2.71	0.59	2.87	1.23
NC[c]	0.0084	0.035	—	0.0391	0.0082	–0.0796	0.0113
t-ratio	2.07	4.07		2.43	0.45	5.49	1.92
$w-\tau_2-p_c$	–0.200	–0.073	–0.565	–0.225	–0.087	–0.338	–0.130
t-ratio	1.88	1.56	3.83	2.79	0.78	2.72	1.62
Standard Error	0.0094	0.0112	0.0174	0.0256	0.0145	0.0163	0.0083
SARGAN[d]	9.97	11.23	10.54	8.25	8.37	6.79	11.41
d.f.	6	7	8	8	6	7	8
LM1[e]	0.27	0.11	0.03	1.07	1.14	1.16	0.49
HETERO[f]	7.26	0.09	0.01	0.16	0.14	0.45	1.29

Notes:

a) These coefficients have been restricted to add up to unity. The restrictions were not rejected at the 5 per cent significance level.

b) The unemployment rate statistics for JA are not a very good measure of labour market conditions (Hamada and Kurosaka, 1986), hence instead the series of the ratio of jobs wanted to jobs offered has been used.

c) For CA and IT, this is the logarithm of the number of days lost through strikes (lagged). For FR, this is the logarithm of the number of conflicts. For the US, this is the logarithm of the number of conflicts (lagged). For the UK, this is an incomes policy dummy for the years 1976-77.

d) Sargan's test for serial correlation of IV residuals (Breusch and Godfrey, 1981, Appendix B).

e) Test for residual serial correlation (Godfrey, 1987)

f) Test for homoskedasticity (White, 1980).

cation, and all coefficients are significant and of the right sign or insignificant at the 5 per cent level. The main point to notice is that the null hypothesis that there is real wage rigidity cannot be rejected at the 5 per cent significance level for FR, GE, IT and JA, because the coefficients on Δw_{-1} (i.e., $1 - \alpha_1$) are insignificantly different from zero. CA, the US and, to a lesser extent, the UK do have a significant degree of nominal inertia. Hence, the European economies (apart from the UK) and the Japanese economies can be characterised by real wage rigidity whilst the Canadian and US economies have a significant degree of nominal wage rigidity.

III. A TWO-COUNTRY WORLD WITH FLOATING EXCHANGE RATES AND UNCOVERED INTEREST PARITY

Consider a two-country world with floating exchange rates, highly integrated and efficient financial markets, and sluggish labour markets. The asset menu consists of home cash, home government bonds and foreign government bonds. There is imperfect substitution between home and foreign goods, but perfect substitution between home and foreign government bonds. Firms produce goods at home and can sell either at home or abroad. The goods and money markets clear instantaneously, but the labour market does not clear due to rigidity of either nominal wages or of real consumers' wages. Indexation of the wage rate to increases in the cost-of-living, arising from increases in consumers' prices or tax rates, is an important feature of the European and Japanese economies whilst nominal wage rigidity is an important feature of the US and Canadian economies (see Section 2). The government has three policy instruments at its disposal, viz. open-market operations (money supply), changes in public spending (fiscal shock) and various forms of supply-side policies (e.g., wage push or marginal tax rates). The residual mode of government finance is bond issues. The analysis abstracts from wealth effects, current-account dynamics, intertemporal government budget constraints and commercial banking systems.

The two-country model consists of the following equations:

$$y = -\bar{\sigma} r + \bar{\delta} c + \bar{f} + \gamma y^*, \qquad 0 \leq \gamma < 1 \tag{3.1}$$

$$y^* = -\bar{\sigma} r^* - \bar{\delta} c + \bar{f}^* + \gamma y \tag{3.2}$$

$$r \equiv i - E\dot{p}_c \tag{3.3}$$

$$r^* \equiv i^* - E\dot{p}_c^* \tag{3.4}$$

$$c \equiv p^* + e - p \tag{3.5}$$

$$m - p = \varphi y - \lambda i \tag{3.6}$$

$$m^* - p^* = \varphi y^* - \lambda i^* \tag{3.7}$$

$$i = i^* + \mathrm{E}\dot{e} \tag{3.8}$$

$$p_c = (1 - \alpha)p + \alpha(p^* + e) \tag{3.9}$$

$$p_c^* = (1 - \alpha)p^* + \alpha(p - e) \tag{3.10}$$

$$y = -\overline{\beta}_1[(w + \tau - p) + \overline{\beta}_2(p_n^* + c)] + \overline{\beta}_3 \tag{3.11}$$

$$y^* = -\overline{\beta}_1^* [(w^* + \tau^* - p^*) + \overline{\beta}_2 p_n^*] + \overline{\beta}_3^* \tag{3.12}$$

$$\dot{w} = \pi + ky \tag{3.13}$$

$$\dot{w}^* = \pi^* + ky^* \tag{3.14}$$

$$\dot{\pi} = \zeta(\dot{p}_c - \pi) \tag{3.15}$$

$$\dot{\pi}^* = \zeta(\dot{p}_e^* - \pi^*) \tag{3.16}$$

where y = real output
p = producers' price level
$\overline{f}$ = real fiscal shock (public deficit)
m = nominal money supply
i = nominal interest rate
r = real interest rate
e = nominal exchange rate
c = real exchange rate (relative price of foreign goods in terms of home goods)
w = nominal wage rate
p_c = consumers' price level
π = core rate of inflation in the cost-of-living index
τ = employers' tax (contributions) rate
p_n^* = real price of imported raw materials.

The variables r, i and τ are ratios expressed as arithmetic differences from their steady-state values. All other variables are expressed as logarithmic deviations from their steady-state values. Foreign variables are denoted by an asterisk.

Equations (3.9) - (3.10) give the cost-of-living indices as weighted averages of home and foreign prices. The share of imports in total expenditures is α, which is constant for Cobb-Douglas preferences. Equations (3.3) - (3.5) define the real rates of interest and the real exchange rate. Equation (3.8) is the uncovered interest parity condition, which says that the differential between the return on home and foreign government bonds must equal the expected depreciation of the exchange rate. It holds when there are no exchange controls and when agents engage in risk-neutral arbitrage. These equations yield

$$r - r^* = (1 - 2\alpha)\, E\dot{c}, \tag{3.17}$$

so that the differential in real interest rates is always zero when the share of foreign goods in total households' expenditures is 50 per cent. Equations (3.1) - (3.2) are the IS-curves, which say that aggregate demand for goods increases when the real interest rate or the relative price of home goods falls, when there is a fiscal expansion, and when there is an expansion of demand abroad. Upon substitution of (3.17) into (3.1) - (3.2), one obtains the *AD*-schedules :

$$y = -\,\sigma r + \delta c + f + \gamma f^* + \gamma \eta E\dot{c} \tag{3.18}$$

$$y^* = -\,\sigma r - \delta c + f^* + \gamma f + \eta E\dot{c} \tag{3.19}$$

where

$\sigma \equiv \bar{\sigma} / (1 - \gamma)$, $\delta \equiv \bar{\delta} / (1 + \gamma)$, $f \equiv \bar{f} / (1 - \gamma^2)$ and $\eta \equiv (1 - 2\alpha)\,\sigma / (1 - \gamma^2)$. Equations (3.6) - (3.7) are the *LM*-curves, which show that the demand for money increases with national income and decreases with the nominal interest rate.

Firms produce at home and sell in both the home and foreign markets. The market environment is one of monopolistic competition. Labour and imported raw materials are the factors of production. It is assumed that the price of the imported input, say oil, is indexed to the foreign (US) price level. This leads to an asymmetry in the specification of aggregate supply for Europe and the US (Canzoneri and Gray, 1985); a real appreciation of the European (home) currency decreases the relative price of raw materials to Europe and therefore increases European production of goods whilst US (foreign) output is unaffected. Obviously, an increase in the real producers' wage, $w + \tau - p$, leads to a reduction in the demand for labour and the supply of goods. The above ideas are captured in equations (3.11) - (3.12).[5] An interesting feature is that, as long as the price elasticities of the demand function for the products of an individual firm are constant, aggregate supply does not depend directly on the real exchange rate despite the fact that allowance has been made for imperfect competition on both the home and foreign markets. Branson and Rotemberg (1980) argue that the relevant producers' price is an average of the price they can fetch on the home market and the price they can fetch on the foreign market, but it is not clear how their model of discriminating monopolists can be consistent with this idea. This means that their argument that an appreciation of the real exchange rate increases the real producers' wage and cuts aggregate supply may not hold.

Equations (3.13) - (3.14) are the expectations-augmented Phillips curves.[6] Equations (3.15) - (3.16) show that the expected rates of inflation adjust gradually to the rates of inflation in the cost-of-living indices. Alternatively, one can interpret the parameters ζ and ζ^* as the speeds of indexation at home and abroad, respectively. The special case of real wage rigidity (*RWR*) corresponds to an infinite speed of indexation to increases in the cost of living. Section 2 showed that *RWR* cannot be rejected at the 5 per cent significance level for the French, German and Italian economies and that the UK economy is very close to *RWR*. The Canadian and US economies display nominal wage rigidity

5. Capital letters denote actual levels (rather than deviations). Firm i maximises its profits, $P_i Y_i - (1 + \tau) W L_i - P_n{}^* E P^* N_i$, subject to the demand function for its products, $Y_i = K(P_i/P) - \eta_1 (P_i/P^*E) - \eta_2$ where the constant K increases with aggregate output (Y) and the real exchange rate (P^*E/P) and the elasticities (η_i) are constant, and its production function, $Y = f(L_i, N_i)$ where $f(.)$ exhibits decreasing returns to scale (as there may be other factors, such as capital, that are fixed). The demand functions imply that each firm competes both with other home firms and with other foreign firms. Profit maximisation yields the conditions that the marginal revenue product of each factor should eaual the real factor price, that is $(1 - \eta^{-1}) f_{L_i}(L_i, N_i) = W(1 + \tau)/P_i$ and $(1 - \eta^{-1}) f_N(L_i, N_i) = P_n{}^* E P^*/P_i$ where $\eta \equiv \eta_1 + \eta_2$. Symmetry yields $P_i = P$. These two first-order conditions yield the optimal demand for labour and raw materials (and thus aggregate output) as functions of the real producers' wage, $W(1 + \tau)/P$, and the real cost of raw materials, $P_n{}^* C$. Obviously, the demand for each factor decreases with the price of the own factor price. When factors are cooperant ($f_{L_i N_i} > 0$), the output effect dominates the substitution effect and therefore the demand for labour (raw materials) decreases with the real price of raw materials (labour). Equations (3.11) — (3.12) follow from log-linearisation and are exact for Cobb-Douglas production functions. The strength of the effects of relative factor prices diminishes when the elasticity of substitution between labour, raw materials and other fixed factors is low.

6. The alternative of overlapping wage contracts (combined with price rigidity) embedded within a numerical two-country model is discussed in Attanasio and van der Ploeg (1988).

(NWR) since the hypothesis of RWR was rejected at the 5 per cent level for these economies. It therefore seems reasonable to distinguish three cases:

(i) $NWR - NWR^*$: $\zeta = \zeta^* = k = 0$, $\dot{w} = \dot{m}$, $\dot{w}^* = \dot{m}^*$, $\bar{\beta}_1 = \bar{\beta}_1^* \to \infty$, $\bar{\beta}_2 = 0$;

(ii) $RWR - RWR^*$: $\zeta = \zeta^* = \infty$, $k = 0$, $w = p_c$, $w^* = p_c^*$, $\bar{\beta}_1 = \bar{\beta}_1^*$, $\bar{\beta}_2 = 0$;

(iii) $RWR - NWR^*$: $\zeta = \infty$, $k = 0$, $w = p_c$, $\zeta^* = 0$, $w^* = \dot{m}^*$, $\bar{\beta}_1^* \to \infty$.

The effects of unemployment on growth in real wages is ignored. Case (i) corresponds most closely to the conventional Mundell-Fleming world and describes the interdependence between, say, the US and Canadian economies (see Section 4). Core inflation is simply equal to the long-run monetary growth rate. Case (ii) describes the interdependence between, say, the French and German economies (see Section 5).[7] Case (iii) allows for real wage rigidity at home and nominal wage rigidity abroad and describes the interactions between, say, the US and European economies (see Section 6).

IV. NOMINAL WAGE RIGIDITY AT HOME AND ABROAD: A MUNDELL - FLEMING WORLD

IV.1 *Spill-over Effects of Fiscal, Monetary and Supply-side Policies*

The case of nominal wage rigidity at home and abroad corresponds most closely to the standard Mundell-Flemming analysis. It is well known that in such a world monetary expansion is a beggar-thy-neighbour policy whilst fiscal expansion is a locomotive policy. The purpose of this section is to examine whether these results carry through when the conventional two-country analysis is extended to allow for aggregate supply and expectational dynamics (cf., Turnovsky, 1985), to analyse the nature of the spill-over effects of supply-side policy, and to develop a convenient diagrammatic exposition that can be used for teaching purposes.

The assumption of $\bar{\beta}_1 \to \infty$ makes matters simple, since the aggregate-supply schedule is replaced by the constant mark-up hypothesis, $p = w + \tau$.

7. Strictly speaking, this does not correspond to an economic model of the interdependence between the French and German economies as the salient features of the European Monetary System have been ignored. Managed intervention in the foreign exchange markets and restricted capital flows also are important in a two-country model of the French and German economies (e.g., Artis and Gazioglu, 1987).

Hence, the nominal interest rate is given by $i = r + \dot{m} + \dot{\tau} + aE\dot{c}$ as wage inflation under *NWR* is simply given by $\dot{w} = \dot{m}$. Upon substitution into (3.6), one obtains the reduced form *LM*-schedule,

$$y = [\lambda(r + \dot{m} + \dot{\tau} + aE\dot{c}) - \tau] / \varphi. \tag{4.1}$$

It slopes upwards in $r - y$ space (see Figure 1), because a higher interest rate chokes off money demand so that a higher level of national income is needed to restore equilibrium in the money market. In the general case (finite $\bar{\beta}_1$), the interpretation is as follows. A higher real interest rate leads to an excess supply of money and thus to a higher price level. This reduces the supply of goods, since workers are locked into nominal wage contracts. Equation (4.1) gives aggregate supply, which should match aggregate demand given by equation (3.18). The result is equilibrium in the goods market, which is captured by the GME-locus :

$$r = [f + \gamma f^* + \delta c + [(\gamma\eta) - (\lambda\alpha / \varphi)] E\dot{c} - (\lambda / \varphi)(\dot{m} + \check{\tau}) + (\tau / \varphi)] / [\sigma + (\lambda / \varphi)]. \tag{4.2}$$

Similarly, the *GME**-locus follows from equations (3.7) and (3.19) and is given by :

$$r = [f^* + \gamma f - \delta c + [\eta + (\lambda(1 - \alpha) / \varphi)] E\dot{c} - (\lambda / \varphi)(\dot{m}^* + \dot{\tau}^*) + (\tau^* / \varphi)] / [\sigma + (\lambda / \varphi)]. \tag{4.3}$$

The *GME*-locus slopes upwards in $r - c$ space (see Figure 1), because a higher interest rate increases the supply and reduces the demand for home goods and goods market equilibrium is then restored by an increase in net exports achieved by an increase in the relative price of foreign goods. Similarly, the *GME**-locus slopes downwards in $r - c$ space.

The equilibrium world interest rate follows from adding (4.2) and (4.3) :

$$r = {}^1/_2[(1 + \gamma)(f + f^* + \bar{\eta}E\dot{c}) - (\lambda / \varphi)(\dot{m} + \dot{m}^* + \dot{\tau} + \check{\tau}^*) + (\tau + \tau^*) / \varphi] / [\sigma + E\lambda / \varphi)] \tag{4.4}$$

where $\bar{\eta} \equiv (1 - 2\alpha)[\sigma(1 - \gamma)^{-1} + (\lambda/\varphi)](1 + \gamma)^{-1} \gtrless 0$. The steady-state world real interest rate decreases when budget deficits at home or abroad decrease, when monetary growth rates at home or abroad increase (the "Mundell effect"), and when reduction in tax rates boost the real supply of money balances.

Subtraction of (4.3) from (4.2) gives the following expression for the expectational dynamics of the real exchange rate:

$$E\dot{c} = [(1-\gamma)(f-f^*) - (\lambda/\varphi)(\dot{m} - \dot{m}^* + \dot{\tau} - \dot{\tau}^*) + \varphi^{-1}(\tau - \tau^*) + 2\delta c] / [(1-\gamma)\eta + (\lambda/\varphi)]. \tag{4.5}$$

The steady-state relative price of foreign goods increases when public deficits (or tax rates) abroad are higher than public deficits (or tax rates) at home, and when monetary growth exceeds foreign monetary growth. The real exchange rate jumps immediately to its new equilibrium value when shocks are permanent and unanticipated, but transient or anticipated shocks lead to expectational dynamics (see for example Figure 2(b) and the associated discussion in Section 5.1). Real liquidities, $m - w$ and $m^* - w^*$, are constant, due to the assumption of $\zeta = \zeta^* = k = 0$, and therefore the adjustment to permanent and unanticipated shocks is instantaneous. Previous studies (e.g., Turnovsky, 1985) allowed for an effect of unemployment on growth in nominal wages ($k \neq 0$), so that the steady-state level of output is always at its natural rate and unaffected by fiscal or monetary policy. This is not so in the present model, since it is concerned with the intermediate run.

The effects of an unanticipated, permanent increase in the home public deficit are presented in Figure 1(a). The resulting excess demand for home goods is choked off by an appreciation of the home real exchange rate and an increase in the world interest rate. The increase in the demand for foreign goods is due to the depreciation of the foreign real exchange rate, but despite

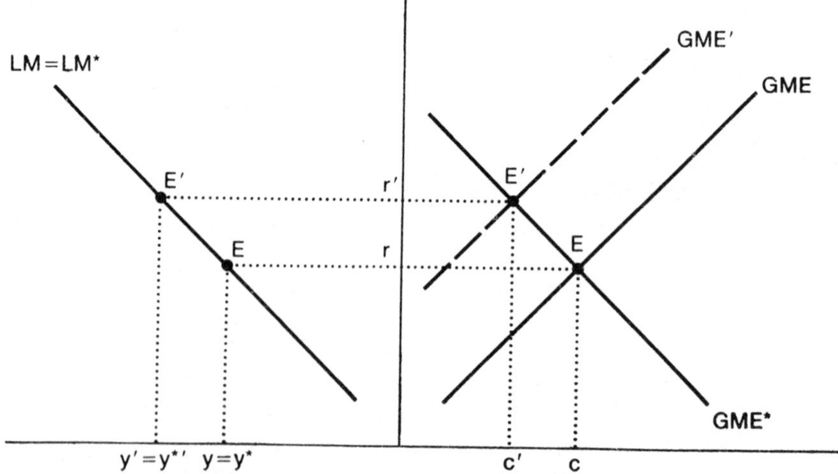

FIGURE 1(a). Wage Rigidity at Home and Abroad (Unanticipated increase in f)

the increase in the world interest rate. Supply at home and abroad increases, because the reduction in the demand for real cash balances boosts the price level and erodes the real value of the nominal wage. It follows that fiscal policy is a *locomotive* policy.

The effects of an unanticipated, permanent increase in the home monetary growth are presented if Figure 1(b). The expected inflation rate increases one-for-one, which reduces the world real interest rate ("Mundell effect") and therefore increases aggregate demand at home and abroad. The home nominal interest rate increases whilst the foreign nominal interest rate decreases, so that the demand for real money balances at home decreases, the home price level rises and home aggregate supply is boosted whilst foreign aggregate supply falls. The resulting excess demand for foreign goods is choked off by an increase in the relative price of foreign goods. Clearly, an expansion of monetary growth is a *beggar-thy-neighbour* policy. Figure 1(b) is also relevant

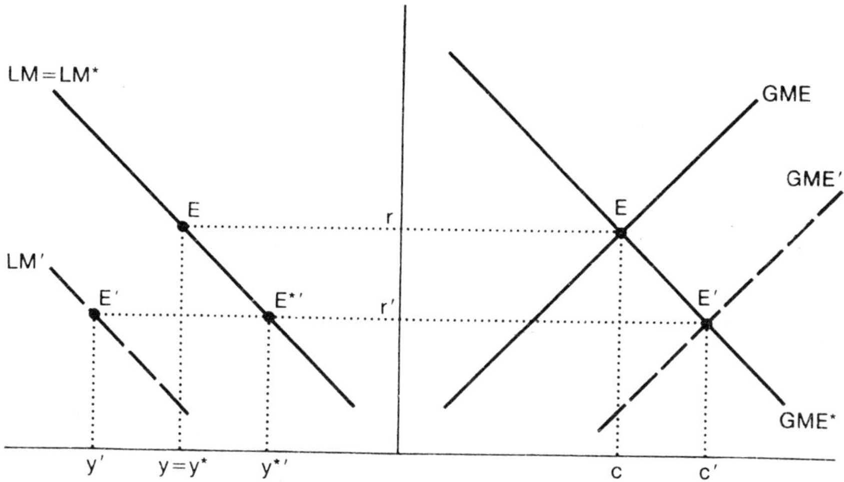

FIGURE 1(b). Nominal Wage Rigidity at Home and Abroad (Unanticipated increase in m or cut in τ)

for an unanticipated, permanent tax incentive, so that supply-side improvements also have negative spill-over effects in a *NWR* – *NWR** world. The reason is that a cut in the employers' tax rate, reduces the price level and boosts the real supply of money balances, which has the same effects as the cut in the real demand for money balances induced by an increase in monetary growth.

So far, it has been argued that, in a Mundell-Fleming world with nominal wage rigidity at home and abroad, monetary expansion is a beggar-thy-neighbour policy. However, some argue that monetary expansion is a locomotive policy (e.g., Minford, 1985). The reason for this is that in the former case one is concerned with a bond-financed monetary expansion, i.e., the government purchases bonds from the private sector, whilst in the latter case a monetary expansion is associated with a looser fiscal stance, i.e., lower taxes or higher government spending. If one ignores interest payments on the public debt, the government budget constraint for the latter case is given by $\log(\dot{m}) = f - (m - p)$ or, under NWR, by $\log(\dot{m}) = f + \tau$ so that a change in monetary growth leads to a change in fiscal change ($df = d\dot{m}/\dot{m}$). In empirical work the locomotive effects of the associated fiscal expansion seem to outweigh the beggar-thy-neighbour effects of the expansion in monetary growth (Minford, 1985).

A joint fiscal expansion shifts up both the GME- and the GME^*-locus, so pushes up the world real interest rate and leaves the real exchange rate unaffected. The resulting fall in the demand for real money balances in each country generates an expansion of employment and output throughout the world. A joint increase in monetary growth has no effect on the real exchange rate, but reduces the world real interest rate and increases nominal interest rates and global activity. A joint improvement in supply-side conditions has similar effects.

An anticipated, permanent increase in the home fiscal deficit leads to an immediate jump appreciation of the real exchange rate followed by further appreciations during the announcement period (see Figure 2(b)). At the time of implementation there is no jump in the real exchange rate, because the news has already been discounted in the financial markets. The result is that home output and employment fall on impact of the news and fall further during the announcement period, whilst foreign output and employment increase on impact and increase further during the announcement period. At the time of implementation, the real interest rate and home output jump up. Hence, an anticipated increase in home demand leads to a current recession at home and boom abroad.

IV.2 *International Coordination of Monetary Policies*

In a $NWR - NWR^*$ world, monetary growth, fiscal expansion and supply-side improvements are, respectively, a beggar-thy-neighbour, locomotive and beggar-thy-neighbour policy, so that in the absence of international policy coordination these policies are, respectively, too expansionary, too tight and too far-reaching. To illustrate these issues, this section concentrates on the determination of (bond-financed) monetary growth when the public deficit and supply-side policies are kept constant (say, $\tau = \tau^* = f = f^* = 0$). There is a recent literature on the international coordination of monetary policies (Miller and Salmon, 1985; Currie and Levine, 1985; Oudiz and Sachs, 1985; and Rogoff 1985), but this literature typically relies on numerical simulation to assess the potential merits of policy coordination. Also, it incorporates the natural rate hypothesis so that there is no long-run trade-off between inflation and output. The present analysis is for the intermediate run and does allow for such a trade-off. To keep matters simple, the share of imports in final expenditures is assumed to be 50 per cent ($\alpha = {}^1/_2$). In such a world $\dot{p} = \dot{w} = \dot{m}$,

$$\dot{p}_c = \dot{m} + {}^1/_2 E\dot{c} = {}^1/_2 (\dot{m} + \dot{m}^*) + (\delta\varphi/\lambda)c, \qquad (4.6)$$

$$r = r^* = -{}^1/_2 \lambda(\sigma\varphi + \lambda)^{-1} (\dot{m} + \dot{m}^*), \qquad (4.7)$$

$$y = \lambda\varphi^{-1}(r + \dot{m} + {}^1/_2 E\dot{c}) = \delta c + \varepsilon(\dot{m} + \dot{m}^*) \qquad (4.8)$$

and

$$E\dot{c} = \dot{m}^* - \dot{m} + (2\delta\varphi/\lambda)c, \quad \varepsilon \equiv {}^1/_2 \tau\lambda(\tau\varphi + \lambda)^{-1} > 0 \qquad (4.9)$$

where $\varepsilon = {}^1/_2\lambda(\sigma\varphi + \lambda)^{-1} > 0$. A joint increase in monetary growth increases world inflation one-for-one and expands global activity.

The policy dilemma of each government is that it wants a high monetary growth rate in order to achieve a high level of activity and that it wants a low monetary growth rate in order to achieve low inflation. For the home government, this is captured by the following social welfare problem :

$$\underset{\dot{m}}{\text{Min}}\ {}^1/_2 \int_0^\infty [\psi(y - \bar{y})^2 + \dot{p}_c^2] \exp(-\rho t)dt, \quad \psi, y, \rho, \geqslant 0., \qquad (4.10)$$

subject to (4.6) - (4.9), where ψ, $\bar{y}$ and ρ denote the relative priority attached to achieving the full-employment target, the full-employment (desired) target of home activity and the social rate of time preference, respectively. The policy dilemma is that a policy of no inflation leads to a too low level of activity ($\bar{y} > 0$). The home country's social welfare problem can be rewritten as :

$$\underset{\dot{m}}{\text{Min}}\ {}^1/_2 \int_0^\infty [\,\psi[\delta c + \varepsilon(\dot{m} + \dot{m}^*) - \bar{y}]^2 + [{}^1/_2(\dot{m} + \dot{m}^*) + (\delta\varphi/\lambda)c]^2] \exp(-\rho t)dt \qquad (4.11)$$

subject to (4.9). The foreign country's social welfare problem can be written as:

$$\underset{\dot{m}^*}{\text{Min}}\ {}^1\!/_2 \int_0^\infty [\psi[-\delta c + \varepsilon(\dot{m} + \dot{m}^*) - \bar{y}]^2 + [{}^1\!/_2(\dot{m} + \dot{m}^*) - (\delta\varphi/\lambda)c]^2] \exp(-\rho t)dt \tag{4.12}$$

subject to (4.9), where the foreign government is assumed to have the same preferences as the home government.

When the two governments decide on their optimal monetary policies in a decentralised fashion and when they cannot pre-commit themselves to these policies vis-à-vis the private sector, the (open-loop) Nash equilibrium with pre-commitment is the appropriate solution concept. The relevant first-order conditions are:

$$\psi\varepsilon[\delta c + \varepsilon(\dot{m} + \dot{m}^*) - \bar{y}] + {}^1\!/_2[{}^1\!/_2(\dot{m} + \dot{m}^*) + (\delta\varphi/\lambda)c] - x = 0 \tag{4.13}$$

$$\psi\varepsilon[-\delta c + \varepsilon(\dot{m} + \dot{m}^*) - \bar{y}] + {}^1\!/_2[{}^1\!/_2(\dot{m} + \dot{m}^*) - (\delta\varphi/\lambda)c] + x^* = 0 \tag{4.14}$$

$$\begin{aligned} \dot{x} = {} & [\rho - 2(\delta\varphi/\lambda)]\, x^* - \psi\delta[-\delta c + \varepsilon(\dot{m} + \dot{m}^*) - \bar{y}] \\ & - (\delta\varphi/\lambda)[{}^1\!/_2(\dot{m} + \dot{m}^*) + (\delta\varphi/\lambda)c], \quad x(0) = 0 \end{aligned} \tag{4.15}$$

$$\begin{aligned} \dot{x}^* = {} & [\rho - 2(\delta\varphi/\lambda)]\, x^* + \psi\delta[-\delta c + \varepsilon(\dot{m} + \dot{m}^*) - \bar{y}] \\ & + (\delta\varphi/\lambda)[{}^1\!/_2(\dot{m} + \dot{m}^*) - (\delta\varphi/\lambda)c], \quad x^*(0) = 0 \end{aligned} \tag{4.16}$$

where x (x^*) denotes the undiscounted shadow price of the real exchange rate to the home (foreign) government. At the beginning of the planning horizon, the real exchange rate is free to jump and therefore its contribution to social welfare at that time must be zero (cf., Calvo, 1978); $x(0) = x^*(0) = 0$. Subtraction of (4.14) and (4.13) and addition of (4.15) and (4.16) yields $x(t) + x^*(t) = c(t) = 0$, for all $t \geqslant 0$. Equation (4.9) then gives $\dot{m} = \dot{m}^*$, so that $y = y^* = 2\,\varepsilon \dot{m}$ and $\dot{p} = \dot{p}_c^* = \dot{m}$. Addition of (4.13) and (4.14) then gives

$$x - x^* = {}^1\!/_2(1 + 4\psi\varepsilon^2)(\dot{m} + \dot{m}^*) - 2\psi\varepsilon\,\bar{y}, \tag{4.17}$$

so that subtraction of (4.16) from (4.15) yields

$$\begin{aligned} \ddot{m} = {} & [\rho - 4(1 + 4\psi\varepsilon^2)^{-1}[(\delta\varphi/\lambda) + \psi\delta\varepsilon(1 + 2\varepsilon\varphi)]]\,\dot{m} + 2\psi(1 + 4\psi\varepsilon^2)^{-1} \\ & [\delta - [\rho - 2(\delta\varphi/\lambda)]\varepsilon]\,\bar{y}, \quad \dot{m}(0) = 2\psi\varepsilon(1 + 4\psi\varepsilon^2)^{-1}\,\bar{y} \equiv \dot{m}_C. \end{aligned} \tag{4.18}$$

The solution of (4.18) is given by

$$\dot{m}(t) = \dot{m}^*(t) = \dot{m}_N + (\dot{m}_C - \dot{m}_N)\exp(-\lambda_N t), \tag{4.19}$$

where the steady-state Nash equilibrium value of monetary growth is given by

$$\dot{m}_N = 2\psi(1 + 4\psi\varepsilon^2)^{-1}\,[\delta - [\rho - 2(\delta\varphi/\lambda)]\,\varepsilon]\,\bar{y}/\lambda_N \tag{4.20}$$

and the speed of policy adjustment under decentralised policy making is given by

$$\lambda_N = 4(1 + 4\psi\varepsilon^2)^{-1}\,[(\delta\varphi/\lambda) + \psi\delta\varepsilon(1 + 2\varepsilon\varphi)] - \rho > 0. \tag{4.21}$$

The outcome under international coordination of monetary policies and pre-commitment is obtained by choosing $\dot{m}$ and $\dot{m}^*$ to minimise the sum of the two countries' welfare loss functions subject to (4.9). This yields $c(t) = 0$, $\dot{p}_c(t) = \dot{m}(t) = \dot{m}_C$, $y(t) = y^*(t) = 2\varepsilon\dot{m}_C$ and $r(t) = r^*(t) = -2\lambda(\sigma\varphi + \lambda)^{-1}\dot{m}_C$, for all $t \geqslant 0$ as the outcomes under international policy coordination.

It can easily be shown that the inequality $\dot{m}_N > \dot{m}_c$ holds, so that the monetary growth rates that prevail in the absence of international policy coordination are excessive. This is due to the fact that an increase in monetary growth is a beggar-thy-neigbour policy and that each government ignores the adverse consequences of such a policy on the rival government. The optimal non-cooperative policies are time inconsistent (Kydland and Prescott, 1977), since if a government reneges and re-optimises at a later date it pays to reduce monetary growth again to its cooperative level and subsequently raise it gradually to its non cooperative level. The "loss of leadership" solution (Buiter, 1984) is an open-loop, time-consistent Nash equilibrium solution, since it assumes that the governments ignore, or do not manipulate, the forward-looking component of the real exchange rate. This means that $x(t) = x^*(t) = 0$, for all $t \geqslant 0$, instead of (4.15)–(4.16), so that $\dot{m}(t) = \dot{m}^*(t) = \dot{m}_C$ is the competitive, time-consistent outcome. The cooperative outcome is time consistent, so that when governments cannot pre-commit there is no gain from international policy coordination. In fact, when the governments cannot pre-commit and the economies eventually return to their natural rates ($k > 0$), international policy coordination is only a transient issue and can be counter-productive (Rogoff, 1985).[8]

8. When the time inconsistency of optimal monetary policies arises in the form of a surprise inflation tax, it can be shown that international coordination can also be counter-productive when governments cannot pre-commit themselves (van der Ploeg, 1988).

V. REAL WAGE RIGIDITY AT HOME AND ABROAD

V.1 *Spill-over Effects of Fiscal and Supply-side Policies*

Now consider case (ii), which assumes real wage rigidity at home and abroad. This might characterise economic interdependence within Europe. Substitution of $w = p_c$, (3.5) and (3.9) into (3.11) yields the *AS*-schedule :

$$y = -\bar{\beta}_1(\alpha c + \tau) + \bar{\beta}_3. \tag{5.1}$$

Aggregate supply increases whenever the wedge between the producers' wage and the consumers' wage, i.e., $\alpha c + \tau$,[9] decreases. Hence, when the real exchange rate depreciates, the cost-of-living for workers and therefore their wage claim increases so that firms employ less labour and produce less output.[10] Similarly, an increase in the employers' tax rate reduces incentives to employ labour and produce output. Both the home and foreign *AS*-schedules are drawn in the bottom half of Figure 2(a).

Intersection of the *AD*-schedule (3.18), and the *AS*-schedule (5.1), yields equilibrium in the home goods market. This gives rise to the *GME*-locus.

$$r = [f + \gamma f^* + \bar{\beta}_1\tau - \bar{\beta}_3 + (\delta + \alpha\bar{\beta}_1)c + \gamma\eta E\dot{c}]/\sigma \tag{5.2}$$

and, similarly, to the *GME**-locus

$$r = [f^* + \gamma f + \bar{\beta}_1\tau^* - \bar{\beta}_3^* - (\delta + \alpha\bar{\beta}_1)c + \eta E\dot{c}]/\sigma \tag{5.3}$$

(see Figure 2(a)). The *GME*-locus slopes upwards, because the excess supply of goods induced by a rise in the real interest rate is choked off by a depreciation of the real exchange rate which boosts net exports and cuts aggregate supply. Intersection of the *GME*-locus and the *GME**-locus yields the relative price of foreign goods in terms of home goods :

$$c = {}^1/_2[(1 - \gamma)(f^* - f + \eta E\dot{c}) + \bar{\beta}_1(\tau^* - \tau) + \bar{\beta}_3 - \bar{\beta}_3^*]/(\delta + \alpha\bar{\beta}_1). \tag{5.4}$$

The real interest rate and output then follow upon substitution of (5.4) into

9. In general, one should also add the employees' tax rate and the indirect tax rate to the wedge.

10. Note that, in contrast to Branson and Rotemberg (1980), aggregate supply never rises when the real exchange rate depreciates (thus excluding their example of the Hong Kong economy).

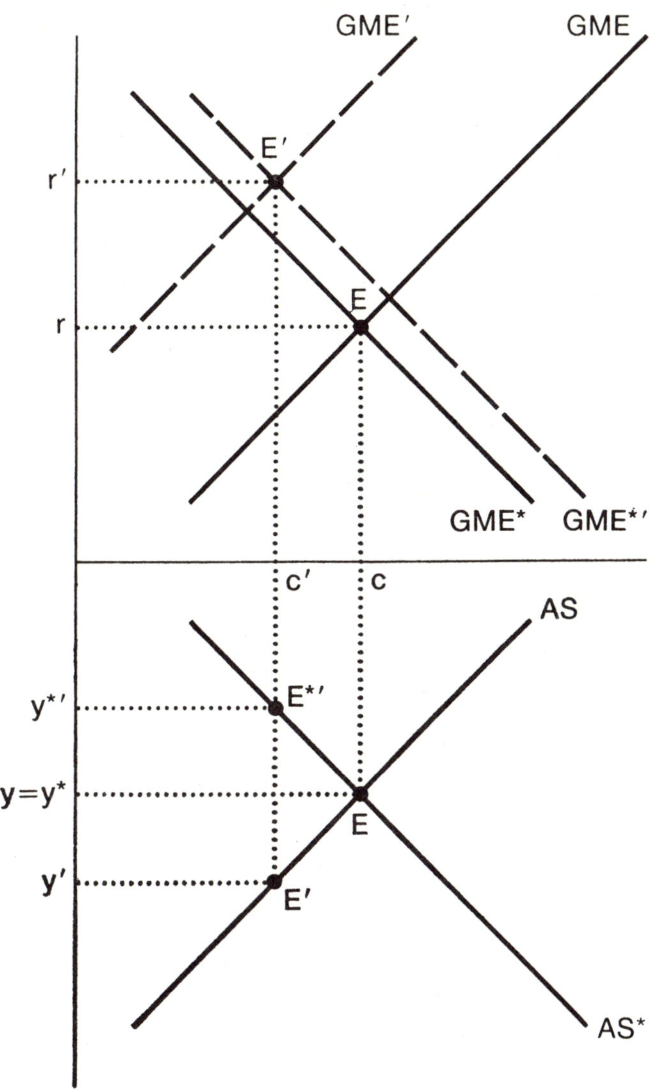

FIGURE 2(a). Real Wage Rigidity at Home and Abroad (Unanticipated increase in f)

(5.2) and (5.1). Alternatively, the comparative statics can be deduced from Figure 2(a).

An unanticipated permanent fiscal expansion at home shifts up the *GME*-locus by more than the *GME**- locus, so that the incipient excess demand for goods is choked off by a rise in the world real interest rate and a fall in the relative price of home goods. The real appreciation of the home currency occurs instantaneously. It reduces the wedge and increases aggregate supply at home, but increases the wedge and reduces aggregate supply abroad. The boost in foreign aggregate demand, due to the real depreciation of the foreign exchange rate and the increase in home activity, and the fall in foreign aggregate supply must be choked off by the rise in the world real interest rate. Clearly, fiscal expansion is a *beggar-thy-neighbour* policy in a *RWR-RWR** world. This contrasts with a *NWR- NWR** (Mundell-Fleming) world, where fiscal expansion is a locomotive policy (see Section 4). The fall in foreign output and the increase in the world interest rate reduces the demand for real foreign money balances, so that the foreign price level must increase. The effect on the home price level is ambiguous. Note that, under purchasing power parity ($\delta \rightarrow \infty$), neither home nor fiscal policy can affect the wedge and consequently output and employment.

The expectational dynamics can be deduced from Figure 2(b). An anticipated permanent fiscal expansion at home leads to a jump appreciation of the real exchange rate and thus to an immediate expansion of home activity and fall in foreign activity. The real exchange rate is expected to appreciate, so that there is a real-interest-rate differential in favour of the home country during the announcement period *AB*. The *GME**-locus shifts down more than the *GME*-locus, so that the home real interest rate falls during the announcement period. This generates the extra demand to choke off the excess supply of goods induced by the real appreciation of the exchange rate. Similarly, the foreign real interest rate must increase during the adjustment period. Obviously, during the adjustment period, home activity continues to increase and foreign activity continues to fall. At the time of implementation of the home fiscal expansion, there is no jump in the real exchange rate and no change in home or foreign activity as the fiscal expansion has already been discounted in the financial markets. Instead, there is an implementation effect leading to an upward jump in the world real interest rate which completely crowds out the increase in demand caused by the fiscal expansion. Since the home real interest rate rises above its original equilibrium value, it is clear that it *misadjusts* when there is an anticipated fiscal expansion.

An unanticipated permanent improvement in home supply, due to a cut in the home tax rate or an increase in home productivity, shifts down the

GME-locus and shifts out the *AS*-schedule. The increase in home supply is partially accommodated by the increase in demand due to the fall in the world real interest rate and the depreciation of the real exchange rate, but obviously the latter effect increases the home wedge and crowds cut some of the initial increase in home suply. The counter-part of this is that the foreign wedge falls and thus foreign activity increases. Foreign demand increases due to the fall in the world interest rate and despite the improvement in foreign net

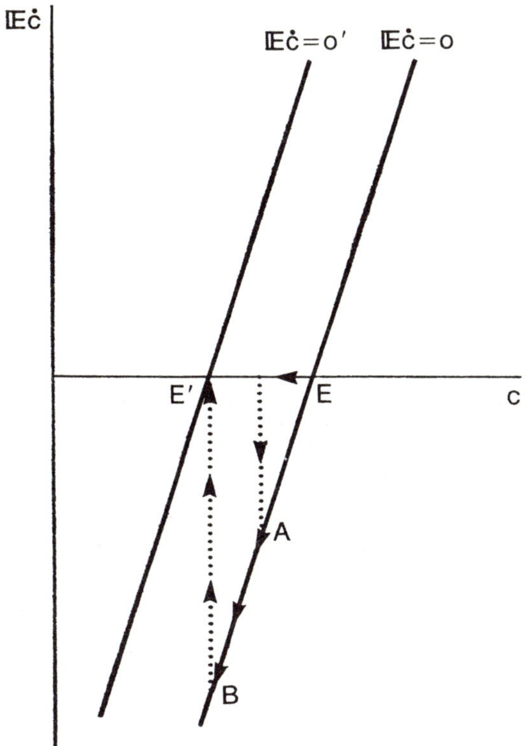

FIGURE 2(b). Real Wage Rigidity at Home and Abroad (Anticipated increase in f)

exports. Hence, supply-side improvements are a *locomotive* policy in a *RWR*-*RWR** world.

A joint fiscal expansion or a joint improvement in supply-side conditions has no real effects whatsoever in this symmetric two-country world, although it does increase world interest rates and reduce price levels. This is in contrast to the effects in a *NWR*-*NWR** world (see Section 4.1). A monetary expansion, either at home or abroad, has no real effects in a *RWR*-*RWR** world

Due to full indexation of wages to the cost-of-living index, a unilateral monetary expansion leads to a one-for-one increase in the home price level, a one-for-one depreciation of the nominal exchange rate and no effect on output and employment. However, if the model is extended to allow for investment and capital accumulation, an interdependent Mundell-Tobin effect emerges. An increase in home monetary growth reduces the world real interest rate and therefore increases capital, employment and output both at home and abroad, so that it is a locomotive policy (van der Ploeg, 1986).

It follows that fully indexed economies are insulated from monetary shocks, but are more responsive to real supply-side (say, tax or oil) shocks.

Finally, it may be useful to consider the special case of perfect substitution between home and foreign goods, i.e., purchasing power parity ($\delta \to \infty$). In that case, the real exchange rate and the wedge between the producers' and consumers' wage are fixed so that output at home and abroad are unaffected by fiscal or supply-side policies (see equations (5.1) and (5.4)).

V.2 *International Coordination of Fiscal Policy*

In a *RWR-RWR** world monetary growth directly affects inflation and has neither a transient nor a persistent effect on real activity. A fiscal expansion at home benefits activity at home and reduces activity abroad. The adverse effects of a fiscal expansion are higher budget deficits, which to the extent that they are financed by an increase in monetary growth have an adverse effect on inflation. The policy dilemma of each country is that they want a high level of government spending for high activity, but a low level of government spending for low inflation. These are exercises in the optimal determination of fiscal policy, so that the effects of supply-side policies are suppressed ($\tau = \tau^* = \bar{\beta}_3 = \bar{\beta}_3^* = 0$). The policy dilemma of the home country is captured by the following social welfare problem:

$$\operatorname*{Min}_{f} \; {}^1\!/_2 \int_0^\infty [\bar{\psi}(y - \bar{y})^2 + f^2] \exp(-\rho t)dt, \qquad \bar{\psi}, \bar{y}, \rho \geqslant 0, \tag{5.5}$$

subject to (5.1) and (5.4), where $\bar{\psi}$ is the relative priority attached to achieving the full-employment target, $\bar{y}$ is the full-employment (desired) level of home activity, and ρ is the government's rate of time preference. The policy dilemma is that a balanced budget or a budget consistent with no inflation leads to a too low level of activity and that achievement of the full-employment target leads to excessive government deficits and inflation. The home country's welfare problem can be rewritten as:

$$\underset{f}{\text{Min}}\ {}^1\!/_2 \int_0^\infty [\psi(c + \bar{c})^2 + f^2] \exp(-\rho t)dt, \quad \psi, \bar{c} \geqslant 0 \tag{5.6}$$

subject to

$$E\dot{c} = (\Gamma c + f - f^*)/\eta, \quad c(0) = \text{free} \tag{5.7}$$

where $\psi \equiv \bar{\psi}(\bar{\beta}_1\alpha)^2$, $\bar{c} \equiv \bar{y}/(\bar{\beta}_1\alpha)$ and $\Gamma \equiv 2(\delta + \bar{\beta}_1\alpha)/(1-\gamma)$ (assumed to exceed $\eta\rho$). The foreign country faces a similar welfare problem :

$$\underset{f^*}{\text{Min}}\ {}^1\!/_2 \int_0^\infty [\psi^*(c - \bar{c})^2 + f^{*2}] \exp(-\rho t)dt, \quad \psi^* \geqslant 0 \tag{5.8}$$

subject to (5.7), where allowance has been made for the possibility that the two countries may attach different priorities to achieving the full-employment target.

When the governments of the two countries can pre-commit and decide on their optimal fiscal policies in a competitive fashion, the Nash equilibrium with pre-commitment is the appropriate solution concept. The relevant first-order conditions can be written as :

$$\dot{f} = -[(\Gamma/\eta) - \rho] f + (\psi/\eta)(c + \bar{c}), \quad f(0) = 0, \tag{5.9}$$

$$\dot{f}^* = -[(\Gamma/\eta) - \rho] f^* - (\psi^*/\eta)(c - \bar{c}), \quad f^*(0) = 0, \tag{5.10}$$

and (5.7), where the adjoint variable associated with the real exchange rate for the home (foreign) country is given by $-\eta f$ (ηf^*). Since the real exchange rate is free to jump at time zero, its marginal contribution to social welfare at that time must be zero (cf., Calvo, 1978) and therefore $f(0) = f^*(0) = 0$ must hold. It follows from subtraction of (5.10) from (5.9) and from (5.7) that, when $\psi = \psi^*$, $c(t) = y(t) = y^*(t) = f(t) - f^*(t) = 0$, for $t \geqslant 0$, so that $r(t) = r^*(t) = (1 + \gamma) f(t)/\sigma$ and

$$f(t) = f^*(t) = f_N\{1 - \exp[-[\Gamma/\eta) - \rho] t]\}, \quad f_N \equiv \psi\bar{c}/(\Gamma - \eta\rho). \tag{5.11}$$

Note that, when the share of imported goods in total expenditures is 50 per cent, the adjustment to the steady-state Nash equilibrium levels of public spending is instantaneous ($f(t) = f^*(t) = f_N$, for $t \geqslant 0$, when $\alpha = {}^1\!/_2$). In general ($\alpha < {}^1\!/_2$), the levels of public deficits are at their no-inflation levels at the start of the planning horizon and afterwards gradually increase towards their steady-state Nash equilibrium levels. This means that the optimal levels of public deficits in the Nash equilibrium with pre-commitment are time inconsistent; when the governments re-optimise after some time they will want to tighten their fiscal policies back to the no-inflation levels.

When the governments of the two countries engage in international policy coordination with pre-commitment, they minimise the global welfare loss and take account of the constraint that the real exchange rate and therefore activity cannot be affected. Hence, when $\psi = \psi^*$, $c(t) = y(t) = y^*(t) = r(t) = r^*(t) = f(t) = f^*(t) = 0$, $t \geqslant 0$, are the cooperative outcomes. There is no problem of time inconsistency when international policy coordination takes place.

The non-cooperative outcomes lead to excessive levels of public deficits relative to the cooperative outcomes. This is a consequence of the beggar-thy-neighbour nature of fiscal policies in a *RWR-RWR** world, since in the non-cooperative outcomes each government ignores the adverse consequences of a fiscal expansion on the other economy. In effect, each country attempts (in vain) to have a high real exchange rate in order to boost employment at home and export unemployment and this is what leads to excessive public deficits. The cooperative outcomes realise the futility of such actions and increase welfare by setting the public deficits at their no-inflation levels. The inefficiencies of the non-cooperative outcomes increase when the priorities attached to achieving the full-employment targets increase, when the desired levels of activity increase, and when the governments' discount rates increase.

When the home country (say, France) attaches a higher priority to the employment target than the foreign country (say, Germany), the steady-state Nash equilibrium levels of the real exchange rate and the fiscal deficit are given by:

$$c_N = (\psi^* - \psi)\bar{c} \,/\, [(\Gamma - \eta\rho)\Gamma + \psi + \psi^*] < 0 \tag{5.12}$$

$$f_N = \psi[2\psi^* + (\Gamma - \eta\rho)\Gamma]\bar{c} \,/\, \{(\Gamma - \rho\eta)[(\Gamma - \eta\rho)\Gamma + \psi + \psi^*]\} > 0 \tag{5.13}$$

so that $y_N > 0 > y_N^*$ and $f_N > f_N^* > 0$. The country that attaches a higher priority to achieving full employment ends up with a higher level of activity, at the expense of a lower level of activity in the other economy, and a higher level of the public deficit and inflation.

As far as supply-side improvements are concerned, they are a locomotive policy in a *RWR-RWR** world. It is clear that, in the absence of international policy coordination, supply-side improvements do not go far enough as each country ignores the beneficial effects on the other country.

It may be useful to relate the analysis of this section to the pioneering work of Hamada (1985, Chapter 5) on the international coordination of monetary policies. Although Hamada was concerned with a full-employment multi-country world, the international trade-offs for monetary policies are similar in a *RWR-RWR** world. Consider the case of floating exchange rates first. Monetary growth has no real effects, so that each country sets its optimal monetary growth to its desired rate of inflation. Since the monetary authorities do not face a policy trade-off, there is no role for international policy coordination. Now consider the case of pegged exchange rates ($e = 0$). Increases in monetary growth ($\dot{m}$) are either due to increases in the rate of domestic credit expansion ($\dot{d}$) or due to balance-of-payments surplusses, expressed as a ratio of the money supply (z). The monetary approach to the balance of payments then gives the balance-of-payments ratio of each country as the excess of the common inflation rate (π) over its rate of domestic credit expansion, i.e., $z = \pi - \dot{d} = \pi_R + {}^1/_2\,(\dot{d}^* - \dot{d})$, where the ratio of the increase in international reserves to the world money supply is denoted by π_R and the world inflation rate is given by $\pi \equiv \dot{p} = \dot{p}^* = \pi_R + {}^1/_2\,(\dot{d} + \dot{d}^*)$. Denote each country's desired inflation rate by $\bar{\pi} = \bar{\pi}^*$ and desired balance of payments ratio by $\bar{z}$. Hamada shows that, in the absence of international policy coordination, world inflation (π) is higher (lower) than desired inflation ($\bar{\pi}$), when the increase in international reserves (π_R) is larger (smaller) than the weighted averages of the desired increases in international reserves (${}^1/_2(\bar{z}+\bar{z}^*)$).

VI. REAL WAGE RIGIDITY IN EUROPE AND NOMINAL WAGE RIGIDITY IN THE U.S.

VI.1 *Asymmetries in International Interdependence*

The interactions between the European (home) and US (foreign) economies are best described by an asymmetric world, that is real wage rigidity is assumed for Europe (and Japan) and nominal wage rigidity for the US and Canada (see Section 2). In that case, the world real interest rate and the real exchange rate follow from the intersection of the *GME*-locus, (5.2), and the *GME**-locus, (4.3), suitably modified to allow for the effects of imported raw materials. European output depends on the real exchange rate and follows from the *AS*-schedule,

$$y = -\bar{\beta}_1(\bar{\alpha}c + \tau) + \bar{\beta}_3 \tag{6.1}$$

where $\overline{\alpha} \equiv \alpha + \overline{\beta}_2$ and $\overline{\beta}_3 \equiv \overline{\beta}_3 - \overline{\beta}_1 \overline{\beta}_2 p_n{}^*$, whilst US output depends on the US interest rate and follows from the reduced-form LM^*-schedule,

$$y^* = [\lambda[r + \dot{m}^* + \dot{\tau}^* + \overline{\beta}_2 \dot{p}_n^* - (1-\alpha) E\dot{c}] - \tau^* - \overline{\beta}_2 p_n^*] / \varphi. \quad (6.2)$$

Hence, both European and US aggregate supply decrease when the price of oil (fixed in terms of US goods) increases. The AS-schedule is steeper than before, because a real depreciation of the European currency not only increases the wedge but also increases the real price of oil to Europe. The comparative statistics of unanticipated, permanent shocks can be deduced by diagrammatic means (see Figure 3). The equilibrium real interest rate is given by

$$\begin{aligned} r = \{ & [\gamma(\delta + \overline{\alpha\beta_1}) + \delta]f + (\delta + \overline{\alpha\beta_1} + \gamma\delta)f^* + \overline{\beta}_1\delta\tau \\ & + (\delta + \overline{\alpha\beta_1})\varphi^{-1}(\tau^* + \overline{\beta}_2 p_n^*) - \lambda(\delta + \overline{\alpha\beta_1})\varphi^{-1}(\dot{m}^* + \dot{\tau}^* + \overline{\beta}_2 \dot{p}_n^*) - \delta\overline{\beta}_3 \\ & + [(\eta + \lambda(1-\alpha)\varphi^{-1})(\delta + \overline{\alpha\beta_1}) + \gamma\eta\delta]E\dot{c}\} / \Delta \end{aligned} \quad (6.3)$$

and the equilibrium real exchange rate follows from

$$\begin{aligned} c = \{ & -[(\sigma + \lambda/\varphi) - \gamma\sigma]f + [-(\sigma + \lambda/\varphi)\gamma + \sigma]f^* - \overline{\beta}_1(\sigma + \lambda/\varphi)\tau \\ & + \varphi^{-1}\sigma[\tau^* + \overline{\beta}_2 p_n^* - \lambda(\dot{m}^* + \dot{\tau}^* + \overline{\beta}_2 \dot{p}_n^*)] + (\sigma + \lambda/\varphi)\overline{\beta}_3 \\ & - [\gamma\eta(\sigma + \lambda/\varphi) - \sigma(\eta + \lambda\varphi^{-1}(1-\alpha))]E\dot{c}\} / \Delta \end{aligned} \quad (6.4)$$

where $\Delta \equiv (\sigma + \lambda\varphi^{-1})(\delta + \overline{\alpha\beta_1}) + \delta\sigma > 0$. The real exchange rate, and consequently all other endogenous variables, jump instantaneously to their new equilibrium values in response to unanticipated permanent shocks, as long as the saddlepoint condition is satisfied ($\sigma\lambda(1-\alpha) + \sigma\eta\varphi(1-\gamma) > \lambda\eta\gamma$), which is definitely the case for $\alpha = {}^1/_2$. Figure 2(b) can be used to analyse the effects of anticipated, permanent shocks.

The effects of an unanticipated permanent increase in the European public deficit are presented in Figure 3(a). The excess demand for European goods is partially choked off by a fall in the relative price of US goods, which induces an increase in European supply and US demand and a fall in European demand for goods, and by a rise in the world interest rate, which induces a fall in the European and US demand for goods and an increase in the US supply of goods. The above is captured by the fact that the upward shift of the GME-locus dominates the upward shift of the GME^*-locus. It shows that a European fiscal expansion increases output and employment in both Europe

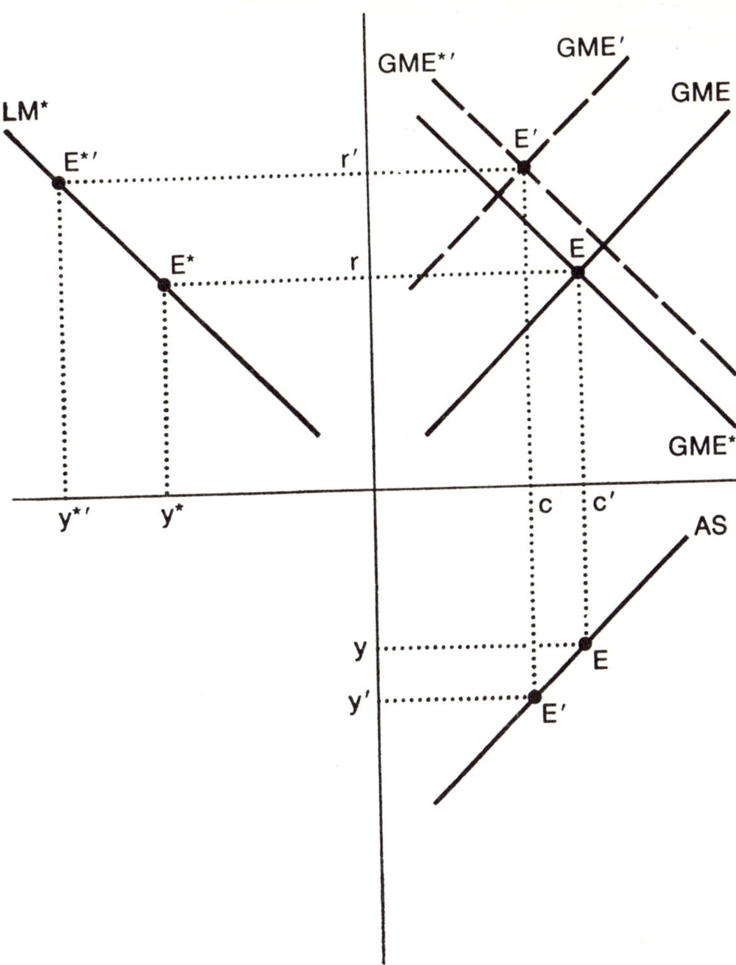

FIGURE 3(a). Interdependence of the European and US Economies (Unanticipated increase in the European public deficit)

and the US and is therefore a *locomotive* policy. For a US fiscal expansion, the shift in the *GME**-locus, typically (as long as $\sigma(1 - \gamma)\varphi > \lambda\gamma$), dominates the shift in the *GME*-locus and therefore results in a rise in the world interest rate and, typically, an increase in the relative price of US goods. Hence, a US fiscal expansion increases output in the US and, typically, leads to a depreciation of the European real exchange rate, an increase in the European wedge and therefore a reduction in European output. It is therefore, typically, a *beggar-thy-neighbour* policy. However, if the negative effects of financial crowding out on European consumption and investment are not too important relative to the positive spill-over effects of US activity on European exports (if $\bar{\sigma}\varphi/\lambda < \gamma$), a US fiscal expansion increases European output and employment and therefore is a *locomotive* policy. Plausible parameter values are $\bar{\sigma} = 0.5$, $\varphi = 1.0$, $\lambda = 0.5$ and $\gamma = 0.3$, which suggests that a US fiscal expansion is a beggar-thy-neighbour policy. It will be assumed that this is the typical case.

An increase in European monetary growth has no real effects, because European wages are indexed to increases in the cost-of-living. It simply increases the European inflation and nominal interest rates one-for-one. The effects of an unanticipated, permanent increase in the US monetary growth rate are presented in Figure 3(b). It increases the US nominal interest rate, cuts US demand for real money balances, exerts an upward pressure on the US price level, erodes the real value of the US wage, and therefore increases US aggregate supply. This is partially accommodated by the increase in the demand for US goods due to a fall in the relative price of US goods and a fall in the US real interest rate. The associated appreciation of the European real exchange rate, reduces the wedge between the European consumers' and producers' wage, and therefore raises European supply. European demand rises due to the fall in the world real interest rate. Clearly, US monetary growth is a *locomotive* policy. A cut in the US tax rate also raises US aggregate supply and therefore raises output and employment in Europe as well as in the US. Hence, a US tax cut is a *locomotive* policy. A cut in the European tax rates shifts out the AS-schedule and shifts down the GME-locus, so that the real interest rate falls, the European real exchange rate appreciates and European output increases. US output falls, so supply-side improvements in Europe are a *beggar-thy-neighbour* policy.

An increase in the real price of oil (in terms of US goods) shifts in the AS- and LM^*-schedules and consequently shifts up the GME- and GME^*-loci. The fall in the world supply of goods induces a rise in the world real interest rate, which attenuates the adverse effects of the oil shock on US supply. The effect on the real exchange rate (and therefore on European output) is ambiguous, but, if $\sigma > \bar{\beta}_1(\sigma\varphi+\lambda)$, the adverse effects on US supply dominate the adverse effects on European supply and then the relative price of US goods increases. In that case, the European real exchange rate depreciates and therefore the adverse effects of an oil shock on European supply are accentuated rather than attenuated. This therefore seems to suggest that an oil shock hits European output and employment much harder than US output and employment.

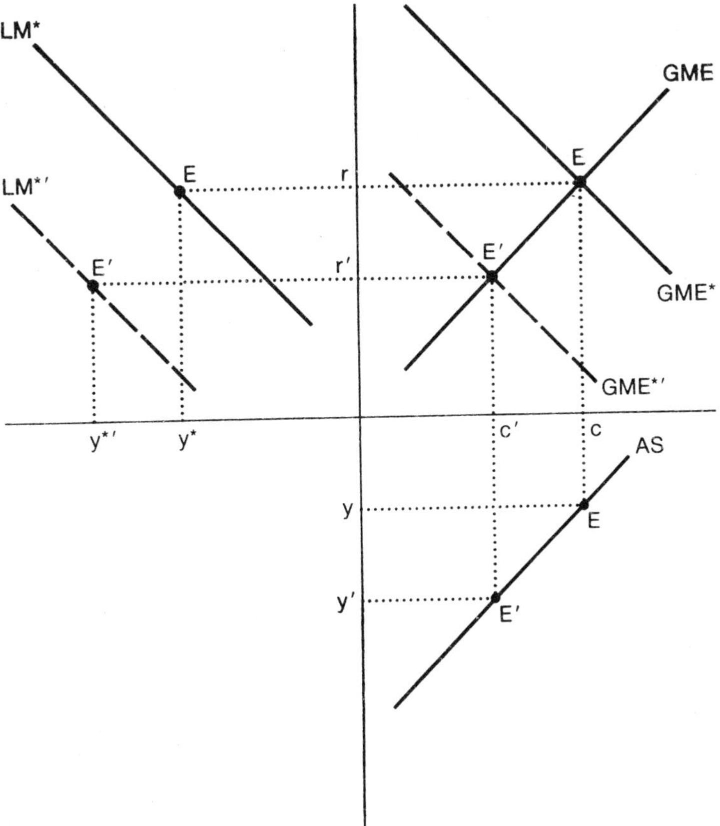

FIGURE 3(b). Interdependence of the European and US Economies (Unanticipated increase in US monetary growth or cut in the US tax rate)

VI.2 *International Economic Policy Coordination*

Section 6.1 showed that a European fiscal expansion, an increase in US monetary growth and a US tax cut stimulate output at home and abroad. This means that, in the absence of international policy coordination, the US (Europe) ignores the beneficial effects on European (US) output and employment of an increase in monetary growth or a supply-side incentive (a fiscal expansion). Hence, the US has a too low monetary growth rate and does not offer enough supply-side improvements whilst Europe's fiscal stance is too tight relative to the outcomes under international policy coordination. Similarly, a cut in European employers' taxes and, typically, a US fiscal expansion have negative spill-over effects. This means that in the absence of internationa policy coordination, European supply-side improvements are too far-reaching and US fiscal policy is, typically, too tight.

Now consider in detail the case of the optimal determination of the European and US public deficits when they are financed by bonds. The social welfare functions are given by (5.5), where after the OPEC shocks $\bar{y} > \bar{y}^*$ as an oil price shock hits Europe harder than the US. The description of the European and US economies follows upon substitution of (6.4) and (6.3) into (6.1) and (6.2) and from (6.4):

$$y = \omega_1 f - \omega_2 f^* + \omega_3 \dot{m}^* - \omega_4 \dot{Ec}, \tag{6.5}$$

$$y^* = \omega_1^* f^* + \omega_2^* f + \omega_3^* \dot{m}^* - \omega_4^* \dot{Ec}, \tag{6.6}$$

$$\dot{Ec} = \omega_5 c + \omega_6 f - \omega_7 f^* + \omega_8 \dot{m}^*, \tag{6.7}$$

where $\omega_1 > 0$, $\omega_i > 0$, $i = 3, 8$, $\omega_i^* > 0$, $i = 1, 4$, sign $(\omega_2) =$ sign (ω_7) and $\omega_5 > \rho$. With the same procedure as used in Sections 4.2 and 5.2, one finds that in the absence of international policy coordination the optimal steady-state public deficits when governments can pre-commit themselves must satisfy:

$$f = -\psi(y - \bar{y}) = \psi(\omega_2 f^* + \bar{y})/(1 + \psi\omega_1) \tag{6.8}$$

$$f^* = \psi^*(y^* - \bar{y}^*) = -\psi^*(\omega_2^* f - \bar{y}^*)/(1 + \psi^*\omega_1^*), \tag{6.9}$$

where $\psi \equiv \bar{\psi}\,[\omega_1 + \rho\omega_4\omega_6(\omega_5 - \rho)^{-1}] > 0$ and $\psi^* \equiv \bar{\psi}\,[\omega_1^* - \rho\omega_4^*\omega_7(\omega_5 - \rho)^{-1}] > 0$. Both countries "lean against the wind", that is the public deficit is increased when output falls below its full-employment level. If Europe reduces its deficit, US output falls and therefore the US government reacts and increases its deficit. The European asymptotic reaction curve is upward- or downward-sloping depending on whether a US fiscal expansion is a beggar-thy-neighbour or a locomotive policy, respectively. If the positive spill-over effect of US activity on European exports is dominated by financial crowding out ($\gamma < \bar{\sigma}\varphi/\lambda$), a US fiscal expansion is a beggar-thy-neighbour policy ($\omega_2 > 0$) and therefore Europe reacts with a fiscal expansion as well. The Nash equilibrium solution corresponds to the intersection of the reaction curves (6.8)-(6.9) and yields:

$$f = [(1 + \psi^*\omega_1^*)\,\psi\,\bar{y} + \psi\,\omega_2\,\psi^*\,\bar{y}^*]\,/\Delta_N \equiv f_N \tag{6.10}$$

$$f^* = [-\psi^*\omega_2^*\,\psi\,\bar{y} + (1 + \psi\omega_1)\,\psi^*\,\bar{y}^*]\,/\Delta_N \equiv f_N^* \tag{6.11}$$

where $\Delta_N \equiv (1 + \psi\omega_1)(1 + \psi^*\omega_1^*) + \psi\, \omega_2\, \psi^*\, \omega_2^* > 0$. Note that, when the desired change in home output increases, each country increases its public sector deficit, and more so when the relative priority on achieving the full-employment target (ψ) is high. An increase in the desired change in output in Europe prompts an increase in the European deficit, which increases US output and therefore the US can afford to have a tighter deficit ($\partial f_N^* / \partial \bar{y} < 0$). An increase in the desired change in US output only leads to a tighter European deficit when a US fiscal expansion is a locomotive policy, but otherwise it leads to a looser European deficit ($\partial f_N / \partial \bar{y}^* \gtrless 0$ when $\omega_2 \gtrless 0$). The optimal public deficits of the Nash equilibrium solution are time-inconsistent, because when the governments re-optimise it pays them to reset the public deficits to (6.10) and (6.11) with ρ set equal to zero. In fact, the "loss-of-leadership" solution (Buiter, 1984) corresponds to (6.10) and (6.11) with ρ set equal to zero. It corresponds to higher public deficits when both countries' policies are locomotive policies ($\omega_2 > 0$), but otherwise the US public deficit may be smaller.

The outcome under international policy coordination minimises a global welfare loss function, where ω is the relative weight of the European welfare loss. The steady-state reactions for the cooperative outcome are:

$$f = -\psi(y - \bar{y}) - \omega^{-1}\psi_*(y^* - \bar{y}^*) \tag{6.12}$$

$$f^* = -\psi^*(y^* - \bar{y}^*) + \omega\psi_*^*(y - \bar{y}) \tag{6.13}$$

where $\psi_* \equiv \bar{\psi}[\omega_2^* + \rho\omega_4^*\omega_6(\omega_5 - \rho)^{-1}] > 0$ and $\psi_*^* \equiv \bar{\psi}[\omega_2 + \rho\omega_4\omega_7 (\omega_5 - \rho)^{-1}]$ is positive (negative) when a US fiscal expansion is a beggar-thy-neighbour (locomotive) policy. Hence, as long as fiscal expansions are locomotive policies, they respond to unemployment at home and abroad. However, if a US fiscal expansion is a beggar-thy-neighbour policy, the US tightens its deficit when there is unemployment in Europe. The resulting asymptotic levels of the public deficit under cooperation are:

$$f = \frac{\{\Delta_N f_N + \psi_*\psi_*^*(\omega_1^*\bar{y} + \omega_2\bar{y}^*) + \omega^{-1}\psi_*\bar{y}^*\}}{\{\Delta_N + \omega_2\psi_*^*(\omega + \psi_*\omega_2^*) + \omega_2^*\psi_*\omega^{-1} + \psi_*^*\,\omega_1^*\psi_*\omega_1\}} \equiv f_c \tag{6.14}$$

$$f^* = \frac{\{\Delta_N f_N^* + \psi_*\psi_*^*(\omega_1\bar{y}^* - \omega_2^*\bar{y}) - \omega\psi_*^*\bar{y}\}}{\{\Delta_N + \omega_2\psi_*^*(\omega + \psi_*\omega_2^*) + \omega_2^*\psi_*\omega^{-1} + \psi_*^*\,\omega_1^*\psi_*\omega_1\}} \equiv f_c^* \tag{6.15}$$

Intuitively, one expects that the European fiscal stance is too tight ($f_N < f_c$)

and that, when a US fiscal expansion is a beggar-thy-neighbour policy, the US fiscal stance is too loose ($f_N^* > f_C^*$). However, this result does not follow immediately. To illustrate the conditions under which this result holds, it is best to consider two special cases.

Consider the case where the world planning authority only cares about US welfare ($\omega \to 0$, $\bar{y} = 0$). In that case, it is easy to show that the planner allows the US to maintain a public sector deficit consistent with no inflation ($f_C^* = 0$) whilst Europe is forced to have an inflationary deficit in order to achieve full employment in the US ($f_C = \bar{y}^*/\omega_2^* > 0$). In the absence of international policy coordination, the US fiscal stance is too loose ($f_N^* > f_C^* = 0$) whilst the European fiscal stance is too tight ($f_N = f_C\,(\omega_2\omega_2^*\psi\psi^*/\Delta_N) < f_C$). This explains why the US urges Europe to expand, especially as this would justify a fiscal contraction in the US (see (6.9)). To understand Europe's reluctance to engage in a fiscal expansion, consider the case where the world planning authority only cares about European welfare ($\omega \to \infty$, $\bar{y}^* = 0$). Now the world planner allows Europe to have a zero-inflation deficit ($f_C = 0$) whilst the US must, typically, have a deflationary deficit in order to achieve full employment in Europe ($f_C^* = -\bar{y}/\omega_2 < 0$ for $\omega_2 > 0$). Now absence of international policy coordination means that the European fiscal stance is too loose ($f_N > f_C = 0$) and the US fiscal stance is, typically, also too loose ($0 > f_N^* = f_C^*(\omega_2\omega_2^*\psi\psi^*/\Delta_N) > f_C^*$ for $\omega_2 > 0$). Since the European fiscal stance is now too loose, it is understandable that the European governments have been reluctant to succumb to US pressure to expand.

It is possible to generalise the above results to allow both countries to have an unemployment problem ($\bar{y}$, $\bar{y}^* > 0$). When the world planner only cares about US welfare ($\omega \to 0$), it can be shown that $f_N < f_C = \bar{y}^*/\omega_2^*$ and (as long as $f_N^* > 0$) $f_N^* > f_C^* = 0$ still holds. Also, when only European welfare matters ($\omega \to \infty$), it can be shown that $f_N > f_C = 0$ and $f_N^* > f_C^* = -\bar{y}/\omega_2$ still hold for the case $\omega_2 > 0$.

It is clear that, whatever the weights the world planner attaches to US and European welfare (or whatever the relative bargaining strengths of the US and Europe), the US fiscal stance is too loose and therefore policy coordination involves a reduction in the US deficit. It is not so clear what policy coordination implies for the European fiscal stance. If the US has its way, international policy coordination implies that Europe would expand. However, if Europe has more bargaining strength, coordination implies that it would reduce its public sector deficit.

So far it has been assumed that a US fiscal expansion is a beggar-thy-neighbour policy ($\omega_2 > 0$). If it is a locomotive policy ($\omega_2 < 0$), a dominant US ($\omega \to 0$, $\bar{y} = 0$) implies, as before, that the US fiscal stance is too loose

($f_N^* > f_C^* = 0$) and the European fiscal is too tight ($f_N < 0 < f_C$) whilst a dominant Europe ($\omega \to \infty$, $\bar{y}^* = 0$) implies that the European fiscal stance is too loose ($f_N > f_C = 0$) and the US fiscal stance is too tight ($f_N^* < 0 < f_C^*$).

So far, the analysis considered bond-financed changes in the public sector deficit. Now consider money-financed changes. For Europe this wil not make much difference, because it is assumed that its economy is fully indexed. For the US the government budget constraint, under money-finance and nominal wage rigidity, can be written as

$$\dot{m}^* = \exp[f^* - (m^* - p^*)] = \exp(f^* + \tau^* + \bar{\beta}_2 p_n^*), \qquad (6.16)$$

where f^* includes interest payments on the government debt. Even if bond-financed increases in the US deficit are a beggar-thy-neighbour policy ($\omega_2 > 0$), it may be, particularly at high rates of monetary growth, that money-financed increases in the US deficit are a locomotive policy (if $\omega_3 \dot{m}^* > \omega_2$). Hence, the optimal US public sector deficits are, in the absence of international policy coordination, more likely to be too tight when they are money-financed than when they are bond-financed.

VII. CONCLUDING REMARKS

Empirical evidence shows that in the eighties US monetary policy has been relatively tight, US fiscal policy has been relatively loose, and European fiscal policy has been relatively tight. This period has also seen a huge rise in European unemployment. Econometric analysis shows that one cannot reject the hypothesis of real wage rigidity for Germany, France, Italy and Japan at the 5 per cent significance level, but that Canada, the UK and the US do display a significant degree of nominal wage rigidity in the short run. Incorporation of these stylistic facts in a two-country model with sluggish output and labour markets, efficient and integrated financial goods shows that a US monetary expansion and a European fiscal expansion are locomotive policies. A US fiscal expansion is, typically, a beggar-thy-neighbour policy, because the negative effects of financial crowding out on European consumption and investment are assumed to dominate the positive spill-over effects of US activity on European exports. Also, an increase in the real price of oil, such as the OPEC oil shocks, leads to a rise in the world real interest rate and, typically, to a depreciation of the European real exchange rate. This means that the adverse effects on aggregate supply are attenuated in the US and accentuated in Europe, so that an oil shock typically hits Europe much harder than the US. It is not surprising that, in the absence of international policy coordination and in the aftermath of the OPEC oil shocks, the European fiscal stance and US monetary growth have been too tight whilst the US fiscal stance has been too loose. It is also clear that each of these three policies have contributed to the recent rise in European unemployment.

The comparative statics results derived in this paper are summarised in Table 2.

TABLE 2

Summary of the Effects of Home Shocks on Home Output (y), Foreign Output (y^*), the Home Real Exchange Rate (c), and the Real Interest Rate (r)

	Section 4	Section 5	Section 6	
	NWR-NWR*	RWR-RWR*	RWR-NWR*	NWR-RWR*
Fiscal expansion	+, +, —, +	+, —, —, +	+, +, —, +	+, ?, ?, +
Expansion in monetary growth	+, —, +, —	0, 0, 0, 0	0, 0, 0, 0	+, +, +, —
Cut in employers' tax rate	+, —, +, —	+, +, +, —	+, —, +, —	+, +, +, —

Note: The effects of a home fiscal expansion in a *NWR-RWR** world are an appreciation (depreciation) of the home real exchange rate and a fall (increase) in foreign output when the negative effect of financial crowding out on foreign consumption and investment dominate (are dominated by) the positive spill-over effects of home activity on foreign exports, that is when $\overline{\sigma\gamma}/\lambda$ exceeds (is less than) γ.

London School of Economics, U.K.

DATA APPENDIX

Standardised unemployment rates. Source: *OECD Employment Outlook*, 1986.

Deflator of consumers' expenditure, P_c. Source: *OECD National Accounts*, various issues.

Inflation in the deflator of consumers' expenditure, Δp_c where $p_c \equiv \log(P_c)$.

Long nominal interest rate, r_L, generally the yield on long-term government bonds. Source: *IMF International Financial Statistics Yearbook*, 1983 and January 1984.

Short nominal interest rate, r_s, generally Central Bank's discount rate or a treasury bill rate. Source: *IMF International Financial Statistics Yearbook*, 1983 and January 1984.

Realised short real interest rate, $r_s - \Delta p_c$.

Real competitiveness, $\log(P_m/P)$.

Deflator of imports, $P_m \equiv MC/MQ$ where MC denotes imports at current prices and MQ denotes imports at 1980 prices. Source: *OECD National Accounts*, various issues.

Deflator of value added, $P \equiv YC/YQ$ where YC denotes GDP at current prices and YQ denotes GDP at 1980 prices. Source: *OECD National Accounts*, various issues.

Actual, structural and inflation-adjusted structural budget balances. Source: *Muller and Price*, 1984, Tables A1.1 - A1.7 and A3.5.

Employers' tax rate, $t_1 \equiv EC/(IE\text{-}EC)$ where EC denotes employers' contributions to social security and private pension schemes and IE denotes income from employment. Source: *OECD National Accounts*, various issues.

Employees' tax rate, $t_2 \equiv DT/HCR$ where DT denotes direct taxes and employees' contributions to social security and HCR denotes households current receipts. Source: *OECD National Accounts*, various issues.

Indirect tax rate, $t_3 \equiv (TX - SB)/YC$ where TX denotes indirect taxes and SB denotes subsidies. Source: *OECD National Accounts*, various issues.

Import price component of the wedge, t_m, defined as the share of imports in final expenditures, $MC/(MC + YC)$, times $\log(P_m/P)$.

Wedge, $t_1 + t_2 + t_3 + t_m$.

Nominal wage, W, which is hourly earnings in manufacturing. Source: *OECD MEI Historical Statistics*, 1955-71 and 1960-79.

Wage inflation, Δw where $w \equiv \log(W)$.

Real producers' wage, $W(1 + t_1)/P$.

Real consumers' wage, $W(1 - t_2)/P_c$.

Unemployment rate, $u \equiv UT/ET$ where UT denotes total unemployment and ET denotes total employment (including armed forces) Source: *OECD Labour Force Statistics*, various issues.

Trend productivity of labour, $PROD \equiv {}^1/_3 \log(YF/ET) + {}^1/_3 \log(YF/ET)_{-1} + {}^1/_3 \log(YF/ET)_{-2}$ where $YF \equiv (YC - TX + SB)YQ/YC$ denotes GDP at factor cost and 1980 prices.

Measure of industrial conflicts, NC (see M. Paldam and Rasmussen, 1981, "Data for Industrial Conflicts in 17 *OECD* countries, 1948-77", Arhus University) Source: *ILO Yearbook of Labour Statistics*, various issues.

All the data, except the structural budget balances, can be found in the *OECD* databank of the Centre for Labour Economics (see A. Newell, 1985, "The Revised *OECD* Data Set", London School of Economics, Working Paper No. 781, which includes D. Grubb, "The *OECD* Data Set").

4

REFERENCES

Argy, V. and Salop, J. (1977) 'Price and Output Effects of Monetary and Fiscal Policy Under Flexible Exchange Rates', *IMF Staff Papers*, pp. 224-256.

—— (1983) 'Price and Output Effects of Monetary and Fiscal Expansion in a Two-Country World Under Flexible Exchange Rates', *Oxford Economic Papers*, 35 : 228-246.

Artis, M. J. and Gazioglu, S. (1987) 'A Two-Country Model with Asymmetric Phillips Curves and Intervention in the Foreign Exchange Market", Centre for Economic Policy Research, Discussion Paper No. 172.

Attanasio, O. and van der Ploeg, F. (1988) : 'Real Effects of Demand- and Supply-Side Policies in Interdependent Economies', *Economic Modelling*, 5 : 151-164.

Attanasio, O., Manasse, P. and van der Ploeg, F. (1987) 'Interdependence in the OECD Economies : An Econometric Model of the Group of Seven', London School of Economics, Centre for Labour Economics, Working Paper No. 914.

Blanchard, O. J. and Summers, L. H. (1987) 'Fiscal Increasing Returns, Hysteresis, Real Wages and Unemployment', *European Economic Review*, 31 : 543-566.

Branson, W. H. and Rotemberg, J. J. (1980) 'International Adjustment with Wage Rigidity', *European Economic Review*, 13 : 309-332.

Breusch, T. S. and Godfrey, L. G. (1981) : 'A Review of Recent Work on Testing for Auto-Correlation in Dynamic Simultaneous Models', in D. Currie, R. Nobay and D. Peel (eds.), *Macroeconomics and Econometrics*, (London : Croom Helm).

Bruno, M. and Sachs, J. D. (1985) *The Economics of Worldwide Stagflation*, (Oxford : Basil Blackwell).

Buiter, W. H. (1984) 'Policy Evaluation and Design for Continuous Time Linear Rational Expectations Models : Some Recent Developments', Centre for Economic Policy Research, Discussion Paper No. 15.

Calvo, G. A. (1978) 'On the Time Consinency of Optimal Policy in a Monetary Economy', *Econometrica*, 46 : 1411-1428.

Canzoneri, M. B. and Gray, J. A. (1985) 'Monetary Policy Games and the Consequences of Non-Cooperative Behaviour', *International Economic Review*, 26 : 547-564.

Canzoneri, M. B. and Henderson, D. W. (1986) *Strategic Aspects of Macroeconomic Policy Making in Interdependent Economies*, mimeo.

Casas, F.R. (1975) 'Efficient Macroeconomic Stabilization Policies under Floating Exchange Rates', *International Economic Review*, 16 : 682-698.

Currie, D. and Levine, P. (1985) 'Macroeconomic Policy Design in an Interdependent World', in W. H. Buiter and R. C. Marston (eds.), *International Economic Policy Coordination*, (Cambridge: Cambridge University Press).

Flemming, J. M. (1962) 'Domestic Financial Policies Under Fixed and Floating Exchange Rates', *IMF Staff Papers*, 9 : 369-379.

Godfrey, L. G. (1987) 'Testing for Higher Order Serial Correlation in Regression Equations When the Regressions Include Lagged Dependent Variables'', *Econometrica*, 46 : 1303-1310.

Grubb, D., Jackman, R. and Layard, R. (1983) 'Wage Rigidity and Unemployment in OECD Countries', *European Economic Review*, 21 : 11-39.

Hamada, K. (1985) *The Political Economy of International Monetary Interdependence*, (Cambridge, Mass : MIT Press).

— and Kurosaka, Y. (1986) 'Trends in Unemployment, Wages and Productivity : The Case of Japan', in C. R. Bean, R. Layard and S. Nickell, (eds.), *The Rise in Unemployment*, (Oxford : Basil Blackwell).

Klundert, Th. van de and Ploeg, F. van der (1989) 'Wage Rigidity and Capital Mobility in an Optimising Model of a Small Open Economy', *De Economist*, 137 : 47-75.

Kydland, F. E. and Prescott, E. C. (1977) 'Rules Rather than Discretions : The Inconsistency of Optimal Plans', *Journal of Political Economy*, 84 : 473-491.

Layard, R., Basevi, G., Blanchard, O., Buiter, W. H. and Dornbusch, R. (1984) 'Europe : The Case for Unsustainable Growth', Centre for European Policy Studies Paper No. 8/9.

McKibbin, W.J. and Sachs, J. D. (1986) 'Coordination of Monetary and Fiscal Policies in the OECD', Cambridge, Massachusetts, National Bureau of Economic Research, Working Paper No. 1800.

Miller, M.H. and Salmon, M., (1985) 'Policy Coordination and Dynamic Games', in W. H. Buiter and R. C. Marston (eds.), *International Economic Policy Coordination*, (Cambridge : Cambridge University Press).

Minford, P. (1985) 'The Effects of American Policies – A New Classical Interpretation', in W. H. Buiter and R.C. Marston, (eds.), *International Economic Policy Coordination*, (Cambridge : Cambridge University Press).

Muller, P. and Price, R. W. R. (1984) 'Structural Budget Deficits and Fiscal Stance', OECD Monetary and Fiscal Policy Division, Working Paper No. 15, Paris.

Mundell, R. A. (1968) *International Economics*, (New York: Macmillan Press).

Newell A. and Symons, J. S. V. (1987) 'Mid 1980s Unemployment', London School of Economics, Centre for Labour Economics, Discussion Paper No. 283.

Oudiz, G. and Sachs, J. (1984) 'Macroeconomic Policy Coordination Among the Industrial Economies', *Brookings Papers on Economic Activity*, 1 : 1-77.

—(1985) 'International Policy Coordination in Dynamic Macroeconomic Models', in W. H. Buiter and R. C. Marston (eds.), *International Economic Policy Coordination*, (Cambridge : Cambridge University Press).

Ploeg, F. van der (1986) 'Capital Accumulation, Inflation and Long-Run Conflict in International Objectives', London School of Economics, Centre for Labour Economics, Discussion Paper No. 250. Forthcoming in *Oxford Economic Papers*.

— (1987) 'International Policy Coordination in Interdependent Monetary Economies', *Journal of International Economics*, 25 : 1-23.

Rogoff, K. (1985) 'Can International Monetary Policy Cooperation be Counterproductive?', *Journal of International Economics*, 18 : 199-217.

Sachs, J. (1980) 'Wages, Flexible Exchange Rates, and Macroeconomic Policy', *Quarterly Journal of Economics*, 94 : 731-747.

Sargan, J. D. (1964) 'Wage and Prices in the U.K.', in P.E. Hart, G. Mills and J. K. Whittaker (eds.), *Econometric Analysis for Economic Planning*, (New York : Macmillan Press).

Turnovsky, S. J. (1985) 'Monetary and Fiscal Policy Under Perfect Foresight : A Symmetric Two-Country Analysis', *Economica*, 53 : 139-158.

White, H. (1980) 'A Heteroskedasticity-Consistent Covariance Matrix Estimator and a Direct Test for Heteroskedasticity', *Econometrica*, 48 : 817-838.